C000182031

BRITISH RAILWAYS

LOCOMOTIVES & COACHING STOCK

2018

The Complete Guide to all Locomotives & Coaching Stock which operate on the National Rail network and Eurotunnel

Robert Pritchard & Peter Hall

Published by Platform 5 Publishing Ltd,
52 Broadfield Road, Sheffield, S8 0XJ, England.

Printed in England by The Lavenham Press, Lavenham, Suffolk.

ISBN 978 1 909431 44 7

CONTENTS

SECTION 1 – LOCOMOTIVES

SECTION 2 – LOCO-HAULED COACHING STOCK

SECTION 3 – DIESEL MULTIPLE UNITS

CONTENTS

CONTENTS 3

SECTION 4 – ELECTRIC MULTIPLE UNITS

SECTION 5 – ON-TRACK MACHINES

SECTION 6 – CODES

COVER PHOTOGRAPHS

Front Cover: In a special Flying Scotsman livery, Virgin Trains East Coast's 91101 "FLYING SCOTSMAN" heads north at Houndwood with the 13.00 London King's Cross–Edinburgh on 17/08/16.   **Neil Gibson**

Back Cover: Brand new South West Trains (now South Western Railway) 707 003 and 707 004 pass Egham with a 5Q38 Staines Up Loop–Ascot test run on 26/05/17.   **Jamie Squibbs**

BRITAIN'S RAILWAY SYSTEM

INFRASTRUCTURE & OPERATION

Britain's national railway infrastructure is owned by a "not for dividend" company, Network Rail. In 2014 Network Rail was reclassified as a public sector company, being described by the Government as a "public sector arm's-length body of the Department for Transport".

Most stations and maintenance depots are leased to and operated by Train Operating Companies (TOCs), but some larger stations are controlled by Network Rail. The only exception is the infrastructure on the Isle of Wight: The Island Line franchise uniquely included maintenance of the infrastructure as well as the operation of passenger services. As Island Line is now part of the South Western Railway franchise, both the infrastructure and trains are operated by South Western Railway.

Trains are operated by TOCs over Network Rail tracks (the National Network), regulated by access agreements between the parties involved. In general, TOCs are responsible for the provision and maintenance of the locomotives, rolling stock and staff necessary for the direct operation of services, whilst Network Rail is responsible for the provision and maintenance of the infrastructure and also for staff to regulate the operation of services.

The Department for Transport (DfT) is the franchising authority for the national network, with Transport Scotland overseeing the award of the ScotRail franchise and the Welsh Government overseeing the Wales & Borders franchise.

A franchise is the right to run specified services within a specified area for a period of time, in return for the right to charge fares and, where appropriate, to receive financial support from the Government. Subsidy is payable in respect of socially necessary services. Service standards are monitored by the DfT throughout the duration of the franchise. Franchisees earn revenue primarily from fares and from subsidy. They generally lease stations from Network Rail and earn rental income by sub-letting parts of them, for example to retailers.

Franchisees' main costs are the track access charges they pay to Network Rail, the costs of leasing stations and rolling stock and of employing staff. Franchisees may do light maintenance work on rolling stock or contract it out to private companies. Heavy maintenance is normally carried out by the Rolling Stock Leasing Companies, according to contracts.

TOCs can take commercial risks, although some franchises are "management contracts", where ticket revenues pass directly to the DfT. Concessions (such as London Overground) see the operator paid a fee to run the service, usually within tightly specified guidelines. Operators running a concession would not normally take commercial risks, although there are usually penalties and rewards in the contract.

Note that a railway "reporting period" is four weeks.

DOMESTIC PASSENGER TRAIN OPERATORS

The majority of passenger trains are operated by Train Operating Companies on fixed-term franchises or concessions. Expiry dates are shown in the list below:

Franchise	Franchisee	Trading Name
Caledonian Sleeper	Serco	**Caledonian Sleeper**
	(until 31 March 2030)	

This new franchise started in April 2015 when operation of the ScotRail and ScotRail Sleeper franchises was separated. Abellio won the ScotRail franchise and Serco the Caledonian Sleeper franchise. Caledonian Sleeper operates four trains nightly between London Euston and Scotland using locomotives hired principally from GBRf. New CAF rolling stock will be introduced in 2018–19 to replace the current Mark 2 and Mark 3 carriages that are used.

Chiltern	Arriva (Deutsche Bahn)	**Chiltern Railways**
	(until 31 December 2021)	

There is an option to extend the franchise by 7 months to July 2022.

Chiltern Railways operates a frequent service between London Marylebone, Banbury and Birmingham Snow Hill, with some peak trains extending to Kidderminster. There are also regular services from Marylebone to Stratford-upon-Avon and to Aylesbury Vale Parkway via Amersham (along the London Underground Metropolitan Line). A new route to Oxford Parkway and then Oxford was added in 2015–16. The fleet consists of DMUs of Classes 165, 168 and 172 plus a number of locomotive-hauled rakes used on some of the Birmingham route trains, worked by Class 68s hired from DRS.

Cross Country	Arriva (Deutsche Bahn)	**CrossCountry**
	(until December 2019)	

There is an option to extend the franchise by 11 months to November 2020.

CrossCountry operates a network of long distance services between Scotland, the North-East of England and Manchester to the South-West of England, Reading, Southampton, Bournemouth and Guildford, centred on Birmingham New Street. These trains are mainly formed of diesel Class 220/221 Voyagers, supplemented by a small number of HSTs on the NE–SW route. Inter-urban services also link Nottingham, Leicester and Stansted Airport with Birmingham and Cardiff. These trains use Class 170 DMUs.

Crossrail	MTR	**TfL Rail**
	(until 30 May 2023)	

There is an option to extend the concession by 2 years to May 2025.

This is a new concession which started in May 2015. Initially Crossrail took over the Liverpool Street–Shenfield stopping service from Greater Anglia, using a fleet of Class 315 EMUs, with the service branded "TfL Rail". New Class 345 EMUs are now being introduced on this route and then from 2018–19 Crossrail will operate through new tunnels beneath central London, from Shenfield and Abbey Wood in the east to Reading and Heathrow Airport in the west. It will then be branded "Elizabeth Line".

East Coast	Stagecoach/Virgin Trains	**Virgin Trains East Coast**
	(until 31 March 2020)	

Franchise originally due to run until 2023, but will now be replaced in 2020 with a new East Coast partnership.

Virgin Trains East Coast operates frequent long distance trains on the East Coast Main Line between London King's Cross, Leeds, York, Newcastle and Edinburgh, with less frequent services to Bradford, Harrogate, Skipton, Hull, Lincoln, Glasgow, Aberdeen and Inverness. A mixed fleet of Class 91s and 30 Mark 4 sets, and 15 HST sets, are used on these lines.

East Midlands	Stagecoach Group (until 3 March 2019)	**East Midlands Trains**

There is an option to extend the franchise until August 2019, with a further option to extend it to August 2020.

EMT operates a mix of long distance high speed services on the Midland Main Line (MML), from London St Pancras to Sheffield (to Leeds at peak times and with some extensions to York/Scarborough) and Nottingham (plus peak-hour trains to Lincoln), and local and regional services ranging from the Norwich–Liverpool route to Nottingham–Skegness, Newark–Mansfield–Worksop, Nottingham–Matlock and Derby–Crewe. It also operates local services in Lincolnshire. Trains on the MML are worked by a fleet of Class 222 DMUs and nine HSTs, whilst the local and regional fleet consists of DMU Classes 153, 156 and 158.

East Anglia	Abellio (Netherlands Railways)/Mitsui Group (until 15 October 2025)	**Greater Anglia**

There is an option to extend the franchise by 1 year to October 2026.

Greater Anglia operates main line trains between London Liverpool Street, Ipswich and Norwich and local trains across Norfolk, Suffolk and parts of Cambridgeshire. It also runs local and commuter services into Liverpool Street from the Great Eastern (including Southend, Braintree and Clacton) and West Anglia (including Cambridge and Stansted Airport) routes. It operates a varied fleet of Class 90s with locomotive-hauled Mark 3 sets, DMUs of Classes 153, 156 and 170 and EMUs of Classes 317, 321, 360 and 379. One locomotive-hauled set, using Class 37s, is currently hired for use on some trains between Norwich and Great Yarmouth/Lowestoft.

Essex Thameside	Trenitalia (until 8 November 2029)	**c2c**

There is an option to extend the franchise by 6 months to May 2030.

c2c operates an intensive, principally commuter, service from London Fenchurch Street to Southend and Shoeburyness via both Upminster and Tilbury. The fleet consists of 74 Class 357 EMUs, plus six Class 387s which arrived in late 2016.

Great Western	First Group (until 1 April 2020)	**Great Western Railway**

Direct Award extension expected to April 2022, with the option of a further 2 year extension to April 2024.

Great Western Railway (until September 2015 branded as First Great Western) operates long distance trains from London Paddington to South Wales, the West Country and Worcester and Hereford. In addition there are frequent trains along the Thames Valley corridor to Newbury/Bedwyn and Oxford, plus local and regional trains throughout the South-West including the Cornish, Devon and Thames Valley branches, the Reading–Gatwick North Downs Line and Cardiff–Portsmouth Harbour and Bristol–Weymouth regional routes. A large fleet of HSTs is used on the long-distance trains, which are currently being replaced by new Class 800 bi-mode InterCity Express Trains. DMUs of Classes 165 and 166 are used on the Thames Valley, Worcester and North Downs routes as well as on local services around Bristol. New Class 387 EMUs are used between Paddington and Didcot Parkway. Classes 143, 150, 153 and 158 are used on local and regional trains in the South-West. A small fleet of Class 57s is maintained to principally work the overnight "Cornish Riviera" Sleeper service between London Paddington and Penzance.

| **London Rail** | Arriva (Deutsche Bahn) | **London Overground** |
| | (until May 2024) | |

This is a concession and is different from other rail franchises, as fares and service levels are set by Transport for London instead of by the DfT. There is an option to extend the concession by 2 years to May 2026.

London Overground operates services on the Richmond–Stratford North London Line and the Willesden Junction–Clapham Junction West London Line, plus the East London Line from Highbury & Islington to New Cross and New Cross Gate, with extensions to Clapham Junction (via Denmark Hill), Crystal Palace and West Croydon. It also runs services from London Euston to Watford Junction. All these use Class 378 EMUs. Class 172 DMUs are used on the Gospel Oak–Barking route, but will be replaced by new Class 710 EMUs in 2018. London Overground also operates some suburban services from London Liverpool Street – to Chingford, Enfield Town and Cheshunt. These use Class 315 and 317 EMUs, but will be replaced by Class 710s from 2018.

| **Merseyrail Electrics** | Serco/Abellio (Netherlands Railways) | **Merseyrail** |
| | (until 19 July 2028) | |

Under the control of Merseytravel PTE instead of the DfT. Franchise reviewed every five years to fit in with the Merseyside Local Transport Plan.

Merseyrail operates services between Liverpool and Southport, Ormskirk, Kirkby, Hunts Cross, New Brighton, West Kirby, Chester and Ellesmere Port, using Class 507 and 508 EMUs.

| **Northern** | Arriva (Deutsche Bahn) | **Northern** |
| | (until 31 March 2025) | |

There is an option to extend the franchise by 1 year to March 2026.

Northern operates a range of inter-urban, commuter and rural services throughout the North of England, including those around the cities of Leeds, Manchester, Sheffield, Liverpool and Newcastle. The network extends from Chathill in the north to Nottingham in the south, and Cleethorpes in the east to St Bees in the west. Long distance services include Leeds–Carlisle, Middlesbrough–Carlisle and York–Blackpool North. The operator uses a large fleet of DMUs of Classes 142, 144, 150, 153, 155, 156 and 158 plus EMU Classes 319, 321, 322, 323 and 333. Class 185s are hired from TransPennine Express for use on some services between Manchester Airport and Blackpool North/Barrow/Windermere. Two locomotive-hauled sets, with Class 37s, are hired from DRS for use on some trains between Carlisle and Barrow-in-Furness/Preston as part of a 4-year contract that started in May 2015.

| **ScotRail** | Abellio (Netherlands Railways) | **ScotRail** |
| | (until 31 March 2022) | |

There is an option to extend the franchise by 3 years to March 2025.

ScotRail provides almost all passenger services within Scotland and also trains from Glasgow to Carlisle via Dumfries, some of which extend to Newcastle (jointly operated with Northern). The company operates a large fleet of DMUs of Classes 156, 158 and 170 and EMU Classes 314, 318, 320, 334 and 380, with Class 385s to be introduced in 2018. Two locomotive-hauled rakes are also used on Fife Circle commuter trains, hauled by Class 68s hired from DRS.

| **South Eastern** | Govia (Go-Ahead/Keolis) | **Southeastern** |
| | (until 31 March 2019) | |

Southeastern operates all services in the South-East London suburbs, the whole of Kent and part of Sussex, which are primarily commuter services to London. It also operates domestic high speed trains on HS1 from London St Pancras to Ashford, Ramsgate, Dover and Faversham with additional peak services on other routes. EMUs of Classes 375, 376, 377, 465 and 466 are used, along with Class 395s on the High Speed trains.

| **South Western** | First Group/MTR
(until 18 August 2024) | **South Western Railway** |

There is an option to extend the franchise by 11 months to July 2025.

South Western Railway operates trains from London Waterloo to destinations across the South and South-West including Woking, Basingstoke, Southampton, Portsmouth, Salisbury, Exeter, Reading and Weymouth as well as suburban services from Waterloo. SWR also runs services between Ryde and Shanklin on the Isle of Wight, using former London Underground 1938 stock (Class 483s). The rest of the fleet consists of DMU Classes 158 and 159 and EMU Classes 444, 450, 455, 456, 458 and 707.

| **Thameslink, Southern &**
Great Northern (TSGN) | Govia (Go-Ahead/Keolis)
(until 19 September 2021) | **Govia Thameslink Railway** |

There is an option to extend the franchise by 2 years to September 2023.

Govia operates this franchise, the largest in the UK, as a management contract. The former Southern franchise was combined with Thameslink/Great Northern in 2015. GTR uses four brands within the franchise: "Thameslink" for trains between Bedford and Brighton via central London and also on the Sutton/Wimbledon loop using new Class 700 EMUs. Some trains to Sevenoaks are jointly operated with Southeastern. "Great Northern" comprises services from London King's Cross and Moorgate to Welwyn Garden City, Hertford North, Peterborough, Cambridge and Kings Lynn using Class 313, 365 and 387 EMUs. "Southern" operates predominantly commuter services between London, Surrey and Sussex and "metro" services in South London, as well as services along the South Coast between Southampton, Brighton, Hastings and Ashford, plus the cross-London service from South Croydon to Milton Keynes. Class 171 DMUs are used on Brighton–Ashford and London Bridge–Uckfield services, whilst all other services are in the hands of Class 313, 377, 455 and 700 EMUs. Finally, the premium "Gatwick Express" operates non-stop trains between London Victoria, Gatwick Airport and Brighton using Class 387/2 EMUs.

| **Trans-Pennine Express** | First Group
(until 31 March 2023) | **TransPennine Express** |

There is an option to extend the franchise by 2 years to March 2025.

TransPennine Express operates predominantly long distance inter-urban services linking major cities across the North of England, along with Edinburgh and Glasgow in Scotland. The main services are Manchester Airport/Manchester Piccadilly–Newcastle/Middlesbrough/Hull plus Liverpool–Scarborough and Liverpool–Newcastle along the North Trans-Pennine route via Huddersfield, Leeds and York, and Manchester Airport–Cleethorpes along the South Trans-Pennine route via Sheffield. TPE also operates Manchester Airport–Edinburgh/Glasgow. The fleet consists of Class 185 DMUs, plus Class 350 EMUs used on Manchester Airport–Scotland services.

| **Wales & Borders** | Arriva (Deutsche Bahn)
(until 14 October 2018) | **Arriva Trains Wales** |

There is an option to extend the franchise by 6 months to April 2019. The Welsh Government is procuring the next Wales & Borders franchise.

Arriva Trains Wales operates a mix of long distance, regional and local services throughout Wales, including the Valley Lines network of lines around Cardiff, and also through services to the English border counties and to Manchester and Birmingham. The fleet consists of DMUs of Classes 142, 143, 150, 158 and 175 and two locomotive-hauled rakes: one used on a premium Welsh Government sponsored service on the Cardiff–Holyhead route, and one used between Manchester/Crewe and Holyhead (both are hauled by a Class 67).

| **West Coast Partnership** | Virgin Rail Group (Virgin/Stagecoach Group) (until 31 March 2019) | **Virgin Trains** |

Virgin Trains operates long distance services along the West Coast Main Line from London Euston to Birmingham/Wolverhampton, Manchester, Liverpool and Glasgow using Class 390 Pendolino EMUs. It also operates Class 221 Voyagers on the Euston–Chester–Holyhead route, whilst a mixture of Class 221s and 390s are used on the Euston–Birmingham–Glasgow/Edinburgh route.

| **West Midlands Trains** | Abellio/JR East/Mitsui (until March 2026) | **West Midlands Railway** **London Northwestern** |

This new franchise started in December 2017. There is an option to extend the franchise by 2 years to March 2028.

West Midlands Trains operates services under two brand names. West Midlands Railway trains are local and regional services around Birmingham, including to Stratford-upon-Avon, Worcester, Hereford, Redditch, Rugeley and Shrewsbury. WMR is managed by a consortium of 16 councils and the Department for Transport. London Northwestern is the brand used for long distance and regional services from London Euston to Northampton and Birmingham/Crewe and also between Birmingham and Liverpool, Bedford–Bletchley and Watford Junction–St Albans Abbey. The fleet consists of DMU Classes 150, 153, 170 and 172 and EMU Classes 319, 323 and 350.

NON-FRANCHISED SERVICES

The following operators run non-franchised, or "open access" services (* special seasonal services):

Operator	*Trading Name*	*Route*
Heathrow Airport Holdings	Heathrow Express	London Paddington–Heathrow Airport

Heathrow Express operates a frequent express passenger service between London Paddington and Heathrow Airport using Class 332 EMUs. A slower stopping service is operated jointly with Great Western Railway, and this uses Class 360 EMUs.

| Hull Trains (part of First) | Hull Trains | London King's Cross–Hull |

Hull Trains operates seven trains a day (weekdays) from Hull to London King's Cross via the East Coast Main Line using Class 180 DMUs. One train in each direction starts back from and extends to Beverley.

| Grand Central (part of Arriva) | Grand Central | London King's Cross–Sunderland/ Bradford Interchange |

Grand Central operates five trains a day from Sunderland and four trains a day from Bradford Interchange to London King's Cross using Class 180 DMUs.

| North Yorkshire Moors Railway Enterprises | North Yorkshire Moors Railway | Pickering–Grosmont–Whitby/ Battersby, Sheringham–Cromer* |

The North Yorkshire Moors Railway operates services on the national network between Grosmont and Whitby or Grosmont and Battersby as an extension of its Pickering–Grosmont services and also operates services between Sheringham and Cromer on behalf of the North Norfolk Railway.

| West Coast Railway Company | West Coast Railway Company | Fort William–Mallaig* York–Settle–Carlisle* |

West Coast Railway Company operates steam-hauled services on these routes on a seasonal basis.

INTERNATIONAL PASSENGER OPERATORS

Eurostar International operates passenger services between the UK and mainland Europe. The company, established in 2010, is jointly owned by SNCF (the national operator of France): 55%, SNCB (the national operator of Belgium): 5% and Patina Rail: 40%. Patina Rail is made up of Canadian-based Caisse de dépôt et placement du Québec (CDPG) and UK-based Hermes Infrastructure (owning 30% and 10% respectively). This 40% was previously owned by the UK Government until it was sold in 2015.

Eurostar uses mainly new Siemens Class 374 trains on its St Pancras–Paris route and on some Brussels trains, with the original Class 373 sets used mainly on the Brussels route. Eight of these sets are being retained and refurbished.

In addition, a service for the conveyance of accompanied road vehicles through the Channel Tunnel is provided by the tunnel operating company, Eurotunnel. All Eurotunnel services are operated in top-and-tail mode by the powerful Class 9 Bo-Bo-Bo locomotives.

FREIGHT TRAIN OPERATORS

The following operators operate freight services or empty passenger stock workings under "Open Access" arrangements:

Colas Rail: Colas Rail operates a number of On-Track Machines and also supplies infrastructure monitoring trains for Network Rail. It also operates a number of different freight flows, including oil and timber. Colas Rail has a small but varied fleet consisting of Class 37s, 56s, 60s, 66s, 67s and 70s.

DB Cargo (UK): Still the biggest freight operator in the country, DBC (EWS until bought by Deutsche Bahn, when it was initially called DB Schenker) provides a large number of infrastructure trains to Network Rail and also operates coal, steel, intermodal and aggregate trains nationwide. The core fleet is Class 66s. Of the original 250 ordered some have moved to DB's French and Polish operations, although some of the French locos do return to the UK when major maintenance is required. A fleet of around 15–20 Class 60s are also used on heavier trains.

DBC's six Class 59/2s are used alongside the Mendip Rail 59/0s and 59/1s on stone traffic from the Mendip quarries and around the South-East. DBC's fleet of Class 67s are used on passenger or standby duties for Arriva Trains Wales and Virgin Trains East Coast and also on excursions or special trains. Class 90s see some use on West Coast Main Line freight traffic and two are also hired to Virgin Trains East Coast on an as-required basis for use on passenger trains. The Class 92s are mainly used on a limited number of overnight freights on High Speed 1.

DBC also operates the Class 325 EMUs for Royal Mail and a number of excursion trains.

Devon & Cornwall Railways (part of Cappagh Construction Contractors (London)): DCRail specialises in short-term freight haulage contracts, mainly using Class 56s.

Direct Rail Services: DRS has built on its original nuclear flask traffic to operate a number of different services. The main flows are intermodal plus the provision of crews and locomotives to Network Rail for autumn Railhead Treatment Trains and also Network Rail infrastructure trains. Its Class 57s and 68s are used on excursion work.

DRS has a varied fleet of locomotives, with Class 20s, 37s, 57s and 66s working alongside new Class 68s and diesel-electric Class 88s. Class 68s are hired to other TOCs such as Chiltern Railways and ScotRail for operating passenger trains.

Freightliner: Freightliner operates container trains from the main Ports at Southampton, Felixstowe, Tilbury and Thamesport to major cities including London, Manchester, Leeds and Birmingham. It also operates trains of coal, cement, infrastructure and aggregates nationwide. Most services are worked by Class 66s, with Class 70s mainly used on some of the heavier intermodal trains. A small fleet of Class 86 and 90 electrics are used on intermodal trains on the Great Eastern and West Coast Main Lines, the Class 86s mainly being used in pairs on the WCML between Crewe and Coatbridge.

GB Railfreight: GBRf, now owned by the Hector Rail group, operates a mixture of traffic types, mainly using Class 66s together with a small fleet of Class 73s on infrastructure duties and test trains in the South-East. A growing fleet of Class 92s is also used on some intermodal flows to/from Dollands Moor or through the Channel Tunnel to Calais. Traffic includes coal, intermodal, biomass, aggregates and gypsum as well as infrastructure services for Network Rail and London Underground. GBRf also supplies locomotives to Caledonian Sleeper and owns three Class 47s.

GBRf also operates some excursion trains, including those using the preserved Class 201 "Hastings" DEMU.

Loram (UK): Loram has a freight license and operates a limited number of trains, most hauling On-Track Machines using hired-in locomotives.

Rail Operations Group: This company mainly facilitates rolling stock movements by providing drivers or using locomotives hired from other companies or by using its own fleet of Class 47s. ROG also operates a small number of excursion trains.

West Coast Railway Company: WCRC has a freight licence but doesn't operate any freight as such – only empty stock movements. Its fleet of Class 47s, supplemented by a smaller number of Class 33s, 37s and 57s, is used on excursion work nationwide.

In addition, Amey, Balfour Beatty Rail, Harsco Rail, South Western Railway, Swietelsky Babcock Rail (SB Rail) and VolkerRail operate trains formed of On-Track Machines.

PROVISION OF INFORMATION

This book has been compiled with care to be as accurate as possible, but some information is not easily available and the publisher cannot be held responsible for any errors or omissions. We would like to thank the companies and individuals who have been helpful in supplying information to us. The authors of this series of books are always pleased to receive notification of any inaccuracies that may be found, to enhance future editions. Please send comments to:

Robert Pritchard, Platform 5 Publishing Ltd, 52 Broadfield Road, Sheffield, S8 0XJ, England.

e-mail: robert.pritchard@platform5.com   **Tel:** 0114 255 2625.

UPDATES

This book is updated to the start of January 2018. The Platform 5 railway magazine **"Today's Railways UK"** publishes Stock Changes every month to update this book. The magazine also contains news and rolling stock information on the railways of Great Britain and Ireland and is published on the second Monday of every month. For further details of **Today's Railways UK**, please contact Platform 5 Publishing Ltd.

1. LOCOMOTIVES

INTRODUCTION

This book contains details of all locomotives which can run on Britain's national railway network, plus those of Eurotunnel.

Locomotives currently approved for use on the national railway network fall into the four broad types: passenger, freight, mixed traffic and shunting.

Passenger
The number of dedicated passenger locomotives has not changed significantly in recent years. However, the number is expected to decline in the future as new multiple unit stock replaces some of the remaining locomotive-hauled or propelled trains. Classes 43 (HST) and 91 and some members of Classes 57, 67, 68, 73/9, 90 and 92 are dedicated to franchised and Open Access passenger operations. Excursion trains have a few dedicated locomotives but mainly use locomotives that are best described as mixed traffic.

Freight
By far the most numerous locomotives are those used solely for bulk commodity and intermodal freight. Since 1998 a large number of new Class 66 locomotives have replaced many former BR designs and in more recent years smaller numbers of Class 70s have also been introduced. There are however a significant number of BR era Class 20, 37, 47, 56, 60, 73/1, 86, 90 and 92 locomotives still in use; their number has increased slightly recently as some locomotives have been reinstated to cope with demand. In addition there is a small fleet of Class 59s acquired privately in the 1980s and 1990s and a small number of re-engined Class 57s in use.

Mixed Traffic
In addition to their use on passenger and commodity freight workings these locomotives are used for stock movements and specialist infrastructure and test trains. The majority, but not all, are fitted with Electric Train Supply. Locomotives from Classes 20, 31, 33, 37, 47, 57, 67, 68, 73/9, 88 and 90 fall into this category. Also included under this heading are preserved locomotives permitted to operate on the national railway network. Although these have in the past solely operated excursion trains they are increasingly seeing occasional use on other types of trains.

Shunting
Very few shunting locomotives are now permitted to operate freely on the National Railway network. The small number that are have to be fitted with a plethora of safety equipment in order to have engineering acceptance. They are mainly used for local workings such as trips between yards or stock movements between depots and stations. Otherwise, shunting locomotives are not permitted to venture from depots or yards onto the National Railway network other than into defined limits within interface infrastructure. Generally such locomotives, which include an increasing number of remotely controlled driverless types, are not included in this

book. However, all ex-BR shunting locomotives are listed in this book under Section 1.1 "Diesel Shunting Locomotives".

Locomotives which are owned by, for example, DB Cargo or Freightliner, which have been withdrawn from service and are awaiting disposal are listed in the main part of the book. Locomotives which are awaiting disposal at scrapyards are listed in the "Locomotives Awaiting Disposal" section.

Only preserved locomotives which are currently used on the National Railway network are included. Others, which may still be Network Rail registered but not at present certified for use, are not included, but can be found in the Platform 5 book, "Preserved Locomotives of British Railways".

LAYOUT OF INFORMATION

Locomotive classes are listed in numerical order of class. Principal details and dimensions are quoted for each class in metric and/or imperial units as considered appropriate bearing in mind common UK usage.

Where numbers actually carried are different from those officially allocated, these are noted in class headings where appropriate. Where locomotives have been recently renumbered, the most immediate previous number is shown in parentheses. Each locomotive entry is laid out as in the following example:

No.	Detail	Livery	Owner	Pool	Allocn.	Name
59206	*b	**DB**	DB	WDAM	MD	John F. Yeoman Rail Pioneer

Detail Differences. Only detail differences which currently affect the areas and types of train which locomotives may work are shown. All other detail differences are excluded. Where such differences occur within a class or part class, they are shown in the "Detail" column alongside the individual locomotive number.

Codes: Codes are used to denote the livery, owner, pool and depot of each locomotive. Details of these will be found in section 6 of this book.

Depot allocation codes for all locomotives are shown in this book (apart from shunting locomotives (Classes 03, 07, 08 & 09) where the actual location of each is shown). It should be noted that today much locomotive maintenance is undertaken away from these depots. This may be undertaken at fuelling points, berthing sidings or similar, or by mobile maintenance teams. Therefore locomotives in particular may not return to their "home" depots as often as in the past.

(S) denotes that the locomotive is stored (the actual location is shown).

Names: Only names carried with official sanction are listed. Names are shown in UPPER/lower case characters as actually shown on the name carried on the locomotive.

Builders: These are shown in class headings. More details and a full list of builders can be found in section 6.7.

GENERAL INFORMATION

CLASSIFICATION AND NUMBERING

All locomotives are classified and allocated numbers under the TOPS numbering system, introduced in 1972. This comprises a two-digit class number followed by a three-digit serial number.

For diesel locomotives, class numbers offer an indication of engine horsepower as shown in the table below.

Class No. Range	Engine hp
01–14	0–799
15–20	800–1000
21–31	1001–1499
32–39	1500–1999
40–54, 57	2000–2999
55–56, 58–70	3000+

For electric locomotives class numbers are allocated in ascending numerical order under the following scheme:

Class 71–80   Direct current and DC/diesel dual system locomotives.
Class 81 onwards   Alternating current and AC/DC dual system locomotives.

Numbers in the 89xxx series are allocated to locomotives which have been deregistered but subsequently re-registered for use on the national railway network and whose original number has already been reused. 89xxx numbers are normally only carried inside locomotive cabs and are not carried externally in normal circumstances.

WHEEL ARRANGEMENT

For main line locomotives the number of driven axles on a bogie or frame is denoted by a letter (A = 1, B = 2, C = 3 etc) and the number of non-powered axles is denoted by a number. The use of the letter "o" after a letter indicates each axle is individually powered, whilst the "+" symbol indicates bogies are inter-coupled.

For shunting locomotives, the Whyte notation is used. In this notation the number of leading wheels are given, followed by the number of driving wheels and then the trailing wheels.

UNITS OF MEASUREMENT

All dimensions and weights are quoted for locomotives in an "as new" condition with all necessary supplies (eg oil, water and sand) on board. Dimensions are quoted in the order length x width. Lengths quoted are over buffers or couplers as appropriate. All widths quoted are maxima. Where two different wheel diameter dimensions are shown, the first refers to powered wheels and the second refers to non-powered wheels. All weights are shown as metric tonnes (t = tonnes).

HAULAGE CAPABILITY OF DIESEL LOCOMOTIVES

The haulage capability of a diesel locomotive depends upon three basic factors:

1. Adhesive weight. The greater the weight on the driving wheels, the greater the adhesion and more tractive power can be applied before wheelslip occurs.

2. The characteristics of its transmission. To start a train the locomotive has to exert a pull at standstill. A direct drive diesel engine cannot do this, hence the need for transmission. This may be mechanical, hydraulic or electric. The present British Standard for locomotives is electric transmission. Here the diesel engine drives a generator or alternator and the current produced is fed to the traction motors. The force produced by each driven wheel depends on the current in its traction motor. In other words, the larger the current, the harder it pulls. As the locomotive speed increases, the current in the traction motor falls, hence the *Maximum Tractive Effort* is the maximum force at its wheels the locomotive can exert at a standstill. The electrical equipment cannot take such high currents for long without overheating. Hence the *Continuous Tractive Effort* is quoted which represents the current which the equipment can take continuously.

3. The power of its engine. Not all power reaches the rail, as electrical machines are approximately 90% efficient. As the electrical energy passes through two such machines (the generator or alternator and the traction motors), the *Power at Rail* is approximately 81% (90% of 90%) of the engine power, less a further amount used for auxiliary equipment such as radiator fans, traction motor blowers, air compressors, battery charging, cab heating, Electric Train Supply (ETS) etc. The power of the locomotive is proportional to the tractive effort times the speed. Hence when on full power there is a speed corresponding to the continuous tractive effort.

HAULAGE CAPABILITY OF ELECTRIC LOCOMOTIVES

Unlike a diesel locomotive, an electric locomotive does not develop its power on board and its performance is determined only by two factors, namely its weight and the characteristics of its electrical equipment. Whereas a diesel locomotive tends to be a constant power machine, the power of an electric locomotive varies considerably. Up to a certain speed it can produce virtually a constant tractive effort. Hence power rises with speed according to the formula given in section three above, until a maximum speed is reached at which tractive effort falls, such that the power also falls. Hence the power at the speed corresponding to the maximum tractive effort is lower than the maximum speed.

BRAKE FORCE

Brake Force (also known as brake power) is a measure of the braking power of a locomotive. The Brake Force available is dependant on the adhesion between the rail and the wheels being braked and the normal reaction of the rail on the wheels being braked (and hence on the weight per braked wheel). A locomotive's Brake Force is shown on its data panels so operating staff can ensure sufficient brake power is available for specific trains.

ELECTRIC TRAIN SUPPLY (ETS)

A number of locomotives are equipped to provide a supply of electricity to the train being hauled to power auxiliaries such as heating, cooling fans, air conditioning and kitchen equipment. ETS is provided from the locomotive by means of a separate alternator (except Class 33 locomotives, which have a DC generator). The ETS index of a locomotive is a measure of the electrical power available for train supply. Class 55 locomotives provide an ETS directly from one of their traction generators into the train supply.

Similarly, most locomotive-hauled carriages also have an ETS index, which in this case is a measure of the power required to operate equipment mounted in the carriage. The sum of the ETS indices of all the hauled vehicles in a train must not exceed the ETS index of the locomotive.

ETS is commonly (but incorrectly) known as ETH (Electric Train Heating), which is a throwback to the days before locomotive-hauled carriages were equipped with electrically powered auxiliary equipment other than for train heating.

ROUTE AVAILABILITY (RA)

This is a measure of a railway vehicle's axle load. The higher the axle load of a vehicle, the higher the RA number on a scale from 1 to 10. Each Network Rail route has a RA number and in general no vehicle with a higher RA number may travel on that route without special clearance.

MULTIPLE WORKING

Multiple working between vehicles (ie two or more powered vehicles being driven from one cab) is facilitated by jumper cables connecting the vehicles. However, not all types of locomotive are compatible with each other, and a number of different systems are in use. Some are compatible with others, some are not. BR used "multiple working codes" to designate which locomotives were compatible. The list below shows which classes of locomotives are compatible with each other – the former BR multiple working code being shown in brackets. It should be noted that some locomotives have had the equipment removed or made inoperable.

With other classes:
Classes 20, 25, 31, 33, 37 40 & 73/1*. (Blue Star)
Classes 56 & 58. (Red Diamond)
Classes 59, 66, 67, 68, 70, 73/9 & 88.
* DRS has since adapted the systems so its Classes 20/3, 37, 47 & 57 can work with each other only.

With other members of same class only:
Class 43, Class 47 (Green Circle), Class 50 (Orange Square), Class 60.

PUSH-PULL OPERATION

Some locomotives are modified to operate passenger and service (formed of laboratory, test and inspection carriages) trains in "push-pull" mode – which allows the train to be driven from either end – either with locomotives at each end (both under power) or with a driving brake van at one end and a locomotive at the other. Various different systems are now in use. Electric locomotive Classes 86, 87, 90 & 91 use a time-division multiplex (TDM) system for push-pull working which utilises the existing Railway Clearing House (RCH) jumper cables fitted to carriages. Previously these cables had only been used to control train lighting and public address systems.

More recently locomotives of Classes 67 and 68 have used the Association of American Railroads (AAR) system.

ABBREVIATIONS

Standard abbreviations used in this section of the book are:

a	Train air brake equipment only.
b	Drophead buckeye couplers.
c	Scharfenberg couplers.
d	Fitted with retractable Dellner couplers.
e	European Railway Traffic Management System (ERTMS) signalling equipment fitted.
k	Fitted with Swinghead Automatic "buckeye" combination couplers.
p	Train air, vacuum and electro-pneumatic brakes.
r	Radio Electric Token Block signalling equipment fitted.
s	Slow Speed Control equipment.
v	Train vacuum brake only.
x	Train air and vacuum brakes ("Dual brakes").
+	Additional fuel tank capacity.
§	Sandite laying equipment.

In all cases use of the above abbreviations indicates the equipment in question is normally operable. The definition of non-standard abbreviations and symbols is detailed in individual class headings.

1.1. DIESEL SHUNTING LOCOMOTIVES

All BR design shunting locomotives still in existence, apart from those considered to be preserved, are now listed together in this section. Preserved shunting locomotives are listed in the Platform 5 publication "Preserved Locomotives of British Railways" (a small number are listed in both that book and in this publication).

Few shunting locomotives have engineering acceptance and are equipped to operate on Network Rail infrastructure (beyond interface infrastructure), but those that are known to be permitted are indicated here.

For shunting locomotives, instead of the two-letter depot code, actual locations at the time of publication are given. Pool codes for shunting locomotives are not shown.

CLASS 03   BR/GARDNER   0-6-0

Built: 1958–62 by BR at Swindon or Doncaster Works.
Engine: Gardner 8L3 of 152 kW (204 hp) at 1200 rpm.
Transmission: Mechanical. Fluidrive type 23 hydraulic coupling to Wilson-Drewry CA5R7 gearbox with SCG type RF11 final drive.
Maximum Tractive Effort: 68 kN (15300 lbf).
Continuous Tractive Effort: 68 kN (15300 lbf) at 3.75 mph.
Train Brakes: Air & vacuum.
Brake Force: 13 t.   **Dimensions:** 7.93 x 2.59 m.
Weight: 31.3 t.   **Wheel Diameter:** 1092 mm.
Design Speed: 28.5 mph.   **Maximum Speed:** 28.5 mph.
Fuel Capacity: 1364 litres.   **Route Availability:** 1.
Train Supply: Not equipped.

Number	Notes	Livery	Owner	Location
03084		G	WC	West Coast Railway Company, Carnforth Depot
03196		B	WC	West Coast Railway Company, Carnforth Depot
D2381	v	G	WC	West Coast Railway Company, Carnforth Depot

CLASS 07   BR/RUSTON & HORNSBY   0-6-0

Built: 1962 by Ruston & Hornsby, Lincoln.
Engine: Paxman 6RPHL Mk III of 205 kW (275 hp) at 1360 rpm.
Transmission: Electric. One AEI RTB 6652 traction motor.
Maximum Tractive Effort: 126 kN (28240 lbf).
Continuous Tractive Effort: 71 kN (15950 lbf) at 4.38 mph.
Train Brakes: Vacuum.
Brake Force: **Dimensions:** 8.17 x 2.59 m.
Weight: 43.6 t.   **Wheel Diameter:** 1067 mm.
Design Speed: 20 mph.   **Maximum Speed:** 20 mph.
Fuel Capacity: 1400 litres.   **Train Supply:** Not equipped.

Number	Notes	Livery	Owner	Location
07007	v	B	AF	Arlington Fleet Services, Eastleigh Works, Hants

CLASS 08   BR/ENGLISH ELECTRIC   0-6-0

Built: 1955–62 by BR at Crewe, Darlington, Derby Locomotive, Doncaster or Horwich Works.
Engine: English Electric 6KT of 298 kW (400 hp) at 680 rpm.
Main Generator: English Electric 801.
Traction Motors: Two English Electric 506.
Maximum Tractive Effort: 156 kN (35000 lbf).
Continuous Tractive Effort: 49 kN (11100 lbf) at 8.8 mph.

Power at Rail: 194 kW (260 hp).	**Train Brakes:** Air & vacuum.
Brake Force: 19 t.	**Dimensions:** 8.92 x 2.59 m.
Weight: 49.6–50.4 t.	**Wheel Diameter:** 1372 mm.
Design Speed: 20 mph.	**Maximum Speed:** 15 mph.
Fuel Capacity: 3037 litres.	**Route Availability:** 5.
Train Supply: Not equipped.	

* Locomotives with engineering acceptence to operate on Network Rail infrastructure. 08850 has acceptance for use between Battersby and Whitby only, for rescue purposes.

† – Fitted with remote control equipment.

§ – On hire from Nottingham Transport Heritage Centre.

Non-standard liveries:

08308	All over ScotRail Caledonian Sleeper purple.
08401	Dark green.
08423	Dark blue.
08442	Dark grey lower bodyside & light grey upper bodyside.
08445	Yellow, blue & green.
08447	Lilac.
08502	Mid blue.
08568	Dark grey lower bodyside & light grey upper bodyside. Red solebar stripe.
08598	Yellow.
08600	Red with a light grey roof.
08678	Light blue & dark blue.
08682	Multi-coloured.
08699	Mid blue.
08774	Red.
08823	Yellow, blue & green.
08870	Light grey.
08899	Crimson lake.
08913	Yellow, blue & green.
08956	Serco Railtest blue.

Number	Notes	Livery	Owner	Location
08220	v	**B**	RS	EMD, Longport Works, Stoke-on-Trent, Staffs§
08308	a	**0**	RL	PD Ports, Teesport, Grangetown, Middlesbrough
08331		**K**	20	Midland Railway-Butterley, Derbyshire
08375	a	**K**	RL	Hanson Cement, Ketton Cement Works, nr Stamford
08389	a†	**E**	HN	Celsa Steel UK, Tremorfa Steelworks, Cardiff

08401	a	O	HU	Hams Hall Distribution Park, Coleshill, Warwickshire
08405	a†	E	RS	East Midlands Trains, Neville Hill Depot, Leeds
08410	* a	GW	GW	Great Western Railway, Long Rock Depot, Penzance
08411	a	B	RS	RSS, Rye Farm, Wishaw, Sutton Coldfield (S)
08417	* a	Y	NR	Loram (UK), RTC Business Park, Derby
08418	a	E	WC	West Coast Railway Company, Carnforth Depot
08423	a	O	RL	PD Ports, Teesport, Grangetown, Middlesbrough
08428	ak	E	HN	Barrow Hill Roundhouse, Chesterfield, Derbys (S)
08441	a	RS	RS	Virgin Trains East Coast, Bounds Green Depot, London
08442	a	O	AV	Arriva TrainCare, Eastleigh Depot, Hampshire (S)
08445	a	O	HU	Daventry International Railfreight Terminal, Crick
08447	a	O	RU	John G Russell (Transport), Hillington, Glasgow
08451	*	B	AM	Alstom, Longsight Depot, Manchester
08454	*	B	AM	Alstom, Widnes Technology Centre, Merseyside
08460	a	RS	RS	Axiom Rail, Stoke-on-Trent Works, Staffordshire
08472	* a	WA	WA	Virgin Trains East Coast, Craigentinny Depot, Edinburgh
08480	a	RS	RS	Greater Anglia, Crown Point Depot, Norwich
08483	* a	K	GW	Great Western Railway, St Philip's Marsh Depot, Bristol
08484	a	RS	RS	Cemex UK, Washwood Heath Stone Terminal, Birmingham
08485	a	B	WC	West Coast Railway Company, Carnforth Depot
08499	a	B	CS	Colas Rail, Canton Depot, Cardiff
08500		E	HN	Nemesis Rail, Burton-upon-Trent, Staffordshire (S)
08502		O	HN	GB Railfreight, Garston Car Terminal, Liverpool
08503	a	B	RS	Barry Rail Centre, Vale of Glamorgan
08507	a	RB	RV	Nemesis Rail, Burton-upon-Trent, Staffordshire
08511	a	RS	RS	Arriva TrainCare, Cambridge Depot
08516	a	LW	AV	Arriva TrainCare, Barton Hill Depot, Bristol
08523	*	B	RL	ScotRail, Inverness Depot
08525		ST	EM	East Midlands Trains, Neville Hill Depot, Leeds
08527		FA	HN	GB Railfreight, Inter Terminals, Immingham East Dock
08530	*	FL	FL	Freightliner, Southampton Maritime FLT
08531	* a	FH	FL	Freightliner, Felixstowe FLT
08536		B	LO	Loram (UK), RTC Business Park, Derby (S)
08567		E	AF	Arlington Fleet Services, Eastleigh Works, Hants
08568	a	O	RS	RSS, Rye Farm, Wishaw, Sutton Coldfield (S)
08571	* a	WA	WA	Daventry International Railfreight Terminal, Crick
08573		K	RL	Bombardier Transportation, Ilford Works, London
08575		FL	FL	Nemesis Rail, Burton-upon-Trent, Staffordshire (S)
08578		E	HN	Quinton Rail Technology Centre, Long Marston, Warks (S)
08580		E	RS	RSS, Rye Farm, Wishaw, Sutton Coldfield (S)
08585	*	FH	FL	Freightliner, Southampton Maritime FLT
08588		RL	RL	Loram (UK), RTC Business Park, Derby
08593		E	RS	RSS, Rye Farm, Wishaw, Sutton Coldfield (S)
08596	* a†	WA	WA	Virgin Trains East Coast, Craigentinny Depot, Edinburgh
08598		O	AD	AV Dawson, Ayrton Rail Terminal, Middlesbrough
08600	a	O	AD	AV Dawson, Ayrton Rail Terminal, Middlesbrough
08602		B	BT	Bombardier Transportation, Derby Works
08605	†	DB	RV	DB Cargo UK, Springs Branch Depot, Wigan
08611	*	B	AM	Alstom, Wembley Depot, London
08613		RL	RL	Weardale Railway, Wolsingham, County Durham
08615	*	WA	WA	LH Group, Barton-under-Needwood, Staffordshire

08616		**LM**	WM	West Midlands Trains, Tyseley Depot, Birmingham
08617	*	**B**	AM	Alstom, Oxley Depot, Wolverhampton
08622		**K**	RL	Weardale Railway, Wolsingham, County Durham
08623		**DB**	HN	Hope Cement, Hope Cement Works, Derbys (S)
08624	*	**FH**	FL	LH Group, Barton-under-Needwood, Staffordshire
08629		**KB**	KB	Knorr-Bremse Rail UK, Wolverton Works, Milton Keynes
08630	†	**K**	HN	Celsa Steel UK, Tremorfa Steelworks, Cardiff
08632	†	**RS**	RS	East Midlands Trains, Neville Hill Depot, Leeds
08641	*	**B**	GW	Great Western Railway, Laira Depot, Plymouth
08643		**B**	MR	Aggregate Industries, Merehead Rail Terminal
08644	*	**B**	GW	Great Western Railway, Laira Depot, Plymouth
08645	*	**DG**	GW	Great Western Railway, Landore Depot, Swansea
08648		**GC**	RL	Northern, Heaton Depot, Newcastle-upon-Tyne
08649		**KB**	KB	Knorr-Bremse Rail UK, Wolverton Works, Milton Keynes
08650		**B**	MR	Hanson Aggregates, Whatley Quarry, near Frome
08652		**B**	MR	Aggregate Industries, Merehead Rail Terminal
08653		**E**	HN	Quinton Rail Technology Centre, Long Marston, Warks (S)
08663	* a	**B**	GW	Great Western Railway, St Philip's Marsh Depot, Bristol
08669	* a	**WA**	WA	Wabtec Rail, Doncaster Works
08670	a	**RS**	RS	Virgin Trains East Coast, Bounds Green Depot, London
08676		**E**	HN	East Kent Light Railway, Shepherdswell, Kent (S)
08678	a	**0**	WC	West Coast Railway Company, Carnforth Depot
08682		**0**	BT	Bombardier Transportation, Derby Works
08683		**RS**	RS	Greater Anglia, Crown Point Depot, Norwich
08685		**E**	HN	East Kent Light Railway, Shepherdswell, Kent (S)
08690		**ST**	EM	East Midlands Trains, Neville Hill Depot, Leeds (S)
08691	*	**FL**	FL	Freightliner, Felixstowe FLT
08696	* a	**B**	AM	Alstom, Wembley Depot, London
08699		**0**	RL	Weardale Railway, Wolsingham, County Durham (S)
08700		**B**	HN	Bombardier Transportation, Ilford Works, London
08701	a	**RX**	HN	Quinton Rail Technology Centre, Long Marston, Warks (S)
08703	a	**E**	RS	DB Cargo UK, Springs Branch Depot, Wigan
08704		**RB**	RV	Nemesis Rail, Burton-upon-Trent, Staffordshire (S)
08706	†	**E**	HN	RSS, Rye Farm, Wishaw, Sutton Coldfield (S)
08709		**E**	RS	RSS, Rye Farm, Wishaw, Sutton Coldfield (S)
08711	k	**RX**	HN	Nemesis Rail, Burton-upon-Trent, Staffordshire (S)
08714		**E**	HN	Hope Cement, Hope Cement Works, Derbys (S)
08721	*	**B**	AM	Alstom, Widnes Technology Centre, Merseyside
08724	*	**WA**	WA	Wabtec Rail, Doncaster Works
08730		**KB**	KB	Knorr-Bremse Rail UK, Springburn Depot, Glasgow
08735	†	**E**	AV	Arriva TrainCare, Eastleigh Depot, Hampshire (S)
08738		**FER**	RS	RSS, Rye Farm, Wishaw, Sutton Coldfield (S)
08742	†	**RX**	HN	Didcot Railway Centre (S)
08743		**B**	SU	SembCorp Utilities UK, Wilton, Middlesbrough
08750	a	**K**	RL	Weardale Railway, Wolsingham, County Durham (S)
08752	†	**E**	RS	RSS, Rye Farm, Wishaw, Sutton Coldfield (S)
08754	*	**B**	RL	Mid Norfolk Railway, East Dereham, Norfolk
08756		**DG**	RL	Weardale Railway, Wolsingham, County Durham
08762		**K**	RL	Weardale Railway, Wolsingham, County Durham
08764	*	**B**	AM	Alstom, Polmadie Depot, Glasgow
08765		**E**	HN	Barrow Hill Roundhouse, Chesterfield, Derbys (S)

08774	a	O	AD	AV Dawson, Ayrton Rail Terminal, Middlesbrough
08782	a†	CU	HN	Barrow HIll Roundhouse, Chesterfield, Derbys (S)
08783		E	ER	European Metal Recycling, Kingsbury, nr Tamworth
08785	* a	FL	FL	Freightliner, Trafford Park FLT
08786	a	DG	HN	Barrow Hill Roundhouse, Chesterfield, Derbys (S)
08787		B	MR	Hanson Aggregates, Machen Quarry, near Newport
08788	*	RL	RL	Tata Steel, Shotton Works, Deeside
08790	*	B	AM	Arlington Fleet Services, Eastleigh Works
08795	*	K	GW	Great Western Railway, Landore Depot, Swansea
08798		E	ER	European Metal Recycling, Attercliffe, Sheffield
08799	a	E	HN	East Kent Light Railway, Shepherdswell, Kent (S)
08802	†	RX	HN	RSS, Rye Farm, Wishaw, Sutton Coldfield (S)
08804	†	E	HN	East Kent Light Railway, Shepherdswell, Kent (S)
08805		FO	WM	West Midlands Trains, Soho Depot, Birmingham
08809		RL	RL	Weardale Railway, Wolsingham, County Durham
08810	a	LW	AV	Arriva TrainCare, Eastleigh Depot, Hampshire
08818		GB	HN	GB Railfreight, Garston Car Terminal, Liverpool
08822	*	IC	GW	Great Western Railway, St Philip's Marsh Depot, Bristol
08823	a	O	HU	LH Group, Barton-under-Needwood, Staffordshire
08824	ak	K	HN	Barrow HIll Roundhouse, Chesterfield, Derbys (S)
08834		HN	HN	Northern, Allerton Depot, Liverpool
08836	*	GW	GW	Great Western Railway, Reading Depot
08846		B	BT	RSS, Rye Farm, Wishaw, Sutton Coldfield
08847	*	CD	RL	Mid Norfolk Railway, East Dereham, Norfolk
08850	*	B	NY	North Yorkshire Moors Railway, Grosmont Depot
08853	* a	WA	WA	Wabtec Rail, Doncaster Works
08865		E	HN	Hope Cement, Hope Cement Works, Derbys (S)
08868		AW	HN	Arriva TrainCare, Crewe Depot, Cheshire
08870		O	RL	Hanson Cement, Ketton Cement Works, nr Stamford
08871		CD	RL	Tata Steel, Trostre Works, Llanelli, Carmarthenshire
08872		E	ER	European Metal Recycling, Attercliffe, Sheffield
08873	*	RX	HU	LH Group, Barton-under-Needwood, Staffordshire
08874	*	SL	RL	Tata Steel, Shotton Works, Deeside
08877		DG	HN	Barrow Hill Roundhouse, Chesterfield, Derbys (S)
08879		E	RX	Arlington Fleet Services, Eastleigh Works
08885		B	RL	Weardale Railway, Wolsingham, County Durham (S)
08887	* a	B	AM	Alstom, Wembley Depot, London
08891	*	FL	FL	Nemesis Rail, Burton-upon-Trent, Staffordshire (S)
08892		DR	HN	Bombardier Transportation, Old Dalby Test Centre, Asfordby
08899		O	EM	East Midlands Trains, Derby Etches Park Depot
08903		B	SU	SembCorp Utilities UK, Wilton, Middlesbrough
08904		E	HN	Celsa Steel UK, Tremorfa Steelworks, Cardiff
08905		E	HN	Hope Cement, Hope Cement Works, Derbys (S)
08908		ST	EM	East Midlands Trains, Neville Hill Depot, Leeds (S)
08912		B	AD	AV Dawson, Ayrton Rail Terminal, Middlesbrough (S)
08913		O	HU	LH Group, Barton-under-Needwood, Staffordshire (S)
08918		DG	HN	Nemesis Rail, Burton-upon-Trent, Staffordshire (S)
08921		E	ER	European Metal Recycling, Kingsbury, nr Tamworth
08924	†	GB	HN	Celsa Steel UK, Tremorfa Steelworks, Cardiff
08925		G	GB	GB Railfreight, Whitemoor Yard, March, Cambs
08927		G	RS	EMD, Roberts Road Depot, Doncaster

08933		**B**	MR	Aggregate Industries, Merehead Rail Terminal
08934	a	**VP**	GB	GB Railfreight, Dagenham Car Terminal, Essex
08936		**B**	RL	Weardale Railway, Wolsingham, County Durham
08937		**G**	BD	Dartmoor Railway, Meldon Quarry, nr Okehampton
08939		**FER**	RS	RSS, Rye Farm, Wishaw, Sutton Coldfield (S)
08943		**HN**	HN	Bombardier Transportation, Central Rivers Depot, Barton-under-Needwood
08947		**B**	MR	Hanson Aggregates, Whatley Quarry, near Frome
08948	c	**EP**	EU	Eurostar, Temple Mills Depot, London
08950		**ST**	EM	East Midlands Trains, Neville Hill Depot, Leeds (S)
08954	*	**B**	AM	Alstom, Polmadie Depot, Glasgow
08956		**O**	LO	Bombardier Transportation, Old Dalby Test Centre, Asfordby

Class 08/9. Reduced height cab. Converted 1985–87 by BR at Landore.

08994	a	**E**	HN	Nemesis Rail, Burton-upon-Trent, Staffordshire (S)

Other numbers or names carried:

08308	"23"	08669	Bob Machin
08375	"21"	08678	ARTILA
08423	"H011" / "14"	08682	Lionheart
08451	LONGSIGHT TMD	08690	DAVID THIRKILL
08460	SPIRIT OF THE OAK	08691	Terri
08484	CAPTAIN NATHANIEL DARELL	08743	Bryan Turner
08499	REDLIGHT	08754	"H041"
08525	DUNCAN BEDFORD	08774	ARTHUR VERNON DAWSON
08568	St. Rollox	08787	"08296"
08585	Vicky	08809	"24"
08588	"H047"	08810	RICHARD J. WENHAM
08602	"004"		EASTLEIGH DEPOT
08605	"WIGAN2"		DECEMBER 1989 – JULY 1999
08613	"H064"	08818	MOLLY / "CELSA 4"
08616	TYSELEY 100 / 3783	08822	Dave Mills
08617	Steve Purser	08823	LIBBIE
08622	"H028" / "19"	08824	"IEMD 01"
08624	Rambo PAUL RAMSEY	08846	"003"
08629	Wolverton	08870	"H024"
08630	Celsa Endeavour / "CELSA 3"	08871	"H074"
08641	Pride of Laira	08874	Catherine
08644	Laira Diesel Depot 50 Years 1962–2012	08885	"H042" / "18"
08645	Mike Baggott	08899	Midland Counties Railway 175 1839–2014
08648	Amanda	08903	John W Antill
08649	Bradwell	08924	"CELSA 2"
08663	St. Silas	08927	D4157
		08937	D4167
		08950	DAVID LIGHTFOOT

CLASS 09   BR/ENGLISH ELECTRIC   0-6-0

Built: 1959–62 by BR at Darlington or Horwich Works.
Engine: English Electric 6KT of 298 kW (400 hp) at 680 rpm.
Main Generator: English Electric 801.
Traction Motors: English Electric 506.
Maximum Tractive Effort: 111 kN (25000 lbf).
Continuous Tractive Effort: 39 kN (8800 lbf) at 11.6 mph.
Power at Rail: 201 kW (269 hp).   **Train Brakes:** Air & vacuum.
Brake Force: 19 t.   **Dimensions:** 8.92 x 2.59 m.
Weight: 49 t.   **Wheel Diameter:** 1372 mm.
Design Speed: 27 mph.   **Maximum Speed:** 27 mph.
Fuel Capacity: 3037 litres.   **Route Availability:** 5.
Train Supply: Not equipped.

Class 09/0. Built as Class 09.

09002	G	GB	GB Railfreight, Whitemoor Yard, March, Cambs
09006	E	HN	Nemesis Rail, Burton-upon-Trent, Staffordshire (S)
09007	G	LN	London Overground, Willesden Depot, London
09009	G	GB	Miles Platting Stone Terminal, Greater Manchester
09014	DG	HN	Nemesis Rail, Burton-upon-Trent, Staffordshire (S)
09015	E	RS	RSS, Rye Farm, Wishaw, Sutton Coldfield (S)
09022	B	VG	Victoria Group, Port of Boston, Boston
09023	E	ER	European Metal Recycling, Attercliffe, Sheffield

Class 09/1. Converted from Class 08 1992–93 by RFS Industries, Kilnhurst.
110 V electrical equipment.

| 09106 | DB | HN | Barrow HIll Roundhouse, Chesterfield, Derbys (S) |

Class 09/2. Converted from Class 08 1992 by RFS Industries, Kilnhurst.
90 V electrical equipment.

| 09201 | DG | HN | Hope Cement, Hope Cement Works, Derbys (S) |
| 09204 | AW | AV | Arriva TrainCare, Crewe Depot, Cheshire |

Other numbers or names carried:

09007   D3671

1.2. MAIN LINE DIESEL LOCOMOTIVES

CLASS 20　　　　　ENGLISH ELECTRIC　　　　Bo-Bo

Built: 1957–68 by English Electric at Vulcan Foundry, Newton-le-Willows or by Robert Stephenson & Hawthorns at Darlington.
Engine: English Electric 8SVT Mk II of 746 kW (1000 hp) at 850 rpm.
Main Generator: English Electric 819/3C.
Traction Motors: English Electric 526/5D or 526/8D.
Maximum Tractive Effort: 187 kN (42000 lbf).
Continuous Tractive Effort: 111 kN (25000 lbf) at 11 mph.
Power at Rail: 574 kW (770 hp).　　　**Train Brakes:** Air & vacuum.
Brake Force: 35 t.　　　　　　　　　**Dimensions:** 14.25 x 2.67 m.
Weight: 73.4–73.5 t.　　　　　　　　**Wheel Diameter:** 1092 mm.
Design Speed: 75 mph.　　　　　　　**Maximum Speed:** 75 mph.
Fuel Capacity: 1727 litres.　　　　　**Route Availability:** 5.
Train Supply: Not equipped.

Non-standard liveries/numbering:

20056　Yellow with grey cabsides and red solebar. Carries No. "81".
20066　Dark blue with yellow stripes. Carries No. "82".
20088　RFS grey. Carries No. 2017.
20110　Carries original number D8110.
20142　LUL Maroon.
20168　White with green cabsides and solebar. Carries No. "2".
20227　LUL Maroon.
20906　White. Carries No. "3".

Class 20/0. Standard Design.

20007	G	20	MOLO	SK	
20016	B	HN	HNRS	LM (S)	
20056	0	HN	HNRL	SC	
20066	0	HN	HNRL	HO	
20081	B	HN	HNRS	LM (S)	
20088	0	HN	HNRS	LM (S)	
20096	B	HN	GBEE	BH	Ian Goddard 1938–2016
20107	B	HN	GBEE	BH	
20110	G	HN	HNRS	BQ (S)	
20118	FO	HN	GBEE	BH	Saltburn-by-the-Sea
20121	HN	HN	HNRL	BH (S)	
20132	FO	HN	GBEE	BH	Barrow Hill Depot
20142	0	20	MOLO	SK	SIR JOHN BETJEMAN
20166	HN	HN	HNRL	Leeming Bar	
20168	0	HN	HNRL	HO	SIR GEORGE EARLE
20189	B	20	MOLO	SK	
20205	B	2L	MOLO	SK	
20227	0	2L	MOLO	SK	

Class 20/3. Direct Rail Services refurbished locomotives. Details as Class 20/0 except:

Refurbished: 15 locomotives were refurbished 1995–96 by Brush Traction at Loughborough (20301–305) or 1997–98 by RFS(E) at Doncaster (20306–315). Disc indicators or headcode panels removed.

Train Brakes: Air.	**Maximum Speed:** 60 mph (+ 75 mph).
Weight: 73 t (+ 76 t).	**Fuel Capacity:** 2909 (+ 4909) litres.
Brake Force: 35 t (+ 31 t).	**RA:** 5 (+ 6).

20301	(20047)	r	**DS**	DR	XHSS	BH (S)
20302	(20084)	r	**DS**	DR	XHSS	BH (S)
20303	(20127)	r	**DS**	DR	XHSS	BH (S) Max Joule 1958–1999
20304	(20120)	r	**DS**	DR	XHSS	BH (S)
20305	(20095)	r	**DS**	DR	XHSS	BH (S) Gresty Bridge
20308	(20187)	r+	**DS**	DR	XHSS	BH (S)
20309	(20075)	r+	**DS**	DR	XHSS	BH (S)
20311	(20102)	r+	**HN**	HN	GBEE	BH
20312	(20042)	r+	**DS**	DR	XHSS	BH (S)
20314	(20117)	r+	**HN**	HN	GBEE	BH

Class 20/9. Harry Needle Railroad Company (former Hunslet-Barclay/ DRS) locomotives. Details as Class 20/0 except:

Refurbished: 1989 by Hunslet-Barclay at Kilmarnock.

Train Brakes: Air.	**Fuel Capacity:** 1727 (+ 4727) litres.
RA: 5 (+ 6).	

20901	(20101)		**GB**	HN	GBEE	BH
20903	(20083)	+	**DR**	HN	HNRS	BU (S)
20904	(20041)		**DR**	HN	HNRS	BU (S)
20905	(20225)	+	**GB**	HN	GBEE	BH
20906	(20219)		**O**	HN	HNRL	HO

CLASS 25   BR/BEYER PEACOCK/SULZER   Bo-Bo

Built: 1965 by Beyer Peacock at Gorton.
Engine: Sulzer 6LDA28-B of 930 kW (1250 hp) at 750 rpm.
Main Generator: AEI RTB15656.   **Traction Motors:** AEI 253AY.
Maximum Tractive Effort: 200 kN (45000 lbf).
Continuous Tractive Effort: 93 kN (20800 lbf) at 17.1 mph.

Power at Rail: 708 kW (949 hp).	**Train Brakes:** Air & vacuum.
Brake Force: 38 t.	**Dimensions:** 15.39 x 2.73 m.
Weight: 71.5 t.	**Wheel Diameter:** 1143 mm.
Design Speed: 90 mph.	**Maximum Speed:** 60 mph.
Fuel Capacity: 2270 litres.	**Route Availability:** 5.
Train Supply: Not equipped.	

Carries original number D7628.

Only certified for use on Network Rail tracks between Whitby and Battersby, as an extension of North Yorkshire Moors Railway services.

25278		**GG**	NY	MBDL	NY	SYBILLA

CLASS 31   BRUSH/ENGLISH ELECTRIC   A1A-A1A

Built: 1958–62 by Brush Traction at Loughborough.
Engine: English Electric 12SVT of 1100 kW (1470 hp) at 850 rpm.
Main Generator: Brush TG160-48.   **Traction Motors:** Brush TM73-68.
Maximum Tractive Effort: 160 kN (35900 lbf).
Continuous Tractive Effort: 83 kN (18700 lbf) at 23.5 mph.
Power at Rail: 872 kW (1170 hp).   **Train Brakes:** Air & vacuum.
Brake Force: 49 t.   **Dimensions:** 17.30 x 2.67 m.
Weight: 106.7–111 t.   **Wheel Diameter:** 1092/1003 mm.
Design Speed: 90 mph.   **Maximum Speed:** 90 mph.
Fuel Capacity: 2409 litres.   **Route Availability:** 5 or 6.
Train Supply: Not equipped.

Class 31/1. Standard Design. RA: 5.

31105		Y	NR	QADD	ZA (S)
31233	a	Y	NR	QADD	ZA (S)
31285		Y	HN	HNRL	BU (S)

Class 31/4. Electric Train Supply equipment. RA: 6.
Train Supply: Electric, index 66.

31459	B	HN	RVLO	WO (S)
31465	Y	HN	HNRL	WO (S)

CLASS 33   BRCW/SULZER   Bo-Bo

Built: 1960–62 by the Birmingham Railway Carriage & Wagon Company at Smethwick.
Engine: Sulzer 8LDA28 of 1160 kW (1550 hp) at 750 rpm.
Main Generator: Crompton Parkinson CG391B1.
Traction Motors: Crompton Parkinson C171C2.
Maximum Tractive Effort: 200 kN (45000 lbf).
Continuous Tractive Effort: 116 kN (26000 lbf) at 17.5 mph.
Power at Rail: 906 kW (1215 hp).   **Train Brakes:** Air & vacuum.
Brake Force: 35 t.   **Dimensions:** 15.47 x 2.82 (2.64 m 33/2).
Weight: 76-78 t.   **Wheel Diameter:** 1092 mm.
Design Speed: 85 mph.   **Maximum Speed:** 85 mph.
Fuel Capacity: 3410 litres.   **Route Availability:** 6.
Train Supply: Electric, index 48 (750 V DC only).

Non-standard numbering: 33012 Carries original number D6515.

Class 33/0. Standard Design.

33012	G	71	MBDL	SW	Lt Jenny Lewis RN
33025	WC	WC	AWCA	CS	
33029	WC	WC	AWCX	CS (S)	
33030	DR	WC	AWCX	CS (S)	

Class 33/2. Built to former Loading Gauge of Tonbridge–Battle Line.
Equipped with slow speed control.

33207	WC	WC	AWCA	CS	Jim Martin

CLASS 37   ENGLISH ELECTRIC   Co-Co

Built: 1960–66 by English Electric at Vulcan Foundry, Newton-le-Willows or by Robert Stephenson & Hawthorns at Darlington.
Engine: English Electric 12CSVT of 1300 kW (1750 hp) at 850 rpm.
Main Generator: English Electric 822/10G.
Traction Motors: English Electric 538/A.
Maximum Tractive Effort: 247 kN (55500 lbf).
Continuous Tractive Effort: 156 kN (35000 lbf) at 13.6 mph.
Power at Rail: 932 kW (1250 hp).   **Train Brakes:** Air & vacuum.
Brake Force: 50 t.   **Dimensions:** 18.75 x 2.74 m.
Weight: 102.8–108.4 t.   **Wheel Diameter:** 1092 mm.
Design Speed: 90 mph.   **Maximum Speed:** 80 mph.
Fuel Capacity: 4046 (+ 7683) litres. **Route Availability:** 5 (§ 6).
Train Supply: Not equipped.

Non-standard numbering:

37057 Also carries original number D6757.
37424 Also carries the number 37558.
37703 Carries the number 37067.
37905 Also carries original number D6838.

Class 37/0. Standard Design.

37025	**BL**	37	COTS	BH	Inverness TMD
37038 a	**DI**	DR	XHNC	KM	
37057	**G**	CS	COTS	BH	
37059 ar+	**DI**	DR	XHNC	KM	
37069 ar+	**DI**	DR	XHNC	KM	
37099	**CS**	CS	COTS	BH	MERL EVANS 1947–2016
37116 +	**CS**	CS	COTS	BH	
37146	**CE**	CS	COLS	Leeming Bar (S)	
37165 a+	**CE**	WC	AWCX	CS (S)	
37175 a	**CS**	CS	COTS	BH	
37188	**F**	CS	COLS	BH (S)	
37198 +	**Y**	NR	MBDL	BU (S)	CHIEF ENGINEER
37207	**B**	CS	COLS	BH (S)	
37218 ar+	**DI**	DR	XHNC	KM	
37219	**CS**	CS	COTS	BH	Jonty Jarvis 8-12-1998 to 18-3-2005
37254	**CS**	CS	COTS	BH	Cardiff Canton
37259 ar	**DS**	DR	XHNC	KM	

Class 37/4. Refurbished with electric train supply equipment. Main generator replaced by alternator. Regeared (CP7) bogies. Details as Class 37/0 except:
Main Alternator: Brush BA1005A.   **Power At Rail:** 935 kW (1254 hp).
Traction Motors: English Electric 538/5A.
Maximum Tractive Effort: 256 kN (57440 lbf).
Continuous Tractive Effort: 184 kN (41250 lbf) at 11.4 mph.
Weight: 107 t.   **Design Speed:** 80 mph.
Fuel Capacity: 7683 litres.
Train Supply: Electric, index 30.

37401 ar	**BL**	DR	XHCC	KM	Mary Queen of Scots

37402 a	**BL**	DR	XHCC	KM	Stephen Middlemore 23.12.1954–8.6.2013
37403	**BL**	SP	XHCC	KM	Isle of Mull
37405 ar	**DS**	DR	XHAC	KM	
37407	**BL**	DR	XHAC	KM	
37409 ar	**DS**	DR	XHSS	ZA (S)	Lord Hinton
37418	**BL**	HN	MBDL	WH (S)	
37419 ar	**DS**	DR	XHAC	KM	Carl Haviland 1954–2012
37421	**CS**	CS	COTS	BH	
37422 ar	**DR**	DR	XHAC	KM	
37423 ar	**DR**	DR	XHAC	KM	Spirit of the Lakes
37424	**BL**	DR	XHCC	KM	Avro Vulcan XH558
37425 ar	**DS**	DR	XHCC	KM	Sir Robert McAlpine/Concrete Bob

Class 37/5. Refurbished without train supply equipment. Main generator replaced by alternator. Regeared (CP7) bogies. Details as Class 37/4 except:
Power At Rail: 932 kW (1250 hp).
Maximum Tractive Effort: 248 kN (55590 lbf).
Weight: 106.1–110.0 t.
Train Supply: Not equipped.

37503 r§	**E**	EP	EPUK	LR (S)	
37510 a	**DS**	EP	EPUK	LR (S)	
37516 s	**WC**	WC	AWCA	CS	Loch Laidon
37517 as	**LH**	WC	AWCX	CS (S)	
37518 ar	**WC**	WC	AWCA	CS	
37521	**CS**	HN	MBDL	WH (S)	

Class 37/6. Originally refurbished for Nightstar services. Main generator replaced by alternator. UIC jumpers. Details as Class 37/5 except:
Maximum Speed: 90 mph.   **Train Brake:** Air.
Train Supply: Not equipped, but electric through wired.

37601 ad	**EX**	EP	GROG	LR	Perseus
37602 ar	**DS**	DR	XHNC	KM	
37603 a	**DS**	DR	XHSS	ZA (S)	
37604 a	**DS**	DR	XHSS	KM (S)	
37605 ar	**DS**	DR	XHNC	KM	
37606 a	**DS**	DR	XHNC	KM	
37607 ar	**DS**	HN	HNRL	BH	
37608 ard	**EX**	EP	GROG	LR	Andromeda
37609 a	**DI**	DR	XHNC	KM	
37610 ar	**DS**	LD	MBDL	CL (S)	
37611 a	**EX**	EP	EPUK	LR	Pegasus
37612 a	**DS**	HN	HNRL	BH (S)	

Class 37/5 continued.

37667 ars	**DS**	LD	MBDL	CL (S)	
37668 e	**WC**	WC	AWCA	CS	
37669 e	**WC**	WC	AWCA	CS	
37670 r	**DB**	EP	EPUK	LR (S)	
37676 a	**WC**	WC	AWCA	CS (S)	Loch Rannoch
37685 a	**WC**	WC	AWCA	CS	Loch Arkaig

Class 37/7. Refurbished locomotives. Main generator replaced by alternator. Regeared (CP7) bogies. Ballast weights added. Details as Class 37/5 except:
Main Alternator: GEC G564AZ (37800) Brush BA1005A (others).
Maximum Tractive Effort: 276 kN (62000 lbf).
Weight: 120 t.   **Route Availability:** 7.

37703	**DR**	DR	XHSS	BO
37706	**WC**	WC	AWCA	CS
37710	**LH**	WC	AWCX	CS (S)
37712 a	**WC**	WC	AWCX	CS (S)
37716	**DI**	DR	XHNC	KM
37800 d	**EX**	EP	GROG	LR
37884 d	**EX**	EP	GROG	LR

Class 37/9. Refurbished locomotives. New power unit. Main generator replaced by alternator. Ballast weights added. Details as Class 37/4 except:
Engine: * Mirrlees 6MB275T of 1340 kW (1800 hp) or † Ruston 6RK270T of 1340 kW (1800 hp) at 900 rpm.
Main Alternator: Brush BA15005A.
Maximum Tractive Effort: 279 kN (62680 lbf).
Weight: 120 t.   **Route Availability:** 7.
Train Supply: Not equipped.

37901 *	**FO**	CS	COLS	SE (S)
37905 †	**G**	UR	UKRM	LR
37906 †	**FO**	UR	UKRM	LR (S)

Class 97/3. Class 37s refurbished for use on the Cambrian Lines which are signalled by ERTMS. Details as Class 37/0.

97301 (37100) e	**Y**	NR	QETS	ZA	
97302 (37170) e	**Y**	NR	QETS	ZA	
97303 (37178) e	**Y**	NR	QETS	ZA	
97304 (37217) e	**Y**	NR	QETS	ZA	John Tiley

CLASS 40   ENGLISH ELECTRIC   1Co-Co1

Built: 1961 by English Electric at Vulcan Foundry, Newton-le-Willows.
Engine: English Electric 16SVT Mk2 of 1492 kW (2000 hp) at 850 rpm.
Main Generator: English Electric 822/4C.
Traction Motors: English Electric 526/5D or EE526/7D.
Maximum Tractive Effort: 231 kN (52000 lbf).
Continuous Tractive Effort: 137 kN (30900 lbf) at 18.8 mph.

Power at Rail: 1160 kW (1550 hp).	**Train Brakes:** Air & vacuum.
Brake Force: 51 t.	**Dimensions:** 21.18 x 2.78 m.
Weight: 132 t.	**Wheel Diameter:** 914/1143 mm.
Design Speed: 90 mph.	**Maximum Speed:** 90 mph.
Fuel Capacity: 3250 litres.	**Route Availability:** 6.
Train Supply: Steam heating.	

Carries original number 345.

40145	**B**	40	CFSL	BQ

CLASS 43   BREL/PAXMAN   Bo-Bo

Built: 1975–82 by BREL at Crewe Works.
Engine: MTU 16V4000R41R of 1680kW (2250 hp) at 1500 rpm.
(* Paxman 12VP185 of 1565 kW (2100 hp) at 1500 rpm.)
Main Alternator: Brush BA1001B.
Traction Motors: Brush TMH68–46 or GEC G417AZ (43124–152); frame mounted.
Maximum Tractive Effort: 80 kN (17980 lbf).
Continuous Tractive Effort: 46 kN (10340 lbf) at 64.5 mph.
Power at Rail: 1320 kW (1770 hp).   **Train Brakes:** Air.
Brake Force: 35 t.   **Dimensions:** 17.79 x 2.74 m.
Weight: 70.25–75.0 t.   **Wheel Diameter:** 1020 mm.
Design Speed: 125 mph.   **Maximum Speed:** 125 mph.
Fuel Capacity: 4500 litres.   **Route Availability:** 5.
Train Supply: Three-phase electric.

† Buffer fitted.

43013, 43014 & 43062 are fitted with measuring apparatus & front-end cameras.

Power cars 43002, 43013, 43048, 43321 and 43423 carry small commemorative plates to celebrate 40 years of the HST, reading "40 YEARS 1976–2016".

Non-standard and advertising liveries:

43002 Original HST BR blue & yellow.
43027 90 Glorious Years (blue).
43144 Building a Greater West.
43172 We Shall Remember Them.
43238 National Railway Museum 40 Years.

43002	**0**	A	EFPC	LA	Sir Kenneth Grange
43003	**FB**	A	EFPC	LA	ISAMBARD KINGDOM BRUNEL
43004	**FB**	A	EFPC	LA	
43005	**GW**	A	EFPC	LA	
43009	**FB**	A	EFPC	LA	
43010	**FB**	A	EFPC	LA	
43012	**FB**	A	HAPC	LB (S)	
43013 †	**Y**	P	QCAR	EC	
43014 †	**Y**	P	QCAR	EC	The Railway Observer
43015	**FB**	A	EFPC	LA	
43016	**GW**	A	EFPC	LA	
43017	**FB**	A	EFPC	LA	Hannahs discoverhannahs.org
43018	**FB**	A	EFPC	LA	
43020	**FB**	A	EFPC	LA	MTU Power. Passion. Partnership
43021	**FB**	A	HAPC	EC	
43022	**FB**	A	EFPC	LA	The Duke of Edinburgh's Award Diamond Anniversary 1956–2016
43023	**FB**	A	EFPC	LA	SQN LDR HAROLD STARR ONE OF THE FEW
43024	**FB**	A	EFPC	LA	Great Western Society 1961–2011 Didcot Railway Centre

43025		**FB**	A	EFPC	LA	IRO The Institution of Railway Operators
						2000–2010 TEN YEARS
						PROMOTING OPERATIONAL EXCELLENCE
43026		**FB**	A	EFPC	LA	Michael Eavis
43027		**AL**	A	EFPC	LA	
43028		**FB**	A	EFPC	LA	
43029		**FB**	A	EFPC	LA	
43030		**FB**	A	EFPC	LA	Christian Lewis Trust
43031		**FB**	A	EFPC	LA	
43032		**FB**	A	EFPC	LA	
43033		**FB**	A	HAPC	LB (S)	
43034		**FB**	A	EFPC	LA	TravelWatch SouthWest
43035		**FB**	A	EFPC	LA	
43036		**FB**	A	HAPC	LB (S)	
43037		**FB**	A	HAPC	HA	
43040		**FB**	A	EFPC	LA	Bristol St. Philip's Marsh
43041		**GW**	A	EFPC	LE	Meningitis Trust Support for Life
43042		**FB**	A	EFPC	LE	
43043	*	**ST**	P	EMPC	NL	
43044	*	**ST**	P	EMPC	NL	
43045	*	**ST**	P	EMPC	NL	
43046	*	**ST**	P	EMPC	NL	
43047	*	**ST**	P	EMPC	NL	
43048	*	**ST**	P	EMPC	NL	T.C.B. Miller MBE
43049	*	**ST**	P	EMPC	NL	Neville Hill
43050	*	**ST**	P	EMPC	NL	
43052	*	**ST**	P	EMPC	NL	
43053		**FB**	P	EFPC	LE	University of Worcester
43054	*	**ST**	P	EMPC	NL	
43055	*	**ST**	P	EMPC	NL	The Sheffield Star 125 Years
43056		**FB**	P	EFPC	LE	The Royal British Legion
43058	*	**ST**	P	EMPC	NL	
43059	*	**ST**	P	EMPC	NL	
43060	*	**ST**	P	EMPC	NL	
43061	*	**ST**	P	EMPC	NL	The Fearless Foxes
43062		**Y**	P	QCAR	EC	John Armitt
43063		**FB**	P	EFPC	LE	
43064	*	**ST**	P	EMPC	NL	
43066	*	**ST**	P	EMPC	NL	
43069		**FB**	P	EFPC	LE	
43070		**FB**	P	EFPC	LE	The Corps of Royal Electrical and
						Mechanical Engineers
43071		**FB**	P	EFPC	LE	
43073	*	**ST**	P	EMPC	NL	
43075	*	**ST**	P	EMPC	NL	
43076	*	**ST**	P	EMPC	NL	IN SUPPORT OF HELP for HEROES
43078		**FB**	P	EFPC	LE	
43079		**FB**	P	EFPC	LE	
43081	*	**ST**	P	EMPC	NL	
43082	*	**ST**	P	EMPC	NL	RAILWAY children – Fighting for
						street children

43083 *	**ST**	P	EMPC	NL	
43086	**FB**	P	EFPC	LE	
43087	**FB**	P	EFPC	LE	11 Explosive Ordnance Disposal Regiment Royal Logistic Corps
43088	**FB**	P	EFPC	LE	
43089 *	**ST**	P	EMPC	NL	
43091	**FB**	P	EFPC	LE	
43092	**FB**	FG	EFPC	LE	
43093	**GW**	FG	EFPC	LE	Old Oak Common HST Depot 1976–2018
43094	**FB**	FG	EFPC	LE	
43097	**FB**	FG	EFPC	LE	Environment Agency
43098	**FB**	FG	EFPC	LE	
43122	**FB**	FG	EFPC	LE	
43124	**FB**	A	EFPC	LE	
43125	**FB**	A	EFPC	LE	
43126	**FB**	A	HAPC	HA	
43127	**FB**	A	EFPC	LE	Sir Peter Parker 1924–2002 Cotswold Line 150
43128	**FB**	A	EFPC	LE	
43129	**FB**	A	EFPC	LE	
43130	**FB**	A	EFPC	LE	
43131	**FB**	A	EFPC	LE	
43132	**FB**	A	HAPC	EC	Aberdeen Station 150th Anniversary
43133	**FB**	A	EFPC	LE	
43134	**FB**	A	HAPC	LB (S)	
43135	**FB**	A	HAPC	HA	
43136	**FB**	A	EFPC	LE	
43137	**FB**	A	EFPC	LE	Newton Abbot 150
43138	**FB**	A	EFPC	LE	
43139	**FB**	A	EFPC	LE	Driver Stan Martin 25 June 1950 – 6 November 2004
43140	**FB**	A	EFPC	LE	Landore Diesel Depot 1963 Celebrating 50 years 2013/ Depo Diesel Glandŵr 1963 Dathlu 50 Mlynedd 2013
43141	**FB**	A	EFPC	LE	Cardiff Panel Signal Box 1966–2016/ Blwch Signalau Panel Caerdydd 1966–2016
43142	**FB**	A	EFPC	LE	Reading Panel Signal Box 1965–2010
43143	**FB**	A	HAPC	LB (S)	
43144	**AL**	A	EFPC	LE	
43145	**FB**	A	EFPC	LE	
43146	**FB**	A	HAPC	LB (S)	
43147	**FB**	A	EFPC	LE	Royal Marines Celebrating 350 Years
43148	**FB**	A	HAPC	LB (S)	
43149	**FB**	A	EFPC	LE	University of Plymouth
43150	**FB**	A	EFPC	LE	
43151	**FB**	A	EFPC	LE	
43152	**FB**	A	EFPC	LE	

43153	**FB**	FG	EFPC	OO	
43154	**FB**	FG	EFPC	OO	
43155	**FB**	FG	EFPC	OO	The Red Arrows
					50 Seasons of Excellence
43156	**FB**	P	EFPC	OO	Dartington International Summer School
43158	**FB**	FG	EFPC	OO	
43159	**FB**	P	EFPC	OO	
43160	**FB**	P	EFPC	OO	Sir Moir Lockhead OBE
43161	**FB**	P	EFPC	OO	
43162	**FB**	P	EFPC	OO	
43163	**FB**	A	HAPC	LB (S)	
43164	**FB**	A	EFPC	OO	
43165	**FB**	A	EFPC	OO	Prince Michael of Kent
43168	**FB**	A	EFPC	OO	
43169	**FB**	A	EFPC	OO	THE NATIONAL TRUST
43170	**FB**	A	EFPC	OO	
43171	**FB**	A	EFPC	OO	
43172	**AL**	A	EFPC	OO	Harry Patch – The last survivor of
					the trenches
43174	**FB**	A	EFPC	OO	
43175	**FB**	A	EFPC	OO	GWR 175TH ANNIVERSARY
43176	**FB**	A	EFPC	OO	
43177	**FB**	A	EFPC	OO	
43179	**FB**	A	HAPC	HA	
43180	**FB**	P	EFPC	OO	
43181	**FB**	A	EFPC	OO	
43182	**FB**	A	EFPC	OO	
43183	**FB**	A	EFPC	OO	
43185	**IC**	A	EFPC	OO	Great Western
43186	**FB**	A	EFPC	OO	
43187	**GW**	A	EFPC	OO	
43188	**GW**	A	EFPC	OO	
43189	**FB**	A	EFPC	OO	RAILWAY HERITAGE TRUST
43190	**FB**	A	EFPC	OO	
43191	**FB**	A	EFPC	OO	
43192	**FB**	A	EFPC	OO	
43193	**FB**	P	EFPC	OO	
43194	**GW**	FG	EFPC	OO	
43195	**FB**	P	EFPC	OO	
43196	**FB**	P	EFPC	OO	
43197	**FB**	P	EFPC	OO	
43198	**GW**	FG	EFPC	OO	Oxfordshire 2007

Class 43/2. Rebuilt Virgin Trains East Coast, CrossCountry and East Midlands Trains (former Grand Central) power cars. Power cars have been renumbered by adding 200 to their original number or 400 to their original number (EMT), except 43123 which became 43423.

43206 (43006)	**VE**	A	IECP	EC	
43207 (43007)	**XC**	A	EHPC	EC	
43208 (43008)	**VE**	A	IECP	EC	Lincolnshire Echo

43238 (43038)	**AL**	A	IECP	EC	National Railway Museum 40 Years 1975–2015
43239 (43039)	**VE**	A	IECP	EC	
43251 (43051)	**VE**	P	IECP	EC	
43257 (43057)	**VE**	P	IECP	EC	Bounds Green
43272 (43072)	**VE**	P	IECP	EC	
43274 (43074)	**VE**	P	IECP	EC	Spirit of Sunderland
43277 (43077)	**VE**	P	IECP	EC	
43285 (43085)	**XC**	P	EHPC	EC	
43290 (43090)	**VE**	P	IECP	EC	mtu fascination of power
43295 (43095)	**VE**	A	IECP	EC	
43296 (43096)	**VE**	A	IECP	EC	
43299 (43099)	**VE**	P	IECP	EC	
43300 (43100)	**VE**	P	IECP	EC	Craigentinny 100 YEARS 1914–2014
43301 (43101)	**XC**	P	EHPC	EC	
43302 (43102)	**VE**	P	IECP	EC	World Speed Record – HST
43303 (43103)	**XC**	P	EHPC	EC	
43304 (43104)	**XC**	A	EHPC	EC	
43305 (43105)	**VE**	A	IECP	EC	
43306 (43106)	**VE**	A	IECP	EC	
43307 (43107)	**VE**	A	IECP	EC	
43308 (43108)	**VE**	A	IECP	EC	HIGHLAND CHIEFTAIN
43309 (43109)	**VE**	A	IECP	EC	
43310 (43110)	**VE**	A	IECP	EC	
43311 (43111)	**VE**	A	IECP	EC	
43312 (43112)	**VE**	A	IECP	EC	
43313 (43113)	**VE**	A	IECP	EC	
43314 (43114)	**VE**	A	IECP	EC	
43315 (43115)	**VE**	A	IECP	EC	
43316 (43116)	**VE**	A	IECP	EC	
43317 (43117)	**VE**	A	IECP	EC	
43318 (43118)	**VE**	A	IECP	EC	
43319 (43119)	**VE**	A	IECP	EC	
43320 (43120)	**VE**	A	IECP	EC	
43321 (43121)	**XC**	P	EHPC	EC	
43357 (43157)	**XC**	P	EHPC	EC	
43366 (43166)	**XC**	A	EHPC	EC	
43367 (43167)	**VE**	A	IECP	EC	DELTIC 50 1955–2005
43378 (43178)	**XC**	A	EHPC	EC	
43384 (43184)	**XC**	A	EHPC	EC	
43423 (43123) †	**GC**	A	EMPC	DY	
43465 (43065) †	**GC**	A	EMPC	DY	
43467 (43067) †	**GC**	A	EMPC	DY	
43468 (43068) †	**GC**	A	EMPC	DY	
43480 (43080) †	**GC**	A	EMPC	DY	
43484 (43084) †	**GC**	A	EMPC	DY	

CLASS 47   BR/BRUSH/SULZER   Co-Co

Built: 1963–67 by Brush Traction, at Loughborough or by BR at Crewe Works.
Engine: Sulzer 12LDA28C of 1920 kW (2580 hp) at 750 rpm.
Main Generator: Brush TG160-60 Mk4 or TM172-50 Mk1.
Traction Motors: Brush TM64-68 Mk1 or Mk1A.
Maximum Tractive Effort: 267 kN (60000 lbf).
Continuous Tractive Effort: 133 kN (30000 lbf) at 26 mph.
Power at Rail: 1550 kW (2080 hp).   **Train Brakes:** Air.
Brake Force: 61 t.   **Dimensions:** 19.38 x 2.79 m.
Weight: 111.5–120.6 t.   **Wheel Diameter:** 1143 mm.
Design Speed: 95 mph.   **Maximum Speed:** 95 mph.
Fuel Capacity: 3273 (+ 5887).   **Route Availability:** 6 or 7.
Train Supply: Not equipped.

Class 47s exported for use abroad are listed in section 1.6 of this book.

Non-standard liveries/numbering:

47270   Also carries original number 1971.
47501   Carries original number D1944.
47773   Also carries original number D1755.
47798   Royal Train claret with Rail Express Systems markings.
47805   Carries original number D1935.
47830   Also carries original number D1645.

Class 47/0. Standard Design. Built with train air and vacuum brakes.

47194	+	**F**	WC	AWCX	CS (S)	
47237	x+	**WC**	WC	AWCA	CS	
47245	x+	**WC**	WC	AWCA	CS	
47270	+	**B**	WC	AWCA	CS	SWIFT

Class 47/3. Built with train air and vacuum brakes. Details as Class 47/0 except: **Weight:** 113.7 t.

| 47355 | a+ | **K** | WC | AWCX | CS (S) |
| 47368 | | **F** | WC | AWCX | CS (S) |

Class 47/4. Electric Train Supply equipment.
Details as Class 47/0 except:

Weight: 120.4–125.1 t.   **Fuel Capacity:** 3273 (+ 5537) litres.
Train Supply: Electric, index 66.   **Route Availability:** 7.

47492	x	**RX**	WC	AWCX	CS (S)	
47500	x	**WC**	WC	AWCX	CS (S)	
47501	x+	**GG**	LD	MBDL	CL	CRAFTSMAN
47526	x	**BL**	WC	AWCX	CS (S)	
47580	x	**BL**	47	MBDL	TM	County of Essex

Class 47/7. Previously fitted with an older form of TDM.
Details as Class 47/4 except:

Weight: 118.7 t.   **Fuel Capacity:** 5887 litres.
Maximum Speed: 100 mph.

| 47703 | **FR** | HN | HNRL | ZB | |
| 47714 | **AR** | HN | HNRL | Old Dalby | |

Class 47/7. Former Railnet dedicated locomotives.
Details as Class 47/0 except:

Fuel Capacity: 5887 litres.

47727	**CA**	GB	GBDF	ZG	
47739	**CS**	GB	GBDF	ZG	
47746 x	**WC**	WC	AWCA	CS	Chris Fudge 29.7.70 – 22.6.10
47749	**CS**	GB	GBDF	ZG	
47760 x	**WC**	WC	AWCA	CS	
47768	**RX**	WC	AWCX	CS (S)	
47769	**V**	HN	HNRS	BH (S)	Resolve
47772 x	**WC**	WC	AWCA	CS	Carnforth TMD
47773 x	**GG**	70	MBDL	TM	
47776 x	**RX**	WC	AWCX	CS (S)	
47786	**WC**	WC	AWCA	CS	Roy Castle OBE
47787	**WC**	WC	AWCX	CS (S)	Windsor Castle
47790	**VN**	LD	MBDL	CL (S)	

Class 47/4 continued. Route Availability: 6.

47798 x	**O**	NM	MBDL	YK	Prince William
47802 +	**WC**	WC	AWCA	CS	
47804	**WC**	WC	AWCA	CS	
47805 +	**GG**	LD	MBDL	CL	
47810 +	**DI**	LD	MBDL	ZG (S)	
47811 +	**GL**	LD	DHLT	CL (S)	
47812 +	**RB**	RO	SROG	LR	
47813 +	**RO**	RO	GROG	LR	
47815 +	**RB**	RO	GROG	LR	
47816 +	**GL**	LD	DHLT	CL (S)	
47818 +	**DS**	AF	MBDL	ZG (S)	
47826 +	**WC**	WC	AWCA	CS	
47830 +	**GG**	FL	DHLT	CB	BEECHING'S LEGACY
47832 +	**WC**	WC	AWCA	CS	
47841 +	**DS**	LD	MBDL	CL (S)	
47843 +	**RB**	RO	SROG	LR (S)	
47847 +	**BL**	RO	SROG	LR (S)	
47848 +	**RB**	RO	SROG	LR	
47851 +	**WC**	WC	AWCA	CS	
47853 +	**DR**	HN	GBHN	BH (S)	
47854 +	**WC**	WC	AWCA	CS	Diamond Jubilee

CLASS 50   ENGLISH ELECTRIC   Co-Co

Built: 1967–68 by English Electric at Vulcan Foundry, Newton-le-Willows.
Engine: English Electric 16CVST of 2010 kW (2700 hp) at 850 rpm.
Main Generator: English Electric 840/4B.
Traction Motors: English Electric 538/5A.
Maximum Tractive Effort: 216 kN (48500 lbf).

Continuous Tractive Effort: 147 kN (33000 lbf) at 23.5 mph.
Power at Rail: 1540 kW (2070 hp).   **Train Brakes:** Air & vacuum.
Brake Force: 59 t.   **Dimensions:** 20.88 x 2.78 m.
Weight: 116.9 t.   **Wheel Diameter:** 1092 mm.
Design Speed: 105 mph.   **Maximum Speed:** 90 mph.
Fuel Capacity: 4796 litres.   **Route Availability:** 6.
Train Supply: Electric, index 61.

Non-standard numbering:

50007 Also carries original number D407.
50050 Also carries original number D400.

50007	B	50	CFOL	KR	Hercules
50008	B	HT	HTLX	ZA	Thunderer
50017	N	NB	MBDL	WH	Royal Oak
50044	B	50	CFOL	KR	Exeter
50049	BL	50	CFOL	KR	Defiance
50050	B	NB	MBDL	WH	Fearless

CLASS 52   BR/MAYBACH   C-C

Built: 1961–64 by BR at Swindon Works.
Engine: Two Maybach MD655 of 1007 kW (1350 hp) each at 1500 rpm.
Transmission: Hydraulic. Voith L630rV.
Maximum Tractive Effort: 297 kN (66700 lbf).
Continuous Tractive Effort: 201 kN (45200 lbf) at 14.5 mph.
Power at Rail: 1490 kW (2000 hp).   **Train Brakes:** Air & vacuum.
Brake Force: 83 t.   **Dimensions:** 20.70 m x 2.78 m.
Weight: 110 t.   **Wheel Diameter:** 1092 mm.
Design Speed: 90 mph.   **Maximum Speed:** 90 mph.
Fuel Capacity: 3900 litres.   **Route Availability:** 6.
Train Supply: Steam heating.

Never allocated a number in the 1972 number series.

| D1015 | M | DT | MBDL | KR | WESTERN CHAMPION |

CLASS 55   ENGLISH ELECTRIC   Co-Co

Built: 1961 by English Electric at Vulcan Foundry, Newton-le-Willows.
Engine: Two Napier-Deltic D18-25 of 1230 kW (1650 hp) each at 1500 rpm.
Main Generators: Two English Electric 829/1A.
Traction Motors: English Electric 538/A.
Maximum Tractive Effort: 222 kN (50000 lbf).
Continuous Tractive Effort: 136 kN (30500 lbf) at 32.5 mph.
Power at Rail: 1969 kW (2640 hp).   **Train Brakes:** Air & vacuum.
Brake Force: 51 t.   **Dimensions:** 21.18 x 2.68 m.
Weight: 100 t.   **Wheel Diameter:** 1092 mm.
Design Speed: 105 mph.   **Maximum Speed:** 100 mph.
Fuel Capacity: 3755 litres.   **Route Availability:** 5.
Train Supply: Electric, index 66.

Non-standard numbering:

55002	Carries orignal number D9002.
55009	Carries orignal number D9009.
55016	Carries orignal number D9016.

55002	**GG**	NM	MBDL		YK	THE KING'S OWN YORKSHIRE
						LIGHT INFANTRY
55009	**B**	DP	MBDL		BH	ALYCIDON
55016	**GG**	LD	MBDL		CL (S)	GORDON HIGHLANDER
55022	**B**	LD	MBDL		CL	ROYAL SCOTS GREY

CLASS 56   BRUSH/BR/RUSTON   Co-Co

Built: 1976–84 by Electroputere at Craiova, Romania (as sub-contractors for Brush) or BREL at Doncaster or Crewe Works.
Engine: Ruston Paxman 16RK3CT of 2460 kW (3250 hp) at 900 rpm.
Main Alternator: Brush BA1101A.
Traction Motors: Brush TM73-62.
Maximum Tractive Effort: 275 kN (61800 lbf).
Continuous Tractive Effort: 240 kN (53950 lbf) at 16.8 mph.

Power at Rail: 1790 kW (2400 hp).	**Train Brakes:** Air.
Brake Force: 60 t.	**Dimensions:** 19.36 x 2.79 m.
Weight: 126 t.	**Wheel Diameter:** 1143 mm.
Design Speed: 80 mph.	**Maximum Speed:** 80 mph.
Fuel Capacity: 5228 litres.	**Route Availability:** 7.
Train Supply: Not equipped.	

All equipped with Slow Speed Control.

Class 56s exported for use abroad are listed in section 1.6 of this book.

Non-standard liveries:

56009 All over blue.
56303 All over dark green.

56007	**B**	UR	UKRS		LR (S)	
56009	**0**	UR	UKRS		BL (S)	
56018	**FER**	UR	UKRS		LB (S)	
56031	**FER**	UR	UKRS		LR (S)	
56032	**FER**	UR	UKRS		LR (S)	
56037	**E**	UR	UKRS		LR (S)	
56038	**FER**	UR	UKRS		LR (S)	
56049	**CS**	CS	COFS		WH	Robin of Templecombe 1938–2013
56051	**CS**	CS	COLS		WH (S)	
56060	**FER**	UR	UKRS		LR (S)	
56065	**FER**	UR	UKRS		LR (S)	
56069	**FER**	UR	UKRS		LR (S)	
56077	**LH**	UR	UKRS		LR (S)	
56078	**CS**	CS	COFS		WH	
56081	**FO**	UR	UKRL		LR	
56087	**CS**	CS	COFS		WH	
56090	**CS**	CS	COLS		WH (S)	

56091	**FER**	BA	HTLX	LR (S)	
56094	**CS**	CS	COFS	WH	
56096	**CS**	CS	COFS	WH	
56098	**FO**	UR	UKRL	LR	Lost Boys 68–88
56103	**FER**	BA	HTLX	LR (S)	
56104	**FO**	UR	UKRL	LR	
56105	**CS**	CS	COFS	WH	
56106	**FER**	UR	UKRS	LR (S)	
56113	**CS**	CS	COFS	WH	

56301 (56045)	**FA**	56	UKRL	LR	
56302 (56124)	**CS**	CS	COFS	WH	PECO The Railway Modeller 2016 70 Years
56303 (56125)	**O**	BA	HTLX	WH	
56311 (56057)	**DC**	ED	HTLX	LR (S)	
56312 (56003)	**DC**	ED	HTLX	LR (S)	Jeremiah Dixon Son of County Durham Surveyor of the Mason-Dixon Line U.S.A.

CLASS 57   BRUSH/GM   Co-Co

Built: 1964–65 by Brush Traction at Loughborough or BR at Crewe Works as Class 47. Rebuilt 1997–2004 by Brush Traction at Loughborough.
Engine: General Motors 12 645 E3 of 1860 kW (2500 hp) at 904 rpm.
Main Alternator: Brush BA1101D (recovered from Class 56).
Traction Motors: Brush TM64-68 Mark 1 or Mark 1A.
Maximum Tractive Effort: 244.5 kN (55000 lbf).
Continuous Tractive Effort: 140 kN (31500 lbf) at ?? mph.
Power at Rail: 1507 kW (2025 hp).   **Train Brakes:** Air.
Brake Force: 80 t.   **Dimensions:** 19.38 x 2.79 m.
Weight: 120.6 t.   **Wheel Diameter:** 1143 mm.
Design Speed: 75 mph.   **Maximum Speed:** 75 mph.
Fuel Capacity: 5550 litres.   **Route Availability:** 6
Train Supply: Not equipped.

Non-standard livery: 57604 Original Great Western Railway green.

Class 57/0. No Train Supply Equipment. Rebuilt 1997–2000.

57001 (47356)	**WC**	WC	AWCA	CS (S)	
57002 (47322)	**DI**	DR	XHCK	KM	RAIL EXPRESS
57003 (47317)	**DI**	DR	XHSS	ZG (S)	
57004 (47347)	**DS**	DR	XHSS	LW (S)	
57005 (47350)	**AZ**	WC	AWCX	CS (S)	
57006 (47187)	**WC**	WC	AWCX	CS (S)	
57007 (47332)	**DI**	DR	XHCK	KM	
57008 (47060)	**DS**	DR	XHSS	LW (S)	
57009 (47079)	**DS**	DR	XHSS	LW (S)	
57010 (47231)	**DI**	DR	XHSS	LW (S)	
57011 (47329)	**DS**	DR	XHSS	ZG (S)	
57012 (47204)	**DS**	DR	XHSS	LW (S)	

Class 57/3. Electric Train Supply Equipment. Former Virgin Trains locomotives fitted with retractable Dellner couplers. Rebuilt 2002–04. Details as Class 57/0 except:

Engine: General Motors 12645F3B of 2050 kW (2750 hp) at 954 rpm.
Main Alternator: Brush BA1101F (recovered from Class 56) or Brush BA1101G.
Fuel Capacity: 5887 litres.   **Train Supply:** Electric, index 100.
Design Speed: 95 mph.   **Maximum Speed:** 95 mph.
Brake Force: 60 t.   **Weight:** 117 t.

57301	(47845)	d	**DI**	P	XHAC	KM	Goliath
57302	(47827)	d	**DS**	DR	XHSS	ZG (S)	Chad Varah
57303	(47705)	d	**DI**	P	XHAC	KM	Pride of Carlisle
57304	(47807)	d	**DI**	DR	XHVT	KM	Pride of Cheshire
57305	(47822)	d	**VN**	P	XHAC	KM	Northern Princess
57306	(47814)	d	**DI**	P	XHAC	KM	Her Majesty's Railway Inspectorate 175
57307	(47225)	d	**DI**	DR	XHVT	KM	LADY PENELOPE
57308	(47846)	d	**DI**	DR	XHVT	KM	Jamie Ferguson
57309	(47806)	d	**DI**	DR	XHVT	KM	Pride of Crewe
57310	(47831)	d	**DI**	P	XHAC	KM	Pride of Cumbria
57311	(47817)	d	**DS**	DR	XHVT	KM	Thunderbird
57312	(47330)	d	**VN**	P	XHAC	KM	Solway Princess
57313	(47371)		**WC**	WC	AWCA	CS	
57314	(47372)		**WC**	WC	AWCA	CS	
57315	(47234)		**WC**	WC	AWCA	CS	
57316	(47290)		**WC**	WC	AWCA	CS	

Class 57/6. Electric Train Supply Equipment. Prototype ETS loco. Rebuilt 2001. Details as Class 57/0 except:

Main Alternator: Brush BA1101E.   **Fuel Capacity:** 3273 litres.
Train Supply: Electric, index 95.   **Weight:** 113 t.
Design Speed: 95 mph.   **Maximum Speed:** 95 mph.
Brake Force: 60 t.

57601	(47825)	**WC**	WC	AWCA	CS

Class 57/6. Electric Train Supply Equipment. Great Western Railway locomotives. Rebuilt 2004. Details as Class 57/3.

57602	(47337)	**GW**	P	EFOO	OO	Restormel Castle
57603	(47349)	**GW**	P	EFOO	OO	Tintagel Castle
57604	(47209)	**0**	P	EFOO	OO	PENDENNIS CASTLE
57605	(47206)	**GW**	P	EFOO	OO	Totnes Castle

CLASS 59   GENERAL MOTORS   Co-Co

Built: 1985 (59001–004) or 1989 (59005) by General Motors, La Grange, Illinois, USA or 1990 (59101–104), 1994 (59201) and 1995 (59202–206) by General Motors, London, Ontario, Canada.
Engine: General Motors 16-645E3C two stroke of 2460 kW (3300 hp) at 904 rpm.
Main Alternator: General Motors AR11 MLD-D14A.
Traction Motors: General Motors D77B.
Maximum Tractive Effort: 506 kN (113550 lbf).
Continuous Tractive Effort: 291 kN (65300 lbf) at 14.3 mph.
Power at Rail: 1889 kW (2533 hp).   **Train Brakes:** Air.
Brake Force: 69 t.   **Dimensions:** 21.35 x 2.65 m.
Weight: 121 t.   **Wheel Diameter:** 1067 mm.
Design Speed: 60 (* 75) mph.   **Maximum Speed:** 60 (* 75) mph.
Fuel Capacity: 4546 litres.   **Route Availability:** 7.
Train Supply: Not equipped.

Class 59/0. Owned by Aggregate Industries and GB Railfreight.

59001	**AI**	AI	XYPO	MD	YEOMAN ENDEAVOUR
59002	**AI**	AI	XYPO	MD	ALAN J DAY
59003	**GB**	GB	GBYH	RR	YEOMAN HIGHLANDER
59004	**AI**	AI	XYPO	MD	PAUL A HAMMOND
59005	**AI**	AI	XYPO	MD	KENNETH J PAINTER

Class 59/1. Owned by Hanson UK.

59101	**HA**	HA	XYPA	MD	Village of Whatley
59102	**HA**	HA	XYPA	MD	Village of Chantry
59103	**HA**	HA	XYPA	MD	Village of Mells
59104	**HA**	HA	XYPA	MD	Village of Great Elm

Class 59/2. Owned by DB Cargo.

59201	*	**DB**	DB	WDAM	MD	
59202	*	**DB**	DB	WDAM	MD	Alan Meddows Taylor MD Mendip Rail Limited
59203	*	**DB**	DB	WDAM	MD	
59204	*	**DB**	DB	WDAM	MD	
59205	*b	**DB**	DB	WDAM	MD	
59206	*b	**DB**	DB	WDAM	MD	John F. Yeoman Rail Pioneer

CLASS 60   BRUSH/MIRRLEES   Co-Co

Built: 1989–93 by Brush Traction at Loughborough.
Engine: Mirrlees 8MB275T of 2310 kW (3100 hp) at 1000 rpm.
Main Alternator: Brush BA1006A.
Traction Motors: Brush TM2161A.
Maximum Tractive Effort: 500 kN (106500 lbf).
Continuous Tractive Effort: 336 kN (71570 lbf) at 17.4 mph.
Power at Rail: 1800 kW (2415 hp).   **Train Brakes:** Air.

Brake Force: 74 t (+ 62 t).   **Dimensions:** 21.34 x 2.64 m.
Weight: 129 t (+ 131 t).   **Wheel Diameter:** 1118 mm.
Design Speed: 62 mph.   **Maximum Speed:** 60 mph.
Fuel Capacity: 4546 (+ 5225) litres. **Route Availability:** 8.
Train Supply: Not equipped.

All equipped with Slow Speed Control.

* Refurbished locomotives.

60034, 60064, 60070, 60072, 60073, 60077, 60084 and 60090 carry their
names on one side only.

60500 originally carried the number 60016.

Non-standard and Advertising liveries:

60066 Powering Drax (silver).
60081 Original Great Western Railway green.
60099 Tata Steel (silver).

60001 *	**DB**	DB	WCAT	TO	
60002 +*	**CS**	CS	COLO	TO	
60003 +	**E**	DB	WQDA	TO (S)	FREIGHT TRANSPORT ASSOCIATION
60004 +	**E**	DB	WQDA	TO (S)	
60005 +	**E**	DB	WQDA	TO (S)	
60006	**CU**	DB	WQDA	TO (S)	
60007 +*	**DB**	DB	WCBT	TO	The Spirit of Tom Kendell
60008	**E**	DB	WQDA	TO (S)	Sir William McAlpine
60009	**E**	DB	WQBA	TO (S)	
60010 +*	**DB**	DB	WQAB	TO	
60011	**DB**	DB	WCAT	TO	
60012 +	**E**	DB	WQBA	TO (S)	
60013	**EG**	DB	WQDA	TO (S)	Robert Boyle
60014	**EG**	DB	WQDA	TO (S)	
60015 +*	**DB**	DB	WCBT	TO	
60017 +*	**DB**	DB	WCBT	TO	
60018	**E**	DB	WQDA	TO (S)	
60019 *	**DB**	DB	WCAT	TO	Port of Grimsby & Immingham
60020 +*	**DB**	DB	WCBT	TO	The Willows
60021 +*	**CS**	CS	COLO	TO	
60022 +	**E**	DB	WQDA	TO (S)	
60023 +	**E**	DB	WQDA	TO (S)	
60024 *	**DB**	DB	WQAB	TO (S)	Clitheroe Castle
60025 +	**E**	DB	WQDA	TO (S)	
60026 +*	**CS**	CS	COLO	TO·	
60027 +	**E**	DB	WQDA	TO (S)	
60028 +	**EG**	DB	WQCA	CE (S)	
60029	**E**	DB	WQCA	CE (S)	
60030 +	**E**	DB	WQDA	TO (S)	
60031	**E**	DB	WQDA	TO (S)	
60032	**F**	DB	WQDA	TO (S)	
60033 +	**CU**	DB	WQCA	TO (S)	Tees Steel Express
60034	**EG**	DB	WQBA	TO (S)	Carnedd Llewelyn

60035	**E**	DB	WQAB	TO (S)	
60036	**E**	DB	WQAB	TO (S)	GEFCO
60037 +	**E**	DB	WQDA	TO (S)	
60038 +	**E**	DB	WQCA	CE (S)	
60039 *	**DB**	DB	WCAT	TO	Dove Holes
60040 *	**DB**	DB	WQAA	TO (S)	The Territorial Army Centenary
60041 +	**E**	DB	WQCA	TO (S)	
60042	**E**	DB	WQDA	TO (S)	
60043	**E**	DB	WQBA	TO (S)	
60044 *	**DB**	DB	WCAT	TO	Dowlow
60045	**E**	DB	WQAB	TO (S)	The Permanent Way Institution
60046 +	**EG**	DB	WQCA	CE (S)	
60047 *	**CS**	CS	COLO	TO	
60048	**E**	DB	WQCA	TO (S)	
60049	**E**	DB	WQAB	TO (S)	
60050	**E**	DB	WQDA	TO (S)	
60051 +	**E**	DB	WQDA	TO (S)	
60052 +	**E**	DB	WQDA	TO (S)	Glofa Twr – The last deep mine in Wales – Tower Colliery
60053	**E**	DB	WQBA	TO (S)	
60054 +*	**DB**	DB	WCBT	TO	
60055 +	**EG**	DB	WQCA	CE (S)	
60056 +*	**CS**	CS	COLO	TO	
60057	**EG**	DB	WQBA	TO (S)	Adam Smith
60058 +	**E**	DB	WQBA	TO (S)	
60059 +*	**DB**	DB	WCBT	TO	Swinden Dalesman
60060	**EG**	DB	WQBA	TO (S)	
60061	**F**	DB	WQCA	TO (S)	
60062 *	**DB**	DB	WQAB	TO (S)	Stainless Pioneer
60063 *	**DB**	DB	WCAT	TO	
60064 +	**EG**	DB	WQBA	TO (S)	Back Tor
60065	**E**	DB	WCAT	TO	Spirit of JAGUAR
60066 *	**AL**	DB	WCAT	TO	
60067	**EG**	DB	WQBA	TO (S)	
60068	**EG**	DB	WQBA	TO (S)	
60069	**E**	DB	WQBA	TO (S)	Slioch
60070 +	**F**	DB	WQBA	TO (S)	John Loudon McAdam
60071 +	**E**	DB	WQAB	TO (S)	Ribblehead Viaduct
60072	**EG**	DB	WQBA	TO (S)	Cairn Toul
60073	**EG**	DB	WQBA	TO (S)	Cairn Gorm
60074 *	**DB**	DB	WCAT	TO	
60075	**E**	DB	WQBA	TO (S)	
60076 *	**CS**	CS	COLO	TO	Dunbar
60077 +	**EG**	DB	WQBA	TO (S)	Canisp
60078	**ML**	DB	WQBA	TO (S)	
60079 *	**DB**	DB	WQAB	TO (S)	
60080 +	**E**	DB	WQBA	TO (S)	
60081 +	**0**	DB	WQBA	TO (S)	
60082	**EG**	DB	WQBA	CE (S)	
60083	**E**	DB	WQBA	TO (S)	
60084	**EG**	DB	WQBA	TO (S)	Cross Fell

60085	*	**CS**	CS	COLO	TO	
60086		**EG**	DB	WQBA	TO (S)	
60087	*	**CS**	CS	COLO	TO	CLIC Sargent www.clicsargent.co.uk
60088		**F**	DB	WQBA	TO (S)	
60089	+	**E**	DB	WQBA	TO (S)	
60090	+	**EG**	DB	WQBA	TO (S)	Quinag
60091	+*	**DB**	DB	WCBT	TO	Barry Needham
60092	+*	**DB**	DB	WQAA	TO (S)	
60093		**E**	DB	WQBA	TO (S)	
60094		**E**	DB	WQBA	TO (S)	Rugby Flyer
60095	*	**CS**	CS	COLO	TO	
60096	+*	**CS**	CS	COLO	TO	
60097	+	**E**	DB	WQBA	TO (S)	
60098	+	**E**	DB	WQBA	TO (S)	
60099		**AL**	DB	WQAB	TO (S)	
60100		**DB**	DB	WCAT	TO	
60500		**E**	DB	WQBA	TO (S)	

CLASS 66   GENERAL MOTORS/EMD   Co-Co

Built: 1998–2008 by General Motors/EMD, London, Ontario, Canada (Model JT42CWR (low emission locomotives Model JT42CWRM)) or 2013–16 by EMD/Progress Rail, Muncie, Indiana (66752–779).
Engine: General Motors 12N-710G3B-EC two stroke of 2385 kW (3200 hp) at 904 rpm.
Main Alternator: General Motors AR8/CA6.
Traction Motors: General Motors D43TR.
Maximum Tractive Effort: 409 kN (92000 lbf).
Continuous Tractive Effort: 260 kN (58390 lbf) at 15.9 mph.
Power at Rail: 1850 kW (2480 hp).   **Train Brakes:** Air.
Brake Force: 68 t.   **Dimensions:** 21.35 x 2.64 m.
Weight: 127 t.   **Wheel Diameter:** 1120 mm.
Design Speed: 87.5 mph.   **Maximum Speed:** 75 mph.
Fuel Capacity: 6550 litres.   **Route Availability:** 7.
Train Supply: Not equipped.

All equipped with Slow Speed Control.

Class 66s previously used in the UK but now in use abroad are listed in section 1.6 of this book. Some of the DBC 66s moved to France return to Great Britain from time to time for maintenance or operational requirements.

Class 66 delivery dates. The Class 66 design and delivery evolved over an 18-year period, with more than 400 locomotives delivered. For clarity the delivery dates (by year) for each batch of locomotives is as follows:

66001–250	EWS (now DB Cargo). 1998–2000 (some now in use in France or Poland and ten sold to GB Railfreight).
66301–305	Fastline. 2008. Now used by DRS.
66401–410	DRS. 2003. Now in use with GB Railfreight or Colas Rail and renumbered 66733–737 and 66742–746 (66734 since scrapped).
66411–420	DRS. 2006. Now leased by Freightliner (66411/412/417 exported to Poland).

66421–430	DRS. 2007
66431–434	DRS. 2008
66501–505	Freightliner. 1999
66506–520	Freightliner. 2000
66521–525	Freightliner. 2000 (66521 since scrapped).
66526–531	Freightliner. 2001
66532–537	Freightliner. 2001
66538–543	Freightliner. 2001
66544–553	Freightliner. 2001
66554	Freightliner. 2002†
66555–566	Freightliner. 2002
66567–574	Freightliner. 2003. 66573–574 now used by Colas Rail and renumbered 66846–847.
66575–577	Freightliner. 2004. Now used by Colas Rail and renumbered 66848–850.
66578–581	Freightliner. 2005. Now used by GBRf and renumbered 66738–741.
66582–594	Freightliner. 2007 (66582/583/584/586 exported to Poland).
66595–599	Freightliner. 2008
66601–606	Freightliner. 2000
66607–612	Freightliner. 2002 (66607/609/611/612 exported to Poland)
66613–618	Freightliner. 2003
66619–622	Freightliner. 2005
66623–625	Freightliner. 2007 (66624/625 exported to Poland).
66701–707	GB Railfreight. 2001
66708–712	GB Railfreight. 2002
66713–717	GB Railfreight. 2003
66718–722	GB Railfreight. 2006
66723–727	GB Railfreight. 2006
66728–732	GB Railfreight. 2008
66747–749	Built in 2008 as 20078968-004/006/007 (DE 6313/15/16) for Crossrail AG in the Netherlands but never used. Sold to GB Railfreight in 2012.
66750–751	Built in 2003 as 20038513-01/04 and have worked in the Netherlands, Germany and Poland. GBRf secured these two locomotives on lease in 2013.
66752–772	GB Railfreight. 2014
66773–779	GB Railfreight. 2016
66780–789	GB Railfreight. 1998–2000. Former DB Cargo locomotives acquired in 2017 that will be renumbered in this GBRf number series.
66951–952	Freightliner. 2004
66953–957	Freightliner. 2008

† Replacement for 66521, written off in the Great Heck accident in 2001.

Advertising and non-standard liveries:

66522	Shanks Waste (one half of loco Freightliner green and one half Shanks' Waste light green).
66623	Bardon Aggregates blue.
66709	MSC – blue with images of a container ship.
66718	London Underground 150, (black).
66720	Day and night (various colours, different on each side).

66721   London Underground 150 (white with tube map images).
66727   Maritime (blue).
66775   Also carries the number F231.
66779   BR dark green.

Class 66/0. DB Cargo-operated locomotives. Ten locomotives have been sold to GB Railfreight and will be renumbered into the 66780–789 series during 2018.

All fitted with Swinghead Automatic "Buckeye" Combination Couplers except 66001 and 66002.

† Fitted with additional lights and drawgear for Lickey banking duties.

t Fitted with tripcocks for working over London Underground tracks between Harrow-on-the-Hill and Amersham.

66001 t	**DB**	DB	WBAE	TO	
66002	**E**	DB	WBAT	TO	
66003	**E**	DB	WBAT	TO	
66004	**E**	DB	WBAE	TO	
66005	**E**	DB	WBAT	TO	
66006	**E**	DB	WBAT	TO	
66007	**E**	DB	WBAR	TO	
66008	**E**	GB	GBOB	RR	*(to be renumbered 66780)*
66009	**DB**	DB	WBAE	TO	
66011	**E**	DB	WBAE	TO	
66012	**E**	DB	WBAT	TO	
66013	**E**	DB	WBAE	TO	
66014	**E**	DB	WBAR	TO	
66015	**E**	DB	WBAR	TO	
66016	**DB**	GB	GBOB	RR	*(to be renumbered 66781)*
66017 t	**DB**	DB	WBAR	TO	
66018	**DB**	DB	WBAE	TO	
66019 t	**DB**	DB	WBAR	TO	
66020	**DB**	DB	WBAE	TO	
66021	**E**	DB	WBAR	TO	
66023	**E**	DB	WBAT	TO	
66024	**E**	DB	WBAE	TO	
66025	**E**	DB	WBAR	TO	
66027	**E**	DB	WBAT	TO	
66030	**E**	DB	WBAR	TO	
66031	**E**	DB	WBAT	TO	
66034	**DB**	DB	WBAE	TO	
66035	**E**	DB	WBAE	TO	
66037	**E**	DB	WBAR	TO	
66039	**E**	DB	WBAE	TO	
66040	**E**	DB	WBAR	TO	
66041	**DB**	DB	WBAE	TO	
66043	**E**	DB	WQAA	TO (S)	
66044	**DB**	DB	WBAE	TO	
66046	**E**	GB	GBOB	RR	*(to be renumbered 66782)*
66047	**E**	DB	WBAT	TO	
66050	**E**	DB	WBAE	TO	EWS Energy

66051	E	DB	WBAR	TO	
66053	E	DB	WBAE	TO	
66054	E	DB	WBAR	TO	
66055 †	**DB**	DB	WBAR	TO	Alain Thauvette
66056 †	E	DB	WBLE	TO	
66057 †	E	DB	WBLT	TO	
66058 †	**DB**	GB	GBOB	RR	*(to be renumbered 66783)*
66059 †	E	DB	WBLE	TO	
66060	E	DB	WBAT	TO	
66061	E	DB	WBAE	TO	
66063	E	DB	WBAE	TO	
66065	E	DB	WBAR	TO	
66066	**DB**	DB	WBAR	TO	Geoff Spencer
66067	E	DB	WBAR	TO	
66068	E	DB	WBAR	TO	
66069	E	DB	WBAR	TO	
66070	E	DB	WBAT	TO	
66074	E	DB	WBAE	TO	
66075	E	DB	WBAT	TO	
66076	E	DB	WBAE	TO	
66077	E	DB	WBAR	TO	
66078	E	DB	WBAE	TO	
66079	E	DB	WBAR	TO	James Nightall G.C.
66080	E	DB	WBAE	TO	
66081	E	GB	GBOB	RR	*(to be renumbered 66784)*
66082	**DB**	DB	WBAE	TO	
66083	E	DB	WBAR	TO	
66084	E	DB	WBAR	TO	
66085	E	DB	WBAR	TO	
66086	E	DB	WBAT	TO	
66087	E	DB	WBAT	TO	
66088	E	DB	WBAE	TO	
66089	E	DB	WBAR	TO	
66090	E	DB	WBAE	TO	
66091	E	DB	WBAR	TO	
66092	E	DB	WBAE	TO	
66093	E	DB	WBAE	TO	
66094	E	DB	WBAE	TO	
66095	E	DB	WBAE	TO	
66096	E	DB	WBAR	TO	
66097	**DB**	DB	WBAE	TO	
66098	E	DB	WBAE	TO	
66099 r	E	DB	WBBE	TO	
66100 r	E	DB	WBBE	TO	
66101 r	**DB**	DB	WBBE	TO	
66102 r	E	DB	WBBE	TO	
66103 r	E	DB	WBBE	TO	
66104 r	E	DB	WBAR	TO	
66105 r	E	DB	WBAR	TO	
66106 r	E	DB	WBBE	TO	
66107 r	E	DB	WBAR	TO	

66108 r	E	DB	WBBE	TO	
66109	E	DB	WBAR	TO	
66110 r	E	DB	WBBE	TO	
66111 r	E	DB	WBBT	TO	
66112 r	E	DB	WBBE	TO	
66113 r	E	DB	WBBE	TO	
66114 r	DB	DB	WBBE	TO	
66115	E	DB	WBAT	TO	
66116	E	DB	WBAE	TO	
66117	E	DB	WBAT	TO	
66118	DB	DB	WBAE	TO	
66119	E	DB	WBAE	TO	
66120	E	DB	WBAE	TO	
66121	E	DB	WBAE	TO	
66122	E	DB	WBAE	TO	
66124	DB	DB	WBAR	TO	
66125	E	DB	WBAE	TO	
66126	E	DB	WBAE	TO	
66127	E	DB	WBAT	TO	
66128	DB	DB	WBAE	TO	
66129	E	DB	WBAR	TO	
66130	DB	DB	WBAR	TO	
66131	E	DB	WBAT	TO	
66132	E	GB	GBOB	RR	*(to be renumbered 66785)*
66133	E	DB	WBAE	TO	
66134	E	DB	WBAE	TO	
66135	E	DB	WBAE	TO	
66136	DB	DB	WBAE	TO	
66137	E	DB	WBAE	TO	
66138	E	DB	WBAR	TO	
66139	E	DB	WBAE	TO	
66140	E	DB	WBAE	TO	
66141	E	GB	GBOB	RR	*(to be renumbered 66786)*
66142	E	DB	WBAR	TO	
66143	E	DB	WBAE	TO	
66144	E	DB	WBAR	TO	
66145	E	DB	WBAE	TO	
66147	E	DB	WBAT	TO	
66148	E	DB	WBAE	TO	
66149	DB	DB	WBAE	TO	
66150	DB	DB	WBAE	TO	
66151	E	DB	WBAE	TO	
66152	DB	DB	WBAE	TO	Derek Holmes Railway Operator
66154	E	DB	WBAE	TO	
66155	E	DB	WBAE	TO	
66156	E	DB	WBAE	TO	
66158	E	DB	WBAE	TO	
66160	E	DB	WBAE	TO	
66161	E	DB	WBAE	TO	
66162	E	DB	WBAR	TO	
66164	E	DB	WBAE	TO	

66165	E	DB	WBAR	TO	
66167	E	DB	WBAE	TO	
66168	E	DB	WBAE	TO	
66169	E	DB	WBAR	TO	
66170	E	DB	WBAE	TO	
66171	E	DB	WBAR	TO	
66172	E	DB	WBAT	TO	PAUL MELLENEY
66174	E	DB	WBAE	TO	
66175	E	DB	WBAE	TO	
66176	E	DB	WBAR	TO	
66177	E	DB	WBAT	TO	
66181	E	DB	WBAR	TO	
66182	E	DB	WBAE	TO	
66183	E	DB	WBAE	TO	
66184	E	GB	GBOB	RR	*(to be renumbered 66787)*
66185	DB	DB	WBAE	TO	DP WORLD London Gateway
66186	E	DB	WBAT	TO	
66187	E	DB	WBAE	TO	
66188	E	DB	WBAR	TO	
66192	DB	DB	WBAR	TO	
66194	E	DB	WBAR	TO	
66197	E	DB	WBAE	TO	
66198	E	DB	WBAE	TO	
66199	E	DB	WBAE	TO	
66200	E	DB	WBAE	TO	
66206	DB	DB	WBAE	TO	
66207	E	DB	WBAE	TO	
66221	E	DB	WBAT	TO	
66230	DB	DB	WBAE	TO	
66238	E	GB	GBOB	RR	*(to be renumbered 66788)*
66250	E	GB	GBOB	RR	*(to be renumbered 66789)*

Class 66/3. Former Fastline-operated locomotives now operated by DRS. Low emission. Details as Class 66/0 except:

Engine: EMD 12N-710G3B-T2 two stroke of 2420 kW (3245 hp) at 904 rpm.
Traction Motors: General Motors D43TRC.
Fuel Capacity: 5150 litres.

66301	DR	BN	XHIM	KM	Kingmoor TMD
66302	DR	BN	XHIM	KM	
66303	DR	BN	XHIM	KM	
66304	DR	BN	XHIM	KM	
66305	DR	BN	XHIM	KM	

Class 66/4. Low emission. Macquarie Group-owned. Details as Class 66/3.

66413	DS	MQ	DFIN	LD	
66414	FH	MQ	DFIN	LD	
66415	DS	MQ	DFIN	LD	
66416	FH	MQ	DFIN	LD	
66418	FH	MQ	DFIN	LD	PATRIOT – IN MEMORY OF FALLEN RAILWAY EMPLOYEES

66419	**DS**	MQ	DFIN	LD	
66420	**FH**	MQ	DFIN	LD	
66421	**DR**	MQ	XHIM	KM	
66422	**DR**	MQ	XHIM	KM	
66423	**DR**	MQ	XHIM	KM	
66424	**DR**	MQ	XHIM	KM	
66425	**DR**	MQ	XHIM	KM	
66426	**DR**	MQ	XHIM	KM	
66427	**DR**	MQ	XHIM	KM	
66428	**DR**	MQ	XHIM	KM	
66429	**DR**	MQ	XHIM	KM	
66430	**DR**	MQ	XHIM	KM	
66431	**DR**	MQ	XHIM	KM	
66432	**DR**	MQ	XHIM	KM	
66433	**DR**	MQ	XHIM	KM	
66434	**DR**	MQ	XHIM	KM	

Class 66/5. Standard design. Freightliner-operated locomotives. Details as Class 66/0.

66501	**FL**	P	DFIM	LD	Japan 2001
66502	**FL**	P	DFIM	LD	Basford Hall Centenary 2001
66503	**FL**	P	DFIM	LD	The RAILWAY MAGAZINE
66504	**FH**	P	DFIM	LD	
66505	**FL**	P	DFIM	LD	
66506	**FL**	E	DFIM	LD	Crewe Regeneration
66507	**FL**	E	DFIM	LD	
66508	**FL**	E	DFIM	LD	
66509	**FL**	E	DFIM	LD	
66510	**FL**	E	DFIM	LD	
66511	**FL**	E	DFIM	LD	
66512	**FL**	E	DFIM	LD	
66513	**FL**	E	DFIM	LD	
66514	**FL**	E	DFIM	LD	
66515	**FL**	E	DFIM	LD	
66516	**FL**	E	DFIM	LD	
66517	**FL**	E	DFIM	LD	
66518	**FL**	E	DFIM	LD	
66519	**FL**	E	DFIM	LD	
66520	**FL**	E	DFIM	LD	
66522	**AL**	E	DFIM	LD	
66523	**FL**	E	DFIM	LD	
66524	**FL**	E	DFIM	LD	
66525	**FL**	E	DFIM	LD	
66526	**FL**	P	DFIM	LD	Driver Steve Dunn (George)
66528	**FH**	P	DFIM	LD	Madge Elliot MBE
					Borders Railway Opening 2015
66529	**FL**	P	DFIM	LD	
66531	**FL**	P	DFIM	LD	
66532	**FL**	P	DFIM	LD	P&O Nedlloyd Atlas
66533	**FL**	P	DFIM	LD	Hanjin Express/Senator Express
66534	**FL**	P	DFIM	LD	OOCL Express

66536	**FL**	P	DFIM	LD	
66537	**FL**	P	DFIM	LD	
66538	**FL**	E	DFIM	LD	
66539	**FL**	E	DFIM	LD	
66540	**FL**	E	DFIM	LD	Ruby
66541	**FL**	E	DFIM	LD	
66542	**FL**	E	DFIM	LD	
66543	**FL**	E	DFIM	LD	
66544	**FL**	P	DFIM	LD	
66545	**FL**	P	DFIM	LD	
66546	**FL**	P	DFIM	LD	
66547	**FL**	P	DFIM	LD	
66548	**FL**	P	DFIM	LD	
66549	**FL**	P	DFIM	LD	
66550	**FL**	P	DFIM	LD	
66551	**FL**	P	DFIM	LD	
66552	**FL**	P	DFIM	LD	Maltby Raider
66553	**FL**	P	DFIM	LD	
66554	**FL**	E	DFIM	LD	
66555	**FL**	E	DFIM	LD	
66556	**FL**	E	DFIM	LD	
66557	**FL**	E	DFIM	LD	
66558	**FL**	E	DFIM	LD	
66559	**FL**	E	DFIM	LD	
66560	**FL**	E	DFIM	LD	
66561	**FL**	E	DFIM	LD	
66562	**FL**	E	DFIM	LD	
66563	**FL**	E	DFIM	LD	
66564	**FL**	E	DFIM	LD	
66565	**FL**	E	DFIM	LD	
66566	**FL**	E	DFIM	LD	
66567	**FL**	E	DFIM	LD	
66568	**FL**	E	DFIM	LD	
66569	**FL**	E	DFIM	LD	
66570	**FL**	E	DFIM	LD	
66571	**FL**	E	DFIM	LD	
66572	**FL**	E	DFIM	LD	

Class 66/5. Freightliner-operated low emission locomotives. Details as Class 66/3.

66585	**FL**	MQ	DFIN	LD	
66586	**FL**	MQ	DFIN	LD	
66587	**FL**	MQ	DFIN	LD	
66588	**FL**	MQ	DFIN	LD	
66589	**FL**	MQ	DFIN	LD	
66590	**FL**	MQ	DFIN	LD	
66591	**FL**	MQ	DFIN	LD	
66592	**FL**	MQ	DFIN	LD	Johnson Stevens Agencies
66593	**FL**	MQ	DFIN	LD	3MG MERSEY MULTIMODAL GATEWAY
66594	**FL**	MQ	DFIN	LD	NYK Spirit of Kyoto
66595	**FL**	BN	DFIN	LD	
66596	**FL**	BN	DFIN	LD	

66597	**FL**	BN	DFIN	LD	Viridor
66598	**FL**	BN	DFIN	LD	
66599	**FL**	BN	DFIN	LD	

Class 66/6. Freightliner-operated locomotives with modified gear ratios.
Details as Class 66/0 except:

Maximum Tractive Effort: 467 kN (105080 lbf).
Continuous Tractive Effort: 296 kN (66630 lbf) at 14.0 mph.
Design Speed: 65 mph.   **Maximum Speed:** 65 mph.

66601	**FL**	P	DFHH	LD	The Hope Valley
66602	**FL**	P	DFHH	LD	
66603	**FL**	P	DFHH	LD	
66604	**FL**	P	DFHH	LD	
66605	**FL**	P	DFHH	LD	
66606	**FL**	P	DFHH	LD	
66607	**FL**	P	DFHH	LD	
66610	**FL**	P	DFHH	LD	
66613	**FL**	E	DFHH	LD	
66614	**FL**	E	DFHH	LD	1916 POPPY 2016
66615	**FL**	E	DFHH	LD	
66616	**FL**	E	DFHH	LD	
66617	**FL**	E	DFHH	LD	
66618	**FL**	E	DFHH	LD	Railways Illustrated Annual Photographic Awards Alan Barnes
66619	**FL**	E	DFHH	LD	Derek W. Johnson MBE
66620	**FL**	E	DFHH	LD	
66621	**FL**	E	DFHH	LD	
66622	**FL**	E	DFHH	LD	

Class 66/6. Freightliner-operated low emission locomotive with modified gear ratios. Details as Class 66/6 except:

Fuel Capacity: 5150 litres.

| 66623 | **0** | MQ | DFHH | LD | Bill Bolsover |

Class 66/7. Standard design. GB Railfreight-operated locomotives. Details as Class 66/0.

66701	**GB**	E	GBBT	RR	
66702	**GB**	E	GBBT	RR	Blue Lightning
66703	**GB**	E	GBBT	RR	Doncaster PSB 1981–2002
66704	**GB**	E	GBBT	RR	Colchester Power Signalbox
66705	**GB**	E	GBBT	RR	Golden Jubilee
66706	**GB**	E	GBBT	RR	Nene Valley
66707	**GB**	E	GBBT	RR	Sir Sam Fay GREAT CENTRAL RAILWAY
66708	**GB**	E	GBBT	RR	Jayne
66709	**AL**	E	GBBT	RR	Sorrento
66710	**GB**	E	GBBT	RR	Phil Packer BRIT
66711	**AI**	E	GBBT	RR	Sence
66712	**GB**	E	GBBT	RR	Peterborough Power Signalbox
66713	**GB**	E	GBBT	RR	Forest City
66714	**GB**	E	GBBT	RR	Cromer Lifeboat

66715	**GB**	E	GBBT	RR	VALOUR – IN MEMORY OF ALL RAILWAY EMPLOYEES WHO GAVE THEIR LIVES FOR THEIR COUNTRY
66716	**GB**	E	GBBT	RR	LOCOMOTIVE & CARRIAGE INSTITUTION CENTENARY 1911–2011
66717	**GB**	E	GBBT	RR	Good Old Boy

66718–751. GB Railfreight locomotives.

Details as Class 66/0 except 66718–732/747–749 as below:

Engine: EMD 12N-710G3B-T2 two stroke of 2420 kW (3245 hp) at 904 rpm.
Traction Motors: General Motors D43TRC.
Fuel Capacity: 5546 litres (66718–722) or 5150 litres (66723–732/747–749).

66747–749 were originally built for Crossrail AG in the Netherlands.

66750/751 were originally built for mainland Europe in 2003.

66718		**AL**	E	GBLT	RR	Sir Peter Hendy CBE
66719		**GB**	E	GBLT	RR	METRO-LAND
66720		**0**	E	GBLT	RR	
66721		**AL**	E	GBLT	RR	Harry Beck
66722		**GB**	E	GBLT	RR	Sir Edward Watkin
66723		**GB**	E	GBLT	RR	Chinook
66724		**GB**	E	GBLT	RR	Drax Power Station
66725		**GB**	E	GBLT	RR	SUNDERLAND
66726		**GB**	E	GBLT	RR	SHEFFIELD WEDNESDAY
66727		**AL**	E	GBLT	RR	Maritime One
66728		**GB**	P	GBLT	RR	Institution of Railway Operators
66729		**GB**	P	GBLT	RR	DERBY COUNTY
66730		**GB**	P	GBLT	RR	Whitemoor
66731		**GB**	P	GBLT	RR	interhub GB
66732		**GB**	P	GBLT	RR	GBRf The First Decade 1999–2009 John Smith – MD
66733	(66401) r	**GB**	P	GBFM	RR	Cambridge PSB
66735	(66403)	**GB**	P	GBBT	RR	
66736	(66404) r	**GB**	P	GBFM	RR	WOLVERHAMPTON WANDERERS
66737	(66405) r	**GB**	P	GBFM	RR	Lesia
66738	(66578) r	**GB**	BN	GBBT	RR	HUDDERSFIELD TOWN
66739	(66579)	**GB**	BN	GBFM	RR	Bluebell Railway
66740	(66580) r	**GB**	BN	GBFM	RR	Sarah
66741	(66581)	**GB**	BN	GBBT	RR	Swanage Railway
66742	(66406, 66841)	**GB**	BN	GBBT	RR	ABP Port of Immingham Centenary 1912–2012
66743	(66407, 66842) r	**M**	BN	GBFM	RR	
66744	(66408, 66843)	**GB**	BN	GBBT	RR	Crossrail
66745	(66409, 66844)	**GB**	BN	GBRT	RR	Modern Railways The first 50 years
66746	(66410, 66845) r	**M**	BN	GBFM	RR	
66747	(20078968-007)	**GB**	GB	GBEB	RR	

66748	(20078968-004)	**GB**	GB	GBEB	RR	West Burton 50
66749	(20078968-006)	**GB**	GB	GBEB	RR	
66750	(20038513-01)	**GB**	BN	GBEB	RR	Bristol Panel Signal Box
66751	(20038513-04) c	**GB**	BN	GBEB	RR	Inspiration Delivered Hitachi Rail Europe

66752–779. Low emission. New build locomotives. Details as Class 66/3.

66752	**GB**	GB	GBEL	RR	The Hoosier State
66753	**GB**	GB	GBEL	RR	EMD Roberts Road
66754	**GB**	GB	GBEL	RR	Northampton Saints
66755	**GB**	GB	GBEL	RR	
66756	**GB**	GB	GBEL	RR	Royal Corps of Signals
66757	**GB**	GB	GBEL	RR	West Somerset Railway
66758	**GB**	GB	GBEL	RR	
66759	**GB**	GB	GBEL	RR	Chippy
66760	**GB**	GB	GBEL	RR	David Gordon Harris
66761	**GB**	GB	GBEL	RR	Wensleydale Railway Association 25 Years 1990–2015
66762	**GB**	GB	GBEL	RR	
66763	**GB**	GB	GBEL	RR	Severn Valley Railway
66764	**GB**	GB	GBEL	RR	
66765	**GB**	GB	GBEL	RR	
66766	**GB**	GB	GBEL	RR	
66767	**GB**	GB	GBEL	RR	
66768	**GB**	GB	GBEL	RR	
66769	**GB**	GB	GBEL	RR	
66770	**GB**	GB	GBEL	RR	
66771	**GB**	GB	GBEL	RR	
66772	**GB**	GB	GBEL	RR	
66773	**GB**	GB	GBNB	RR	
66774	**GB**	GB	GBNB	RR	
66775	**GB**	GB	GBNB	RR	HMS Argyll
66776	**GB**	GB	GBNB	RR	Joanne
66777	**GB**	GB	GBNB	RR	Annette
66778	**GB**	GB	GBNB	RR	Darius Cheskin
66779	**0**	GB	GBEL	RR	EVENING STAR

66780–789. Standard design. Former DB Cargo locomotives acquired by GB Railfreight in 2017. Details as Class 66/0.

66780	(66008)	GB
66781	(66016)	GB
66782	(66046)	GB
66783	(66058)	GB
66784	(66081)	GB
66785	(66132)	GB
66786	(66141)	GB
66787	(66184)	GB
66788	(66238)	GB
66789	(66250)	GB

Class 66/8. Standard design. Colas Rail locomotives. Details as Class 66/0.

66846	(66573)	**CS**	CS	COLO	HJ	
66847	(66574)	**CS**	CS	COLO	HJ	
66848	(66575)	**CS**	CS	COLO	HJ	
66849	(66576)	**CS**	CS	COLO	HJ	Wylam Dilly
66850	(66577)	**CS**	CS	COLO	HJ	David Maidment OBE

Class 66/9. Freightliner locomotives. Low emission "demonstrator" locomotives. Details as Class 66/3.

* **Fuel Capacity:** 5905 litres.

66951	*	**FL**	E	DFIN	LD
66952		**FL**	E	DFIN	LD

Class 66/5. Freightliner-operated low emission locomotives. Owing to the 665xx number range being full, subsequent deliveries of 66/5s were numbered from 66953 onwards. Details as Class 66/5 (low emission).

66953	**FL**	BN	DFIN	LD	
66954	**FL**	BN	DFIN	LD	
66955	**FL**	BN	DFIN	LD	
66956	**FL**	BN	DFIN	LD	
66957	**FL**	BN	DFIN	LD	Stephenson Locomotive Society 1909–2009

CLASS 67   ALSTOM/GENERAL MOTORS   Bo-Bo

Built: 1999–2000 by Alstom at Valencia, Spain, as sub-contractors for General Motors (General Motors model JT42 HW-HS).
Engine: GM 12N-710G3B-EC two stroke of 2385 kW (3200 hp) at 904 rpm.
Main Alternator: General Motors AR9A/HEP7/CA6C.
Traction Motors: General Motors D43FM.
Maximum Tractive Effort: 141 kN (31770 lbf).
Continuous Tractive Effort: 90 kN (20200 lbf) at 46.5 mph.
Power at Rail: 1860 kW.   **Train Brakes:** Air.
Brake Force: 78 t.   **Dimensions:** 19.74 x 2.72 m.
Weight: 90 t.   **Wheel Diameter:** 965 mm.
Design Speed: 125 mph.   **Maximum Speed:** 125 mph (* 80 mph).
Fuel Capacity: 4927 litres.   **Route Availability:** 8.
Train Supply: Electric, index 66.

All equipped with Slow Speed Control and Swinghead Automatic "Buckeye" Combination Couplers.

67004, 67007, 67009 and 67011 were fitted with cast iron brake blocks for working the Fort William Sleeper.

Non-standard liveries:

67026 Diamond Jubilee silver.
67029 All over silver with DB logos.

67001	**AB**	DB	WQAA	TO (S)	
67002	**AB**	DB	WAAC	CE	
67003	**AB**	DB	WAAC	CE	
67004 r*	**DB**	DB	WQAA	TO (S)	
67005	**RZ**	DB	WAAC	CE	Queen's Messenger
67006	**RZ**	DB	WAAC	CE	Royal Sovereign
67007 r*	**E**	DB	WABC	CE	
67008	**E**	DB	WAAC	CE	
67009 r*	**E**	DB	WQAA	CE (S)	
67010	**DB**	DB	WAAC	CE	
67011 r*	**E**	DB	WQAB	CE (S)	
67012	**CM**	DB	WAAC	CE	
67013	**DB**	DB	WAAC	CE	
67014	**CM**	DB	WAAC	CE	
67015	**DB**	DB	WAWC	CE	
67016	**E**	DB	WAWC	CE	
67017	**E**	DB	WQAB	CE (S)	Arrow
67018	**DB**	DB	WAAC	CE	Keith Heller
67019	**E**	DB	WQBA	TO (S)	
67020	**E**	DB	WAAC	CE	
67021	**PC**	DB	WAAC	CE	
67022	**E**	DB	WAAC	CE	
67023	**CS**	CS	COTS	RU	Stella
67024	**PC**	DB	WAAC	CE	
67025	**E**	DB	WQBA	CE (S)	Western Star
67026	**O**	DB	WAAC	CE (S)	Diamond Jubilee
67027	**CS**	CS	COTS	RU	Charlotte
67028	**DB**	DB	WAAC	CE	
67029	**O**	DB	WACC	CE	Royal Diamond
67030 r	**E**	DB	WABC	CE	

CLASS 68   VOSSLOH/STADLER   Bo-Bo

New Vossloh/Stadler mixed-traffic locomotives now in service with DRS.

Built: 2012–16 by Vossloh/Stadler, Valencia, Spain.
Engine: Caterpillar C175-16 of 2800 kW (3750 hp) at 1740 rpm.
Main Alternator: ABB WGX560.
Traction Motors: 4 x AC frame mounted ABB 4FRA6063.
Maximum Tractive Effort: 317 kN (71260 lbf).
Continuous Tractive Effort: 250 kN (56200 lbf) at 20.5 mph.

Power at Rail:	**Train Brakes:** Air.
Brake Force: 73 t.	**Dimensions:** 20.50 x 2.69 m.
Weight: 85 t.	**Wheel Diameter:** 1100 mm.
Design Speed: 100 mph.	**Maximum Speed:** 100 mph.
Fuel Capacity: 6000 litres.	**Route Availability:** 7.
Train Supply: Electric, index 96.	

68008–015 have been modified to operate in push-pull mode on the Chiltern
Railways locomotive-hauled sets.

68019–034 are to be modified to operate with the new TransPennine Express Mark 5A stock from late 2018.

68001	**DI**	BN	XHVE	CR	Evolution
68002	**DI**	BN	XHVE	CR	Intrepid
68003	**DI**	BN	XHVE	CR	Astute
68004	**DI**	BN	XHVE	CR	Rapid
68005	**DI**	BN	XHVE	CR	Defiant
68006	**SR**	BN	XHVE	CR	Daring
68007	**SR**	BN	XHVE	CR	Valiant
68008	**DI**	BN	XHVE	CR	Avenger
68009	**DI**	BN	XHVE	CR	Titan
68010	**CM**	BN	XHCE	CR	Oxford Flyer
68011	**CM**	BN	XHCE	CR	
68012	**CM**	BN	XHCE	CR	
68013	**CM**	BN	XHCE	CR	
68014	**CM**	BN	XHCE	CR	
68015	**CM**	BN	XHCE	CR	
68016	**DI**	BN	XHVE	CR	Fearless
68017	**DI**	BN	XHVE	CR	Hornet
68018	**DI**	BN	XHVE	CR	Vigilant
68019	**TP**	BN	XHTP	CR	Brutus
68020	**DI**	BN	XHTP	CR	Reliance
68021	**TP**	BN	XHTP	CR	Tireless
68022	**DI**	BN	XHTP	CR	Resolution
68023	**DI**	BN	XHTP	CR	Achilles
68024	**DI**	BN	XHTP	CR	Centaur
68025	**DI**	BN	XHTP	CR	Superb
68026	**DR**	BN	XHTP	CR	
68027	**DR**	BN	XHTP	CR	
68028	**DR**	BN	XHTP	CR	
68029	**DR**	BN	XHVE	CR	
68030	**DR**	BN	XHTP	CR	
68031	**DR**	BN	XHTP	CR	
68032	**DR**	BN	XHVE	CR	
68033	**DI**	BN	XHVE	CR	
68034	**DI**	BN	XHVE	CR	

CLASS 70   GENERAL ELECTRIC   Co-Co

GE "PowerHaul" locomotives. 70012 was badly damaged whilst being unloaded in 2011 and was returned to Pennsylvania.

70801 (built as 70099) is a Turkish-built demonstrator that arrived in Britain in 2012. Colas Rail leased this locomotive and then in 2013 ordered a further nine locomotives (70802–810) that were delivered in 2014. 70811–817 followed in 2017.

Built: 2009–17 by General Electric, Erie, Pennsylvania, USA or by TÜLOMSAS, Eskişehir, Turkey (70801).
Engine: General Electric PowerHaul P616LDA1 of 2848 kW (3820 hp) at 1500 rpm.

Main Alternator: General Electric GTA series.
Traction Motors: AC-GE 5GEB30.
Maximum Tractive Effort: 544 kN (122000 lbf).
Continuous Tractive Effort: 427 kN (96000 lbf) at ?? mph.
Power at Rail: **Train Brakes:** Air.
Brake Force: 96.7 t.   **Dimensions:** 21.71 x 2.64 m.
Weight: 129 t.   **Wheel Diameter:** 1066 mm.
Design Speed: 75 mph.   **Maximum Speed:** 75 mph.
Fuel Capacity: 6000 litres.   **Route Availability:** 7.
Train Supply: Not equipped.

Class 70/0. Freightliner locomotives.

70001	**FH**	MQ	DHLT	LD (S)	PowerHaul
70002	**FH**	MQ	DHLT	LD (S)	
70003	**FH**	MQ	DFGI	LD	
70004	**FH**	MQ	DFGI	LD	The Coal Industry Society
70005	**FH**	MQ	DFGI	LD	
70006	**FH**	MQ	DFGI	LD	
70007	**FH**	MQ	DFGI	LD	
70008	**FH**	MQ	DFGI	LD	
70009	**FH**	MQ	DHLT	LD (S)	
70010	**FH**	MQ	DFGI	LD	
70011	**FH**	MQ	DFGI	LD	
70013	**FH**	MQ	DHLT	LD (S)	
70014	**FH**	MQ	DFGI	LD	
70015	**FH**	MQ	DFGI	LD	
70016	**FH**	MQ	DHLT	LD (S)	
70017	**FH**	MQ	DFGI	LD	
70018	**FH**	MQ	DHLT	LD (S)	
70019	**FH**	MQ	DFGI	LD	
70020	**FH**	MQ	DFGI	LD	

Class 70/8. Colas Rail locomotives.

70801	**CS**	LF	COLO	CF
70802	**CS**	LF	COLO	CF
70803	**CS**	LF	COLO	CF
70804	**CS**	LF	COLO	CF
70805	**CS**	LF	COLO	CF
70806	**CS**	LF	COLO	CF
70807	**CS**	LF	COLO	CF
70808	**CS**	LF	COLO	CF
70809	**CS**	LF	COLO	CF
70810	**CS**	LF	COLO	CF
70811	**CS**	CS	COLO	CF
70812	**CS**	CS	COLO	CF
70813	**CS**	CS	COLO	CF
70814	**CS**	CS	COLO	CF
70815	**CS**	CS	COLO	CF
70816	**CS**	CS	COLO	CF
70817	**CS**	CS	COLO	CF

1.3. ELECTRO-DIESEL & ELECTRIC LOCOMOTIVES

CLASS 73/1   BR/ENGLISH ELECTRIC   Bo-Bo

Electro-diesel locomotives which can operate either from a DC supply or using power from a diesel engine.

Built: 1965–67 by English Electric Co. at Vulcan Foundry, Newton-le-Willows.
Engine: English Electric 4SRKT of 447 kW (600 hp) at 850 rpm.
Main Generator: English Electric 824/5D.
Electric Supply System: 750 V DC from third rail.
Traction Motors: English Electric 546/1B.
Maximum Tractive Effort (Electric): 179 kN (40000 lbf).
Maximum Tractive Effort (Diesel): 160 kN (36000 lbf).
Continuous Rating (Electric): 1060 kW (1420 hp) giving a tractive effort of 35 kN (7800 lbf) at 68 mph.
Continuous Tractive Effort (Diesel): 60 kN (13600 lbf) at 11.5 mph.
Maximum Rail Power (Electric): 2350 kW (3150 hp) at 42 mph.
Train Brakes: Air, vacuum & electro-pneumatic († Air & electro-pneumatic).
Brake Force: 31 t.   **Dimensions:** 16.36 x 2.64 m.
Weight: 77 t.   **Wheel Diameter:** 1016 mm.
Design Speed: 90 mph.   **Maximum Speed:** 90 mph.
Fuel Capacity: 1409 litres.   **Route Availability:** 6.
Train Supply: Electric, index 66 (on electric power only).

Formerly numbered E6007–E6020/E6022–E6026/E6028–E6049 (not in order).

Locomotives numbered in the 732xx series are classed as 73/2 and were originally dedicated to Gatwick Express services.

There have been two separate Class 73 rebuild projects. For GBRf 11 locomotives were rebuilt at Brush, Loughborough with a 1600 hp MTU engine (renumbered 73961–971). For Network Rail 73104/211 were rebuilt at RVEL Derby (now Loram) with 2 x QSK19 750 hp engines (now 73951/952).

Non-standard liveries and numbering:

73110   Carries original number E6016.
73128   Two-tone grey.
73139   Light blue & light grey.
73235   Plain dark blue.

73101	**PC**	LO	RVLO	ZA (S)	
73107	**GB**	GB	GBED	SE	Tracy
73109	**GB**	GB	GBED	SE	
73110	**B**	GB	GBBR	ZG (S)	
73119	**GB**	GB	GBED	SE	Borough of Eastleigh
73128	**GB**	GB	GBED	SE	O.V.S. BULLEID C.B.E.
73133	**TT**	TT	MBED	ZG	
73134	**IC**	GB	GBBR	LB (S)	Woking Homes 1885–1985

▲ BR Blue-liveried 07007 shunts London Underground stock in Eastleigh Works on 08/03/07. **Brian Denton**

▼ 08600 is seen at AV Dawson, Ayrton Rail Terminal, Middlesbrough during a Branch Line Society railtour of the site on 25/06/17. **Courtesy Branch Line Society**

▲ Wabtec black-liveried 08853 shunts 91131 outside Doncaster Works on 27/04/17.　　**Robin Ralston**

▼ HNRC-liveried 20314 and 20311 haul a train of LUL S Stock from Banbury to Derby Litchurch Lane at Whitacre Junction on 15/08/17.　　**Steven Harrow**

▲ DCR Green-liveried 31452 passes Elford, near Tamworth, with 4Z02 12.34 Derby RTC–Okehampton on 05/05/17 hauling a new Rail Grinding Machine for testing.

Kevin Payne

▲ BR Green liveried 33012 approaches Worgret Junction with the 16.23 Swanage–Wareham on 15/06/17, one of the new seasonal through services from the Swanage Railway onto the National Rail network. **Robert Pritchard**

▲ Colas Rail-liveried 37219 and 37421 top-and-tail 1Z22 12.00 Mossend–Derby test train near Lanark Junction on 23/10/16. **Robin Ralston**

▼ BR Blue-liveried 40145 passes Deganwy with a 1Z37 18.18 Llandudno–Preston railtour on 10/06/17. **Kevin Payne**

▲ CrossCountry-liveried 43285 and 43384 are seen near Cobbinshaw, between Carstairs and Edinburgh, with the 06.01 Glasgow Central–Paignton on 03/06/17. **Robin Ralston**

▲ Virgin Trains East Coast-liveried 43314 leads the 11.30 Edinburgh–London King's Cross through Grantham on 23/04/17. **Robert Pritchard**

▼ Rail Operations Group-liveried 47813 passes Northolt Park with the 12.53 London Marylebone–Birmingham Moor Street additional on 26/08/17. **Jamie Squibbs**

▲ BR Blue-liveried 50007 and BR Revised blue-liveried 50049 haul 20059 and 20188 as a 08.56 Bishops Lydeard–Butterley near Cogload Junction on 14/06/17. **Tony Christie**

▼ Colas Rail-liveried 56302 and 56087 top-and-tail a set of RHTT wagons from York to Gloucester, seen at Eckington, Worcs, on 30/09/16. **Dave Gommersall**

▲ Belmond Northern Belle-liveried 57305 passes Kidsgrove with a Preston–Rugeley Northern Belle tour on 23/04/17. **Cliff Beeton**

▼ Hanson-liveried 59103 passes Burghfield, west of Reading, with 7C77 12.40 Acton Yard–Merehead on 02/11/16. **Brian Denton**

▲ DB Cargo-liveried 60059 passes Barrow-upon-Trent heading towards Stenson Junction with 6M00 14.27 Humber–Kingsbury oil tanks on 04/08/17. **Paul Biggs**

▼ Freightliner Powerhaul-liveried 66418 is seen near Melton Mowbray with 4M20 10.14 Felixstowe–Lawley Street intermodal on 25/03/17. **Paul Biggs**

▲ Direct Rail Services-liveried 66431 passes Larbert Junction with 4H47 05.04 Mossend–Inverness intermodal on 14/07/17. **Ian Lothian**

▼ Colas Rail-liveried 67027 and 67023 top-and-tail a 1Z12 High Marnham–Derby test train at Trowell Junction on 21/06/17. **Steve Donald**

▲ New Direct Rail Services-liveried 68003 and 68024 arrive at Great Yarmouth (while on hire to Greater Anglia) with the 08.09 from Norwich on 14/06/17.

Robert Pritchard

▲ The first Class 68 in the new TransPennine Express livery is 68021, seen here at Crewe Gresty Bridge depot on 04/09/17. **Courtesy TransPennine Express**

▼ Freightliner PowerHaul-liveried 70019 passes Thurmaston heading for Leicester with the diverted 4M67 12.13 Felixstowe–Crewe on 15/04/17. **Paul Biggs**

▲ Caledonian Sleeper-liveried 73968 passes Dalrigh with the 10.30 Oban–Polmadie empty Sleeper stock on 25/03/17. **Andrew Wills**

▼ Caledonian Sleeper-liveried 86101 is seen at London Euston on 13/08/17.
Brian Garvin

▲ New DRS-liveried 88002 passes Wandel, near Abington, with 4M48 19.04 Mossend–Daventry intermodal on 20/06/17. **Robin Ralston**

▼ Freightliner PowerHaul-liveried 90045 passes Old Linslade with the 20.44 Inverness–London Euston Sleeper on 21/03/17. **Nigel Gibbs**

▲ Virgin Trains East Coast-liveried 91132 passes Ganwick, near Hadley Wood, with the 18.27 London King's Cross–Newcastle on 18/06/17.　**Robert Pritchard**

▼ Caledonian Sleeper-liveried 92010 crosses Slateford Viaduct with the 06.40 Carstairs–Edinburgh Sleeper portion on 18/07/17.　**Ian Lothian**

73136	**GB**	GB	GBED	SE	Mhairi
73138	**Y**	NR	QADD	ZA	
73139	**0**	LO	RVLO	ZA (S)	
73141	**GB**	GB	GBED	SE	Charlotte
73201 †	**B**	GB	GBED	SE	Broadlands
73202 †	**SN**	P	MBED	SL	Graham Stenning
73212 †	**GB**	GB	GBED	SE	Fiona
73213 †	**GB**	GB	GBED	SE	Rhodalyn
73235 †	**0**	P	HYWD	BM	

CLASS 73/9 (RVEL)   BR/RVEL   Bo-Bo

The 7395x number series is reserved for rebuilt Network Rail locomotives.

Rebuilt: Re-engineered by RVEL Derby 2013–15.
Engine: 2 x QSK19 of 560 kW (750 hp) at 1800 rpm (total 1120 kw (1500 hp)).
Main Alternator: 2 x Marathon Magnaplus.
Electric Supply System: 750 V DC from third rail.
Traction Motors: English Electric 546/1B.
Maximum Tractive Effort (Electric): 179 kN (40000 lbf).
Maximum Tractive Effort (Diesel): 179 kN (40000 lbf).
Continuous Rating (Electric): 1060 kW (1420 hp) giving a tractive effort of 35 kN (7800 lbf) at 68 mph.
Continuous Tractive Effort (Diesel): 990 kW (1328 hp) giving a tractive effort of 33 kN (7420 lbf) at 68 mph.
Maximum Rail Power (Electric): 2350 kW (3150 hp) at 42 mph.
Train Brakes: Air.   **Brake Force:** 31 t.
Weight: 77 t.   **Dimensions:** 16.36 x 2.64 m.
Maximum Speed: 90 mph.   **Wheel Diameter:** 1016 mm.
Fuel Capacity: 2260 litres.   **Route Availability:** 6.
Train Supply: Not equipped.

| 73951 (73104) | **Y** | LO | QADD | ZA | Malcolm Brinded |
| 73952 (73211) | **Y** | LO | QADD | ZA | Janis Kong |

CLASS 73/9 (GBRf)   BR/BRUSH   Bo-Bo

GBRf Class 73s rebuilt at Brush Loughborough. 73961–965 are normally used on Network Rail contracts and 73966–971 are used by Caledonian Sleeper.

Rebuilt: Re-engineered by Brush, Loughborough 2014–16.
Engine: MTU 8V4000 R43L of 1195 kW (1600 hp) at 1800 rpm.
Main Alternator: Lechmotoren SDV 87.53-12.
Electric Supply System: 750 V DC from third rail (73961–965 only).
Traction Motors: English Electric 546/1B.
Maximum Tractive Effort (Electric): 179 kN (40000 lbf).
Maximum Tractive Effort (Diesel): 179 kN (40000 lbf).
Continuous Rating (Electric): 1060 kW (1420 hp) giving a tractive effort of 35 kN (7800 lbf) at 68 mph.
Continuous Tractive Effort (Diesel):
Maximum Rail Power (Electric): 2350 kW (3150 hp) at 42 mph.
Train Brakes: Air.   **Brake Force:** 31 t.

Weight: 77 t.
Maximum Speed: 90 mph.
Fuel Capacity: 1409 litres.
Dimensions: 16.36 x 2.64 m.
Wheel Diameter: 1016 mm.
Route Availability: 6.
Train Supply: Electric, index 38 (electric & diesel).

73961	(73209)	**GB** GB	GBNR	SE	Alison
73962	(73204)	**GB** GB	GBNR	SE	Dick Mabbutt
73963	(73206)	**GB** GB	GBNR	SE	Janice
73964	(73205)	**GB** GB	GBNR	SE	Jeanette
73965	(73208)	**GB** GB	GBNR	SE	

73966–971 have been rebuilt for Caledonian Sleeper but their third rail electric capability has been retained. They have a higher Train Supply index and a slightly higher fuel capacity. Details as 73961–965 except:
Fuel Capacity: 1509 litres.   **Train Supply:** Electric, index 96.

73005 and 73006 were originally assembled at Eastleigh Works.

73966	(73005) d	**CA** GB	GBCS	EC
73967	(73006) d	**CA** GB	GBCS	EC
73968	(73117) d	**CA** GB	GBCS	EC
73969	(73105) d	**CA** GB	GBCS	EC
73970	(73103) d	**CA** GB	GBCS	EC
73971	(73207) d	**CA** GB	GBCS	EC

CLASS 86   BR/ENGLISH ELECTRIC   Bo-Bo

Built: 1965–66 by English Electric Co at Vulcan Foundry, Newton-le-Willows or by BR at Doncaster Works.
Electric Supply System: 25 kV AC 50 Hz overhead.
Traction Motors: AEI 282BZ axle hung.
Maximum Tractive Effort: 207 kN (46500 lbf).
Continuous Rating: 3010 kW (4040 hp) giving a tractive effort of 85 kN (19200 lbf) at 77.5 mph.
Maximum Rail Power: 4550 kW (6100 hp) at 49.5 mph.
Train Brakes: Air.
Dimensions: 17.83 x 2.65 m.
Wheel Diameter: 1156 mm.
Design Speed: 110–125 mph.
Route Availability: 6.
Brake Force: 40 t.
Weight: 83–86.8 t.
Train Supply: Electric, index 74.
Maximum Speed: 100 mph.

Formerly numbered E3101–E3200 (not in order).

Class 86s exported for use abroad are listed in section 1.6 of this book.

Class 86/1. Class 87-type bogies & motors. Details as above except:

Traction Motors: GEC 412AZ frame mounted.
Maximum Tractive Effort: 258 kN (58000 lbf).
Continuous Rating: 3730 kW (5000 hp) giving a tractive effort of 95 kN (21300 lbf) at 87 mph.
Maximum Rail Power: 5860 kW (7860 hp) at 50.8 mph.
Wheel Diameter: 1150 mm.
Design Speed: 110 mph.   **Maximum Speed:** 110 mph.

86101	**CA** EL	GBCH	WN	Sir William A Stanier FRS	

Class 86/2. Standard design rebuilt with resilient wheels & Flexicoil suspension. Details as in main class heading.

Non-standard livery:

86259 BR "Electric blue". Also carries number E3137.

86229		**V**	FL	EPEX	LM (S)	
86251		**V**	FL	EPEX	LM (S)	
86259	x	**0**	PP	MBEL	WN	Les Ross

Class 86/4. Details as Class 86/2 except:

Traction Motors: AEI 282AZ axle hung.
Maximum Tractive Effort: 258 kN (58000 lbf).
Continuous Rating: 2680 kW (3600 hp) giving a tractive effort of 89 kN (20000 lbf) at 67 mph.
Maximum Rail Power: 4400 kW (5900 hp) at 38 mph.
Weight: 83–83.9 t.
Design Speed: 100 mph.   **Maximum Speed:** 100 mph.

86401	**CA**	EL	GBCH	WN	Mons Meg

Class 86/6. Freightliner-operated locomotives.

Previously numbered in the Class 86/0 and 86/4 series'. 86608 was also regeared and renumbered 86501 between 2000 and 2016.

Details as Class 86/4 except:
Traction Motors: AEI 282AZ axle hung.
Maximum Speed: 75 mph.   **Train Supply:** Electric, isolated.

86604	**FL**	FL	DFNC	CB
86605	**FL**	FL	DFNC	CB
86607	**FL**	FL	DFNC	CB
86608	**FL**	FL	DFNC	CB
86609	**FL**	FL	DFNC	CB
86610	**FL**	FL	DFNC	CB
86612	**FL**	FL	DFNC	CB
86613	**FL**	FL	DFNC	CB
86614	**FL**	FL	DFNC	CB
86622	**FH**	FL	DFNC	CB
86627	**FL**	FL	DFNC	CB
86628	**FL**	FL	DFNC	CB
86632	**FL**	FL	DFNC	CB
86637	**FH**	FL	DFNC	CB
86638	**FL**	FL	DFNC	CB
86639	**FL**	FL	DFNC	CB

CLASS 87   BREL/GEC   Bo-Bo

Built: 1973–75 by BREL at Crewe Works.
Electric Supply System: 25 kV AC 50 Hz overhead.
Traction Motors: GEC G412AZ frame mounted.
Maximum Tractive Effort: 258 kN (58000 lbf).

Continuous Rating: 3730 kW (5000 hp) giving a tractive effort of 95 kN (21300 lbf) at 87 mph.
Maximum Rail Power: 5860 kW (7860 hp) at 50.8 mph.

Train Brakes: Air.	**Brake Force:** 40 t.
Dimensions: 17.83 x 2.65 m.	**Weight:** 83.3 t.
Wheel Diameter: 1150 mm.	**Train Supply:** Electric, index 95.
Design Speed: 110 mph.	**Maximum Speed:** 110 mph.

Route Availability: 6.

Class 87s exported for use abroad are listed in section 1.6 of this book.

87002	**CA** EL	GBCH	WN	Royal Sovereign

CLASS 88   VOSSLOH/STADLER   Bo-Bo

Ten new Vossloh/Stadler bi-mode locomotives for DRS.

Built: 2015–16 by Vossloh/Sladler, Valencia, Spain.
Electric Supply System: 25 kV AC 50 Hz overhead.
Engine: Caterpillar C27 12-cylinder 708 kW (950 hp) at 1750 rpm.
Main Alternator: ABB AMXL400.
Traction Motors: ABB AMXL400.
Maximum Tractive Effort (Electric): 317 kN (71 260 lbf).
Maximum Tractive Effort (Diesel): 317 kN (71 260 lbf).
Continuous Rating: 4000 kW (5360 hp) giving a tractive effort of 250 kN (56200 lbf) at 28 mph (electric) or 4.5 mph (diesel).
Maximum Rail Power:
Train Brakes: Air, regenerative & rheostatic.

Brake Force: 73 t.	**Dimensions:** 20.50 x 2.69 m.
Weight: 85 t.	**Wheel Diameter:** 1100 mm.
Fuel Capacity: 1800 litres.	**Train Supply:** Electric, index 96.
Design Speed: 100 mph.	**Maximum Speed:** 100 mph.

Route Availability: 7.

88001	**DI**	BN	XHVE	KM	Revolution
88002	**DI**	BN	XHVE	KM	Prometheus
88003	**DI**	BN	XHVE	KM	Genesis
88004	**DI**	BN	XHVE	KM	Pandora
88005	**DI**	BN	XHVE	KM	Minerva
88006	**DI**	BN	XHVE	KM	Juno
88007	**DI**	BN	XHVE	KM	Electra
88008	**DI**	BN	XHVE	KM	Ariadne
88009	**DI**	BN	XHVE	KM	Diana
88010	**DI**	BN	XHVE	KM	Aurora

CLASS 90   GEC   Bo-Bo

Built: 1987–90 by BREL at Crewe Works (as sub-contractors for GEC).
Electric Supply System: 25 kV AC 50 Hz overhead.
Traction Motors: GEC G412CY frame mounted.
Maximum Tractive Effort: 258 kN (58000 lbf).
Continuous Rating: 3730 kW (5000 hp) giving a tractive effort of 95 kN (21300 lbf) at 87 mph.

Maximum Rail Power: 5860 kW (7860 hp) at 68.3 mph.
Train Brakes: Air.
Brake Force: 40 t.
Weight: 84.5 t.
Design Speed: 110 mph.
Train Supply: Electric, index 95.

Dimensions: 18.80 x 2.74 m.
Wheel Diameter: 1150 mm.
Maximum Speed: 110 mph.
Route Availability: 7.

Advertising livery: 90024 Malcolm Logistics (blue).

90001 b	**GA**	P	IANA	NC	Crown Point
90002 b	**GA**	P	IANA	NC	Eastern Daily Press 1870–2010
					SERVING NORFOLK FOR 140 YEARS
90003 b	**GA**	P	IANA	NC	
90004 b	**GA**	P	IANA	NC	City of Chelmsford
90005 b	**GA**	P	IANA	NC	Vice-Admiral Lord Nelson
90006 b	**GA**	P	IANA	NC	Modern Railways Magazine/
					Roger Ford
90007 b	**GA**	P	IANA	NC	Sir John Betjeman
90008 b	**GA**	P	IANA	NC	The East Anglian
90009 b	**GA**	P	IANA	NC	
90010 b	**GA**	P	IANA	NC	
90011 b	**GA**	P	IANA	NC	East Anglian Daily Times Suffolk & Proud
90012 b	**GA**	P	IANA	NC	Royal Anglian Regiment
90013 b	**GA**	P	IANA	NC	
90014 b	**GA**	P	IANA	NC	Norfolk and Norwich Festival
90015 b	**GA**	P	IANA	NC	Colchester Castle
90016	**FL**	FL	DFLC	CB	
90017	**E**	DB	WQBA	CE (S)	
90018	**DB**	DB	WEAC	CE	The Pride of Bellshill
90019	**DB**	DB	WEDC	CE	Multimodal
90020	**E**	DB	WEDC	CE	Collingwood
90021	**FS**	DB	WQAB	CE (S)	
90022	**EG**	DB	WQBA	CE (S)	Freightconnection
90023	**E**	DB	WQBA	CE (S)	
90024	**AL**	DB	WEAC	CE	
90025	**F**	DB	WQBA	CE (S)	
90026	**E**	DB	WQAB	CE (S)	
90027	**F**	DB	WQBA	CE (S)	Allerton T&RS Depot
90028	**E**	DB	WEAC	CE	
90029	**DB**	DB	WEDC	CE	
90030	**E**	DB	WQBA	CE (S)	
90031	**E**	DB	WQBA	CE (S)	The Railway Children Partnership
					Working For Street Children Worldwide
90032	**E**	DB	WQBA	CE (S)	
90033	**FE**	DB	WQBA	CE (S)	
90034	**DR**	DB	WEDC	CE	
90035	**E**	DB	WEAC	CE	
90036	**DB**	DB	WQAA	CE (S)	Driver Jack Mills
90037	**E**	DB	WEAC	CE	Spirit of Dagenham
90038	**FE**	DB	WQBA	CE (S)	
90039	**E**	DB	WEDC	CE	
90040	**DB**	DB	WEAC	CE	

90041	**FL**	FL	DFLC	CB
90042	**FH**	FL	DFLC	CB
90043	**FH**	FL	DFLC	CB
90044	**FF**	FL	DFLC	CB
90045	**FH**	FL	DFLC	CB
90046	**FL**	FL	DFLC	CB
90047	**FF**	FL	DFLC	CB
90048	**FF**	FL	DFLC	CB
90049	**FH**	FL	DFLC	CB
90050	**FF**	AV	DHLT	CB (S)

CLASS 91   GEC   Bo-Bo

Built: 1988–91 by BREL at Crewe Works (as sub-contractors for GEC).
Electric Supply System: 25 kV AC 50 Hz overhead.
Traction Motors: GEC G426AZ.
Maximum Tractive Effort: 190 kN (43 000 lbf).
Continuous Rating: 4540 kW (6090 hp) giving a tractive effort of 170 kN at 96 mph.
Maximum Rail Power: 4700 kW (6300 hp) at ?? mph.
Train Brakes: Air.
Brake Force: 45 t.   **Dimensions:** 19.41 x 2.74 m.
Weight: 84 t.   **Wheel Diameter:** 1000 mm.
Design Speed: 140 mph.   **Maximum Speed:** 125 mph.
Train Supply: Electric, index 95.   **Route Availability:** 7.

Locomotives were originally numbered in the 910xx series, but were renumbered upon completion of overhauls at Bombardier, Doncaster by the addition of 100 to their original number. The exception to this rule was 91023 which was renumbered 91132.

91114 has been fitted with a second pantograph for evaluation purposes.

Advertising liveries:

91101 Flying Scotsman (red, white & purple).
91110 Battle of Britain (black and grey).
91111 For the fallen (various with poppy and Union Jack vinyls).

91101	**AL**	E	IECA	BN	FLYING SCOTSMAN
91102	**VE**	E	IECA	BN	City of York
91103	**VE**	E	IECA	BN	
91104	**VE**	E	IECA	BN	
91105	**VE**	E	IECA	BN	
91106	**VE**	E	IECA	BN	
91107	**VE**	E	IECA	BN	SKYFALL
91108	**VE**	E	IECA	BN	
91109	**VE**	E	IECA	BN	Sir Bobby Robson
91110	**AL**	E	IECA	BN	BATTLE OF BRITAIN MEMORIAL FLIGHT
91111	**AL**	E	IECA	BN	For the Fallen
91112	**VE**	E	IECA	BN	
91113	**VE**	E	IECA	BN	
91114	**VE**	E	IECA	BN	Durham Cathedral

91115	**VE**	E	IECA	BN	Blaydon Races
91116	**VE**	E	IECA	BN	
91117	**VE**	E	IECA	BN	WEST RIDING LIMITED
91118	**VE**	E	IECA	BN	
91119	**VE**	E	IECA	BN	Bounds Green INTERCITY Depot 1977–2017
91120	**VE**	E	IECA	BN	
91121	**VE**	E	IECA	BN	
91122	**VE**	E	IECA	BN	
91124	**VE**	E	IECA	BN	
91125	**VE**	E	IECA	BN	
91126	**VE**	E	IECA	BN	Darlington Hippodrome
91127	**VE**	E	IECA	BN	
91128	**VE**	E	IECA	BN	INTERCITY 50
91129	**VE**	E	IECA	BN	
91130	**VE**	E	IECA	BN	Lord Mayor of Newcastle
91131	**VE**	E	IECA	BN	
91132	**VE**	E	IECA	BN	

CLASS 92   BRUSH   Co-Co

Built: 1993–96 by Brush Traction at Loughborough.
Electric Supply System: 25 kV AC 50 Hz overhead or 750 V DC third rail.
Traction Motors: Asea Brown Boveri design. Model 6FRA 7059B (Asynchronous 3-phase induction motors).
Maximum Tractive Effort: 400 kN (90 000 lbf).
Continuous Rating: 5040 kW (6760 hp) on AC, 4000 kW (5360 hp) on DC.

Maximum Rail Power:	**Train Brakes:** Air.
Brake Force: 63 t.	**Dimensions:** 21.34 x 2.67 m.
Weight: 126 t.	**Wheel Diameter:** 1070 mm.
Design Speed: 140 km/h (87 mph).	**Maximum Speed:** 145 km/h (90 mph).

Train Supply: Electric, index 108 (AC), 70 (DC).
Route Availability: 7.

* Fitted with TVM430 signalling equipment to operate on High Speed 1.

Class 92s exported for use abroad are listed in section 1.6 of this book.

Advertising livery: 92017 Stobart Rail (two-tone blue & white).

92004		**EG**	DB	WQBA	CE (S)	Jane Austen
92006		**EP**	GB	GBET	LB (S)	Louis Armand
92007		**EG**	DB	WQBA	CE (S)	Schubert
92008		**EG**	DB	WQBA	CE (S)	Jules Verne
92009	*	**DB**	DB	WQBA	CE (S)	Marco Polo
92010	*	**CA**	GB	GBST	WN	
92011	*	**EG**	DB	WFBC	CE	Handel
92013		**EG**	DB	WQAA	CE (S)	Puccini
92014		**CA**	GB	GBSL	WN	
92015	*	**DB**	DB	WFBC	CE	
92016	*	**DB**	DB	WQAA	CE (S)	
92017		**AL**	DB	WQBA	CE (S)	Bart the Engine

92018 *	CA	GB	GBST	WN	
92019 *	EG	DB	WFBC	CE	Wagner
92020	GB	GB	GBET	LB (S)	
92021	EP	GB	GBET	CO (S)	Purcell
92023 *	CA	GB	GBST	WN	
92028	GB	GB	GBSL	WN	
92029	EG	DB	WQBA	CE (S)	Dante
92031 *	DB	DB	WQAB	CE (S)	
92032 *	GB	GB	GBST	WN	IMechE Railway Division
92033	CA	GB	GBSL	WN	
92035	EP	DB	WQBA	CE (S)	Mendelssohn
92036 *	EG	DB	WFBC	CE	Bertolt Brecht
92037	EG	DB	WQAB	CE (S)	Sullivan
92038 *	CA	GB	GBST	WN	
92040	EP	GB	GBET	CO (S)	Goethe
92041 *	EG	DB	WQAA	CE (S)	Vaughan Williams
92042 *	DB	DB	WFBC	CE	
92043 *	GB	GB	GBST	WN	
92044 *	EP	GB	GBST	WN	Couperin
92045	EP	GB	GBET	LB (S)	Chaucer
92046	EP	GB	GBET	LB (S)	Sweelinck

1.4. EUROTUNNEL LOCOMOTIVES

DIESEL LOCOMOTIVES

0001–10 are registered on TOPS as 21901–910.

0001–0005　　　　MaK　　　　　　　　　　Bo-Bo

Channel Tunnel maintenance and rescue train locomotives.
Built: 1991–92 by MaK at Kiel, Germany (Model DE 1004).
Engine: MTU 12V396 TC 13 of 950 kW (1275 hp) at 1800 rpm.
Main Alternator: ABB.　　　　**Traction Motors:** ABB.
Maximum Tractive Effort: 305 kN (68600 lbf).
Continuous Tractive Effort: 140 kN (31500 lbf) at 20 mph.
Power At Rail: 750 kW (1012 hp).　**Dimensions:** 14.40 x ?? m.
Brake Force: 120 kN.　　　　　**Wheel Diameter:** 1000 mm.
Train Brakes: Air.　　　　　　**Weight:** 90 t.
Maximum Speed: 100 km/h.　　**Design Speed:** 120 km/h.
Fuel Capacity: 3500 litres.　　**Multiple Working:** Within class.
Train Supply: Not equipped.　**Signalling System:** TVM430 cab signalling.

0001	**GY**	ET	CO		0004	**GY**	ET	CO
0002	**GY**	ET	CO		0005	**GY**	ET	CO
0003	**GY**	ET	CO					

0006–0010　　　　MaK　　　　　　　　　　Bo-Bo

Channel Tunnel maintenance and rescue locomotives. Rebuilt from Netherlands Railways/DB Cargo Nederland Class 6400. 0006/07 were added to the ET fleet in 2011, and 0008–10 in 2016. 0010 is used for shunting at Coquelles.

Built: 1990–91 by MaK at Kiel, Germany (Model DE 6400).
Engine: MTU 12V396 TC 13 of 1180 kW (1580 hp) at 1800 rpm.
Main Alternator: ABB.　　　　**Traction Motors:** ABB.
Maximum Tractive Effort: 290 kN (65200 lbf).
Continuous Tractive Effort: 140 kN (31500 lbf) at 20 mph.
Power At Rail: 750 kW (1012 hp).　**Dimensions:** 14.40 x ?? m.
Brake Force: 120 kN.　　　　　**Wheel Diameter:** 1000 mm.
Train Brakes: Air.　　　　　　**Weight:** 80 t.
Maximum Speed: 120 km/h.　　**Design Speed:** 120 km/h.
Fuel Capacity: 2900 litres.　　**Multiple Working:** Within class.
Train Supply: Not equipped.

Not fitted with TVM 430 cab signalling so have to operate with another locomotive/s when used on HS1.

0006	(6456)	**GY**	ET	CO		0009	(6451)	**GY**	ET	CO
0007	(6457)	**GY**	ET	CO		0010	(6447)	**EB**	ET	CO
0008	(6450)	**GY**	ET	CO						

0031–0042   HUNSLET/SCHÖMA   0-4-0

Built: 1989–90 by Hunslet Engine Company at Leeds as 900 mm gauge.
Rebuilt: 1993–94 by Schöma in Germany to 1435 mm gauge.
Engine: Deutz FL10L 413FW of 170 kW (230 hp) at 2300 rpm.
Transmission: Mechanical Clark 5000 series.

Maximum Tractive Effort:	**Continuous Tractive Effort:**
Power At Rail:	
Brake Force:	**Dimensions:** 6.63 x 2.69 m.
Weight: 26–28 t.	**Wheel Diameter:**
Design Speed: 48 km/h.	**Maximum Speed:** 50 km/h.
Fuel Capacity:	**Train Brakes:** Air.
Train Supply: Not equipped.	**Multiple Working:** Not equipped.

* Rebuilt with inspection platforms to check overhead catenary.

0031	**GY**	ET	CO	FRANCES
0032	**GY**	ET	CO	ELISABETH
0033	**GY**	ET	CO	SILKE
0034	**GY**	ET	CO	AMANDA
0035	**GY**	ET	CO	MARY
0036	**GY**	ET	CO	LAURENCE
0037	**GY**	ET	CO	LYDIE
0038	**GY**	ET	CO	JENNY
0039	*	**GY**	ET	CO	PACITA
0040		**GY**	ET	CO	JILL
0041	*	**GY**	ET	CO	KIM
0042		**GY**	ET	CO	NICOLE

ELECTRIC LOCOMOTIVES

9005–9840   BRUSH/ABB   Bo-Bo-Bo

Built: 1993–2002 by Brush Traction, Loughborough.
Electric Supply System: 25 kV AC 50 Hz overhead.
Traction Motors: Asea Brown Boveri design. Asynchronous 3-phase motors.
Model 6FHA 7059 (as built). Model 6FHA 7059C (7000 kW rated locos).
Maximum Tractive Effort: 400kN (90 000 lbf).
Continuous Rating: Class 9/0: 5760 kW (7725 hp). Class 9/7 and 9/8:
7000 kW (9387 hp).

Maximum Rail Power:	**Multiple Working:** TDM system.
Brake Force: 50 t.	**Dimensions:** 22.01 x 2.97 x 4.20 m.
Weight: 136 t.	**Wheel Diameter:** 1250 mm.
Maximum Speed: 100 mph.	**Design Speed:** 100 mph.
Train Supply: Electric.	**Train Brakes:** Air.

Class 9/0 Original build locos. Built 1993–94.

9005	**EB**	ET	CO	JESSYE NORMAN
9007	**EB**	ET	CO	DAME JOAN SUTHERLAND
9011	**EB**	ET	CO	JOSÉ VAN DAM

9013	**EB**	ET	CO	MARIA CALLAS
9015	**EB**	ET	CO	LÖTSCHBERG 1913
9018	**EB**	ET	CO	WILHELMENIA FERNANDEZ
9022	**EB**	ET	CO	DAME JANET BAKER
9024	**EB**	ET	CO	GOTTHARD 1882
9026	**EB**	ET	CO	FURKATUNNEL 1982
9029	**EB**	ET	CO	THOMAS ALLEN
9033	**EB**	ET	CO	MONTSERRAT CABALLE
9036	**EB**	ET	CO	ALAIN FONDARY
9037	**EB**	ET	CO	GABRIEL BACQUIER

Class 9/7. Increased power freight shuttle locos. Built 2001–02 (9711–23 built 1998–2001 as 9101–13 and rebuilt as 9711–23 2010–12).

9701	**EB**	ET	CO
9702	**EB**	ET	CO
9703	**EB**	ET	CO
9704	**EB**	ET	CO
9705	**EB**	ET	CO
9706	**EB**	ET	CO
9707	**EB**	ET	CO

9711	(9101)	**EB**	ET	CO
9712	(9102)	**EB**	ET	CO
9713	(9103)	**EB**	ET	CO
9714	(9104)	**EB**	ET	CO
9715	(9105)	**EB**	ET	CO
9716	(9106)	**EB**	ET	CO
9717	(9107)	**EB**	ET	CO
9718	(9108)	**EB**	ET	CO
9719	(9109)	**EB**	ET	CO
9720	(9110)	**EB**	ET	CO
9721	(9111)	**EB**	ET	CO
9722	(9112)	**EB**	ET	CO
9723	(9113)	**EB**	ET	CO

Class 9/8 Locos rebuilt from Class 9/0 by adding 800 to the loco number. Uprated to 7000 kW.

9801	**EB**	ET	CO		LESLEY GARRETT
9802	**EB**	ET	CO		STUART BURROWS
9803	**EB**	ET	CO		BENJAMIN LUXON
9804	**EB**	ET	CO		VICTORIA DE LOS ANGELES
9806	**EB**	ET	CO		REGINE CRESPIN
9808	**EB**	ET	CO		ELISABETH SODERSTROM
9809	**EB**	ET	CO		FRANÇOISE POLLET
9810	**EB**	ET	CO		JEAN-PHILIPPE COURTIS
9812	**EB**	ET	CO		LUCIANO PAVAROTTI
9814	**EB**	ET	CO		LUCIA POPP
9816	**EB**	ET	CO		WILLARD WHITE
9817	**EB**	ET	CO	(S)	JOSÉ CARRERAS
9819	**EB**	ET	CO		MARIA EWING

9820	**EB**	ET	CO	NICOLAI GHIAROV
9821	**EB**	ET	CO	TERESA BERGANZA
9823	**EB**	ET	CO	DAME ELISABETH LEGGE-SCHWARZKOPF
9825	**EB**	ET	CO	
9827	**EB**	ET	CO	BARBARA HENDRICKS
9828	**EB**	ET	CO	DAME KIRI TE KANAWA
9831	**EB**	ET	CO	
9832	**EB**	ET	CO	RENATA TEBALDI
9834	**EB**	ET	CO	MIRELLA FRENI
9835	**EB**	ET	CO	NICOLAI GEDDA
9838	**EB**	ET	CO	HILDEGARD BEHRENS
9840	**EB**	ET	CO	

1.5. LOCOMOTIVES AWAITING DISPOSAL

Locomotives that are still extant but best classed as awaiting disposal are listed here.

Class 56

56128	CF Booth, Rotherham

Class 58

58012	Battlefield Line
58023	Battlefield Line

Class 66

66048	EMD, Longport Works

Class 86

86901	Freightliner, Crewe Basford Hall Yard

1.6. LOCOMOTIVES EXPORTED FOR USE ABROAD

This section details former British Railways (plus privatisation era) diesel and electric locomotives that have been exported from the UK for use in industrial locations or with a main line operator abroad. Not included are locos that are "preserved" abroad, which are included in the Platform 5 "Preserved Locomotives of British Railways" publication. (S) denotes locomotives that are stored.

Number	Other no./name	Location
Class 03		
03156		Ferramenta Pugliese, Terlizzi, Bari, Italy
Class 04		
D2289		Lonato SpA, Lonato Steelworks, Lonato, Brescia, Italy
Class 47		
47375	92 70 00 47375-5	Continental Railway Solution, Hungary
Class 56		
56101	92 55 0659 001-5	FLOYD, Hungary
56115	92 55 0659 002-3	FLOYD, Hungary
56117	92 55 0659 003-1	FLOYD, Hungary (S) Budapest Keleti
Class 58		
58001		DB, France, (S) Alizay
58004		DB, France, (S) Alizay
58005		DB, France, (S) Alizay
58006		DB, France, (S) Alizay
58007		DB, France, (S) Alizay
58009		DB, France, (S) Alizay
58010		DB, France, (S) Alizay
58011		DB, France, (S) Alizay
58013		DB, France, (S) Alizay
58015	L54	Transfesa, Spain, Monforte del Cid, Alicante
58018		DB, France, (S) Alizay
58020	L43	Transfesa, Spain, Monforte del Cid, Alicante
58021		DB, France, (S) Alizay
58024	L42	Transfesa, Spain, Monforte del Cid, Alicante
58025		DB, Spain, (S) Albacete
58026		DB, France, (S) Alizay
58027	L52	DB, Spain, (S) Albacete
58029	L44	Transfesa, Spain, (S) Monforte del Cid, Alicante
58030	L46	Transfesa, Spain, Monforte del Cid, Alicante
58031	L45	Transfesa, Spain, Monforte del Cid, Alicante
58032		DB, France, (S) Alizay
58033		DB, France, (S) Alizay
58034		DB, France, (S) Alizay

58035		DB, France, (S) Alizay
58036		DB, France, (S) Alizay
58038		DB, France, (S) Alizay
58039		DB, France, (S) Alizay
58040		DB, France, (S) Alizay
58041	L36	Transfesa, Spain, (S) Albacete
58042		DB, France, (S) Alizay
58043	L37	Transfesa, Spain, Monforte del Cid, Alicante
58044		DB, France, (S) Woippy, Metz
58046		DB, France, (S) Alizay
58047	L51	Transfesa, Spain, Monforte del Cid, Alicante
58049		DB, France, (S) Alizay
58050	L53	DB, Spain, (S) Albacete

Class 66

66010	Euro Cargo Rail, France		66202	Euro Cargo Rail, France
66022	Euro Cargo Rail, France		66203	Euro Cargo Rail, France
66026	Euro Cargo Rail, France		66204	Euro Cargo Rail, France
66028	Euro Cargo Rail, France		66205	Euro Cargo Rail, France
66029	Euro Cargo Rail, France		66208	Euro Cargo Rail, France
66032	Euro Cargo Rail, France		66209	Euro Cargo Rail, France
66033	Euro Cargo Rail, France		66210	Euro Cargo Rail, France
66036	Euro Cargo Rail, France		66211	Euro Cargo Rail, France
66038	Euro Cargo Rail, France		66212	Euro Cargo Rail, France
66042	Euro Cargo Rail, France		66213	Euro Cargo Rail, France
66045	Euro Cargo Rail, France		66214	Euro Cargo Rail, France
66049	Euro Cargo Rail, France		66215	Euro Cargo Rail, France
66052	Euro Cargo Rail, France		66216	Euro Cargo Rail, France
66062	Euro Cargo Rail, France		66217	Euro Cargo Rail, France
66064	Euro Cargo Rail, France		66218	Euro Cargo Rail, France
66071	Euro Cargo Rail, France		66219	Euro Cargo Rail, France
66072	Euro Cargo Rail, France		66220	DB Cargo Polska, Poland
66073	Euro Cargo Rail, France		66222	Euro Cargo Rail, France
66123	Euro Cargo Rail, France		66223	Euro Cargo Rail, France
66146	DB Cargo Polska, Poland		66224	Euro Cargo Rail, France
66153	DB Cargo Polska, Poland		66225	Euro Cargo Rail, France
66157	DB Cargo Polska, Poland		66226	Euro Cargo Rail, France
66159	DB Cargo Polska, Poland		66227	DB Cargo Polska, Poland
66163	DB Cargo Polska, Poland		66228	Euro Cargo Rail, France
66166	DB Cargo Polska, Poland		66229	Euro Cargo Rail, France
66173	DB Cargo Polska, Poland		66231	Euro Cargo Rail, France
66178	DB Cargo Polska, Poland		66232	Euro Cargo Rail, France
66179	Euro Cargo Rail, France		66233	Euro Cargo Rail, France
66180	DB Cargo Polska, Poland		66234	Euro Cargo Rail, France
66189	DB Cargo Polska, Poland		66235	Euro Cargo Rail, France
66190	Euro Cargo Rail, France		66236	Euro Cargo Rail, France
66191	Euro Cargo Rail, France		66237	DB Cargo Polska, Poland
66193	Euro Cargo Rail, France		66239	Euro Cargo Rail, France
66195	Euro Cargo Rail, France		66240	Euro Cargo Rail, France
66196	DB Cargo Polska, Poland		66241	Euro Cargo Rail, France
66201	Euro Cargo Rail, France		66242	Euro Cargo Rail, France

66243		Euro Cargo Rail, France
66244		Euro Cargo Rail, France
66245		Euro Cargo Rail, France
66246		Euro Cargo Rail, France
66247		Euro Cargo Rail, France
66248		DB Cargo Polska, Poland
66249		Euro Cargo Rail, France
66411	66013	Freightliner, Poland
66412	66015	Freightliner, Poland
66417	66014	Freightliner, Poland
66527	66016	Freightliner, Poland
66530	66017	Freightliner, Poland
66535	66018	Freightliner, Poland
66582	66009	Freightliner, Poland
66583	66010	Freightliner, Poland
66584	66011	Freightliner, Poland
66586	66008	Freightliner, Poland
66608	66603	Freightliner, Poland
66609	66605	Freightliner, Poland
66611	66604	Freightliner, Poland
66612	66606	Freightliner, Poland
66624	66602	Freightliner, Poland
66625	66601	Freightliner, Poland

Class 86

86213	91 52 00 87703-2	Lancashire Witch	Bulmarket, Bulgaria
86215	91 55 0450 005-8		FLOYD, Hungary
86217	91 55 0450 006-6		FLOYD, Hungary
86218	91 55 0450 004-1		FLOYD, Hungary
86228	91 55 0450 007-4		FLOYD, Hungary
86231	91 52 00 85005-4	Lady of the Lake	Bulmarket, Bulgaria
86232	91 55 0450 003-3		FLOYD, Hungary
86233			Bulmarket, Bulgaria (S) Ruse
86234			Bulmarket, Bulgaria
86235	91 52 00 87704-0	Novelty	Bulmarket, Bulgaria
86242	91 55 0450 008-2		FLOYD, Hungary
86248	91 55 0450 001-7		FLOYD, Hungary
86250	91 55 0450 002-5		FLOYD, Hungary
86424	91 55 0450 009-0		FLOYD, Hungary (S) Budapest
86701	91 52 00 87701-6	Orion	Bulmarket, Bulgaria
86702	91 52 00 87702-4	Cassiopeia	Bulmarket, Bulgaria

Class 87

87003	91 52 00 87003-7		BZK, Bulgaria
87004	91 52 00 87004-5	Britannia	BZK, Bulgaria
87006	91 52 00 87006-0		BZK, Bulgaria
87007	91 52 00 87007-8		BZK, Bulgaria
87008	87008-9		BZK, Bulgaria (S) Ruse
87009	91 52 00 87009-4		Bulmarket, Bulgaria
87010	91 52 00 87010-2		BZK, Bulgaria
87012	91 52 00 87012-8		BZK, Bulgaria
87013	91 52 00 87013-6		BZK, Bulgaria
87014	87014-7		BZK, Bulgaria (S) Sofia
87017	91 52 00 87017-7	Iron Duke	Bulmarket, Bulgaria
87019	91 52 00 87019-3		BZK, Bulgaria
87020	91 52 00 87020-1		BZK, Bulgaria
87022	91 52 00 87022-7		BZK, Bulgaria
87023	91 52 00 87023-5	Velocity	Bulmarket, Bulgaria
87025	91 52 00 87025-0		Bulmarket, Bulgaria
87026	91 52 00 87026-8		BZK, Bulgaria
87028	91 52 00 87028-4		BZK, Bulgaria

87029	91 52 00 87029-2		BZK, Bulgaria
87033	91 52 00 87033-4		BZK, Bulgaria
87034	91 52 00 87034-2		BZK, Bulgaria

Class 92

92001	91 53 0 472 002-1	Mircea Eliade	DB Cargo, Romania
92002	91 53 0 472 003-9	Lucian Blaga	DB Cargo, Romania
92003		Beethoven	DB Cargo, Bulgaria
92005	91 53 0 472-005-4		Transagent Špedicija, Croatia
92012	91 53 0 472 001-3	Mihai Eminescu	DB Cargo, Romania
92022		Charles Dickens	DB Cargo, Bulgaria
92024	91 53 0 472 004-7	Marin Preda	DB Cargo, Romania
92025	91 52 1 688 025-1	Oscar Wilde	DB Cargo, Bulgaria
92026		Britten	DB Cargo, Bulgaria
92027	91 52 1 688 027-7	George Eliot	DB Cargo, Bulgaria
92030	91 52 1 688 030-1	Ashford	DB Cargo, Bulgaria
92034	91 52 1 688 034-3	Kipling	DB Cargo, Bulgaria
92039	91 53 0 472 006-2	Eugen Ionescu	DB Cargo, Romania

2. LOCO-HAULED COACHING STOCK

This section contains details of all locomotive-hauled or propelled coaching stock, often referred to as carriages, which can run on Britain's national railway network.

The number of locomotive-hauled or propelled carriages in use on the national railway network is much fewer than was once the case. Those that remain fall into two distinct groups.

Firstly, there are those used by franchised and open access operators for regular timetabled services. Most of these are formed in fixed or semi-fixed formations with either locomotives or a locomotive and Driving Brake Carriage at either end which allows for push-pull operation. There are also a small number of mainly overnight and peak-hour trains with variable formations that use conventional locomotive haulage.

Secondly there are those used for what can best be described as excursion trains. These include a wide range of carriage types ranging from luxurious saloons to those more suited to the "bucket and spade" seaside type of excursion. These are formed into sets to suit the requirements of the day. From time to time some see limited use with franchised and open access operators to cover for stock shortages and times of exceptional demand such as major sporting events.

In addition, there remain a small number of carriages referred to as "Service Stock" which are used internally within the railway industry and are not used to convey passengers.

FRANCHISED & OPEN ACCESS OPERATORS

For each operator regularly using locomotive-hauled carriages brief details are given here of the sphere of operation. For details of operators using HSTs see Section 2.2.

Arriva Trains Wales
The Monday–Friday Welsh Government sponsored train between Cardiff and Holyhead uses Mark 3 carriages in push-pull mode with a Class 67. A second similarly formed set is used for weekday trains between Crewe or Manchester and Chester/North Wales. These carriages are also used for relief trains, particularly in connection with sports fixtures at Cardiff and busy ferry sailings to/from Holyhead.

Caledonian Sleeper
This franchise, operated by Serco, started in 2015 when the Anglo-Scottish Sleeper operation was split from the ScotRail franchise. Caledonian Sleeper comprises seating and sleeping car services between London Euston and Scotland using sets of Mark 3 Sleeping Cars and Mark 2 seating and catering carriages. These are soon to be replaced with a fleet of newly built CAF Mark 5 carriages.

GBRf is contracted to supply the motive power for the Sleepers. Class 92s are normally used between London Euston and Edinburgh/Glasgow Central. Rebuilt Class 73/9s are used between Edinburgh and Inverness. Aberdeen and Fort William, although at the time of writing Class 67s were also being hired in from DB Cargo to cover for unavailable Class 73/9s. A Class 47 is also used in Scotland, mainly for empty stock workings.

Chiltern Railways
Chiltern operates four sets of Mark 3 carriages with DRS Class 68 locomotives on its Mainline services between London Marylebone and Birmingham Moor Street/Kidderminster (plus one train to Oxford). Another set is used on a peak-hour commuter service between Marylebone and Bicester North or Banbury. All trains operate as push-pull sets.

Greater Anglia
The Inter-City service between London Liverpool Street and Norwich is operated using 12 sets of Mark 3 carriages with Class 90 locomotives in push-pull formations. In addition one set of Mark 2 carriages supplied by DRS is used between Norwich and Great Yarmouth/Lowestoft, using Class 37s in push-pull mode.

Great Western Railway
The "Night Riviera" seating and sleeping car service between London Paddington and Penzance uses sets of Mark 3 carriages hauled by Class 57/6 locomotives.

Northern
Northern operates two sets of Mark 2 carriages hired from DRS on the Cumbrian Coast route (between Carlisle and Barrow-in-Furness/Preston) with Class 37/4s in push-pull mode.

North Yorkshire Moors Railway
In addition to operating the North Yorkshire Moors Railway between Pickering and Grosmont the company operates through services to Whitby and occasionally Battersby. A fleet of Mark 1 passenger carriages and Pullman Cars are used for these services. It also operates the "North Norfolkman" services on behalf of the North Norfolk Railway between Sheringham and Cromer.

ScotRail
ScotRail operates two sets of Mark 2 carriages supplied by DRS on peak-hour services between Edinburgh and Fife using Class 68s.

Virgin Trains East Coast
VTEC operates 30 sets of Mark 4 carriages with Class 91 locomotives in push-pull formations on its Inter-City services between London King's Cross and Yorkshire, North-East England and Scotland.

West Coast Railway Company
WCRC operates two sets of Mark 1/2 carriages on its steam-hauled "Jacobite" trains between Fort William and Mallaig. These trains normally operate between late April and late October.

EXCURSION TRAIN OPERATORS

Usually, three types of companies will be involved in the operation of an excursion train. There will be the promoter, the rolling stock provider and the train operator. In many cases two or more of these roles may be undertaken by the same or associated companies. Only a small number of Train Operating Companies facilitate the operation of excursion trains. This takes various forms ranging from the complete package of providing and operating the train, through offering a "hook up and haul" service, to operating the train for a third party rolling stock custodian.

DB Cargo UK
DBC currently operates its own luxurious train of Mark 3 carriages, called the Company Train. It also offers a hook up and haul service and regularly operates the Royal Train and the Belmond British Pullman as well as trains for Riviera Trains and Locomotives Services and their client promoters. An excursion train fleet of Mark 2 carriages is owned by DBC but these are now awaiting disposal.

Direct Rail Services
DRS operates a fleet of Mark 2 carriages originally intended for use on excursion trains. These are currently hired to Greater Anglia, Northern and ScotRail for use on regular timetabled services. The company also offers a hook up and haul service operating the Northern Belle as well as trains for Riviera Trains and their client promoters.

GB Railfreight
GBRf initially operated excursion trains using the preserved Class 201 "Hastings" DEMU. It now also operates a small number of company excursions using hired carriages. The company also offers a hook up and haul service operating the Royal Scotsman luxury train, as well as trains for Riviera Trains and its client promoters.

Locomotive Services
This vertically integrated company gained a restricted license in 2017. Currently its operations are bounded by Crewe, Chester, North Wales and Shrewsbury. Excursion trains are operated in this area using its fleet of steam and diesel locomotives and carriages.

Rail Operations Group
This company operates a small number of excursion trains using hired in carriages. It also offers a hook up and haul service.

West Coast Railway Company
This vertically integrated company has its own fleet of steam and diesel locomotives as well as a full range of different carriage types. It operates its own regular trains, such as the "Jacobite" steam service between Fort William and Mallaig and numerous excursion trains for itself and client promoters. In addition, it offers a hook up and haul service operating trains for Vintage Trains, The Princess Royal Locomotive Trust, Locomotives Services and the Scottish Railway Preservation Society.

LAYOUT OF INFORMATION

Carriages are listed in numerical order of painted number in batches according to type.

Where a carriage has been renumbered, the former number is shown in parentheses. If a carriage has been renumbered more than once, the original number is shown first in parentheses, followed by the most recent previous number.

Each carriage entry is laid out as in the following example (previous number(s) column may be omitted where not applicable):

No.	Prev. No.	Notes	Livery	Owner	Operator	Depot/Location
42346	(41053)	*h	**FD**	A	*GW*	LA

Codes: Codes are used to denote the livery, owner, operator and depot/location of each carriage. Details of codes used can be found in Section 6 of this book.

The owner is the responsible custodian of the carriage and this may not always be the legal owner. Actual ownership can be very complicated. Some vehicles are owned by finance/leasing companies. Others are owned by subsidiary companies of a holding company or by an associate company of the responsible custodian or operator.

The operator is the organisation which facilitates the use of the carriage and may not be the actual train operating company which runs the train. If no operator is shown the carriage is considered to be not in use.

The depot is the facility primarily responsible for the carriages maintenance. Light maintenance and heavy overhauls may be carried out elsewhere.

The location is where carriages not in use are currently being kept/stored.

GENERAL INFORMATION

CLASSIFICATION AND NUMBERING

Seven different numbering systems were in use on British Rail. These were the British Rail series, the four pre-nationalisation companies' series', the Pullman Car Company's series and the UIC (International Union of Railways) series. In this book BR number series carriages and former Pullman Car Company series are listed separately. There is also a separate listing of "Saloon" type carriages, that includes pre-nationalisation survivors, which are permitted to run on the national railway system, Locomotive Support Carriages and Service Stock. Please note the Mark 2 Pullman carriages were ordered after the Pullman Car Company had been nationalised and are therefore numbered in the British Rail series. The new CAF Mark 5 carriages currently being built have been allocated numbers in the British Rail series.

Also listed separately are the British Rail and Pullman Car Company number series carriages used on North Yorkshire Moors Railway and North Norfolk Railway services on the national railway network. This is due to their very restricted sphere of operation.

The BR number series grouped carriages of a particular type together in chronological order. Major modifications affecting type of accommodation resulted in renumbering into a more appropriate or new number series. Since privatisation such renumbering has not always taken place resulting in renumbering which has been more haphazard and greater variations within numbering groups.

With the introduction of the TOPS numbering system, coaching stock (including multiple unit vehicles) retained their original BR number unless this conflicted with a locomotive number. Carriages can be one–five digits, although no one or two digit examples remain in use on the national network. BR generally numbered "Service Stock" in a six-digit wagon number series.

UNITS OF MEASUREMENT

All dimensions and weights are quoted for carriages in an "as new" condition or after a major modification, such as fitting with new bogies etc. Dimensions are quoted in the order length x width. Lengths quoted are over buffers or couplers as appropriate. All widths quoted are maxima. All weights are shown as metric tonnes (t = tonnes).

DETAILED INFORMATION & CODES

Under each type heading, the following details are shown:

- "Mark" of carriage (see below).
- Descriptive text.
- Number of First Class seats, Standard Class seats, lavatory compartments and wheelchair spaces shown as F/S nT nW respectively. A number in brackets indicates tip-up seats (in addition to the regular seats).
- Bogie type (see below).
- Additional features.
- ETS Index.
- Weight: All weights are shown as metric tonnes.

BOGIE TYPES

Gresley. LNER design of bogie first used in the "Gresley" era. Used by BR on some Mark 1 catering carriages. Now used for some saloons.

BR Mark 1 (BR1). Double bolster leaf spring bogie. Generally 90 mph, but Mark 1 bogies may be permitted to run at 100 mph with special maintenance. Weight: 6.1 t.

BR Mark 2 (BR2). Single bolster leaf-spring bogie used on certain types of non-passenger stock and suburban stock (all now withdrawn). Weight: 5.3 t.

COMMONWEALTH (C). Heavy, cast steel coil spring bogie. 100 mph. Weight: 6.75 t.

B4. Coil spring fabricated bogie. Generally 100 mph, but B4 bogies may be permitted to run at 110 mph with special maintenance. Weight: 5.2 t.

B5. Heavy duty version of B4. 100 mph. Weight: 5.3 t.

B5 (SR). A bogie originally used on Southern Region EMUs, similar in design to B5. Now also used on locomotive-hauled carriages. 100 mph.

BT10. A fabricated bogie designed for 125 mph. Air suspension.

T4. A 125 mph bogie designed by BREL (now Bombardier Transportation).

BT41. Fitted to Mark 4 carriages, designed by SIG in Switzerland. At present limited to 125 mph, but designed for 140 mph.

CAF. Fitted to CAF Mark 5 and Mark 5A carriages.

BRAKES

Air braking is now standard on British main line trains. Carriages with other equipment are denoted:

b   Air braked, through vacuum pipe.
v   Vacuum braked.
x   Dual braked (air and vacuum).

HEATING & VENTILATION

Electric heating and ventilation is now standard on British main-line trains. Certain carriages for use on excursion services may also have steam heating facilities, or be steam heated only. All carriages used on North Yorkshire Moors Railway and North Norfolk Railway trains have steam heating.

NOTES ON ELECTRIC TRAIN SUPPLY

The sum of ETS indices in a train must not be more than the ETS index of the locomotive or generator van. The normal voltage on British trains is 1000 V. Suffix "X" denotes 600 amp wiring instead of 400 amp. Trains whose ETS index is higher than 66 must be formed completely of 600 amp wired stock. Class 33 and 73/1 locomotives cannot provide a suitable electric train supply for Mark 2D, Mark 2E, Mark 2F, Mark 3, Mark 3A, Mark 3B or Mark 4 carriages. Class 55 locomotives provide an ETS directly from one of their traction generators into the train line. Consequently voltage fluctuations can result in motor-alternator flashover. Thus these locomotives are not suitable for use with Mark 2D, Mark 2E, Mark 2F, Mark 3, Mark 3A, Mark 3B or Mark 4 carriages unless modified motor-alternators are fitted. Such motor alternators were fitted to Mark 2D and 2F carriages used on the East Coast Main Line, but few remain fitted.

PUBLIC ADDRESS

It is assumed all carriages are now fitted with public address equipment, although certain stored carriages may not have this feature. In addition, it is assumed all carriages with a conductor's compartment have public address transmission facilities, as have catering carriages.

COOKING EQUIPMENT

It is assumed that Mark 1 catering carriages have gas powered cooking equipment, whilst Mark 2, 3 and 4 catering carriages have electric powered cooking equipment unless stated otherwise.

ADDITIONAL FEATURE CODES

d	Central Door Locking.
dg	Driver–Guard communication equipment.
f	Facelifted or fluorescent lighting.
h	"High density" seating.
k	Composition brake blocks (instead of cast iron).
n	Day/night lighting.
pg	Public address transmission and driver-guard communication.
pt	Public address transmission facility.
q	Catering staff to shore telephone.
w	Wheelchair space.

BUILD DETAILS

Lot Numbers
Carriages ordered under the auspices of BR were allocated a lot (batch) number when ordered and these are quoted in class headings and sub-headings.

Builders
These are shown for each lot. More details and a full list of builders can be found in section 6.7.

Information on sub-contracting works which built parts of carriages eg the underframes etc is not shown.

In addition to the above, certain vintage Pullman cars were built or rebuilt at the following works:

Metropolitan Carriage & Wagon Company, Birmingham (later Alstom).
Midland Carriage & Wagon Company, Birmingham.
Pullman Car Company, Preston Park, Brighton.
Conversions have also been carried out at the Railway Technical Centre, Derby, LNWR Crewe and Blakes Fabrications, Edinburgh.

2.1. BRITISH RAILWAYS NUMBER SERIES COACHING STOCK

KITCHEN FIRST

Mark 1. Spent most of its life as a Royal Train vehicle and was numbered 2907 for a time. 24/–. B5 bogies. ETS 2.

Lot No. 30633 Swindon 1961. 41 t.

| 325 | **VN** WC *NB* | KR | DUART |

PULLMAN KITCHEN

Mark 2. Pressure Ventilated. Built with First Class seating but this has been replaced with a servery area. Gas cooking. 2T. B5 bogies. ETS 6.

Lot No. 30755 Derby 1966. 40 t.

| 504 | **PC** WC *WC* | CS | ULLSWATER |
| 506 | **PC** WC *WC* | CS | WINDERMERE |

PULLMAN OPEN FIRST

Mark 2. Pressure Ventilated. 36/– 2T. B4 bogies. ETS 5.

Lot No. 30754 Derby 1966. 35 t.

Non-standard livery: 546 Maroon & beige.

546	**O** WC	CS	CITY OF MANCHESTER
548	**PC** WC *WC*	CS	GRASMERE
549	**PC** WC *WC*	CS	BASSENTHWAITE
550	**PC** WC *WC*	CS	RYDAL WATER
551	**PC** WC *WC*	CS	BUTTERMERE
552	**PC** WC *WC*	CS	ENNERDALE WATER
553	**PC** WC *WC*	CS	CRUMMOCK WATER

PULLMAN OPEN BRAKE FIRST

Mark 2. Pressure Ventilated. 30/– 2T. B4 bogies. ETS 4.

Lot No. 30753 Derby 1966. 35 t.

| 586 | **PC** WC *WC* | CS | DERWENTWATER |

BUFFET FIRST

Mark 2F. Air conditioned. Converted 1988–89/91 at BREL, Derby from Mark 2F Open Firsts. 1200/01/03/11/20/21 have Stones equipment, others have Temperature Ltd. 25/– 1T 1W. B4 bogies. d. ETS 6X.

1200/03/11/20. Lot No. 30845 Derby 1973. 33 t.
1201/07/10/12/21. Lot No. 30859 Derby 1973–74. 33 t.

1200	(3287, 6459)	**BG** RV	*RV*	BU
1201	(3361, 6445)	**CH** VT		TM
1203	(3291)	**IC** LS		ZG
1207	(3328, 6422)	**V** WC		CS
1210	(3405, 6462)	**FS** CA	*CA*	PO
1211	(3305)	**PC** LS	*LS*	CL
1212	(3427, 6453)	**V** RV	*RV*	BU
1220	(3315, 6432)	**FS** CA	*CA*	PO
1221	(3371)	**IC** WC		CS

KITCHEN WITH BAR

Mark 1. Built with no seats but three Pullman-style seats now fitted in bar area. B5 bogies. ETS 1.

Lot No. 30624 Cravens 1960–61. 41 t.

1566	**VN** WC *NB*	KR	CAERDYDD

KITCHEN BUFFET UNCLASSIFIED

Mark 1. Built with 23 loose chairs. All remaining vehicles were refurbished with 23 fixed polypropylene chairs and fluorescent lighting. 1683/91 were further refurbished with 21 chairs, wheelchair space and carpets. ETS 2 (* 2X).

Now used on excursion trains with the seating area adapted to various uses including servery and food preparation areas, with some or all seating removed.

1651–91. Lot No. 30628 Pressed Steel 1960–61. Commonwealth bogies. 39 t.
1730. Lot No. 30512 BRCW 1960–61. B5 bogies. 37 t.

1651		**CC** RV	*RV*	ZG	1671 x*	**CH** RV	*RV*	ZG
1657		**BG** RV	*RV*	BU	1683	**RB** RV		BU
1659		**PC** LS		CL	1691	**CC** RV	*RV*	ZG
1666	x	**M** RP	*WC*	CS	1730 x	**M** SP	*SP*	BO

BUFFET STANDARD

Mark 1. These carriages are basically an open standard with two full window spaces removed to accommodate a buffet counter, and four seats removed to allow for a stock cupboard. All remaining vehicles now have fluorescent lighting. –/44 2T. Commonwealth bogies. ETS 3.

1861 has had its toilets replaced with store cupboards.

1813–32. Lot No. 30520 Wolverton 1960. 38 t.
1840. Lot No. 30507 Wolverton 1960. 37 t.
1859–63. Lot No. 30670 Wolverton 1961–62. 38 t.
1882. Lot No. 30702 Wolverton 1962. 38 t.

1813	x	**CH**	RV	*RV*	ZG		1860	x	**M**	WC	*WC*	CS
1832	x	**CC**	RV	*RV*	ZG		1861	x	**M**	WC	*WC*	CS
1840	v	**M**	WC	*WC*	CS		1863	x	**CH**	LS		CL
1859	x	**M**	SP	*SP*	BO		1882	x	**M**	WC	*WC*	CS

KITCHEN UNCLASSIFIED

Mark 1. These carriages were built as Unclassified Restaurants. They were rebuilt with buffet counters and 23 fixed polypropylene chairs, then further refurbished by fitting fluorescent lighting. Further modified for use as servery vehicle with seating removed and kitchen extended. ETS 2X.

1953. Lot No. 30575 Swindon 1960. B4/B5 bogies. 36.5 t.
1961. Lot No. 30632 Swindon 1961. Commonwealth bogies. 39 t.

1953		**VN**	WC	*NB*	KR		1961	x	**M**	WC	*WC*	CS

HM THE QUEEN'S SALOON

Mark 3. Converted from an Open First built 1972. Consists of a lounge, bedroom and bathroom for HM The Queen, and a combined bedroom and bathroom for the Queen's dresser. One entrance vestibule has double doors. Air conditioned. BT10 bogies. ETS 9X.

Lot No. 30886 Wolverton 1977. 36 t.

2903	(11001)	**RP**	NR	*RT*		ZN

HRH THE DUKE OF EDINBURGH'S SALOON

Mark 3. Converted from an Open Standard built 1972. Consists of a combined lounge/dining room, a bedroom and a shower room for the Duke, a kitchen and a valet's bedroom and bathroom. Air conditioned. BT10 bogies. ETS 15X.

Lot No. 30887 Wolverton 1977. 36 t.

2904	(12001)	**RP**	NR	*RT*		ZN

ROYAL HOUSEHOLD SLEEPING CAR

Mark 3A. Built to similar specification as Sleeping Cars 10647–729. 12 sleeping compartments for use of Royal Household with a fixed lower berth and a hinged upper berth. 2T plus shower room. Air conditioned. BT10 bogies. ETS 11X.

Lot No. 31002 Derby/Wolverton 1985. 44 t.

| 2915 | | **RP** | NR | *RT* | ZN |

HRH THE PRINCE OF WALES'S DINING CAR

Mark 3. Converted from HST TRUK (kitchen car) built 1976. Large kitchen retained, but dining area modified for Royal use seating up to 14 at central table(s). Air conditioned. BT10 bogies. ETS 13X.

Lot No. 31059 Wolverton 1988. 43 t.

| 2916 | (40512) | **RP** | NR | *RT* | ZN |

ROYAL KITCHEN/HOUSEHOLD DINING CAR

Mark 3. Converted from HST TRUK built 1977. Large kitchen retained and dining area slightly modified with seating for 22 Royal Household members. Air conditioned. BT10 bogies. ETS 13X.

Lot No. 31084 Wolverton 1990. 43 t.

| 2917 | (40514) | **RP** | NR | *RT* | ZN |

ROYAL HOUSEHOLD CARS

Mark 3. Converted from HST TRUKs built 1976/77. Air conditioned. BT10 bogies. ETS 10X.

Lot Nos. 31083 (* 31085) Wolverton 1989. 41.05 t.

| 2918 | (40515) | | **RP** | NR | ZN |
| 2919 | (40518) | * | **RP** | NR | ZN |

ROYAL HOUSEHOLD COUCHETTES

Mark 2B. Converted from Corridor Brake First built 1969. Consists of luggage accommodation, guard's compartment, workshop area, 350 kW diesel generator and staff sleeping accommodation. B5 bogies. ETS 2X (when generator not in use). ETS index ?? (when generator in use).

Lot No. 31044 Wolverton 1986. 48 t.

| 2920 | (14109, 17109) | **RP** | NR | *RT* | ZN |

Mark 2B. Converted from Corridor Brake First built 1969. Consists of luggage accommodation, kitchen, brake control equipment and staff accommodation. B5 bogies. ETS 7X.

Lot No. 31086 Wolverton 1990. 41.5 t.

2921   (14107, 17107)   **RP**   NR   *RT*   ZN

HRH THE PRINCE OF WALES'S SLEEPING CAR

Mark 3B. Air conditioned. BT10 bogies. ETS 7X.

Lot No. 31035 Derby/Wolverton 1987.

2922   **RP**   NR   *RT*   ZN

ROYAL SALOON

Mark 3B. Air conditioned. BT10 bogies. ETS 6X.

Lot No. 31036 Derby/Wolverton 1987.

2923   **RP**   NR   *RT*   ZN

OPEN FIRST

Mark 1. 42/– 2T. ETS 3. Many now fitted with table lamps.

3058 was numbered DB 975313, 3068 was numbered DB 975606 and 3093 was numbered DB 977594 for a time when in departmental service for BR.

3058–68. Lot No. 30169 Doncaster 1955. B4 bogies. 33 t (* Commonwealth bogies 35 t).
3093. Lot No. 30472 BRCW 1959. B4 bogies. 33 t.
3096–3100. Lot No. 30576 BRCW 1959. B4 bogies. 33 t.

3058	*x **M**	WC	*WC*	CS	FLORENCE	3096	x **M**	SP	*SP*	BO	
3066	**CC**	RV	*RV*	ZG		3097	x **CH**	RV	*RV*	ZG	
3068	**CC**	RV	*RV*	ZG		3098	x **CH**	RV	*RV*	ZG	
3093	x **M**	WC	*WC*	CS	FLORENCE	3100	x **CC**	LS	*LS*	CL	

Later design with fluorescent lighting, aluminium window frames and Commonwealth bogies.

3128/36/41/43/46/47/48 were renumbered 1058/60/63/65/68/69/70 when reclassified Restaurant Open First, then 3600/05/08/09/06/04/10 when declassified to Open Standard, but have since regained their original numbers. 3136 was numbered DB 977970 for a time when in use with Serco Railtest as a Brake Force Runner.

3105 has had its luggage racks removed and has tungsten lighting.

3105–28. Lot No. 30697 Swindon 1962–63. 36 t.
3130–50. Lot No. 30717 Swindon 1963. 36 t.

3105	x	**M**	WC	*WC*	CS		3125	x	**CH**	LS	CL
3106	x	**M**	WC	*WC*	CS		3128	x	**M**	WC	*WC*	CS
3107	x	**CH**	LS		CL		3130	x	**M**	WC	*WC*	CS
3110	x	**CH**	RV	*RV*	ZG		3136	x	**M**	WC	*WC*	CS
3112	x	**CH**	LS		CL		3140	x	**CH**	LS		CL
3113	x	**M**	WC	*WC*	CS		3141		**M**	RV		ZG
3115	x	**M**	SP	*SP*	BO		3143	x	**M**	WC	*WC*	CS
3117	x	**M**	WC	*WC*	CS		3146		**M**	RV		ZG
3119		**CH**	RV	*RV*	ZG		3147		**CH**	RV	*RV*	ZG
3120		**CC**	RV	*RV*	ZG		3148		**CC**	LS	*LS*	CL
3121		**CH**	RV	*RV*	ZG		3149		**CH**	RV	*RV*	ZG
3122	x	**CH**	LS		CL		3150		**M**	SP	*SP*	BO
3123		**CC**	RV	*RV*	ZG							

Names:

3105	JULIA		3128	VICTORIA
3106	ALEXANDRA		3130	PAMELA
3113	JESSICA		3136	DIANA
3117	CHRISTINA		3143	PATRICIA

OPEN FIRST

Mark 2D. Air conditioned. Stones equipment. 42/– 2T. B4 bogies. ETS 5.

† Interior modified to Pullman Car standards with new seating, new panelling, tungsten lighting and table lights.

Lot No. 30821 Derby 1971–72. 34 t.

3174	†	**VN**	WC	*NB*	KR	GLAMIS
3182	†	**VN**	WC	*NB*	KR	WARWICK
3188		**PC**	LS	*LS*	CL	CADAIR IDRIS

OPEN FIRST

Mark 2E. Air conditioned. Stones equipment. 42/– 2T (* 36/– 2T). B4 bogies. ETS 5.

r Refurbished with new seats.
† Interior modified to Pullman Car standards with new seating, new panelling, tungsten lighting and table lights.

Lot No. 30843 Derby 1972–73. 32.5 t. († 35.8 t).

3223		**RV**	LS		CL	DIAMOND
3231	*	**PC**	LS	*LS*	CL	BEN CRUACHAN
3232	dr	**BG**	WC		SH	
3240		**RV**	LS		CL	SAPPHIRE
3247	†	**VN**	WC	*NB*	KR	CHATSWORTH
3267	†	**VN**	WC	*NB*	KR	BELVOIR
3273	†	**VN**	WC	*NB*	KR	ALNWICK
3275	†	**VN**	WC	*NB*	KR	HARLECH

OPEN FIRST

Mark 2F. Air conditioned. 3277–3314/3359–79 have Stones equipment, others have Temperature Ltd. All refurbished in the 1980s with power-operated vestibule doors, new panels and new seat trim. 42/– 2T. B4 bogies. d. ETS 5X.

r Further refurbished with table lamps and modified seats with burgundy seat trim.
u Fitted with power supply for Mark 1 Kitchen Buffet Unclassified.

3277–3314. Lot No. 30845 Derby 1973. 33.5 t.
3325–3426. Lot No. 30859 Derby 1973–74. 33.5 t.
3431–3438. Lot No. 30873 Derby 1974–75. 33.5 t.

3277		**AR**	LS		CL	3351		**CH**	VT		TM
3278	r	**BG**	RV	*RV*	BU	3352	r	**M**	WC	*WC*	CS
3295		**AR**	LS		CL	3356	r	**BG**	RV	*RV*	BU
3304	r	**BG**	RV	*RV*	BU	3359	r	**M**	WC	*WC*	CS
3312		**PC**	LS	*LS*	CL	3360	r	**PC**	WC	*WC*	CS
3313	r	**M**	WC	*WC*	CS	3362	r	**PC**	WC	*WC*	CS
3314	r	**BG**	RV	*RV*	BU	3364	r	**BG**	RV	*RV*	BU
3325	r	**V**	RV	*RV*	BU	3379	u	**AR**	RV		DE
3326	r	**M**	WC	*WC*	CS	3384	r	**PC**	LS	*LS*	CL
3330	r	**CC**	LS	*LS*	CL	3386	r	**BG**	RV	*RV*	BU
3333	r	**BG**	RV	*RV*	BU	3390	r	**BG**	RV	*RV*	BU
3334		**AR**	RV		DE	3392	r	**M**	WC	*WC*	CS
3336	u	**AR**	RV		DE	3395	r	**M**	WC	*WC*	CS
3340	r	**V**	RV	*RV*	BU	3397	r	**BG**	RV	*RV*	BU
3344	r	**V**	RV	*RV*	BU	3417		**AR**	RV		DE
3345	r	**BG**	RV	*RV*	BU	3426	r	**CC**	LS	*LS*	CL
3348	r	**PC**	LS	*LS*	CL	3431	r	**M**	WC	*WC*	CS
3350	r	**M**	WC	*WC*	CS	3438	r	**PC**	LS	*LS*	CL

Names:

3312	HELVELLYN		3426	ELGAR
3348	INGLEBOROUGH		3438	BEN LOMOND
3384	PEN-Y-GHENT			

OPEN STANDARD

Mark 1. –/64 2T. ETS 4.

4831–36. Lot No. 30506 Wolverton 1959. Commonwealth bogies. 33 t.
4854/56. Lot No. 30525 Wolverton 1959–60. B4 bogies. 33 t.

4831	x	**M**	SP	*SP*	BO	4854	x	**M**	WC	*WC*	CS
4832	x	**M**	SP	*SP*	BO	4856	x	**M**	SP	*SP*	BO
4836	x	**M**	SP	*SP*	BO						

OPEN STANDARD

Mark 1. Commonwealth bogies. –/64 2T. ETS 4.

4905. Lot No. 30646 Wolverton 1961. 36 t.
4927–5044. Lot No. 30690 Wolverton 1961–62. 37 t.

4905	x	**M**	WC	*WC*	CS	4984	x	**M**	WC	*WC*	CS
4927	x	**CC**	RV	*RV*	ZG	4991		**CH**	RV	*RV*	ZG
4931	v	**M**	WC	*WC*	CS	4994	x	**M**	WC	*WC*	CS
4940	x	**M**	WC	*WC*	CS	4998		**CH**	RV	*RV*	ZG
4946	x	**CH**	RV	*RV*	ZG	5009	x	**CH**	RV		BU
4949	x	**CH**	RV	*RV*	ZG	5027		**G**	RV		BU
4951	x	**M**	WC	*WC*	CS	5028	x	**M**	SP	*SP*	BO
4954	v	**M**	WC	*WC*	CS	5032	x	**M**	WC	*WC*	CS
4959		**CH**	RV	*RV*	ZG	5033	x	**M**	WC	*WC*	CS
4960	x	**M**	WC	*WC*	CS	5035	x	**M**	WC	*WC*	CS
4973	x	**M**	WC	*WC*	CS	5044	x	**M**	WC	*WC*	CS

OPEN STANDARD

Mark 2. Pressure ventilated. –/64 2T. B4 bogies. ETS 4.

Lot No. 30751 Derby 1965–67. 32 t.

5157	v	**CH**	VT	*VT*	TM	5200	v	**M**	WC	*WC*	CS
5171	v	**M**	WC	*WC*	CS	5212	v	**CH**	VT	*VT*	TM
5177	v	**CH**	VT	*VT*	TM	5216	v	**M**	WC	*WC*	CS
5191	v	**CH**	VT	*VT*	TM	5222	v	**M**	WC	*WC*	CS
5198	v	**CH**	VT	*VT*	TM						

OPEN STANDARD

Mark 2. Pressure ventilated. –/48 2T. B4 bogies. ETS 4.

Lot No. 30752 Derby 1966. 32 t.

5229		**M**	WC	*WC*	CS	5239		**M**	WC	*WC*	CS
5236	v	**M**	WC	*WC*	CS	5249	v	**M**	WC	*WC*	CS
5237	v	**M**	WC	*WC*	CS						

OPEN STANDARD

Mark 2A. Pressure ventilated. –/64 2T (w –/62 2T). B4 bogies. ETS 4.

f Facelifted vehicles.

5278–5341. Lot No. 30776 Derby 1967–68. 32 t.
5366–5419. Lot No. 30787 Derby 1968. 32 t.

5278		**M**	WC	*WC*	CS	5366	f	**CH**	RV	*RV*	ZG
5292	f	**CC**	RV		BU	5419	w	**M**	WC	*WC*	CS
5341	f	**CC**	RV		BU						

OPEN STANDARD

Mark 2B. Pressure ventilated. –/62. B4 bogies. ETS 4.

Lot No. 30791 Derby 1969. 32 t.

| 5487 | | **M** | WC | *WC* | CS |

OPEN STANDARD

Mark 2E. Air conditioned. Stones equipment. Refurbished with new interior panelling. –/64 2T. B4 bogies. d. ETS 5.

s   Modified design of seat headrest and centre luggage stack. –/60 2T.

5787–97. Lot No. 30837 Derby 1972. 33.5 t.
5810. Lot No. 30844 Derby 1972–73. 33.5 t.

| 5787 | s | **DS** | DR | *GA* | KM | | 5810 | | **DS** | DR | *GA* | KM |
| 5797 | | **IC** | LS | | CL | | | | | | | |

OPEN STANDARD

Mark 2F. Air conditioned. Temperature Ltd equipment. InterCity 70 seats. All were refurbished in the 1980s with power-operated vestibule doors, new panels and seat trim. They have subsequently undergone a second refurbishment with carpets and new seat trim. –/64 2T. B4 bogies. d. ETS 5X.

q   Fitted with two wheelchair spaces. –/60 2T 2W.
s   Fitted with centre luggage stack. –/60 2T.
t   Fitted with centre luggage stack and wheelchair space. –/58 2T 1W.
†   Retention toilets.

5910–55. Lot No. 30846 Derby 1973. 33 t.
5959–6158. Lot No. 30860 Derby 1973–74. 33 t.
6173–83. Lot No. 30874 Derby 1974–75. 33 t.

5910	q	**V**	RV		ZA		5987		**SR**	RV	*SR*	ML
5912		**PC**	LS	*LS*	CL		5991		**PC**	LS	*LS*	CL
5919	† pt	**DS**	DR	*NO*	KM		5995	†	**DS**	DR	*NO*	KM
5921		**AR**	RV	*RV*	BU		5998		**BG**	RV	*RV*	BU
5928		**CH**	VT		TM		6000	t	**M**	WC	*WC*	CS
5929		**AR**	RV	*RV*	BU		6001	†	**DS**	DR	*NO*	KM
5937		**DS**	DR	*GA*	KM		6006		**AR**	RV		BU
5945		**SR**	RV	*SR*	ML		6008	† s	**DS**	DR	*NO*	KM
5950		**AR**	RV	*RV*	BU		6012		**M**	WC	*WC*	CS
5952		**SR**	RV	*SR*	ML		6021		**M**	WC	*WC*	CS
5955		**SR**	RV	*SR*	ML		6022	s	**M**	WC	*WC*	CS
5961	pt	**BG**	RV	*RV*	BU		6024		**BG**	RV	*RV*	BU
5964		**AR**	RV	*RV*	BU		6027	q	**SR**	RV	*SR*	ML
5965	t	**SR**	RV	*SR*	ML		6042		**AR**	RV	*RV*	BU
5971	†	**DS**	DR	*NO*	KM		6046	†	**DS**	DR	*NO*	KM
5976	t	**SR**	RV	*SR*	ML		6051		**BG**	RV	*RV*	BU
5985		**AR**	RV	*RV*	BU		6054	s	**BG**	RV	*RV*	BU

6064	†	**DS**	DR	*NO*	KM
6067	pt	**BG**	RV	*RV*	BU
6103		**M**	WC	*WC*	CS
6115	s	**M**	WC	*WC*	CS
6117	†	**DS**	DR	*NO*	KM
6122	†	**DS**	DR	*NO*	KM
6137	s pt	**SR**	RV	*SR*	ML

6141	q	**V**	RV		BU
6158		**BG**	RV	*RV*	BU
6173	†	**DS**	DR	*NO*	KM
6176	t	**SR**	RV	*SR*	ML
6177	s	**SR**	RV	*SR*	ML
6183	s	**SR**	RV	*SR*	ML

BRAKE GENERATOR VAN

Mark 1. Renumbered 1989 from BR departmental series. Converted from Gangwayed Brake Van in 1973 to three-phase supply brake generator van for use with HST trailers. Modified 1999 for use with locomotive-hauled stock. B5 bogies. ETS index ??.

Lot No. 30400 Pressed Steel 1958.

6310	(81448, 975325)	**CH**	RV	*RV*	BU

GENERATOR VAN

Mark 1. Converted from Gangwayed Brake Vans in 1992. B4 (* B5) bogies. ETS index 75.

6311. Lot No. 30162 Pressed Steel 1958. 37.25 t.
6312. Lot No. 30224 Cravens 1956. 37.25 t.
6313. Lot No. 30484 Pressed Steel 1958. 37.25 t.

6311	(80903, 92911)		**B**	LS		CL
6312	(81023, 92925)		**M**	WC	*WC*	CS
6313	(81553, 92167)	*	**PC**	BE	*BP*	SL

BUFFET STANDARD

Mark 2C. Converted from Open Standard by removal of one seating bay and replacing this with a counter with a space for a trolley, now replaced with a more substantial buffet. Adjacent toilet removed and converted to steward's washing area/store. Pressure ventilated. –/55 1T. B4 bogies. ETS 4.

Lot No. 30795 Derby 1969–70. 32.5 t.

6528	(5592)	**M**	WC	*WC*	CS

SLEEPER RECEPTION CAR

Mark 2F. Converted from Open First. These vehicles consist of pantry, microwave cooking facilities, seating area for passengers (with loose chairs, staff toilet plus two bars). Now refurbished again with new "sofa" seating as well as the loose chairs. Converted at RTC, Derby (6700), Ilford (6701–05) and Derby (6706–08). Air conditioned. 6700/01/03/05–08 have Stones equipment and 6702/04 have Temperature Ltd equipment. The number of seats per coach can vary but typically is 25/– 1T (12 seats as "sofa" seating and 13 loose chairs). B4 bogies. d. ETS 5X.

6700–02/04/08. Lot No. 30859 Derby 1973–74. 33.5 t.
6703/05–07. Lot No. 30845 Derby 1973. 33.5 t.

6700	(3347)	**FS**	CA	*CA*	PO
6701	(3346)	**CA**	CA	*CA*	PO
6702	(3421)	**FS**	CA	*CA*	PO
6703	(3308)	**FS**	CA	*CA*	PO
6704	(3341)	**FS**	CA	*CA*	PO
6705	(3310, 6430)	**FS**	CA	*CA*	PO
6706	(3283, 6421)	**FS**	CA	*CA*	PO
6707	(3276, 6418)	**FS**	CA	*CA*	PO
6708	(3370)	**FS**	CA	*CA*	PO

BUFFET FIRST

Mark 2D. Converted from Buffet Standard by the removal of another seating bay and fitting a more substantial buffet counter with boiler and microwave oven. Now converted to First Class with new seating and end luggage stacks. Air conditioned. Stones equipment. 30/– 1T. B4 bogies. d. ETS 5. Lot No. 30822 Derby 1971. 33 t.

6722	(5736, 6661)	**FP**	E		LM
6723	(5641, 6662)	**M**	WC		CS
6724	(5721, 6665)	**M**	WC	*WC*	CS

OPEN BRAKE STANDARD WITH TROLLEY SPACE

Mark 2. This vehicle uses the same bodyshell as Mark 2 Corridor Brake Firsts and has First Class seat spacing and wider tables. Converted from Open Brake Standard by removal of one seating bay and replacing this with a counter with a space for a trolley. Adjacent toilet removed and converted to a steward's washing area/store. –/23. B4 bogies. ETS 4.

Lot No. 30757 Derby 1966. 31 t.

9101	(9398)	v	**CH**	VT	*VT*	TM

OPEN BRAKE STANDARD

Mark 2. These vehicles use the same bodyshell as Mark 2 Corridor Brake Firsts and have First Class seat spacing and wider tables. Pressure ventilated. –/31 1T. B4 bogies. ETS 4.

9104 was originally numbered 9401. It was renumbered when converted to Open Brake Standard with trolley space. Now returned to original layout.

Lot No. 30757 Derby 1966. 31.5 t.

9104	v	**M**	WC	*WC*	CS	9392	v	**M**	WC	*WC*	CS
9391		**M**	WC	*WC*	CS						

OPEN BRAKE STANDARD

Mark 2D. Air conditioned. Stones Equipment. B4 bogies. d. pg. ETS 5.

r Refurbished with new interior panelling –/31 1T.
s Refurbished with new seating –/22 1TD.

Lot No. 30824 Derby 1971. 33 t.

9479	r	**PC**	LS	*LS*	CL	9493	s	**M**	WC	*WC*	CS
9488	s	**SR**	DR	*SR*	ML						

OPEN BRAKE STANDARD

Mark 2E. Air conditioned. Stones Equipment. Refurbished with new interior panelling. –/32 1T (* –/30 1T 1W). B4 bogies. d. pg. ETS 5.

Lot No. 30838 Derby 1972. 33 t.

Non-standard livery: 9502 Pullman umber & cream.

s Modified design of seat headrest.

9496		**M**	VT		TM	9507	s	**BG**	RV	*CA*	PO
9502	s	**0**	BE	*BP*	SL	9509	s	**AV**	RV		BU
9504	s*	**BG**	RV	*RV*	BU						

OPEN BRAKE STANDARD

Mark 2F. Air conditioned. Temperature Ltd equipment. All were refurbished in the 1980s with power-operated vestibule doors, new panels and seat trim. All now further refurbished with carpets. –/32 1T (w –/30 1T 1W). B4 bogies. d. pg. ETS 5X.

9537 has had all its seats removed for the purpose of carrying luggage.

Lot No. 30861 Derby 1974. 34 t.

9520	nw	**AR**	RV	*RV*	BU	9527	n	**SR**	RV	*SR*	ML
9521		**DS**	RV	*GA*	KM	9537	n	**V**	RV		BU
9525		**DS**	DR	*GA*	KM	9539		**SR**	RV	*SR*	ML
9526	n	**BG**	RV	*RV*	BU						

DRIVING OPEN BRAKE STANDARD

Mark 2F. Air conditioned. Temperature Ltd equipment. Push & pull (tdm system). Converted from Open Brake Standard, these vehicles originally had half cabs at the brake end. They have since been refurbished and have had their cabs widened and the cab-end gangways removed. Five vehicles (9701–03/08/14) have been converted for use in Network Rail test trains and can be found in the Service Stock section of this book. –/30(+1) 1W. B4 bogies. d. pg. Cowcatchers. ETS 5X.

Lot No. 30861 Derby 1974. Converted Glasgow 1979. Disc brakes. 34 t.

9704	(9512)	**DS**	DR	*NO*	KM	9709	(9515)	**DS**	DR	*NO*	KM
9705	(9519)	**DS**	DR	*GA*	KM	9710	(9518)	**DS**	DR	*NO*	KM
9707	(9511)	**DS**	DR	*NO*	KM						

OPEN BRAKE UNCLASSIFIED

Mark 2E. Converted from Open Standard with new seating by Railcare, Wolverton. Air conditioned. Stones equipment. –/31 2T. B4 bogies. d. ETS 4X.

9800–03. Lot No. 30837 Derby 1972. 33.5 t.
9804–10. Lot No. 30844 Derby 1972–73. 33.5 t.

9800	(5751)	**FS**	CA	*CA*	PO	9806	(5840)	**FS**	CA	*CA*	PO
9801	(5760)	**FS**	CA	*CA*	PO	9807	(5851)	**FS**	CA	*CA*	PO
9802	(5772)	**CA**	CA	*CA*	PO	9808	(5871)	**FS**	CA	*CA*	PO
9803	(5799)	**FS**	CA	*CA*	PO	9809	(5890)	**FS**	CA	*CA*	PO
9804	(5826)	**FS**	CA	*CA*	PO	9810	(5892)	**FS**	CA	*CA*	PO
9805	(5833)	**FS**	CA	*CA*	PO						

KITCHEN BUFFET FIRST

Mark 3A. Air conditioned. Converted from HST catering vehicles and Mark 3 Open Firsts. Refurbished with table lamps and burgundy seat trim (except *). 18/– plus two seats for staff use (* 24/–, † 24/–, § 24/–, t 23/– 1T 1W). BT10 bogies. d. ETS 14X.

§ Great Western Railway Sleeper "day coaches" that have been fitted with former HST First Class seats to a 2+1 layout.

Non-standard liveries:

10211 EWS dark maroon.
10241 Livery trials.

10202–211. Lot No. 30884 Derby 1977. 39.8 t.
10212–229. Lot No. 30878 Derby 1975–76. 39.8 t.
10232–259. Lot No. 30890 Derby 1979. 39.8 t.

10202	(40504) †	**BG**	AV		LM
10211	(40510)	**O**	DB	*DB*	TO
10212	(11049)	**VT**	P	*TP*	CP
10215	(11032)	**BG**	AV		LM
10217	(11051)	**VT**	P		ZN
10219	(11047) §	**GW**	P	*GW*	PZ
10222	(11063)	**BG**	AV		LM
10225	(11014) §	**GW**	P	*GW*	PZ
10226	(11015)	**V**	AV		LM
10229	(11059) *	**GA**	P	*TP*	CP
10232	(10027) §	**FD**	P	*GW*	PZ
10233	(10013)	**V**	AV		LM
10235	(10015) †	**BG**	AV		LM
10237	(10022)	**DR**	AV		LM
10241	(10009) *	**O**	P		IL
10242	(10002)	**BG**	AV		LM
10246	(10014) †	**BG**	AV		LM
10249	(10012)	**AW**	AV	*AW*	CF
10250	(10020)	**V**	AV		LM
10257	(10007) †	**BG**	AV		LM
10259	(10025) t	**AW**	AV	*AW*	CF

KITCHEN BUFFET FIRST

Mark 3A. Air conditioned. Rebuilt 2011–12 and fitted with sliding plug doors. Interiors originally refurbished for Wrexham & Shropshire with Primarius seating, a new kitchen area and universal-access toilet. Retention toilets. 30/– 1TD 1W. BT10 bogies. ETS 14X.

10271/273/274. Lot No. 30890 Derby 1979. 41.3 t.
10272. Lot No. 30884 Derby 1977. 41.3 t.

10271	(10018, 10236)	**CM**	AV	*CR*	AL
10272	(40517, 10208)	**CM**	AV	*CR*	AL
10273	(10021, 10230)	**CM**	AV	*CR*	AL
10274	(10010, 10255)	**CM**	AV	*CR*	AL

KITCHEN BUFFET STANDARD

Mark 4. Air conditioned. Rebuilt from First to Standard Class with bar adjacent to seating area instead of adjacent to end of coach. Retention toilets. –/30 1T. BT41 bogies. ETS 6X.

Lot No. 31045 Metro-Cammell 1989–92. 43.2 t.

10300	**VE**	E	*VE*	BN	10317	**VE**	E	*VE*	BN
10301	**VE**	E	*VE*	BN	10318	**VE**	E	*VE*	BN
10302	**VE**	E	*VE*	BN	10319	**VE**	E	*VE*	BN
10303	**VE**	E	*VE*	BN	10320	**VE**	E	*VE*	BN
10304	**VE**	E	*VE*	BN	10321	**VE**	E	*VE*	BN
10305	**VE**	E	*VE*	BN	10323	**VE**	E	*VE*	BN
10306	**VE**	E	*VE*	BN	10324	**VE**	E	*VE*	BN
10307	**VE**	E	*VE*	BN	10325	**VE**	E	*VE*	BN
10308	**VE**	E	*VE*	BN	10326	**VE**	E	*VE*	BN
10309	**VE**	E	*VE*	BN	10328	**VE**	E	*VE*	BN
10310	**VE**	E	*VE*	BN	10329	**VE**	E	*VE*	BN
10311	**VE**	E	*VE*	BN	10330	**VE**	E	*VE*	BN
10312	**VE**	E	*VE*	BN	10331	**VE**	E	*VE*	BN
10313	**VE**	E	*VE*	BN	10332	**VE**	E	*VE*	BN
10315	**VE**	E	*VE*	BN	10333	**VE**	E	*VE*	BN

BUFFET STANDARD

Mark 3A. Air conditioned. Converted from Mark 3 Open Standard at Derby 2006. –/54. d. ETS 13X.

Lot No. 30877 Derby 1975–77. 37.8 t.

10401	(12168)	**GA**	P	*GA*	NC	10404	(12068)	**GA**	P	*GA*	NC
10402	(12010)	**GA**	P	*GA*	NC	10405	(12157)	**GA**	P	*GA*	NC
10403	(12135)	**GA**	P	*GA*	NC	10406	(12020)	**GA**	P	*GA*	NC

BUFFET STANDARD

Mark 3A. Air conditioned. Converted from Mark 3 Kitchen Buffet First 2015–16. –/54. BT10 bogies. d. ETS 13X.

10411–412. Lot No. 30884 Derby 1977. 37.8 t.
10413–416. Lot No. 30878 Derby 1975–76. 37.8 t.
10417. Lot No. 30890 Derby 1979. 37.8 t.

10411	(40519, 10200)	**GA**	P	*GA*	NC
10412	(40506, 10203)	**GA**	P	*GA*	NC
10413	(11034, 10214)	**GA**	P	*GA*	NC
10414	(11041, 10216)	**GA**	P	*GA*	NC
10415	(11043, 10223)	**GA**	P	*GA*	NC
10416	(11035, 10228)	**GA**	P	*GA*	NC
10417	(10011, 10247)	**GA**	P	*GA*	NC

SLEEPING CAR WITH PANTRY

Mark 3A. Air conditioned. Retention toilets. 12 compartments with a fixed lower berth and a hinged upper berth, plus an attendant's compartment. 2T. BT10 bogies. d. ETS 7X.

Non-standard livery: 10546 EWS dark maroon.

Lot No. 30960 Derby 1981–83. 41 t.

10501	**FS**	P	*CA*	PO	10531	**FS**	P	*CA*	PO
10502	**FS**	P	*CA*	PO	10532	**GW**	P	*GW*	PZ
10504	**FS**	P	*CA*	PO	10534	**GW**	P	*GW*	PZ
10506	**FS**	P	*CA*	PO	10542	**FS**	P	*CA*	PO
10507	**FS**	P	*CA*	PO	10543	**FS**	P	*CA*	PO
10508	**FS**	P	*CA*	PO	10544	**FS**	P	*CA*	PO
10513	**FS**	P	*CA*	PO	10546	**0**	DB	*DB*	TO
10516	**FS**	P	*CA*	PO	10548	**FS**	P	*CA*	PO
10519	**FS**	P	*CA*	PO	10551	**FS**	P	*CA*	PO
10520	**FS**	P	*CA*	PO	10553	**FS**	P	*CA*	PO
10522	**FS**	P	*CA*	PO	10561	**FS**	P	*CA*	PO
10523	**FS**	P	*CA*	PO	10562	**FS**	P	*CA*	PO
10526	**FS**	P	*CA*	PO	10563	**GW**	P	*GW*	PZ
10527	**FS**	P	*CA*	PO	10565	**FS**	P	*CA*	PO
10529	**FS**	P	*CA*	PO	10580	**CA**	P	*CA*	PO

10584	**GW** P	*GW*	PZ		10605	**FS** P	*CA*	PO
10589	**GW** P	*GW*	PZ		10607	**FS** P	*CA*	PO
10590	**GW** P	*GW*	PZ		10610	**FS** P	*CA*	PO
10594	**GW** P	*GW*	PZ		10612	**GW** P	*GW*	PZ
10596	**GW** P	*GW*	PZ		10613	**FS** P	*CA*	PO
10597	**FS** P	*CA*	PO		10614	**FS** P	*CA*	PO
10598	**FS** P	*CA*	PO		10616	**GW** P	*GW*	PZ
10600	**FS** P	*CA*	PO		10617	**FS** P	*CA*	PO
10601	**GW** P	*GW*	PZ					

SLEEPING CAR

Mark 3A. Air conditioned. Retention toilets. 13 compartments with a fixed lower berth and a hinged upper berth (* 11 compartments with a fixed lower berth and a hinged upper berth + one compartment for a disabled person. 1TD). 2T. BT10 bogies. ETS 6X.

10734 was originally 2914 and used as a Royal Train staff sleeping car. It has 12 berths and a shower room and is ETS 11X.

10648–729. Lot No. 30961 Derby 1980–84. 43.5 t.
10734. Lot No. 31002 Derby/Wolverton 1985. 42.5 t.

10648 d*	**FS**	P	*CA*	PO		10699 d*	**FS**	P	*CA*	PO
10650 d*	**FS**	P	*CA*	PO		10703 d	**FS**	P	*CA*	PO
10666 d*	**FS**	P	*CA*	PO		10706 d*	**FS**	P	*CA*	PO
10675 d	**FS**	P	*CA*	PO		10714 d*	**FS**	P	*CA*	PO
10680 d*	**FS**	P	*CA*	PO		10718 d*	**FS**	P	*CA*	PO
10683 d	**FS**	P	*CA*	PO		10719 d*	**FS**	P	*CA*	PO
10688 d	**FS**	P	*CA*	PO		10722 d*	**FS**	P	*CA*	PO
10689 d*	**FS**	P	*CA*	PO		10723 d*	**FS**	P	*CA*	PO
10690 d	**FS**	P	*CA*	PO		10729	**VN**	WC	*NB*	KR
10693 d	**CA**	P	*CA*	PO		10734	**VN**	WC	*NB*	KR

Names:

10729	CREWE		10734	BALMORAL

OPEN FIRST

Mark 3A. Air conditioned. All refurbished with table lamps and new seat cushions and trim. 48/– 2T. BT10 bogies. d. ETS 6X.

† Reseated with Standard Class seats: –/68 2T 2W.

11007 was open composite 11907 for a time.

Non-standard livery: 11039 EWS dark maroon.

Lot No. 30878 Derby 1975–76. 34.3 t.

11007	**VT** P		LA		11031 †	**CM** AV	*CR*	AL
11018	**VT** P	*TP*	CP		11033	**DR** AV		LM
11028	**V** AV		ZB		11039	**O** DB	*DB*	TO
11029 †	**CM** AV	*CR*	AL		11048	**VT** P	*TP*	CP

OPEN FIRST

Mark 3B. Air conditioned. InterCity 80 seats. All refurbished with table lamps and new seat cushions and trim. Retention toilets. 48/– 1T. BT10 bogies. d. ETS 6X.

† Fitted with disabled toilet and reduced seating, including three Compin Pegasus seats. 37/– 1TD 2W.

Lot No. 30982 Derby 1985. 36.5 t.

11066	**GA**	P	*GA*	NC	11085 †	**GA**	P	*GA*	NC
11067	**GA**	P	*GA*	NC	11087 †	**GA**	P	*GA*	NC
11068	**GA**	P	*GA*	NC	11088 †	**GA**	P	*GA*	NC
11069	**GA**	P	*GA*	NC	11090 †	**GA**	P	*GA*	NC
11070	**GA**	P	*GA*	NC	11091	**GA**	P	*GA*	NC
11072	**GA**	P	*GA*	NC	11092 †	**GA**	P	*GA*	NC
11073	**GA**	P	*GA*	NC	11093 †	**GA**	P	*GA*	NC
11075	**GA**	P	*GA*	NC	11094 †	**GA**	P	*GA*	NC
11076	**GA**	P	*GA*	NC	11095 †	**GA**	P	*GA*	NC
11077	**GA**	P	*GA*	NC	11096 †	**GA**	P	*GA*	NC
11078 †	**GA**	P	*GA*	NC	11098 †	**GA**	P	*GA*	NC
11080	**GA**	P	*GA*	NC	11099 †	**GA**	P	*GA*	NC
11081	**GA**	P	*GA*	NC	11100 †	**GA**	P	*GA*	NC
11082	**GA**	P	*GA*	NC	11101 †	**GA**	P	*GA*	NC

OPEN FIRST

Mark 4. Air conditioned. Rebuilt with new interior by Bombardier Wakefield 2003–05 (some converted from Standard Class vehicles). Retention toilets. 41/– 1T (plus 2 seats for staff use). BT41 bogies. ETS 6X.

11201–11273. Lot No. 31046 Metro-Cammell 1989–92. 41.3 t.
11277–11299. Lot No. 31049 Metro-Cammell 1989–92. 41.3 t.

11201		**VE**	E	*VE*	BN	11284 (12487)	**VE**	E	*VE*	BN
11219		**VE**	E	*VE*	BN	11285 (12537)	**VE**	E	*VE*	BN
11229		**VE**	E	*VE*	BN	11286 (12482)	**VE**	E	*VE*	BN
11237		**VE**	E	*VE*	BN	11287 (12527)	**VE**	E	*VE*	BN
11241		**VE**	E	*VE*	BN	11288 (12517)	**VE**	E	*VE*	BN
11244		**VE**	E	*VE*	BN	11289 (12528)	**VE**	E	*VE*	BN
11273		**VE**	E	*VE*	BN	11290 (12530)	**VE**	E	*VE*	BN
11277 (12408)	**VE**	E	*VE*	BN	11291 (12535)	**VE**	E	*VE*	BN
11278 (12479)	**VE**	E	*VE*	BN	11292 (12451)	**VE**	E	*VE*	BN
11279 (12521)	**VE**	E	*VE*	BN	11293 (12536)	**VE**	E	*VE*	BN
11280 (12523)	**VE**	E	*VE*	BN	11294 (12529)	**VE**	E	*VE*	BN
11281 (12418)	**VE**	E	*VE*	BN	11295 (12475)	**VE**	E	*VE*	BN
11282 (12524)	**VE**	E	*VE*	BN	11298 (12416)	**VE**	E	*VE*	BN
11283 (12435)	**VE**	E	*VE*	BN	11299 (12532)	**VE**	E	*VE*	BN

OPEN FIRST (DISABLED)

Mark 4. Air conditioned. Rebuilt from Open First by Bombardier Wakefield 2003–05. Retention toilets. 42/– 1TD 1W. BT41 bogies. ETS 6X.

Lot No. 31046 Metro-Cammell 1989–92. 40.7 t.

11301	(11215)	**VE**	E	*VE*	BN			
11302	(11203)	**VE**	E	*VE*	BN			
11303	(11211)	**VE**	E	*VE*	BN			
11304	(11257)	**VE**	E	*VE*	BN			
11305	(11261)	**VE**	E	*VE*	BN			
11306	(11276)	**VE**	E	*VE*	BN			
11307	(11217)	**VE**	E	*VE*	BN			
11308	(11263)	**VE**	E	*VE*	BN			
11309	(11259)	**VE**	E	*VE*	BN			
11310	(11272)	**VE**	E	*VE*	BN			
11311	(11221)	**VE**	E	*VE*	BN			
11312	(11225)	**VE**	E	*VE*	BN			
11313	(11210)	**VE**	E	*VE*	BN			
11314	(11207)	**VE**	E	*VE*	BN			
11315	(11238)	**VE**	E	*VE*	BN			

11316	(11227)	**VE**	E	*VE*	BN
11317	(11223)	**VE**	E	*VE*	BN
11318	(11251)	**VE**	E	*VE*	BN
11319	(11247)	**VE**	E	*VE*	BN
11320	(11255)	**VE**	E	*VE*	BN
11321	(11245)	**VE**	E	*VE*	BN
11322	(11228)	**VE**	E	*VE*	BN
11323	(11235)	**VE**	E	*VE*	BN
11324	(11253)	**VE**	E	*VE*	BN
11325	(11231)	**VE**	E	*VE*	BN
11326	(11206)	**VE**	E	*VE*	BN
11327	(11236)	**VE**	E	*VE*	BN
11328	(11274)	**VE**	E	*VE*	BN
11329	(11243)	**VE**	E	*VE*	BN
11330	(11249)	**VE**	E	*VE*	BN

OPEN FIRST

Mark 4. Air conditioned. Rebuilt from Open First by Bombardier Wakefield 2003–05. Separate area for 7 smokers, although smoking is no longer allowed. Retention toilets. 46/– 1TD 1W. BT41 bogies. ETS 6X.

Lot No. 31046 Metro-Cammell 1989–92. 42.1 t.

11401	(11214)	**VE**	E	*VE*	BN
11402	(11216)	**VE**	E	*VE*	BN
11403	(11258)	**VE**	E	*VE*	BN
11404	(11202)	**VE**	E	*VE*	BN
11405	(11204)	**VE**	E	*VE*	BN
11406	(11205)	**VE**	E	*VE*	BN
11407	(11256)	**VE**	E	*VE*	BN
11408	(11218)	**VE**	E	*VE*	BN
11409	(11262)	**VE**	E	*VE*	BN
11410	(11260)	**VE**	E	*VE*	BN
11411	(11240)	**VE**	E	*VE*	BN
11412	(11209)	**VE**	E	*VE*	BN
11413	(11212)	**VE**	E	*VE*	BN
11414	(11246)	**VE**	E	*VE*	BN
11415	(11208)	**VE**	E	*VE*	BN

11416	(11254)	**VE**	E	*VE*	BN
11417	(11226)	**VE**	E	*VE*	BN
11418	(11222)	**VE**	E	*VE*	BN
11419	(11250)	**VE**	E	*VE*	BN
11420	(11242)	**VE**	E	*VE*	BN
11421	(11220)	**VE**	E	*VE*	BN
11422	(11232)	**VE**	E	*VE*	BN
11423	(11230)	**VE**	E	*VE*	BN
11424	(11239)	**VE**	E	*VE*	BN
11425	(11234)	**VE**	E	*VE*	BN
11426	(11252)	**VE**	E	*VE*	BN
11427	(11200)	**VE**	E	*VE*	BN
11428	(11233)	**VE**	E	*VE*	BN
11429	(11275)	**VE**	E	*VE*	BN
11430	(11248)	**VE**	E	*VE*	BN

OPEN FIRST

CAF Mark 5A. Air conditioned. Under construction by CAF for TransPennine Express for delivery 2018. Full details awaited. Retention toilets. 30/– 1TD 2W.

11501	**TP**	BN		11508	**TP**	BN
11502	**TP**	BN		11509	**TP**	BN
11503	**TP**	BN		11510	**TP**	BN
11504	**TP**	BN		11511	**TP**	BN
11505	**TP**	BN		11512	**TP**	BN
11506	**TP**	BN		11513	**TP**	BN
11507	**TP**	BN				

OPEN FIRST

Mark 4. Air conditioned. Converted from Kitchen Buffet Standard with new interior by Bombardier Wakefield 2005. Retention toilets. 46/– 1T. BT41 bogies. ETS 6X.

Lot No. 31046 Metro-Cammell 1989–92. 41.3 t.

11998	(10314)	**VE**	E	*VE*	BN			
11999	(10316)	**VE**	E	*VE*	BN			

OPEN STANDARD

Mark 3A. Air conditioned. All refurbished with modified seat backs and new layout and further refurbished with new seat trim. –/76 2T († –/70 2T 1W, t –/72 2T, z –/70 1TD 1T 2W). BT10 bogies. d. ETS 6X.

* Further refurbished with more unidirectional seating and one toilet removed. Retention toilets. –/80 1T.

s Refurbished Sleeper day coaches fitted with new Transcal seating to a 2+2 layout and a universal access toilet. Retention toilets. –/65 1TD 1W.

12170/171 were converted from Open Composites 11909/910, formerly Open Firsts 11009/010.

12005–167. Lot No. 30877 Derby 1975–77. 34.3 t.
12170/171. Lot No. 30878 Derby 1975–76. 34.3 t.

12005	*	**GA**	P	*GA*	NC		12031	*	**GA**	P	*GA*	NC
12009	*	**GA**	P	*GA*	NC		12032	*	**GA**	P	*GA*	NC
12011		**VT**	P	*TP*	CP		12034	*	**GA**	P	*GA*	NC
12012	*	**GA**	P	*GA*	NC		12035	*	**GA**	P	*GA*	NC
12013	*	**GA**	P	*GA*	NC		12036	†	**CM**	AV	*CR*	AL
12015	*	**GA**	P	*GA*	NC		12037	*	**GA**	P	*GA*	NC
12016	*	**GA**	P	*GA*	NC		12040	*	**GA**	P	*GA*	NC
12017	t	**CM**	AV	*CR*	AL		12041	*	**GA**	P	*GA*	NC
12019	*	**GA**	P	*GA*	NC		12042	*	**GA**	P	*GA*	NC
12021	*	**GA**	P	*GA*	NC		12043	†	**CM**	AV	*CR*	AL
12024	*	**GA**	P	*GA*	NC		12046	*	**GA**	P	*GA*	NC
12026	*	**GA**	P	*GA*	NC		12049	*	**GA**	P	*GA*	NC
12027	*	**GA**	P	*GA*	NC		12051	*	**GA**	P	*GA*	NC
12030	*	**GA**	P	*GA*	NC		12054	†	**CM**	AV	*CR*	AL

12056	*	**GA**	P	*GA*	NC		12115	*	**GA**	P	*GA*	NC

12056	*	**GA**	P	*GA*	NC
12057	*	**GA**	P	*GA*	NC
12058		**V**	AV		LM
12060	*	**GA**	P	*GA*	NC
12061	*	**GA**	P	*GA*	NC
12062	*	**GA**	P	*GA*	NC
12064	*	**GA**	P	*GA*	NC
12066	*	**GA**	P	*GA*	NC
12067	*	**GA**	P	*GA*	NC
12073	*	**GA**	P	*GA*	NC
12078		**VT**	P	*TP*	CP
12079	*	**GA**	P	*GA*	NC
12081	*	**GA**	P	*GA*	NC
12082	*	**GA**	P	*GA*	NC
12084	*	**GA**	P	*GA*	NC
12089	*	**GA**	P	*GA*	NC
12090	*	**GA**	P	*GA*	NC
12091	*	**GA**	P	*GA*	NC
12093	*	**GA**	P	*GA*	NC
12094		**CM**	AV	*CR*	AL
12097	*	**GA**	P	*GA*	NC
12098	*	**GA**	P	*GA*	NC
12099	*	**GA**	P	*GA*	NC
12100	s	**GW**	P	*GW*	PZ
12103	*	**GA**	P	*GA*	NC
12104		**V**	AV		LM
12105	*	**GA**	P	*GA*	NC
12107	*	**GA**	P	*GA*	NC
12108	*	**GA**	P	*GA*	NC
12109	*	**GA**	P	*GA*	NC
12110	*	**GA**	P	*GA*	NC
12111	*	**GA**	P	*GA*	NC
12114	*	**GA**	P	*GA*	NC
12115	*	**GA**	P	*GA*	NC
12116	*	**GA**	P	*GA*	NC
12118	*	**GA**	P	*GA*	NC
12119	t	**CM**	AV	*CR*	AL
12120	*	**GA**	P	*GA*	NC
12122	z	**VT**	P	*TP*	CP
12125	*	**GA**	P	*GA*	NC
12126	*	**GA**	P	*GA*	NC
12129	*	**GA**	P	*GA*	NC
12130	*	**GA**	P	*GA*	NC
12132	*	**GA**	P	*GA*	NC
12133		**VT**	P	*TP*	CP
12137	*	**GA**	P	*GA*	NC
12138		**VT**	P	*TP*	CP
12139	*	**GA**	P	*GA*	NC
12141	*	**GA**	P	*GA*	NC
12142	s	**GW**	P	*GW*	PZ
12143	*	**GA**	P	*GA*	NC
12146	*	**GA**	P	*GA*	NC
12147	*	**GA**	P	*GA*	NC
12148	*	**GA**	P	*GA*	NC
12150	*	**GA**	P	*GA*	NC
12151	*	**GA**	P	*GA*	NC
12153	*	**GA**	P	*GA*	NC
12154	*	**GA**	P	*GA*	NC
12159	*	**GA**	P	*GA*	NC
12161	s	**GW**	P	*GW*	PZ
12164	*	**GA**	P	*GA*	NC
12165		**V**	AV		LM
12166	*	**GA**	P	*GA*	NC
12167	*	**GA**	P	*GA*	NC
12170	*	**GA**	P	*GA*	NC
12171	*	**GA**	P	*GA*	NC

OPEN STANDARD

Mark 3A (†) or Mark 3B. Air conditioned. Converted from Mark 3A or 3B Open First. Fitted with new Grammer seating. –/70 2T 1W. BT10 bogies. d. ETS 6X.

12176–181/185. Mark 3B. Lot No. 30982 Derby 1985. 38.5 t.
12182–184. Mark 3A. Lot No. 30878 Derby 1975–76. 38.5 t.

12176	(11064)		**AW**	AV	*AW*	CF
12177	(11065)		**AW**	AV	*AW*	CF
12178	(11071)		**AW**	AV	*AW*	CF
12179	(11083)		**AW**	AV	*AW*	CF
12180	(11084)		**AW**	AV	*AW*	CF
12181	(11086)		**AW**	AV	*AW*	CF
12182	(11013)	†	**AW**	AV	*AW*	CF
12183	(11027)	†	**AW**	AV	*AW*	CF
12184	(11044)	†	**AW**	AV	*AW*	CF
12185	(11089)		**AW**	AV	*AW*	CF

OPEN STANDARD (END)

Mark 4. Air conditioned. Rebuilt with new interior by Bombardier Wakefield 2003–05. Separate area for 26 smokers, although smoking is no longer allowed. Retention toilets. –/76 1T. BT41 bogies. ETS 6X.

12232 was converted from the original 12405.

12200–231. Lot No. 31047 Metro-Cammell 1989–91. 39.5 t.
12232. Lot No. 31049 Metro-Cammell 1989–92. 39.5 t.

12200	**VE**	E	*VE*	BN	12217	**VE**	E	*VE*	BN
12201	**VE**	E	*VE*	BN	12218	**VE**	E	*VE*	BN
12202	**VE**	E	*VE*	BN	12219	**VE**	E	*VE*	BN
12203	**VE**	E	*VE*	BN	12220	**VE**	E	*VE*	BN
12204	**VE**	E	*VE*	BN	12222	**VE**	E	*VE*	BN
12205	**VE**	E	*VE*	BN	12223	**VE**	E	*VE*	BN
12207	**VE**	E	*VE*	BN	12224	**VE**	E	*VE*	BN
12208	**VE**	E	*VE*	BN	12225	**VE**	E	*VE*	BN
12209	**VE**	E	*VE*	BN	12226	**VE**	E	*VE*	BN
12210	**VE**	E	*VE*	BN	12227	**VE**	E	*VE*	BN
12211	**VE**	E	*VE*	BN	12228	**VE**	E	*VE*	BN
12212	**VE**	E	*VE*	BN	12229	**VE**	E	*VE*	BN
12213	**VE**	E	*VE*	BN	12230	**VE**	E	*VE*	BN
12214	**VE**	E	*VE*	BN	12231	**VE**	E	*VE*	BN
12215	**VE**	E	*VE*	BN	12232	**VE**	E	*VE*	BN
12216	**VE**	E	*VE*	BN					

OPEN STANDARD (DISABLED)

Mark 4. Air conditioned. Rebuilt with new interior by Bombardier Wakefield 2003–05. Retention toilets. –/68 2W 1TD. BT41 bogies. ETS 6X.

12331 was converted from Open Standard 12531.

12300–330. Lot No. 31048 Metro-Cammell 1989–91. 39.4 t.
12331. Lot No. 31049 Metro-Cammell 1989–92. 39.4 t.

12300	**VE**	E	*VE*	BN	12317	**VE**	E	*VE*	BN
12301	**VE**	E	*VE*	BN	12318	**VE**	E	*VE*	BN
12302	**VE**	E	*VE*	BN	12319	**VE**	E	*VE*	BN
12303	**VE**	E	*VE*	BN	12320	**VE**	E	*VE*	BN
12304	**VE**	E	*VE*	BN	12321	**VE**	E	*VE*	BN
12305	**VE**	E	*VE*	BN	12322	**VE**	E	*VE*	BN
12307	**VE**	E	*VE*	BN	12323	**VE**	E	*VE*	BN
12308	**VE**	E	*VE*	BN	12324	**VE**	E	*VE*	BN
12309	**VE**	E	*VE*	BN	12325	**VE**	E	*VE*	BN
12310	**VE**	E	*VE*	BN	12326	**VE**	E	*VE*	BN
12311	**VE**	E	*VE*	BN	12327	**VE**	E	*VE*	BN
12312	**VE**	E	*VE*	BN	12328	**VE**	E	*VE*	BN
12313	**VE**	E	*VE*	BN	12329	**VE**	E	*VE*	BN
12315	**VE**	E	*VE*	BN	12330	**VE**	E	*VE*	BN
12316	**VE**	E	*VE*	BN	12331	**VE**	E	*VE*	BN

OPEN STANDARD

Mark 4. Air conditioned. Rebuilt with new interior by Bombardier Wakefield 2003–05. Retention toilets. –/76 1T. BT41 bogies. ETS 6X.

12405 is the second coach to carry that number. It was built from the bodyshell originally intended for 12221. The original 12405 is now 12232.

Lot No. 31049 Metro-Cammell 1989–92. 40.8 t.

12400	**VE**	E	*VE*	BN	12448	**VE**	E	*VE*	BN
12401	**VE**	E	*VE*	BN	12449	**VE**	E	*VE*	BN
12402	**VE**	E	*VE*	BN	12450	**VE**	E	*VE*	BN
12403	**VE**	E	*VE*	BN	12452	**VE**	E	*VE*	BN
12404	**VE**	E	*VE*	BN	12453	**VE**	E	*VE*	BN
12405	**VE**	E	*VE*	BN	12454	**VE**	E	*VE*	BN
12406	**VE**	E	*VE*	BN	12455	**VE**	E	*VE*	BN
12407	**VE**	E	*VE*	BN	12456	**VE**	E	*VE*	BN
12409	**VE**	E	*VE*	BN	12457	**VE**	E	*VE*	BN
12410	**VE**	E	*VE*	BN	12458	**VE**	E	*VE*	BN
12411	**VE**	E	*VE*	BN	12459	**VE**	E	*VE*	BN
12414	**VE**	E	*VE*	BN	12460	**VE**	E	*VE*	BN
12415	**VE**	E	*VE*	BN	12461	**VE**	E	*VE*	BN
12417	**VE**	E	*VE*	BN	12462	**VE**	E	*VE*	BN
12419	**VE**	E	*VE*	BN	12463	**VE**	E	*VE*	BN
12420	**VE**	E	*VE*	BN	12464	**VE**	E	*VE*	BN
12421	**VE**	E	*VE*	BN	12465	**VE**	E	*VE*	BN
12422	**VE**	E	*VE*	BN	12466	**VE**	E	*VE*	BN
12423	**VE**	E	*VE*	BN	12467	**VE**	E	*VE*	BN
12424	**VE**	E	*VE*	BN	12468	**VE**	E	*VE*	BN
12425	**VE**	E	*VE*	BN	12469	**VE**	E	*VE*	BN
12426	**VE**	E	*VE*	BN	12470	**VE**	E	*VE*	BN
12427	**VE**	E	*VE*	BN	12471	**VE**	E	*VE*	BN
12428	**VE**	E	*VE*	BN	12472	**VE**	E	*VE*	BN
12429	**VE**	E	*VE*	BN	12473	**VE**	E	*VE*	BN
12430	**VE**	E	*VE*	BN	12474	**VE**	E	*VE*	BN
12431	**VE**	E	*VE*	BN	12476	**VE**	E	*VE*	BN
12432	**VE**	E	*VE*	BN	12477	**VE**	E	*VE*	BN
12433	**VE**	E	*VE*	BN	12478	**VE**	E	*VE*	BN
12434	**VE**	E	*VE*	BN	12480	**VE**	E	*VE*	BN
12436	**VE**	E	*VE*	BN	12481	**VE**	E	*VE*	BN
12437	**VE**	E	*VE*	BN	12483	**VE**	E	*VE*	BN
12438	**VE**	E	*VE*	BN	12484	**VE**	E	*VE*	BN
12439	**VE**	E	*VE*	BN	12485	**VE**	E	*VE*	BN
12440	**VE**	E	*VE*	BN	12486	**VE**	E	*VE*	BN
12441	**VE**	E	*VE*	BN	12488	**VE**	E	*VE*	BN
12442	**VE**	E	*VE*	BN	12489	**VE**	E	*VE*	BN
12443	**VE**	E	*VE*	BN	12513	**VE**	E	*VE*	BN
12444	**VE**	E	*VE*	BN	12514	**VE**	E	*VE*	BN
12445	**VE**	E	*VE*	BN	12515	**VE**	E	*VE*	BN
12446	**VE**	E	*VE*	BN	12518	**VE**	E	*VE*	BN
12447	**VE**	E	*VE*	BN	12519	**VE**	E	*VE*	BN

12520	**VE**	E	*VE*	BN		12533	**VE**	E	*VE*	BN
12522	**VE**	E	*VE*	BN		12534	**VE**	E	*VE*	BN
12526	**VE**	E	*VE*	BN		12538	**VE**	E	*VE*	BN

OPEN STANDARD

Mark 3A. Air conditioned. Rebuilt 2011–13 and fitted with sliding plug doors. Original InterCity 70 seating retained but mainly arranged around tables. Retention toilets. –/72(+6) or * –/69(+4) 1T. BT10 bogies. ETS 6X.

12602–609/614–616/618/620. Lot No. 30877 Derby 1975–77. 36.2 t (* 37.1 t).
12601/613/617–619/621/623/625/627. Lot No. 30878 Derby 1975–76. 36.2 t (* 37.1 t).

12602	(12072)		**CM**	AV	*CR*	AL
12603	(12053)	*	**CM**	AV	*CR*	AL
12604	(12131)		**CM**	AV	*CR*	AL
12605	(11040)	*	**CM**	AV	*CR*	AL
12606	(12048)		**CM**	AV	*CR*	AL
12607	(12038)	*	**CM**	AV	*CR*	AL
12608	(12069)		**CM**	AV	*CR*	AL
12609	(12014)	*	**CM**	AV	*CR*	AL
12610	(12117)		**CM**	AV	*CR*	AL
12613	(11042, 12173)	*	**CM**	AV	*CR*	AL
12614	(12145)		**CM**	AV	*CR*	AL
12615	(12059)	*	**CM**	AV	*CR*	AL
12616	(12127)		**CM**	AV	*CR*	AL
12617	(11052, 12174)	*	**CM**	AV	*CR*	AL
12618	(11008, 12169)		**CM**	AV	*CR*	AL
12619	(11058, 12175)	*	**CM**	AV	*CR*	AL
12620	(12124)		**CM**	AV	*CR*	AL
12621	(11046)	*	**CM**	AV	*CR*	AL
12623	(11019)	*	**CM**	AV	*CR*	AL
12625	(11030)	*	**CM**	AV	*CR*	AL
12627	(11054)	*	**CM**	AV	*CR*	AL

OPEN STANDARD

CAF Mark 5A. Air conditioned. Under construction by CAF for TransPennine Express for delivery 2018. Retention toilets. Full details awaited.

12701	**TP**	BN		12712	**TP**	BN
12702	**TP**	BN		12713	**TP**	BN
12703	**TP**	BN		12714	**TP**	BN
12704	**TP**	BN		12715	**TP**	BN
12705	**TP**	BN		12716	**TP**	BN
12706	**TP**	BN		12717	**TP**	BN
12707	**TP**	BN		12718	**TP**	BN
12708	**TP**	BN		12719	**TP**	BN
12709	**TP**	BN		12720	**TP**	BN
12710	**TP**	BN		12721	**TP**	BN
12711	**TP**	BN		12722	**TP**	BN

12723	**TP**	BN		12732	**TP**	BN
12724	**TP**	BN		12733	**TP**	BN
12725	**TP**	BN		12734	**TP**	BN
12726	**TP**	BN		12735	**TP**	BN
12727	**TP**	BN		12736	**TP**	BN
12728	**TP**	BN		12737	**TP**	BN
12729	**TP**	BN		12738	**TP**	BN
12730	**TP**	BN		12739	**TP**	BN
12731	**TP**	BN				

DRIVING OPEN BRAKE STANDARD

CAF Mark 5A. Air conditioned. Under construction by CAF for TransPennine Express for delivery 2018. Full details awaited. –/64.

12801	**TP**	BN		12808	**TP**	BN
12802	**TP**	BN		12809	**TP**	BN
12803	**TP**	BN		12810	**TP**	BN
12804	**TP**	BN		12811	**TP**	BN
12805	**TP**	BN		12812	**TP**	BN
12806	**TP**	BN		12813	**TP**	BN
12807	**TP**	BN		12814	**TP**	BN

CORRIDOR FIRST

Mark 1. Seven compartments. 42/– 2T. B4 bogies. ETS 3.

Lot No. 30381 Swindon 1959. 33 t.

13227	x	**CH**	LS		CL		13230	xk	**M**	SP	*SP*		BO
13229	xk	**M**	SP	*SP*	BO								

OPEN FIRST

Mark 1 converted from Corridor First in 2013–14. 42/– 2T. Commonwealth bogies. ETS 3.

Lot No. 30667 Swindon 1962. 35 t.

13320	x	**M**	WC	*WC*	CS	ANNA

CORRIDOR FIRST

Mark 2A. Seven compartments. Pressure ventilated. 42/– 2T. B4 bogies. ETS 4.

Lot No. 30774 Derby 1968. 33 t.

13440	v	**M**	WC	*WC*	CS

SLEEPER SEATED CARRIAGE WITH BRAKE

CAF Mark 5. Air conditioned. Under construction by CAF for Caledonian Sleeper for delivery 2018. Retention toilets. –/31 1TD 1W. CAF bogies. ETS XX. 32.5 t.

15001	**CA**	LF	15007	**CA**	LF
15002	**CA**	LF	15008	**CA**	LF
15003	**CA**	LF	15009	**CA**	LF
15004	**CA**	LF	15010	**CA**	LF
15005	**CA**	LF	15011	**CA**	LF
15006	**CA**	LF			

SLEEPER LOUNGE CAR

CAF Mark 5. Air conditioned. Under construction by CAF for Caledonian Sleeper for delivery 2018. –/30 or –/28 1W. CAF bogies. ETS XX. 35.5 t.

15101	**CA**	LF	15106	**CA**	LF
15102	**CA**	LF	15107	**CA**	LF
15103	**CA**	LF	15108	**CA**	LF
15104	**CA**	LF	15109	**CA**	LF
15105	**CA**	LF	15110	**CA**	LF

SLEEPING CAR (FULLY ACCESSIBLE)

CAF Mark 5. Air conditioned. Under construction by CAF for Caledonian Sleeper for delivery 2018. Retention toilets. Two fully accessible berths (one with double bed, one with foldable upper bed), two berths with double beds and en-suite toilets and showers, two berths with foldable upper beds. 2TD 2T, plus two showers. CAF bogies. ETS XX. 35.5 t.

15201	**CA**	LF	15208	**CA**	LF
15202	**CA**	LF	15209	**CA**	LF
15203	**CA**	LF	15210	**CA**	LF
15204	**CA**	LF	15211	**CA**	LF
15205	**CA**	LF	15212	**CA**	LF
15206	**CA**	LF	15213	**CA**	LF
15207	**CA**	LF	15214	**CA**	LF

SLEEPING CAR

CAF Mark 5. Air conditioned. Under construction by CAF for Caledonian Sleeper for delivery 2018. Retention toilets. 6 en-suite toilet/shower and 4 non en-suite compartments with a fixed lower berth and hinged upper berth. 7T. CAF bogies. ETS XX. 38.0 t.

15301	**CA**	LF		15321	**CA**	LF
15302	**CA**	LF		15322	**CA**	LF
15303	**CA**	LF		15323	**CA**	LF
15304	**CA**	LF		15324	**CA**	LF
15305	**CA**	LF		15325	**CA**	LF
15306	**CA**	LF		15326	**CA**	LF
15307	**CA**	LF		15327	**CA**	LF
15308	**CA**	LF		15328	**CA**	LF
15309	**CA**	LF		15329	**CA**	LF
15310	**CA**	LF		15330	**CA**	LF
15311	**CA**	LF		15331	**CA**	LF
15312	**CA**	LF		15332	**CA**	LF
15313	**CA**	LF		15333	**CA**	LF
15314	**CA**	LF		15334	**CA**	LF
15315	**CA**	LF		15335	**CA**	LF
15316	**CA**	LF		15336	**CA**	LF
15317	**CA**	LF		15337	**CA**	LF
15318	**CA**	LF		15338	**CA**	LF
15319	**CA**	LF		15339	**CA**	LF
15320	**CA**	LF		15340	**CA**	LF

CORRIDOR BRAKE FIRST

Mark 1. Four compartments. 24/– 1T. Commonwealth bogies. ETS 2.

Lot No. 30668 Swindon 1961. 36 t.

17018 (14018)	v	**CH**	VT	*VT*	TM	BOTAURUS

CORRIDOR BRAKE FIRST

Mark 2A. Four compartments. Pressure ventilated. 24/– 1T. B4 bogies. ETS 4.

17080/090 were numbered 35516/503 for a time when declassified.

17056. Lot No. 30775 Derby 1967–68. 32 t.
17080–102. Lot No. 30786 Derby 1968. 32 t.

17056 (14056)		**CC**	LS	*LS*	CL	
17080 (14080)		**PC**	LS		CL	
17090 (14090)	v	**CH**	VT		TM	
17102 (14102)		**M**	WC	*WC*	CS	

COUCHETTE/GENERATOR COACH

Mark 2B. Formerly part of Royal Train. Converted from Corridor Brake First built 1969. Consists of luggage accommodation, guard's compartment, 350 kW diesel generator and staff sleeping accommodation. Pressure ventilated. B5 bogies. ETS 5X (when generator not in use). ETS index ?? (when generator in use).

Lot No. 30888 Wolverton 1977. 46 t.

17105 (14105, 2905)		**RB**	RV	*RV*	BU

CORRIDOR BRAKE FIRST

Mark 2D. Four compartments. Air conditioned. Stones equipment. 24/– 1T. B4 Bogies. ETS 5.

Lot No. 30823 Derby 1971–72. 33.5 t.

17159 (14159)	d	**CC**	LS	*LS*	CL	
17167 (14167)		**VN**	WC	*NB*	KR	MOW COP

OPEN BRAKE UNCLASSIFIED

Mark 3B. Air conditioned. Fitted with hydraulic handbrake. Used as Sleeper day coaches. Fitted with former HST First Class seats to a 2+1 layout (effectively unclassified). 36/– 1T. BT10 bogies. pg. d. ETS 6X.

Lot No. 30990 Derby 1986. 35.81 t.

17173	**GW**	P	*GW*	PZ		17175	**GW**	P	*GW*	PZ
17174	**GW**	P	*GW*	PZ						

CORRIDOR STANDARD

Mark 1. –/48 2T. Eight Compartments. Commonwealth bogies. ETS 4.

Currently in use as part of the Harry Potter World exhibition at Leavesden, near Watford.

Lot No. 30685 Derby 1961–62. 36 t.

18756 (25756)	x	**M**	WC		SH

CORRIDOR BRAKE COMPOSITE

Mark 1. There are two variants depending upon whether the Standard Class compartments have armrests. Each vehicle has two First Class and three Standard Class compartments. 12/18 2T (* 12/24 2T). Commonwealth bogies. ETS 2.

21241–245. Lot No. 30669 Swindon 1961–62. 36 t.
21256. Lot No. 30731 Derby 1963. 37 t.
21266–272. Lot No. 30732 Derby 1964. 37 t.

21241	x	**M**	SP	*SP*	BO	21266	x*	**M**	WC	*WC*	CS
21245	x	**M**	RV		ZG	21269	*	**CC**	RV	*RV*	ZG
21256	x	**M**	WC	*WC*	CS	21272	x*	**CH**	RV	*RV*	ZG

CORRIDOR BRAKE STANDARD

Mark 1. Four compartments. –/24 1T. ETS 2.

35185. Lot No. 30427 Wolverton 1959. B4 bogies. 33 t.
35459. Lot No. 30721 Wolverton 1963. Commonwealth bogies. 37 t.

| 35185 | x | **M** | SP | *SP* | BO |
| 35459 | x | **M** | WC | *WC* | CS |

CORRIDOR BRAKE GENERATOR STANDARD

Mark 1. Four compartments. –/24 1T. Fitted with an ETS generator in the former luggage compartment. ETS 2 (when generator not in use). ETS index ?? (when generator in use).

Lot No. 30721 Wolverton 1963. Commonwealth bogies. 37 t.

| 35469 | x | **CH** | RV | *RV* | ZG |

BRAKE/POWER KITCHEN

Mark 2C. Pressure ventilated. Converted from Corridor Brake First (declassified to Corridor Brake Standard) built 1970. Converted by West Coast Railway Company 2000–01. Consists of 60 kVA generator, guard's compartment and electric kitchen. B5 bogies. ETS ? (when generator not in use). ETS index ?? (when generator in use).

Non-standard livery: Brown.

Lot No. 30796 Derby 1969–70. 32.5 t.

| 35511 | (14130, 17130) | **0** | LS | | CL |

KITCHEN CAR

Mark 1. Converted 1989/2006/2017 from Kitchen Buffet Unclassified. Buffet and seating area replaced with additional kitchen and food preparation area. Fluorescent lighting. Commonwealth bogies. ETS 2X.

Lot No. 30628 Pressed Steel 1960–61. 39 t.

80041 (1690) x	**M**	RV		ZG
80042 (1646)	**BG**	RV	*RV*	BU
80043 (1680)	**PC**	LS	*LS*	CL

DRIVING BRAKE VAN (110 mph)

Mark 3B. Air conditioned. T4 bogies. dg. ETS 5X. Driving Brake Vans converted for use by Network Rail can be found in the Service Stock section of this book.

Non-standard liveries:

82113 Light blue
82146 All over silver with DB logos.

Lot No. 31042 Derby 1988. 45.2 t.

82101	**V**	DR		LW		82123	**V**	AV		LM
82102	**GA**	P	*GA*	NC		82126	**VT**	DR		LW
82103	**GA**	P	*GA*	NC		82127	**GA**	P	*GA*	NC
82105	**GA**	P	*GA*	NC		82132	**GA**	P	*GA*	NC
82106	**V**	AV		LM		82133	**GA**	P	*GA*	NC
82107	**GA**	P	*GA*	NC		82136	**GA**	P	*GA*	NC
82110	**V**	AV		LM		82137	**V**	AV		LM
82112	**GA**	P	*GA*	NC		82138	**V**	AV		LM
82113	**0**	AV		BO		82139	**GA**	P	*GA*	NC
82114	**GA**	P	*GA*	NC		82141	**V**	AV		LM
82115	**B**	NR		ZN		82143	**GA**	P	*GA*	NC
82116	**V**	AV		LM		82146	**0**	DB	*DB*	TO
82118	**GA**	P	*GA*	NC		82148	**V**	AV		LM
82120	**V**	AV		LM		82150	**V**	AV		LM
82121	**GA**	P	*GA*	NC		82152	**GA**	P	*GA*	NC
82122	**V**	AV		LM						

DRIVING BRAKE VAN (140 mph)

Mark 4. Air conditioned. Swiss-built (SIG) bogies. dg. ETS 6X.

Advertising livery: 82205 Flying Scotsman (red, white & purple).

Lot No. 31043 Metro-Cammell 1988. 43.5 t.

82200	**VE**	E	*VE*	BN		82204	**VE**	E	*VE*	BN
82201	**VE**	E	*VE*	BN		82205	**AL**	E	*VE*	BN
82202	**VE**	E	*VE*	BN		82206	**VE**	E	*VE*	BN
82203	**VE**	E	*VE*	BN		82207	**VE**	E	*VE*	BN

82208	**VE**	E	*VE*	BN	82220	**VE**	E	*VE*	BN
82209	**VE**	E	*VE*	BN	82222	**VE**	E	*VE*	BN
82210	**VE**	E	*VE*	BN	82223	**VE**	E	*VE*	BN
82211	**VE**	E	*VE*	BN	82224	**VE**	E	*VE*	BN
82212	**VE**	E	*VE*	BN	82225	**VE**	E	*VE*	BN
82213	**VE**	E	*VE*	BN	82226	**VE**	E	*VE*	BN
82214	**VE**	E	*VE*	BN	82227	**VE**	E	*VE*	BN
82215	**VE**	E	*VE*	BN	82228	**VE**	E	*VE*	BN
82216	**VE**	E	*VE*	BN	82229	**VE**	E	*VE*	BN
82217	**VE**	E	*VE*	BN	82230	**VE**	E	*VE*	BN
82218	**VE**	E	*VE*	BN	82231	**VE**	E	*VE*	BN
82219	**VE**	E	*VE*	BN					

DRIVING BRAKE VAN (110 mph)

Mark 3B. Air conditioned. T4 bogies. dg. ETS 6X.

82301–305 originally converted 2008. 82306–308 converted 2011–12. 82309 converted 2013.

g Fitted with a diesel generator for use while stabled in terminal stations or at depots. 48.5 t.

Lot No. 31042 Derby 1988. 45.2 t.

82301	(82117)	g	**CM**	AV	*CR*	AL
82302	(82151)	g	**CM**	AV	*CR*	AL
82303	(82135)	g	**CM**	AV	*CR*	AL
82304	(82130)	g	**CM**	AV	*CR*	AL
82305	(82134)	g	**CM**	AV	*CR*	AL
82306	(82144)		**AW**	AV	*AW*	CF
82307	(82131)		**AW**	AV	*AW*	CF
82308	(82108)		**AW**	AV	*AW*	CF
82309	(82104)	g	**CM**	AV	*CR*	AL

GANGWAYED BRAKE VAN (100 mph)

Mark 1. Short frame (57 ft). Load 10 t. Adapted 199? for use as Brake Luggage Van. Guard's compartment retained and former baggage area adapted for secure stowage of passengers' luggage. B4 bogies. 100 mph. ETS 1X.

Lot No. 30162 Pressed Steel 1956–57. 30.5 t.

92904	(80867, 99554)	**VN**	WC	*NB*	KR

HIGH SECURITY GENERAL UTILITY VAN

Mark 1. Short frame (57 ft). Load 14 t. Modified with new floors, three roller shutter doors per side and the end doors removed. Commonwealth bogies. ETS 0X.

Lot No. 30616 Pressed Steel 1959–60. 32 t.

94225	(86849, 93849)	**M**	WC	*WC*	CS

GENERAL UTILITY VAN (100 mph)

Mark 1. Short frame (57 ft). Load 14 t. Screw couplers. Adapted 2013/2010 for use as a water carrier with 3000 gallon capacity. ETS 0.

Non-standard livery: 96100 GWR Brown.

96100. Lot No. 30565 Pressed Steel 1959. 30 t. B5 bogies.
96175. Lot No. 30403 York/Glasgow 1958–60. 32 t. Commonwealth bogies.

96100	(86734, 93734)	x	**0**	VT	*VT*	TM
96175	(86628, 93628)	x	**M**	WC	*WC*	CS

KITCHEN CAR

Mark 1 converted from Corridor First in 2008 with staff accommodation. Commonwealth bogies. ETS 3.

Lot No. 30667 Swindon 1961. 35 t.

99316	(13321)	x	**M**	WC	*WC*	CS

BUFFET STANDARD

Mark 1 converted from Open Standard in 2013 by the removal of two seating bays and fitting of a buffet. –/48 2T. Commonwealth bogies. ETS 4.

Lot No. 30646 Wolverton 1961. 36 t.

99318	(4912)	x	**M**	WC	*WC*	CS

KITCHEN CAR

Mark 1 converted from Corridor Standard in 2011 with staff accommodation. Commonwealth bogies. ETS 3.

Lot No. 30685 Derby 1961–62. 34 t.

99712	(18893)	x	**M**	WC	*WC*	CS

OPEN STANDARD

Mark 1 Corridor Standard rebuilt in 1997 as Open Standard using components from 4936. –/64 2T. Commonwealth bogies. ETS 4.

Lot No. 30685 Derby 1961–62. 36 t.

99722	(25806, 18806)	x	**M**	WC	*WC*	CS

NNR REGISTERED CARRIAGES

These carriages are permitted to operate on the national railway network only between Sheringham and Cromer as an extension of North Norfolk Railway (NNR) "North Norfolkman" services. Only NNR coaches currently registered for use on the national railway network are listed.

KITCHEN BUFFET STANDARD

Mark 1. Built as Unclassified Restaurant. Rebuilt with Buffet Counter and seating reduced. –/23. Commonwealth bogies. Lot No. 30632 Swindon 1960–61. 39 t.

1969   v   **CC**   NN   *NY*   NO

OPEN FIRST

Mark 1. 42/–. Commonwealth bogies. Lot No. 30697 Swindon 1962–63. 36 t.

3116   v   **CC**   NN   *NY*   NO

OPEN STANDARD

Mark 1. –/48 2T. BR Mark 1 bogies. Lot No. 30121 Eastleigh 1953–55. 32 t.

4372   v   **CC**   NN   *NY*   NO

GANGWAYED BRAKE VAN

Mark 1. Short frame (57 ft). Now fitted with a kitchen. BR Mark 1 bogies. Lot No. 30224 Cravens 1955–56. 31.5 t.

81033   v   **CC**   NN   *NY*   NO

NYMR REGISTERED CARRIAGES

These carriages are permitted to operate on the national railway network but may only be used to convey fare-paying passengers between Middlesbrough and Whitby on the Esk Valley branch as an extension of North Yorkshire Moors Railway services between Pickering and Grosmont. Only NYMR coaches currently registered for use on the national railway network are listed.

RESTAURANT FIRST

Mark 1. 24/–. Commonwealth bogies. Lot No. 30633 Swindon 1961. 42.5 t.

| 324 | x | **PC** | NY | *NY* | NY | | JOS de CRAU |

BUFFET STANDARD

Mark 1. –/44 2T. Commonwealth bogies.
Lot No. 30520 Wolverton 1960. 38 t.

| 1823 | v | **M** | NY | *NY* | NY |

OPEN STANDARD

Mark 1. –/64 2T (* –/60 2W 2T, † –/60 3W 1T). BR Mark 1 bogies.

3798/3801. Lot No. 30079 York 1953. 33 t.
3860/72. Lot No. 30080 York 1954. 33 t.
3948. Lot No. 30086 Eastleigh 1954–55. 33 t.
4198/4252. Lot No. 30172 York 1956. 33 t.
4286/90. Lot No. 30207 BRCW 1956. 33 t.
4455. Lot No. 30226 BRCW 1957. 33 t.

3798	v	**M**	NY	*NY*	NY		4198	v	**CC**	NY	*NY*	NY
3801	v	**CC**	NY	*NY*	NY		4252	v*	**CC**	NY	*NY*	NY
3860	v*	**M**	NY	*NY*	NY		4286	v	**CC**	NY	*NY*	NY
3872	v†	**BG**	NY	*NY*	NY		4290	v	**M**	NY	*NY*	NY
3948	v	**CC**	NY	*NY*	NY		4455	v	**CC**	NY	*NY*	NY

OPEN STANDARD

Mark 1. –/48 2T. BR Mark 1 bogies.

4786. Lot No. 30376 York 1957. 33 t.
4817. Lot No. 30473 BRCW 1959. 33 t.

| 4786 | v | **CH** | NY | *NY* | NY | | 4817 | v | **M** | NY | *NY* | NY |

OPEN STANDARD

Mark 1. Later vehicles built with Commonwealth bogies. –/64 2T.
Lot No. 30690 Wolverton 1961–62. Aluminium window frames. 37 t.

| 4990 | v | **M** | NY | *NY* | NY | | 5029 | v | **CH** | NY | *NY* | NY |
| 5000 | v | **M** | NY | *NY* | NY | | | | | | | |

OPEN BRAKE STANDARD

Mark 1. –/39 1T. BR Mark 1 bogies.

Lot No. 30170 Doncaster 1956. 34 t.

| 9225 | v | **M** | NY | *NY* | NY | | 9274 | v | **M** | NY | *NY* | NY |

CORRIDOR COMPOSITE

Mark 1. 24/18 1T. BR Mark 1 bogies.

15745. Lot No. 30179 Metro Cammell 1956. 36 t.
16156. Lot No. 30665 Derby 1961. 36 t.

| 15745 | v | **M** | NY | *NY* | NY | | 16156 | v | **CC** | NY | *NY* | NY |

CORRIDOR BRAKE COMPOSITE

Mark 1. Two First Class and three Standard Class compartments. 12/18 2T. BR Mark 1 bogies.

Lot No. 30185 Metro Cammell 1956. 36 t.

| 21100 | v | **CC** | NY | *NY* | NY |

CORRIDOR BRAKE STANDARD

Mark 1. –/24 1T. BR Mark 1 bogies.

Lot No. 30233 Gloucester 1957. 35 t.

| 35089 | v | **CC** | NY | *NY* | NY |

PULLMAN BRAKE THIRD

Built 1928 by Metropolitan Carriage & Wagon Company. –/30. Gresley bogies. 37.5 t.

| 232 | v | **PC** | NY | *NY* | NY | CAR No. 79 |

PULLMAN KITCHEN FIRST

Built by Metro-Cammell 1960–61 for East Coast Main Line services. 20/– 2T. Commonwealth bogies. 41.2 t.

| 318 | x | **PC** | NY | *NY* | NY | ROBIN |

PULLMAN PARLOUR FIRST

Built by Metro-Cammell 1960–61 for East Coast Main Line services. 29/– 2T. Commonwealth bogies. 38.5 t.

| 328 | x | **PC** | NY | *NY* | NY | OPAL |

2.2. HIGH SPEED TRAIN TRAILER CARS

HSTs consist of a number of trailer cars (usually between six and nine) with a power car at each end. All trailers are classified Mark 3 and have BT10 bogies with disc brakes and central door locking. Heating is by a 415 V three-phase supply and vehicles have air conditioning. Maximum speed is 125 mph.

The trailer cars have one standard 23m bodyshell for both First and Standard Class, thus facilitating easy conversion from one class to the other. As built all cars had facing seating around tables with Standard Class carriages having nine bays of seats per side which did not line up with the eight windows per side. This created a new unwelcome trend in British rolling stock of seats not lining up with windows.

All vehicles underwent a mid-life refurbishment in the 1980s with Standard Class seating layouts revised to incorporate unidirectional seating in addition to facing, in a somewhat higgledy-piggledy layout where seats did not line up either side of the aisle.

A further refurbishment programme was completed in November 2000, with each Train Operating Company having a different scheme as follows:

Great Western Trains (later First Great Western). Green seat covers and extra partitions between seat bays.

Great North Eastern Railway. New ceiling lighting panels and brown seat covers.

Virgin CrossCountry. Green seat covers. Standard Class vehicles had four seats in the centre of each carriage replaced with a luggage stack. All have now passed to other operators.

Midland Mainline. Grey seat covers, redesigned seat squabs, side carpeting and two seats in the centre of each Standard Class carriage and one in First Class carriages replaced with a luggage stack.

Since then the remaining three operators of HSTs embarked on separate, and very different, refurbishment projects:

Midland Mainline was first to refurbish its vehicles a second time during 2003–04. This involved fitting new fluorescent and halogen ceiling lighting, although the original seats were retained in First and Standard Class, but with blue upholstery.

London St Pancras–Sheffield/Leeds and Nottingham services are now operated by **East Midlands Trains** and in late 2009 this operator embarked on another, less radical, refurbishment which included retention of the original seats but with red upholstery in Standard Class and blue in First Class. This programme was completed in 2010.

First Great Western (now **Great Western Railway**) started a major rebuild of its HST sets in late 2006, with the programme completed in 2008. With an increased fleet of 54 sets the new interiors feature new lighting and seating throughout. First Class seats have leather upholstery, and are made by Primarius UK. Standard Class seats are of high-back design by Grammer. A number of sets operate without a full buffet or kitchen car, instead using one of 19 TS vehicles converted to include a "mini buffet" counter for use on shorter distance services. During 2012 15 402xx or 407xx buffet vehicles were converted to Trailer Standards to make the rakes formed as 7-cars up to 8-cars. During 2014–15 further changes to the FGW sets included the conversion of one First Class carriage from each set to Standard Class.

Great Western Railway is now starting to withdrawn its sets, but will retain 11 short 4-car sets for local and regional services. Trailers for these sets will be fitted with sliding doors and renumbered.

Having increased its sets to 9-car sets in 2004, at the end of 2006 **GNER** embarked on a major rebuild of its HSTs. All vehicles have similar interiors to the Mark 4 "Mallard" fleet, with new Primarius seats throughout. The refurbishment of the 13 sets was completed by **National Express East Coast** in late 2009, these trains are now operated by **Virgin Trains East Coast**. VTEC refurbished its sets in 2015–16, with the same seats retained but with new upholstery, and leather in First Class.

Ten sets ex-Virgin CrossCountry, and some spare vehicles, were temporarily allocated to Midland Mainline for the interim service to Manchester during 2003–04. Buffet cars were converted from TSB to TFKB and renumbered in the 408xx series. Most of these vehicles are now in use with GWR.

Open access operator **Grand Central** started operation in December 2007 with a new service from Sunderland to London King's Cross. This operator had three sets mostly using stock converted from loco-hauled Mark 3s. The seats in Standard Class have First Class spacing and in most vehicles are all facing. These sets were withdrawn in December 2017 for transfer to East Midlands Trains.

CrossCountry reintroduced HSTs to the Cross-Country network from 2008. Five sets were refurbished at Wabtec, Doncaster principally for use on the Plymouth–Edinburgh route. Three of these sets use stock mostly converted from loco-hauled Mark 3s and two are sets ex-Midland Mainline. The interiors are similar to refurbished East Coast sets, although the seating layout is different and one toilet per carriage has been removed in favour of a luggage stack. These sets are currently being fitted with sliding doors.

ScotRail is to start operating HSTs from spring 2018. The operator will use refurbished former GWR power cars and trailers (with sliding doors) to form 17 5-car sets and nine 4-car sets for use between Glasgow/Edinburgh and Aberdeen/Inverness, as well as Aberdeen–Inverness.

Operator Codes

Operator codes are shown in the heading before each set of vehicles. The first letter is always "T" for HST carriages, denoting a Trailer vehicle. The second letter denotes the passenger accommodation in that vehicle, for example "F" for First. "GS" denotes Guards accommodation and Standard Class seating. This is followed by catering provision, with "B" for buffet, and "K" for a kitchen and buffet:

TC	Trailer Composite	TFKB	Trailer Kitchen Buffet First
TCK	Trailer Composite Kitchen	TSB	Trailer Buffet Standard
TF	Trailer First	TS	Trailer Standard
TFB	Trailer Buffet First	TGS	Trailer Guard's Standard

TRAILER BUFFET STANDARD   TSB

19 vehicles converted at Laira 2009–10 from HST TSs for First Great Western. Refurbished with Grammer seating.

40101–119. For Lot No. details see TS. –/70 1T. 35.5 t.

40101	(42170)	**FD**	P *GW*	LA
40102	(42223)	**FD**	P *GW*	LA
40103	(42316)	**FD**	P *GW*	LA
40104	(42254)	**FD**	P *GW*	LA
40105	(42084)	**FD**	P *GW*	LA
40106	(42162)	**FD**	P *GW*	LA
40107	(42334)	**FD**	P *GW*	LA
40108	(42314)	**FD**	P *GW*	LA
40109	(42262)	**FD**	P *GW*	LA
40110	(42187)	**FD**	P *GW*	LA
40111	(42248)	**FD**	P *GW*	LA
40112	(42336)	**FD**	P *GW*	LA
40113	(42309)	**FD**	P *GW*	LA
40114	(42086)	**FD**	P *GW*	LA
40115	(42320)	**FD**	P *GW*	LA
40116	(42147)	**FD**	P *GW*	LA
40117	(42249)	**FD**	P *GW*	LA
40118	(42338)	**FD**	P *GW*	LA
40119	(42090)	**FD**	P *GW*	LA

TRAILER BUFFET FIRST   TFB

Converted from TSB by fitting First Class seats. Renumbered from 404xx series by subtracting 200. All refurbished by First Great Western and fitted with Primarius leather seating. 23/–.

40204–221. Lot No. 30883 Derby 1976–77. 36.12 t.
40231. Lot No. 30899 Derby 1978–79. 36.12 t.

40204	**FD**	A	*SR*	HA		40210	**FD**	A	*SR*	HA
40205	**FD**	A		EP		40221	**FD**	A		EP
40207	**FD**	A	*SR*	HA		40231	**FD**	A	*GW*	LA

TRAILER BUFFET STANDARD   TSB

Renumbered from 400xx series by adding 400. –/33 1W.

40433 was numbered 40233 for a time when fitted with 23 First Class seats.

40402–426. Lot No. 30883 Derby 1976–77. 36.12 t.
40433. Lot No. 30899 Derby 1978–79. 36.12 t.

40402	**V**	AV		ZR		40426	**GC**	A	*EM*	DY
40419	**V**	AV		LM		40433	**GC**	A	*EM*	DY
40424	**GC**	A	*EM*	DY						

TRAILER KITCHEN BUFFET FIRST   TFKB

These vehicles have larger kitchens than the 402xx and 404xx series vehicles, and are used in trains where a full meal service is required. They were renumbered from the 403xx series (in which the seats were unclassified) by adding 400 to the previous number. 17/–.

* Refurbished Great Western Railway vehicles. Primarius leather seating.
m Refurbished Virgin Trains East Coast vehicles with Primarius seating.

40700–721. Lot No. 30921 Derby 1978–79. 38.16 t.
40722–735. Lot No. 30940 Derby 1979–80. 38.16 t.
40737–753. Lot No. 30948 Derby 1980–81. 38.16 t.
40754–757. Lot No. 30966 Derby 1982. 38.16 t.

40700		**ST**	P	*EM*	NL	40732		**VE**	P	*VE*	EC
40701	m	**VE**	P	*VE*	EC	40733	*	**FD**	A	*GW*	LA
40702	m	**VE**	P	*VE*	EC	40734	*	**FD**	A	*GW*	LA
40703	*	**FD**	A	*GW*	LA	40735	m	**VE**	A	*VE*	EC
40704	m	**VE**	A	*VE*	EC	40737	m	**VE**	A	*VE*	EC
40705	m	**VE**	A	*VE*	EC	40739	*	**FD**	A	*GW*	LA
40706	m	**VE**	A	*VE*	EC	40740	m	**VE**	A	*VE*	EC
40707	*	**FD**	A	*GW*	LA	40741		**ST**	P	*EM*	NL
40708	m	**VE**	P	*VE*	EC	40742	m	**VE**	A	*VE*	EC
40710	*	**FD**	A	*GW*	LA	40743	*	**GW**	A	*GW*	LA
40711	m	**VE**	A	*VE*	EC	40746		**ST**	P	*EM*	NL
40713	*	**FD**	A	*GW*	LA	40748	m	**VE**	A	*VE*	EC
40715	*	**GW**	A	*GW*	LA	40749		**ST**	P	*EM*	NL
40716	*	**FD**	A	*GW*	LA	40750	m	**VE**	A	*VE*	EC
40718	*	**FD**	A	*GW*	LA	40751		**VE**	P	*VE*	NL
40720	m	**VE**	A	*VE*	EC	40752	*	**FD**	A	*GW*	LA
40721	*	**FD**	A	*GW*	LA	40753		**ST**	P	*EM*	NL
40722	*	**FD**	A	*GW*	LA	40754		**ST**	P	*EM*	NL
40727	*	**FD**	A	*GW*	LA	40755	*	**GW**	A	*GW*	LA
40728		**ST**	P	*EM*	NL	40756		**ST**	P	*EM*	NL
40730		**ST**	P	*EM*	NL	40757	*	**FD**	A	*GW*	LA

TRAILER KITCHEN BUFFET FIRST   TFKB

These vehicles have been converted from TSBs in the 404xx series to be similar to the 407xx series vehicles. 17/–.

40802/804/811 were numbered 40212/232/211 for a time when fitted with 23 First Class seats.

* Refurbished Great Western Railway vehicles. Primarius leather seating.
m Refurbished Virgin Trains East Coast vehicle with Primarius seating.

40801–803/805/808/809/811. Lot No. 30883 Derby 1976–77. 38.16 t.
40804/806/807/810. Lot No. 30899 Derby 1978–79. 38.16 t.

40801	(40027, 40427)	*	**GW**	P	*GW*	LA
40802	(40012, 40412)	*	**FD**	P	*GW*	LA

40803 (40018, 40418)	*	**GW**	P	*GW*	LA
40804 (40032, 40432)	*	**FD**	P	*GW*	LA
40805 (40020, 40420)	m	**VE**	P	*VE*	EC
40806 (40029, 40429)	*	**FD**	P	*GW*	LA
40807 (40035, 40435)	*	**FD**	P	*GW*	LA
40808 (40015, 40415)	*	**FD**	P	*GW*	LA
40809 (40014, 40414)	*	**FD**	P	*GW*	LA
40810 (40030, 40430)	*	**FD**	P	*GW*	LA
40811 (40011, 40411)	*	**FD**	P	*GW*	LA

TRAILER BUFFET FIRST   TFB

Converted from TSB by First Great Western. Refurbished with Primarius leather seating. 23/–.

40900/902/904. Lot No. 30883 Derby 1976–77. 36.12 t.
40901/903. Lot No. 30899 Derby 1978–79. 36.12 t.

40900 (40022, 40422)	**FD**	FG	*GW*	LA
40901 (40036, 40436)	**FD**	FG	*GW*	LA
40902 (40023, 40423)	**FD**	FG	*GW*	LA
40903 (40037, 40437)	**FD**	FG	*GW*	LA
40904 (40001, 40401)	**FD**	FG	*GW*	LA

TRAILER FIRST   TF

As built and m 48/– 2T (mt 48/– 1T – one toilet removed for trolley space).
* Refurbished Great Western Railway vehicles. Primarius leather seating.
c Refurbished CrossCountry vehicles with Primarius seating and 2 tip-up seats. One toilet removed. 40/– 1TD 1W.
m Refurbished Virgin Trains East Coast vehicles with Primarius seating.
s Fitted with centre luggage stack, disabled toilet and wheelchair space. 46/– 1T 1TD 1W.
w Wheelchair space. 47/– 2T 1W. (41154 47/– 1TD 1T 1W).
x Toilet removed for trolley space (FGW). 48/– 1T.

41004–056. Lot No. 30881 Derby 1976–77. 33.66 t.
41057–120. Lot No. 30896 Derby 1977–78. 33.66 t.
41122–146. Lot No. 30938 Derby 1979–80. 33.66 t.
41149–166. Lot No. 30947 Derby 1980. 33.66 t.
41167/169. Lot No. 30963 Derby 1982. 33.66 t.
41170. Lot No. 30967 Derby 1982. Former prototype vehicle. 33.66 t.
41176. Lot No. 30897 Derby 1977. 33.66 t.
41180. Lot No. 30884 Derby 1976–77. 33.66 t.
41182/183/189. Lot No. 30939 Derby 1979–80. 33.66 t.
41185–187. Lot No. 30969 Derby 1982. 33.66 t.
41190. Lot No. 30882 Derby 1976–77. 33.60 t.
41192. Lot No. 30897 Derby 1977–79. 33.60 t.
41193–195/201–206. Lot No. 30878 Derby 1975–76. 34.3 t. Converted from Mark 3A Open First.

▲ Royal Train-liveried Royal Household Couchette Mark 2B 2920 is seen being shunted at Wolverton Works on 09/06/17. **Mark Beal**

▼ BR Carmine & Cream-liveried Mark 1 Open First 3066 at Kingswear on 02/07/17. **Tony Christie**

▲ BR Blue & Grey-liveried Mark 2F Open First 3386 at Birmingham Moor Street on 26/08/17. **Robert Pritchard**

▼ West Coast Railway Company Maroon-liveried Mark 1 Open Standard 5035 is seen at Worgret Junction (near Wareham) on 15/06/17. **Robert Pritchard**

▲ Revised Direct Rail Services-liveried Mark 2F Open Standard 5937 at Great Yarmouth on 14/06/17. **Robert Pritchard**

▼ ScotRail Saltire-liveried Mark 2F Open Standard 6027 is seen near Whifflet on 05/10/16. **Robin Ralston**

▲ Caledonian Sleeper-liveried Mark 2F Sleeper Reception Car 6701 is seen near Auchengray on 12/07/17. **Robin Ralston**

▼ Pullman Car Company-liveried Mark 2D Open Brake Standard 9479 at Waterside (between Churston and Goodrington on the Dartmouth Steam Railway) on 26/08/17. **Tony Christie**

▲ Old Anglia Railways-liveried Mark 2F Open Brake Standard 9520 at Great Yarmouth on 14/06/17, while on hire to Greater Anglia.   **Robert Pritchard**

▼ Chiltern Railways Mainline-liveried Mark 3A Kitchen Buffet Standard 10272 is seen at Neasden on 05/07/16.   **Robert Pritchard**

▲ Virgin Trains East Coast-liveried Mark 4 Kitchen Buffet Standard 10312 at Grantham on 23/04/17. **Robert Pritchard**

▼ First Group-liveried Mark 3A Sleeping Car With Pantry 10508 is seen near Auchengray on 12/07/17. **Robin Ralston**

▲ Greater Anglia-liveried Mark 3B Open First 11099 at Manningtree on 14/06/17. **Robert Pritchard**

▼ Arriva Trains Wales-liveried Mark 3B Open Standard 12181 at Cardiff Central on 14/06/16. **Robert Pritchard**

▲ One of the brand new CAF Mark 5 Sleeping cars for Caledonian Sleeper, 15301, is seen at the Velim test centre in the Czech Republic on 26/08/17. **Quintus Vosman**

▼ Great Western Railway Green-liveried Mark 3B Open Brake Unclassified 17175 at Plymouth on 05/08/17. **Tony Christie**

▲ West Coast Railway Company Maroon-liveried Mark 1 Corridor Brake Composite 21266 at Carlisle on 22/07/17. **Robert Pritchard**

▼ Arriva Trains Wales-liveried Mark 3B Driving Brake Van 82308 at Bangor leading the 13.07 Holyhead–Manchester Piccadilly on 14/08/17. **Tony Christie**

▲ Great Western Railway Green-liveried HST Trailer Kitchen Buffet First 40715 at St Germans on 16/08/16. **Tony Christie**

▼ Stagecoach East Midlands Trains-liveried HST Trailer First 41067 is seen at Nottingham on 17/07/16. **Robert Pritchard**

▲ Grand Central-liveried HST Trailer First 41205 at York on 02/10/16.
Robert Pritchard

▼ First Great Western Dynamic Lines-liveried Trailer Standard 42502 at Plymouth on 16/06/17.
Robert Pritchard

▲ CrossCountry-liveried HST Trailer Guard's Standard 44021 at Plymouth on 16/06/17. **Robert Pritchard**

▼ West Coast Railway Company Maroon-liveried Pullman Parlour Second 347 (carrying number 99347) at Cogload Junction on 26/05/17. **Tony Christie**

▲ BR Carmine & Cream Mark 1 Locomotive Support Coach 35317 (converted from Corridor Brake Standard) is seen at Dainton on 30/07/17.   **Tony Christie**

▼ West Coast Railway Company Maroon-liveried Mark 2C Locomotive Support Coach 35508 (converted from Corridor Brake First) is seen at Romiley on 06/11/16.   **Robert Pritchard**

▲ Revised Direct Rail Services-liveried Escort Coach 9419 (converted from a Mark 2A Open Brake Standard) is seen at Taunton on 08/03/17. **Stephen Ginn**

▼ Network Rail Yellow-liveried Brake Force Runner 96606 (converted from a Motorail Van) is seen near Carluke on 03/08/17. **Robin Ralston**

▲ Network Rail Yellow-liveried Ultrasonic Test Coach 62384 (converted from a Class 421 EMU MBSO) is seen at Exeter depot on 08/08/17. **Tony Christie**

▼ Network Rail Yellow-liveried Overhead Line Equipment Test Coach ("MENTOR") 975091 (converted from a Mark 1 Corridor Brake Standard) is seen at Saxilby on 19/08/17. **Robert Pritchard**

▲ Network Rail Yellow-liveried Structure Gauging Train Coach 977985 (converted from a Mark 2F Open Standard) is seen at Derby on 01/09/16. **Robert Pritchard**

▼ Former Newspaper Van 94006, now used as an internal user Stores Van, at Old Oak Common HST depot on 02/09/17. **Andy Barclay**

41004	*x	**FD**	A	*GW*	LA
41006	*w	**FD**	A	*GW*	LA
41008	*w	**FD**	A	*GW*	LA
41010	*w	**FD**	A	*GW*	LA
41012	*w	**GW**	A	*GW*	LA
41016	*w	**FD**	A	*GW*	LA
41018	*w	**FD**	A	*GW*	LA
41020	*w	**FD**	A	*GW*	LA
41022	*w	**FD**	A	*GW*	LA
41024	*w	**FD**	A		ZB
41026	c	**XC**	A	*XC*	EC
41028	*w	**FD**	A	*GW*	LA
41030	*w	**FD**	A	*GW*	LA
41032	*w	**FD**	A		ZB
41034	*w	**FD**	A	*GW*	LA
41035	c	**XC**	A	*XC*	EC
41038	*w	**FD**	A		ZB
41039	m†	**VE**	A	*VE*	EC
41040	mw	**VE**	A	*VE*	EC
41041	s	**ST**	P	*EM*	NL
41044	mw	**VE**	A	*VE*	EC
41046	s	**ST**	P	*EM*	NL
41052	*w	**FD**	A		EP
41056	*w	**FD**	A	*GW*	LA
41057		**ST**	P	*EM*	NL
41059	*w	**FD**	FG	*GW*	LA
41061	w	**ST**	P	*EM*	NL
41062		**VE**	P	*VE*	EC
41063		**ST**	P	*EM*	NL
41064	s	**ST**	P	*EM*	NL
41066	m†	**VE**	A	*VE*	EC
41067	s	**ST**	P	*EM*	NL
41068	w	**VE**	P	*VE*	NL
41069	s	**ST**	P	*EM*	NL
41070	s	**ST**	P	*EM*	NL
41071		**ST**	P	*EM*	NL
41072	s	**ST**	P	*EM*	NL
41075		**ST**	P	*EM*	NL
41076	s	**ST**	P	*EM*	NL
41077		**ST**	P	*EM*	NL
41079		**ST**	P	*EM*	NL
41083	mw	**VE**	P	*VE*	EC
41084	s	**ST**	P	*EM*	NL
41087	m†	**VE**	A	*VE*	EC
41088	mw	**VE**	A	*VE*	EC
41089	*w	**FD**	A	*GW*	LA
41090	m†	**VE**	A	*VE*	EC
41091	m†	**VE**	A	*VE*	EC
41092	mw	**VE**	A	*VE*	EC
41094	*w	**FD**	A		ZB
41095	mw	**VE**	P	*VE*	EC
41097	m†	**VE**	A	*VE*	EC
41098	mw	**VE**	A	*VE*	EC
41099	m†	**VE**	A	*VE*	EC
41100	mw	**VE**	A	*VE*	EC
41102	*w	**FD**	A	*GW*	LA
41103	*x	**FD**	A	*GW*	LA
41104	*w	**FD**	A	*SR*	HA
41106	*w	**FD**	A	*GW*	LA
41108	*w	**FD**	P	*GW*	LA
41110	*w	**FD**	A	*GW*	LA
41111		**ST**	P	*EM*	NL
41112		**VE**	P	*VE*	NL
41113	s	**ST**	P	*EM*	NL
41115	m†	**VE**	P	*VE*	EC
41116	*x	**FD**	A	*GW*	LA
41117		**ST**	P	*EM*	NL
41118	mw	**VE**	A	*VE*	EC
41120	m†	**VE**	A	*VE*	EC
41122	*w	**FD**	A	*GW*	LA
41124	*w	**FD**	A	*GW*	LA
41126	*w	**FD**	A	*GW*	LA
41128	*w	**FD**	A	*GW*	LA
41130	*w	**FD**	A	*GW*	LA
41132	*w	**FD**	A	*GW*	LA
41134	*w	**FD**	A	*GW*	LA
41135	*w	**FD**	A	*GW*	LA
41136	*w	**FD**	A		EP
41137	*x	**FD**	A	*GW*	LA
41138	*w	**FD**	A	*GW*	LA
41140	*w	**FD**	A	*GW*	LA
41142	*w	**FD**	A	*GW*	LA
41144	*w	**FD**	A	*GW*	LA
41146	*w	**GW**	A	*GW*	LA
41149	*w	**FD**	P	*GW*	LA
41150	mw	**VE**	A	*VE*	EC
41151	m†	**VE**	A	*VE*	EC
41152	mw	**VE**	A	*VE*	EC
41154	w	**VE**	P	*VE*	EC
41156		**ST**	P	*EM*	NL
41158	*w	**GW**	A	*GW*	LA
41159	m†	**VE**	P	*VE*	EC
41160	*w	**FD**	FG	*GW*	LA
41161	*w	**FD**	P	*GW*	LA
41162	*w	**FD**	FG	*GW*	LA
41164	mw	**VE**	A	*VE*	EC
41165	mw	**VE**	P	*VE*	EC
41166	*w	**FD**	FG	*GW*	LA
41167	*w	**FD**	FG	*GW*	LA
41169	*w	**FD**	P	*GW*	LA

41170	(41001)	m†	**VE**	A	*VE*	EC
41176	(42142, 42352)	*w	**FD**	P	*GW*	LA
41180	(40511)	*w	**FD**	A	*GW*	LA
41182	(42278)	*w	**GW**	P	*GW*	LA
41183	(42274)	*w	**GW**	P	*GW*	LA
41185	(42313)	m†	**VE**	P	*VE*	EC
41186	(42312)	*w	**FD**	P	*GW*	LA
41187	(42311)	*w	**FD**	P	*GW*	LA
41189	(42298)	*w	**FD**	P	*GW*	LA
41190	(42088)	m†	**VE**	P	*VE*	EC
41192	(42246)	*w	**FD**	P	*GW*	LA

The following carriages have been converted from loco-hauled Mark 3 vehicles.

41193	(11060)	c	**XC**	P	*XC*	EC
41194	(11016)	c	**XC**	P	*XC*	EC
41195	(11020)	c	**XC**	P	*XC*	EC
41201	(11045)		**GC**	A	*EM*	DY
41202	(11017)		**GC**	A	*EM*	DY
41203	(11038)		**GC**	A	*EM*	DY
41204	(11023)		**GC**	A	*EM*	DY
41205	(11036)		**GC**	A	*EM*	DY
41206	(11055)		**GC**	A	*EM*	DY

TRAILER STANDARD   TS

42158 was numbered 41177 for a time when fitted with First Class seats.
42310 was numbered 41188 for a time when fitted with First Class seats.

Standard seating and m –/76 2T.
* Refurbished Great Western Railway vehicles. Grammer seating. –/80 2T (unless h – high density).
c Refurbished CrossCountry vehicles with Primarius seating. One toilet removed. –/82 1T.
§c Refurbished CrossCountry vehicles with Primarius seating and 2 tip-up seats. One toilet removed. –/66 1TD 2W. 42379/380 are –/71 1TD 1T 2W.
d Great Western Railway vehicles with disabled persons toilet and 5, 6 or 7 tip-up seats. –/68 1T 1TD 2W.
h "High density" Great Western Railway vehicles. –/84 2T.
k "High density" Great Western Railway refurbished vehicle with disabled persons toilet and 5, 6 or 7 tip-up seats. –/72 1T 1TD 2W.
m Refurbished Virgin Trains East Coast vehicles with Primarius seating.
u Centre luggage stack (EMT) –/74 2T.
w Centre luggage stack and wheelchair space (EMT) –72 2T 1W.
† Disabled persons toilet (VTEC) –/62 1T 1TD 1W.

42003–089/362. Lot No. 30882 Derby 1976–77. 33.6 t.
42091–250. Lot No. 30897 Derby 1977–79. 33.6 t.
42251–305. Lot No. 30939 Derby 1979–80. 33.6 t.
42306–322. Lot No. 30969 Derby 1982. 33.6 t.
42323–341. Lot No. 30983 Derby 1984–85. 33.6 t.

42342/360. Lot No. 30949 Derby 1982. 33.47 t. Converted from TGS.
42343/345. Lot No. 30970 Derby 1982. 33.47 t. Converted from TGS.
42344/361. Lot No. 30964 Derby 1982. 33.47 t. Converted from TGS.
42346/347/350/351/379/380/551–564. Lot No. 30881 Derby 1976–77. 33.66 t. Converted from TF.
42348/349/363–365/381/565–570. Lot No. 30896 Derby 1977–78. 33.66 t. Converted from TF.
42354. Lot No. 30897 Derby 1977. Was TF from 1983 to 1992. 33.66 t.
42353/355–357. Lot No. 30967 Derby 1982. Ex-prototype vehicles. 33.66 t.
42366–378/382/383/401–409. Lot No. 30877 Derby 1975–77. 34.3 t. Converted from Mark 3A Open Standard.
42384. Lot No. 30896 Derby 1977–78. 33.66 t. Converted from TF.
42501/509/513/515/517. Lot No. 30948 Derby 1980–81. 34.8 t. Converted from TFKB.
42502/506/508/514/516. Lot No. 30940 Derby 1979–80. 34.8 t. Converted from TFKB.
42503/504/510/511. Lot No. 30921 Derby 1978–79. 34.8 t. Converted from TFKB.
42505/507/512/518/519. Lot No. 30883 Derby 1976–77. 34.8 t. Converted from TSB.
42520. Lot No. 30899 Derby 1978–79. 34.8 t. Converted from TSB.
42571–579. Lot No. 30938 Derby 1979–80. 33.66 t. Converted from TF.
42580–583. Lot No. 30947 Derby 1980. 33.66 t. Converted from TF.

42003	*h	**FD**	A	*GW*	LA		42036	c	**XC**	A	*XC*	EC
42004	*d	**FD**	A		ZB		42037	c	**XC**	A	*XC*	EC
42005	*h	**GW**	A	*GW*	LA		42038	c	**XC**	A	*XC*	EC
42006	*h	**FD**	A	*GW*	LA		42039	*h	**FD**	A	*GW*	LA
42007	*d	**FD**	A		ZB		42040	*h	**FD**	A	*GW*	LA
42008	*k	**GW**	A	*GW*	LA		42041	*h	**FD**	A	*GW*	LA
42009	*h	**FD**	A	*GW*	LA		42042	*h	**FD**	A	*GW*	LA
42010	*h	**FD**	A	*GW*	LA		42043	*h	**FD**	A	*GW*	LA
42012	*k	**FD**	A	*GW*	LA		42044	*h	**FD**	A	*GW*	LA
42013	*h	**FD**	A	*GW*	LA		42045	*	**FD**	A		ZB
42014	*h	**FD**	A	*GW*	LA		42046	*	**FD**	A		ZB
42015	*k	**GW**	A	*GW*	LA		42047	*	**FD**	A	*SR*	HA
42016	*h	**GW**	A	*GW*	LA		42048	*h	**FD**	A	*GW*	LA
42019	*	**FD**	A	*GW*	LA		42049	*h	**FD**	A	*GW*	LA
42021	*k	**FD**	A	*GW*	LA		42050	*h	**FD**	A	*GW*	LA
42023	*h	**FD**	A	*GW*	LA		42051	c	**XC**	A	*XC*	EC
42024	*k	**FD**	A	*GW*	LA		42052	c	**XC**	A	*XC*	EC
42025	*h	**FD**	A	*GW*	LA		42053	c	**XC**	A	*XC*	EC
42026	*h	**FD**	A	*GW*	LA		42054	*	**FD**	A	*SR*	HA
42027	*h	**FD**	A	*GW*	LA		42055	*	**FD**	A		ZB
42028	*h	**FD**	A	*GW*	LA		42056	*	**FD**	A		EP
42029	*h	**FD**	A	*GW*	LA		42057	m	**VE**	A	*VE*	EC
42030	*k	**FD**	A	*GW*	LA		42058	m	**VE**	A	*VE*	EC
42031	*h	**FD**	A	*GW*	LA		42059	m	**VE**	A	*VE*	EC
42032	*h	**FD**	A	*GW*	LA		42060	*h	**FD**	A	*GW*	LA
42033	*	**FD**	A	*SR*	HA		42061	*h	**FD**	A	*GW*	LA
42034		**FD**	A		ZB		42062	*k	**FD**	A	*GW*	LA
42035	*	**FD**	A	*SR*	HA		42063	m	**VE**	A	*VE*	EC

42064	m	**VE**	A	*VE*	EC	42123		**VE**	P	*VE*	EC

42064 m	**VE**	A	*VE*	EC
42065 m	**VE**	A	*VE*	EC
42066 *k	**FD**	A	*GW*	LA
42067 *h	**FD**	A	*GW*	LA
42068 *h	**FD**	A	*GW*	LA
42069 *k	**FD**	A	*GW*	LA
42070 *h	**FD**	A	*GW*	LA
42071 *h	**FD**	A	*GW*	LA
42072 *	**FD**	A	*GW*	LA
42073 *h	**FD**	A	*GW*	LA
42074 *h	**FD**	A	*GW*	LA
42075 *	**FD**	A	*GW*	LA
42076 *	**FD**	A	*SR*	HA
42077 *	**FD**	A		EP
42078 *	**FD**	A		EP
42079 *h	**FD**	A	*GW*	LA
42080 *h	**FD**	A	*GW*	LA
42081 *k	**FD**	A	*GW*	LA
42083 *h	**FD**	A	*GW*	LA
42085 *h	**FD**	P	*GW*	LA
42087 *h	**FD**	P	*GW*	LA
42089 *h	**FD**	A	*GW*	LA
42091 m†	**VE**	A	*VE*	EC
42092 *k	**FD**	FG	*GW*	LA
42094 *h	**FD**	FG	*GW*	LA
42095 *	**FD**	FG	*GW*	LA
42096 *h	**FD**	A	*GW*	LA
42097 c	**XC**	A	*XC*	EC
42098 *h	**FD**	A	*GW*	LA
42099 *h	**FD**	A	*GW*	LA
42100 u	**ST**	P	*EM*	NL
42101 *h	**FD**	P	*GW*	LA
42103 *k	**FD**	P	*GW*	LA
42104 m	**VE**	A	*VE*	EC
42105 *k	**FD**	FG	*GW*	LA
42106 m	**VE**	A	*VE*	EC
42107 *	**FD**	A		LR
42108 *h	**FD**	FG	*GW*	LA
42109 m	**VE**	P	*VE*	EC
42110 m	**VE**	P	*VE*	EC
42111 u	**ST**	P	*EM*	NL
42112 u	**ST**	P	*EM*	NL
42113 u	**ST**	P	*EM*	NL
42115 *h	**FD**	P	*GW*	LA
42116 m†	**VE**	A	*VE*	EC
42117 m	**VE**	P	*VE*	EC
42118 *h	**FD**	A	*GW*	LA
42119 u	**ST**	P	*EM*	NL
42120 u	**ST**	P	*EM*	NL
42121 u	**ST**	P	*EM*	NL
42122 m	**VE**	A	*VE*	EC
42123	**VE**	P	*VE*	EC
42124 u	**ST**	P	*EM*	NL
42125	**VE**	P	*VE*	EC
42126 *h	**FD**	A	*GW*	LA
42127 m†	**VE**	A	*VE*	EC
42128 m†	**VE**	A	*VE*	EC
42129 *	**GW**	A	*GW*	LA
42130 m	**VE**	P	*VE*	EC
42131 u	**ST**	P	*EM*	NL
42132 w	**ST**	P	*EM*	NL
42133 u	**ST**	P	*EM*	NL
42134 m	**VE**	A	*VE*	EC
42135 u	**ST**	P	*EM*	NL
42136 u	**ST**	P	*EM*	NL
42137 u	**ST**	P	*EM*	NL
42138 *k	**FD**	A	*GW*	LA
42139 u	**ST**	P	*EM*	NL
42140 u	**ST**	P	*EM*	NL
42141 u	**ST**	P	*EM*	NL
42143 *	**FD**	A	*SR*	HA
42144 *	**FD**	A		EP
42145 *	**FD**	A	*SR*	HA
42146 m	**VE**	A	*VE*	EC
42148 u	**ST**	P	*EM*	NL
42149 u	**ST**	P	*EM*	NL
42150 m	**VE**	A	*VE*	EC
42151 w	**ST**	P	*EM*	NL
42152 u	**ST**	P	*EM*	NL
42153 u	**ST**	P	*EM*	NL
42154 m	**VE**	A	*VE*	EC
42155 w	**ST**	P	*EM*	NL
42156 u	**ST**	P	*EM*	NL
42157 u	**ST**	P	*EM*	NL
42158 m	**VE**	A	*VE*	EC
42159 m†	**VE**	P	*VE*	EC
42160 m	**VE**	P	*VE*	EC
42161 m†	**VE**	A	*VE*	EC
42163 m	**VE**	P	*VE*	EC
42164	**ST**	P	*EM*	NL
42165	**ST**	P	*EM*	NL
42166 *h	**FD**	P	*GW*	LA
42167 *h	**FD**	FG	*GW*	LA
42169 *h	**FD**	FG	*GW*	LA
42171 m	**VE**	A	*VE*	EC
42172 m	**VE**	A	*VE*	EC
42173 *k	**FD**	P	*GW*	LA
42174 *k	**FD**	P	*GW*	LA
42175 *h	**FD**	FG	*GW*	LA
42176 *h	**FD**	FG	*GW*	LA
42178 *h	**FD**	P	*GW*	LA
42179 m	**VE**	A	*VE*	EC

42180	m	**VE**	A	*VE*	EC
42181	m	**VE**	A	*VE*	EC
42182	m	**VE**	A	*VE*	EC
42183	*d	**FD**	A		ZB
42184	*	**FD**	A		ZB
42185	*	**FD**	A		LR
42186	m	**VE**	A	*VE*	EC
42188	m†	**VE**	A	*VE*	EC
42189	m†	**VE**	A	*VE*	EC
42190	m	**VE**	A	*VE*	EC
42191	m	**VE**	A	*VE*	EC
42192	m	**VE**	A	*VE*	EC
42193	m	**VE**	A	*VE*	EC
42194	u	**VE**	P	*VE*	NL
42195	*k	**FD**	P	*GW*	LA
42196	*h	**FD**	A	*GW*	LA
42197	*h	**FD**	A	*GW*	LA
42198	m	**VE**	A	*VE*	EC
42199	m	**VE**	A	*VE*	EC
42200	*d	**GW**	A	*GW*	LA
42201	*k	**FD**	A	*GW*	LA
42202	*k	**FD**	A	*GW*	LA
42203	*h	**FD**	A	*GW*	LA
42204	*h	**FD**	A	*GW*	LA
42205		**VE**	P	*VE*	EC
42206	*d	**FD**	A	*SR*	HA
42207	*d	**FD**	A	*SR*	HA
42208	*	**FD**	A	*SR*	HA
42209	*	**FD**	A	*SR*	HA
42210		**VE**	P	*VE*	EC
42211	*k	**FD**	A	*GW*	LA
42212	*h	**FD**	A	*GW*	LA
42213	*h	**FD**	A	*GW*	LA
42214	*h	**FD**	A	*GW*	LA
42215	m	**VE**	A	*VE*	EC
42216	*h	**FD**	A	*GW*	LA
42217	*k	**FD**	P	*GW*	LA
42218	*k	**FD**	P	*GW*	LA
42219	m	**VE**	A	*VE*	EC
42220	w	**ST**	P	*EM*	NL
42221	*h	**FD**	A	*GW*	LA
42222	*h	**FD**	P	*GW*	LA
42224	*k	**FD**	P	*GW*	LA
42225		**VE**	P	*VE*	NL
42226	m	**VE**	A	*VE*	EC
42227		**VE**	P	*VE*	NL
42228	m	**VE**	P	*VE*	EC
42229		**VE**	P	*VE*	NL
42230	u	**ST**	P	*EM*	NL
42231	*h	**FD**	FG	*GW*	LA
42232	*h	**FD**	FG	*GW*	LA
42233	*h	**FD**	FG	*GW*	LA
42234	c	**XC**	P	*XC*	EC
42235	m	**VE**	A	*VE*	EC
42236	*h	**FD**	A	*GW*	LA
42237	m	**VE**	P	*VE*	EC
42238	m†	**VE**	A	*VE*	EC
42239	m†	**VE**	A	*VE*	EC
42240	m	**VE**	A	*VE*	EC
42241	m	**VE**	A	*VE*	EC
42242	m	**VE**	A	*VE*	EC
42243	m	**VE**	A	*VE*	EC
42244	m	**VE**	A	*VE*	EC
42245	*	**GW**	A	*GW*	LA
42247	*h	**FD**	P	*GW*	LA
42250	*	**GW**	A	*GW*	LA
42251	*k	**FD**	A	*GW*	LA
42252	*	**FD**	A	*GW*	LA
42253	*	**FD**	A	*GW*	LA
42255	*d	**FD**	A	*GW*	LA
42256	*	**FD**	A	*GW*	LA
42257	*	**FD**	A	*GW*	LA
42258	*h	**FD**	P	*GW*	LA
42259	*k	**FD**	A	*GW*	LA
42260	*h	**FD**	A	*GW*	LA
42261	*h	**FD**	A	*GW*	LA
42263	*	**FD**	A	*GW*	LA
42264	*k	**FD**	A	*GW*	LA
42265	*	**FD**	A	*GW*	LA
42266	*k	**FD**	P	*GW*	LA
42267	*d	**FD**	A	*GW*	LA
42268	*d	**FD**	A		EP
42269	*	**FD**	A	*GW*	LA
42271	*k	**FD**	A	*GW*	LA
42272	*h	**FD**	A	*GW*	LA
42273	*h	**FD**	A	*GW*	LA
42275	*d	**FD**	A	*GW*	LA
42276	*	**FD**	A	*GW*	LA
42277	*	**FD**	A	*GW*	LA
42279	*d	**FD**	A	*GW*	LA
42280	*	**FD**	A	*GW*	LA
42281	*	**FD**	A	*GW*	LA
42283	*h	**FD**	A	*GW*	LA
42284	*h	**FD**	A	*GW*	LA
42285	*h	**FD**	A	*GW*	LA
42286	m†	**VE**	P	*VE*	EC
42287	*k	**FD**	A	*GW*	LA
42288	*h	**FD**	A	*GW*	LA
42289	*h	**FD**	A	*GW*	LA
42290	c	**XC**	P	*XC*	EC
42291	*d	**FD**	A	*GW*	LA
42292	*d	**FD**	A		ZB

42293	*	**FD**	A	*GW*	LA	42319	*h	**FD**	P	*GW*	LA
42294	*	**FD**	P	*GW*	LA	42321	*h	**FD**	P	*GW*	LA
42295	*d	**FD**	A	*GW*	LA	42322	m	**VE**	P	*VE*	EC
42296	*	**FD**	A	*GW*	LA	42323	m	**VE**	A	*VE*	EC
42297	*	**FD**	A	*GW*	LA	42325	*	**FD**	A	*GW*	LA
42299	*d	**GW**	A	*GW*	LA	42326	m	**VE**	P	*VE*	EC
42300	*	**GW**	A	*GW*	LA	42327	w	**ST**	P	*EM*	NL
42301	*	**GW**	A	*GW*	LA	42328	w	**ST**	P	*EM*	NL
42302	*k	**FD**	P	*GW*	LA	42329	w	**ST**	P	*EM*	NL
42303	*h	**FD**	FG	*GW*	LA	42330	m	**VE**	P	*VE*	EC
42304	*h	**FD**	FG	*GW*	LA	42331	u	**ST**	P	*EM*	NL
42305	*h	**FD**	FG	*GW*	LA	42332	*	**FD**	A	*GW*	LA
42306	m	**VE**	P	*VE*	EC	42333	*	**FD**	A	*GW*	LA
42307	m	**VE**	P	*VE*	EC	42335	w	**VE**	P	*VE*	EC
42308	*h	**FD**	P	*GW*	LA	42337	w	**ST**	P	*EM*	NL
42310	*k	**FD**	P	*GW*	LA	42339	w	**ST**	P	*EM*	NL
42315	*h	**FD**	P	*GW*	LA	42340	w	**VE**	A	*VE*	EC
42317	*k	**FD**	P	*GW*	LA	42341	u	**ST**	P	*EM*	NL

42342	(44082)	c	**XC**	A	*XC*	EC
42343	(44095)	*	**FD**	A		ZB
42344	(44092)	*k	**FD**	A	*GW*	LA
42345	(44096)	*d	**FD**	A	*GW*	LA
42346	(41053)	*h	**FD**	A	*GW*	LA
42347	(41054)	*k	**FD**	A	*GW*	LA
42348	(41073)	*k	**FD**	A	*GW*	LA
42349	(41074)	*h	**FD**	A	*GW*	LA
42350	(41047)	*	**FD**	A	*GW*	LA
42351	(41048)	*	**GW**	A	*GW*	LA
42353	(42001, 41171)	*k	**FD**	FG	*GW*	LA
42354	(42114, 41175)	m	**VE**	A	*VE*	EC
42355	(42000, 41172)	m	**VE**	A	*VE*	EC
42356	(42002, 41173)	*k	**FD**	A	*GW*	LA
42357	(41002, 41174)	m	**VE**	A	*VE*	EC
42360	(44084, 45084)	*h	**FD**	A	*GW*	LA
42361	(44099, 42000)	*h	**GW**	A	*GW*	LA
42362	(42011, 41178)	*h	**FD**	A	*GW*	LA
42363	(41082)	m†	**VE**	A	*VE*	EC
42364	(41080)	*k	**FD**	P	*GW*	LA
42365	(41107)	*h	**FD**	P	*GW*	LA

42366–378 were converted from loco-hauled Mark 3 vehicles for CrossCountry and 42382/383 for First Great Western.

42366	(12007)	§c	**XC**	P	*XC*	EC
42367	(12025)	c	**XC**	P	*XC*	EC
42368	(12028)	c	**XC**	P	*XC*	EC
42369	(12050)	c	**XC**	P	*XC*	EC
42370	(12086)	c	**XC**	P	*XC*	EC
42371	(12052)	§c	**XC**	P	*XC*	EC
42372	(12055)	c	**XC**	P	*XC*	EC
42373	(12071)	c	**XC**	P	*XC*	EC

42374	(12075)	c	**XC**	P	*XC*	EC
42375	(12113)	c	**XC**	P	*XC*	EC
42376	(12085)	§c	**XC**	P	*XC*	EC
42377	(12102)	c	**XC**	P	*XC*	EC
42378	(12123)	c	**XC**	P	*XC*	EC
42379	(41036)	§c	**XC**	A	*XC*	EC
42380	(41025)	§c	**XC**	A	*XC*	EC
42381	(41058)	*k	**FD**	P	*GW*	LA
42382	(12128)	*h	**FD**	P	*GW*	LA
42383	(12172)	*h	**FD**	P	*GW*	LA
42384	(41078)	w	**ST**	P	*EM*	NL

The following carriages were converted from loco-hauled Mark 3 vehicles for Grand Central. They have a lower density seating layout (most seats arranged around tables). –/64 2T († –/60 1TD 1T 2W).

42401	(12149)		**GC**	A	*EM*	DY
42402	(12155)		**GC**	A	*EM*	DY
42403	(12033) †	**GC**	A	*EM*	DY
42404	(12152)		**GC**	A	*EM*	DY
42405	(12136)		**GC**	A	*EM*	DY
42406	(12112) †	**GC**	A	*EM*	DY
42407	(12044)		**GC**	A	*EM*	DY
42408	(12121)		**GC**	A	*EM*	DY
42409	(12088) †	**GC**	A	*EM*	DY

These carriages have been converted from TFKB or TSB buffet cars to TS vehicles in 2011–12 (42501–515) and 2013–14 (42516–520) at Wabtec Kilmarnock for FGW. Refurbished with Grammer seating. –/84 1T. 34.8 t.

42501	(40344, 40744)	**FD**	A	*GW*	LA
42502	(40331, 40731)	**FD**	A	*GW*	LA
42503	(40312, 40712)	**FD**	A	*GW*	LA
42504	(40314, 40714)	**FD**	A	*GW*	LA
42505	(40428, 40228)	**FD**	A	*GW*	LA
42506	(40324, 40724)	**FD**	A	*GW*	LA
42507	(40409, 40209)	**FD**	A	*GW*	LA
42508	(40325, 40725)	**FD**	A	*GW*	LA
42509	(40336, 40736)	**FD**	A	*GW*	LA
42510	(40317, 40717)	**FD**	A	*GW*	LA
42511	(40309, 40709)	**FD**	A	*SR*	HA
42512	(40408, 40208)	**FD**	A	*GW*	LA
42513	(40338, 40738)	**FD**	A	*GW*	LA
42514	(40326, 40726)	**FD**	A	*GW*	LA
42515	(40347, 40747)	**FD**	A	*GW*	LA
42516	(40323, 40723)	**FD**	A	*GW*	LA
42517	(40345, 40745)	**FD**	A	*GW*	LA
42518	(40003, 40403)	**FD**	P	*GW*	LA
42519	(40016, 40416)	**FD**	P	*GW*	LA
42520	(40234, 40434)	**FD**	P	*GW*	LA

These carriages have been converted from TF to TS vehicles in 2014 at Wabtec Kilmarnock for FGW. Refurbished with Grammer seating. –/80 1T. 35.5 t.

42551	(41003)	**FD**	A		EP
42552	(41007)	**FD**	A	*GW*	LA
42553	(41009)	**FD**	A	*GW*	LA
42554	(41011)	**GW**	A	*GW*	LA
42555	(41015)	**FD**	A	*GW*	LA
42556	(41017)	**FD**	A	*GW*	LA
42557	(41019)	**FD**	A	*GW*	LA
42558	(41021)	**FD**	A	*GW*	LA
42559	(41023)	**FD**	A		ZB
42560	(41027)	**FD**	A	*GW*	LA
42561	(41031)	**FD**	A		ZB
42562	(41037)	**FD**	A		ZB
42563	(41045)	**FD**	FG	*GW*	LA
42564	(41051)	**FD**	A		EP
42565	(41085)	**FD**	FG	*GW*	LA
42566	(41086)	**FD**	FG	*GW*	LA
42567	(41093)	**FD**	A		ZB
42568	(41101)	**FD**	A	*GW*	LA
42569	(41105)	**FD**	A	*GW*	LA
42570	(41114)	**FD**	FG	*GW*	LA
42571	(41121)	**FD**	A	*GW*	LA
42572	(41123)	**FD**	A	*GW*	LA
42573	(41127)	**FD**	A	*GW*	LA
42574	(41129)	**FD**	A	*GW*	LA
42575	(41131)	**FD**	A	*GW*	LA
42576	(41133)	**FD**	A	*GW*	LA
42577	(41141)	**FD**	A	*GW*	LA
42578	(41143)	**FD**	A	*GW*	LA
42579	(41145)	**GW**	A	*GW*	LA
42580	(41155)	**FD**	P	*GW*	LA
42581	(41157)	**GW**	A	*GW*	LA
42582	(41163)	**FD**	FG	*GW*	LA
42583	(41153, 42385)	**GW**	P	*GW*	LA

TRAILER GUARD'S STANDARD   TGS

As built and m –/65 1T.
* Refurbished Great Western Railway vehicles. Grammer seating and toilet removed for trolley store. –/67 (unless h).
c Refurbished CrossCountry vehicles with Primarius seating. –/67 1T.
h "High density" Great Western Railway vehicles. –/71.
m Refurbished Virgin Trains East Coast vehicles with Primarius seating.
s Fitted with centre luggage stack (EMT) –/63 1T. 44027 is –/64 1T.
t Fitted with centre luggage stack –/61 1T.

44000. Lot No. 30953 Derby 1980. 33.47 t.
44001–090. Lot No. 30949 Derby 1980–82. 33.47 t.
44091–094. Lot No. 30964 Derby 1982. 33.47 t.
44097–101. Lot No. 30970 Derby 1982. 33.47 t.

44000	*h	**FD**	P	*GW*	LA		44046	s	**ST**	P	*EM*	NL
44001	*	**FD**	A		LR		44047	s	**ST**	P	*EM*	NL
44002	*h	**FD**	A	*GW*	LA		44048	s	**ST**	P	*EM*	NL
44003	*h	**FD**	A	*GW*	LA		44049	*	**FD**	A		EP
44004	*h	**FD**	A	*GW*	LA		44050	m	**VE**	P	*VE*	EC
44005		**GW**	A	*GW*	LA		44051	s	**ST**	P	*EM*	NL
44007	*h	**FD**	A	*GW*	LA		44052	c	**XC**	P	*XC*	EC
44008	*h	**FD**	A	*GW*	LA		44054	s	**ST**	P	*EM*	NL
44009	*h	**FD**	A	*GW*	LA		44056	m	**VE**	A	*VE*	EC
44010	*h	**FD**	A	*GW*	LA		44057	m	**VE**	A	*VE*	EC
44011	*	**FD**	A	*SR*	HA		44058	m	**VE**	A	*VE*	EC
44012	c	**XC**	A	*XC*	EC		44059	*	**FD**	A	*GW*	LA
44013	*h	**FD**	A	*GW*	LA		44060	*h	**FD**	P	*GW*	LA
44014	*h	**FD**	A	*GW*	LA		44061	m	**VE**	A	*VE*	EC
44015	*	**FD**	A	*SR*	EC		44063	m	**VE**	A	*VE*	EC
44016	*h	**FD**	A	*GW*	LA		44064	*h	**FD**	A	*GW*	LA
44017	c	**XC**	A	*XC*	EC		44065	t	**V**	AV		LM
44018	*	**FD**	A		EP		44066	*	**FD**	A	*SR*	HA
44019	m	**VE**	A	*VE*	EC		44067	*h	**FD**	A	*GW*	LA
44020	*h	**FD**	A	*GW*	LA		44068	*h	**FD**	FG	*GW*	LA
44021	c	**XC**	P	*XC*	EC		44069	*h	**FD**	P	*GW*	LA
44022	*h	**FD**	A	*GW*	LA		44070	s	**ST**	P	*EM*	NL
44023	*h	**FD**	A	*GW*	LA		44071	s	**ST**	P	*EM*	NL
44024	*h	**FD**	A	*GW*	LA		44072	c	**XC**	P	*XC*	EC
44025	*	**FD**	A		LR		44073	†	**VE**	P	*VE*	EC
44026	*h	**FD**	A	*GW*	LA		44074	m	**FD**	FG	*GW*	LA
44027	s	**VE**	P	*VE*	NL		44075	m	**VE**	P	*VE*	EC
44028	*	**FD**	A	*GW*	LA		44076	*h	**FD**	FG	*GW*	LA
44029	*	**FD**	A	*GW*	LA		44077	m	**VE**	A	*VE*	EC
44030	*h	**FD**	A	*GW*	LA		44078	*h	**FD**	P	*GW*	LA
44031	m	**VE**	A	*VE*	EC		44080	m	**VE**	A	*VE*	EC
44032	*	**FD**	A	*GW*	LA		44081	*h	**FD**	FG	*GW*	LA
44033	*h	**FD**	A	*GW*	LA		44083	*h	**FD**	P	*GW*	LA
44034	*	**FD**	A	*GW*	LA		44085	s	**ST**	P	*EM*	NL
44035	*	**FD**	A	*GW*	LA		44086	*	**GW**	A	*GW*	LA
44036	*h	**FD**	A	*GW*	LA		44089	t	**V**	AV		ZR
44037	*h	**FD**	A	*GW*	LA		44090	*h	**FD**	P	*GW*	LA
44038	*	**FD**	A	*GW*	LA		44091	*h	**FD**	P	*GW*	LA
44039	*	**FD**	A	*GW*	LA		44093	*h	**FD**	A	*GW*	LA
44040	*	**GW**	A	*GW*	LA		44094	m	**VE**	A	*VE*	EC
44041	s	**ST**	P	*EM*	NL		44097	*h	**FD**	P	*GW*	LA
44042	*h	**FD**	P	*GW*	LA		44098	m	**VE**	A	*VE*	EC
44043	*h	**FD**	A	*GW*	LA		44100	*h	**FD**	FG	*GW*	PM
44044	s	**ST**	P	*EM*	NL		44101	*h	**FD**	P	*GW*	LA
44045	m	**VE**	A	*VE*	EC							

TRAILER COMPOSITE KITCHEN   TCK

Converted from Mark 3A Open Standard. Refurbished CrossCountry vehicles with Primarius seating. Small kitchen for the preparation of hot food and stowage space for two trolleys between First and Standard Class.

One toilet removed. 30/10 1T.

45001–005. Lot No. 30877 Derby 1975–77. 34.3 t.

45001	(12004)	**XC**	P	*XC*	EC
45002	(12106)	**XC**	P	*XC*	EC
45003	(12076)	**XC**	P	*XC*	EC
45004	(12077)	**XC**	P	*XC*	EC
45005	(12080)	**XC**	P	*XC*	EC

TRAILER COMPOSITE   TC

Converted from TF for First Great Western 2014–15. Refurbished with Grammer seating. 24/39 1T.

46001–004. Lot No. 30881 Derby 1976–77. 35.6 t. Converted from TF.
46005–009. Lot No. 30896 Derby 1977–78. 35.6 t. Converted from TF.
46010–013. Lot No. 30938 Derby 1979–80. 35.6 t. Converted from TF.
46014. Lot No. 30963 Derby 1982. 35.6 t. Converted from TF.
46015. Lot No. 30884 Derby 1976–77. 35.6 t. Converted from TF.
46016/017. Lot No. 30939 Derby 1979–80. 35.6 t. Converted from TF.
46018. Lot No. 30969 Derby 1982. 35.6 t. Converted from TF.

46001	(41005)	**FD**	A	*GW*	LA
46002	(41029)	**FD**	A	*GW*	LA
46003	(41033)	**FD**	A	*GW*	LA
46004	(41055)	**FD**	A	*GW*	LA
46005	(41065)	**FD**	A	*GW*	LA
46006	(41081)	**FD**	P	*GW*	LA
46007	(41096)	**FD**	P	*GW*	LA
46008	(41109)	**FD**	P	*GW*	LA
46009	(41119)	**FD**	P	*GW*	LA
46010	(41125)	**FD**	A	*GW*	LA
46011	(41139)	**FD**	A	*GW*	LA
46012	(41147)	**FD**	P	*GW*	LA
46013	(41148)	**FD**	P	*GW*	LA
46014	(41168)	**FD**	P	*GW*	LA
46015	(40505, 41179)	**FD**	A	*GW*	LA
46016	(42282, 41181)	**FD**	P	*GW*	LA
46017	(42270, 41184)	**FD**	P	*GW*	LA
46018	(42318, 41191)	**FD**	P	*GW*	LA

TRAILER STANDARD   TS

Refurbished for Great Western Railway 2017–18 and fitted with sliding doors and retention toilets. Planned for use in 4-car sets on local and regional services in the South-West. Full details awaited.

48101–107/111/114/119/120/122–126/132. Lot No. 30897 Derby 1977–79.
48108/109. Lot No. 30969 Derby 1982.
48110/127. Lot No. 30896 Derby 1977–78.
48112/113/128/129/131/134/135. Lot No. 30939 Derby 1979–80.
48115–118/121/130/133. Lot No. 30882 Derby 1976–77.

48101	(42168)	**GW**	FG	*GW*	LA
48102	(42177)	**GW**	FG	*GW*	LA
48103	(42218)	**GW**			
48104	(42102)	**GW**	FG	*GW*	LA
48105	(42224)	**GW**			
48106	(42222)	**GW**			
48107	(42101)	**GW**			
48108	(42317)	**GW**			
48109	(42315)	**GW**			
48110	(41107, 42365)	**GW**			
48111	(42093)	**GW**	FG	*GW*	LA
48112	(42266)	**GW**			
48113	(42258)	**GW**			
48114	(42174)	**GW**			
48115	(42085)	**GW**			
48116	(42044)	**GW**			
48117	(42008)	**GW**			
48118	(42042)	**GW**			
48119	(42204)	**GW**			
48120	(42201)	**GW**			
48121	(42027)	**GW**			
48122	(42214)	**GW**			
48123	(42211)	**GW**			
48124	(42212)	**GW**			
48125	(42203)	**GW**			
48126	(42138)	**GW**			
48127	(41074, 42349)	**GW**			
48128	(42273)	**GW**			
48129	(42271)	**GW**			
48130	(42073)	**GW**			
48131	(42285)	**GW**			
48132	(42202)	**GW**			
48133	(42003)	**GW**			
48134	(42264)	**GW**			
48135	(42251)	**GW**			

TRAILER GUARD'S STANDARD   TGS

Refurbished for Great Western Railway 2017–18 and fitted with sliding doors and retention toilets. Full details awaited.

49101/103/104/106–113. Lot No. 30949 Derby 1980–82.
49102/105. Lot No. 30970 Derby 1982.

49101	(44055)	**GW**	FG	*GW*	LA		49108	(44067)	**GW**			
49102	(44101)	**GW**					49109	(44003)	**GW**			
49103	(44090)	**GW**					49110	(44033)	**GW**			
49104	(44083)	**GW**					49111	(44036)	**GW**			
49105	(44097)	**GW**					49112	(44079)	**GW**	FG	*GW*	LA
49106	(44014)	**GW**					49113	(44034)	**GW**			
49107	(44064)	**GW**										

2.3. HST SET FORMATIONS

GREAT WESTERN RAILWAY

The largest operator of HSTs is Great Western Railway with (at the start of 2018), 47 sets to cover 44 diagrams.

The sets are split into three types, "low density", "high density" and "super high density", as shown below.

Although some sets are prefixed "OC" for Old Oak Common, for maintenance purposes all trailers are now based at Laira apart from one spare vehicle.

By summer 2015 all GWR HSTs were 8-car rakes with one full First Class carriage and either a First Class buffet car or one of the newly converted Composite vehicles – essentially both carrying 1½ coaches of First Class, although withdrawals have meant four sets running as 7-cars at the time of writing.

New Class 800 and 802 units are taking over GWR's InterCity services between autumn 2017 and spring 2019, replacing all of the full-length HSTs which will be stored or transferred to ScotRail during 2018, although GWR will retain and refurbish 11 4-car sets for local and regional services in the South-West.

Number of sets: 47.
Maximum number of daily diagrams: 44.
Formations: 8-cars.
Allocation: Laira (Plymouth).
Other maintenance and servicing depots: Landore (Swansea), St Philip's Marsh (Bristol), Long Rock (Penzance).
Operation: London Paddington–Exeter/Paignton/Plymouth/(Newquay in the summer)/Penzance, Bristol, Cardiff/Swansea/West Wales, Oxford/Hereford/Great Malvern/Cheltenham Spa.

Set	L	K	F	E	D	C	B	A	density
LA07	41122	40722	42252	42571	42019	42345	42253	44028	L
LA08	41124	40739	42256	42572	42263	42255	42257	44029	L
LA09	41130	40716	42072	42574	42325	42267	42269	44032	L
LA10	41134	40721	42276	42576	42332	42275	42277	44034	L
LA11	41135	40703	42280	42502	42265	42279	42281	44035	L
LA13	41142	40734	42333	42577	42075	42291	42293	44038	L
LA14	41144	40733	42296	42578	42350	42295	42297	44039	L
LA15	41146	40715	42300	42579	42351	42299	42301	44040	L
LA16	41158	40743	42245	42581	42129	42200	42250	44086	L
OC30	41008	40807	42079	42552	42236	42251	42080	44026	H
OC31	41128	40804	42060	42573	42197	42347	42061	44020	H
OC32	41018	40801	42025	42556	42362	42024	42026	44008	H
OC33	41028	40806	42040	42560	42039	42348	42041	44013	H
OC34	41102	40803	42203	42568	42027	42201	42204	44064	H
OC35	41106	40808	42213	42569	42212	42211	42214	44067	H
OC36	41110	40809	42346	42517	42349	42138	42089	44003	H

Set	L	K	F	E	D	C	B	A	density
OC37	41132	40802	42272	42575	42073	42271	42273	44033	H
OC38	41138	40810	42284	42505	42003	42202	42285	44036	H
LA60	41162	40900	42231	42570	42232	42353	42233	44074	H
LA61	41160	40901	42304	42566	42303	42302	42305	44068	H
LA62	41167	40902	42167	42565		42103	42169	44002	H
LA63	41059	40903	42175	42563	42176	42105		44081	H
LA64	41166	40904	42094	42582		42092	42108	44076	H
LA71	41010	40707	42013	42553	42360	42012	42014	44004	H
LA72	41012	40755	42016	42554	42005	42015	42361	44005	H
LA73	41016	40727	42006	42555	42096	42021	42023	44007	H
LA74	41020	40757	42028	42557	42009	42259	42029	44009	H
LA75	41022	40231	42031	42558	42010	42030	42032	44010	H
LA80	41137	40718		42083	42071	42356	42049	44083	H

Set	L	K	F	E	D	C	B	A	density
OC40	41149	46016	40106	42580	42166	42218		44024	SH
OC41	41182	46008	40107	42520	42222	42224	42382	44101	SH
OC42	41183	46014	40108	42519	42315	42317	42383	44090	SH
OC43	41186	46012	40109	42515	42258	42266	42365	44000	SH
OC44	41192	46018	40110	42514	42115	42174	42288	44097	SH
OC45	41187	46009	40111	42501	42247	42173	42260	44078	SH
OC46	41161	46007	40112	42512	42178	42195	42043	44042	SH
OC47	41108	46006	40113	42509	42308	42217	42067	44060	SH
OC48	41189	46017	40114	42518	42085	42310	42087	44069	SH
OC49	41169	46013	40115	42583	42319	42364	42321	44091	SH
OC50	41180	46015	40101	42516	42098	42264	42283	44093	SH
OC51	41006	46001	40103	42513	42070	42069	42118	44023	SH
OC52	41030	46002	40102	42510	42042	42008	42244	44014	SH
OC53	41034	46003	40118	42506	42048	42066	42050	44016	SH
OC54	41056	46004	40117	42503	42074	42081	42126	44043	SH
OC55	41089	46005	40104	42504	42221	42062	42068	44022	SH
OC56	41126	46010	40116	42508	42216	42344	42261	44030	SH
OC57	41140	46011	40105	42507	42099	42287	42289	44037	SH

L = Low density; H = High density; SH = Super High density.

Spares:

LA:	40119	40710	40713	40752	40811	41004	41103	41116	41176
	42095	42101	42196	42294	42381	44059			
PM:	44100								

VIRGIN TRAINS EAST COAST

Virgin Trains East Coast operates 15 HST sets on the ECML. As well as serving non-electrified destinations such as Hull and Inverness the VTEC HSTs also work alongside Class 91s and Mark 4 sets on services to Leeds, Newcastle and Edinburgh. Set EC64 (ex-NL05) transferred from East Midlands Trains in 2011 and set NL65 (ex-NL02) as an 8-car followed in 2015.

Number of sets: 15.
Maximum number of daily diagrams: 14.
Formations: 9-cars.
Allocation: Craigentinny (Edinburgh).
Other maintenance depot: Neville Hill (Leeds).
Operation: London King's Cross–Leeds/Harrogate/Skipton/Hull/Lincoln/Newcastle/Edinburgh/Aberdeen/Inverness.

Set	M	L	J	G	F	E	D	C	B
EC51	41120	41150	40748	42215	42091	42146	42150	42154	44094
EC52	41039	41040	40735	42323	42189	42057	42058	42059	44019
EC53	41090	41044	40737	42340	42127	42063	42064	42065	44045
EC54	41087	41088	40706	42104	42161	42171	42172	42219	44056
EC55	41091	41092	40704	42179	42188	42180	42181	42106	44058
EC56	41170	41118	40720	42241	42363	42242	42243	42244	44098
EC57	41151	41152	40740	42226	42128	42182	42186	42190	44080
EC58	41097	41098	40750	42158	42238	42191	42192	42193	44061
EC59	41099	41100	40711	42235	42239	42240	42198	42199	44063
EC60	41066	41164	40742	42122	42116	42357	42134	42355	44031
EC61	41115	41165	40702	42117	42159	42160	42109	42110	44057
EC62	41185	41095	40701	42306	42326	42330	42237	42307	44075
EC63	41083	41043	40708	42163	42286	42228	42130	42322	44050
EC64	41062	41154	40705	42125	42335	42123	42205	42210	44073
NL65	41112	41068	40805	42194	42229	42227	42225		44027

Spares:

EC: 40732   40805   41190   42354   44077

EAST MIDLANDS TRAINS

East Midlands Trains HSTs are concentrated on the St Pancras–Nottingham corridor during the day, with early morning and evening services to Leeds for servicing at Neville Hill.

The three 6-car sets were transferred from Grand Central at the end of 2017 and are due to enter traffic in spring 2018.

Number of sets: 12.
Maximum number of daily diagrams: 8 (to increase in spring 2018).
Formations: 8-cars or 6-cars.
Allocation: Neville Hill (Leeds) or Derby Etches Park.
Operation: London St Pancras–Nottingham, Sheffield/Leeds.

Set	J	G	F	E	D	C	B	A
NL01	41057	41084	40730	42327	42111	42112	42113	44041
NL03	41061	41067	40741	42337	42119	42120	42121	44054
NL04	41077	41064	40749	42151	42164	42165	42153	44047
NL06	41156	41041	40746	42132	42131	42331	42133	44046
NL07	41111	41070	40754	42339	42135	42136	42137	44044
NL08	41071	41072	40753	42329	42139	42140	42141	44048
NL10	41075	41076	40756	42328	42341	42148	42149	44051
NL11	41117	41046	40728	42220	42100	42230	42124	44085
NL12	41079	41069	40700	42155	42156	42157	42152	44070
DY21	41201	40424	42403	42402	42401	41204		
DY22	41202	40426	42406	42405	42404	41205		
DY23	41203	40433	42409	42408	42407	41206		

Spares:

NL: 41063   41113   42384   44071

CROSSCOUNTRY

CrossCountry reintroduced regular HST diagrams on its services from the December 2008 timetable. Trains run in 7-car formation with the spare TS coaches regularly used in traffic as coaches "C", "D" or "E". At the time of wiriting formations were in a state of flux as trailers are being fitted with sliding doors (the first being XC03).

Number of sets: 5.
Maximum number of daily diagrams: 4.
Formations: 7-cars.
Allocation: Craigentinny (Edinburgh).
Other maintenance depots: Laira (Plymouth) or Neville Hill (Leeds).
Operation: Edinburgh–Leeds–Plymouth is the core route with some services extending to Dundee or Penzance.

Set	A	B	C	D	E	F	G
XC01	41193	45001	42368	42374	42367	42366	44021
XC02	41194	45002	42375	42373	42372	42371	44072
XC03	41195	45003	42369	42378	42377	42376	44052
XC04	41026	45004	42038	42037	42036	42380	44012
XC05	41035	45005	42051	42053	42052	42379	44017

Spares:

EC: 42097   42234   42290   42342   42370

2.4. SALOONS

Several specialist passenger carrying carriages, normally referred to as saloons are permitted to run on the national railway system. Many of these are to pre-nationalisation designs.

WCJS FIRST CLASS SALOON

Built 1892 by LNWR, Wolverton. Originally dining saloon mounted on six-wheel bogies. Rebuilt with new underframe with four-wheel bogies in 1927. Rebuilt 1960 as observation saloon with DMU end. Gangwayed at other end. The interior has a saloon, kitchen, guards vestibule and observation lounge. 19/– 1T. Gresley bogies. 28.5 t. 75 mph. ETS x.

41   (484, 45018) x   **M**   WC *WC*   CS

LNWR DINING SALOON

Built 1890 by LNWR, Wolverton. Mounted on the underframe of LMS General Utility Van 37908 in the 1980s. Contains kitchen and dining area seating 12 at tables for two. 12/–. Gresley bogies. 75 mph. 25.4 t. ETS x.

159   (5159)   x   **M**   WC *WC*   CS

GNR FIRST CLASS SALOON

Built 1912 by GNR, Doncaster. Contains entrance vestibule, lavatory, two separate saloons, library and luggage space. 19/– 1T. Gresley bogies. 75 mph. 29.4 t. ETS x.

Non-standard livery: Teak.

807   (4807)   x   **0**   WC *WC*   CS

LNER GENERAL MANAGERS SALOON

Built 1945 by LNER, York. Gangwayed at one end with a veranda at the other. The interior has a dining saloon seating 12, kitchen, toilet, office and nine seat lounge. 21/– 1T. B4 bogies. 75 mph. 35.7 t. ETS 3.

1999   (902260)   **M**   WC   CS   DINING CAR No. 2

GENERAL MANAGER'S SALOON

Renumbered 1989 from London Midland Region departmental series. Formerly the LMR General Manager's saloon. Rebuilt from LMS period 1 Corridor Brake First M5033M to dia 1654 and mounted on the underframe of BR suburban Brake Standard M43232. Screw couplings have been removed. B4 bogies. 100 mph. ETS 2X.

LMS Lot No. 326 Derby 1927. 27.5 t.

6320 (5033, DM 395707) x **M** PR *PR* SK

BELMOND BRITISH PULLMAN SUPPORT CAR

Converted 199? from Courier vehicle converted from Mark 1 Corridor Brake Standard 1986–87. Toilet retained and former compartment area replaced with train manager's office, crew locker room, linen store and dry goods store. The former luggage area has been adapted for use as an engineers' compartment and workshop. B5 bogies. 100 mph. ETS 2.

Lot No. 30721 Wolverton 1963. 35.5 t.

99545 (35466, 80207) **PC** BE *BP* SL BAGGAGE CAR No. 11

SERVICE CAR

Converted from BR Mark 1 Corridor Brake Standard. Commonwealth bogies. 100 mph. ETS 2.

Lot No. 30721 Wolverton 1963.

99886 (35407) x **M** WC *WC* CS 86 SERVICE CAR No. 1

ROYAL SCOTSMAN SALOONS

Built 1960 by Metro-Cammell as Pullman Kitchen Second for East Coast Main Line Services. Rebuilt 2016 as a Spa Car with two large bedrooms with bathroom/spa areas. Commonwealth bogies. xx t. ETS ?.

99337 (CAR No. 337) **M** BE *RS* ZG SPA STATEROOM

Built 1960 by Metro-Cammell as Pullman Kitchen First for East Coast Main Line services. Rebuilt 2013 as dining car. Commonwealth bogies. 38.5 t. ETS ?.

99960 (321 SWIFT) **M** BE *RS* ZG DINING CAR No. 2

Built 1960 by Metro-Cammell as Pullman Parlour First (§ Pullman Kitchen First) for East Coast Main Line services. Rebuilt 1990 as sleeping cars with four twin sleeping rooms (*§ three twin sleeping rooms and two single sleeping rooms at each end). Commonwealth bogies. 38.5 t. ETS ?.

99961 (324 AMBER) *	**M**	BE	*RS*	ZG	STATE CAR 1
99962 (329 PEARL)	**M**	BE	*RS*	ZG	STATE CAR 2
99963 (331 TOPAZ)	**M**	BE	*RS*	ZG	STATE CAR 3
99964 (313 FINCH) §	**M**	BE	*RS*	ZG	STATE CAR 4

Built 1960 by Metro-Cammell as Pullman Kitchen First for East Coast Main Line services. Rebuilt 1990 as observation car with open verandah seating 32. B4 bogies. 36.95 t. ETS ?.

| 99965 (319 SNIPE) | **M** | BE | *RS* | ZG | OBSERVATION CAR |

Built 1960 by Metro-Cammell as Pullman Kitchen First for East Coast Main Line services. Rebuilt 1993 as dining car. Commonwealth bogies. 38.5 t. ETS ?.

| 99967 (317 RAVEN) | **M** | BE | *RS* | ZG | DINING CAR No. 1 |

Mark 3A. Converted 1997 from a Sleeping Car at Carnforth Railway Restoration & Engineering Services. BT10 bogies. Attendant's and adjacent two sleeping compartments converted to generator room containing a 160 kW Volvo unit. In 99968 four sleeping compartments remain for staff use with another converted for use as a staff shower and toilet. The remaining five sleeping compartments have been replaced by two passenger cabins. In 99969 seven sleeping compartments remain for staff use. A further sleeping compartment, along with one toilet, have been converted to store rooms. The other two sleeping compartments have been combined to form a crew mess. 41.5 t. 99968 ETS index ?. 99969 ETS 7X (when generator not in use). ETS index ?? (when generator in use).

Lot No. 30960 Derby 1981–83.

| 99968 (10541) | **M** | BE | *RS* | ZG | STATE CAR 5 |
| 99969 (10556) | **M** | BE | *RS* | ZG | SERVICE CAR |

"LMS CLUB CAR"

Converted from BR Mark 1 Open Standard at Carnforth Railway Restoration & Engineering Services in 1994. Contains kitchen, pantry and two dining saloons. 20/– 1T. Commonwealth bogies. 100 mph. ETS 4.

Lot No. 30724 York 1963. 37 t.

| 99993 (5067) | x | **M** | LS | | CL | LMS CLUB CAR |

BR INSPECTION SALOON

Mark 1. Short frames. Non-gangwayed. Observation windows at each end. The interior layout consists of two saloons interspersed by a central lavatory/kitchen/guards/luggage section. 90 mph. ETS x.

BR Wagon Lot No. 3095 Swindon 1957. B4 bogies. 30.5 t.

| 999506 | **M** | WC | *WC* | CS | |

2.5. PULLMAN CAR COMPANY SERIES

Pullman cars have never generally been numbered as such, although many have carried numbers, instead they have carried titles. However, a scheme of schedule numbers exists which generally lists cars in chronological order. In this section those numbers are shown followed by the car's title. Cars described as "kitchen" contain a kitchen in addition to passenger accommodation and have gas cooking unless otherwise stated. Cars described as "parlour" consist entirely of passenger accommodation. Cars described as "brake" contain a compartment for the use of the guard and a luggage compartment in addition to passenger accommodation.

PULLMAN PARLOUR FIRST

Built 1927 by Midland Carriage & Wagon Company. 26/– 2T. Gresley bogies. 41 t. ETS 2.

213	MINERVA	**PC**	BE	*BP*	SL

PULLMAN KITCHEN FIRST

Built 1928 by Metropolitan Carriage & Wagon Company. 20/– 1T. Gresley bogies. 42 t. ETS 4.

238	PHYLISS	**PC**	BE		SL

PULLMAN PARLOUR FIRST

Built 1928 by Metropolitan Carriage & Wagon Company. 24/– 2T. Gresley bogies. 40 t. ETS 4.

239	AGATHA	**PC**	BE		SL
243	LUCILLE	**PC**	BE	*BP*	SL

PULLMAN KITCHEN FIRST

Built 1925 by BRCW. Rebuilt by Midland Carriage & Wagon Company in 1928. 20/– 1T. Gresley bogies. 41 t. ETS 4.

245	IBIS	**PC**	BE	*BP*	SL

PULLMAN PARLOUR FIRST

Built 1928 by Metropolitan Carriage & Wagon Company. 24/– 2T. Gresley bogies. ETS 4.

254	ZENA	**PC**	BE	*BP*	SL

PULLMAN KITCHEN FIRST

Built 1928 by Metropolitan Carriage & Wagon Company. 20/– 1T. Gresley bogies. 42 t. ETS 4.

255	IONE		**PC**	BE	*BP*	SL

PULLMAN KITCHEN COMPOSITE

Built 1932 by Metropolitan Carriage & Wagon Company. Originally included in 6-Pul EMU. Electric cooking. 12/16 1T. EMU bogies. ETS x.

264	RUTH		**PC**	BE		SL

PULLMAN KITCHEN FIRST

Built 1932 by Metropolitan Carriage & Wagon Company. Originally included in "Brighton Belle" EMUs but now used as hauled stock. Electric cooking. 20/– 1T. B5 (SR) bogies (§ EMU bogies). 44 t. ETS 2.

280	AUDREY		**PC**	BE	*BP*	SL
281	GWEN		**PC**	BE	*BP*	SL
283	MONA	§	**PC**	BE		SL
284	VERA		**PC**	BE	*BP*	SL

PULLMAN PARLOUR THIRD

Built 1932 by Metropolitan Carriage & Wagon Company. Originally included in "Brighton Belle" EMUs. –/56 2T. EMU bogies. ETS x.

Non-standard livery: BR Revised Pullman (blue & white lined out in white).

286	CAR No. 86	**0**	BE		SL

PULLMAN BRAKE THIRD

Built 1932 by Metropolitan Carriage & Wagon Company. Originally driving motor cars in "Brighton Belle" EMUs. Traction and control equipment removed for use as hauled stock. –/48 1T. EMU bogies. ETS x.

292	CAR No. 92	**PC**	BE	SL
293	CAR No. 93	**PC**	BE	SL

PULLMAN PARLOUR FIRST

Built 1951 by Birmingham Railway Carriage & Wagon Company. 32/– 2T. Gresley bogies. 39 t. ETS 3.

301	PERSEUS	**PC**	BE	*BP*	SL

Built 1952 by Pullman Car Company, Preston Park using underframe and bogies from 176 RAINBOW, the body of which had been destroyed by fire. 26/– 2T. Gresley bogies. 38 t. ETS 4.

302	PHOENIX	**PC**	BE	*BP*	SL

PULLMAN PARLOUR FIRST

Built 1951 by Birmingham Railway Carriage & Wagon Company. 32/– 2T. Gresley bogies. 39 t. ETS 3.

308	CYGNUS	**PC**	BE	*BP*	SL

PULLMAN BAR FIRST

Built 1951 by Birmingham Railway Carriage & Wagon Company. Rebuilt 1999 by Blake Fabrications, Edinburgh with original timber-framed body replaced by a new fabricated steel body. Contains kitchen, bar, dining saloon and coupé. Electric cooking. 14/– 1T. Gresley bogies. ETS 3.

310	PEGASUS	x	**PC**	LS	*LS*	CL

Also carries "THE TRIANON BAR" branding.

PULLMAN PARLOUR FIRST

Built 1960–61 by Metro-Cammell for East Coast Main Line services. –/36 2T. Commonwealth bogies. 38.5 t. ETS x.

325	AMBER	x	**PC**	WC	*WC*	CS
326	EMERALD	x	**PC**	WC	*WC*	CS

PULLMAN KITCHEN SECOND

Built 1960–61 by Metro-Cammell for East Coast Main Line services. Commonwealth bogies. –/30 1T. 40 t. ETS x.

335	CAR No. 335	x	**PC**	VT	*VT*	TM

PULLMAN PARLOUR SECOND

Built 1960–61 by Metro-Cammell for East Coast Main Line services. 347 is used as an Open First. –/42 2T. Commonwealth bogies. 38.5 t. ETS x.

347	CAR No. 347	x	**M**	WC	*WC*	CS
348	TOPAZ	x	**PC**	WC	*WC*	CS
349	CAR No. 349	x	**PC**	VT	*VT*	TM
350	TANZANITE	x	**PC**	WC	*WC*	CS
351	SAPPHIRE	x	**PC**	WC	*WC*	CS
352	AMETHYST	x	**PC**	WC	*WC*	CS
353	CAR No. 353	x	**PC**	VT	*VT*	TM

PULLMAN SECOND BAR

Built 1960–61 by Metro-Cammell for East Coast Main Line services. –/24+17 bar seats. Commonwealth bogies. 38.5 t. ETS x.

354	THE HADRIAN BAR	x	**PC**	WC	*WC*	CS

2.6. LOCOMOTIVE SUPPORT CARRIAGES

These carriages have been adapted from Mark 1s and Mark 2s for use as support carriages for heritage steam and diesel locomotives. Some seating is retained for the use of personnel supporting the locomotives operation with the remainder of the carriage adapted for storage, workshop, dormitory and catering purposes. These carriages can spend considerable periods of time off the national railway system when the locomotives they support are not being used on that system. No owner or operator details are included in this section. After the depot code, the locomotive(s) each carriage is usually used to support is given.

CORRIDOR BRAKE FIRST

Mark 1. Commonwealth bogies. ETS 2.

14007. Lot No. 30382 Swindon 1959. 35 t.
17025. Lot No. 30718 Swindon 1963. Metal window frames. 36 t.

14007	(14007, 17007)	x	**M**	NY	LNER 61264
17025	(14025)	v	**M**	CS	LMS 45690

CORRIDOR BRAKE FIRST

Mark 2A. Pressure ventilated. B4 bogies. ETS 4.

14064. Lot No. 30775 Derby 1967–68. 32 t.
14099/17096. Lot No. 30786 Derby 1968. 32 t.

14064	(14064, 17064)	x	**M**	CS	LMS 45305/BR 70013	
14099	(14099, 17099)	v	**M**	CS	LMS 45305/BR 70013	
17096	(14096)		**PC**	SL	SR 35028	MERCATOR

CORRIDOR BRAKE COMPOSITE

Mark 1. ETS 2.

21096. Lot No. 30185 Metro-Cammell 1956. BR Mark 1 bogies. 32.5 t.
21232. Lot No. 30574 GRCW 1960. B4 bogies. 34 t.
21249. Lot No. 30669 Swindon 1961–62. Commonwealth bogies. 36 t.

21096	x	**M**	NY	LNER 60007
21232	x	**M**	SK	LMS 46201
21249	x	**CC**	SL	New Build 60163

CORRIDOR BRAKE STANDARD

Mark 1. Metal window frames and melamine interior panelling. ETS 2.

35317–322. Lot No. 30699 Wolverton 1962–63. Commonwealth bogies. 37 t.
35449. Lot No. 30728 Wolverton 1963. Commonwealth bogies. 37 t.
35451–486. Lot No. 30721 Wolverton 1963. Commonwealth bogies. 37 t.

35317	x	**CC**	SH	LMS 46100
35322	x	**M**	CS	WCRC Carnforth-based locomotives
35449	x	**M**	CL	LMS 45231
35451	x	**CC**	SH	SR 34046
35461	x	**CH**	CL	GWR 5029
35463	v	**M**	CS	WCRC Carnforth-based locomotives
35465	x	**CC**	SH	BR 70000
35468	x	**M**	YK	National Railway Museum locomotives
35470	v	**CH**	TM	Tyseley Locomotive Works-based locos
35476	x	**M**	SK	LMS 46233
35479	v	**M**	SH	LNER 61306
35486	x	**M**	TN	LNER 60009

CORRIDOR BRAKE FIRST

Mark 2C. Pressure ventilated. Renumbered when declassified. B4 bogies. ETS 4.

Lot No. 30796 Derby 1969–70. 32.5 t.

35508 (14128, 17128)	**M**	BQ	LMS 44871/45212/45407

CORRIDOR BRAKE FIRST

Mark 2A. Pressure ventilated. Renumbered when declassified. B4 bogies. ETS 4.

Lot No. 30786 Derby 1968. 32 t.

35517 (14088, 17088)	b	**M**	BQ	LMS 44871/45212/45407
35518 (14097, 17097)	b	**G**	SH	SR 34067

COURIER VEHICLE

Mark 1. Converted 1986–87 from Corridor Brake Standards. ETS 2.

80204/217. Lot No. 30699 Wolverton 1962. Commonwealth bogies. 37 t.
80220. Lot No. 30573 Gloucester 1960. B4 bogies. 33 t.

80204 (35297)	**M**	CS	WCRC Carnforth-based locomotives
80217 (35299)	**M**	CS	WCRC Carnforth-based locomotives
80220 (35276)	**M**	NY	LNER 62005

2.7. 95xxx & 99xxx RANGE NUMBER CONVERSION TABLE

The following table is presented to help readers identify carriages which may still carry numbers in the 95xxx and 99xxx number ranges of the former private owner number series, which is no longer in general use.

9xxxx	BR No.	9xxxx	BR No.	9xxxx	BR No.
95402	Pullman 326	99350	Pullman 350	99673	550
99025	Pullman 325	99351	Pullman 351	99674	551
99035	35322	99352	Pullman 352	99675	552
99040	21232	99353	Pullman 353	99676	553
99041	35476	99354	Pullman 354	99677	586
99052	Saloon 41	99361	Pullman 335	99678	504
99121	3105	99371	3128	99679	506
99122	3106	99405	35486	99680	17102
99125	3113	99530	Pullman 301	99710	18767
99127	3117	99531	Pullman 302	99716 *	18808
99128	3130	99532	Pullman 308	99718	18862
99131	Saloon 1999	99534	Pullman 245	99721	18756
99241	35449	99535	Pullman 213	99723	35459
99302	13323	99536	Pullman 254	99880	Saloon 159
99304	21256	99537	Pullman 280	99881	Saloon 807
99311	1882	99539	Pullman 255	99883	2108
99312	35463	99541	Pullman 243	99885	2110
99319	17168	99543	Pullman 284	99887	2127
99326	4954	99546	Pullman 281	99953	35468
99327	5044	99547	Pullman 292	99966	34525
99328	5033	99548	Pullman 293	99970	Pullman 232
99329	4931	99670	546	99972	Pullman 318
99347	Pullman 347	99671	548	99973	324
99348	Pullman 348	99672	549	99974	Pullman 328
99349	Pullman 349				

* The number 99716 has also been applied to 3416 for filming purposes.

2.8. SET FORMATIONS

VIRGIN TRAINS EAST COAST MARK 4 SET FORMATIONS

The Virgin Trains East Coast Mark 4 sets generally run in fixed formations since their refurbishment at Bombardier, Wakefield in 2003–05. These rakes are listed below. Class 91 locomotives are positioned next to Coach B.

Set	B	C	D	E	F	H	K	L	M	DVT
BN01	12207	12417	12415	12414	12307	10307	11298	11301	11401	82207
BN02	12232	12402	12450	12448	12302	10302	11299	11302	11402	82202
BN03	12201	12401	12459	12478	12301	10320	11277	11303	11403	82219
BN04	12202	12480	12421	12518	12327	10303	11278	11304	11404	82209
BN05	12209	12486	12520	12522	12300	10326	11219	11305	11405	82210
BN06	12208	12406	12420	12422	12313	10309	11279	11306	11406	82208
BN07	12231	12411	12405	12489	12329	10323	11280	11307	11407	82204
BN08	12205	12481	12485	12407	12328	10300	11229	11308	11408	82211
BN09	12230	12513	12483	12514	12304	10304	11281	11309	11409	82215
BN10	12214	12419	12488	12443	12305	10331	11282	11310	11410	82205
BN11	12203	12437	12436	12484	12315	10308	11283	11311	11411	82218
BN12	12212	12431	12404	12426	12330	10333	11284	11312	11412	82212
BN13	12228	12469	12430	12424	12311	10313	11285	11313	11413	82213
BN14	12229	12410	12526	12423	12312	10332	11201	11314	11414	82206
BN15	12226	12442	12409	12515	12309	10306	11286	11315	11415	82214
BN16	12213	12428	12445	12433	12304	10315	11287	11316	11416	82222
BN17	12223	12444	12427	12432	12303	10324	11288	11317	11417	82225
BN18	12215	12453	12468	12467	12324	10305	11289	11318	11418	82222
BN19	12211	12434	12400	12470	12310	10318	11290	11319	11419	82201
BN20	12224	12477	12439	12440	12326	10321	11241	11320	11420	82200
BN21	12222	12461	12441	12476	12323	10330	11244	11321	11421	82227
BN22	12210	12452	12460	12473	12316	10301	11291	11322	11422	82230
BN23	12225	12454	12456	12455	12318	10325	11292	11323	11423	82226
BN24	12219	12447	12425	12403	12319	10328	11293	11324	11424	82229
BN25	12217	12446	12519	12464	12322	10312	11294	11325	11425	82216
BN26	12220	12474	12465	12429	12325	10311	11295	11326	11426	82223
BN27	12216	12449	12466	12538	12317	10319	11237	11327	11427	82228
BN28	12218	12458	12463	12533	12320	10310	11273	11328	11428	82217
BN29	12204	12462	12457	12438	12321	10317	11998	11329	11429	82231
BN30	12227	12471	12534	12472	12331	10329	11999	11330	11430	82203
Spare	12200									82224

2.9. SERVICE STOCK

Carriages in this section are used for internal purposes within the railway industry, ie they do not generate revenue from outside the industry. Most are numbered in the former BR departmental number series.

BARRIER, ESCORT & TRANSLATOR VEHICLES

These vehicles are used to move multiple unit, HST and other vehicles around the national railway system.

HST Barrier Vehicles. Mark 1/2A. Renumbered from BR departmental series, or converted from various types. B4 bogies (* Commonwealth bogies).

Non-standard livery: 6340, 6344, 6346 All over dark blue.

6330. Mark 2A. Lot No. 30786 Derby 1968.
6336/38/44. Mark 1. Lot No. 30715 Gloucester 1962.
6340. Mark 1. Lot No. 30669 Swindon 1962.
6346. Mark 2A. Lot No. 30777 Derby 1967.
6348. Mark 1. Lot No. 30163 Pressed Steel 1957.

6330	(14084, 975629)		**FB**	A	*GW*	LA
6336	(81591, 92185)		**FB**	A	*GW*	LA
6338	(81581, 92180)		**FB**	A	*GW*	LA
6340	(21251, 975678)	*	**O**	A	*VE*	EC
6344	(81263, 92080)		**O**	A	*VE*	EC
6346	(9422)		**O**	A	*VE*	EC
6348	(81233, 92963)		**FB**	A	*GW*	LA

Mark 4 Barrier Vehicles. Mark 2A/2C. Converted from Corridor First (*) or Open Brake Standard. B4 bogies.

Non-standard livery: 6358 All over dark blue.

6352/53. Mark 2A. Lot No. 30774 Derby 1968.
6354/55. Mark 2C. Lot No. 30820 Derby 1970.
6358/59. Mark 2A. Lot No. 30788 Derby 1968.

6352	(13465, 19465)	*	**HB**	E	*VE*	BN
6353	(13478, 19478)	*	**HB**	E	*VE*	BN
6354	(9459)		**GN**	DR		LW
6355	(9477)		**GN**	DR		LW
6358	(9432)		**O**	DR		LW
6359	(9429)		**GN**	DR		LW

EMU Translator Vehicles. Mark 1. Converted 1980 from Restaurant Unclassified Opens. 6376/77 have Tightlock couplers and 6378/79 Dellner couplers. Commonwealth bogies.

Lot No. 30647 Wolverton 1959–61.

6376	(1021, 975973)	**PB**	P	*DB*	TO *(works with 6377)*
6377	(1042, 975975)	**PB**	P	*DB*	TO *(works with 6376)*
6378	(1054, 975971)	**PB**	P	*DB*	TO *(works with 6379)*
6379	(1059, 975972)	**PB**	P	*DB*	TO *(works with 6378)*

Brake Force Runners. Mark 1. Previously used as HST Barrier Vehicles. Converted from Gangwayed Brake Vans in 1994–95. B4 bogies.

6392. Lot No. 30715 Gloucester 1962.
6397. Lot No. 30716 Gloucester 1962.

6392	(81588, 92183)	**PB**	CS	*CS*	ZA
6397	(81600, 92190)	**PB**	CS	*CS*	ZA

HST Barrier Vehicles. Mark 1. Converted from Gangwayed Brake Vans in 1994–95. B4 bogies.

6393. Lot No. 30716 Gloucester 1962.
6394. Lot No. 30162 Pressed Steel 1956–57.
6398/99. Lot No. 30400 Pressed Steel 1957–58.

6393	(81609, 92196)	**PB**	P	*VE*	EC
6394	(80878, 92906)	**PB**	P	*VE*	EC
6398	(81471, 92126)	**PB**	EM	*EM*	NL
6399	(81367, 92994)	**PB**	EM	*EM*	NL

Escort Coaches. Converted from Mark 2A (* Mark 2E) Open Brake Standards. 9419/28 use the same bodyshell as the Mark 2A Corridor Brake First. B4 bogies.

9419. Lot No.30777 Derby 1970.
9428. Lot No.30820 Derby 1970.
9506/08. Lot No.30838 Derby 1972.

9419		**DS**	DR	*DR*	KM
9428		**DS**	DR	*DR*	KM
9506	*	**DS**	DR	*DR*	KM
9508	*	**DS**	DR	*DR*	KM

EMU Translator Vehicles. Converted from Class 508 driving cars.

64664. Lot No. 30979 York 1979–80.
64707. Lot No. 30981 York 1979–80.

64664	**AG**	A	*GB*	ZG	Liwet	*(works with 64707)*
64707	**AG**	A	*GB*	ZG	Labezerin	*(works with 64664)*

Eurostar Barrier Vehicles. Mark 1. Converted from General Utility Vans with bodies removed. Fitted with B4 bogies for use as Eurostar barrier vehicles.

96380/381. Lot No. 30417 Pressed Steel 1958–59.
96383. Lot No. 30565 Pressed Steel 1959.
96384. Lot No. 30616 Pressed Steel 1959–60.

96380	(86386, 6380)	**B**	EU	*EU*	TI
96381	(86187, 6381)	**B**	EU	*EU*	TI
96383	(86664, 6383)	**B**	EU	*EU*	TI
96384	(86955, 6384)	**B**	EU	*EU*	TI

Brake Force Runners. Converted from Motorail vans built 1998–99 by Marcroft Engineering using underframe and running gear from Motorail General Utility Vans. B5 bogies.

Lot No. 30417 Pressed Steel 1958–59.

96604	(86337, 96156)	**Y**	CS	*CS*	ZA	
96606	(86324, 96213)	**Y**	CS	*CS*	ZA	
96608	(86385, 96216)	**Y**	CS	*CS*	ZA	
96609	(86327, 96217)	**Y**	CS	*CS*	ZA	

EMU Translator Vehicles. Converted from various Mark 1s.

Non-standard livery: All over blue.

975864. Lot No. 30054 Eastleigh 1951–54. Commonwealth bogies.
975867. Lot No. 30014 York 1950–51. Commonwealth bogies.
975875. Lot No. 30143 Charles Roberts 1954–55. Commonwealth bogies.
975974/978. Lot No. 30647 Wolverton 1959–61. B4 bogies.
977087. Lot No. 30229 Metro–Cammell 1955–57. Commonwealth bogies.

975864	(3849)	**HB**	E	*GB*	ZH		*(works with 975867)*
975867	(1006)	**HB**	E	*GB*	ZH		*(works with 975864)*
975875	(34643)	**0**	E	*RG*	LR		*(works with 977087)*
975974	(1030)	**AG**	A	*GB*	ZG	Paschar	*(works with 975978)*
975978	(1025)	**AG**	A	*GB*	ZG	Perpetiel	*(works with 975974)*
977087	(34971)	**0**	E	*RG*	LR		*(works with 975875)*

LABORATORY, TESTING & INSPECTION COACHES

These coaches are used for research, development, testing and inspection on the national railway system. Many are fitted with sophisticated technical equipment.

Plain Line Pattern Recognition Coaches. Converted from BR Mark 2F Buffet First (*) or Open Standard. B4 bogies.

1256. Lot No. 30845 Derby 1973.
5981. Lot No. 30860 Derby 1973–74.

1256	(3296)	*	**Y**	NR	*CS*	ZA
5981			**Y**	NR	*CS*	ZA

Generator Vans. Mark 1. Converted from BR Mark 1 Gangwayed Brake Vans. B5 bogies.

6260. Lot No. 30400 Pressed Steel 1957–58.
6261. Lot No. 30323 Pressed Steel 1957.
6262. Lot No. 30228 Metro-Cammell 1957–58.
6263. Lot No. 30163 Pressed Steel 1957.
6264. Lot No. 30173 York 1956.

6260	(81450, 92116)	**Y**	NR	*CS*	ZA	
6261	(81284, 92988)	**Y**	NR	*CS*	ZA	
6262	(81064, 92928)	**Y**	NR	*CS*	ZA	
6263	(81231, 92961)	**Y**	NR	*CS*	ZA	
6264	(80971, 92923)	**Y**	NR	*CS*	ZA	

Staff Coach. Mark 2D. Converted from BR Mark 2D Open Brake Standard. Lot No. 30824 Derby 1971. B4 bogies.

9481	**Y**	NR	*CS*	ZA

Test Train Brake Force Runners. Mark 2F. Converted from BR Mark 2F Open Brake Standard. Lot No. 30861 Derby 1974. B4 bogies.

9516	Y	NR	CS	ZA
9523	Y	NR	CS	ZA

Driving Trailer Coaches. Converted 2008 at Serco, Derby from Mark 2F Driving Open Brake Standards. Fitted with generator. Disc brakes. B4 bogies.

9701–08. Lot No. 30861 Derby 1974. Converted to Driving Open Brake Standard Glasgow 1974.
9714. Lot No. 30861 Derby 1974. Converted to Driving Open Brake Standard Glasgow 1986.

9701	(9528)	Y	NR	CS	ZA
9702	(9510)	Y	NR	CS	ZA
9703	(9517)	Y	NR	CS	ZA
9708	(9530)	Y	NR	CS	ZA
9714	(9536)	Y	NR	CS	ZA

Ultrasonic Test Coach. Converted from Class 421 EMU MBSO.

62287. Lot No. 30808. York 1970. SR Mark 6 bogies.
62384. Lot No. 30816. York 1970. SR Mark 6 bogies.

62287	Y	NR	CS	ZA
62384	Y	NR	CS	ZA

Test Train Brake Force Runners. Converted from Mark 2F Open Standard converted to Class 488/3 EMU TSOLH. These vehicles are included in test trains to provide brake force and are not used for any other purposes. Lot No. 30860 Derby 1973–74. B4 bogies.

72612	(6156)	Y	NR	CS	ZA
72616	(6007)	Y	NR	CS	ZA

Structure Gauging Train Coach. Converted from Mark 2F Open Standard converted to Class 488/3 EMU TSOLH. Lot No. 30860 Derby 1973–74. B4 bogies.

72630	(6094)	Y	NR	CS	ZA	*(works with 99666)*

Plain Line Pattern Recognition Coaches. Converted from BR Mark 2F Open Standard converted to Class 488/3 EMU TSOLH. Lot No. 30860 Derby 1973–74. B4 bogies.

72631	(6096)	Y	NR	CS	ZA
72639	(6070)	Y	NR	CS	ZA

Driving Trailer Coaches. Converted from Mark 3B 110 mph Driving Brake Vans. Fitted with diesel generator. Lot No. 31042 Derby 1988.

82111	Y	NR	ZA
82124	Y	NR	ZA
82129	Y	NR	ZA
82145	Y	NR	ZA

Structure Gauging Train Coach. Converted from BR Mark 2E Open First then converted to exhibition van. Lot No. 30843 Derby 1972–73. B4 bogies.

99666	(3250)	Y	NR	CS	ZA	*(works with 72630)*

Inspection Saloon. Converted from Class 202 DEMU TRB at Stewarts Lane for use as a BR Southern Region General Manager's Saloon. Overhauled at FM Rail, Derby 2004–05 for use as a New Trains Project Saloon. Can be used in push-pull mode with suitably equipped locomotives. Eastleigh 1958. SR Mark 4 bogies.

| 975025 | (60755) | **G** | NR | *CS* | ZA | CAROLINE |

Overhead Line Equipment Test Coach ("MENTOR"). Converted from BR Mark 1 Corridor Brake Standard. Lot No. 30142 Gloucester 1954–55. Fitted with pantograph. B4 bogies.

| 975091 | (34615) | **Y** | NR | *CS* | ZA |

New Measurement Train Conference Coach. Converted from prototype HST TF Lot No. 30848 Derby 1972. BT10 bogies.

| 975814 | (11000, 41000) | **Y** | NR | *CS* | EC |

New Measurement Train Lecture Coach. Converted from prototype HST catering vehicle. Lot No. 30849 Derby 1972–73. BT10 bogies.

| 975984 | (10000, 40000) | **Y** | NR | *CS* | EC |

Radio Survey Coach. Converted from BR Mark 2E Open Standard. Lot No. 30844 Derby 1972–73. B4 bogies.

| 977868 | (5846) | **Y** | NR | *CS* | ZA |

Staff Coach. Converted from Royal Household couchette Lot No. 30889, which in turn had been converted from BR Mark 2B Corridor Brake First. Lot No. 30790 Derby 1969. B5 bogies.

| 977969 | (14112, 2906) | **Y** | NR | *CS* | ZA |

Track Inspection Train Coach. Converted from BR Mark 2E Open Standard. Lot No. 30844 Derby 1972–73. B4 bogies.

| 977974 | (5854) | **Y** | NR | *CS* | ZA |

Electrification Measurement Coach. Converted from BR Mark 2F Open First converted to Class 488/2 EMU TFOH. Lot No. 30859 Derby 1973–74. B4 bogies.

| 977983 | (3407, 72503) | **Y** | NR | *CS* | ZA |

New Measurement Train Staff Coach. Converted from HST catering vehicle. Lot No. 30884 Derby 1976–77. BT10 bogies.

| 977984 | (40501) | **Y** | P | *CS* | EC |

Structure Gauging Train Coaches. Converted from Mark 2F Open Standard converted to Class 488/3 EMU TSOLH or from BR Mark 2D Open First subsequently declassified to Open Standard and then converted to exhibition van. B4 bogies.

977985. Lot No. 30860 Derby 1973–74.
977986. Lot No. 30821 Derby 1971.

| 977985 | (6019, 72715) | **Y** | NR | *CS* | ZA | *(works with 977986)* |
| 977986 | (3189, 99664) | **Y** | NR | *CS* | ZA | *(works with 977985)* |

New Measurement Train Overhead Line Equipment Test Coach. Converted from HST TGS. Lot No. 30949 Derby 1982. Fitted with pantograph. BT10 bogies.

977993	(44053)	Y	P	*CS*	EC

New Measurement Train Track Recording Coach. Converted from HST TGS. Lot No. 30949 Derby 1982. BT10 bogies.

977994	(44087)	Y	P	*CS*	EC

New Measurement Train Coach. Converted from HST catering vehicle. Lot No. 30921 Derby 1978–79. BT10 bogies. Fitted with generator.

977995	(40719, 40619)	Y	P	*CS*	EC

Radio Survey Coach. Converted from Mark 2F Open Standard converted to Class 488/3 EMU TSOLH. Lot No. 30860 Derby 1973–74.

977997	(72613, 6126)	Y	NR	*CS*	ZA

Track Recording Coach. Purpose built Mark 2. B4 bogies.

999550		Y	NR	*CS*	ZA

Ultrasonic Test Coaches. Converted from Class 421 EMU MBSO and Class 432 EMU MSO.

999602/605. Lot No. 30862 York 1974. SR Mk 6 bogies.
999606. Lot No. 30816. York 1970. SR Mk 6 bogies.

999602	(62483)	Y	NR	*CS*	ZA
999605	(62482)	Y	NR	*CS*	ZA
999606	(62356)	Y	NR	*CS*	ZA

BREAKDOWN TRAIN COACHES

These coaches are formed in trains used for the recovery of derailed railway vehicles and were converted from BR Mark 1 Corridor Brake Standard and General Utility Van. The current use of each vehicle is given.

971001/003/004. Lot No. 30403 York/Glasgow 1958–60. Commonwealth bogies.
971002. Lot No. 30417 Pressed Steel 1958–59. Commonwealth bogies.
975087. Lot No. 30032 Wolverton 1951–52. BR Mark 1 bogies.
975464. Lot No. 30386 Charles Roberts 1956–58. Commonwealth bogies.
975471. Lot No. 30095 Wolverton 1953–55. Commonwealth bogies.
975477. Lot No. 30233 GRCW 1955–57. BR Mark 1 bogies.
975486. Lot No. 30025 Wolverton 1950–52. Commonwealth bogies.

971001	(86560, 94150)	Y	NR	*DB*	BS	Tool & Generator Van
971002	(86624, 94190)	Y	NR	*DB*	SP	Tool Van
971003	(86596, 94191)	Y	NR	*DB*	BS	Tool Van
971004	(86194, 94168)	Y	NR	*DB*	SP	Tool Van
975087	(34289)	Y	NR	*DB*	SP	Tool & Generator Van
975464	(35171)	Y	NR	*DB*	SP	Staff Coach
975471	(34543)	Y	NR	*DB*	BS	Staff Coach
975477	(35108)	Y	NR	*DB*	SP	Staff Coach
975486	(34100)	Y	NR	*DB*	SP	Tool & Generator Van

6364	Barry	80404	CS	94410	WE	96164	CS
6365	Barry	80414	SL	94420	CS	96165	CS
6412	CL	82125	LM	94422	TO	96170	CS
6720	FA	92114	ZA	94423	BS	96178	CS
7204	CL	92159	CS	94427	WE	96182	CS
7931	BU	92303	BU	94428	CS	96191	CS
9440	SH	92908	CS	94429	HM	96192	CS
9489	CS	92936	BU	94431	CS	96371	LR
9490	BU	93723	BY	94434	CL	96372	LM
9494	ZG	94058	BU	94435	TO	96373	LM
9522	ZG	94101	CS	94445	WE	96374	ZB
9529	DR	94104	TO	94450	WE	96375	LM
9531	DR	94106	BU	94451	WE	96602	Barry
10201	LM	94116	BU	94470	TO	96603	CF
10245	CS	94153	WE	94479	TO	96605	Barry
10530	ZN	94166	BS	94482	CS	96607	Barry
10578	ZN	94170	CL	94488	BU	99019	CS
10588	ZN	94176	BS	94490	BU	99884	CL
10656	ZN	94177	TO	94492	WE	889400	ZA
10682	LM	94195	BS	94495	Hellifield	975081	ZR
11005	LM	94196	CS	94498	CS	975280	ZR
11006	BU	94197	BS	94501	TO	975454	TO
11021	LM	94207	TO	94504	Hellifield	975484	CS
11079	LM	94208	TO	94512	CS	975490	BU
11097	LM	94214	CS	94515	Eastleigh	975639	CS
12008	LM	94222	CS		East Yard	975681	Portobello
12029	LM	94227	HM	94517	BU	975682	Portobello
12095	LM	94229	CL	94520	BU	975685	Portobello
12096	ZN	94302	Hellifield	94522	CL	975686	Portobello
12101	CS	94303	Hellifield	94525	CS	975687	Portobello
12144	LM	94304	MH	94526	CS	975688	Portobello
12156	LM	94306	Hellifield	94527	Hellifield	975920	Portobello
12160	LM	94308	CS	94530	CS	977077	Ripple Lane
12163	LM	94310	WE	94531	BU	977085	BU
13306	CS	94311	WE	94538	CL	977095	CS
13323	CS	94313	WE	94539	CS	977111	Ripple Lane
13508	CL	94316	TO	94540	TJ	977112	Ripple Lane
17013	CL	94317	TO	94542	CS	977169	CL
17168	CS	94322	CS	94545	HM	977241	BU
18767	SH	94323	Hellifield	94546	Hellifield	977618	BY
18808	SH	94326	Hellifield	94547	CS	999509	CL
18862	CS	94332	CS	94548	CS		
21268	CL	94333	Hellifield	95300	CS	083439	BU
34525	CS	94335	CL	95410	CS		
35333	ZG	94336	CL	95727	WE	DS70220 Western
35467	CL	94337	WE	95754	CS	Trading Estate
40729	NL	94338	WE	95761	WE	Siding, North Acton
41043	LB	94344	TO	95763	BS	
80212	CS	94401	CS	96110	CS	Pullman 315 CS
80374	BU	94406	CS	96132	CS	Pullman 316 CS
80403	CS	94408	CS	96135	CS	

3. DIESEL MULTIPLE UNITS

INTRODUCTION

This section contains details of all Diesel Multiple Units, usually referred to as DMUs, which can run on Britain's national railway network.

Since the 1980s DMUs have replaced more traditional locomotive-hauled trains on many routes. DMUs today work a wide variety of services, from long distance Intercity to inter-urban and suburban duties.

LAYOUT OF INFORMATION

DMUs are listed in numerical order of set – using current numbers as allocated by the Rolling Stock Library. Individual "loose" vehicles are listed in numerical order after vehicles formed into fixed formations. Where sets or vehicles have been renumbered in recent years, former numbering detail is shown in parentheses. Each entry is laid out as in the following example:

Set No.	Detail	Livery	Owner	Operator	Depot	Formation	Name
153 309	cr	**GA**	P	*GA*	NC	52309	GERALD FIENNES

Codes: Codes are used to denote the livery, owner, operator and depot allocation of each Diesel Multiple Unit. Details of these can be found in section 6 of this book. Where a unit or spare car is off-lease, the operator column is left blank.

Detail Differences: Detail differences which currently affect the areas and types of train which vehicles may work are shown, plus differences in interior layout. Where such differences occur within a class, these are shown either in the heading information or alongside the individual set or vehicle number. The following standard abbreviations are used:

e European Railway Traffic Management System (ERTMS) signalling equipment fitted.

r Radio Electric Token Block signalling equipment fitted.

Use of the above abbreviations indicates the equipment fitted is normally operable. Meaning of non-standard abbreviations is detailed in individual class headings.

Set Formations: Regular set formations are shown where these are normally maintained. Readers should note set formations might be temporarily varied from time to time to suit maintenance and/or operational requirements. Vehicles shown as "Spare" are not formed in any regular set formation.

Names: Only names carried with official sanction are listed. Names are shown in UPPER/lower case characters as actually shown on the name carried on the vehicle(s). Unless otherwise shown, complete units are regarded as named rather than just the individual car(s) which carry the name.

GENERAL INFORMATION

CLASSIFICATION AND NUMBERING

DMU Classes are listed in class number order.

First generation ("Heritage") DMUs were classified in the series 100–139.
Parry People Movers (not technically DMUs) are classified in the series 139.
Second generation DMUs are classified in the series 140–199.
Diesel Electric Multiple Units are classified in the series 200–249.
Service units are classified in the series 930–999.

First and second generation individual cars are numbered in the series 50000–59999 and 79000–79999.

Parry People Mover cars are numbered in the 39000 series.

DEMU individual cars are numbered in the series 60000–60999, except for a few former EMU vehicles which retain their EMU numbers.

For all new vehicles allocated by the Rolling Stock Library since 2014 6-digit vehicle numbers are being used. The Class 230 D-Train DEMU individual cars are numbered in the 300xxx series.

WHEEL ARRANGEMENT

A system whereby the number of powered axles on a bogie or frame is denoted by a letter (A = 1, B = 2, C= 3 etc) and the number of unpowered axles is denoted by a number is used in this publication. The letter "o" after a letter indicates that each axle is individually powered.

UNITS OF MEASUREMENT

Principal details and dimensions are quoted for each class in metric and/or imperial units as considered appropriate bearing in mind common UK usage.

All dimensions and weights are quoted for vehicles in an "as new" condition with all necessary supplies (eg oil, water, sand) on board. Dimensions are quoted in the order Length – Width. All lengths quoted are over buffers or couplers as appropriate. Where two lengths are quoted, the first refers to outer vehicles in a set and the second to inner vehicles. All width dimensions quoted are maxima. All weights are shown as metric tonnes (t = tonnes).

OPERATING CODES

These codes are used by train operating company staff to describe the various different types of vehicles and normally appear on data panels on the inner (ie non driving) ends of vehicles.

The first part of the code describes whether the car has a motor or a driving cab as follows:

DM Driving motor   DT Driving trailer   M   Motor   T   Trailer

The next letter is a "B" for cars with a brake compartment.
This is followed by the saloon details:

F	First	L	denotes a vehicle with a toilet.
S	Standard	W	denotes a Wheelchair space.
C	Composite		

Finally vehicles with a buffet or kitchen area are suffixed RB or RMB for a miniature buffet counter.

Where two vehicles of the same type are formed within the same unit, the above codes may be suffixed by (A) and (B) to differentiate between the vehicles.

A composite is a vehicle containing both First and Standard Class accommodation, whilst a brake vehicle is a vehicle containing separate specific accommodation for the conductor.

Where vehicles have been declassified, the correct operating code which describes the actual vehicle layout is quoted in this publication.

BUILD DETAILS

Lot Numbers

Vehicles ordered under the auspices of BR were allocated a Lot (batch) number when ordered and these are quoted in class headings and sub-headings. Vehicles ordered since 1995 have no Lot Numbers, but the manufacturer and location that they were built is given.

Builders

These are shown for each lot. More details and a full list of builders can be found in section 6.7.

Information on sub-contracting works which built parts of carriages eg the underframes etc is not shown.

ACCOMMODATION

The information given in class headings and sub-headings is in the form F/S nT (or TD) nW. For example 12/54 1T 1W denotes 12 First Class and 54 Standard Class seats, one toilet and one space for a wheelchair. A number in brackets (ie (+2)) denotes tip-up seats (in addition to the fixed seats). Tip-up seats in vestibules do not count. The seating layout of open saloons is shown as 2+1, 2+2 or 3+2 as the case may be. Where units have First Class accommodation as well as Standard Class and the layout is different for each class then these are shown separately prefixed by "1:" and "2:". TD denotes a universal access toilet suitable for use by a disabled person.

NEW DMUS ON ORDER

DMUs that are on order but <u>are not shown in this book</u> are summarised in the table below:

Class	Manufacturer	Operator	Quantity	Delivery dates
tbc	CAF	West Midlands Trains	14 x 4-car	2020
tbc	CAF	West Midlands Trains	12 x 2-car	2020

3.1. DIESEL MECHANICAL & DIESEL HYDRAULIC UNITS

3.1.1 FIRST GENERATION UNIT

CLASS 121   PRESSED STEEL SUBURBAN

First generation unit. Used by Chiltern Railways until 2017, and then sold to Locomotives Services for use as a route learning vehicle.
Construction: Steel.
Engines: Two Leyland 1595 of 112 kW (150 hp) at 1800 rpm.
Transmission: Mechanical. Cardan shaft and freewheel to a four-speed epicyclic gearbox and final drive.
Bogies: DD10.
Brakes: Vacuum.
Couplers: Screw.
Dimensions: 20.45 x 2.82 m.
Gangways: Non gangwayed single cars with cabs at each end.
Wheel arrangement: 1-A + A-1.
Doors: Manually-operated slam.
Maximum Speed: 70 mph.
Seating Layout: 3+2 facing.
Multiple Working: "Blue Square" coupling code. First Generation vehicles cannot be coupled to Second Generation units.

Fitted with central door locking.

Formerly in departmental use as 977828.

DMBS. Lot No. 30518 1960. –/65. 38.0 t.

| 121 034 | **G** | LS | *LS* | CL | 55034 |

3.1.2. PARRY PEOPLE MOVERS

CLASS 139   PPM-60

Gas/flywheel hybrid drive Railcars used on the Stourbridge Junction–
Stourbridge Town branch.

Body construction: Stainless steel framework.

Chassis construction: Welded mild steel box section.

Primary Drive: Ford MVH420 2.3 litre 64 kW (86 hp) LPG fuel engine driving
through Newage marine gearbox, Tandler bevel box and 4 "V" belt driver
to flywheel.

Flywheel Energy Store: 500 kg, 1 m diameter, normal operational speed
range 1000–1500 rpm.

Final transmission: 4 "V" belt driver from flywheel to Tandler bevel box,
Linde hydrostatic transmission and spiral bevel gearbox at No. 2 end axle.

Braking: Normal service braking by regeneration to flywheel (1 m/s/s);
emergency/parking braking by sprung-on, air-off disc brakes (3 m/s/s).

Maximum Speed: 45 mph.

Dimensions: 8.7 x 2.4 m.

Doors: Deans powered doors, double-leaf folding (one per side).

Seating Layout: 1+1 unidirectional/facing.

Multiple Working: Not applicable.

39001–002. DMS. Main Road Sheet Metal, Leyland 2007–08. –/17(+4) 1W.
12.5 t.

139 001	**LM** P	*WM*	SJ	39001
139 002	**LM** P	*WM*	SJ	39002

3.1.3. SECOND GENERATION UNITS

All units in this section have air brakes and are equipped with public
address, with transmission equipment on driving vehicles and flexible
diaphragm gangways. Except where otherwise stated, transmission is
Voith 211r hydraulic with a cardan shaft to a Gmeinder GM190 final drive.

CLASS 142   PACER   BREL DERBY/LEYLAND

DMS–DMSL.

Construction: Steel underframe, rivetted steel body and roof. Built from
Leyland National bus parts on Leyland Bus four-wheeled underframes.

Engines: One Cummins LT10-R of 165 kW (225 hp) at 1950 rpm.

Couplers: BSI at outer ends, bar within unit.

Dimensions: 15.55 x 2.80 m.

Gangways: Within unit only.   **Wheel Arrangement:** 1-A + A-1.

Doors: Twin-leaf inward pivoting.   **Maximum Speed:** 75 mph.

Seating Layout: 3+2 mainly unidirectional bus/bench style unless stated.

Multiple Working: Within class and with Classes 143, 144, 150, 153, 155,
156, 158 and 159.

c Refurbished Arriva Trains Wales units. Fitted with 2+2 individual Chapman seating.
s Fitted with 2+2 individual high-back seating.
t Former First North Western facelifted units – DMS fitted with a luggage/bicycle rack and wheelchair space.
u Merseytravel units – Fitted with 3+2 individual low-back seating.

55542–591. DMS. Lot No. 31003 1985–86. –/62 (c –/46(+6) 2W, s –/56, t –/53 or 55 1W, u –/52 or 54 1W). 24.5 t.
55592–641. DMSL. Lot No. 31004 1985–86. –/59 1T (c –/44(+6) 1T 2W, s –/50 1T, u –/60 1T). 25.0 t.
55701–746. DMS. Lot No. 31013 1986–87. –/62 (c –/46(+6) 2W, s –/56, t –/53 or 55 1W, u –/52 or 54 1W). 24.5 t.
55747–792. DMSL. Lot No. 31014 1986–87. –/59 1T (c –/44(+6) 1T 2W, s –/50 1T, u –/60 1T). 25.0 t.

142 001	t	**NO**	A	*NO*	NH	55542	55592
142 002	c	**AV**	A	*AW*	CF	55543	55593
142 003		**NO**	A	*NO*	NH	55544	55594
142 004	t	**NO**	A	*NO*	NH	55545	55595
142 005	t	**NO**	A	*NO*	NH	55546	55596
142 006	c	**AV**	A	*AW*	CF	55547	55597
142 007	t	**NO**	A	*NO*	NH	55548	55598
142 009	t	**NO**	A	*NO*	HT	55550	55600
142 010	c	**AV**	A	*AW*	CF	55551	55601
142 011	t	**NO**	A	*NO*	NH	55552	55602
142 012	t	**NO**	A	*NO*	NH	55553	55603
142 013		**NO**	A	*NO*	NH	55554	55604
142 014	t	**NO**	A	*NO*	NH	55555	55605
142 015	s	**NO**	A	*NO*	HT	55556	55606
142 016	s	**NO**	A	*NO*	HT	55557	55607
142 017	s	**NO**	A	*NO*	HT	55558	55608
142 018	s	**NO**	A	*NO*	HT	55559	55609
142 019	s	**NO**	A	*NO*	HT	55560	55610
142 020	s	**NO**	A	*NO*	HT	55561	55611
142 021	s	**NO**	A	*NO*	HT	55562	55612
142 022	s	**NO**	A	*NO*	HT	55563	55613
142 023	t	**NO**	A	*NO*	HT	55564	55614
142 024	s	**NO**	A	*NO*	HT	55565	55615
142 025	s	**NO**	A	*NO*	HT	55566	55616
142 026	s	**NO**	A	*NO*	HT	55567	55617
142 027	t	**NO**	A	*NO*	NH	55568	55618
142 028	t	**NO**	A	*NO*	NH	55569	55619
142 029		**NO**	A	*NO*	NH	55570	55620
142 030		**NO**	A	*NO*	NH	55571	55621
142 031	t	**NO**	A	*NO*	NH	55572	55622
142 032	t	**NO**	A	*NO*	NH	55573	55623
142 033	t	**NO**	A	*NO*	NH	55574	55624
142 034	t	**NO**	A	*NO*	NH	55575	55625
142 035	t	**NO**	A	*NO*	NH	55576	55626
142 036	t	**NO**	A	*NO*	NH	55577	55627
142 037	t	**NO**	A	*NO*	NH	55578	55628

142 038	t	**NO**	A	*NO*	NH	55579	55629
142 039	t	**NO**	A	*NO*	NH	55580	55630
142 040	t	**NO**	A	*NO*	NH	55581	55631
142 041	u	**NO**	A	*NO*	NH	55582	55632
142 042	u	**NO**	A	*NO*	NH	55583	55633
142 043	u	**NO**	A	*NO*	NH	55584	55634
142 044	u	**NO**	A	*NO*	NH	55585	55635
142 045	u	**NO**	A	*NO*	NH	55586	55636
142 046	u	**NO**	A	*NO*	NH	55587	55637
142 047	u	**NO**	A	*NO*	NH	55588	55638
142 048	u	**NO**	A	*NO*	NH	55589	55639
142 049	u	**NO**	A	*NO*	NH	55590	55640
142 050	s	**NO**	A	*NO*	HT	55591	55641
142 051	u	**NO**	A	*NO*	NH	55701	55747
142 052	u	**NO**	A	*NO*	NH	55702	55748
142 053	u	**NO**	A	*NO*	NH	55703	55749
142 054	u	**NO**	A	*NO*	NH	55704	55750
142 055	u	**NO**	A	*NO*	NH	55705	55751
142 056	u	**NO**	A	*NO*	NH	55706	55752
142 057	u	**NO**	A	*NO*	NH	55707	55753
142 058	u	**NO**	A	*NO*	NH	55708	55754
142 060	t	**NO**	A	*NO*	NH	55710	55756
142 061	t	**NO**	A	*NO*	NH	55711	55757
142 062	t	**NO**	A	*NO*	NH	55712	55758
142 063	t	**NO**	A	*NO*	NH	55713	55759
142 064	t	**NO**	A	*NO*	HT	55714	55760
142 065	s	**NO**	A	*NO*	HT	55715	55761
142 066	s	**NO**	A	*NO*	HT	55716	55762
142 067		**NO**	A	*NO*	HT	55717	55763
142 068	t	**NO**	A	*NO*	HT	55718	55764
142 069	c	**AV**	A	*AW*	CF	55719	55765
142 070	t	**NO**	A	*NO*	HT	55720	55766
142 071	s	**NO**	A	*NO*	HT	55721	55767
142 072	c	**AV**	A	*AW*	CF	55722	55768
142 073	c	**AV**	A	*AW*	CF	55723	55769
142 074	c	**AV**	A	*AW*	CF	55724	55770
142 075	c	**AV**	A	*AW*	CF	55725	55771
142 076	c	**AV**	A	*AW*	CF	55726	55772
142 077	c	**AV**	A	*AW*	CF	55727	55773
142 078	s	**NO**	A	*NO*	HT	55728	55774
142 079	s	**NO**	A	*NO*	HT	55729	55775
142 080	c	**AV**	A	*AW*	CF	55730	55776
142 081	c	**AV**	A	*AW*	CF	55731	55777
142 082	c	**AV**	A	*AW*	CF	55732	55778
142 083	c	**AV**	A	*AW*	CF	55733	55779
142 084	s	**NO**	A	*NO*	HT	55734	55780
142 085	c	**AV**	A	*AW*	CF	55735	55781
142 086	s	**NO**	A	*NO*	HT	55736	55782
142 087	s	**NO**	A	*NO*	HT	55737	55783
142 088	s	**NO**	A	*NO*	HT	55738	55784
142 089	s	**NO**	A	*NO*	HT	55739	55785

142 090	s	**NO**	A	*NO*	HT	55740	55786
142 091	s	**NO**	A	*NO*	HT	55741	55787
142 092	s	**NO**	A	*NO*	HT	55742	55788
142 093	s	**NO**	A	*NO*	HT	55743	55789
142 094	s	**NO**	A	*NO*	HT	55744	55790
142 095	s	**NO**	A	*NO*	HT	55745	55791
142 096	s	**NO**	A	*NO*	HT	55746	55792

CLASS 143   PACER   ALEXANDER/BARCLAY

DMS–DMSL. Similar design to Class 142, but bodies built by W Alexander with Barclay underframes.

Construction: Steel underframe, aluminium alloy body and roof. Alexander bus bodywork on four-wheeled underframes.
Engines: One Cummins LT10-R of 165 kW (225 hp) at 1950 rpm.
Couplers: BSI at outer ends, bar within unit.
Dimensions: 15.45 x 2.80 m.
Gangways: Within unit only.   **Wheel Arrangement:** 1-A + A-1.
Doors: Twin-leaf inward pivoting.   **Maximum Speed:** 75 mph.
Seating Layout: 2+2 high-back Chapman seating, mainly unidirectional.
Multiple Working: Within class and with Classes 142, 144, 150, 153, 155, 156, 158 and 159.

DMS. Lot No. 31005 Andrew Barclay 1985–86. –/48(+6) 2W. 24.0 t.
DMSL. Lot No. 31006 Andrew Barclay 1985–86. –/44(+6) 1T 2W. 24.5 t.

143 601	**AV**	MG	*AW*	CF	55642	55667	
143 602	**AW**	P	*AW*	CF	55651	55668	
143 603	**GW**	P	*GW*	EX	55658	55669	
143 604	**AW**	P	*AW*	CF	55645	55670	
143 605	**AW**	P	*AW*	CF	55646	55671	
143 606	**AW**	P	*AW*	CF	55647	55672	
143 607	**AW**	P	*AW*	CF	55648	55673	
143 608	**AW**	P	*AW*	CF	55649	55674	
143 609	**AV**	SG	*AW*	CF	55650	55675	Sir Tom Jones
143 610	**AV**	MG	*AW*	CF	55643	55676	
143 611	**GW**	P	*GW*	EX	55652	55677	
143 612	**GW**	P	*GW*	EX	55653	55678	
143 614	**AV**	MG	*AW*	CF	55655	55680	
143 616	**AW**	P	*AW*	CF	55657	55682	
143 617	**GW**	GW	*GW*	EX	55644	55683	
143 618	**GW**	GW	*GW*	EX	55659	55684	
143 619	**GW**	GW	*GW*	EX	55660	55685	
143 620	**GW**	P	*GW*	EX	55661	55686	
143 621	**GW**	P	*GW*	EX	55662	55687	
143 622	**AW**	P	*AW*	CF	55663	55688	
143 623	**AW**	P	*AW*	CF	55664	55689	
143 624	**AW**	P	*AW*	CF	55665	55690	
143 625	**AW**	P	*AW*	CF	55666	55691	

CLASS 144   PACER   ALEXANDER/BREL DERBY

DMS–DMSL or DMS–MS–DMSL. As Class 143, but underframes built by BREL.

Construction: Steel underframe, aluminium alloy body and roof. Alexander bus bodywork on four-wheeled underframes.
Engines: One Cummins LT10-R of 165 kW (225 hp) at 1950 rpm.
Couplers: BSI at outer ends, bar within unit.
Dimensions: 15.45/15.43 x 2.80 m.
Gangways: Within unit only.   **Wheel Arrangement:** 1-A + A-1.
Doors: Twin-leaf inward pivoting.   **Maximum Speed:** 75 mph.
Seating Layout: 2+2 high-back Richmond seating, mainly unidirectional.
Multiple Working: Within class and with Classes 142, 143, 150, 153, 155, 156, 158 and 159.

† Prototype demonstrator unit, refurbished by RVEL for Porterbrook as a trial, with new Fainsa seating and a universal access toilet to meet the 2020 accessibility regulations. Details are as follows:
DMS 55812: Lot No. 31015 BREL Derby 1986–87. –/43(+3). 27.2 t.
DMSL 55835: Lot No. 31016 BREL Derby 1986–87. –/35 1TD 2W. 28.0 t.

Non-standard livery: 144 012 144evolution (blue & purple).

DMS. Lot No. 31015 BREL Derby 1986–87. –/45(+3) 1W 24.0 t.
MS. Lot No. 31037 BREL Derby 1987. –/58. 23.5 t.
DMSL. Lot No. 31016 BREL Derby 1986–87. –/41(+3) 1T. 24.5 t.

144 001		**NO**	P	*NO*	NL	55801		55824
144 002		**NO**	P	*NO*	NL	55802		55825
144 003		**NO**	P	*NO*	NL	55803		55826
144 004		**NO**	P	*NO*	NL	55804		55827
144 005		**NO**	P	*NO*	NL	55805		55828
144 006		**NO**	P	*NO*	NL	55806		55829
144 007		**NO**	P	*NO*	NL	55807		55830
144 008		**NO**	P	*NO*	NL	55808		55831
144 009		**NO**	P	*NO*	NL	55809		55832
144 010		**NO**	P	*NO*	NL	55810		55833
144 011		**NO**	P	*NO*	NL	55811		55834
144 012	†	**0**	P	*NO*	NL	55812		55835
144 013		**NO**	P	*NO*	NL	55813		55836
144 014		**NO**	P	*NO*	NL	55814	55850	55837
144 015		**NO**	P	*NO*	NL	55815	55851	55838
144 016		**NO**	P	*NO*	NL	55816	55852	55839
144 017		**NO**	P	*NO*	NL	55817	55853	55840
144 018		**NO**	P	*NO*	NL	55818	55854	55841
144 019		**NO**	P	*NO*	NL	55819	55855	55842
144 020		**NO**	P	*NO*	NL	55820	55856	55843
144 021		**NO**	P	*NO*	NL	55821	55857	55844
144 022		**NO**	P	*NO*	NL	55822	55858	55845
144 023		**NO**	P	*NO*	NL	55823	55859	55846

Name: 144 001 THE PENISTONE LINE PARTNERSHIP

CLASS 150/0   SPRINTER   BREL YORK

DMSL–MS–DMS. Prototype Sprinter.

Construction: Steel.
Engines: One Cummins NT855R5 of 213 kW (285 hp) at 2100 rpm.
Bogies: BX8P (powered), BX8T (non-powered).
Couplers: BSI at outer end of driving vehicles, bar non-driving ends.
Dimensions: 19.93/19.92 x 2.73 m.
Gangways: Within unit only.   **Wheel Arrangement:** 2-B + 2-B + B-2.
Doors: Twin-leaf sliding.   **Maximum Speed:** 75 mph.
Seating Layout: 3+2 (mainly unidirectional).
Multiple Working: Within class and with Classes 142, 143, 144, 153, 155, 156, 158, 159, 170 and 172.

Fitted with a new universal access toilet to meet the 2020 accessibility regulations. Full details awaited.

DMSL. Lot No. 30984 1984. –/72 1T. 35.4 t.
MS. Lot No. 30986 1984. –/92. 35.0 t.
DMS. Lot No. 30985 1984. –/69(+6). 34.7 t.

150 001	**GW**	A	*GW*	PM	55200	55400	55300
150 002	**GW**	A	*GW*	PM	55201	55401	55301

CLASS 150/1   SPRINTER   BREL YORK

DMSL–DMS.

Construction: Steel.
Engines: One Cummins NT855R5 of 213 kW (285 hp) at 2100 rpm.
Bogies: BP38 (powered), BT38 (non-powered).
Couplers: BSI.
Dimensions: 19.74 x 2.82 m.
Gangways: Within unit only.   **Wheel Arrangement:** 2-B (+ 2-B) + B-2.
Doors: Twin-leaf sliding.   **Maximum Speed:** 75 mph.
Seating Layout: 3+2 facing as built but Centro units were reseated with mainly unidirectional seating.
Multiple Working: Within class and with Classes 142, 143, 144, 153, 155, 156, 158, 159, 170 and 172.

c 3+2 Chapman seating.
* Northern units fitted with a new universal access toilet to meet the 2020 accessibility regulations. Full details awaited.

DMSL. Lot No. 31011 1985–86. –/72 1T (c –/59 1TD (except 52144 –/62 1TD), t –/71 1T, u –/71 1T). 38.3 t.
DMS. Lot No. 31012 1985–86. –/76 (c –/65, t –/73, u –/70(+6)). 38.1 t.

150 101	u	**FB**	A	*GW*	PM	52101	57101
150 102	u*	**FB**	A	*NO*	NH	52102	57102
150 103	u	**NO**	A	*NO*	NH	52103	57103
150 104	u	**FB**	A	*GW*	PM	52104	57104

150 105	u	**LM**	A	*WM*	TS	52105	57105
150 106	u	**FB**	A	*GW*	PM	52106	57106
150 107	u	**LM**	A	*WM*	TS	52107	57107
150 108	u	**FB**	A	*GW*	PM	52108	57108
150 109	u	**LM**	A	*WM*	TS	52109	57109
150 110	u	**NO**	A	*NO*	NH	52110	57110
150 111	u	**NO**	A	*NO*	NH	52111	57111
150 112	u	**NO**	A	*NO*	NH	52112	57112
150 113	u	**NO**	A	*NO*	NH	52113	57113
150 114	u	**NO**	A	*NO*	NH	52114	57114
150 115	u	**NO**	A	*NO*	NH	52115	57115
150 116	u	**NO**	A	*NO*	NH	52116	57116
150 117	u	**NO**	A	*NO*	NH	52117	57117
150 118	u	**NO**	A	*NO*	NH	52118	57118
150 119	u	**NO**	A	*NO*	NH	52119	57119
150 120	t	**FB**	A	*GW*	EX	52120	57120
150 121	u	**FB**	A	*GW*	EX	52121	57121
150 122	u	**FB**	A	*NO*	NH	52122	57122
150 123	t	**FB**	A	*GW*	EX	52123	57123
150 124	u*	**NR**	A	*NO*	NH	52124	57124
150 127	u	**FB**	A	*GW*	EX	52127	57127
150 128	t	**FB**	A	*GW*	EX	52128	57128
150 129	t	**FB**	A	*GW*	EX	52129	57129
150 130	t	**FB**	A	*GW*	EX	52130	57130
150 131	t	**FB**	A	*GW*	EX	52131	57131
150 132	u	**NO**	A	*NO*	NH	52132	57132
150 133	c	**NO**	A	*NO*	NH	52133	57133
150 134	c*	**NR**	A	*NO*	NH	52134	57134
150 135	c	**NO**	A	*NO*	NH	52135	57135
150 136	c*	**NR**	A	*NO*	NH	52136	57136
150 137	c*	**NR**	A	*NO*	NH	52137	57137
150 138	c	**NO**	A	*NO*	NH	52138	57138
150 139	c	**NO**	A	*NO*	NH	52139	57139
150 140	c*	**NR**	A	*NO*	NH	52140	57140
150 141	c	**NO**	A	*NO*	NH	52141	57141
150 142	c*	**NR**	A	*NO*	NH	52142	57142
150 143	c	**NO**	A	*NO*	NH	52143	57143
150 144	c*	**NR**	A	*NO*	NH	52144	57144
150 145	c	**NO**	A	*NO*	NH	52145	57145
150 146	c	**NO**	A	*NO*	NH	52146	57146
150 147	c	**NO**	A	*NO*	NH	52147	57147
150 148	c	**NO**	A	*NO*	NH	52148	57148
150 149	c*	**NR**	A	*NO*	NH	52149	57149
150 150	c	**NO**	A	*NO*	NH	52150	57150

Names:

150 129	Devon & Cornwall RAIL PARTNERSHIP
150 130	Severnside Community Rail Partnership

CLASS 150/2   SPRINTER   BREL YORK

DMSL–DMS.

Construction: Steel.
Engines: One Cummins NT855R5 of 213 kW (285 hp) at 2100 rpm.
Bogies: BP38 (powered), BT38 (non-powered).
Couplers: BSI.
Dimensions: 19.74 x 2.82 m.
Gangways: Throughout.   **Wheel Arrangement:** 2-B + B-2.
Doors: Twin-leaf sliding.   **Maximum Speed:** 75 mph.
Seating Layout: 3+2 mainly unidirectional seating as built, but most units
have now been refurbished with new 2+2 seating.
Multiple Working: Within class and with Classes 142, 143, 144, 153, 155,
156, 158, 159, 170 and 172.

c   Former First North Western units with 3+2 Chapman seating.
p   Refurbished Arriva Trains Wales units with 2+2 Primarius seating.
v   Units refurbished for Valley Lines with 2+2 Chapman seating.
w   Units refurbished for First Great Western with 2+2 Chapman seating.
*   Refurbished units for Great Western Railway with 2+2 Chapman seating
    and a new universal access toilet to meet the 2020 accessibility regulations.
†   Refurbished units for Northern with a new universal access toilet to meet
    the 2020 accessibility regulations. 3+2 Chapman seating.
§   Refurbished units for Northern with new universal access toilet to meet the
    2020 accessibility regulations. Orignal Ashbourne seating. Full detais awaited.

Northern promotional vinyls:

150 203/205/207/211/215/218/222/223/225/228/268–271/273/277
Welcome to Yorkshire.
150 272 R&B Festival week, Colne.

DMSL. Lot No. 31017 1986–87. * –/50(+4) 1TD 2W, † –/58(+3) 1TD 2W, c –/62
1TD, p –/60(+4) 1T, s –/68 1T 1W, u –/71 1T), v –/60(+8) 1T, w –/60(+8) 1T.
37.5 t (* 35.8 t, † 38.1 t).
DMS. Lot No. 31018 1986–87. * –/58(10), † –/70(+6), c –/70, p –/56(+10) 1W,
s –/71(+3), †u –/70(+6), v –/56(+15) 2W, w –/56(+17) 2W. 36.5 t.

150 201	c	**NO**	A	*NO*	NH	52201	57201
150 202	u	**GW**	A	*GW*	PM	52202	57202
150 203	†	**NR**	A	*NO*	NH	52203	57203
150 204	†	**NO**	A	*NO*	NH	52204	57204
150 205	†	**NR**	A	*NO*	NH	52205	57205
150 206	†	**NR**	A	*NO*	NH	52206	57206
150 207	c	**NO**	A	*NO*	NH	52207	57207
150 208	p	**AW**	P	*AW*	CF	52208	57208
150 210	u	**NO**	A	*NO*	NH	52210	57210
150 211	†	**NR**	A	*NO*	NH	52211	57211
150 213	p	**AW**	P	*AW*	CF	52213	57213
150 214	u	**NO**	A	*NO*	NH	52214	57214
150 215	c	**NO**	A	*NO*	NH	52215	57215
150 216	u	**GW**	A	*GW*	PM	52216	57216

150 217	p	**AW**	P	*AW*	CF	52217	57217
150 218	c	**NO**	A	*NO*	NH	52218	57218
150 219	*	**FB**	P	*GW*	PM	52219	57219
150 220	†	**NR**	A	*NO*	NH	52220	57220
150 221	*	**GW**	P	*GW*	PM	52221	57221
150 222	†	**NR**	A	*NO*	NH	52222	57222
150 223	†	**NO**	A	*NO*	NH	52223	57223
150 224	c	**NO**	A	*NO*	NH	52224	57224
150 225	c	**NO**	A	*NO*	NH	52225	57225
150 226	u	**NO**	A	*NO*	NH	52226	57226
150 227	p	**AW**	P	*AW*	CF	52227	57227
150 228	s	**NO**	P	*NO*	NH	52228	57228
150 229	p	**AW**	P	*AW*	CF	52229	57229
150 230	w	**AW**	P	*AW*	CF	52230	57230
150 231	p	**AW**	P	*AW*	CF	52231	57231
150 232	*	**GW**	P	*GW*	PM	52232	57232
150 233	*	**GW**	P	*GW*	PM	52233	57233
150 234	*	**GW**	P	*GW*	PM	52234	57234
150 235	p	**AW**	P	*AW*	CF	52235	57235
150 236	w	**AW**	P	*AW*	CF	52236	57236
150 237	p	**AW**	P	*AW*	CF	52237	57237
150 238	*	**FB**	P	*GW*	PM	52238	57238
150 239	*	**GW**	P	*GW*	PM	52239	57239
150 240	w	**AW**	P	*AW*	CF	52240	57240
150 241	w	**AW**	P	*AW*	CF	52241	57241
150 242	w	**AW**	P	*AW*	CF	52242	57242
150 243	*	**GW**	P	*GW*	PM	52243	57243
150 244	*	**GW**	P	*GW*	PM	52244	57244
150 245	p	**AV**	P	*AW*	CF	52245	57245
150 246	*	**GW**	P	*GW*	PM	52246	57246
150 247	*	**GW**	P	*GW*	PM	52247	57247
150 248	*	**GW**	P	*GW*	PM	52248	57248
150 249	*	**GW**	P	*GW*	PM	52249	57249
150 250	p	**AW**	P	*AW*	CF	52250	57250
150 251	w	**AW**	P	*AW*	CF	52251	57251
150 252	p	**AW**	P	*AW*	CF	52252	57252
150 253	w	**AW**	P	*AW*	CF	52253	57253
150 254	w	**AW**	P	*AW*	CF	52254	57254
150 255	p	**AW**	P	*AW*	CF	52255	57255
150 256	p	**AW**	P	*AW*	CF	52256	57256
150 257	p	**AW**	P	*AW*	CF	52257	57257
150 258	p	**AW**	P	*AW*	CF	52258	57258
150 259	p	**AW**	P	*AW*	CF	52259	57259
150 260	p	**AW**	P	*AW*	CF	52260	57260
150 261	*	**GW**	P	*GW*	PM	52261	57261
150 262	p	**AW**	P	*AW*	CF	52262	57262
150 263	*	**GW**	P	*GW*	PM	52263	57263
150 264	p	**AV**	P	*AW*	CF	52264	57264
150 265	*	**GW**	P	*GW*	PM	52265	57265
150 266	*	**GW**	P	*GW*	PM	52266	57266
150 267	v	**AW**	P	*AW*	CF	52267	57267

150 268	s	**NO**	P	*NO*	NH	52268	57268
150 269	s	**NO**	P	*NO*	NH	52269	57269
150 270	s	**NO**	P	*NO*	NH	52270	57270
150 271	s	**NO**	P	*NO*	NH	52271	57271
150 272	s	**NO**	P	*NO*	NH	52272	57272
150 273	s	**NO**	P	*NO*	NH	52273	57273
150 274	§	**NR**	P	*NO*	NH	52274	57274
150 275	§	**NR**	P	*NO*	NH	52275	57275
150 276	§	**NR**	P	*NO*	NH	52276	57276
150 277	s	**NO**	P	*NO*	NH	52277	57277
150 278	v	**AW**	P	*AW*	CF	52278	57278
150 279	v	**AW**	P	*AW*	CF	52279	57279
150 280	v	**AW**	P	*AW*	CF	52280	57280
150 281	v	**AW**	P	*AW*	CF	52281	57281
150 282	v	**AW**	P	*AW*	CF	52282	57282
150 283	p	**AW**	P	*AW*	CF	52283	57283
150 284	p	**AV**	P	*AW*	CF	52284	57284
150 285	p	**AV**	P	*AW*	CF	52285	57285

Name:

150 275   The Yorkshire Regiment Yorkshire Warrior

CLASS 150/9   SPRINTER   BREL YORK

3-car Great Western Railway hybrids formed of a Class 150/1 with a 150/2 centre vehicle. DMSL–DMS–DMS. For details see Class 150/1 or Class 150/2.

150 925	u	**FB**	A	*GW*	PM	52125	57209	57125
150 926	u	**FB**	A	*GW*	PM	52126	57212	57126

Name:

150 925   THE HEART OF WESSEX LINE

CLASS 153   SUPER SPRINTER   LEYLAND BUS

DMSL. Converted by Hunslet-Barclay, Kilmarnock from Class 155 2-car units.

Construction: Steel underframe, rivetted steel body and roof. Built from Leyland National bus parts on Leyland Bus bogied underframes.
Engine: One Cummins NT855R5 of 213 kW (285 hp) at 2100 rpm.
Bogies: One P3-10 (powered) and one BT38 (non-powered).
Couplers: BSI.
Dimensions: 23.21 x 2.70 m.
Gangways: Throughout.   **Wheel Arrangement:** 2-B.
Doors: Single-leaf sliding plug.   **Maximum Speed:** 75 mph.
Seating Layout: 2+2 facing/unidirectional.
Multiple Working: Within class and with Classes 142, 143, 144, 150, 155, 156, 158, 159, 170 and 172.

Cars numbered in the 573xx series were renumbered by adding 50 to their original number so that the last two digits correspond with the set number.

c Chapman seating.
d Richmond seating.

Non-standard and Advertising liveries:

153 305 Light grey.
153 325 Citizens Rail (pink).
153 333 Visit South Devon by train (dark blue).

52301–52335. DMSL. Lot No. 31026 1987–88. Converted under Lot No. 31115 1991–92. –/72(+3) 1T 1W. (s –/72 1T 1W, t –/72(+2) 1T 1W). 41.2 t.
57301–57335. DMSL. Lot No. 31027 1987–88. Converted under Lot No. 31115 1991–92. –/72(+3) 1T 1W (s –/72 1T 1W). 41.2 t.

153 301	d	NO	A	NO	NL	52301	
153 302	c	EM	A	EM	NM	52302	
153 303	c	AW	A	AW	CF	52303	
153 304	ds	NO	A	NO	NL	52304	
153 305	d	O	A	GW	EX	52305	
153 306	cr	GA	P	GA	NC	52306	
153 307	d	NO	A	NO	NL	52307	
153 308	c	EM	A	EM	NM	52308	
153 309	cr	GA	P	GA	NC	52309	GERARD FIENNES
153 310	c	EM	P	EM	NM	52310	
153 311	c	EM	P	EM	NM	52311	
153 312	s	AW	A	AW	CF	52312	
153 313	cs	EM	P	EM	NM	52313	
153 314	cr	GA	P	GA	NC	52314	
153 315	ds	NO	A	NO	NL	52315	
153 316	c	NO	P	NO	NL	52316	John "Longitude" Harrison Inventor of the Marine Chronometer
153 317	ds	NO	A	NO	NL	52317	
153 318	d	GW	A	GW	EX	52318	
153 319	c	EM	A	EM	NM	52319	
153 320	c	AV	P	AW	CF	52320	
153 321	ct	EM	P	EM	NM	52321	
153 322	cr	GA	P	GA	NC	52322	BENJAMIN BRITTEN
153 323	c	AV	P	AW	CF	52323	
153 324	c	NO	P	NO	NL	52324	
153 325	c	AL	P	GW	EX	52325	
153 326	c	EM	P	EM	NM	52326	
153 327	c	AW	A	AW	CF	52327	
153 328	ds	NO	A	NO	NL	52328	
153 329	c	FB	P	GW	EX	52329	
153 330	cs	NO	P	NO	NL	52330	
153 331	d	NO	A	NO	NL	52331	
153 332	c	NO	P	NO	NL	52332	
153 333	cs	AL	P	GW	EX	52333	
153 334	ct	LM	P	WM	TS	52334	
153 335	cr	GA	P	GA	NC	52335	MICHAEL PALIN
153 351	d	NO	A	NO	NL	57351	
153 352	ds	NO	A	NO	NL	57352	
153 353	c	AW	A	AW	CF	57353	

153 354	c	**LM**	P	*WM*	TS	57354	
153 355	c	**EM**	A	*EM*	NM	57355	
153 356	c	**LM**	P	*WM*	TS	57356	
153 357	c	**EM**	A	*EM*	NM	57357	
153 358	c	**NO**	P	*NO*	NL	57358	
153 359	c	**NO**	P	*NO*	NL	57359	
153 360	c	**NO**	P	*NO*	NL	57360	
153 361	cs	**FB**	P	*GW*	EX	57361	
153 362	cs	**AW**	A	*AW*	CF	57362	
153 363	cs	**NO**	P	*NO*	NL	57363	
153 364	c	**LM**	P	*WM*	TS	57364	
153 365	c	**LM**	P	*WM*	TS	57365	
153 366	c	**LM**	P	*WM*	TS	57366	
153 367	cs	**AV**	P	*AW*	CF	57367	
153 368	d	**GW**	A	*GW*	EX	57368	
153 369	c	**FB**	P	*GW*	EX	57369	
153 370	d	**GW**	A	*GW*	EX	57370	
153 371	c	**LM**	P	*WM*	TS	57371	
153 372	d	**GW**	A	*GW*	EX	57372	
153 373	d	**GW**	A	*GW*	EX	57373	
153 374	c	**EM**	A	*EM*	NM	57374	
153 375	c	**LM**	P	*WM*	TS	57375	
153 376	c	**EM**	P	*EM*	NM	57376	X24-EXPEDITIOUS
153 377	d	**GW**	A	*GW*	EX	57377	
153 378	d	**NO**	A	*NO*	NL	57378	
153 379	c	**EM**	P	*EM*	NM	57379	
153 380	d	**GW**	A	*GW*	EX	57380	
153 381	c	**EM**	P	*EM*	NM	57381	
153 382	d	**GW**	A	*GW*	EX	57382	
153 383	c	**EM**	P	*EM*	NM	57383	Ecclesbourne Valley Railway 150 Years
153 384	c	**EM**	P	*EM*	NM	57384	
153 385	c	**EM**	P	*EM*	NM	57385	

CLASS 155   SUPER SPRINTER   LEYLAND BUS

DMSL–DMS.

Construction: Steel underframe, rivetted steel body and roof. Built from Leyland National bus parts on Leyland Bus bogied underframes.
Engines: One Cummins NT855R5 of 213 kW (285 hp) at 2100 rpm.
Bogies: One P3-10 (powered) and one BT38 (non-powered).
Couplers: BSI.
Dimensions: 23.21 x 2.70 m.
Gangways: Throughout.   **Wheel Arrangement:** 2-B + B-2.
Doors: Single-leaf sliding plug.   **Maximum Speed:** 75 mph.
Seating Layout: 2+2 facing/unidirectional Chapman seating.
Multiple Working: Within class and with Classes 142, 143, 144, 150, 153, 156, 158, 159, 170 and 172.

Northern promotional vinyls:

155 341–344 Leeds–Bradford–Manchester route (the "Calder Valley").

DMSL. Lot No. 31057 1988. –/76 1TD 1W. 39.0 t.
DMS. Lot No. 31058 1988. –/80. 38.6 t.

155 341	**NO**	P	*NO*	NL	52341	57341
155 342	**NO**	P	*NO*	NL	52342	57342
155 343	**NO**	P	*NO*	NL	52343	57343
155 344	**NO**	P	*NO*	NL	52344	57344
155 345	**NR**	P	*NO*	NL	52345	57345
155 346	**NR**	P	*NO*	NL	52346	57346
155 347	**NR**	P	*NO*	NL	52347	57347

CLASS 156   SUPER SPRINTER   METRO-CAMMELL

DMSL–DMS.

Construction: Steel.
Engines: One Cummins NT855R5 of 213 kW (285 hp) at 2100 rpm.
Bogies: One P3-10 (powered) and one BT38 (non-powered).
Couplers: BSI.
Dimensions: 23.03 x 2.73 m.

Gangways: Throughout.	**Wheel Arrangement:** 2-B + B-2.
Doors: Single-leaf sliding.	**Maximum Speed:** 75 mph.

Seating Layout: 2+2 facing/unidirectional.
Multiple Working: Within class and with Classes 142, 143, 144, 150, 153, 155, 158, 159, 170 and 172.

† Greater Anglia units fitted with a new universal access toilet to meet the 2020 accessibility regulations.
* Angel-owned Northern units fitted with a new universal access toilet to meet the 2020 accessibility regulations.
b Refurbished as a demonstrator unit by Brodies, Kilmarnock with a new universal access toilet to meet the 2020 accessibility regulations. Full details awaited.
c Chapman seating.
d Richmond seating.
v ScotRail units fitted with a new universal access toilet to meet the 2020 accessibility regulations (but still with original seating).
w Fully refurbished ScotRail units with new Fainsa seating and universal access toilet. Full details awaited.

Northern promotional vinyls:

156441 Manchester and Liverpool
156461 Ravenglass & Eskdale Railway
156464 Lancashire DalesRail

DMSL. Lot No. 31028 1988–89. –/74 1TD 1W († –/62 1TD 2W, * –/64(+2) 1TD 2W, c –/70, s –/72, t –/68 1W, u –/68, v –/64(+3) 1TD 2W). 38.6 t.
DMS. Lot No. 31029 1987–89. –/76 († –/74, *–/76, d –/78, t & u –/72, v –/76). 36.1 t.

156 401	cs **EM**	P	*EM*	DY	52401	57401
156 402	†cr **GA**	P	*GA*	NC	52402	57402
156 403	cs **EM**	P	*EM*	DY	52403	57403
156 404	cs **EM**	P	*EM*	DY	52404	57404

156 405	cs	**EM**	P	*EM*	DY	52405	57405
156 406	cs	**EM**	P	*EM*	DY	52406	57406
156 407	†cr	**GA**	P	*GA*	NC	52407	57407
156 408	cs	**EM**	P	*EM*	DY	52408	57408
156 409	†cr	**GA**	P	*GA*	NC	52409	57409
156 410	cs	**EM**	P	*EM*	DY	52410	57410
156 411	cs	**EM**	P	*EM*	DY	52411	57411
156 412	†cr	**GA**	P	*GA*	NC	52412	57412
156 413	cs	**EM**	P	*EM*	DY	52413	57413
156 414	cs	**EM**	P	*EM*	DY	52414	57414
156 415	cs	**EM**	P	*EM*	DY	52415	57415
156 416	†cr	**GA**	P	*GA*	NC	52416	57416
156 417	†cr	**GA**	P	*GA*	NC	52417	57417
156 418	†cr	**GA**	P	*GA*	NC	52418	57418
156 419	†cr	**GA**	P	*GA*	NC	52419	57419
156 420	c	**NO**	P	*NO*	AN	52420	57420
156 421	c	**NO**	P	*NO*	AN	52421	57421
156 422	†cr	**GA**	P	*GA*	NC	52422	57422
156 423	c	**NO**	P	*NO*	AN	52423	57423
156 424	c	**NO**	P	*NO*	AN	52424	57424
156 425	c	**NO**	P	*NO*	AN	52425	57425
156 426	c	**NO**	P	*NO*	AN	52426	57426
156 427	c	**NO**	P	*NO*	AN	52427	57427
156 428	c	**NO**	P	*NO*	AN	52428	57428
156 429	c	**NO**	P	*NO*	AN	52429	57429
156 430	w	**SR**	A	*SR*	CK	52430	57430
156 431	t	**SR**	A	*SR*	CK	52431	57431
156 432	v	**SR**	A	*SR*	CK	52432	57432
156 433	t	**SR**	A	*SR*	CK	52433	57433
156 434	t	**SR**	A	*SR*	CK	52434	57434
156 435	t	**SR**	A	*SR*	CK	52435	57435
156 436	†	**SR**	A	*SR*	CK	52436	57436
156 437	t	**SR**	A	*SR*	CK	52437	57437
156 438	*d	**NR**	A	*NO*	HT	52438	57438
156 439	t	**SR**	A	*SR*	CK	52439	57439
156 440	c	**NO**	P	*NO*	AN	52440	57440
156 441	c	**NO**	P	*NO*	AN	52441	57441
156 442	t	**SR**	A	*SR*	CK	52442	57442
156 443	*d	**NR**	A	*NO*	HT	52443	57443
156 444	*d	**NR**	A	*NO*	HT	52444	57444
156 445	ru	**SR**	A	*SR*	CK	52445	57445
156 446	t	**FS**	A	*SR*	CK	52446	57446
156 447	ru	**FS**	A	*SR*	CK	52447	57447
156 448	*d	**NO**	A	*NO*	HT	52448	57448
156 449	u	**FS**	A	*SR*	CK	52449	57449
156 450	ru	**FS**	A	*SR*	CK	52450	57450
156 451	*d	**NR**	A	*NO*	HT	52451	57451
156 452	c	**NO**	P	*NO*	AN	52452	57452
156 453	ru	**FS**	A	*SR*	CK	52453	57453
156 454	*d	**NR**	A	*NO*	HT	52454	57454
156 455	c	**NO**	P	*NO*	AN	52455	57455

156 456	rt	**FS**	A	*SR*	CK	52456	57456
156 457	rt	**FS**	A	*SR*	CK	52457	57457
156 458	rt	**FS**	A	*SR*	CK	52458	57458
156 459	c	**NO**	P	*NO*	AN	52459	57459
156 460	c	**NO**	P	*NO*	AN	52460	57460
156 461	c	**NO**	P	*NO*	AN	52461	57461
156 462		**SR**	A	*SR*	CK	52462	57462
156 463	*d	**NR**	A	*NO*	HT	52463	57463
156 464	c	**NO**	P	*NO*	AN	52464	57464
156 465	ru	**FS**	A	*SR*	CK	52465	57465
156 466	c	**NO**	P	*NO*	AN	52466	57466
156 467	rv	**SR**	A	*SR*	CK	52467	57467
156 468	d	**NO**	A	*NO*	AN	52468	57468
156 469	d	**NO**	A	*NO*	HT	52469	57469
156 470	c	**EM**	A	*EM*	DY	52470	57470
156 471	*d	**NR**	A	*NO*	AN	52471	57471
156 472	*d	**NR**	A	*NO*	AN	52472	57472
156 473	c	**EM**	A	*EM*	DY	52473	57473
156 474	rt	**FS**	A	*SR*	CK	52474	57474
156 475	*d	**NO**	A	*NO*	HT	52475	57475
156 476	rt	**FS**	A	*SR*	CK	52476	57476
156 477	t	**FS**	A	*SR*	CK	52477	57477
156 478	b	**SR**	BR	*SR*	CK	52478	57478
156 479	*d	**NR**	A	*NO*	HT	52479	57479
156 480	*d	**NO**	A	*NO*	HT	52480	57480
156 481	*d	**NR**	A	*NO*	HT	52481	57481
156 482	*d	**NR**	A	*NO*	AN	52482	57482
156 483	*d	**NR**	A	*NO*	AN	52483	57483
156 484	*d	**NR**	A	*NO*	HT	52484	57484
156 485	ru	**FS**	A	*SR*	CK	52485	57485
156 486	*d	**NR**	A	*NO*	AN	52486	57486
156 487	*d	**NR**	A	*NO*	AN	52487	57487
156 488	*d	**NR**	A	*NO*	AN	52488	57488
156 489	*d	**NR**	A	*NO*	AN	52489	57489
156 490	*d	**NR**	A	*NO*	HT	52490	57490
156 491	*d	**NO**	A	*NO*	AN	52491	57491
156 492	rs	**SR**	A	*SR*	CK	52492	57492
156 493	rt	**FS**	A	*SR*	CK	52493	57493
156 494	u	**SR**	A	*SR*	CK	52494	57494
156 495	v	**SR**	A	*SR*	CK	52495	57495
156 496	ru	**FS**	A	*SR*	CK	52496	57496
156 497	c	**EM**	A	*EM*	DY	52497	57497
156 498	c	**EM**	A	*EM*	DY	52498	57498
156 499	rt	**SR**	A	*SR*	CK	52499	57499
156 500	ru	**SR**	A	*SR*	CK	52500	57500
156 501	v	**SR**	A	*SR*	CK	52501	57501
156 502	v	**SR**	A	*SR*	CK	52502	57502
156 503	v	**SR**	A	*SR*	CK	52503	57503
156 504		**SR**	A	*SR*	CK	52504	57504
156 505	v	**SR**	A	*SR*	CK	52505	57505
156 506	v	**SR**	A	*SR*	CK	52506	57506

156 507	v	**SR**	A	*SR*	CK	52507	57507
156 508	v	**SR**	A	*SR*	CK	52508	57508
156 509	v	**SR**	A	*SR*	CK	52509	57509
156 510	w	**SR**	A	*SR*	CK	52510	57510
156 511	v	**SR**	A	*SR*	CK	52511	57511
156 512		**SR**	A	*SR*	CK	52512	57512
156 513	v	**SR**	A	*SR*	CK	52513	57513
156 514	v	**SR**	A	*SR*	CK	52514	57514

Names:

156 416	Saint Edmund
156 418	ESTA 1965–2015
156 420	LA' AL RATTY Ravenglass & Eskdale Railway
156 440	George Bradshaw
156 441	William Huskisson MP
156 448	Bram Stoker Creator of Dracula
156 459	Benny Rothman – The Manchester Rambler
156 460	Driver John Axon G.C.
156 464	Lancashire DalesRail
156 466	Gracie Fields
156 469	The Royal Northumberland Fusiliers (The Fighting Fifth)

CLASS 158/0   BREL

DMSL(B)–DMSL(A) or DMCL–DMSL or DMSL–MSL–DMSL.

Construction: Welded aluminium.
Engines: 158 701–813/158 880–890/158 950–961: One Cummins NTA855R1 of 260 kW (350 hp) at 2100 rpm.
158 815–862: One Perkins 2006-TWH of 260 kW (350 hp) at 2100 rpm.
158 863–872: One Cummins NTA855R3 of 300 kW (400 hp) at 1900 rpm.
Bogies: One BREL P4 (powered) and one BREL T4 (non-powered) per car.
Couplers: BSI.   **Dimensions:** 22.57 x 2.70 m.
Gangways: Throughout.   **Wheel Arrangement:** 2-B + B-2.
Doors: Twin-leaf swing plug.   **Maximum Speed:** 90 mph.
Seating Layout: 2+2 facing/unidirectional in all Standard and First Class except 2+1 in South West Trains First Class.
Multiple Working: Within class and with Classes 142, 143, 144, 150, 153, 155, 156, 159, 170 and 172.

ScotRail 158s 158 701–736/738–741 are "fitted" for RETB. When a unit arrives at Inverness the cab display unit is clipped on and plugged in.

Arriva Trains Wales units have ERTMS plugged in at Shrewsbury for working the Cambrian Lines.

*   Refurbished ScotRail units fitted with Grammer seating, additional luggage racks and cycle stowage areas.
        ScotRail units 158 726–736/738–741 are fitted with Richmond seating.
†   Refurbished East Midlands Trains units with Grammer seating.
§   Northern 3-car units with modifications for operation beyond 2020.
c   Chapman seating.

s   Refurbished Arriva Trains Wales units with Grammer seating.
t   East Midlands Trains units with modifications for operation beyond 2020.
u   Refurbished former South West Trains units with Class 159-style interiors, including First Class seating.
v   Northern units with modifications for operation beyond 2020.
w   Refurbished Great Western Railway units. Units 158 745–749/751/762/767 (now formed into 3-car sets) have Richmond seating.

Advertising livery:

158 798   Springboard Opportunity Group (light blue).

Northern promotional vinyls:

158 784 PTEG: 40 years.
158 787, 158 792–796: Sheffield–Leeds fast service.
158 790/842/843/844/845/848/849/850/853/855: We Are Northern.
158 860: Keighley & Brontë Country.
158 901–910: Leeds–Bradford–Manchester route (the "Calder Valley").

DMSL(B). Lot No. 31051 BREL Derby 1989–92. –/68 1TD 1W. († –/72 1TD 1W, §, v –/64 1TD 1W, c, w –/66 1TD 1W, s –/64(+4) 1TD 2W, t – 68(+3) 1TD 2W, z –/62 1TD 2W). 38.5 t.
MSL. Lot No. 31050 BREL Derby 1991. –/66(+3) 1T. 38.5 t.
DMSL(A). Lot No. 31052 BREL Derby 1989–92. –/70 1T († –/74, c, w –/68 1T, * –/64(+2) 1T plus cycle stowage area). 38.5 t.

The above details refer to the "as built" condition. The following DMSL(B) have now been converted to DMCL as follows:
52701–736/738–741 (ScotRail). 15/53 1TD 1W (* refurbished sets –/60(+6) 1TD 1W plus cycle stowage area).
52786/789 (Former South West Trains units). 13/44 1TD 1W.

158 701	*	**SR**	P	*SR*	IS	52701	57701
158 702	*	**SR**	P	*SR*	IS	52702	57702
158 703	*	**SR**	P	*SR*	IS	52703	57703
158 704	*	**SR**	P	*SR*	IS	52704	57704
158 705	*	**SR**	P	*SR*	IS	52705	57705
158 706	*	**SR**	P	*SR*	IS	52706	57706
158 707	*	**SR**	P	*SR*	IS	52707	57707
158 708	*	**SR**	P	*SR*	IS	52708	57708
158 709	*	**SR**	P	*SR*	IS	52709	57709
158 710	*	**SR**	P	*SR*	IS	52710	57710
158 711	*	**SR**	P	*SR*	IS	52711	57711
158 712	*	**SR**	P	*SR*	IS	52712	57712
158 713	*	**SR**	P	*SR*	IS	52713	57713
158 714	*	**SR**	P	*SR*	IS	52714	57714
158 715	*	**SR**	P	*SR*	IS	52715	57715
158 716	*	**SR**	P	*SR*	IS	52716	57716
158 717	*	**SR**	P	*SR*	IS	52717	57717
158 718	*	**SR**	P	*SR*	IS	52718	57718
158 719	*	**SR**	P	*SR*	IS	52719	57719
158 720	*	**SR**	P	*SR*	IS	52720	57720

158 721	*	**SR**	P	*SR*	IS	52721	57721
158 722	*	**SR**	P	*SR*	IS	52722	57722
158 723	*	**SR**	P	*SR*	IS	52723	57723
158 724	*	**SR**	P	*SR*	IS	52724	57724
158 725	*	**SR**	P	*SR*	IS	52725	57725
158 726		**FS**	P	*SR*	HA	52726	57726
158 727		**FS**	P	*SR*	HA	52727	57727
158 728		**FS**	P	*SR*	HA	52728	57728
158 729		**SR**	P	*SR*	HA	52729	57729
158 730		**FS**	P	*SR*	HA	52730	57730
158 731		**SR**	P	*SR*	HA	52731	57731
158 732		**FS**	P	*SR*	HA	52732	57732
158 733		**FS**	P	*SR*	HA	52733	57733
158 734		**FS**	P	*SR*	HA	52734	57734
158 735		**FS**	P	*SR*	HA	52735	57735
158 736		**FS**	P	*SR*	HA	52736	57736
158 738		**FS**	P	*SR*	HA	52738	57738
158 739		**FS**	P	*SR*	HA	52739	57739
158 740		**SR**	P	*SR*	HA	52740	57740
158 741		**FS**	P	*SR*	HA	52741	57741
158 752	§	**NR**	P	*NO*	NL	52752	58716	57752
158 753	§	**NR**	P	*NO*	NL	52753	58710	57753
158 754	§	**NR**	P	*NO*	NL	52754	58708	57754
158 755	§	**NR**	P	*NO*	NL	52755	58702	57755
158 756	§	**NR**	P	*NO*	NL	52756	58712	57756
158 757	§	**NR**	P	*NO*	NL	52757	58706	57757
158 758		**NO**	P	*NO*	NL	52758	58714	57758
158 759		**NO**	P	*NO*	NL	52759	58713	57759
158 763	w	**FI**	P	*GW*	PM	52763	57763
158 766	w	**GW**	P	*GW*	PM	52766	57766
158 770	†	**ST**	P	*EM*	NM	52770	57770
158 773	†	**ST**	P	*EM*	NM	52773	57773
158 774	†	**ST**	P	*EM*	NM	52774	57774
158 777	†	**ST**	P	*EM*	NM	52777	57777
158 780	††	**ST**	A	*EM*	NM	52780	57780
158 782		**SR**	A	*SR*	HA	52782	57782
158 783	††	**ST**	A	*EM*	NM	52783	57783
158 784		**NO**	A	*NO*	NL	52784	57784
158 785	††	**ST**	A	*EM*	NM	52785	57785
158 786	u	**SR**	A	*SR*	HA	52786	57786
158 787		**NO**	A	*NO*	NL	52787	57787
158 788	†	**ST**	A	*EM*	NM	52788	57788
158 789	u	**SR**	A	*SR*	HA	52789	57789
158 790		**NO**	A	*NO*	NL	52790	57790
158 791		**NO**	A	*NO*	NL	52791	57791
158 792		**NO**	A	*NO*	NL	52792	57792
158 793		**NO**	A	*NO*	NL	52793	57793
158 794		**NO**	A	*NO*	NL	52794	57794
158 795		**NO**	A	*NO*	NL	52795	57795
158 796		**NO**	A	*NO*	NL	52796	57796
158 797		**NO**	A	*NO*	NL	52797	57797

158 798	w	**AL**	P	*GW*	PM	52798	58715	57798
158 799	†	**ST**	P	*EM*	NM	52799	57799
158 806	†	**ST**	P	*EM*	NM	52806	57806
158 810	†	**ST**	P	*EM*	NM	52810	57810
158 812	†	**ST**	P	*EM*	NM	52812	57812
158 813	†	**ST**	P	*EM*	NM	52813	57813
158 815	c	**NO**	A	*NO*	NL	52815	57815
158 816	c	**NO**	A	*NO*	NL	52816	57816
158 817	c	**NO**	A	*NO*	NL	52817	57817
158 818	es	**AW**	A	*AW*	MN	52818	57818
158 819	es	**AW**	A	*AW*	MN	52819	57819
158 820	es	**AW**	A	*AW*	MN	52820	57820
158 821	es	**AW**	A	*AW*	MN	52821	57821
158 822	es	**AW**	A	*AW*	MN	52822	57822
158 823	es	**AW**	A	*AW*	MN	52823	57823
158 824	es	**AW**	A	*AW*	MN	52824	57824
158 825	es	**AW**	A	*AW*	MN	52825	57825
158 826	es	**AW**	A	*AW*	MN	52826	57826
158 827	es	**AW**	A	*AW*	MN	52827	57827
158 828	es	**AW**	A	*AW*	MN	52828	57828
158 829	es	**AW**	A	*AW*	MN	52829	57829
158 830	es	**AW**	A	*AW*	MN	52830	57830
158 831	es	**AW**	A	*AW*	MN	52831	57831
158 832	es	**AW**	A	*AW*	MN	52832	57832
158 833	es	**AW**	A	*AW*	MN	52833	57833
158 834	es	**AW**	A	*AW*	MN	52834	57834
158 835	es	**AW**	A	*AW*	MN	52835	57835
158 836	es	**AW**	A	*AW*	MN	52836	57836
158 837	es	**AW**	A	*AW*	MN	52837	57837
158 838	es	**AW**	A	*AW*	MN	52838	57838
158 839	es	**AW**	A	*AW*	MN	52839	57839
158 840	es	**AW**	A	*AW*	MN	52840	57840
158 841	es	**AW**	A	*AW*	MN	52841	57841
158 842	c	**NO**	A	*NO*	NL	52842	57842
158 843	c	**NO**	A	*NO*	NL	52843	57843
158 844		**NO**	A	*NO*	NL	52844	57844
158 845	v	**NO**	A	*NO*	NL	52845	57845
158 846	tt	**ST**	A	*EM*	NM	52846	57846
158 847	tt	**ST**	A	*EM*	NM	52847	57847
158 848	v	**NO**	A	*NO*	NL	52848	57848
158 849	v	**NO**	A	*NO*	NL	52849	57849
158 850	v	**NO**	A	*NO*	NL	52850	57850
158 851		**NO**	A	*NO*	NL	52851	57851
158 852	tt	**ST**	A	*EM*	NM	52852	57852
158 853		**NO**	A	*NO*	NL	52853	57853
158 854	†	**ST**	A	*EM*	NM	52854	57854
158 855		**NO**	A	*NO*	NL	52855	57855
158 856	†	**ST**	A	*EM*	NM	52856	57856
158 857	†	**ST**	A	*EM*	NM	52857	57857
158 858	†	**ST**	A	*EM*	NM	52858	57858
158 859		**NO**	A	*NO*	NL	52859	57859

158 860	v	**NO**	A	*NO*	NL	52860	57860
158 861		**NO**	A	*NO*	NL	52861	57861
158 862	†	**ST**	A	*EM*	NM	52862	57862
158 863	†	**ST**	A	*EM*	NM	52863	57863
158 864	†	**ST**	A	*EM*	NM	52864	57864
158 865	†	**ST**	A	*EM*	NM	52865	57865
158 866	†	**ST**	A	*EM*	NM	52866	57866
158 867	c	**SR**	A	*SR*	HA	52867	57867
158 868	c	**SR**	A	*SR*	HA	52868	57868
158 869	c	**SR**	A	*SR*	HA	52869	57869
158 870	c	**SR**	A	*NO*	NL	52870	57870
158 871	c	**SR**	A	*NO*	NL	52871	57871
158 872	c	**NO**	A	*NO*	NL	52872	57872

Names:

158 773	EASTCROFT DEPOT
158 784	Barbara Castle
158 791	County of Nottinghamshire
158 796	Fred Trueman Cricketing Legend
158 797	Jane Tomlinson
158 847	Lincoln Castle Explorer
158 854	The Station Volunteer
158 860	Ian Dewhirst
158 861	Magna Carta 800 Lincoln 2015

Class 158/8. Refurbished South Western Railway and East Midlands Trains units. Converted from former TransPennine Express units at Wabtec, Doncaster in 2007. 2+1 seating in First Class. Refurbished with modifications for operation beyond 2020.

158 885 has been fitted with new ZF transmission as a trial.

Details as Class 158/0 except:

DMCL. Lot No. 31051 BREL Derby 1989–92. * 13/40(+2) 1TD 1W. 38.5 t.
DMSL. Lot No. 31052 BREL Derby 1989–92. –/70 1T. 38.5 t.

158 880	(158 737)	**ST**	P	*SW*	SA	52737	57737
158 881	(158 742)	**ST**	P	*SW*	SA	52742	57742
158 882	(158 743)	**ST**	P	*SW*	SA	52743	57743
158 883	(158 744)	**ST**	P	*SW*	SA	52744	57744
158 884	(158 772)	**ST**	P	*SW*	SA	52772	57772
158 885	(158 775)	**ST**	P	*SW*	SA	52775	57775
158 886	(158 779)	**ST**	P	*SW*	SA	52779	57779
158 887	(158 781)	**SW**	P	*SW*	SA	52781	57781
158 888	(158 802)	**SW**	P	*SW*	SA	52802	57802
158 889	(158 808)	**ST**	P	*EM*	NM	52808	57808
158 890	(158 814)	**SW**	P	*SW*	SA	52814	57814

CLASS 158/9   BREL

DMSL–DMS. Units leased by West Yorkshire PTE but managed by Eversholt Rail. Details as Class 158/0 except for seating and toilets.

DMSL. Lot No. 31051 BREL Derby 1990–92. –/70 1TD 1W. 38.5 t.
DMS. Lot No. 31052 BREL Derby 1990–92. –/72 and parcels area. 38.5 t.

158 901	**NO**	E	*NO*	NL	52901	57901	
158 902	**NO**	E	*NO*	NL	52902	57902	
158 903	**NO**	E	*NO*	NL	52903	57903	
158 904	**NO**	E	*NO*	NL	52904	57904	
158 905	**NO**	E	*NO*	NL	52905	57905	
158 906	**NO**	E	*NO*	NL	52906	57906	
158 907	**NO**	E	*NO*	NL	52907	57907	
158 908	**NO**	E	*NO*	NL	52908	57908	
158 909	**NO**	E	*NO*	NL	52909	57909	
158 910	**NO**	E	*NO*	NL	52910	57910	William Wilberforce

CLASS 158/0   BREL

DMSL(A)–DMS(B)–DMSL(A). Units reformed as 3-car hybrid sets for Great Western Railway, mainly used between Cardiff and Portsmouth. For vehicle details see above. Formations can be flexible depending on when unit exams become due.

z – refurbished Great Western Railway units with modifications to comply with the 2020 accessibility regulations.

158 950	z	**GW**	P	*GW*	PM	57751	52761	57761
158 951	z	**GW**	P	*GW*	PM	52751	52764	57764
158 952	z	**GW**	P	*GW*	PM	57745	52762	57762
158 953	w	**FI**	P	*GW*	PM	52745	52750	57750
158 954	w	**FI**	P	*GW*	PM	52747	52760	57760
158 955	w	**FI**	P	*GW*	PM	52747	52765	57765
158 956	z	**GW**	P	*GW*	PM	52748	52768	57768
158 957	z	**GW**	P	*GW*	PM	57748	52771	57771
158 958	w	**FI**	P	*GW*	PM	57746	52776	57776
158 959	w	**FI**	P	*GW*	PM	52746	52778	57778
158 960	w	**FI**	P	*GW*	PM	57749	52769	57769
158 961	z	**GW**	P	*GW*	PM	52749	52767	57767

CLASS 159/0   BREL

DMCL–MSL–DMSL. Built as Class 158. Converted before entering passenger service to Class 159 by Rosyth Dockyard.

Construction: Welded aluminium.
Engines: One Cummins NTA855R3 of 300 kW (400 hp) at 1900 rpm.
Bogies: One BREL P4 (powered) and one BREL T4 (non-powered) per car.
Couplers: BSI.   **Dimensions:** 22.16 x 2.70 m.
Gangways: Throughout.   **Wheel Arrangement:** 2-B + B-2 + B-2.

Doors: Twin-leaf swing plug.   **Maximum Speed:** 90 mph.
Seating Layout: 1: 2+1 facing, 2: 2+2 facing/unidirectional.
Multiple Working: Within class and with Classes 142, 143, 144, 150, 153, 155, 156, 158 and 170.

DMCL. Lot No. 31051 BREL Derby 1992–93. 23/28 1TD 1W. 38.5 t.
MSL. Lot No. 31050 BREL Derby 1992–93. –/70(+6) 1T. 38.5 t.
DMCL. Lot No. 31052 BREL Derby 1992–93. –/72 1T. 38.5 t.

159 001	**ST**	P	*SW*	SA	52873	58718	57873	CITY OF EXETER
159 002	**ST**	P	*SW*	SA	52874	58719	57874	CITY OF SALISBURY
159 003	**ST**	P	*SW*	SA	52875	58720	57875	TEMPLECOMBE
159 004	**ST**	P	*SW*	SA	52876	58721	57876	BASINGSTOKE AND DEANE
159 005	**ST**	P	*SW*	SA	52877	58722	57877	WEST OF ENGLAND LINE
159 006	**ST**	P	*SW*	SA	52878	58723	57878	THE SEATON TRAMWAY Seaton–Colyford–Colyton
159 007	**ST**	P	*SW*	SA	52879	58724	57879	
159 008	**ST**	P	*SW*	SA	52880	58725	57880	
159 009	**ST**	P	*SW*	SA	52881	58726	57881	
159 010	**ST**	P	*SW*	SA	52882	58727	57882	
159 011	**ST**	P	*SW*	SA	52883	58728	57883	
159 012	**ST**	P	*SW*	SA	52884	58729	57884	
159 013	**ST**	P	*SW*	SA	52885	58730	57885	
159 014	**ST**	P	*SW*	SA	52886	58731	57886	
159 015	**ST**	P	*SW*	SA	52887	58732	57887	
159 016	**ST**	P	*SW*	SA	52888	58733	57888	
159 017	**ST**	P	*SW*	SA	52889	58734	57889	
159 018	**ST**	P	*SW*	SA	52890	58735	57890	
159 019	**ST**	P	*SW*	SA	52891	58736	57891	
159 020	**ST**	P	*SW*	SA	52892	58737	57892	
159 021	**ST**	P	*SW*	SA	52893	58738	57893	
159 022	**ST**	P	*SW*	SA	52894	58739	57894	

CLASS 159/1   BREL

DMCL–MSL–DMSL. Units converted from Class 158s at Wabtec, Doncaster in 2006–07 for South West Trains. Refurbished with modifications for operation beyond 2020.

Details as Class 158/0 except:
Seating Layout: 1: 2+1 facing, 2: 2+2 facing/unidirectional.

DMCL. Lot No. 31051 BREL Derby 1989–92. 24/24(+2) 1TD 2W. 38.5 t.
MSL. Lot No. 31050 BREL Derby 1989–92. –/70 1T. 38.5 t.
DMSL. Lot No. 31052 BREL Derby 1989–92. –/72 1T. 38.5 t.

159 101	(158 800)	**ST**	P	*SW*	SA	52800	58717	57800
159 102	(158 803)	**ST**	P	*SW*	SA	52803	58703	57803
159 103	(158 804)	**ST**	P	*SW*	SA	52804	58704	57804
159 104	(158 805)	**ST**	P	*SW*	SA	52805	58705	57805
159 105	(158 807)	**ST**	P	*SW*	SA	52807	58707	57807

159 106	(158 809)	**ST**	P	*SW*	SA	52809	58709	57809
159 107	(158 811)	**ST**	P	*SW*	SA	52811	58711	57811
159 108	(158 801)	**ST**	P	*SW*	SA	52801	58701	57801

CLASS 165/0   NETWORK TURBO   BREL

DMSL–DMS and DMSL–MS–DMS. Chiltern Railways units. Refurbished 2003–05 with First Class seats removed and air conditioning fitted.
Construction: Welded aluminium.
Engines: One Perkins 2006-TWH of 260 kW (350 hp) at 2100 rpm.
Bogies: BREL P3-17 (powered), BREL T3-17 (non-powered).
Couplers: BSI.
Dimensions: 23.50/23.25 x 2.81 m.
Gangways: Within unit only.   **Wheel Arrangement:** 2-B (+ B-2) + B-2.
Doors: Twin-leaf swing plug.   **Maximum Speed:** 75 mph.
Seating Layout: 2+2/3+2 facing/unidirectional.
Multiple Working: Within class and with Classes 166, 168, 170 and 172.

Fitted with tripcocks for working over London Underground tracks between Harrow-on-the-Hill and Amersham.

* Refurbished with a new universal access toilet to comply with the 2020 accessibility regulations.

58801–822/58873–878. DMSL. Lot No. 31087 BREL York 1990. –/82(+7) 1T 2W (* –/77(+7) 1TD 2W). 42.1 t.
58823–833. DMSL. Lot No. 31089 BREL York 1991–92. –/82(+7) 1T 2W (* –/77(+7) 1TD 2W). 40.1 t.
MS. Lot No. 31090 BREL York 1991–92. –/106. 37.0 t.
DMS. Lot No. 31088 BREL York 1991–92. –/94. 41.5 t.

165 001	*	**CR**	A	*CR*	AL	58801	58834
165 002		**CR**	A	*CR*	AL	58802	58835
165 003		**CR**	A	*CR*	AL	58803	58836
165 004	*	**CR**	A	*CR*	AL	58804	58837
165 005		**CR**	A	*CR*	AL	58805	58838
165 006		**CR**	A	*CR*	AL	58806	58839
165 007		**CR**	A	*CR*	AL	58807	58840
165 008	*	**CR**	A	*CR*	AL	58808	58841
165 009		**CR**	A	*CR*	AL	58809	58842
165 010	*	**CR**	A	*CR*	AL	58810	58843
165 011	*	**CR**	A	*CR*	AL	58811	58844
165 012		**CR**	A	*CR*	AL	58812	58845
165 013		**CR**	A	*CR*	AL	58813	58846
165 014	*	**CR**	A	*CR*	AL	58814	58847
165 015	*	**CR**	A	*CR*	AL	58815	58848
165 016	*	**CR**	A	*CR*	AL	58816	58849
165 017	*	**CR**	A	*CR*	AL	58817	58850
165 018	*	**CR**	A	*CR*	AL	58818	58851
165 019		**CR**	A	*CR*	AL	58819	58852
165 020	*	**CR**	A	*CR*	AL	58820	58853
165 021	*	**CR**	A	*CR*	AL	58821	58854
165 022	*	**CR**	A	*CR*	AL	58822	58855

165 023		CR	A	CR	AL	58873		58867
165 024	*	CR	A	CR	AL	58874		58868
165 025	*	CR	A	CR	AL	58875		58869
165 026	*	CR	A	CR	AL	58876		58870
165 027		CR	A	CR	AL	58877		58871
165 028	*	CR	A	CR	AL	58878		58872
165 029	*	CR	A	CR	AL	58823	55404	58856
165 030	*	CR	A	CR	AL	58824	55405	58857
165 031	*	CR	A	CR	AL	58825	55406	58858
165 032	*	CR	A	CR	AL	58826	55407	58859
165 033	*	CR	A	CR	AL	58827	55408	58860
165 034	*	CR	A	CR	AL	58828	55409	58861
165 035		CR	A	CR	AL	58829	55410	58862
165 036	*	CR	A	CR	AL	58830	55411	58863
165 037		CR	A	CR	AL	58831	55412	58864
165 038	*	CR	A	CR	AL	58832	55413	58865
165 039		CR	A	CR	AL	58833	55414	58866

CLASS 165/1   NETWORK TURBO   BREL

Great Western Railway units. DMSL–MS–DMS or DMSL–DMS. In 2015 GWR removed First Class from all its Class 165s: all are now Standard Class only.

Construction: Welded aluminium.
Engines: One Perkins 2006-TWH of 260 kW (350 hp) at 2100 rpm.
Bogies: BREL P3-17 (powered), BREL T3-17 (non-powered).
Couplers: BSI.
Dimensions: 23.50/23.25 x 2.81 m.
Gangways: Within unit only.   **Wheel Arrangement:** 2-B (+ B-2) + B-2.
Doors: Twin-leaf swing plug.   **Maximum Speed:** 90 mph.
Seating Layout: 3+2/2+2 facing/unidirectional.
Multiple Working: Within class and with Classes 166, 168, 170 and 172.

* Refurbished with a new universal access toilet to comply with the 2020 accessibility regulations.

58953–969. DMSL. Lot No. 31098 BREL York 1992. –/82 1T (* –/67 1TD 2W). 38.0 t (* 40.8 t).
58879–898. DMSL. Lot No. 31096 BREL York 1992. –/88 1T. 38.0 t.
MS. Lot No. 31099 BREL 1992. –/106. 38.1 t.
DMS. Lot No. 31097 BREL 1992. –/98. 37.0 t.

165 101		GW	A	GW	RG	58953	55415	58916
165 102		GW	A	GW	RG	58954	55416	58917
165 103		GW	A	GW	RG	58955	55417	58918
165 104	*	GW	A	GW	RG	58956	55418	58919
165 105	*	GW	A	GW	RG	58957	55419	58920
165 106	*	GW	A	GW	RG	58958	55420	58921
165 107	*	GW	A	GW	RG	58959	55421	58922
165 108	*	GW	A	GW	RG	58960	55422	58923
165 109	*	GW	A	GW	RG	58961	55423	58924
165 110	*	GW	A	GW	RG	58962	55424	58925
165 111	*	GW	A	GW	RG	58963	55425	58926

165 112	*	**GW**	A	*GW*	RG	58964	55426	58927
165 113	*	**GW**	A	*GW*	RG	58965	55427	58928
165 114	*	**GW**	A	*GW*	RG	58966	55428	58929
165 116	*	**GW**	A	*GW*	RG	58968	55430	58931
165 117	*	**GW**	A	*GW*	RG	58969	55431	58932
165 118		**FD**	A	*GW*	RG	58879		58933
165 119	*	**GW**	A	*GW*	RG	58880		58934
165 120		**FD**	A	*GW*	RG	58881		58935
165 121	*	**GW**	A	*GW*	RG	58882		58936
165 122		**FD**	A	*GW*	RG	58883		58937
165 123		**FD**	A	*GW*	RG	58884		58938
165 124		**FD**	A	*GW*	RG	58885		58939
165 125		**FD**	A	*GW*	RG	58886		58940
165 126		**FD**	A	*GW*	RG	58887		58941
165 127		**FD**	A	*GW*	RG	58888		58942
165 128		**FD**	A	*GW*	RG	58889		58943
165 129		**FD**	A	*GW*	RG	58890		58944
165 130		**FD**	A	*GW*	RG	58891		58945
165 131		**FD**	A	*GW*	RG	58892		58946
165 132		**FD**	A	*GW*	RG	58893		58947
165 133		**FD**	A	*GW*	RG	58894		58948
165 134		**FD**	A	*GW*	RG	58895		58949
165 135		**FD**	A	*GW*	RG	58896		58950
165 136		**FD**	A	*GW*	RG	58897		58951
165 137		**FD**	A	*GW*	RG	58898		58952

CLASS 166   NETWORK EXPRESS TURBO   ABB

DMCL–MS–DMSL. Great Western Railway units, built for Paddington–Oxford/Newbury services. Air conditioned and with additional luggage space compared to the Class 165s. The DMSL vehicles have had their 16 First Class seats declassified. Refurbished with a new universal access toilet to comply with the 2020 accessibility regulations.

Construction: Welded aluminium.
Engines: One Perkins 2006-TWH of 260 kW (350 hp) at 2100 rpm.
Bogies: BREL P3-17 (powered), BREL T3-17 (non-powered).
Couplers: BSI.
Dimensions: 23.50 x 2.81 m.
Gangways: Within unit only.   **Wheel Arrangement:** 2-B + B-2 + B-2.
Doors: Twin-leaf swing plug.   **Maximum Speed:** 90 mph.
Seating Layout: 1: 2+2 facing, 2: 2+2/3+2 facing/unidirectional.
Multiple Working: Within class and with Classes 165, 168, 170 and 172.

DMCL. Lot No. 31116 ABB York 1992–93. 16/53 1TD 2W. 41.2 t.
MS. Lot No. 31117 ABB York 1992–93. –/91. 39.9 t.
DMSL. Lot No. 31116 ABB York 1992–93. –/84 1T. 39.6 t.

166 201	**FB**	A	*GW*	RG	58101	58601	58122
166 202	**FB**	A	*GW*	PM	58102	58602	58123
166 203	**FB**	A	*GW*	RG	58103	58603	58124
166 204	**GW**	A	*GW*	PM	58104	58604	58125

166 205	GW	A	GW	PM	58105	58605	58126
166 206	GW	A	GW	PM	58106	58606	58127
166 207	FB	A	GW	PM	58107	58607	58128
166 208	GW	A	GW	PM	58108	58608	58129
166 209	FB	A	GW	PM	58109	58609	58130
166 210	GW	A	GW	PM	58110	58610	58131
166 211	FB	A	GW	RG	58111	58611	58132
166 212	GW	A	GW	PM	58112	58612	58133
166 213	GW	A	GW	RG	58113	58613	58134
166 214	GW	A	GW	PM	58114	58614	58135
166 215	FB	A	GW	RG	58115	58615	58136
166 216	GW	A	GW	PM	58116	58616	58137
166 217	GW	A	GW	RG	58117	58617	58138
166 218	GW	A	GW	RG	58118	58618	58139
166 219	GW	A	GW	PM	58119	58619	58140
166 220	GW	A	GW	RG	58120	58620	58141
166 221	FB	A	GW	RG	58121	58621	58142

Names:

166 204	Norman Topsom MBE
166 220	Roger Watkins THE GWR MASTER TRAIN PLANNER
166 221	Reading Train Care Depot/READING TRAIN CARE DEPOT *(alt sides)*

CLASS 168   CLUBMAN   ADTRANZ/BOMBARDIER

Air conditioned.

Construction: Welded aluminium bodies with bolt-on steel ends.
Engines: One MTU 6R183TD13H of 315 kW (422 hp) at 1900 rpm.
Transmission: Hydraulic. Voith T211rzze to ZF final drive.
Bogies: One Adtranz P3–23 and one BREL T3–23 per car.
Couplers: BSI at outer ends, bar within unit.
Dimensions: Class 168/0: 24.10/23.61 x 2.69 m. Others: 23.62/23.61 x 2.69 m.
Gangways: Within unit only.   **Wheel Arrangement:** 2-B (+ B-2 + B-2) + B-2.
Doors: Twin-leaf swing plug.   **Maximum Speed:** 100 mph.
Seating Layout: 2+2 facing/unidirectional.
Multiple Working: Within class and with Classes 165 and 166.

Fitted with tripcocks for working over London Underground tracks between Harrow-on-the-Hill and Amersham.

Class 168/0. Original Design. DMSL(A)–MS–MSL–DMSL(B) or DMSL(A)–MSL–MS–DMSL(B).

58451–455 were numbered 58656–660 for a time when used in 168 106–110.

58151–155. DMSL(A). Adtranz Derby 1997–98. –/57 1TD 1W. 44.0 t.
58651–655. MSL. Adtranz Derby 1998. –/73 1T. 41.0 t.
58451–455. MS. Adtranz Derby 1998. –/77. 41.0 t.
58251–255. DMSL(B). Adtranz Derby 1998. –/68 1T. 43.6 t.

168 001	CL	P	CR	AL	58151	58651	58451	58251
168 002	CL	P	CR	AL	58152	58652	58452	58252
168 003	CL	P	CR	AL	58153	58453	58653	58253

▲ London Midland-liveried Parry People Mover 139 002 arrives at Stourbridge Junction with a shuttle from Stourbridge Town on 21/09/14. **Robert Pritchard**

▼ Arriva Trains-liveried 142 076 is seen at Tenby with the 11.50 Swansea–Pembroke Dock on 11/04/15. **Tom McAtee**

▲ Ex-works in Great Western Railway Green livery, 143 603 is seen with 153 373 at Newton Abbot on 22/07/17 with the 09.04 Paignton–Exmouth. **Tony Christie**

▼ Northern-liveried 144 002 arrives at Saxilby with the 09.19 Scunthorpe–Lincoln Central on 29/12/16. **Robert Pritchard**

▲ Arriva Trains Wales dark blue-liveried 150 240 stands at Blaenau Ffestiniog with the 15.03 to Llandudno Junction on 13/08/17.

Tony Christie

▲ In the new Northern livery, 150 137 is seen at York with the 08.47 to Leeds via Harrogate on 13/07/17. **Gavin Morrison**

▼ Greater Anglia-liveried 153 335 arrives at Great Yarmouth with the 07.36 from Norwich on 14/06/17. **Robert Pritchard**

▲ New Northern-liveried 155 346 stands at Leeds on 02/08/17. **James Stokes**

▼ ScotRail Saltire-liveried 156 442 is seen near Breich with the 19.27 Edinburgh Waverley–Glasgow Central on 11/07/17. **Robin Ralston**

▲ Great Western Railway Green-liveried 158 957 approaches Southampton Central with the 13.30 Cardiff Central–Portsmouth Harbour on 17/06/17. **Robert Pritchard**

▼ South West Trains-liveried 159 103 and 159 001 are seen near Wimbledon with the 06.19 Honiton–London Waterloo on 19/06/17. **Robert Pritchard**

▲ Chiltern Railways-liveried 165 020 leaves Kings Sutton with the 14.47 Banbury–London Marylebone on 22/05/17. **Brian Denton**

▼ Great Western Railway Green-liveried 166 217 calls at Ealing Broadway with the 10.48 Reading–London Paddington on 02/09/17. **Robert Pritchard**

▲ Chiltern Railways Mainline-liveried 168 112 and 168 321 pass Neasden with the 16.18 London Marylebone–Oxford on 05/07/16. **Robert Pritchard**

▼ Greater Anglia-liveried 170 270 arrives at March with the 13.58 Ipswich–Peterborough on 12/07/17. **Antony Guppy**

▲ Southern-liveried 171 722 and 171 402 approach Norwood Junction with the 09.02 London Bridge–Uckfield on 19/06/17. **Brian Denton**

▼ Chiltern Railways-liveried 172 101 passes West Hampstead (LUL) with the 19.36 London Marylebone–Gerrards Cross on 05/07/16. **Robert Pritchard**

▲ Arriva Trains-liveried 175 113 is seen between Oxford Road and Piccadilly stations in Manchester with the 08.54 Llandudno Junction–Manchester Airport on 29/11/16. **Robert Pritchard**

▼ First Hull Trains Dynamic Lines-liveried 180 111 passes Claypole with the 15.48 London King's Cross–Hull on 10/08/17. **Paul Biggs**

▲ TransPennine Express liveried 185 138 leaves Lancaster with the 08.29 Manchester Airport–Windermere on 22/04/17. **Robert Pritchard**

▼ CrossCountry-liveried 220 008 arrives in the turnback siding just beyond Southampton Central station on 17/06/17. **Robert Pritchard**

▲ Virgin Trains-liveried 221 101 arrives at Milton Keynes Central on 26/02/17 with the 11.58 Lancaster–London Euston. **Robert Pritchard**

▼ East Midlands Trains-liveried 222 011 passes Cossington with the 07.04 Lincoln–London St Pancras on 19/08/17. **Paul Biggs**

▲ Vivarail-liveried D-Train prototype 230 001 is seen at Honeybourne running empty stock from Long Marston to Moreton-in-Marsh on 14/06/17.
Dave Gommersall

▼ Colas Rail Plasser & Theurer 08-4x4/4S-RT Tamper DR 73906 crosses Dent Head Viaduct with a 10.52 Garsdale–Guide Bridge Sidings on 03/05/17. **Paul Biggs**

▲ Volker Rail Matisa R 24 S Ballast Regulator DR 77802 is seen at Sutton Bonington with a 10.00 Melton Mowbray–Scunthorpe Frodingham on 06/02/15.
Paul Biggs

▼ Brand new Network Rail Loram C44 Rail Grinding Train 99 70 9427 042-5 + 99 70 9427 043-3 + 99 70 9427 044-1 + 99 70 9427 045-8 ("DR 79401–404") is seen on test at Okehampton on the Dartmoor Railway on 10/05/17. **David Hunt**

▲ Network Rail Harsco Track Technologies Multi-purpose Stoneblower DR 80303 passes Virginia Water whilst running from Bristol Kingsland Road to Woking Up Yard on 19/06/17. **Robert Pritchard**

▼ Network Rail Plasser & Theurer NB-PW Ballast System Propulsion Machine DR 92264 is seen on the rear of a Taunton Fairwater Yard–Westbury train at Cogload Junction on 03/08/17. **Tony Christie**

▲ Network Rail Robel Type 69.70 Mobile Maintenance Train 99 70 9481 005-5 + 99 70 9559 005-2 + 99 70 9580 005-5 ("DR 97505/605/805") is seen at Sheffield on 05/07/16. **Andy Barclay**

▼ Track Assessment unit 999600+999601 ("950 001") (based on the BREL Class 150/1 design) passes Trowell heading for Derby RTC on 14/03/17. **Steve Donald**

| 168 004 | **CL** | P | *CR* | AL | 58154 | 58654 | 58454 | 58254 |
| 168 005 | **CL** | P | *CR* | AL | 58155 | 58655 | 58455 | 58255 |

Class 168/1. These units are effectively Class 170s. DMSL(A)–MSL–MS–DMSL(B) or DMSL(A)–MS–DMSL(B).

58461–463 have been renumbered from 58661–663.

58156–163. DMSL(A). Adtranz Derby 2000. –/57 1TD 2W. 45.2 t.
58456–460. MS. Bombardier Derby 2002. –/76. 41.8 t.
58756–757. MSL. Bombardier Derby 2002. –/73 1T. 42.9 t.
58461–463. MS. Adtranz Derby 2000. –/76. 42.4 t.
58256–263. DMSL(B). Adtranz Derby 2000. –/69 1T. 45.2 t.

168 106	**CL**	P	*CR*	AL	58156	58756	58456	58256
168 107	**CL**	P	*CR*	AL	58157	58757	58457	58257
168 108	**CL**	P	*CR*	AL	58158		58458	58258
168 109	**CL**	P	*CR*	AL	58159		58459	58259
168 110	**CL**	P	*CR*	AL	58160		58460	58260
168 111	**CL**	E	*CR*	AL	58161		58461	58261
168 112	**CL**	E	*CR*	AL	58162		58462	58262
168 113	**CL**	E	*CR*	AL	58163		58463	58263

Class 168/2. These units are effectively Class 170s. DMSL(A)–(MS)–MS–DMSL(B).

58164–169. DMSL(A). Bombardier Derby 2003–04. –/57 1TD 2W. 45.4 t.
58365–367. MS. Bombardier Derby 2006. –/76. 43.3 t.
58464/468/469. MS. Bombardier Derby 2003–04. –/76. 44.0 t.
58465–467. MS. Bombardier Derby 2006. –/76. 43.3 t.
58264–269. DMSL(B). Bombardier Derby 2003–04. –/69 1T. 45.5 t.

168 214	**CL**	P	*CR*	AL	58164		58464	58264
168 215	**CL**	P	*CR*	AL	58165	58365	58465	58265
168 216	**CL**	P	*CR*	AL	58166	58366	58466	58266
168 217	**CL**	P	*CR*	AL	58167	58367	58467	58267
168 218	**CL**	P	*CR*	AL	58168		58468	58268
168 219	**CL**	P	*CR*	AL	58169		58469	58269

Class 168/3. Former South West Trains/TransPennine Express Class 170s taken on by Chiltern Railways in 2015–16 and renumbered in the 168 3xx series. 170 309 was originally numbered 170 399. DMSL(A)–DMSL(B).

50301–308/399. DMCL. Adtranz Derby 2000–01. –/59 1TD 2W. 45.8 t.
79301–308/399. DMSL. Adtranz Derby 2000–01. –/69 1T. 45.8 t.

168 321	(170 301)	**CL**	P	*CR*	AL	50301	79301
168 322	(170 302)	**CL**	P	*CR*	AL	50302	79302
168 323	(170 303)	**CL**	P	*CR*	AL	50303	79303
168 324	(170 304)	**CL**	P	*CR*	AL	50304	79304
168 325	(170 305)	**CL**	P	*CR*	AL	50305	79305
168 326	(170 306)	**CL**	P	*CR*	AL	50306	79306
168 327	(170 307)	**CL**	P	*CR*	AL	50307	79307
168 328	(170 308)	**CL**	P	*CR*	AL	50308	79308
168 329	(170 309)	**CL**	P	*CR*	AL	50399	79399

CLASS 170 TURBOSTAR ADTRANZ/BOMBARDIER

Various formations. Air conditioned.

Construction: Welded aluminium bodies with bolt-on steel ends.
Engines: One MTU 6R183TD13H of 315 kW (422 hp) at 1900 rpm.
Transmission: Hydraulic. Voith T211rzze to ZF final drive.
Bogies: One Adtranz P3–23 and one BREL T3–23 per car.
Couplers: BSI at outer ends, bar within later build units.
Dimensions: 23.62/23.61 x 2.69 m.
Gangways: Within unit only.   **Wheel Arrangement:** 2-B (+ B-2) + B-2.
Doors: Twin-leaf sliding plug.   **Maximum Speed:** 100 mph.
Seating Layout: 1: 2+1 facing/unidirectional. 2: 2+2 unidirectional/facing.
Multiple Working: Within class and with Classes 150, 153, 155, 156, 158, 159 and 172.

Class 170/1. CrossCountry (former Midland Mainline) units. Lazareni seating. DMSL–MS–DMCL/DMSL–DMCL.

DMSL. Adtranz Derby 1998–99. –/59 1TD 2W. 45.0 t.
MS. Adtranz Derby 2001. –/80. 43.0 t.
DMCL. Adtranz Derby 1998–99. 9/52 1T. 44.8 t

170 101	**XC**	P	*XC*	TS	50101	55101	79101
170 102	**XC**	P	*XC*	TS	50102	55102	79102
170 103	**XC**	P	*XC*	TS	50103	55103	79103
170 104	**XC**	P	*XC*	TS	50104	55104	79104
170 105	**XC**	P	*XC*	TS	50105	55105	79105
170 106	**XC**	P	*XC*	TS	50106	55106	79106
170 107	**XC**	P	*XC*	TS	50107	55107	79107
170 108	**XC**	P	*XC*	TS	50108	55108	79108
170 109	**XC**	P	*XC*	TS	50109	55109	79109
170 110	**XC**	P	*XC*	TS	50110	55110	79110
170 111	**XC**	P	*XC*	TS	50111		79111
170 112	**XC**	P	*XC*	TS	50112		79112
170 113	**XC**	P	*XC*	TS	50113		79113
170 114	**XC**	P	*XC*	TS	50114		79114
170 115	**XC**	P	*XC*	TS	50115		79115
170 116	**XC**	P	*XC*	TS	50116		79116
170 117	**XC**	P	*XC*	TS	50117		79117

Class 170/2. Greater Anglia 3-car units. Chapman seating. DMCL–MSL–DMSL.

DMCL. Adtranz Derby 1999. 7/39 1TD 2W. 45.0 t.
MSL. Adtranz Derby 1999. –/68 1T. Guard's office. 45.3 t.
DMSL. Adtranz Derby 1999. –/66 1T. 43.4 t.

170 201	r	**GA**	P	*GA*	NC	50201	56201	79201
170 202	r	**GA**	P	*GA*	NC	50202	56202	79202
170 203	r	**GA**	P	*GA*	NC	50203	56203	79203
170 204	r	**1**	P	*GA*	NC	50204	56204	79204
170 205	r	**1**	P	*GA*	NC	50205	56205	79205
170 206	r	**GA**	P	*GA*	NC	50206	56206	79206
170 207	r	**1**	P	*GA*	NC	50207	56207	79207

170 208	r	**GA**	P	*GA*	NC	50208	56208	79208

Class 170/2. Greater Anglia 2-car units. Chapman seating. DMSL–DMCL.

DMSL. Bombardier Derby 2002. –/57 1TD 2W. 45.7 t.
DMCL. Bombardier Derby 2002. 9/53 1T. 45.7 t.

170 270	r	**GA**	P	*GA*	NC	50270	79270
170 271	r	**AN**	P	*GA*	NC	50271	79271
170 272	r	**AN**	P	*GA*	NC	50272	79272
170 273	r	**AN**	P	*GA*	NC	50273	79273

Class 170/3. Units built for Hull Trains, now in use with ScotRail. Chapman seating. DMSL–MSLRB–DMSL.

DMSL(A). Bombardier Derby 2004. –/55 1TD 2W. 46.5 t.
MSLRB. Bombardier Derby 2004. –/57 1T. Buffet and guard's office 44.7 t.
DMSL(B). Bombardier Derby 2004. –/67 1T. 47.0 t.

170 393	**SR**	P	*SR*	HA	50393	56393	79393
170 394	**SR**	P	*SR*	HA	50394	56394	79394
170 395	**SR**	P	*SR*	HA	50395	56395	79395
170 396	**SR**	P	*SR*	HA	50396	56396	79396

Class 170/3. CrossCountry units. Lazareni seating. DMSL–MS–DMCL.

DMSL. Bombardier Derby 2002. –/59 1TD 2W. 45.4 t.
MS. Bombardier Derby 2002. –/80. 43.0 t.
DMCL. Bombardier Derby 2002. 9/52 1T. 45.8 t.

170 397	**XC**	P	*XC*	TS	50397	56397	79397
170 398	**XC**	P	*XC*	TS	50398	56398	79398

Class 170/4. ScotRail "express" units. Chapman seating. DMCL–MS–DMCL.

170 416–420 are sub-leased from Southern to ScotRail.

170 421–424 have been renumbered as Southern 171 201/202 and 171 401/402.

Non-standard/Advertising liveries:

170 407   BTP text number 61016 (blue).
170 416, 170 417, 170 419, 170 420 Unbranded Saltire blue with grey doors.

DMCL(A). Adtranz Derby 1999–2001. 9/43 1TD 2W. 45.2 t.
MS. Adtranz Derby 1999–2001. –/76. 42.5 t.
DMCL(B). Adtranz Derby 1999–2001. 9/49 1T. 45.2 t.

170 401	**SR**	P	*SR*	HA	50401	56401	79401
170 402	**SR**	P	*SR*	HA	50402	56402	79402
170 403	**SR**	P	*SR*	HA	50403	56403	79403
170 404	**SR**	P	*SR*	HA	50404	56404	79404
170 405	**SR**	P	*SR*	HA	50405	56405	79405
170 406	**SR**	P	*SR*	HA	50406	56406	79406
170 407	**AL**	P	*SR*	HA	50407	56407	79407
170 408	**SR**	P	*SR*	HA	50408	56408	79408
170 409	**SR**	P	*SR*	HA	50409	56409	79409
170 410	**SR**	P	*SR*	HA	50410	56410	79410
170 411	**SR**	P	*SR*	HA	50411	56411	79411

170 412	**SR**	P	*SR*	HA	50412	56412	79412
170 413	**SR**	P	*SR*	HA	50413	56413	79413
170 414	**SR**	P	*SR*	HA	50414	56414	79414
170 415	**SR**	P	*SR*	HA	50415	56415	79415
170 416	**0**	E	*SR*	HA	50416	56416	79416
170 417	**0**	E	*SR*	HA	50417	56417	79417
170 418	**SR**	E	*SR*	HA	50418	56418	79418
170 419	**0**	E	*SR*	HA	50419	56419	79419
170 420	**0**	E	*SR*	HA	50420	56420	79420

Class 170/4. ScotRail "express" units. Chapman seating. DMCL–MS–DMCL.

DMCL. Bombardier Derby 2003–05. 9/43 1TD 2W. 46.8 t.
MS. Bombardier Derby 2003–05. –/76. 43.7 t.
DMCL. Bombardier Derby 2003–05. 9/49 1T. 46.5 t.

170 425	**SR**	P	*SR*	HA	50425	56425	79425
170 426	**SR**	P	*SR*	HA	50426	56426	79426
170 427	**SR**	P	*SR*	HA	50427	56427	79427
170 428	**SR**	P	*SR*	HA	50428	56428	79428
170 429	**SR**	P	*SR*	HA	50429	56429	79429
170 430	**SR**	P	*SR*	HA	50430	56430	79430
170 431	**SR**	P	*SR*	HA	50431	56431	79431
170 432	**SR**	P	*SR*	HA	50432	56432	79432
170 433	**SR**	P	*SR*	HA	50433	56433	79433
170 434	**SR**	P	*SR*	HA	50434	56434	79434

Class 170/4. ScotRail units. Originally built as Standard Class only units.
170 450–457 have been retro-fitted with First Class. Chapman seating.
DMSL–MS–DMSL or † DMCL–MS–DMCL.

DMSL. Bombardier Derby 2004–05. –/55 1TD 2W († 9/47 1TD 2W). 46.3 t.
MS. Bombardier Derby 2004–05. –/76. 43.4 t.
DMSL. Bombardier Derby 2004–05. –/67 1T († 9/49 1T 1W). 46.4 t.

170 450	†	**SR**	P	*SR*	HA	50450	56450	79450
170 451	†	**SR**	P	*SR*	HA	50451	56451	79451
170 452	†	**SR**	P	*SR*	HA	50452	56452	79452
170 453	†	**SR**	P	*SR*	HA	50453	56453	79453
170 454	†	**SR**	P	*SR*	HA	50454	56454	79454
170 455	†	**SR**	P	*SR*	HA	50455	56455	79455
170 456	†	**SR**	P	*SR*	HA	50456	56456	79456
170 457	†	**SR**	P	*SR*	HA	50457	56457	79457
170 458		**SR**	P	*SR*	HA	50458	56458	79458
170 459		**SR**	P	*SR*	HA	50459	56459	79459
170 460		**SR**	P	*SR*	HA	50460	56460	79460
170 461		**SR**	P	*SR*	HA	50461	56461	79461

Class 170/4. ScotRail units. Standard Class only units. Chapman seating.
DMSL–MS–DMSL.

50470–471. DMSL(A). Adtranz Derby 2001. –/55 1TD 2W. 45.1 t.
50472–478. DMSL(A). Bombardier Derby 2004–05. –/57 1TD 2W. 46.3 t.
56470–471. MS. Adtranz Derby 2001. –/76. 42.4 t.
56472–478. MS. Bombardier Derby 2004–05. –/76. 43.4 t.

79470–471. DMSL(B). Adtranz Derby 2001. –/67 1T. 45.1 t.
79472–478. DMSL(B). Bombardier Derby 2004–05. –/67 1T. 46.4 t.

170 470	**SR**	P	*SR*	HA	50470	56470	79470
170 471	**SR**	P	*SR*	HA	50471	56471	79471
170 472	**SR**	P	*SR*	HA	50472	56472	79472
170 473	**SR**	P	*SR*	HA	50473	56473	79473
170 474	**SR**	P	*SR*	HA	50474	56474	79474
170 475	**SR**	P	*SR*	HA	50475	56475	79475
170 476	**SR**	P	*SR*	HA	50476	56476	79476
170 477	**SR**	P	*SR*	HA	50477	56477	79477
170 478	**SR**	P	*SR*	HA	50478	56478	79478

Class 170/5. West Midlands Trains and CrossCountry 2-car units. Lazareni seating. DMSL–DMSL or * DMSL–DMCL (CrossCountry).

DMSL(A). Adtranz Derby 1999–2000. –/55 1TD 2W (* –/59 1TD 2W). 45.8 t.
DMSL(B). Adtranz Derby 1999–2000. –/67 1T (* DMCL 9/52 1T). 45.9 t.

170 501		**LM**	P	*WM*	TS	50501	79501
170 502		**LM**	P	*WM*	TS	50502	79502
170 503		**LM**	P	*WM*	TS	50503	79503
170 504		**LM**	P	*WM*	TS	50504	79504
170 505		**LM**	P	*WM*	TS	50505	79505
170 506		**LM**	P	*WM*	TS	50506	79506
170 507		**LM**	P	*WM*	TS	50507	79507
170 508		**LM**	P	*WM*	TS	50508	79508
170 509		**LM**	P	*WM*	TS	50509	79509
170 510		**LM**	P	*WM*	TS	50510	79510
170 511		**LM**	P	*WM*	TS	50511	79511
170 512		**LM**	P	*WM*	TS	50512	79512
170 513		**LM**	P	*WM*	TS	50513	79513
170 514		**LM**	P	*WM*	TS	50514	79514
170 515		**LM**	P	*WM*	TS	50515	79515
170 516		**LM**	P	*WM*	TS	50516	79516
170 517		**LM**	P	*WM*	TS	50517	79517
170 518	*	**XC**	P	*XC*	TS	50518	79518
170 519	*	**XC**	P	*XC*	TS	50519	79519
170 520	*	**XC**	P	*XC*	TS	50520	79520
170 521	*	**XC**	P	*XC*	TS	50521	79521
170 522	*	**XC**	P	*XC*	TS	50522	79522
170 523	*	**XC**	P	*XC*	TS	50523	79523

Class 170/6. West Midlands Trains and CrossCountry 3-car units. Lazareni seating. DMSL–MS–DMSL or * DMSL–MS–DMCL (CrossCountry).

DMSL(A). Adtranz Derby 2000. –/55 1TD 2W (* –/59 1TD 2W). 45.8 t.
MS. Adtranz Derby 2000. –/74 (* –/80). 42.4 t.
DMSL(B). Adtranz Derby 2000. –/67 1T (* DMCL 9/52 1T). 45.9 t.

170 630	**LM**	P	*WM*	TS	50630	56630	79630
170 631	**LM**	P	*WM*	TS	50631	56631	79631
170 632	**LM**	P	*WM*	TS	50632	56632	79632
170 633	**LM**	P	*WM*	TS	50633	56633	79633

170 634	**LM**	P	*WM*	TS	50634	56634	79634
170 635	**LM**	P	*WM*	TS	50635	56635	79635
170 636	* **XC**	P	*XC*	TS	50636	56636	79636
170 637	* **XC**	P	*XC*	TS	50637	56637	79637
170 638	* **XC**	P	*XC*	TS	50638	56638	79638
170 639	* **XC**	P	*XC*	TS	50639	56639	79639

CLASS 171   TURBOSTAR   BOMBARDIER

DMCL–DMSL or DMCL–MS–MS–DMCL. Southern units. Air conditioned. Chapman seating.

Construction: Welded aluminium bodies with bolt-on steel ends.
Engines: One MTU 6R183TD13H of 315 kW (422 hp) at 1900 rpm.
Transmission: Hydraulic. Voith T211rzze to ZF final drive.
Bogies: One Adtranz P3–23 and one BREL T3–23 per car.
Couplers: Dellner 12 at outer ends, bar within unit (Class 171/8).
Dimensions: 23.62/23.61 x 2.69 m.
Gangways: Within unit only.   **Wheel Arrangement:** 2-B (+ B-2 + B-2) + B-2.
Doors: Twin-leaf swing plug.   **Maximum Speed:** 100 mph.
Seating Layout: 1: 2+1 facing/unidirectional. 2: 2+2 facing/unidirectional.
Multiple Working: Within class and with EMU Classes 375 and 377 in an emergency.

Class 171/2. 2-car units rebuilt from ScotRail Class 170s. Full details awaited. DMCL–DMSL.

Originally built as 3-car units 170 421/423, but renumbered as Class 171 on fitting with Dellner couplers.

DMCL. Adtranz Derby 1999–2001.
DMSL. Adtranz Derby 1999–2001.

171 201	**SN**	E	*SN*	SU	50421	79421
171 202	**SN**	E	*SN*	SU	50423	79423

Class 171/4. 4-car units rebuilt from ScotRail Class 170s. Full details awaited. DMCL(A)–MS–MS–DMCL(B).

Reformed and renumbered Class 171s in 2016 using vehicles from ScotRail 3-car Class 170s 170 421–424.

DMCL(A). Adtranz Derby 1999–2001.
MS. Adtranz Derby 1999–2001.
DMCL(B). Adtranz Derby 1999–2001.

171 401	**SN**	E	*SN*	SU	50422	56421	56422	79422
171 402	**SN**	E	*SN*	SU	50424	56423	56424	79424

Class 171/7. 2-car units. DMCL–DMSL.

171 721–726 were built as Class 170s (170 721–726), but renumbered as Class 171 on fitting with Dellner couplers.

171 730 was formerly South West Trains unit 170 392, before transferring to Southern in 2007.

50721–726. DMCL. Bombardier Derby 2003. 9/43 1TD 2W. 47.6 t.
50727–729. DMCL. Bombardier Derby 2005. 9/43 1TD 2W. 46.3 t.
50392. DMCL. Bombardier Derby 2003. 9/43 1TD 2W. 46.6 t.
79721–726. DMSL. Bombardier Derby 2003. –/64 1T. 47.8 t.
79727–729. DMSL. Bombardier Derby 2005. –/64 1T. 46.2 t.
79392. DMSL. Bombardier Derby 2003. –/64 1T. 46.5 t.

171 721	**SN**	P	*SN*	SU	50721	79721
171 722	**SN**	P	*SN*	SU	50722	79722
171 723	**SN**	P	*SN*	SU	50723	79723
171 724	**SN**	P	*SN*	SU	50724	79724
171 725	**SN**	P	*SN*	SU	50725	79725
171 726	**SN**	P	*SN*	SU	50726	79726
171 727	**SN**	P	*SN*	SU	50727	79727
171 728	**SN**	P	*SN*	SU	50728	79728
171 729	**SN**	P	*SN*	SU	50729	79729
171 730	**SN**	P	*SN*	SU	50392	79392

Class 171/8. 4-car units. DMCL(A)–MS–MS–DMCL(B).

DMCL(A). Bombardier Derby 2004. 9/43 1TD 2W. 46.5 t.
MS. Bombardier Derby 2004. –/74. 43.7 t.
DMCL(B). Bombardier Derby 2004. 9/50 1T. 46.5 t.

171 801	**SN**	P	*SN*	SU	50801	54801	56801	79801
171 802	**SN**	P	*SN*	SU	50802	54802	56802	79802
171 803	**SN**	P	*SN*	SU	50803	54803	56803	79803
171 804	**SN**	P	*SN*	SU	50804	54804	56804	79804
171 805	**SN**	P	*SN*	SU	50805	54805	56805	79805
171 806	**SN**	P	*SN*	SU	50806	54806	56806	79806

CLASS 172   TURBOSTAR   BOMBARDIER

New generation London Overground, Chiltern Railways and West Midlands Trains Turbostars. Air conditioned.

Construction: Welded aluminium bodies with bolt-on steel ends.
Engines: One MTU 6H1800R83 of 360 kW (483 hp) at 1800 rpm.
Transmission: Mechanical. Supplied by ZF, Germany.
Bogies: B5006 type "lightweight" bogies.
Couplers: BSI at outer ends, bar within unit.
Dimensions: 23.62/23.0 x 2.69 m.
Gangways: London Overground & Chiltern units: Within unit only. West Midlands Trains units: Throughout.
Wheel Arrangement: 2-B (+ B-2) + B-2.
Doors: Twin-leaf sliding plug.
Maximum Speed: 100 mph (London Overground units 75 mph).
Seating Layout: 2+2 facing/unidirectional.
Multiple Working: Within class and with Classes 150, 153, 155, 156, 158, 159, 165, 166 and 170.

Class 172/0. London Overground units. Used on the Gospel Oak–Barking line. To transfer to West Midlands Trains during 2018. DMS–DMS.

59311–318. DMS(W). Bombardier Derby 2009–10. –/60 2W. 41.6 t.
59411–418. DMS. Bombardier Derby 2009–10. –/64. 41.5 t.

172 001	**LO**	A	*LO*	WN	59311	59411
172 002	**LO**	A	*LO*	WN	59312	59412
172 003	**LO**	A	*LO*	WN	59313	59413
172 004	**LO**	A	*LO*	WN	59314	59414
172 005	**LO**	A	*LO*	WN	59315	59415
172 006	**LO**	A	*LO*	WN	59316	59416
172 007	**LO**	A	*LO*	WN	59317	59417
172 008	**LO**	A	*LO*	WN	59318	59418

Class 172/1. Chiltern Railways units. DMSL–DMS.

59111–114. DMSL. Bombardier Derby 2009–10. –/60(+5) 1TD 2W. 42.4 t.
59211–214. DMS. Bombardier Derby 2009–10. –/80. 41.8 t.

172 101	**CR**	A	*CR*	AL	59111	59211
172 102	**CR**	A	*CR*	AL	59112	59212
172 103	**CR**	A	*CR*	AL	59113	59213
172 104	**CR**	A	*CR*	AL	59114	59214

Class 172/2. West Midlands Trains 2-car units. DMSL–DMS. Used on local services via Birmingham Snow Hill.

50211–222. DMSL. Bombardier Derby 2010–11. –/52(+11) 1TD 2W. 42.5 t.
79211–222. DMS. Bombardier Derby 2010–11. –/68(+8). 41.9 t.

172 211	**LM**	P	*WM*	TS	50211	79211
172 212	**LM**	P	*WM*	TS	50212	79212
172 213	**LM**	P	*WM*	TS	50213	79213
172 214	**LM**	P	*WM*	TS	50214	79214
172 215	**LM**	P	*WM*	TS	50215	79215
172 216	**LM**	P	*WM*	TS	50216	79216
172 217	**LM**	P	*WM*	TS	50217	79217
172 218	**LM**	P	*WM*	TS	50218	79218
172 219	**LM**	P	*WM*	TS	50219	79219
172 220	**LM**	P	*WM*	TS	50220	79220
172 221	**LM**	P	*WM*	TS	50221	79221
172 222	**LM**	P	*WM*	TS	50222	79222

Class 172/3. West Midlands Trains 3-car units. DMSL–MS–DMS. Used on local services via Birmingham Snow Hill.

50331–345. DMSL. Bombardier Derby 2010–11. –/52(+11) 1TD 2W. 42.5 t.
56331–345. MS. Bombardier Derby 2010–11. –/72(+8). 38.8 t.
79331–345. DMS. Bombardier Derby 2010–11. –/68(+8). 41.9 t.

172 331	**LM**	P	*WM*	TS	50331	56331	79331
172 332	**LM**	P	*WM*	TS	50332	56332	79332
172 333	**LM**	P	*WM*	TS	50333	56333	79333
172 334	**LM**	P	*WM*	TS	50334	56334	79334
172 335	**LM**	P	*WM*	TS	50335	56335	79335
172 336	**LM**	P	*WM*	TS	50336	56336	79336

172 337	**LM**	P	*WM*	TS	50337	56337	79337
172 338	**LM**	P	*WM*	TS	50338	56338	79338
172 339	**WM**	P	*WM*	TS	50339	56339	79339
172 340	**LM**	P	*WM*	TS	50340	56340	79340
172 341	**LM**	P	*WM*	TS	50341	56341	79341
172 342	**LM**	P	*WM*	TS	50342	56342	79342
172 343	**LM**	P	*WM*	TS	50343	56343	79343
172 344	**LM**	P	*WM*	TS	50344	56344	79344
172 345	**LM**	P	*WM*	TS	50345	56345	79345

CLASS 175   CORADIA 1000   ALSTOM

Air conditioned.

Construction: Steel.
Engines: One Cummins N14 of 335 kW (450 hp).
Transmission: Hydraulic. Voith T211rzze to ZF Voith final drive.
Bogies: ACR (Alstom FBO) – LTB-MBS1, TB-MB1, MBS1-LTB.
Couplers: Scharfenberg outer ends and bar within unit (Class 175/1).
Dimensions: 23.7 x 2.73 m.
Gangways: Within unit only.   **Wheel Arrangement:** 2-B (+ B-2) + B-2.
Doors: Single-leaf swing plug.   **Maximum Speed:** 100 mph.
Seating Layout: 2+2 facing/unidirectional.
Multiple Working: Within class and with Class 180.

Class 175/0. DMSL–DMSL. 2-car units.

DMSL(A). Alstom Birmingham 1999–2000. –/54 1TD 2W. 48.8 t.
DMSL(B). Alstom Birmingham 1999–2000. –/64 1T. 50.7 t.

175 001	**AV**	A	*AW*	CH	50701	79701
175 002	**AV**	A	*AW*	CH	50702	79702
175 003	**AV**	A	*AW*	CH	50703	79703
175 004	**AV**	A	*AW*	CH	50704	79704
175 005	**AV**	A	*AW*	CH	50705	79705
175 006	**AV**	A	*AW*	CH	50706	79706
175 007	**AV**	A	*AW*	CH	50707	79707
175 008	**AV**	A	*AW*	CH	50708	79708
175 009	**AV**	A	*AW*	CH	50709	79709
175 010	**AV**	A	*AW*	CH	50710	79710
175 011	**AV**	A	*AW*	CH	50711	79711

Class 175/1. DMSL–MSL–DMSL. 3-car units.

DMSL(A). Alstom Birmingham 1999–2001. –/54 1TD 2W. 50.7 t.
MSL. Alstom Birmingham 1999–2001. –/68 1T. 47.5 t.
DMSL(B). Alstom Birmingham 1999–2001. –/64 1T. 49.5 t.

175 101	**AV**	A	*AW*	CH	50751	56751	79751
175 102	**AV**	A	*AW*	CH	50752	56752	79752
175 103	**AV**	A	*AW*	CH	50753	56753	79753
175 104	**AV**	A	*AW*	CH	50754	56754	79754
175 105	**AV**	A	*AW*	CH	50755	56755	79755
175 106	**AV**	A	*AW*	CH	50756	56756	79756
175 107	**AV**	A	*AW*	CH	50757	56757	79757

175 108	**AV**	A	*AW*	CH	50758	56758	79758
175 109	**AV**	A	*AW*	CH	50759	56759	79759
175 110	**AV**	A	*AW*	CH	50760	56760	79760
175 111	**AV**	A	*AW*	CH	50761	56761	79761
175 112	**AV**	A	*AW*	CH	50762	56762	79762
175 113	**AV**	A	*AW*	CH	50763	56763	79763
175 114	**AV**	A	*AW*	CH	50764	56764	79764
175 115	**AV**	A	*AW*	CH	50765	56765	79765
175 116	**AV**	A	*AW*	CH	50766	56766	79766

CLASS 180   CORADIA 1000   ALSTOM

Air conditioned.

Construction: Steel.
Engines: One Cummins QSK19 of 560 kW (750 hp) at 2100 rpm.
Transmission: Hydraulic. Voith T312br to Voith final drive.
Bogies: ACR (Alstom FBO): LTB1-MBS2, TB1-MB2, TB1-MB2, TB2-MB2, MBS2-LTB1.
Couplers: Scharfenberg outer ends, bar within unit.
Dimensions: 23.71/23.03 x 2.73 m.
Gangways: Within unit only.
Wheel Arrangement: 2-B + B-2 + B-2 + B-2 + B-2.
Doors: Single-leaf swing plug.   **Maximum Speed:** 125 mph.
Seating Layout: 1: 2+1 facing/unidirectional, 2: 2+2 facing/unidirectional.
Multiple Working: Within class and with Class 175.
DMSL(A). Alstom Birmingham 2000–01. –/46 2W 1TD. 51.7 t.
MFL. Alstom Birmingham 2000–01. 42/– 1T 1W + catering point. 49.6 t.
MSL. Alstom Birmingham 2000–01. –/68 1T. 49.5 t.
MSLRB. Alstom Birmingham 2000–01. –/56 1T. 50.3 t.
DMSL(B). Alstom Birmingham 2000–01. –/56 1T. 51.4 t.

180 101	**GC**	A	*GC*	HT	50901	54901	55901	56901	59901
180 102	**FD**	A	*GC*	HT	50902	54902	55902	56902	59902
180 103	**FD**	A	*GC*	HT	50903	54903	55903	56903	59903
180 104	**FD**	A	*GC*	HT	50904	54904	55904	56904	59904
180 105	**GC**	A	*GC*	HT	50905	54905	55905	56905	59905
180 106	**FD**	A	*GC*	HT	50906	54906	55906	56906	59906
180 107	**GC**	A	*GC*	HT	50907	54907	55907	56907	59907
180 108	**GC**	A	*GC*	HT	50908	54908	55908	56908	59908
180 109	**FD**	A	*HT*	OO	50909	54909	55909	56909	59909
180 110	**FD**	A	*HT*	OO	50910	54910	55910	56910	59910
180 111	**FD**	A	*HT*	OO	50911	54911	55911	56911	59911
180 112	**GC**	A	*GC*	HT	50912	54912	55912	56912	59912
180 113	**FD**	A	*HT*	OO	50913	54913	55913	56913	59913
180 114	**GC**	A	*GC*	HT	50914	54914	55914	56914	59914

Names (carried on DMSL(A):

180 105	THE YORKSHIRE ARTIST ASHLEY JACKSON
180 107	HART OF THE NORTH
180 112	JAMES HERRIOT CELEBRATING 100 YEARS 1916–2016
180 114	KIRKGATE CALLING

CLASS 185   DESIRO UK   SIEMENS

Air conditioned. Grammer seating.

Construction: Aluminium.
Engines: One Cummins QSK19 of 560 kW (750 hp) at 2100 rpm.
Transmission: Voith.
Bogies: Siemens.
Couplers: Dellner 12.   **Dimensions:** 23.76/23.75 x 2.66 m.
Gangways: Within unit only.   **Wheel Arrangement:** 2-B + 2-B + B-2.
Doors: Double-leaf sliding plug.   **Maximum Speed:** 100 mph.
Seating Layout: 1: 2+1 facing/unidirectional, 2: 2+2 facing/unidirectional.
Multiple Working: Within class only.

DMCL. Siemens Krefeld 2005–06. 15/18(+8) 2W 1TD + catering point. 55.4 t.
MSL. Siemens Krefeld 2005–06. –/72 1T. 52.7 t.
DMS. Siemens Krefeld 2005–06. –/64(4). 54.9 t.

185 101	**TP**	E	*TP*	AK	51101	53101	54101
185 102	**TP**	E	*TP*	AK	51102	53102	54102
185 103	**TP**	E	*TP*	AK	51103	53103	54103
185 104	**TP**	E	*TP*	AK	51104	53104	54104
185 105	**TP**	E	*TP*	AK	51105	53105	54105
185 106	**TP**	E	*TP*	AK	51106	53106	54106
185 107	**TP**	E	*TP*	AK	51107	53107	54107
185 108	**TP**	E	*TP*	AK	51108	53108	54108
185 109	**TP**	E	*TP*	AK	51109	53109	54109
185 110	**TP**	E	*TP*	AK	51110	53110	54110
185 111	**TP**	E	*TP*	AK	51111	53111	54111
185 112	**TP**	E	*TP*	AK	51112	53112	54112
185 113	**TP**	E	*TP*	AK	51113	53113	54113
185 114	**TP**	E	*TP*	AK	51114	53114	54114
185 115	**TP**	E	*TP*	AK	51115	53115	54115
185 116	**TP**	E	*TP*	AK	51116	53116	54116
185 117	**TP**	E	*TP*	AK	51117	53117	54117
185 118	**TP**	E	*TP*	AK	51118	53118	54118
185 119	**TP**	E	*TP*	AK	51119	53119	54119
185 120	**TP**	E	*TP*	AK	51120	53120	54120
185 121	**TP**	E	*TP*	AK	51121	53121	54121
185 122	**TP**	E	*TP*	AK	51122	53122	54122
185 123	**TP**	E	*TP*	AK	51123	53123	54123
185 124	**TP**	E	*TP*	AK	51124	53124	54124
185 125	**TP**	E	*TP*	AK	51125	53125	54125
185 126	**TP**	E	*TP*	AK	51126	53126	54126
185 127	**TP**	E	*TP*	AK	51127	53127	54127
185 128	**TP**	E	*TP*	AK	51128	53128	54128
185 129	**TP**	E	*TP*	AK	51129	53129	54129
185 130	**TP**	E	*TP*	AK	51130	53130	54130
185 131	**TP**	E	*TP*	AK	51131	53131	54131
185 132	**TP**	E	*TP*	AK	51132	53132	54132
185 133	**TP**	E	*TP*	AK	51133	53133	54133
185 134	**TP**	E	*TP*	AK	51134	53134	54134

185 135	**TP**	E	*TP*	AK	51135	53135	54135
185 136	**TP**	E	*TP*	AK	51136	53136	54136
185 137	**TP**	E	*TP*	AK	51137	53137	54137
185 138	**TP**	E	*TP*	AK	51138	53138	54138
185 139	**TP**	E	*TP*	AK	51139	53139	54139
185 140	**TP**	E	*TP*	AK	51140	53140	54140
185 141	**TP**	E	*TP*	AK	51141	53141	54141
185 142	**TP**	E	*TP*	AK	51142	53142	54142
185 143	**TP**	E	*TP*	AK	51143	53143	54143
185 144	**TP**	E	*TP*	AK	51144	53144	54144
185 145	**TP**	E	*TP*	AK	51145	53145	54145
185 146	**TP**	E	*TP*	AK	51146	53146	54146
185 147	**TP**	E	*TP*	AK	51147	53147	54147
185 148	**TP**	E	*TP*	AK	51148	53148	54148
185 149	**TP**	E	*TP*	AK	51149	53149	54149
185 150	**TP**	E	*TP*	AK	51150	53150	54150
185 151	**TP**	E	*TP*	AK	51151	53151	54151

CLASS 195   CIVITY   CAF

DMS–DMS or DMS–MS–DMS. New units under construction for Northern, for delivery 2018–19. Air conditioned. Full details awaited.

Construction: Aluminium.
Engines: One Rolls-Royce MTU 6H 1800 R85L of 390 kW (523 hp) per car.
Transmission: ZF.
Bogies: CAF.
Couplers: Dellner.
Gangways: Within unit only.
Doors:
Seating Layout:
Multiple Working: Within class only.

Dimensions:
Wheel Arrangement:
Maximum Speed: 100 mph.

Class **195**/0. DMS–DMS. 2-car units.

DMS(A). CAF Irun 2017–19.
DMS(B). CAF Irun 2017–19.

195 001	E	101001	103001
195 002	E	101002	103002
195 003	E	101003	103003
195 004	E	101004	103004
195 005	E	101005	103005
195 006	E	101006	103006
195 007	E	101007	103007
195 008	E	101008	103008
195 009	E	101009	103009
195 010	E	101010	103010
195 011	E	101011	103011
195 012	E	101012	103012

195 013	E	101013	103013
195 014	E	101014	103014
195 015	E	101015	103015
195 016	E	101016	103016
195 017	E	101017	103017
195 018	E	101018	103018
195 019	E	101019	103019
195 020	E	101020	103020
195 021	E	101021	103021
195 022	E	101022	103022
195 023	E	101023	103023
195 024	E	101024	103024
195 025	E	101025	103025

Class 195/1. DMS–MS–DMS. 3-car units.

DMS(A). CAF Irun 2017–19.
MS. CAF Irun 2017–19.
DMS(B). CAF Irun 2017–19.

195 101	E	101101	102101	103101
195 102	E	101102	102102	103102
195 103	E	101103	102103	103103
195 104	E	101104	102104	103104
195 105	E	101105	102105	103105
195 106	E	101106	102106	103106
195 107	E	101107	102107	103107
195 108	E	101108	102108	103108
195 109	E	101109	102109	103109
195 110	E	101110	102110	103110
195 111	E	101111	102111	103111
195 112	E	101112	102112	103112
195 113	E	101113	102113	103113
195 114	E	101114	102114	103114
195 115	E	101115	102115	103115
195 116	E	101116	102116	103116
195 117	E	101117	102117	103117
195 118	E	101118	102118	103118
195 119	E	101119	102119	103119
195 120	E	101120	102120	103120
195 121	E	101121	102121	103121
195 122	E	101122	102122	103122
195 123	E	101123	102123	103123
195 124	E	101124	102124	103124
195 125	E	101125	102125	103125
195 126	E	101126	102126	103126
195 127	E	101127	102127	103127
195 128	E	101128	102128	103128
195 129	E	101129	102129	103129
195 130	E	101130	102130	103130

3.2. DIESEL ELECTRIC UNITS

CLASS 201/202   PRESERVED "HASTINGS" UNIT   BR

DMBS–TSL–TSL–TSRB–TSL–DMBS.

Preserved unit made up from two Class 201 short-frame cars and three Class 202 long-frame cars. The "Hastings" units were made with narrow body-profiles for use on the section between Tonbridge and Battle which had tunnels of restricted loading gauge. These tunnels were converted to single track operation in the 1980s thus allowing standard loading gauge stock to be used. The set also contains a Class 411 EMU trailer (not Hastings line gauge) and a Class 422 EMU buffet car.

Construction: Steel.
Engine: One English Electric 4SRKT Mk. 2 of 450 kW (600 hp) at 850 rpm.
Main Generator: English Electric EE824.
Traction Motors: Two English Electric EE507 mounted on the inner bogie.
Bogies: SR Mk 4. (Former EMU TSL vehicles have Commonwealth bogies).
Couplers: Drophead buckeye.
Dimensions: 18.40 x 2.50 m (60000), 20.35 x 2.50 m (60116/118/529), 18.36 x 2.50 m (60501), 20.35 x 2.82 m (69337), 20.30 x 2.82 m (70262).
Gangways: Within unit only.   **Doors:** Manually operated slam.
Wheel arrangement: 2-Bo + 2-2 + 2-2 + 2-2- + 2-2- + Bo-2.
Brakes: Electro-pneumatic and automatic air.
Maximum Speed: 75 mph.   **Seating Layout:** 2+2 facing.
Multiple Working: Other ex-BR Southern Region DEMU vehicles.

60000. DMBS. Lot No. 30329 Eastleigh 1957. –/22. 55.0 t.
60116. DMBS. Lot No. 30395 Eastleigh 1957. –/31. 56.0 t.
60118. DMBS. Lot No. 30395 Eastleigh 1957. –/30. 56.0 t.
60501. TSL. Lot No. 30331 Eastleigh 1957. –/52 2T. 29.5 t.
60529. TSL. Lot No. 30397 Eastleigh 1957. –/60 2T. 30.5 t.
69337. TSRB (ex-Class 422 EMU). Lot No. 30805 York 1970. –/40. 35.0 t.
70262. TSL (ex-Class 411/5 EMU). Lot No. 30455 Eastleigh 1958. –/64 2T. 31.5 t.

201 001	**G**	HD	*HD*	SE	60116	60529	70262	69337	60501	60118
Spare	**G**	HD	*HD*	SE	60000					

Names:

60000	Hastings	60118	Tunbridge Wells
60116	Mountfield		

CLASS 220   VOYAGER   BOMBARDIER

DMS–MS–MS–DMF. All engines have been derated from 750 hp to 700 hp.

Construction: Steel.
Engine: Cummins QSK19 of 520 kW (700 hp) at 1800 rpm.
Transmission: Two Alstom Onix 800 three-phase traction motors of 275 kW.
Braking: Rheostatic and electro-pneumatic.

Bogies: Bombardier B5005.
Couplers: Dellner 12 at outer ends, bar within unit.
Dimensions: 23.85/23.00 (602xx) x 2.73 m.
Gangways: Within unit only.
Wheel Arrangement: 1A-A1 + 1A-A1 + 1A-A1 + 1A-A1.
Doors: Single-leaf swing plug.
Maximum Speed: 125 m.p.h.
Seating Layout: 1: 2+1 facing/unidirectional, 2: 2+2 mainly unidirectional.
Multiple Working: Within class and with Classes 221 and 222 (in an emergency). Also can be controlled from Class 57/3 locomotives.

DMS. Bombardier Bruges/Wakefield 2000–01. –/42 1TD 1W. 51.1 t.
MS(A). Bombardier Bruges/Wakefield 2000–01. –/66. 45.9 t.
MS(B). Bombardier Bruges/Wakefield 2000–01. –/66 1TD. 46.7 t.
DMF. Bombardier Bruges/Wakefield 2000–01. 26/– 1TD 1W. 50.9 t.

220 001	**XC**	BN	*XC*	CZ	60301	60701	60201	60401
220 002	**XC**	BN	*XC*	CZ	60302	60702	60202	60402
220 003	**XC**	BN	*XC*	CZ	60303	60703	60203	60403
220 004	**XC**	BN	*XC*	CZ	60304	60704	60204	60404
220 005	**XC**	BN	*XC*	CZ	60305	60705	60205	60405
220 006	**XC**	BN	*XC*	CZ	60306	60706	60206	60406
220 007	**XC**	BN	*XC*	CZ	60307	60707	60207	60407
220 008	**XC**	BN	*XC*	CZ	60308	60708	60208	60408
220 009	**XC**	BN	*XC*	CZ	60309	60709	60209	60409
220 010	**XC**	BN	*XC*	CZ	60310	60710	60210	60410
220 011	**XC**	BN	*XC*	CZ	60311	60711	60211	60411
220 012	**XC**	BN	*XC*	CZ	60312	60712	60212	60412
220 013	**XC**	BN	*XC*	CZ	60313	60713	60213	60413
220 014	**XC**	BN	*XC*	CZ	60314	60714	60214	60414
220 015	**XC**	BN	*XC*	CZ	60315	60715	60215	60415
220 016	**XC**	BN	*XC*	CZ	60316	60716	60216	60416
220 017	**XC**	BN	*XC*	CZ	60317	60717	60217	60417
220 018	**XC**	BN	*XC*	CZ	60318	60718	60218	60418
220 019	**XC**	BN	*XC*	CZ	60319	60719	60219	60419
220 020	**XC**	BN	*XC*	CZ	60320	60720	60220	60420
220 021	**XC**	BN	*XC*	CZ	60321	60721	60221	60421
220 022	**XC**	BN	*XC*	CZ	60322	60722	60222	60422
220 023	**XC**	BN	*XC*	CZ	60323	60723	60223	60423
220 024	**XC**	BN	*XC*	CZ	60324	60724	60224	60424
220 025	**XC**	BN	*XC*	CZ	60325	60725	60225	60425
220 026	**XC**	BN	*XC*	CZ	60326	60726	60226	60426
220 027	**XC**	BN	*XC*	CZ	60327	60727	60227	60427
220 028	**XC**	BN	*XC*	CZ	60328	60728	60228	60428
220 029	**XC**	BN	*XC*	CZ	60329	60729	60229	60429
220 030	**XC**	BN	*XC*	CZ	60330	60730	60230	60430
220 031	**XC**	BN	*XC*	CZ	60331	60731	60231	60431
220 032	**XC**	BN	*XC*	CZ	60332	60732	60232	60432
220 033	**XC**	BN	*XC*	CZ	60333	60733	60233	60433
220 034	**XC**	BN	*XC*	CZ	60334	60734	60234	60434

CLASS 221   SUPER VOYAGER   BOMBARDIER

* DMS–MS–MS–MSRMB–DMF (Virgin Trains units) or DMS–MS–(MS)–
MS–DMF (CrossCountry units). Built as tilting units but tilt now isolated on
CrossCountry sets. All engines have been derated from 750 hp to 700 hp.

Construction: Steel.
Engine: Cummins QSK19 of 520 kW (700 hp) at 1800 rpm.
Transmission: Two Alstom Onix 800 three-phase traction motors of 275 kW.
Braking: Rheostatic and electro-pneumatic.
Bogies: Bombardier HVP.
Couplers: Dellner 12 at outer ends, bar within unit.
Dimensions: 23.67 x 2.73 m.
Gangways: Within unit only.
Wheel Arrangement: 1A-A1 + 1A-A1 + 1A-A1 (+ 1A-A1) + 1A-A1.
Doors: Single-leaf swing plug.
Maximum Speed: 125 mph.
Seating Layout: 1: 2+1 facing/unidirectional, 2: 2+2 mainly unidirectional.
Multiple Working: Within class and with Classes 220 and 222 (in an
emergency). Also can be controlled from Class 57/3 locomotives.

* Virgin Trains units. MSRMB moved adjacent to the DMF. The seating in
this vehicle (2+2 facing) can be used by First or Standard Class passengers
depending on demand.

Advertising livery: 221 115 Dark grey Bombardier branding on end vehicles.

DMS. Bombardier Bruges/Wakefield 2001–02. –/42 1TD 1W. 58.5 t (* 58.9 t.)
60751–794 MS (* MSRMB). Bombardier Bruges/Wakefield 2001–02. –/66
(* –/52). 54.1 t (* 55.9 t.)
60951–994. MS. Bombardier Bruges/Wakefield 2001–02. –/66 1TD (* –/68
1TD). 54.8 t (* 54.3 t.)
60851–890. MS. Bombardier Bruges/Wakefield 2001–02. –/62 1TD (* –/68
1TD). 54.4 t (* 55.0 t.)
DMF. Bombardier Bruges/Wakefield 2001–02. 26/– 1TD 1W. 58.9 t (* 59.1 t.)

221 101	*	**VT**	BN	*VW*	CZ	60351	60951	60851	60751	60451
221 102	*	**VT**	BN	*VW*	CZ	60352	60952	60852	60752	60452
221 103	*	**VT**	BN	*VW*	CZ	60353	60953	60853	60753	60453
221 104	*	**VT**	BN	*VW*	CZ	60354	60954	60854	60754	60454
221 105	*	**VT**	BN	*VW*	CZ	60355	60955	60855	60755	60455
221 106	*	**VT**	BN	*VW*	CZ	60356	60956	60856	60756	60456
221 107	*	**VT**	BN	*VW*	CZ	60357	60957	60857	60757	60457
221 108	*	**VT**	BN	*VW*	CZ	60358	60958	60858	60758	60458
221 109	*	**VT**	BN	*VW*	CZ	60359	60959	60859	60759	60459
221 110	*	**VT**	BN	*VW*	CZ	60360	60960	60860	60760	60460
221 111	*	**VT**	BN	*VW*	CZ	60361	60961	60861	60761	60461
221 112	*	**VT**	BN	*VW*	CZ	60362	60962	60862	60762	60462
221 113	*	**VT**	BN	*VW*	CZ	60363	60963	60863	60763	60463
221 114	*	**VT**	BN	*VW*	CZ	60364	60964	60864	60764	60464
221 115	*	**AL**	BN	*VW*	CZ	60365	60965	60865	60765	60465
221 116	*	**VT**	BN	*VW*	CZ	60366	60966	60866	60766	60466
221 117	*	**VT**	BN	*VW*	CZ	60367	60967	60867	60767	60467

221 118	*	VT	BN	VW	CZ	60368	60968	60868	60768	60468
221 119		XC	BN	XC	CZ	60369	60769	60969	60869	60469
221 120		XC	BN	XC	CZ	60370	60770	60970	60870	60470
221 121		XC	BN	XC	CZ	60371	60771	60971	60871	60471
221 122		XC	BN	XC	CZ	60372	60772	60972	60872	60472
221 123		XC	BN	XC	CZ	60373	60773	60973	60873	60473
221 124		XC	BN	XC	CZ	60374	60774	60974	60874	60474
221 125		XC	BN	XC	CZ	60375	60775	60975	60875	60475
221 126		XC	BN	XC	CZ	60376	60776	60976	60876	60476
221 127		XC	BN	XC	CZ	60377	60777	60977	60877	60477
221 128		XC	BN	XC	CZ	60378	60778	60978	60878	60478
221 129		XC	BN	XC	CZ	60379	60779	60979	60879	60479
221 130		XC	BN	XC	CZ	60380	60780	60980	60880	60480
221 131		XC	BN	XC	CZ	60381	60781	60981	60881	60481
221 132		XC	BN	XC	CZ	60382	60782	60982	60882	60482
221 133		XC	BN	XC	CZ	60383	60783	60983	60883	60483
221 134		XC	BN	XC	CZ	60384	60784	60984	60884	60484
221 135		XC	BN	XC	CZ	60385	60785	60985	60885	60485
221 136		XC	BN	XC	CZ	60386	60786		60886	60486
221 137		XC	BN	XC	CZ	60387	60787	60987	60887	60487
221 138		XC	BN	XC	CZ	60388	60788	60988	60888	60488
221 139		XC	BN	XC	CZ	60389	60789	60989	60889	60489
221 140		XC	BN	XC	CZ	60390	60790		60890	60490
221 141		XC	BN	XC	CZ	60391	60791	60991		60491
221 142	*	VT	BN	VW	CZ	60392	60992	60986	60792	60492
221 143	*	VT	BN	VW	CZ	60393	60993	60994	60793	60493
221 144		XC	BN	XC	CZ	60394	60794	60990		60494

Names (carried on MS No. 609xx):

221 101	Louis Bleriot	221 110	James Cook
221 102	John Cabot	221 111	Roald Amundsen
221 103	Christopher Columbus	221 112	Ferdinand Magellan
221 104	Sir John Franklin	221 113	Sir Walter Raleigh
221 105	William Baffin	221 115	Polmadie Depot
221 106	Willem Barents	221 117	The Wrekin Giant
221 107	Sir Martin Frobisher	221 142	BOMBARDIER Voyager
221 108	Sir Ernest Shackleton	221 143	Auguste Picard
221 109	Marco Polo		

CLASS 222   MERIDIAN   BOMBARDIER

Construction: Steel.
Engine: Cummins QSK19 of 560 kW (750 hp) at 1800 rpm.
Transmission: Two Alstom Onix 800 three-phase traction motors of 275 kW.
Braking: Rheostatic and electro-pneumatic.
Bogies: Bombardier B5005.   **Dimensions:** 23.85/23.00 x 2.73 m.
Couplers: Dellner at outer ends, bar within unit.
Gangways: Within unit only.   **Wheel Arrangement:** All cars 1A-A1.
Doors: Single-leaf swing plug.   **Maximum Speed:** 125 mph.
Seating Layout: 1: 2+1, 2: 2+2 facing/unidirectional.
Multiple Working: Within class and with Classes 220 and 221 (in an emergency).

222 001–006. 7-car units. DMF–MF–MF–MSRMB–MS–MS–DMS.

The 7-car units were built as 9-car units, before being reduced to 8-car sets and then later to 7-car sets to strengthen all 4-car units to 5-cars. 222 007 was built as a 9-car unit but later reduced to a 5-car unit.

DMRF. Bombardier Bruges 2004–05. 22/– 1TD 1W. 52.8 t.
MF. Bombardier Bruges 2004–05. 42/– 1T. 46.8 t.
MSRMB. Bombardier Bruges 2004–05. –/62. 48.0 t.
MS. Bombardier Bruges 2004–05. –/68 1T. 47.0 t.
DMS. Bombardier Bruges 2004–05. –/38 1TD 1W. 49.4 t.

222 001	**ST**	E	*EM*	DY	60241	60445	60341	60621
					60561	60551	60161	
222 002	**ST**	E	*EM*	DY	60242	60346	60342	60622
					60562	60544	60162	
222 003	**ST**	E	*EM*	DY	60243	60446	60343	60623
					60563	60553	60163	
222 004	**ST**	E	*EM*	DY	60244	60345	60344	60624
					60564	60554	60164	
222 005	**ST**	E	*EM*	DY	60245	60347	60443	60625
					60555	60565	60165	
222 006	**ST**	E	*EM*	DY	60246	60447	60441	60626
					60566	60556	60166	

Names (carried on MSRMB or DMS (222 003)):

222 001   THE ENTREPRENEUR EXPRESS
222 002   THE CUTLERS' COMPANY
222 003   TORNADO
222 004   CHILDREN'S HOSPITAL SHEFFIELD
222 006   THE CARBON CUTTER

222 007–023. 5-car units. DMF–MC–MSRMB–MS–DMS.

DMRF. Bombardier Bruges 2003–04. 22/– 1TD 1W. 52.8 t.
MC. Bombardier Bruges 2003–04. 28/22 1T. 48.6 t.
MSRMB. Bombardier Bruges 2003–04. –/62. 49.6 t.
MS. Bombardier Bruges 2004–05. –/68 1T. 47.0 t.
DMS. Bombardier Bruges 2003–04. –/40 1TD 1W. 51.0 t.

222 007	**ST**	E	*EM*	DY	60247	60442	60627	60567	60167

222 008	**ST**	E	*EM*	DY	60248 60918 60628 60545 60168
222 009	**ST**	E	*EM*	DY	60249 60919 60629 60557 60169
222 010	**ST**	E	*EM*	DY	60250 60920 60630 60546 60170
222 011	**ST**	E	*EM*	DY	60251 60921 60631 60531 60171
222 012	**ST**	E	*EM*	DY	60252 60922 60632 60532 60172
222 013	**ST**	E	*EM*	DY	60253 60923 60633 60533 60173
222 014	**ST**	E	*EM*	DY	60254 60924 60634 60534 60174
222 015	**ST**	E	*EM*	DY	60255 60925 60635 60535 60175
222 016	**ST**	E	*EM*	DY	60256 60926 60636 60536 60176
222 017	**ST**	E	*EM*	DY	60257 60927 60637 60537 60177
222 018	**ST**	E	*EM*	DY	60258 60928 60638 60444 60178
222 019	**ST**	E	*EM*	DY	60259 60929 60639 60547 60179
222 020	**ST**	E	*EM*	DY	60260 60930 60640 60543 60180
222 021	**ST**	E	*EM*	DY	60261 60931 60641 60552 60181
222 022	**ST**	E	*EM*	DY	60262 60932 60642 60542 60182
222 023	**ST**	E	*EM*	DY	60263 60933 60643 60541 60183

Names (carried on MSRMB or DMS):

222 008 Derby Etches Park
222 011 Sheffield City Battalion 1914–1918
222 015 175 YEARS OF DERBY'S RAILWAYS 1839–2014
222 017 LIONS CLUB INTERNATIONAL CENTENARY 1917–2017
222 022 INVEST IN NOTTINGHAM

222 101–104. 4-car former Hull Trains units. DMF–MC–MSRMB–DMS.

DMRF. Bombardier Bruges 2005. 22/– 1TD 1W. 52.8 t.
MC. Bombardier Bruges 2005. 11/46 1T. 47.1 t.
MSRMB. Bombardier Bruges 2005. –/62. 48.0 t.
DMS. Bombardier Bruges 2005. –/40 1TD 1W. 49.4 t.

222 101	**ST**	E	*EM*	DY	60271 60571 60681 60191
222 102	**ST**	E	*EM*	DY	60272 60572 60682 60192
222 103	**ST**	E	*EM*	DY	60273 60573 60683 60193
222 104	**ST**	E	*EM*	DY	60274 60574 60684 60194

CLASS 230 D-TRAIN METRO-CAMMELL/VIVARAIL

The Class 230 D-Train is a prototype 3-car DEMU rebuilt from former London Underground D78 Stock by Vivarail at Long Marston. The D-Train uses the bodyshells, bogies and electric traction motors of D78 Stock. Instead of being powered by electricity the motors are instead powered by new underfloor-mounted diesel engines – two per driving car. Modern IGBT electronic controls replace the previous mechanical camshaft controllers, incorporating the latest automotive stop-start technology and dynamic braking.

The prototype was due to commence trial operation on the Coventry–Nuneaton line in 2017, but following fire damage sustained during test running in December 2016 this trial was cancelled. West Midlands Trains has ordered three sets for use on the Bedford–Bletchley Marston Vale Line from late 2018 (numbering details awaited).

Vivarail has acquired more than 200 redundant D78 Stock vehicles that are stored at Long Marston and it is hoped that orders for further conversions will be forthcoming.

Construction: Aluminium.
Engine: 2 x Ford Duratorq 3.2 litre engines of 150 kW (200 hp).
Control System: IGBT Inverter.   **Braking:** Rheostatic & Dynamic.
Bogies: Bombardier Flex1000 flexible-frame.
Dimensions: 18.37/18.12 x 2.85 m.
Couplers: LUL automatic wedgelock. **Gangways:** Within unit only.
Wheel Arrangement: Bo-Bo + 2-2 + Bo-Bo.
Doors: Sliding.   **Maximum Speed:** 60 mph.
Seating Layout: Longitudinal or 2+2 facing.
Multiple Working: Within class.

Rebuilt from former London Underground D78 Stock:
300001 rebuilt from Driving Motor 7058; redesignated DMSO(A).
300101 rebuilt from Driving Motor 7511; redesignated DMSO(B).
300201 rebuilt from Trailer 17128; redesignated TSO.

DMSO(A). Metro-Cammell Birmingham 1979–83. 28 t.
TSO. Metro-Cammell Birmingham 1979–83. 20 t.
DMSO(B). Metro-Cammell Birmingham 1979–83. 28 t.

230 001   **VI**   VI   LM   300001 300201 300101

4. ELECTRIC MULTIPLE UNITS

INTRODUCTION

This section contains details of all Electric Multiple Units, usually referred to as EMUs, which can run on Britain's national railway network.

The number of EMUs in operation has been steadily increasing in recent years as both more lines have been opened or have been electrified and as the number of passengers travelling on the network has increased. EMUs work a wide variety of services, from long distance Intercity (such as the Class 390 Pendolinos) to inter-urban and suburban duties.

LAYOUT OF INFORMATION

25 kV AC 50 Hz overhead EMUs and dual voltage EMUs are listed in numerical order of set numbers. Individual "loose" vehicles are listed in numerical order after vehicles formed into fixed formations.

750 V DC third rail EMUs are listed in numerical order of class number, then in numerical order of set number. Some of these use the former Southern Region four-digit set numbers. These are derived from theoretical six digit set numbers which are the four-digit set number prefixed by the first two numbers of the class.

Where sets or vehicles have been renumbered in recent years, former numbering detail is shown alongside current detail. Each entry is laid out as in the following example:

Set No.	Detail	Livery	Owner	Operator	Allocation	Formation
5912	*	SS	P	SW	WD	77835 62837 67400 77836

Codes: Codes are used to denote the livery, owner, operator and depot allocation of each Electric Multiple Unit. Details of these can be found in section 6 of this book. Where a unit or spare car is off-lease, the operator column is left blank.

Detail Differences: Detail differences which currently affect the areas and types of train which vehicles may work are shown, plus differences in interior layout. Where such differences occur within a class, these are shown either in the heading information or alongside the individual set or vehicle number.

Set Formations: Regular set formations are shown where these are normally maintained. Readers should note set formations might be temporarily varied from time to time to suit maintenance and/or operational requirements. Vehicles shown as "Spare" are not formed in any regular set formation.

Names: Only names carried with official sanction are listed. Names are shown in UPPER/lower case characters as actually shown on the name carried on the vehicle(s). Unless otherwise shown, complete units are regarded as named rather than just the individual car(s) which carry the name.

GENERAL INFORMATION

CLASSIFICATION AND NUMBERING

25 kV AC 50 Hz overhead and "Versatile" EMUs are classified in the series 300–399. 750 V DC third rail EMUs are classified in the series 400–599. More recently dual-voltage units have been numbered in the 700+ series and Hitachi IEP units in the 800+ series. Classes 800 and 802 are bi-mode units which can operate under both diesel or electric power.

Until 2014 EMU individual cars were numbered in the series 61000–78999, except for vehicles used on the Isle of Wight – which are numbered in a separate series, and the Class 378s, 380s and 395s, which took up the 38xxx and 39xxx series'.

For all new vehicles allocated by the Rolling Stock Library since 2014 6-digit vehicle numbers are being used.

Any vehicle constructed or converted to replace another vehicle following accident damage and carrying the same number as the original vehicle is denoted by the suffix[II] in this publication

WHEEL ARRANGEMENT

A system whereby the number of powered axles on a bogie or frame is denoted by a letter (A = 1, B = 2, C= 3 etc) and the number of unpowered axles is denoted by a number is used in this publication. The letter "o" after a letter indicates that each axle is individually powered.

UNITS OF MEASUREMENT

Principal details and dimensions are quoted for each class in metric and/or imperial units as considered appropriate bearing in mind common UK usage.

All dimensions and weights are quoted for vehicles in an "as new" condition with all necessary supplies (eg oil, water, sand) on board. Dimensions are quoted in the order Length – Width. All lengths quoted are over buffers or couplers as appropriate. Where two lengths are quoted, the first refers to outer vehicles in a set and the second to inner vehicles. All width dimensions quoted are maxima. All weights are shown as metric tonnes (t = tonnes).

Bogie Types are quoted in the format motored/non-motored (eg BP20/BT13 denotes BP20 motored bogies and BT non-motored bogies).

Unless noted to the contrary, all vehicles listed have bar couplers at non-driving ends.

Traction motors power details refer to each motored car per unit.

Vehicles ordered under the auspices of BR were allocated a Lot (batch) number when ordered and these are quoted in class headings and sub-headings. Vehicles ordered since 1995 have no Lot Numbers, but the manufacturer and location that they were built is given.

OPERATING CODES

These codes are used by train operating company staff to describe the various different types of vehicles and normally appear on data panels on the inner (ie non driving) ends of vehicles.

A "B" prefix indicates a battery vehicle.

A "P" prefix indicates a trailer vehicle on which is mounted the pantograph, instead of the default case where the pantograph is mounted on a motor vehicle.

The first part of the code describes whether or not the car has a motor or a driving cab as follows:

DM Driving motor   DT Driving trailer   M   Motor   T   Trailer

The next letter is a "B" for cars with a brake compartment.
This is followed by the saloon details:

F   First   S   Standard   C Composite

The next letter denotes the style of accommodation, which is "O" for Open for all EMU vehicles still in service.

Finally vehicles with a buffet or kitchen area are suffixed RB or RMB for a miniature buffet counter.

Where two vehicles of the same type are formed within the same unit, the above codes may be suffixed by (A) and (B) to differentiate between vehicles.

A composite is a vehicle containing both First and Standard Class accommodation, whilst a brake vehicle is a vehicle containing separate specific accommodation for the conductor.

ACCOMMODATION

The information given in class headings and sub-headings is in the form F/S nT (or TD) nW. For example 12/54 1T 1W denotes 12 First Class and 54 Standard Class seats, one toilet and one space for a wheelchair. A number in brackets (ie (+2)) denotes tip-up seats (in addition to the fixed seats). Tip-up seats in vestibules do not count. The seating layout of open saloons is shown as 2+1, 2+2 or 3+2 as the case may be. Where units have First Class accommodation as well as Standard Class and the layout is different for each class then these are shown separately prefixed by "1:" and "2:". TD denotes a universal access toilet suitable for use by a disabled person.

NEW EMUS ON ORDER

Where possible all EMUs for which firm orders have been placed are
listed in this book, where numbers have been allocated. However there
are several orders for new EMUs for which the unit number and/or vehicle
number series' have not yet been confirmed. EMUs or bi-mode units that
are on order but are not shown in this book are summarised in the table
below:

Class	Manufacturer	Operator	Quantity	Delivery dates
701	Bombardier	South Western Railway	60 x 10-car	2019–20
701	Bombardier	South Western Railway	30 x 5-car	2019–20
720	Bombardier	c2c	6 x 10-car	2021
745	Stadler	Greater Anglia	20 x 12-car	2019
755	Stadler	Greater Anglia (bi-mode)	14 x 3-car	2019
755	Stadler	Greater Anglia (bi-mode)	24 x 4-car	2019
777	Stadler	Merseyrail	52 x 4-car	2019–20
tbc	Bombardier	West Midlands Trains	45 x 5-car	2020–21
tbc	Bombardier	West Midlands Trains	36 x 3-car	2020–21

4.1. 25 kV AC 50 Hz OVERHEAD & DUAL VOLTAGE UNITS

Except where otherwise stated, all units in this section operate on 25 kV AC 50 Hz overhead only.

CLASS 313   BREL YORK

Inner suburban units.

Formation: DMSO–PTSO–BDMSO or DMSO–TSO–BDMSO.
Systems: 25 kV AC overhead/750 V DC third rail.
Construction: Steel underframe, aluminium alloy body and roof.
Traction Motors: Four GEC G310AZ of 82.125 kW.
Wheel Arrangement: Bo-Bo + 2-2 + Bo-Bo.
Braking: Disc & rheostatic.   **Dimensions:** 20.33/20.18 x 2.82 m.
Bogies: BX1.   **Couplers:** Tightlock.
Gangways: Within unit + end doors. **Control System:** Camshaft.
Doors: Sliding.   **Maximum Speed:** 75 mph.
Seating Layout: Various, see sub-class headings.
Multiple Working: Within class.

DMSO. Lot No. 30879 1976–77. –/74. 36.0 t.
PTSO. Lot No. 30880 1976–77. –/83. 31.0 t.
BDMSO. Lot No. 30885 1976–77. –/74. 37.5 t.

Class 313/0. Standard Design. Refurbished with high-back seating (3+2 facing).
Fitted with tripcocks for operating between Moorgate and Drayton Park.

313018	**FU**	E	*GN*	HE	62546	71230	62610
313024	**FU**	E	*GN*	HE	62552	71236	62616
313025	**FU**	E	*GN*	HE	62553	71237	62617
313026	**FU**	E	*GN*	HE	62554	71238	62618
313027	**FU**	E	*GN*	HE	62555	71239	62619
313028	**FU**	E	*GN*	HE	62556	71240	62620
313029	**FU**	E	*GN*	HE	62557	71241	62621
313030	**FU**	E	*GN*	HE	62558	71242	62622
313031	**FU**	E	*GN*	HE	62559	71243	62623
313032	**FU**	E	*GN*	HE	62560	71244	62643
313033	**FU**	E	*GN*	HE	62561	71245	62625
313035	**FU**	E	*GN*	HE	62563	71247	62627
313036	**FU**	E	*GN*	HE	62564	71248	62628
313037	**FU**	E	*GN*	HE	62565	71249	62629
313038	**FU**	E	*GN*	HE	62566	71250	62630
313039	**FU**	E	*GN*	HE	62567	71251	62631
313040	**FU**	E	*GN*	HE	62568	71252	62632
313041	**FU**	E	*GN*	HE	62569	71253	62633
313042	**FU**	E	*GN*	HE	62570	71254	62634
313043	**FU**	E	*GN*	HE	62571	71255	62635
313044	**FU**	E	*GN*	HE	62572	71256	62636
313045	**FU**	E	*GN*	HE	62573	71257	62637

313046	**FU**	E	*GN*	HE	62574	71258	62638
313047	**FU**	E	*GN*	HE	62575	71259	62639
313048	**FU**	E	*GN*	HE	62576	71260	62640
313049	**FU**	E	*GN*	HE	62577	71261	62641
313050	**FU**	E	*GN*	HE	62578	71262	62649
313051	**FU**	E	*GN*	HE	62579	71263	62624
313052	**FU**	E	*GN*	HE	62580	71264	62644
313053	**FU**	E	*GN*	HE	62581	71265	62645
313054	**FU**	E	*GN*	HE	62582	71266	62646
313055	**FU**	E	*GN*	HE	62583	71267	62647
313056	**FU**	E	*GN*	HE	62584	71268	62648
313057	**FU**	E	*GN*	HE	62585	71269	62642
313058	**FU**	E	*GN*	HE	62586	71270	62650
313059	**FU**	E	*GN*	HE	62587	71271	62651
313060	**FU**	E	*GN*	HE	62588	71272	62652
313061	**FU**	E	*GN*	HE	62589	71273	62653
313062	**FU**	E	*GN*	HE	62590	71274	62654
313063	**FU**	E	*GN*	HE	62591	71275	62655
313064	**FU**	E	*GN*	HE	62592	71276	62656

Name (carried on PTSO): 313054   Captain William Leefe Robinson V.C.

Class 313/1. Former London Overground units. Original low back seating (3+2 facing). Fitted with tripcocks for operating between Moorgate and Drayton Park. Details as Class 313/0.

313122	**FU**	E	*GN*	HE	62550	71234	62614
313123	**FU**	E	*GN*	HE	62551	71235	62615
313134	**FU**	E	*GN*	HE	62562	71246	62626

Names (carried on PTSO):

313122   Eric Roberts 1946–2012 "The Flying Nottsman"
313134   City of London

Class 313/2. Southern units. Refurbished for Brighton Coastway services. Fitted with 2+2 mainly facing high-back seating. 750 V DC only (pantographs removed).

DMSO. Lot No. 30879 1976–77. –/64. 37.0 t.
TSO. Lot No. 30880 1976–77. –/64(+2). 31.0 t.
BDMSO. Lot No. 30885 1976–77. –/64. 37.0 t.

313201	(313101)	**BG**	BN	*SN*	BI	62529	71213	62593
313202	(313102)	**SN**	BN	*SN*	BI	62530	71214	62594
313203	(313103)	**SN**	BN	*SN*	BI	62531	71215	62595
313204	(313104)	**SN**	BN	*SN*	BI	62532	71216	62596
313205	(313105)	**SN**	BN	*SN*	BI	62533	71217	62597
313206	(313106)	**SN**	BN	*SN*	BI	62534	71218	62598
313207	(313107)	**SN**	BN	*SN*	BI	62535	71219	62599
313208	(313108)	**SN**	BN	*SN*	BI	62536	71220	62600
313209	(313109)	**SN**	BN	*SN*	BI	62537	71221	62601
313210	(313110)	**SN**	BN	*SN*	BI	62538	71222	62602
313211	(313111)	**SN**	BN	*SN*	BI	62539	71223	62603
313212	(313112)	**SN**	BN	*SN*	BI	62540	71224	62604

313213	(313113)	**SN**	BN	*SN*	BI	62541	71225	62605
313214	(313114)	**SN**	BN	*SN*	BI	62542	71226	62606
313215	(313115)	**SN**	BN	*SN*	BI	62543	71227	62607
313216	(313116)	**SN**	BN	*SN*	BI	62544	71228	62608
313217	(313117)	**SN**	BN	*SN*	BI	62545	71229	62609
313219	(313119)	**SN**	BN	*SN*	BI	62547	71231	62611
313220	(313120)	**SN**	BN	*SN*	BI	62548	71232	62612

CLASS 314   BREL YORK

Inner suburban units.

Formation: DMSO–PTSO–DMSO.
Construction: Steel underframe, aluminium alloy body and roof.
Traction Motors: Four GEC G310AZ (* Brush TM61-53) of 82.125 kW.
Wheel Arrangement: Bo-Bo + 2-2 + Bo-Bo.
Braking: Disc & rheostatic.   **Dimensions:** 20.33/20.18 x 2.82 m.
Bogies: BX1.   **Couplers:** Tightlock.
Gangways: Within unit + end doors. **Control System:** Thyristor.
Doors: Sliding.   **Maximum Speed:** 70 mph.
Seating Layout: 3+2 low-back facing.
Multiple Working: Within class and with Class 315.

DMSO. Lot No. 30912 1979. –/68. 34.5 t.
64588[II]. **DMSO.** Lot No. 30908 1978–80. Rebuilt Railcare Glasgow 1996 from
Class 507 No. 64426. The original 64588 was scrapped. –/74. 34.5 t.
PTSO. Lot No. 30913 1979. –/76. 33.0 t.

314201	*	**SC**	A	*SR*	GW	64583	71450	64584
314202	*	**SC**	A	*SR*	GW	64585	71451	64586
314203	*	**SR**	A	*SR*	GW	64587	71452	64588[II]
314204	*	**SR**	A	*SR*	GW	64589	71453	64590
314205	*	**SC**	A	*SR*	GW	64591	71454	64592
314206	*	**SC**	A	*SR*	GW	64593	71455	64594
314207		**SC**	A	*SR*	GW	64595	71456	64596
314208		**SR**	A	*SR*	GW	64597	71457	64598
314209		**SR**	A	*SR*	GW	64599	71458	64600
314210		**SC**	A	*SR*	GW	64601	71459	64602
314211		**SR**	A	*SR*	GW	64603	71460	64604
314212		**SR**	A	*SR*	GW	64605	71461	64606
314213		**SC**	A	*SR*	GW	64607	71462	64608
314214		**SR**	A	*SR*	GW	64609	71463	64610
314215		**SC**	A	*SR*	GW	64611	71464	64612
314216		**SC**	A	*SR*	GW	64613	71465	64614

CLASS 315   BREL YORK

Inner suburban units.

Formation: DMSO–TSO–PTSO–DMSO.
Construction: Steel underframe, aluminium alloy body and roof.
Traction Motors: Four Brush TM61-53 (* GEC G310AZ) of 82.125 kW.

Wheel Arrangement: Bo-Bo + 2-2 + 2-2 + Bo-Bo.
Braking: Disc & rheostatic.   **Dimensions:** 20.18 x 2.82 m.
Bogies: BX1.   **Couplers:** Tightlock.
Gangways: Within unit + end doors. **Control System:** Thyristor.
Doors: Sliding.   **Maximum Speed:** 75 mph.
Seating Layout: 3+2 low-back facing.
Multiple Working: Within class and with Class 314 and 317.

DMSO. Lot No. 30902 1980–81. –/74. 38.2 t.
TSO. Lot No. 30904 1980–81. –/86. 27.4 t.
PTSO. Lot No. 30903 1980–81. –/75(+7) 2W. 33.8 t.

315801	**LO**	E	*LO*	IL	64461	71281	71389	64462
315802	**LO**	E	*LO*	IL	64463	71282	71390	64464
315803	**LO**	E	*LO*	IL	64465	71283	71391	64466
315804	**LO**	E	*LO*	IL	64467	71284	71392	64468
315805	**LO**	E	*LO*	IL	64469	71285	71393	64470
315806	**LO**	E	*LO*	IL	64471	71286	71394	64472
315807	**LO**	E	*LO*	IL	64473	71287	71395	64474
315808	**LO**	E	*LO*	IL	64475	71288	71396	64476
315809	**LO**	E	*LO*	IL	64477	71289	71397	64478
315810	**LO**	E	*LO*	IL	64479	71290	71398	64480
315811	**LO**	E	*LO*	IL	64481	71291	71399	64482
315812	**LO**	E	*LO*	IL	64483	71292	71400	64484
315813	**LO**	E	*LO*	IL	64485	71293	71401	64486
315814	**LO**	E	*LO*	IL	64487	71294	71402	64488
315815	**LO**	E	*LO*	IL	64489	71295	71403	64490
315816	**LO**	E	*LO*	IL	64491	71296	71404	64492
315817	**LO**	E	*LO*	IL	64493	71297	71405	64494
315818	**TF**	E	*XR*	IL	64495	71298	71406	64496
315819	**TF**	E	*XR*	IL	64497	71299	71407	64498
315820	**TF**	E	*XR*	IL	64499	71300	71408	64500
315821	**TF**	E	*XR*	IL	64501	71301	71409	64502
315822	**TF**	E	*XR*	IL	64503	71302	71410	64504
315823	**TF**	E	*XR*	IL	64505	71303	71411	64506
315824	**TF**	E	*XR*	IL	64507	71304	71412	64508
315825	**TF**	E	*XR*	IL	64509	71305	71413	64510
315826	**TF**	E	*XR*	IL	64511	71306	71414	64512
315827	**TF**	E	*XR*	IL	64513	71307	71415	64514
315828	**TF**	E	*XR*	IL	64515	71308	71416	64516
315829	**TF**	E	*XR*	IL	64517	71309	71417	64518
315830	**TF**	E	*XR*	IL	64519	71310	71418	64520
315831	**TF**	E	*XR*	IL	64521	71311	71419	64522
315832	**TF**	E		ZN	64523	71312	71420	64524
315833	**TF**	E	*XR*	IL	64525	71313	71421	64526
315834	**TF**	E	*XR*	IL	64527	71314	71422	64528
315835	**TF**	E		ZN	64529	71315	71423	64530
315836	**TF**	E	*XR*	IL	64531	71316	71424	64532
315837	**TF**	E	*XR*	IL	64533	71317	71425	64534
315838	**TF**	E	*XR*	IL	64535	71318	71426	64536
315839	**TF**	E	*XR*	IL	64537	71319	71427	64538
315840	**TF**	E		ZN	64539	71320	71428	64555

315841		TF	E	XR	IL	64541	71321	71429	64542
315842	*	TF	E	XR	IL	64543	71322	71430	64544
315843	*	TF	E	XR	IL	64545	71323	71431	64546
315844	*	TF	E	XR	IL	64547	71324	71432	64548
315845	*	TF	E	XR	IL	64549	71325	71433	64550
315846	*	TF	E	XR	IL	64551	71326	71434	64552
315847	*	TF	E	XR	IL	64553	71327	71435	64554
315848	*	TF	E	XR	IL	64540	71328	71436	64556
315849	*	TF	E	XR	IL	64557	71329	71437	64558
315850	*	TF	E		ZN	64559	71330	71438	64560
315851	*	TF	E	XR	IL	64561	71331	71439	64562
315852	*	TF	E	XR	IL	64563	71332	71440	64564
315853	*	TF	E	XR	IL	64565	71333	71441	64566
315854	*	TF	E	XR	IL	64567	71334	71442	64568
315855	*	TF	E	XR	IL	64569	71335	71443	64570
315856	*	TF	E	XR	IL	64571	71336	71444	64572
315857	*	TF	E	XR	IL	64573	71337	71445	64574
315858	*	TF	E	XR	IL	64575	71338	71446	64576
315859	*	TF	E	XR	IL	64577	71339	71447	64578
315860	*	TF	E		ZN	64579	71340	71448	64580
315861	*	TF	E		ZN	64581	71341	71449	64582

Names (carried on DMSO):

315817	Transport for London
315829	London Borough of Havering Celebrating 40 years
315845	Herbie Woodward

CLASS 317   BREL YORK/DERBY

Outer suburban units.

Formation: Various, see sub-class headings.
Construction: Steel.
Traction Motors: Four GEC G315BZ of 247.5 kW (except 317 722, see below).
Wheel Arrangement: 2-2 + Bo-Bo + 2-2 + 2-2.
Braking: Disc.   **Dimensions:** 19.83/20.18 x 2.82 m.
Bogies: BP20 (MSO), BT13 (others).   **Couplers:** Tightlock.
Gangways: Throughout   **Control System:** Thyristor.
Doors: Sliding.   **Maximum Speed:** 100 mph.
Seating Layout: Various, see sub-class headings.
Multiple Working: Within class & with Classes 315, 318, 319, 320, 321, 322 and 323.

Class 317/1. Pressure ventilated.

Formation: DTSO–MSO–TCO–DTSO.
Seating Layout: 1: 2+2 facing, 2: 3+2 facing.

DTSO(A) Lot No. 30955 York 1981–82. –/74. 29.5 t.
MSO. Lot No. 30958 York 1981–82. –/79. 49.0 t.
TCO. Lot No. 30957 Derby 1981–82. 22/46 2T. 29.0 t.
DTSO(B) Lot No. 30956 York 1981–82. –/71. 29.5 t.

317337	**TL**	A	*GA*	IL	77036	62671	71613	77084
317338	**TL**	A	*GA*	IL	77037	62698	71614	77085
317339	**TL**	A	*GA*	IL	77038	62699	71615	77086
317340	**TL**	A	*GA*	IL	77039	62700	71616	77087
317341	**TL**	A	*GA*	IL	77040	62701	71617	77088
317342	**TL**	A	*GA*	IL	77041	62702	71618	77089
317343	**TL**	A	*GA*	IL	77042	62703	71619	77090
317344	**GA**	A	*GA*	IL	77029	62690	71620	77091
317345	**GA**	A	*GA*	IL	77044	62705	71621	77092
317346	**GA**	A	*GA*	IL	77045	62706	71622	77093
317347	**GA**	A	*GA*	IL	77046	62707	71623	77094
317348	**TL**	A	*GA*	IL	77047	62708	71624	77095

Names (carried on TCO):

317345 Driver John Webb | 317348 Richard A Jenner

Class 317/5. Pressure ventilated. Units renumbered from Class 317/1 in 2005 for West Anglia Metro services. Refurbished with new upholstery and Passenger Information Systems. Details as Class 317/1.

The original DTSO 77048 was written off after the Cricklewood accident of 1983. A replacement vehicle was built at Wolverton in 1987 and given the same number.

317501	**GA**	A	*GA*	IL	77024	62661	71577	77048[ll]
317502	**GA**	A	*GA*	IL	77001	62662	71578	77049
317503	**GA**	A	*GA*	IL	77002	62663	71579	77050
317504	**GA**	A	*GA*	IL	77003	62664	71580	77051
317505	**GA**	A	*GA*	IL	77004	62665	71581	77052
317506	**GA**	A	*GA*	IL	77005	62666	71582	77053
317507	**GA**	A	*GA*	IL	77006	62667	71583	77054
317508	**GA**	A	*GA*	IL	77010	62697	71587	77058
317509	**GA**	A	*GA*	IL	77011	62672	71588	77059
317510	**GA**	A	*GA*	IL	77012	62673	71589	77060
317511	**NC**	A	*GA*	IL	77014	62675	71591	77062
317512	**NC**	A	*GA*	IL	77015	62676	71592	77063
317513	**GA**	A	*GA*	IL	77016	62677	71593	77064
317514	**GA**	A	*GA*	IL	77017	62678	71594	77065
317515	**GA**	A	*GA*	IL	77019	62680	71596	77067

Name (carried on TCO):

317507 University of Cambridge 800 Years 1209–2009

Class 317/6. Convection heating. Units converted from Class 317/2 by Railcare, Wolverton 1998–99 with Chapman seating.

Formation: DTSO–MSO–TSO–DTCO.
Seating Layout: 2+2 facing.

77200–219. DTSO. Lot No. 30994 York 1985–86. –/64. 29.5 t.
77280–283. DTSO. Lot No. 31007 York 1987. –/64. 29.5 t.
62846–865. MSO. Lot No. 30996 York 1985–86. –/71. 49.0 t.
62886–889. MSO. Lot No. 31009 York 1987. –/71. 49.0 t.
71734–753. TSO. Lot No. 30997 York 1985–86. –/60(+3) 2T. 29.0 t.

71762–765. TSO. Lot No. 31010 York 1987. –/60(+3) 2T. 29.0 t.
77220–239. DTCO. Lot No. 30995 York 1985–86. 24/36. 29.5 t.
77284–287. DTCO. Lot No. 31008 York 1987. 24/36. 29.5 t.

317649	**NC**	A	*GA*	IL	77200	62846	71734	77220
317650	**NC**	A	*GA*	IL	77201	62847	71735	77221
317651	**NC**	A	*GA*	IL	77202	62848	71736	77222
317652	**NC**	A	*GA*	IL	77203	62849	71739	77223
317653	**NC**	A	*GA*	IL	77204	62850	71738	77224
317654	**NC**	A	*GA*	IL	77205	62851	71737	77225
317655	**GA**	A	*GA*	IL	77206	62852	71740	77226
317656	**NC**	A	*GA*	IL	77207	62853	71742	77227
317657	**NC**	A	*GA*	IL	77208	62854	71741	77228
317658	**GA**	A	*GA*	IL	77209	62855	71743	77229
317659	**GA**	A	*GA*	IL	77210	62856	71744	77230
317660	**GA**	A	*GA*	IL	77211	62857	71745	77231
317661	**GA**	A	*GA*	IL	77212	62858	71746	77232
317662	**GA**	A	*GA*	IL	77213	62859	71747	77233
317663	**GA**	A	*GA*	IL	77214	62860	71748	77234
317664	**GA**	A	*GA*	IL	77215	62861	71749	77235
317665	**GA**	A	*GA*	IL	77216	62862	71750	77236
317666	**NC**	A	*GA*	IL	77217	62863	71752	77237
317667	**GA**	A	*GA*	IL	77218	62864	71751	77238
317668	**GA**	A	*GA*	IL	77219	62865	71753	77239
317669	**NC**	A	*GA*	IL	77280	62886	71762	77284
317670	**GA**	A	*GA*	IL	77281	62887	71763	77285
317671	**NC**	A	*GA*	IL	77282	62888	71764	77286
317672	**GA**	A	*GA*	IL	77283	62889	71765	77287

Name (carried on DTCO): 317654   Richard Wells

Class 317/7. Units converted from Class 317/1 by Railcare, Wolverton 2000 for Stansted Express services between London Liverpool Street and Stansted. Air conditioning. Fitted with luggage stacks. Displaced from Stansted services in 2011 by Class 379s – most units are now operated by London Overground.

* 317722 has received new Bombardier MJA 280-8 AC traction motors as part of an Angel trial. Two vehicles (77021 and 62682, now in **GA** livery) have also received an interior refurbishment with new Fainsa seating whilst the other two vehicles have been left in their former Stansted Express condition (and still in **NX** livery). Leased to Greater Anglia as a demonstrator unit.

Formation: DTSO–MSO–TSO–DTCO.
Seating Layout: 1: 2+1 facing, 2: 2+2 facing.

DTSO Lot No. 30955 York 1981–82. –/52 + catering point. 31.4 t.
MSO. Lot No. 30958 York 1981–82. –/62 (* –/64). 51.3 t.
TSO. Lot No. 30957 Derby 1981–82. –/42(+5) 1W 1T 1TD. 30.2 t.
DTCO Lot No. 30956 York 1981–82. 22/16 + catering point. 31.6 t.

317708	**LO**	A	*LO*	IL	77007	62668	71584	77055
317709	**LO**	A	*LO*	IL	77008	62669	71585	77056
317710	**LO**	A	*LO*	IL	77009	62670	71586	77057

317714	LO	A	LO	IL	77013	62674	71590	77061
317719	LO	A	LO	IL	77018	62679	71595	77066
317722	* GA/NX	A	GA	IL	77021	62682	71598	77069
317723	LO	A	LO	IL	77022	62683	71599	77070
317729	LO	A	LO	IL	77028	62689	71605	77076
317732	LO	A	LO	IL	77031	62692	71608	77079

Class 317/8. Pressure Ventilated. Units refurbished and renumbered from Class 317/1 in 2005–06 at Wabtec, Doncaster for use on Stansted Express services. Displaced from Stansted services in 2011.

Formation: DTSO–MSO–TCO–DTSO.
Seating Layout: 1: 2+2 facing, 2: 3+2 facing.

DTSO(A) Lot No. 30955 York 1981–82. –/66. 29.5 t.
MSO. Lot No. 30958 York 1981–82. –/71. 49.0 t.
TCO. Lot No. 30957 Derby 1981–82. 20/42 2T († –/62 2T). 29.0 t.
DTSO(B) Lot No. 30956 York 1981–82. –/66. 29.5 t.

317881		GA	A	GA	IL	77020	62681	71597	77068	
317882		GA	A	GA	IL	77023	62684	71600	77071	
317883		GA	A	GA	IL	77000	62685	71601	77072	
317884		NC	A	GA	IL	77025	62686	71602	77073	
317885		GA	A	GA	IL	77026	62687	71603	77074	
317886		NC	A	GA	IL	77027	62688	71604	77075	
317887	†	LO	A	LO	IL	77043	62704	71606	77077	
317888	†	LO	A	LO	IL	77030	62691	71607	77078	
317889	†	LO	A	LO	IL	77032	62693	71609	77080	
317890	†	LO	A	LO	IL	77033	62694	71610	77081	
317891	†	LO	A	LO	IL	77034	62695	71611	77082	
317892	†	LO	A	LO	IL	77035	62696	71612	77083	Ilford Depot

CLASS 318   BREL YORK

Outer suburban units. Fitted with a universal access toilet to comply with the 2020 accessibility regulations.

Formation: DTSO–MSO–DTSO.
Construction: Steel.
Traction Motors: Four Brush TM 2141 of 268 kW.
Wheel Arrangement: 2-2 + Bo-Bo + 2-2.
Braking: Disc.   **Dimensions:** 19.83/19.92 x 2.82 m.
Bogies: BP20 (MSO), BT13 (others).   **Couplers:** Tightlock.
Gangways: Within unit.   **Control System:** Thyristor.
Doors: Sliding.   **Maximum Speed:** 90 mph.
Seating Layout: 3+2 facing.
Multiple Working: Within class & with Classes 317, 319, 320, 321, 322 and 323.

77240–259. DTSO. Lot No. 30999 1985–86. –/55 1TD 2W. 32.0 t.
77288. DTSO. Lot No. 31020 1987. –/55 1TD 2W. 32.0 t.
62866–885. MSO. Lot No. 30998 1985–86. –/79. 53.0 t.
62890. MSO. Lot No. 31019 1987. –/79. 53.0 t.
77260–279. DTSO. Lot No. 31000 1985–86. –/74. 31.6 t.
77289. DTSO. Lot No. 31021 1987. –/74. 31.6 t.

TL	P		LM	77295	62893	71774	77294
TL	P		ZN	77297	62894	71775	77296
TL	P		ZN	77299	62895	71776	77298
TL	P		LM	77301	62896	71777	77300
TL	P		ZN	77303	62897	71778	77302
TL	P		LM	77305	62898	71779	77304
TL	P		LM	77307	62899	71780	77306
TL	P		LM	77309	62900	71781	77308
TL	P		LM	77311	62901	71782	77310
TL	P		CP	77313	62902	71783	77312
LM	P	WM	NN	77315	62903	71784	77314

arried on TSO):

river Mick Winnett	319009 Coquelles
heriton	319011 John Ruskin College

2. DTSO–MSO–TSO–DTCO. Units converted from Class 319/0.

ayout: 1: 2+1 facing, 2: 2+2/3+2 facing.

No. 31022 (odd nos.) 1987–88. –/64. 30.0 t.
No. 31023 1987–88. –/73. 51.0 t.
No. 31024 1987–88. –/52 1T 1TD. 31.0 t.
No. 31025 (even nos.) 1987–88. 18/36. 30.0 t.

*	TL	P		LM	77317	62904	71785	77316
*	TL	P		LM	77319	62905	71786	77318
*	LM	P	WM	NN	77321	62906	71787	77320
*	TL	P		LM	77323	62907	71788	77322 Brighton
*	TL	P		LM	77325	62908	71789	77324
*	TL	P		LM	77327	62909	71790	77326
*	TL	P		CP	77329	62910	71791	77328

9/3. DTSO–MSO–TSO–DTSO. Converted from Class 319/1 by
First Class seats with Standard Class seats.

shed with a new universal access toilet to comply with the 2020
lity regulations. Full details awaited.

ayout: 3+2 facing.

Lot No. 31063 1990. –/72. 29.0 t.
No. 31064 1990. –/79. 50.6 t.
No. 31065 1990. –/74 2T. 31.0 t.
Lot No. 31066 1990. –/77 2W. 29.7 t.

*	NR	P	NO	AN	77459	63043	71929	77458
*	NR	P	NO	AN	77461	63044	71930	77460
*	NR	P	NO	AN	77463	63045	71931	77462
*	NR	P	NO	AN	77465	63046	71932	77464
*	NR	P	NO	AN	77467	63047	71933	77466
*	NR	P	NO	AN	77469	63048	71934	77468
*	NR	P	NO	AN	77471	63049	71935	77470
*	NR	P	NO	AN	77473	63050	71936	77472
*	NR	P	NO	AN	77475	63051	71937	77474

318250	**SR**	E	*SR*	GW	77240	62
318251	**SR**	E	*SR*	GW	77241	62
318252	**SR**	E	*SR*	GW	77242	62
318253	**SR**	E	*SR*	GW	77243	62
318254	**SR**	E	*SR*	GW	77244	62
318255	**SR**	E	*SR*	GW	77245	62
318256	**SR**	E	*SR*	GW	77246	62:
318257	**SR**	E	*SR*	GW	77247	62:
318258	**SR**	E	*SR*	GW	77248	628
318259	**SR**	E	*SR*	GW	77249	628
318260	**SR**	E	*SR*	GW	77250	628
318261	**SR**	E	*SR*	GW	77251	628
318262	**SR**	E	*SR*	GW	77252	628
318263	**SR**	E	*SR*	GW	77253	628
318264	**SR**	E	*SR*	GW	77254	628
318265	**SR**	E	*SR*	GW	77255	628
318266	**SR**	E	*SR*	GW	77256	628
318267	**SR**	E	*SR*	GW	77257	628:
318268	**SR**	E	*SR*	GW	77258	628:
318269	**SR**	E	*SR*	GW	77259	628:
318270	**SR**	E	*SR*	GW	77288	628!

CLASS 319

Express and outer suburban units. Units shown * ⊂
access toilet to comply with the 2020 accessibility
are being rebuilt as bi-mode units and will be renu
number series.

Formation: Various, see sub-class headings.
Systems: 25 kV AC overhead/750 V DC third rail.
Construction: Steel.
Traction Motors: Four GEC G315BZ of 268 kW.
Wheel Arrangement: 2-2 + Bo-Bo + 2-2 + 2-2.
Braking: Disc.   **Dimensions:**
Bogies: P7-4 (MSO), T3-7 (others).   **Couplers:** Tig
Gangways: Within unit + end doors. **Control Syste**
Doors: Sliding.   **Maximum Spe**
Seating Layout: Various, see sub-class headings.
Multiple Working: Within class & with Classes 317, 31:

Class 319/0. DTSO–MSO–TSO–DTSO.

Seating Layout: 3+2 facing.

DTSO(A). Lot No. 31022 (odd nos.) 1987–88. –/82 (* –
MSO. Lot No. 31023 1987–88. –/82 (* –/81). 49.2 t (* 5
TSO. Lot No. 31024 1987–88. –/77 2T (* –/63 1TD 2W
(*† 32.5 t).
DTSO(B). Lot No. 31025 (even nos.) 1987–88. –/78 (*

| 319001 | | **TL** | P | | LM | 77291 | 62891 |
| 319002 | * | **TL** | P | | LM | 77293 | 62892 |

| 319003 |
| 319004 |
| 319005 |
| 319006 |
| 319007 |
| 319008 |
| 319009 |
| 319010 |
| 319011 |
| 319012 |
| 319013 |

Names

319001
319008

Class 31

Seating

DTSO. L
MSO. L
TSO. Lc
DTCO. L

319214
319215
319216
319217
319218
319219
319220

Class :
replaci

* Refur
access

Seatin

DTSO(
MSO. L
TSO. L
DTSO

319362
319362
319362
319364
319364
319364
319364
319364

319370	*	**NR**	P	*NO*	AN	77477	63052	71938	77476
319371	*	**NR**	P	*NO*	AN	77479	63053	71939	77478
319372		**TL**	P		LM	77481	63054	71940	77480
319373		**TL**	P		LM	77483	63055	71941	77482
319374	*	**NR**	P	*NO*	AN	77485	63056	71942	77484
319375	*	**NR**	P	*NO*	AN	77487	63057	71943	77486
319376	*	**NR**	P	*NO*	AN	77489	63058	71944	77488
319377	*	**NR**	P	*NO*	AN	77491	63059	71945	77490
319378	*	**NR**	P	*NO*	AN	77493	63060	71946	77492
319379	*	**NR**	P	*NO*	AN	77495	63061	71947	77494
319380	*	**NR**	P	*NO*	AN	77497	63062	71948	77496
319381	*	**NR**	P	*NO*	AN	77973	63093	71979	77974
319382	*	**NR**	P	*NO*	AN	77975	63094	71980	77976
319383	*	**NR**	P	*NO*	AN	77977	63095	71981	77978
319384	*	**NR**	P	*NO*	AN	77979	63096	71982	77980
319385	*	**NR**	P	*NO*	AN	77981	63097	71983	77982
319386	*	**NR**	P	*NO*	AN	77983	63098	71984	77984

Class 319/4. DTCO–MSO–TSO–DTSO. Converted from Class 319/0. Refurbished with carpets. DTSO(A) converted to composite.

319424/434/456 are at Brush, Loughborough for conversion to Class 769 bi-mode units, with diesel engines fitted. 319431/442/448/450/458 will follow.

Seating Layout: 1: 2+1 facing 2: 2+2/3+2 facing.

77331–381. DTCO. Lot No. 31022 (odd nos.) 1987–88. 12/51 (* 12/50). 30.0t (* 31.0 t).
77431–457. DTCO. Lot No. 31038 (odd nos.) 1988. 12/51 (* 12/50). 30.0t (* 31.0 t).
62911–936. MSO. Lot No. 31023 1987–88. –/74 (* –/75). 49.2t (* 52.4 t).
62961–974. MSO. Lot No. 31039 1988. –/74 (* –/75). 49.2 t (* 52.4 t).
71792–817. TSO. Lot No. 31024 1987–88. –/67 2T (* –/58 1TD 2W). 31.0t (* 33.7 t).
71866–879. TSO. Lot No. 31040 1988. –67 2T (* –/58 1TD 2W). 31.0t (* 33.7 t).
77330–380. DTSO. Lot No. 31025 (even nos.) 1987–88. –/71 1W (* –/73). 28.1t (* 30.7 t).
77430–456. DTSO. Lot No. 31041 (even nos.) 1988. –/71 1W (* –/73). 28.1t (* 30.7 t).

319421	*	**TL**	P		LM	77331	62911	71792	77330
319422	*	**TL**	P		LM	77333	62912	71793	77332
319423	*	**TL**	P		LM	77335	62913	71794	77334
319424	*	**NR**	P		LB	77337	62914	71795	77336
319425	*	**TL**	P		LM	77339	62915	71796	77338
319426	*	**TL**	P		LM	77341	62916	71797	77340
319427	*	**TL**	P		ZN	77343	62917	71798	77342
319428	*	**TL**	P		LM	77345	62918	71799	77344
319429	*	**LM**	P	*WM*	NN	77347	62919	71800	77346
319430	*	**TL**	P		LM	77349	62920	71801	77348
319431	*	**NR**	P	*NO*	AN	77351	62921	71802	77350
319432	*	**TL**	P		LM	77353	62922	71803	77352
319433	*	**LM**	P	*WM*	NN	77355	62923	71804	77354
319434	*	**NR**	P		LB	77357	62924	71805	77356
319435	*	**TL**	P		LM	77359	62925	71806	77358
319436	*	**TL**	P		LM	77361	62926	71807	77360
319437	*	**TL**	P		LM	77363	62927	71808	77362
319438	*	**TL**	P		LM	77365	62928	71809	77364

319439	*	TL	P		LM	77367	62929	71810	77366
319440	*	TL	P		LM	77369	62930	71811	77368
319441	*	LM	P	WM	NN	77371	62931	71812	77370
319442	*	NR	P	NO	AN	77373	62932	71813	77372
319443	*	TL	P		LM	77375	62933	71814	77374
319444	*	TL	P		LM	77377	62934	71815	77376
319445	*	TL	P		LM	77379	62935	71816	77378
319446	*	TL	P		LM	77381	62936	71817	77380
319447	*	TL	P		LM	77431	62961	71866	77430
319448	*	NR	P	NO	AN	77433	62962	71867	77432
319449	*	TL	P		LM	77435	62963	71868	77434
319450	*	NR	P	NO	AN	77437	62964	71869	77436
319451		FU	P		LM	77439	62965	71870	77438
319452	*	TL	P		LM	77441	62966	71871	77440
319453		FU	P		LM	77443	62967	71872	77442
319454		FU	P		LM	77445	62968	71873	77444
319455		FU	P		LM	77447	62969	71874	77446
319456	*	NR	P		LB	77449	62970	71875	77448
319457	*	LM	P	WM	NN	77451	62971	71876	77450
319458	*	NR	P	NO	AN	77453	62972	71877	77452
319459	*	TL	P		LM	77455	62973	71878	77454
319460	*	LM	P	WM	NN	77457	62974	71879	77456

Name (carried on TSO): 319444 City of St Albans

CLASS 320   BREL YORK

Suburban units. All 320/3s refurbished 2011–13 and fitted with a new universal access toilet to comply with the 2020 accessibility regulations. In 2016 ScotRail received 320411–417 (ex-321 411–417), reformed as 3-cars and also refurbished with a new universal access toilet.

Formation: DTSO–MSO–DTSO.
Construction: Steel
Traction Motors: Four Brush TM2141B of 268 kW.
Wheel Arrangement: 2-2 + Bo-Bo + 2-2.
Braking: Disc.   **Dimensions:** 19.95 x 2.82 m.
Bogies: P7-4 (MSO), T3-7 (others). **Couplers:** Tightlock.
Gangways: Within unit.   **Control System:** Thyristor.
Doors: Sliding.   **Maximum Speed:** 90 mph.
Seating Layout: 3+2 facing.
Multiple Working: Within class & with Classes 317, 318, 319, 321, 322 and 323.

Class 320/3. Original build.

DTSO (A). Lot No. 31060 1990. –/51(+4) 1TD 2W. 31.7 t.
MSO. Lot No. 31062 1990. –/78. 52.6 t.
DTSO (B). Lot No. 31061 1990. –/77. 31.6 t.

320301	SR	E	SR	GW	77899	63021	77921
320302	SR	E	SR	GW	77900	63022	77922
320303	SR	E	SR	GW	77901	63023	77923
320304	SR	E	SR	GW	77902	63024	77924

320305	**SR**	E	*SR*	GW	77903	63025	77925
320306	**SR**	E	*SR*	GW	77904	63026	77926
320307	**SR**	E	*SR*	GW	77905	63027	77927
320308	**SR**	E	*SR*	GW	77906	63028	77928
320309	**SR**	E	*SR*	GW	77907	63029	77929
320310	**SR**	E	*SR*	GW	77908	63030	77930
320311	**SR**	E	*SR*	GW	77909	63031	77931
320312	**SR**	E	*SR*	GW	77910	63032	77932
320313	**SR**	E	*SR*	GW	77911	63033	77933
320314	**SR**	E	*SR*	GW	77912	63034	77934
320315	**SR**	E	*SR*	GW	77913	63035	77935
320316	**SR**	E	*SR*	GW	77914	63036	77936
320317	**SR**	E	*SR*	GW	77915	63037	77937
320318	**SR**	E	*SR*	GW	77916	63038	77938
320319	**SR**	E	*SR*	GW	77917	63039	77939
320320	**SR**	E	*SR*	GW	77918	63040	77940
320321	**SR**	E	*SR*	GW	77919	63041	77941
320322	**SR**	E	*SR*	GW	77920	63042	77942

Class 320/4. Former London Midland Class 321s reduced to 3-car formation and refurbished as Class 320/4s by Wabtec Doncaster 2015–16.

DTSO (A). Lot No. 31060 1990. –/54(+4) 1TD 1W. 32.0 t.
MSO. Lot No. 31062 1990. –/79. 52.2 t.
DTSO (B). Lot No. 31061 1990. –/74(+2) 1W. 32.0 t.

320411	(321411)	**SR**	E	*SR*	GW	78105	63073	77953
320412	(321412)	**SR**	E	*SR*	GW	78106	63074	77954
320413	(321413)	**SR**	E	*SR*	GW	78107	63075	77955
320414	(321414)	**SR**	E	*SR*	GW	78108	63076	77956
320415	(321415)	**SR**	E	*SR*	GW	78109	63077	77957
320416	(321416)	**SR**	E	*SR*	GW	78110	63078	77958
320417	(321417)	**SR**	E	*SR*	GW	78111	63079	77959

CLASS 321   BREL YORK

Outer suburban units.

Formation: DTCO (DTSO on Class 321/9)–MSO–TSO–DTSO.
Construction: Steel.
Traction Motors: Four Brush TM2141C of 268 kW († Four TSA010163 AC motors of 300 kW).
Wheel Arrangement: 2-2 + Bo-Bo + 2-2 + 2-2.
Braking: Disc († and regenerative).   **Dimensions:** 19.95 x 2.82 m.
Bogies: P7-4 (MSO), T3-7 (others).   **Couplers:** Tightlock.
Gangways: Within unit.
Control System: Thyristor († IGBT Inverter).
Doors: Sliding.   **Maximum Speed:** 100 mph.
Seating Layout: 1: 2+2 facing, 2: 3+2 facing.
Multiple Working: Within class & with Classes 317, 318, 319, 320, 322 and 323.

Class 321/3.

* "Renatus" rebuilt units with completely new interiors and Quantum seating, still arranged to a 3+2 layout in Standard Class. 30 Class 321/3 units are due to be refurbished by late 2018.

† "Renatus" rebuilt units also fitted with new TSA AC traction motors.

DTCO. Lot No. 31053 1988–90. 16/57 (321 347–366 16/56) (* 16/31(+4) 1TD 2W. 29.7 t.
MSO. Lot No. 31054 1988–90. –/82 (* –/80). 51.5 t.
TSO. Lot No. 31055 1988–90. –/75 2T (* –/78 1T). 29.1 t.
DTSO. Lot No. 31056 1988–90. –/78 (* –/76). 29.7 t.

321301	*†	**GR**	E	*GA*	IL	78049	62975	71880	77853
321302	*†	**GR**	E	*GA*	IL	78050	62976	71881	77854
321303	*†	**GR**	E	*GA*	IL	78051	62977	71882	77855
321304	*†	**GR**	E	*GA*	IL	78052	62978	71883	77856
321305	*	**GR**	E	*GA*	IL	78053	62979	71884	77857
321306	*	**GR**	E	*GA*	IL	78054	62980	71885	77858
321307	*	**GR**	E	*GA*	IL	78055	62981	71886	77859
321308	*†	**GR**	E	*GA*	IL	78056	62982	71887	77860
321309	*†	**GR**	E	*GA*	IL	78057	62983	71888	77861
321310	†	**NX**	E	*GA*	IL	78058	62984	71889	77862
321311	*†	**GR**	E	*GA*	IL	78059	62985	71890	77863
321312	*†	**GR**	E	*GA*	IL	78060	62986	71891	77864
321313	*†	**GR**	E	*GA*	IL	78061	62987	71892	77865
321314	†	**NX**	E	*GA*	IL	78062	62988	71893	77866
321315	†	**NX**	E	*GA*	IL	78063	62989	71894	77867
321316	*†	**GR**	E	*GA*	IL	78064	62990	71895	77868
321317	*†	**NX**	E	*GA*	IL	78065	62991	71896	77869
321318	†	**NX**	E	*GA*	IL	78066	62992	71897	77870
321319	†	**NX**	E	*GA*	IL	78067	62993	71898	77871
321320	†	**NX**	E	*GA*	IL	78068	62994	71899	77872
321321	*†	**GR**	E	*GA*	IL	78069	62995	71900	77873
321322		**NX**	E	*GA*	IL	78070	62996	71901	77874
321323		**NX**	E	*GA*	IL	78071	62997	71902	77875
321324	†	**NX**	E	*GA*	IL	78072	62998	71903	77876
321325		**NX**	E	*GA*	IL	78073	62999	71904	77877
321326		**NX**	E	*GA*	IL	78074	63000	71905	77878
321327		**NC**	E	*GA*	IL	78075	63001	71906	77879
321328		**NX**	E	*GA*	IL	78076	63002	71907	77880
321329	†	**NX**	E	*GA*	IL	78077	63003	71908	77881
321330		**NC**	E	*GA*	IL	78078	63004	71909	77882
321331		**NC**	E	*GA*	IL	78079	63005	71910	77883
321332		**NC**	E	*GA*	IL	78080	63006	71911	77884
321333		**NC**	E	*GA*	IL	78081	63007	71912	77885
321334		**NC**	E	*GA*	IL	78082	63008	71913	77886
321335		**NC**	E	*GA*	IL	78083	63009	71914	77887
321336		**NC**	E	*GA*	IL	78084	63010	71915	77888
321337		**NC**	E	*GA*	IL	78085	63011	71916	77889
321338		**NC**	E	*GA*	IL	78086	63012	71917	77890
321339		**NC**	E	*GA*	IL	78087	63013	71918	77891

321340	NC	E	GA	IL	78088	63014	71919	77892
321341	NC	E	GA	IL	78089	63015	71920	77893
321342	NC	E	GA	IL	78090	63016	71921	77894
321343	NC	E	GA	IL	78091	63017	71922	77895
321344	NC	E	GA	IL	78092	63018	71923	77896
321345	NC	E	GA	IL	78093	63019	71924	77897
321346	NC	E	GA	IL	78094	63020	71925	77898
321347	NC	E	GA	IL	78131	63105	71991	78280
321348	NC	E	GA	IL	78132	63106	71992	78281
321349	NC	E	GA	IL	78133	63107	71993	78282
321350	NC	E	GA	IL	78134	63108	71994	78283
321351	NC	E	GA	IL	78135	63109	71995	78284
321352	NC	E	GA	IL	78136	63110	71996	78285
321353	NC	E	GA	IL	78137	63111	71997	78286
321354	NC	E	GA	IL	78138	63112	71998	78287
321355	NC	E	GA	IL	78139	63113	71999	78288
321356	NC	E	GA	IL	78140	63114	72000	78289
321357	NC	E	GA	IL	78141	63115	72001	78290
321358	NC	E	GA	IL	78142	63116	72002	78291
321359	GA	E	GA	IL	78143	63117	72003	78292
321360	NC	E	GA	IL	78144	63118	72004	78293
321361	GA	E	GA	IL	78145	63119	72005	78294
321362	GA	E	GA	IL	78146	63120	72006	78295
321363	GA	E	GA	IL	78147	63121	72007	78296
321364	GA	E	GA	IL	78148	63122	72008	78297
321365	GA	E	GA	IL	78149	63123	72009	78298
321366	GA	E	GA	IL	78150	63124	72010	78299

Names (carried on TSO):

321334 Amsterdam
321336 GEOFFREY FREEMAN ALLEN
321342 R. Barnes
321343 RSA RAILWAY STUDY ASSOCIATION
321351 London Southend Airport
321361 Phoenix

Class 321/4.

The original vehicles 71966 and 77960 from 321418 and 78114 and 63082 from 321420 were written off after the Watford Junction accident in 1996. The undamaged vehicles were formed together as 321418 whilst four new vehicles were built in 1997, taking the same numbers as the scrapped vehicles, and these became the second 321420.

The DTCOs of 321421–437 have had 12 First Class seats declassified.

Units 321 411–417 have been refurbished as Class 320/4 3-car units for ScotRail (their TSO vehicles are stored). In 2018 321401/403/404 plus two further units are due to transfer to ScotRail as 3-car units. 321401/403 are on short-term lease to Greater Anglia at the time of writing.

† 321448 received an interior refurbishment as an Eversholt demonstrator unit. Fitted with two different types of interior using seats supplied by

Quantum it acted as the pilot unit for the "Renatus" work being carried out on the Class 321/3s. 78130 and 63104 have a "suburban" interior with a 3+2 seating layout and 78279 and 71990 have a "metro" interior with 2+2 seating. It is also fitted with the new TSA AC traction motors.

Non-standard livery: 321448 Eversholt demonstrator (silver with blue doors and multi-coloured stripes).

DTCO. Lot No. 31067 1989–90. 28/40 (321 421–437 16/52, 321 438–447 16/56). 29.8 t. († 16/30(+4) 1TD 2W 33.9 t).
MSO. Lot No. 31068 1989–90. –/79 (321 438–447 –/82). 51.6 t († –/82. 54.0 t).
TSO. Lot No. 31069 1989–90. –/74 2T (321 438–447 –/75 2T). 29.2 t († –/62 1T. 31.7 t).
DTSO. Lot No. 31070 1989–90. –/78. 29.8 t. († –/58. 33.2 t).

321401	**FU**	E	*GA*	IL	78095	63063	71949	77943
321402	**FB**	E	*GA*	IL	78096	63064	71950	77944
321403	**FU**	E	*GA*	IL	78097	63065	71951	77945
321404	**FU**	E		ZK	78098	63066	71952	77946
321405	**FB**	E	*GA*	IL	78099	63067	71953	77947
321406	**FB**	E	*GA*	IL	78100	63068	71954	77948
321407	**FB**	E	*GA*	IL	78101	63069	71955	77949
321408	**FB**	E	*GA*	IL	78102	63070	71956	77950
321409	**FB**	E	*GA*	IL	78103	63071	71957	77951
321410	**FB**	E	*GA*	IL	78104	63072	71958	77952
321418	**FB**	E	*GA*	IL	78112	63080	71968	77962
321419	**FB**	E	*GA*	IL	78113	63081	71967	77961
321420	**FB**	E	*GA*	IL	78114[II]	63082[II]	71966[II]	77960[II]
321421	**NC**	E	*GA*	IL	78115	63083	71969	77963
321422	**NC**	E	*GA*	IL	78116	63084	71970	77964
321423	**NC**	E	*GA*	IL	78117	63085	71971	77965
321424	**NX**	E	*GA*	IL	78118	63086	71972	77966
321425	**NC**	E	*GA*	IL	78119	63087	71973	77967
321426	**NX**	E	*GA*	IL	78120	63088	71974	77968
321427	**NX**	E	*GA*	IL	78121	63089	71975	77969
321428	**NX**	E	*GA*	IL	78122	63090	71976	77970
321429	**NX**	E	*GA*	IL	78123	63091	71977	77971
321430	**NX**	E	*GA*	IL	78124	63092	71978	77972
321431	**NX**	E	*GA*	IL	78151	63125	72011	78300
321432	**NC**	E	*GA*	IL	78152	63126	72012	78301
321433	**NC**	E	*GA*	IL	78153	63127	72013	78302
321434	**NC**	E	*GA*	IL	78154	63128	72014	78303
321435	**NC**	E	*GA*	IL	78155	63129	72015	78304
321436	**NC**	E	*GA*	IL	78156	63130	72016	78305
321437	**NC**	E	*GA*	IL	78157	63131	72017	78306
321438	**GA**	E	*GA*	IL	78158	63132	72018	78307
321439	**GA**	E	*GA*	IL	78159	63133	72019	78308
321440	**GA**	E	*GA*	IL	78160	63134	72020	78309
321441	**GA**	E	*GA*	IL	78161	63135	72021	78310
321442	**GA**	E	*GA*	IL	78162	63136	72022	78311
321443	**GA**	E	*GA*	IL	78125	63099	71985	78274
321444	**NC**	E	*GA*	IL	78126	63100	71986	78275
321445	**NC**	E	*GA*	IL	78127	63101	71987	78276

321446	**NC**	E	*GA*	IL	78128	63102	71988	78277
321447	**0**	E	*GA*	IL	78129	63103	71989	78278
321448 †	**0**	E	*GA*	IL	78130	63104	71990	78279
Spare	**LM**	E		ZB (S)	71959			
Spare	**LM**	E		LM (S)	71960	71963	71964	71965
Spare	**LO**	E		LM (S)	71961	71962		

Names (carried on TSO):

321403 Stewart Fleming Signalman King's Cross
321409 Dame Alice Owen's School 400 Years of Learning
321428 The Essex Commuter
321442 Crouch Valley 1889–2014
321444 Essex Lifeboats
321446 George Mullings

Class 321/9. DTSO(A)–MSO–TSO–DTSO(B). Refurbished 2015 with a new universal access toilet to comply with the 2020 accessibility regulations.

DTSO(A). Lot No. 31108 1991. –/45(+6) 1TD 2W. 31.7 t.
MSO. Lot No. 31109 1991. –/79. 52.1 t.
TSO. Lot No. 31110 1991. –/78. 30.6 t.
DTSO(B). Lot No. 31111 1991. –/79. 30.6 t.

321901	**NB**	E	*NO*	NL	77990	63153	72128	77993
321902	**NB**	E	*NO*	NL	77991	63154	72129	77994
321903	**NB**	E	*NO*	NL	77992	63155	72130	77995

CLASS 322   BREL YORK

Units built for use on Stansted Airport services, used for a number of years with ScotRail before transfer to Northern. Refurbished 2014–15 with a universal access toilet to comply with the 2020 accessibility regulations.

Formation: DTSO–MSO–TSO–DTSO.
Construction: Steel.
Traction Motors: Four Brush TM2141C of 268 kW.
Wheel Arrangement: 2-2 + Bo-Bo + 2-2 + 2-2.
Braking: Disc.   **Dimensions:** 19.95/19.92 x 2.82 m.
Bogies: P7-4 (MSO), T3-7 (others).   **Couplers:** Tightlock.
Gangways: Within unit.   **Control System:** Thyristor.
Doors: Sliding.   **Maximum Speed:** 100 mph.
Seating Layout: 3+2 facing.
Multiple Working: Within class & with Classes 317, 318, 319, 320, 321 and 323.

DTSO(A). Lot No. 31094 1990. –/54(+4) 1TD 2W. 31.7 t.
MSO. Lot No. 31092 1990. –/83. 52.1 t.
TSO. Lot No. 31093 1990. –/80 1T. 30.6 t.
DTSO(B). Lot No. 31091 1990. –/79. 30.6 t.

322481	**NB**	E	*NO*	NL	78163	63137	72023	77985
322482	**NB**	E	*NO*	NL	78164	63138	72024	77986
322483	**NB**	E	*NO*	NL	78165	63139	72025	77987
322484	**NB**	E	*NO*	NL	78166	63140	72026	77988
322485	**NB**	E	*NO*	NL	78167	63141	72027	77989

CLASS 323 HUNSLET TRANSPORTATION PROJECTS

Suburban units.

Formation: DMSO–PTSO–DMSO.
Construction: Welded aluminium alloy.
Traction Motors: Four Holec DMKT 52/24 asynchronous of 146 kW.
Wheel Arrangement: Bo-Bo + 2-2 + Bo-Bo.
Braking: Disc & regenerative.   **Dimensions:** 23.37/23.44 x 2.80 m.
Bogies: SRP BP62 (DMSO), BT52 (PTSO). **Couplers:** Tightlock.
Gangways: Within unit.   **Control System:** IGBT Inverter.
Doors: Sliding plug.   **Maximum Speed:** 90 mph.
Seating Layout: 3+2 facing/unidirectional.
Multiple Working: Within class & with Classes 317, 318, 319, 320, 321 and 322.

DMSO(A). Lot No. 31112 Hunslet 1992–93. –/98 († –/82). 41.0 t.
TSO. Lot No. 31113 Hunslet 1992–93. –/88(+5) 1T 2W. († –/80(+5) 1T 2W).
39.4 t.
DMSO(B). Lot No. 31114 Hunslet 1992–93. –/98 († –/82). 41.0 t.

323 201		**LM**	P	*WM*	SO	64001	72201	65001
323 202		**LM**	P	*WM*	SO	64002	72202	65002
323 203		**LM**	P	*WM*	SO	64003	72203	65003
323 204		**LM**	P	*WM*	SO	64004	72204	65004
323 205		**LM**	P	*WM*	SO	64005	72205	65005
323 206		**LM**	P	*WM*	SO	64006	72206	65006
323 207		**LM**	P	*WM*	SO	64007	72207	65007
323 208		**LM**	P	*WM*	SO	64008	72208	65008
323 209		**LM**	P	*WM*	SO	64009	72209	65009
323 210		**LM**	P	*WM*	SO	64010	72210	65010
323 211		**LM**	P	*WM*	SO	64011	72211	65011
323 212		**LM**	P	*WM*	SO	64012	72212	65012
323 213		**LM**	P	*WM*	SO	64013	72213	65013
323 214		**LM**	P	*WM*	SO	64014	72214	65014
323 215		**LM**	P	*WM*	SO	64015	72215	65015
323 216		**LM**	P	*WM*	SO	64016	72216	65016
323 217		**LM**	P	*WM*	SO	64017	72217	65017
323 218		**LM**	P	*WM*	SO	64018	72218	65018
323 219		**LM**	P	*WM*	SO	64019	72219	65019
323 220		**LM**	P	*WM*	SO	64020	72220	65020
323 221		**LM**	P	*WM*	SO	64021	72221	65021
323 222		**LM**	P	*WM*	SO	64022	72222	65022
323 223	†	**NO**	P	*NO*	LG	64023	72223	65023
323 224	†	**NO**	P	*NO*	LG	64024	72224	65024
323 225	†	**NO**	P	*NO*	LG	64025	72225	65025
323 226		**NO**	P	*NO*	LG	64026	72226	65026
323 227		**NO**	P	*NO*	LG	64027	72227	65027
323 228		**NO**	P	*NO*	LG	64028	72228	65028
323 229		**NO**	P	*NO*	LG	64029	72229	65029
323 230		**NO**	P	*NO*	LG	64030	72230	65030
323 231		**NO**	P	*NO*	LG	64031	72231	65031
323 232		**NO**	P	*NO*	LG	64032	72232	65032

323233	**NO**	P	*NO*	LG	64033	72233	65033
323234	**NO**	P	*NO*	LG	64034	72234	65034
323235	**NO**	P	*NO*	LG	64035	72235	65035
323236	**NO**	P	*NO*	LG	64036	72236	65036
323237	**NO**	P	*NO*	LG	64037	72237	65037
323238	**NO**	P	*NO*	LG	64038	72238	65038
323239	**NO**	P	*NO*	LG	64039	72239	65039
323240	**LM**	P	*WM*	SO	64040	72340	65040
323241	**LM**	P	*WM*	SO	64041	72341	65041
323242	**LM**	P	*WM*	SO	64042	72342	65042
323243	**LM**	P	*WM*	SO	64043	72343	65043

CLASS 325   ABB DERBY

Postal units based on Class 319s. Compatible with diesel or electric locomotive haulage. Built for dual voltage use, but 750 V DC third rail shoe gear has been removed as it is not required on current duties.

Formation: DTPMV–MPMV–TPMV–DTPMV.
System: 25 kV AC overhead.
Construction: Steel.
Traction Motors: Four GEC G315BZ of 268 kW.
Wheel Arrangement: 2-2 + Bo-Bo + 2-2 + 2-2.
Braking: Disc.   **Dimensions:** 19.33 x 2.82 m.
Bogies: P7-4 (MSO), T3-7 (others).   **Couplers:** Drop-head buckeye.
Gangways: None.   **Control System:** GTO Chopper.
Doors: Roller shutter.   **Maximum Speed:** 100 mph.
Multiple Working: Within class.

DTPMV. Lot No. 31144 1995. 29.1 t.
MPMV. Lot No. 31145 1995. 49.5 t.
TPMV. Lot No. 31146 1995. 30.7 t.

325001	**RM**	RM	*DB*	CE	68300	68340	68360	68301
325002	**RM**	RM	*DB*	CE	68302	68341	68361	68303
325003	**RM**	RM	*DB*	CE	68304	68342	68362	68305
325004	**RM**	RM	*DB*	CE	68306	68343	68363	68307
325005	**RM**	RM	*DB*	CE	68308	68344	68364	68309
325006	**RM**	RM	*DB*	CE	68310	68345	68365	68311
325007	**RM**	RM	*DB*	CE	68312	68346	68366	68313
325008	**RM**	RM	*DB*	CE	68314	68347	68367	68315
325009	**RM**	RM	*DB*	CE	68316	68349	68368	68317
325011	**RM**	RM	*DB*	CE	68320	68350	68370	68321
325012	**RM**	RM	*DB*	CE	68322	68351	68371	68323
325013	**RM**	RM	*DB*	CE	68324	68352	68372	68325
325014	**RM**	RM	*DB*	CE	68326	68353	68373	68327
325015	**RM**	RM	*DB*	CE	68328	68354	68374	68329
325016	**RM**	RM	*DB*	CE	68330	68355	68375	68331

CLASS 331   CIVITY   CAF

New units under construction for Northern, for delivery 2018–20. Full details awaited.

Formation: DMSO–PTSO–DMSO or DMSO–PTSO–TSO–DMSO.
Construction: Aluminium.
Traction Motors:
Wheel Arrangement:

Braking:	**Dimensions:**
Bogies: CAF.	**Couplers:** Dellner.
Gangways: Within unit.	**Control System:** IGBT Inverter.
Doors:	**Maximum Speed:** 100 mph.
Heating & ventilation: Air conditioning.	
Seating:	**Multiple Working:** Within class.

Class 331/0. DMSO–PTSO–DMSO. 3-car units.

DMSO. CAF Zaragoza 2017–20.
PTSO. CAF Zaragoza 2017–20.
DMSO. CAF Zaragoza 2017–20.

331001	E	463001	464001	466001
331002	E	463002	464002	466002
331003	E	463003	464003	466003
331004	E	463004	464004	466004
331005	E	463005	464005	466005
331006	E	463006	464006	466006
331007	E	463007	464007	466007
331008	E	463008	464008	466008
331009	E	463009	464009	466009
331010	E	463010	464010	466010
331011	E	463011	464011	466011
331012	E	463012	464012	466012
331013	E	463013	464013	466013
331014	E	463014	464014	466014
331015	E	463015	464015	466015
331016	E	463016	464016	466016
331017	E	463017	464017	466017
331018	E	463018	464018	466018
331019	E	463019	464019	466019
331020	E	463020	464020	466020
331021	E	463021	464021	466021
331022	E	463022	464022	466022
331023	E	463023	464023	466023
331024	E	463024	464024	466024
331025	E	463025	464025	466025
331026	E	463026	464026	466026
331027	E	463027	464027	466027
331028	E	463028	464028	466028
331029	E	463029	464029	466029
331030	E	463030	464030	466030
331031	E	463031	464031	466031

Class 331/1. DMSO–PTSO–TSO–DMSO. 4-car units.

DMSO. CAF Zaragoza 2017–20.
PTSO. CAF Zaragoza 2017–20.
TSO. CAF Zaragoza 2017–20.
DMSO. CAF Zaragoza 2017–20.

331 101	E	463101	464101	465101	466101
331 102	E	463102	464102	465102	466102
331 103	E	463103	464103	465103	466103
331 104	E	463104	464104	465104	466104
331 105	E	463105	464105	465105	466105
331 106	E	463106	464106	465106	466106
331 107	E	463107	464107	465107	466107
331 108	E	463108	464108	465108	466108
331 109	E	463109	464109	465109	466109
331 110	E	463110	464110	465110	466110
331 111	E	463111	464111	465111	466111
331 112	E	463112	464112	465112	466112

CLASS 332   HEATHROW EXPRESS CAF/SIEMENS

Dedicated Heathrow Express units. Five units were increased from 4-car to 5-car in 2002. Usually operate in coupled pairs. This class is unique in not being fitted with TPWS equipment (as the route operated is ATP only).

Formations: DMSO–TSO–PTSO–(TSO)–DMFO.
Construction: Steel.
Traction Motors: Two Siemens monomotors asynchronous of 350 kW.
Wheel Arrangement: B-B + 2-2 + 2-2 (+ 2-2) + B-B.
Braking: Disc.   **Dimensions:** 23.74/23.35/23.14 x 2.75 m.
Bogies: CAF.   **Couplers:** Scharfenberg 10L.
Gangways: Within unit.   **Control System:** IGBT Inverter.
Doors: Sliding plug.   **Maximum Speed:** 100 mph.
Heating & ventilation: Air conditioning.
Seating: 1: 1+1 facing/unidirectional, 2: 2+2 mainly unidirectional.
Multiple Working: Within class.

Advertising livery: Tata Communications (blue).

DMSO. CAF 1997–98. –/43(+8). 49.9 t.
72400–413. TSO. CAF 1997–98. –/64(+11). 38.4 t.
72414–418. TSO. CAF 2002. –/56 35.8 t.
PTSO. CAF 1997–98. –/39(+11) 1TD 2W. 47.6 t.
DMFO. CAF 1997–98. 20/–. 49.5 t.

332001	**AL**	HE	*HE*	OH	78400	72412	63400		78401
332002	**AL**	HE	*HE*	OH	78402	72409	63406		78403
332003	**AL**	HE	*HE*	OH	78404	72407	63402		78405
332004	**AL**	HE	*HE*	OH	78406	72405	63403		78407
332005	**AL**	HE	*HE*	OH	78408	72411	63404	72417	78409
332006	**AL**	HE	*HE*	OH	78410	72410	63405	72415	78411
332007	**AL**	HE	*HE*	OH	78412	72401	63401	72414	78413

332008	**AL**	HE	*HE*	OH	78414	72413	63407	72418	78415
332009	**AL**	HE	*HE*	OH	78416	72400	63408	72416	78417
332010	**AL**	HE	*HE*	OH	78418	72402	63409		78419
332011	**AL**	HE	*HE*	OH	78420	72403	63410		78421
332012	**AL**	HE	*HE*	OH	78422	72404	63411		78423
332013	**AL**	HE	*HE*	OH	78424	72408	63412		78425
332014	**AL**	HE	*HE*	OH	78426	72406	63413		78427

CLASS 333   CAF/SIEMENS

West Yorkshire area suburban units.

Formation: DMSO–PTSO–TSO–DMSO.
Construction: Steel.
Traction Motors: Two Siemens monomotors asynchronous of 350 kW.
Wheel Arrangement: B-B + 2-2 + 2-2 + B-B.
Braking: Disc.
Dimensions: 23.74 (outer ends)/23.35 (TSO) x 2.75 m.
Bogies: CAF.   **Couplers:** Dellner 10L.
Gangways: Within unit.   **Control System:** IGBT Inverter.
Doors: Sliding plug.   **Maximum Speed:** 100 mph.
Heating & ventilation: Air conditioning. **Multiple Working:** Within class.
Seating Layout: 3+2 facing/unidirectional.

333001–008 were made up to 4-car units from 3-car units in 2002.

333009–016 were made up to 4-car units from 3-car units in 2003.

DMSO(A). (Odd Nos.) CAF 2001. –/90. 50.0 t.
PTSO. CAF 2001. –/73(+7) 1TD 2W. 46.0 t.
TSO. CAF 2002–03. –/100. 38.5 t.
DMSO(B). (Even Nos.) CAF 2001. –/90. 50.0 t.

333001	**YR**	A	*NO*	NL	78451	74461	74477	78452
333002	**YR**	A	*NO*	NL	78453	74462	74478	78454
333003	**YR**	A	*NO*	NL	78455	74463	74479	78456
333004	**YR**	A	*NO*	NL	78457	74464	74480	78458
333005	**YR**	A	*NO*	NL	78459	74465	74481	78460
333006	**YR**	A	*NO*	NL	78461	74466	74482	78462
333007	**YR**	A	*NO*	NL	78463	74467	74483	78464
333008	**YR**	A	*NO*	NL	78465	74468	74484	78466
333009	**YR**	A	*NO*	NL	78467	74469	74485	78468
333010	**YR**	A	*NO*	NL	78469	74470	74486	78470
333011	**YR**	A	*NO*	NL	78471	74471	74487	78472
333012	**YR**	A	*NO*	NL	78473	74472	74488	78474
333013	**YR**	A	*NO*	NL	78475	74473	74489	78476
333014	**YR**	A	*NO*	NL	78477	74474	74490	78478
333015	**YR**	A	*NO*	NL	78479	74475	74491	78480
333016	**YR**	A	*NO*	NL	78481	74476	74492	78482

Names (carried on end cars):

333007 Alderman J Arthur Godwin First Lord Mayor of Bradford 1907
333011 Olicana Ilkley's Roman Fort

CLASS 334   JUNIPER   ALSTOM BIRMINGHAM

Outer suburban units.

Formation: DMSO–PTSO–DMSO.
Construction: Steel.
Traction Motors: Two Alstom ONIX 800 asynchronous of 270 kW.
Wheel Arrangement: 2-Bo + 2-2 + Bo-2.
Braking: Disc.   **Dimensions:** 21.01/19.94 x 2.80 m.
Bogies: Alstom LTB3/TBP3.   **Couplers:** Dellner.
Gangways: Within unit.   **Control System:** IGBT Inverter.
Doors: Sliding plug.   **Maximum Speed:** 90 mph.
Heating & ventilation: Pressure heating and ventilation.
Seating Layout: 2+2 facing/unidirectional (3+2 in PTSO).
Multiple Working: Within class.

DMSO(A). Alstom Birmingham 1999–2001. –/64. 42.6 t.
PTSO. Alstom Birmingham 1999–2001. –/55 1TD 1W. 39.4 t.
DMSO(B). Alstom Birmingham 1999–2001. –/64. 42.6 t.

334001	**SR**	E	*SR*	GW	64101	74301	65101
334002	**SR**	E	*SR*	GW	64102	74302	65102
334003	**SR**	E	*SR*	GW	64103	74303	65103
334004	**SR**	E	*SR*	GW	64104	74304	65104
334005	**SR**	E	*SR*	GW	64105	74305	65105
334006	**SR**	E	*SR*	GW	64106	74306	65106
334007	**SR**	E	*SR*	GW	64107	74307	65107
334008	**SR**	E	*SR*	GW	64108	74308	65108
334009	**SR**	E	*SR*	GW	64109	74309	65109
334010	**SR**	E	*SR*	GW	64110	74310	65110
334011	**SR**	E	*SR*	GW	64111	74311	65111
334012	**SR**	E	*SR*	GW	64112	74312	65112
334013	**SR**	E	*SR*	GW	64113	74313	65113
334014	**SR**	E	*SR*	GW	64114	74314	65114
334015	**SR**	E	*SR*	GW	64115	74315	65115
334016	**SR**	E	*SR*	GW	64116	74316	65116
334017	**SR**	E	*SR*	GW	64117	74317	65117
334018	**SR**	E	*SR*	GW	64118	74318	65118
334019	**SR**	E	*SR*	GW	64119	74319	65119
334020	**SR**	E	*SR*	GW	64120	74320	65120
334021	**SR**	E	*SR*	GW	64121	74321	65121
334022	**SR**	E	*SR*	GW	64122	74322	65122
334023	**SR**	E	*SR*	GW	64123	74323	65123
334024	**SR**	E	*SR*	GW	64124	74324	65124
334025	**SR**	E	*SR*	GW	64125	74325	65125
334026	**SR**	E	*SR*	GW	64126	74326	65126
334027	**SR**	E	*SR*	GW	64127	74327	65127
334028	**SR**	E	*SR*	GW	64128	74328	65128
334029	**SR**	E	*SR*	GW	64129	74329	65129
334030	**SR**	E	*SR*	GW	64130	74330	65130
334031	**SR**	E	*SR*	GW	64131	74331	65131
334032	**SR**	E	*SR*	GW	64132	74332	65132

334033	**SR**	E	*SR*	GW	64133	74333	65133
334034	**SR**	E	*SR*	GW	64134	74334	65134
334035	**SR**	E	*SR*	GW	64135	74335	65135
334036	**SR**	E	*SR*	GW	64136	74336	65136
334037	**SR**	E	*SR*	GW	64137	74337	65137
334038	**SR**	E	*SR*	GW	64138	74338	65138
334039	**SR**	E	*SR*	GW	64139	74339	65139
334040	**SR**	E	*SR*	GW	64140	74340	65140

CLASS 345   AVENTRA   BOMBARDIER DERBY

9-car units currently under construction for London's Crossrail/Elizabeth Line. The first 17 units are entering service as 7-car units on Liverpool Street–Shenfield services. Subsequent units will enter service as 9-cars on services between Paddington and Heathrow Airport from May 2018, and then on the cross-London Elizabeth Line services from December 2018. The design is marketed as "Aventra" by Bombardier and is a development on the successful Electrostar design. There is an option for a further 14 9-car units.

Formations: DMSO–PMSO–MSO–MSO*–TSO–MSO*–MSO–PMSO–DMSO.
* Initially these MSO vehicles are missing from units 345001–017.
Systems: 25 kV AC overhead.
Construction: Aluminium.
Traction Motors: Two Bombardier asynchronous of 250 kW.
Wheel Arrangement: 2-Bo + Bo-2 + Bo-Bo (+ Bo-2) + 2-2 (+ 2-Bo) + Bo-Bo + 2-Bo + Bo-2.

Braking: Disc & regenerative.	**Dimensions:** 23.62/22.50 m x 2.78 m.
Bogies: Inside-frame.	**Couplers:** Dellner.
Gangways: Within unit.	**Control System:** IGBT Inverter.
Doors: Sliding plug.	**Maximum Speed:** 90 mph.

Heating & ventilation: Air conditioning.
Seating Layout: Mostly longitudinal, with some 2+2 facing.
Multiple Working: Within class.

DMSO(A). Bombardier Derby 2015–18. –/46. 39.0 t.
PMSO(A). Bombardier Derby 2015–18. –/46(+6). 37.1 t.
MSO(A). Bombardier Derby 2015–18. –/46(+6). 36.5 t.
MSO(B). Bombardier Derby 2015–18.
TSO. Bombardier Derby 2015–18. –/38(+12). 26.7 t.
MSO(C). Bombardier Derby 2015–18.
MSO(D). Bombardier Derby 2015–18. –/46(+6). 37.3 t.
PMSO(B). Bombardier Derby 2015–18. –/46(+6). 37.1 t.
DMSO(B). Bombardier Derby 2015–18. –/46. 39.0 t.

345001	**XR**	XR	340101	340201	340301	*340401*	340501
			340601	340701	340801	340901	
345002	**XR**	XR	340102	340202	340302	*340402*	340502
			340602	340702	340802	340902	
345003	**XR**	XR	340103	340203	340303	*340403*	340503
			340603	340703	340803	340903	

345 004	**XR**	XR			340104	340204	340304	*340404*	340504
					340604	340704	340804	340904	
345 005	**XR**	XR	*XR*	IL	340105	340205	340305	*340405*	340505
					340605	340705	340805	340905	
345 006	**XR**	XR	*XR*	IL	340106	340206	340306	*340406*	340506
					340606	340706	340806	340906	
345 007	**XR**	XR	*XR*	IL	340107	340207	340307	*340407*	340507
					340607	340707	340807	340907	
345 008	**XR**	XR	*XR*	IL	340108	340208	340308	*340408*	340508
					340608	340708	340808	340908	
345 009	**XR**	XR	*XR*	IL	340109	340209	340309	340409	340509
					340609	340709	340809	340909	
345 010	**XR**	XR	*XR*	IL	340110	340210	340310	*340410*	340510
					340610	340710	340810	340910	
345 011	**XR**	XR	*XR*	IL	340111	340211	340311	*340411*	340511
					340611	340711	340811	340911	
345 012	**XR**	XR	*XR*	IL	340112	340212	340312	*340412*	340512
					340612	340712	340812	340912	
345 013	**XR**	XR			340113	340213	340313	*340413*	340513
					340613	340713	340813	340913	
345 014	**XR**	XR	*XR*	IL	340114	340214	340314	*340414*	340514
					340614	340714	340814	340914	
345 015	**XR**	XR	*XR*	IL	340115	340215	340315	340415	340515
					340615	340715	340815	340915	
345 016	**XR**	XR	*XR*	IL	340116	340216	340316	*340416*	340516
					340616	340716	340816	340916	
345 017	**XR**	XR	*XR*	IL	340117	340217	340317	*340417*	340517
					340617	340717	340817	340917	
345 018	**XR**	XR			340118	340218	340318	340418	340518
					340618	340718	340818	340918	
345 019	**XR**	XR			340119	340219	340319	340419	340519
					340619	340719	340819	340919	
345 020	**XR**	XR			340120	340220	340320	340420	340520
					340620	340720	340820	340920	
345 021	**XR**	XR			340121	340221	340321	340421	340521
					340621	340721	340821	340921	
345 022	**XR**	XR			340122	340222	340322	340422	340522
					340622	340722	340822	340922	
345 023	**XR**	XR			340123	340223	340323	340423	340523
					340623	340723	340823	340923	
345 024	**XR**	XR			340124	340224	340324	340424	340524
					340624	340724	340824	340924	
345 025	**XR**	XR			340125	340225	340325	340425	340525
					340625	340725	340825	340925	
345 026	**XR**	XR			340126	340226	340326	340426	340526
					340626	340726	340826	340926	
345 027	**XR**	XR			340127	340227	340327	340427	340527
					340627	340727	340827	340927	
345 028	**XR**	XR			340128	340228	340328	340428	340528
					340628	340728	340828	340928	

345 029	**XR**	XR	340129	340229	340329	340429	340529
			340629	340729	340829	340929	
345 030	**XR**	XR	340130	340230	340330	340430	340530
			340630	340730	340830	340930	
345 031	**XR**	XR	340131	340231	340331	340431	340531
			340631	340731	340831	340931	
345 032	**XR**	XR	340132	340232	340332	340432	340532
			340632	340732	340832	340932	
345 033	**XR**	XR	340133	340233	340333	340433	340533
			340633	340733	340833	340933	
345 034	**XR**	XR	340134	340234	340334	340434	340534
			340634	340734	340834	340934	
345 035	**XR**	XR	340135	340235	340335	340435	340535
			340635	340735	340835	340935	
345 036	**XR**	XR	340136	340236	340336	340436	340536
			340636	340736	340836	340936	
345 037	**XR**	XR	340137	340237	340337	340437	340537
			340637	340737	340837	340937	
345 038	**XR**	XR	340138	340238	340338	340438	340538
			340638	340738	340838	340938	
345 039	**XR**	XR	340139	340239	340339	340439	340539
			340639	340739	340839	340939	
345 040	**XR**	XR	340140	340240	340340	340440	340540
			340640	340740	340840	340940	
345 041	**XR**	XR	340141	340241	340341	340441	340541
			340641	340741	340841	340941	
345 042	**XR**	XR	340142	340242	340342	340442	340542
			340642	340742	340842	340942	
345 043	**XR**	XR	340143	340243	340343	340443	340543
			340643	340743	340843	340943	
345 044	**XR**	XR	340144	340244	340344	340444	340544
			340644	340744	340844	340944	
345 045	**XR**	XR	340145	340245	340345	340445	340545
			340645	340745	340845	340945	
345 046	**XR**	XR	340146	340246	340346	340446	340546
			340646	340746	340846	340946	
345 047	**XR**	XR	340147	340247	340347	340447	340547
			340647	340747	340847	340947	
345 048	**XR**	XR	340148	340248	340348	340448	340548
			340648	340748	340848	340948	
345 049	**XR**	XR	340149	340249	340349	340449	340549
			340649	340749	340849	340949	
345 050	**XR**	XR	340150	340250	340350	340450	340550
			340650	340750	340850	340950	
345 051	**XR**	XR	340151	340251	340351	340451	340551
			340651	340751	340851	340951	
345 052	**XR**	XR	340152	340252	340352	340452	340552
			340652	340752	340852	340952	
345 053	**XR**	XR	340153	340253	340353	340453	340553
			340653	340753	340853	340953	

345 054	**XR**	XR	340154	340254	340354	340454	340554
			340654	340754	340854	340954	
345 055	**XR**	XR	340155	340255	340355	340455	340555
			340655	340755	340855	340955	
345 056	**XR**	XR	340156	340256	340356	340456	340556
			340656	340756	340856	340956	
345 057	**XR**	XR	340157	340257	340357	340457	340557
			340657	340757	340857	340957	
345 058	**XR**	XR	340158	340258	340358	340458	340558
			340658	340758	340858	340958	
345 059	**XR**	XR	340159	340259	340359	340459	340559
			340659	340759	340859	340959	
345 060	**XR**	XR	340160	340260	340360	340460	340560
			340660	340760	340860	340960	
345 061	**XR**	XR	340161	340261	340361	340461	340561
			340661	340761	340861	340961	
345 062	**XR**	XR	340162	340262	340362	340462	340562
			340662	340762	340862	340962	
345 063	**XR**	XR	340163	340263	340363	340463	340563
			340663	340763	340863	340963	
345 064	**XR**	XR	340164	340264	340364	340464	340564
			340664	340764	340864	340964	
345 065	**XR**	XR	340165	340265	340365	340465	340565
			340665	340765	340865	340965	
345 066	**XR**	XR	340166	340266	340366	340466	340566
			340666	340766	340866	340966	
345 067	**XR**	XR	340167	340267	340367	340467	340567
			340667	340767	340867	340967	
345 068	**XR**	XR	340168	340268	340368	340468	340568
			340668	340768	340868	340968	
345 069	**XR**	XR	340169	340269	340369	340469	340569
			340669	340769	340869	340969	
345 070	**XR**	XR	340170	340270	340370	340470	340570
			340670	340770	340870	340970	

CLASS 350   DESIRO UK   SIEMENS

Outer suburban and long distance units.

Formation: DMCO–TCO–PTSO–DMCO.
Systems: 25 kV AC overhead (350/1s built with 750 V DC, but equipment currently decommissioned).
Construction: Welded aluminium.
Traction Motors: 4 Siemens 1TB2016-0GB02 asynchronous of 250 kW.
Wheel Arrangement: Bo-Bo + 2-2 + 2-2 + Bo-Bo.
Braking: Disc & regenerative.   **Dimensions:** 20.34 x 2.79 m.
Bogies: SGP SF5000.   **Couplers:** Dellner 12.
Gangways: Throughout.   **Control System:** IGBT Inverter.
Doors: Sliding plug.
Maximum Speed: 110 mph (350/1, 350/3 & 350/4) or 100 mph (350/2). Class 350/2 being upgraded to 110 mph 2017–18.

Heating & ventilation: Air conditioning.
Seating Layout: Various, see sub-class headings.
Multiple Working: Within class.

Class 350/1. Original-build units owned by Angel Trains. Formerly part of an aborted South West Trains 5-car Class 450/2 order. 2+2 seating.

Seating Layout: 1: 2+2 facing, 2: 2+2 facing/unidirectional.

Advertising livery: 350 110 Project 110 (silver centre cars).

DMSO(A). Siemens Krefeld 2004–05. –/60. 48.7 t.
TCO. Siemens Krefeld/Prague 2004–05. 24/32 1T. 36.2 t.
PTSO. Siemens Krefeld/Prague 2004–05. –/50(+9) 1TD 2W. 45.2 t.
DMSO(B). Siemens Krefeld 2004–05. –/60. 49.2 t.

350 101	**LM**	A	*WM*	NN	63761	66811	66861	63711
350 102	**LM**	A	*WM*	NN	63762	66812	66862	63712
350 103	**LM**	A	*WM*	NN	63765	66813	66863	63713
350 104	**LM**	A	*WM*	NN	63764	66814	66864	63714
350 105	**LM**	A	*WM*	NN	63763	66815	66868	63715
350 106	**LM**	A	*WM*	NN	63766	66816	66866	63716
350 107	**LM**	A	*WM*	NN	63767	66817	66867	63717
350 108	**LM**	A	*WM*	NN	63768	66818	66865	63718
350 109	**LM**	A	*WM*	NN	63769	66819	66869	63719
350 110	**AL**	A	*WM*	NN	63770	66820	66870	63720
350 111	**LM**	A	*WM*	NN	63771	66821	66871	63721
350 112	**LM**	A	*WM*	NN	63772	66822	66872	63722
350 113	**LM**	A	*WM*	NN	63773	66823	66873	63723
350 114	**LM**	A	*WM*	NN	63774	66824	66874	63724
350 115	**LM**	A	*WM*	NN	63775	66825	66875	63725
350 116	**LM**	A	*WM*	NN	63776	66826	66876	63726
350 117	**LM**	A	*WM*	NN	63777	66827	66877	63727
350 118	**LM**	A	*WM*	NN	63778	66828	66878	63728
350 119	**LM**	A	*WM*	NN	63779	66829	66879	63729
350 120	**LM**	A	*WM*	NN	63780	66830	66880	63730
350 121	**LM**	A	*WM*	NN	63781	66831	66881	63731
350 122	**LM**	A	*WM*	NN	63782	66832	66882	63732
350 123	**LM**	A	*WM*	NN	63783	66833	66883	63733
350 124	**LM**	A	*WM*	NN	63784	66834	66884	63734
350 125	**LM**	A	*WM*	NN	63785	66835	66885	63735
350 126	**LM**	A	*WM*	NN	63786	66836	66886	63736
350 127	**LM**	A	*WM*	NN	63787	66837	66887	63737
350 128	**LM**	A	*WM*	NN	63788	66838	66888	63738
350 129	**LM**	A	*WM*	NN	63789	66839	66889	63739
350 130	**LM**	A	*WM*	NN	63790	66840	66890	63740

Class 350/2. Owned by Porterbrook Leasing.

Seating Layout: 1: 2+2 facing, 2: 3+2 facing/unidirectional.

DMSO(A). Siemens Krefeld 2008–09. –/70. 43.7 t.
TCO. Siemens Prague 2008–09. 24/42 1T. 35.3 t.
PTSO. Siemens Prague 2008–09. –/61(+9) 1TD 2W. 42.9 t.
DMSO(B). Siemens Krefeld 2008–09. –/70. 44.2 t.

350231	**LM**	P	*WM*	NN	61431	65231	67531	61531
350232	**LM**	P	*WM*	NN	61432	65232	67532	61532
350233	**LM**	P	*WM*	NN	61433	65233	67533	61533
350234	**LM**	P	*WM*	NN	61434	65234	67534	61534
350235	**LM**	P	*WM*	NN	61435	65235	67535	61535
350236	**LM**	P	*WM*	NN	61436	65236	67536	61536
350237	**LM**	P	*WM*	NN	61437	65237	67537	61537
350238	**LM**	P	*WM*	NN	61438	65238	67538	61538
350239	**LM**	P	*WM*	NN	61439	65239	67539	61539
350240	**LM**	P	*WM*	NN	61440	65240	67540	61540
350241	**LM**	P	*WM*	NN	61441	65241	67541	61541
350242	**LM**	P	*WM*	NN	61442	65242	67542	61542
350243	**LM**	P	*WM*	NN	61443	65243	67543	61543
350244	**LM**	P	*WM*	NN	61444	65244	67544	61544
350245	**LM**	P	*WM*	NN	61445	65245	67545	61545
350246	**LM**	P	*WM*	NN	61446	65246	67546	61546
350247	**LM**	P	*WM*	NN	61447	65247	67547	61547
350248	**LM**	P	*WM*	NN	61448	65248	67548	61548
350249	**LM**	P	*WM*	NN	61449	65249	67549	61549
350250	**LM**	P	*WM*	NN	61450	65250	67550	61550
350251	**LM**	P	*WM*	NN	61451	65251	67551	61551
350252	**LM**	P	*WM*	NN	61452	65252	67552	61552
350253	**LM**	P	*WM*	NN	61453	65253	67553	61553
350254	**LM**	P	*WM*	NN	61454	65254	67554	61554
350255	**LM**	P	*WM*	NN	61455	65255	67555	61555
350256	**LM**	P	*WM*	NN	61456	65256	67556	61556
350257	**LM**	P	*WM*	NN	61457	65257	67557	61557
350258	**LM**	P	*WM*	NN	61458	65258	67558	61558
350259	**LM**	P	*WM*	NN	61459	65259	67559	61559
350260	**LM**	P	*WM*	NN	61460	65260	67560	61560
350261	**LM**	P	*WM*	NN	61461	65261	67561	61561
350262	**LM**	P	*WM*	NN	61462	65262	67562	61562
350263	**LM**	P	*WM*	NN	61463	65263	67563	61563
350264	**LM**	P	*WM*	NN	61464	65264	67564	61564
350265	**LM**	P	*WM*	NN	61465	65265	67565	61565
350266	**LM**	P	*WM*	NN	61466	65266	67566	61566
350267	**LM**	P	*WM*	NN	61467	65267	67567	61567

Name (carried on one side of PTSO): 350232   Chad Varah

Class 350/3. Owned by Angel Trains. West Midlands Trains units built for 110 mph operation.

Seating Layout: 1: 2+2 facing, 2: 2+2 facing/unidirectional.

DMSO(A). Siemens Krefeld 2014. –/60. 44.2 t.
TCO. Siemens Krefeld 2014. 24/36 1T. 36.3 t.
PTSO. Siemens Krefeld 2014. –/50(+9) 1TD 2W. 44.0 t.
DMSO(B). Siemens Krefeld 2014. –/60. 45.0 t.

350368	**LM**	A	*WM*	NN	60141	60511	60651	60151
350369	**LM**	A	*WM*	NN	60142	60512	60652	60152
350370	**LM**	A	*WM*	NN	60143	60513	60653	60153

350371	**LM**	A	*WM*	NN	60144	60514	60654	60154
350372	**LM**	A	*WM*	NN	60145	60515	60655	60155
350373	**LN**	A	*WM*	NN	60146	60516	60656	60156
350374	**LM**	A	*WM*	NN	60147	60517	60657	60157
350375	**LM**	A	*WM*	NN	60148	60518	60658	60158
350376	**LM**	A	*WM*	NN	60149	60519	60659	60159
350377	**LM**	A	*WM*	NN	60150	60520	60660	60160

Names (carried on one side of PTSO):

350370   Lichfield Festival
350377   Graham Taylor OBE

Class 350/4. Owned by Angel Trains. TransPennine Express units used on the Manchester Airport–Edinburgh/Glasgow route.

Seating Layout: 1: 2+1 facing, 2: 2+2 facing/unidirectional.

DMSO(A). Siemens Krefeld 2013–14. –/56. 44.2 t.
TCO. Siemens Krefeld 2013–14. 19/24 1T. 36.2 t.
PTSO. Siemens Krefeld 2013–14. –/42 1TD 1T. 44.6 t.
DMSO(B). Siemens Krefeld 2013–14. –/56. 45.0 t.

350401	**TP**	A	*TP*	AK	60691	60901	60941	60671
350402	**TP**	A	*TP*	AK	60692	60902	60942	60672
350403	**TP**	A	*TP*	AK	60693	60903	60943	60673
350404	**TP**	A	*TP*	AK	60694	60904	60944	60674
350405	**TP**	A	*TP*	AK	60695	60905	60945	60675
350406	**TP**	A	*TP*	AK	60696	60906	60946	60676
350407	**TP**	A	*TP*	AK	60697	60907	60947	60677
350408	**TP**	A	*TP*	AK	60698	60908	60948	60678
350409	**TP**	A	*TP*	AK	60699	60909	60949	60679
350410	**TP**	A	*TP*	AK	60700	60910	60950	60680

CLASS 357 ELECTROSTAR
ADTRANZ/BOMBARDIER DERBY

Provision for 750 V DC supply if required.
Formation: DMSO–MSO–PTSO–DMSO.
Construction: Welded aluminium alloy underframe, sides and roof with steel ends. All sections bolted together.
Traction Motors: Two Adtranz asynchronous of 250 kW.
Wheel Arrangement: 2-Bo + 2-Bo + 2-2 + Bo-2.
Braking: Disc & regenerative.   **Dimensions:** 20.40/19.99 x 2.80 m.
Bogies: Adtranz P3-25/T3-25.   **Couplers:** Tightlock.
Gangways: Within unit.   **Control System:** IGBT Inverter.
Doors: Sliding plug.   **Maximum Speed:** 100 mph.
Heating & ventilation: Air conditioning.
Seating Layout: 3+2 facing/unidirectional.
Multiple Working: Within class.

Class 357/0. Owned by Porterbrook Leasing.

DMSO(A). Adtranz Derby 1999–2001. –/71. 40.7 t.
MSO. Adtranz Derby 1999–2001. –/78. 36.7 t.
PTSO. Adtranz Derby 1999–2001. –/58(+4) 1TD 2W. 39.5 t.
DMSO(B). Adtranz Derby 1999–2001. –/71. 40.7 t.

357001	**C2**	P	*C2*	EM	67651	74151	74051	67751
357002	**C2**	P	*C2*	EM	67652	74152	74052	67752
357003	**C2**	P	*C2*	EM	67653	74153	74053	67753
357004	**C2**	P	*C2*	EM	67654	74154	74054	67754
357005	**C2**	P	*C2*	EM	67655	74155	74055	67755
357006	**C2**	P	*C2*	EM	67656	74156	74056	67756
357007	**C2**	P	*C2*	EM	67657	74157	74057	67757
357008	**C2**	P	*C2*	EM	67658	74158	74058	67758
357009	**C2**	P	*C2*	EM	67659	74159	74059	67759
357010	**C2**	P	*C2*	EM	67660	74160	74060	67760
357011	**C2**	P	*C2*	EM	67661	74161	74061	67761
357012	**C2**	P	*C2*	EM	67662	74162	74062	67762
357013	**C2**	P	*C2*	EM	67663	74163	74063	67763
357014	**C2**	P	*C2*	EM	67664	74164	74064	67764
357015	**C2**	P	*C2*	EM	67665	74165	74065	67765
357016	**C2**	P	*C2*	EM	67666	74166	74066	67766
357017	**C2**	P	*C2*	EM	67667	74167	74067	67767
357018	**C2**	P	*C2*	EM	67668	74168	74068	67768
357019	**C2**	P	*C2*	EM	67669	74169	74069	67769
357020	**C2**	P	*C2*	EM	67670	74170	74070	67770
357021	**C2**	P	*C2*	EM	67671	74171	74071	67771
357022	**C2**	P	*C2*	EM	67672	74172	74072	67772
357023	**C2**	P	*C2*	EM	67673	74173	74073	67773
357024	**C2**	P	*C2*	EM	67674	74174	74074	67774
357025	**C2**	P	*C2*	EM	67675	74175	74075	67775
357026	**C2**	P	*C2*	EM	67676	74176	74076	67776
357027	**C2**	P	*C2*	EM	67677	74177	74077	67777
357028	**C2**	P	*C2*	EM	67678	74178	74078	67778
357029	**C2**	P	*C2*	EM	67679	74179	74079	67779
357030	**C2**	P	*C2*	EM	67680	74180	74080	67780
357031	**C2**	P	*C2*	EM	67681	74181	74081	67781
357032	**C2**	P	*C2*	EM	67682	74182	74082	67782
357033	**C2**	P	*C2*	EM	67683	74183	74083	67783
357034	**C2**	P	*C2*	EM	67684	74184	74084	67784
357035	**C2**	P	*C2*	EM	67685	74185	74085	67785
357036	**C2**	P	*C2*	EM	67686	74186	74086	67786
357037	**C2**	P	*C2*	EM	67687	74187	74087	67787
357038	**C2**	P	*C2*	EM	67688	74188	74088	67788
357039	**C2**	P	*C2*	EM	67689	74189	74089	67789
357040	**C2**	P	*C2*	EM	67690	74190	74090	67790
357041	**C2**	P	*C2*	EM	67691	74191	74091	67791
357042	**C2**	P	*C2*	EM	67692	74192	74092	67792
357043	**C2**	P	*C2*	EM	67693	74193	74093	67793
357044	**C2**	P	*C2*	EM	67694	74194	74094	67794
357045	**C2**	P	*C2*	EM	67695	74195	74095	67795

| 357046 | **C2** | P | *C2* | EM | 67696 | 74196 | 74096 | 67796 |

Names (carried on DMSO(A) and DMSO(B) (one plate on each)):

357001	BARRY FLAXMAN
357002	ARTHUR LEWIS STRIDE 1841–1922
357003	SOUTHEND city.on.sea
357004	TONY AMOS
357005	SOUTHEND: 2017 Alternative City of Culture
357006	DIAMOND JUBILEE 1952–2012
357007	Sir Andrew Foster
357011	JOHN LOWING
357028	London, Tilbury & Southend Railway 1854–2004
357029	THOMAS WHITELEGG 1840–1922
357030	ROBERT HARBEN WHITELEGG 1871–1957

Class 357/2. Owned by Angel Trains.

DMSO(A). Bombardier Derby 2001–02. –/71. 40.7 t.
MSO. Bombardier Derby 2001–02. –/78. 36.7 t.
PTSO. Bombardier Derby 2001–02. –/58(+4) 1TD 2W. 39.5 t.
DMSO(B). Bombardier Derby 2001–02. –/71. 40.7 t.

357201	**C2**	A	*C2*	EM	68601	74701	74601	68701
357202	**C2**	A	*C2*	EM	68602	74702	74602	68702
357203	**C2**	A	*C2*	EM	68603	74703	74603	68703
357204	**C2**	A	*C2*	EM	68604	74704	74604	68704
357205	**C2**	A	*C2*	EM	68605	74705	74605	68705
357206	**C2**	A	*C2*	EM	68606	74706	74606	68706
357207	**C2**	A	*C2*	EM	68607	74707	74607	68707
357208	**C2**	A	*C2*	EM	68608	74708	74608	68708
357209	**C2**	A	*C2*	EM	68609	74709	74609	68709
357210	**C2**	A	*C2*	EM	68610	74710	74610	68710
357211	**C2**	A	*C2*	EM	68611	74711	74611	68711

Names (carried on DMSO(A) and DMSO(B) (one plate on each)):

357201	KEN BIRD	357206	MARTIN AUNGIER
357202	KENNY MITCHELL	357207	JOHN PAGE
357203	HENRY PUMFRETT	357208	DAVE DAVIS
357204	DEREK FOWERS	357209	JAMES SNELLING
357205	JOHN D'SILVA		

Class 357/3. Owned by Angel Trains. In 2015–16 17 Class 357/2s (357 212–228) were reconfigured as "high density" units 357 312–328 with fewer seats and more standing room for shorter distance workings.

Seating Layout: 2+2 facing/unidirectional.

DMSO(A). Bombardier Derby 2001–02. –/56. 40.7 t.
MSO. Bombardier Derby 2001–02. –/60. 36.7 t.
PTSO. Bombardier Derby 2001–02. –/50 1TD 2W. 39.5 t.
DMSO(B). Bombardier Derby 2001–02. –/56. 40.7 t.

| 357312 | (357212) | **C2** | A | *C2* | EM | 68612 | 74712 | 74612 | 68712 |
| 357313 | (357213) | **C2** | A | *C2* | EM | 68613 | 74713 | 74613 | 68713 |

357314	(357214)	**C2**	A	*C2*	EM	68614 74714 74614 68714
357315	(357215)	**C2**	A	*C2*	EM	68615 74715 74615 68715
357316	(357216)	**C2**	A	*C2*	EM	68616 74716 74616 68716
357317	(357217)	**C2**	A	*C2*	EM	68617 74717 74617 68717
357318	(357218)	**C2**	A	*C2*	EM	68618 74718 74618 68718
357319	(357219)	**C2**	A	*C2*	EM	68619 74719 74619 68719
357320	(357220)	**C2**	A	*C2*	EM	68620 74720 74620 68720
357321	(357221)	**C2**	A	*C2*	EM	68621 74721 74621 68721
357322	(357222)	**C2**	A	*C2*	EM	68622 74722 74622 68722
357323	(357223)	**C2**	A	*C2*	EM	68623 74723 74623 68723
357324	(357224)	**C2**	A	*C2*	EM	68624 74724 74624 68724
357325	(357225)	**C2**	A	*C2*	EM	68625 74725 74625 68725
357326	(357226)	**C2**	A	*C2*	EM	68626 74726 74626 68726
357327	(357227)	**C2**	A	*C2*	EM	68627 74727 74627 68727
357328	(357228)	**C2**	A	*C2*	EM	68628 74728 74628 68728

Names (carried on DMSO(A) and DMSO(B) (one plate on each)):

357313 UPMINSTER I.E.C.C. 357327 SOUTHEND UNITED
357317 ALLAN BURNELL

CLASS 360/0   DESIRO UK   SIEMENS

Outer suburban/express units.

Formation: DMCO–PTSO–TSO–DMCO.
Construction: Welded aluminium.
Traction Motors: Four Siemens 1TB2016-0GB02 asynchronous of 250 kW.
Wheel Arrangement: Bo-Bo + 2-2 + 2-2 + Bo-Bo.
Braking: Disc & regenerative.   **Dimensions:** 20.34 x 2.80 m.
Bogies: SGP SF5000.   **Couplers:** Dellner 12.
Gangways: Within unit.   **Control System:** IGBT Inverter.
Doors: Sliding plug.   **Maximum Speed:** 100 mph.
Heating & ventilation: Air conditioning.
Seating Layout: 1: 2+2 facing, 2: 3+2 facing/unidirectional.
Multiple Working: Within class.

DMCO(A). Siemens Krefeld 2002–03. 8/59. 45.0 t.
PTSO. Siemens Vienna 2002–03. –/60(+9) 1TD 2W. 43.0 t.
TSO. Siemens Vienna 2002–03. –/78. 35.0 t.
DMCO(B). Siemens Krefeld 2002–03. 8/59. 45.0 t.

360101	**FB**	A	*GA*	IL	65551 72551 74551 68551
360102	**FB**	A	*GA*	IL	65552 72552 74552 68552
360103	**FB**	A	*GA*	IL	65553 72553 74553 68553
360104	**FB**	A	*GA*	IL	65554 72554 74554 68554
360105	**FB**	A	*GA*	IL	65555 72555 74555 68555
360106	**FB**	A	*GA*	IL	65556 72556 74556 68556
360107	**FB**	A	*GA*	IL	65557 72557 74557 68557
360108	**FB**	A	*GA*	IL	65558 72558 74558 68558
360109	**FB**	A	*GA*	IL	65559 72559 74559 68559
360110	**FB**	A	*GA*	IL	65560 72560 74560 68560

360 111	**FB**	A	*GA*	IL	65561	72561	74561	68561
360 112	**FB**	A	*GA*	IL	65562	72562	74562	68562
360 113	**FB**	A	*GA*	IL	65563	72563	74563	68563
360 114	**FB**	A	*GA*	IL	65564	72564	74564	68564
360 115	**FB**	A	*GA*	IL	65565	72565	74565	68565
360 116	**FB**	A	*GA*	IL	65566	72566	74566	68566
360 117	**FB**	A	*GA*	IL	65567	72567	74567	68567
360 118	**FB**	A	*GA*	IL	65568	72568	74568	68568
360 119	**FB**	A	*GA*	IL	65569	72569	74569	68569
360 120	**FB**	A	*GA*	IL	65570	72570	74570	68570
360 121	**FB**	A	*GA*	IL	65571	72571	74571	68571

CLASS 360/2   DESIRO UK   SIEMENS

4-car Class 350 testbed units rebuilt for use by Heathrow Express on Paddington–Heathrow Airport stopping services ("Heathrow Connect").

Original 4-car sets 360201–204 were made up to 5-cars during 2007 using additional TSOs. A fifth unit (360205) was delivered in late 2005 as a 5-car set. This set is normally used on Terminals 1&3–Terminal 4 shuttle services.

Formation: DMSO–PTSO–TSO–TSO–DMSO.
Construction: Welded aluminium.
Traction Motors: Four Siemens 1TB2016-0GB02 asynchronous of 250 kW.
Wheel Arrangement: Bo-Bo + 2-2 + 2-2 + 2-2 + Bo-Bo.
Braking: Disc & regenerative.   **Dimensions:** 20.34 x 2.80 m.
Bogies: SGP SF5000.   **Couplers:** Dellner 12.
Gangways: Within unit.   **Control System:** IGBT Inverter.
Doors: Sliding plug.   **Maximum Speed:** 100 mph.
Heating & ventilation: Air conditioning.
Seating Layout: 3+2 (* 2+2) facing/unidirectional.
Multiple Working: Within class.

DMSO(A). Siemens Krefeld 2002–06. –/63 (* –/54). 44.8 t.
PTSO. Siemens Krefeld 2002–06. –/57(+9) 1TD 2W (* –/48(+9) 2W). 44.2 t.
TSO. Siemens Krefeld 2005–06. –/74 (* –/62). 35.3 t.
TSO. Siemens Krefeld 2002–06. –/74 (* –/62). 34.1 t.
DMSO(B). Siemens Krefeld 2002–06. –/63 (* –/54). 44.4 t.

360 201		**HC**	HE	*HC*	OH	78431	63421	72431	72421	78441
360 202		**HC**	HE	*HC*	OH	78432	63422	72432	72422	78442
360 203		**HC**	HE	*HC*	OH	78433	63423	72433	72423	78443
360 204		**HC**	HE	*HC*	OH	78434	63424	72434	72424	78444
360 205	*	**HE**	HE	*HE*	OH	78435	63425	72435	72425	78445

CLASS 365   NETWORKER EXPRESS   ABB YORK

Outer suburban units. Fitted with a universal access toilet to comply with the 2020 accessibility regulations.

Formations: DMCO–TSO–PTSO–DMCO.
Systems: 25 kV AC overhead but with 750 V DC third rail capability (units 365 501–516 were formerly used on DC lines in the South-East).
Construction: Welded aluminium alloy.
Traction Motors: Four GEC-Alsthom G354CX asynchronous of 157 kW.
Wheel Arrangement: Bo-Bo + 2-2 + 2-2 + Bo-Bo.
Braking: Disc & rheostatic.   **Dimensions:** 20.89/20.06 x 2.81 m.
Bogies: ABB P3-16/T3-16.   **Couplers:** Tightlock.
Gangways: Within unit.   **Control System:** GTO Inverter.
Doors: Sliding plug.   **Maximum Speed:** 100 mph.
Seating Layout: 1: 2+2 facing, 2: 2+2 facing.
Multiple Working: Within class only.

DMCO(A). Lot No. 31133 1994–95. 12/56. 41.7 t.
TSO. Lot No. 31134 1994–95. –/58 1TD 2W 32.9 t.
PTSO. Lot No. 31135 1994–95. –/70 1T. 35.2 t.
DMCO(B). Lot No. 31136 1994–95. 12/56. 41.7 t.

365 501	**TL**	E	*GN*	HE	65894	72241	72240	65935
365 502	**TL**	E	*GN*	HE	65895	72243	72242	65936
365 503	**TL**	E	*GN*	HE	65896	72245	72244	65937
365 504	**TL**	E	*GN*	HE	65897	72247	72246	65938
365 505	**TL**	E	*GN*	HE	65898	72249	72248	65939
365 506	**TL**	E	*GN*	HE	65899	72251	72250	65940
365 507	**TL**	E	*GN*	HE	65900	72253	72252	65941
365 508	**TL**	E	*GN*	HE	65901	72255	72254	65942
365 509	**TL**	E	*GN*	HE	65902	72257	72256	65943
365 510	**TL**	E	*GN*	HE	65903	72259	72258	65944
365 511	**TL**	E	*GN*	HE	65904	72261	72260	65945
365 512	**TL**	E	*GN*	HE	65905	72263	72262	65946
365 513	**TL**	E	*GN*	HE	65906	72265	72264	65947
365 514	**TL**	E	*GN*	HE	65907	72267	72266	65948
365 515	**TL**	E	*GN*	HE	65908	72269	72268	65949
365 516	**TL**	E	*GN*	HE	65909	72271	72270	65950
365 517	**TL**	E	*GN*	HE	65910	72273	72272	65951
365 518	**TL**	E	*GN*	HE	65911	72275	72274	65952
365 519	**TL**	E	*GN*	HE	65912	72277	72276	65953
365 520	**TL**	E	*GN*	HE	65913	72279	72278	65954
365 521	**TL**	E	*GN*	HE	65914	72281	72280	65955
365 522	**TL**	E	*GN*	HE	65915	72283	72282	65956
365 523	**TL**	E	*GN*	HE	65916	72285	72284	65957
365 524	**TL**	E	*GN*	HE	65917	72287	72286	65958
365 525	**TL**	E	*GN*	HE	65918	72289	72288	65959
365 527	**TL**	E	*GN*	HE	65920	72293	72292	65961
365 528	**TL**	E	*GN*	HE	65921	72295	72294	65962
365 529	**TL**	E	*GN*	HE	65922	72297	72296	65963
365 530	**TL**	E	*GN*	HE	65923	72299	72298	65964

365531	TL	E	GN	HE	65924	72301	72300	65965
365532	TL	E	GN	HE	65925	72303	72302	65966
365533	TL	E	GN	HE	65926	72305	72304	65967
365534	TL	E	GN	HE	65927	72307	72306	65968
365535	TL	E	GN	HE	65928	72309	72308	65969
365536	TL	E	GN	HE	65929	72311	72310	65970
365537	TL	E	GN	HE	65930	72313	72312	65971
365538	TL	E	GN	HE	65931	72315	72314	65972
365539	TL	E	GN	HE	65932	72317	72316	65973
365540	TL	E	GN	HE	65933	72319	72318	65974
365541	TL	E	GN	HE	65934	72321	72320	65975

Names (carried on each DMCO):

365517 Supporting Red Balloon
365533 Max Appeal
365537 Daniel Edwards (1974–2010) Cambridge Driver

CLASS 375 ELECTROSTAR
ADTRANZ/BOMBARDIER DERBY

Express and outer suburban units.

Formations: Various.
Systems: 25 kV AC overhead/750 V DC third rail (some third rail only with provision for retro-fitting of AC equipment).
Construction: Welded aluminium alloy underframe, sides and roof with steel ends. All sections bolted together.
Traction Motors: Two Adtranz asynchronous of 250 kW.
Wheel Arrangement: 2-Bo (+ 2-Bo) + 2-2 + Bo-2.
Braking: Disc & regenerative.   **Dimensions:** 20.40/19.99 x 2.80 m.
Bogies: Adtranz P3-25/T3-25.   **Couplers:** Dellner 12.
Gangways: Throughout.   **Control System:** IGBT Inverter.
Doors: Sliding plug.   **Maximum Speed:** 100 mph.
Heating & ventilation: Air conditioning.
Seating Layout: 1: 2+2 facing/unidirectional. 2: 2+2 facing/unidirectional (except 375/9 – 3+2 facing/unidirectional).
Multiple Working: Within class and with Classes 376, 377, 378 and 379.

Class 375/3. Express units. 750 V DC only. DMSO–TSO–DMCO.

DMSO. Bombardier Derby 2001–02. –/60. 43.8 t.
TSO. Bombardier Derby 2001–02. –/56 1TD 2W. 35.5 t.
DMCO. Bombardier Derby 2001–02. 12/48. 43.8 t.

375301	SB	E	SE	RM	67921	74351	67931
375302	SB	E	SE	RM	67922	74352	67932
375303	SB	E	SE	RM	67923	74353	67933
375304	SB	E	SE	RM	67924	74354	67934
375305	SB	E	SE	RM	67925	74355	67935
375306	SB	E	SE	RM	67926	74356	67936
375307	SB	E	SE	RM	67927	74357	67937
375308	SB	E	SE	RM	67928	74358	67938

375 309	**SB**	E	*SE*	RM	67929	74359	67939	
375 310	**SB**	E	*SE*	RM	67930	74360	67940	

Class 375/6. Express units. 25 kV AC/750 V DC. DMSO–MCO–PTSO–DMSO.

DMSO(A). Adtranz Derby 1999–2001. –/60. 46.2 t.
MCO. Adtranz Derby 1999–2001. 16/50 1T. 40.5 t.
PTSO. Adtranz Derby 1999–2001. –/56 1TD 2W. 40.7 t.
DMSO(B). Adtranz Derby 1999–2001. –/60. 46.2 t.

375 601	**SB**	E	*SE*	RM	67801	74251	74201	67851
375 602	**SB**	E	*SE*	RM	67802	74252	74202	67852
375 603	**SB**	E	*SE*	RM	67803	74253	74203	67853
375 604	**SB**	E	*SE*	RM	67804	74254	74204	67854
375 605	**SB**	E	*SE*	RM	67805	74255	74205	67855
375 606	**SB**	E	*SE*	RM	67806	74256	74206	67856
375 607	**SB**	E	*SE*	RM	67807	74257	74207	67857
375 608	**SB**	E	*SE*	RM	67808	74258	74208	67858
375 609	**SB**	E	*SE*	RM	67809	74259	74209	67859
375 610	**SB**	E	*SE*	RM	67810	74260	74210	67860
375 611	**SB**	E	*SE*	RM	67811	74261	74211	67861
375 612	**SB**	E	*SE*	RM	67812	74262	74212	67862
375 613	**SB**	E	*SE*	RM	67813	74263	74213	67863
375 614	**SB**	E	*SE*	RM	67814	74264	74214	67864
375 615	**SB**	E	*SE*	RM	67815	74265	74215	67865
375 616	**SB**	E	*SE*	RM	67816	74266	74216	67866
375 617	**SB**	E	*SE*	RM	67817	74267	74217	67867
375 618	**SB**	E	*SE*	RM	67818	74268	74218	67868
375 619	**SB**	E	*SE*	RM	67819	74269	74219	67869
375 620	**SB**	E	*SE*	RM	67820	74270	74220	67870
375 621	**SB**	E	*SE*	RM	67821	74271	74221	67871
375 622	**SB**	E	*SE*	RM	67822	74272	74222	67872
375 623	**SB**	E	*SE*	RM	67823	74273	74223	67873
375 624	**SB**	E	*SE*	RM	67824	74274	74224	67874
375 625	**SB**	E	*SE*	RM	67825	74275	74225	67875
375 626	**SB**	E	*SE*	RM	67826	74276	74226	67876
375 627	**SB**	E	*SE*	RM	67827	74277	74227	67877
375 628	**SB**	E	*SE*	RM	67828	74278	74228	67878
375 629	**SB**	E	*SE*	RM	67829	74279	74229	67879
375 630	**SB**	E	*SE*	RM	67830	74280	74230	67880

Names (carried on one side of each MCO or TSO):

375 619 Hospice in the Weald | 375 623 Driver John Neve

Class 375/7. Express units. 750 V DC only. DMSO–MCO–TSO–DMSO.

DMSO(A). Bombardier Derby 2001–02. –/60. 43.8 t.
MCO. Bombardier Derby 2001–02. 16/50 1T. 36.4 t.
TSO. Bombardier Derby 2001–02. –/56 1TD 2W. 34.1 t.
DMSO(B). Bombardier Derby 2001–02. –/60. 43.8 t.

375 701	**SB**	E	*SE*	RM	67831	74281	74231	67881
375 702	**SB**	E	*SE*	RM	67832	74282	74232	67882
375 703	**SB**	E	*SE*	RM	67833	74283	74233	67883

375704	**SB**	E	*SE*	RM	67834	74284	74234	67884
375705	**SB**	E	*SE*	RM	67835	74285	74235	67885
375706	**SB**	E	*SE*	RM	67836	74286	74236	67886
375707	**SB**	E	*SE*	RM	67837	74287	74237	67887
375708	**SB**	E	*SE*	RM	67838	74288	74238	67888
375709	**SB**	E	*SE*	RM	67839	74289	74239	67889
375710	**SB**	E	*SE*	RM	67840	74290	74240	67890
375711	**SB**	E	*SE*	RM	67841	74291	74241	67891
375712	**SB**	E	*SE*	RM	67842	74292	74242	67892
375713	**SB**	E	*SE*	RM	67843	74293	74243	67893
375714	**SB**	E	*SE*	RM	67844	74294	74244	67894
375715	**SB**	E	*SE*	RM	67845	74295	74245	67895

Names (carried on one side of each MCO or TSO):

375701	Kent Air Ambulance Explorer	375714	Rochester Cathedral
375710	Rochester Castle		

Class 375/8. Express units. 750 V DC only. DMCO–MSO–TSO–DMCO or † DMSO–MCO–TSO–DMSO.

375 801–820 are fitted with de-icing equipment. TSO weighs 36.5 t.

DMCO(A) († DMSO(A)). Bombardier Derby 2004. 12/48 († –/60). 43.3 t.
MSO († MCO). Bombardier Derby 2004. –/66 1T († 16/50 1T). 39.8 t.
TSO. Bombardier Derby 2004. –/52 1TD 2W. 35.9 t.
DMCO(B) († DMSO(B)). Bombardier Derby 2004. 12/52 († –/64). 43.3 t.

375801	†	**SB**	E	*SE*	RM	73301	79001	78201	73701
375802	†	**SB**	E	*SE*	RM	73302	79002	78202	73702
375803	†	**SB**	E	*SE*	RM	73303	79003	78203	73703
375804	†	**SB**	E	*SE*	RM	73304	79004	78204	73704
375805	†	**SB**	E	*SE*	RM	73305	79005	78205	73705
375806	†	**SB**	E	*SE*	RM	73306	79006	78206	73706
375807	†	**SB**	E	*SE*	RM	73307	79007	78207	73707
375808	†	**SB**	E	*SE*	RM	73308	79008	78208	73708
375809	†	**SB**	E	*SE*	RM	73309	79009	78209	73709
375810	†	**SB**	E	*SE*	RM	73310	79010	78210	73710
375811	†	**SB**	E	*SE*	RM	73311	79011	78211	73711
375812	†	**SB**	E	*SE*	RM	73312	79012	78212	73712
375813	†	**SB**	E	*SE*	RM	73313	79013	78213	73713
375814	†	**SB**	E	*SE*	RM	73314	79014	78214	73714
375815	†	**SB**	E	*SE*	RM	73315	79015	78215	73715
375816	†	**SB**	E	*SE*	RM	73316	79016	78216	73716
375817	†	**SB**	E	*SE*	RM	73317	79017	78217	73717
375818	†	**SB**	E	*SE*	RM	73318	79018	78218	73718
375819	†	**SB**	E	*SE*	RM	73319	79019	78219	73719
375820	†	**SB**	E	*SE*	RM	73320	79020	78220	73720
375821	†	**SB**	E	*SE*	RM	73321	79021	78221	73721
375822	†	**SB**	E	*SE*	RM	73322	79022	78222	73722
375823	†	**SB**	E	*SE*	RM	73323	79023	78223	73723
375824		**CN**	E	*SE*	RM	73324	79024	78224	73724
375825	†	**SB**	E	*SE*	RM	73325	79025	78225	73725
375826		**CN**	E	*SE*	RM	73326	79026	78226	73726

375827 †	**SB**	E	*SE*	RM	73327	79027	78227	73727
375828	**CN**	E	*SE*	RM	73328	79028	78228	73728
375829	**CN**	E	*SE*	RM	73329	79029	78229	73729
375830	**CN**	E	*SE*	RM	73330	79030	78230	73730

Names (carried on one side of each MSO or TSO):

375823 Ashford Proudly Served by Rail for 175 years
375830 City of London

Class 375/9. Outer suburban units. 750 V DC only. DMCO–MSO–TSO–DMCO.

DMCO(A). Bombardier Derby 2003–04. 12/59. 43.4 t.
MSO. Bombardier Derby 2003–04. –/73 1T. 39.3 t.
TSO. Bombardier Derby 2003–04. –/62 1TD 2W. 35.6 t.
DMCO(B). Bombardier Derby 2003–04. 12/59. 43.4 t.

375901	**SB**	E	*SE*	RM	73331	79031	79061	73731
375902	**SB**	E	*SE*	RM	73332	79032	79062	73732
375903	**SB**	E	*SE*	RM	73333	79033	79063	73733
375904	**SB**	E	*SE*	RM	73334	79034	79064	73734
375905	**SB**	E	*SE*	RM	73335	79035	79065	73735
375906	**SB**	E	*SE*	RM	73336	79036	79066	73736
375907	**SB**	E	*SE*	RM	73337	79037	79067	73737
375908	**SB**	E	*SE*	RM	73338	79038	79068	73738
375909	**SB**	E	*SE*	RM	73339	79039	79069	73739
375910	**SB**	E	*SE*	RM	73340	79040	79070	73740
375911	**SB**	E	*SE*	RM	73341	79041	79071	73741
375912	**SB**	E	*SE*	RM	73342	79042	79072	73742
375913	**SB**	E	*SE*	RM	73343	79043	79073	73743
375914	**SB**	E	*SE*	RM	73344	79044	79074	73744
375915	**SB**	E	*SE*	RM	73345	79045	79075	73745
375916	**SB**	E	*SE*	RM	73346	79046	79076	73746
375917	**SB**	E	*SE*	RM	73347	79047	79077	73747
375918	**SB**	E	*SE*	RM	73348	79048	79078	73748
375919	**SB**	E	*SE*	RM	73349	79049	79079	73749
375920	**CN**	E	*SE*	RM	73350	79050	79080	73750
375921	**SB**	E	*SE*	RM	73351	79051	79081	73751
375922	**SB**	E	*SE*	RM	73352	79052	79082	73752
375923	**SB**	E	*SE*	RM	73353	79053	79083	73753
375924	**SB**	E	*SE*	RM	73354	79054	79084	73754
375925	**CN**	E	*SE*	RM	73355	79055	79085	73755
375926	**CN**	E	*SE*	RM	73356	79056	79086	73756
375927	**CN**	E	*SE*	RM	73357	79057	79087	73757

CLASS 376   ELECTROSTAR   BOMBARDIER DERBY

Inner suburban units.

Formation: DMSO–MSO–TSO–MSO–DMSO.
System: 750 V DC third rail.
Construction: Welded aluminium alloy underframe, sides and roof with steel ends. All sections bolted together.
Traction Motors: Two Bombardier asynchronous of 200 kW.

Wheel Arrangement: 2-Bo + 2-Bo + 2-2 + Bo-2 + Bo-2.
Braking: Disc & regenerative.   **Dimensions:** 20.40/19.99 x 2.80 m.
Bogies: Bombardier P3-25/T3-25.   **Couplers:** Dellner 12.
Gangways: Within unit.   **Control System:** IGBT Inverter.
Doors: Sliding.   **Maximum Speed:** 75 mph.
Heating & ventilation: Pressure heating and ventilation.
Seating Layout: 2+2 low density facing.
Multiple Working: Within class and with Classes 375, 377, 378 and 379.

DMSO(A). Bombardier Derby 2004–05. –/36(+6) 1W. 42.1 t.
MSO. Bombardier Derby 2004–05. –/48. 36.2 t.
TSO. Bombardier Derby 2004–05. –/48. 36.3 t.
DMSO(B). Bombardier Derby 2004–05. –/36(+6) 1W. 42.1 t.

376001	**CN**	E	*SE*	SG	61101	63301	64301	63501	61601
376002	**CN**	E	*SE*	SG	61102	63302	64302	63502	61602
376003	**CN**	E	*SE*	SG	61103	63303	64303	63503	61603
376004	**CN**	E	*SE*	SG	61104	63304	64304	63504	61604
376005	**CN**	E	*SE*	SG	61105	63305	64305	63505	61605
376006	**CN**	E	*SE*	SG	61106	63306	64306	63506	61606
376007	**CN**	E	*SE*	SG	61107	63307	64307	63507	61607
376008	**CN**	E	*SE*	SG	61108	63308	64308	63508	61608
376009	**CN**	E	*SE*	SG	61109	63309	64309	63509	61609
376010	**CN**	E	*SE*	SG	61110	63310	64310	63510	61610
376011	**CN**	E	*SE*	SG	61111	63311	64311	63511	61611
376012	**CN**	E	*SE*	SG	61112	63312	64312	63512	61612
376013	**CN**	E	*SE*	SG	61113	63313	64313	63513	61613
376014	**CN**	E	*SE*	SG	61114	63314	64314	63514	61614
376015	**CN**	E	*SE*	SG	61115	63315	64315	63515	61615
376016	**CN**	E	*SE*	SG	61116	63316	64316	63516	61616
376017	**CN**	E	*SE*	SG	61117	63317	64317	63517	61617
376018	**CN**	E	*SE*	SG	61118	63318	64318	63518	61618
376019	**CN**	E	*SE*	SG	61119	63319	64319	63519	61619
376020	**CN**	E	*SE*	SG	61120	63320	64320	63520	61620
376021	**CN**	E	*SE*	SG	61121	63321	64321	63521	61621
376022	**CN**	E	*SE*	SG	61122	63322	64322	63522	61622
376023	**CN**	E	*SE*	SG	61123	63323	64323	63523	61623
376024	**CN**	E	*SE*	SG	61124	63324	64324	63524	61624
376025	**CN**	E	*SE*	SG	61125	63325	64325	63525	61625
376026	**CN**	E	*SE*	SG	61126	63326	64326	63526	61626
376027	**CN**	E	*SE*	SG	61127	63327	64327	63527	61627
376028	**CN**	E	*SE*	SG	61128	63328	64328	63528	61628
376029	**CN**	E	*SE*	SG	61129	63329	64329	63529	61629
376030	**CN**	E	*SE*	SG	61130	63330	64330	63530	61630
376031	**CN**	E	*SE*	SG	61131	63331	64331	63531	61631
376032	**CN**	E	*SE*	SG	61132	63332	64332	63532	61632
376033	**CN**	E	*SE*	SG	61133	63333	64333	63533	61633
376034	**CN**	E	*SE*	SG	61134	63334	64334	63534	61634
376035	**CN**	E	*SE*	SG	61135	63335	64335	63535	61635
376036	**CN**	E	*SE*	SG	61136	63336	64336	63536	61636

Name (carried on TSO): 376001   Alan Doggett

▲ London Overground-liveried 315 804 is seen at Silver Street with the 16.22 Enfield Town–London Liverpool Street on 14/08/16. **Robert Pritchard**

▼ ScotRail Saltire-liveried 318 270 and 318 264 pass Craigenhill with the 13.51 Lanark–Glasgow Central on 13/04/17. **Robin Ralston**

▲ In the full new Northern livery, 319 374 leaves Crewe on its way from Wolverton Works to Allerton depot following overhaul on 22/07/17. **Cliff Beeton**

▼ Greater Anglia "Renatus"-liveried 321 321 passes South Kenton working back from Wolverton to Ilford on 10/05/17. **Antony Guppy**

▲ Royal Mail-liveried 325 013, 325 011 and 325 003 form a 12-car set near Law Junction with 1M44 16.17 Shieldmuir–Warrington on 16/03/17. **Robin Ralston**

▼ West Yorkshire PTE-liveried 333 006 arrives at Bradford Forster Square with the 08.00 from Skipton on 30/04/16. **Robert Pritchard**

▲ ScotRail Saltire-liveried 334 035 is seen near Caldercruix with the 17.56 Helensburgh Central–Edinburgh Waverley on 01/06/13. **Robert Pritchard**

▼ Elizabeth Line-liveried 345 005 stands at Shenfield after arrival with the 10.35 from London Liverpool Street on 22/06/17. **Jonathan Webb**

▲ TransPennine Express-liveried 350 401 passes Lamington with the 18.13 Edinburgh–Manchester Airport on 12/07/17. **Robin Ralston**

▼ c2c-liveried 357 004 leaves Leigh-on-Sea with the 11.11 London Fenchurch Street–Southend on 11/11/16. 387 301 can be seen alongside on driving training. **Robert Pritchard**

▲ Still in First Group dark blue, 360 110 and 360 114 arrive at Kelvedon with the 18.12 Colchester–London Liverpool Street on 14/06/17. **Robert Pritchard**

▼ Southeastern blue-liveried 375 618 approaches Shortlands with the 17.02 Ashford International–London Victoria on 19/06/17. **Robert Pritchard**

▲ Still in the old Connex white livery, 376 028 leads the 11.51 Dartford–London Charing Cross into Barnehurst on 20/12/16. **Brian Denton**

▼ Southern-liveried 377 404 and 377 143 leave East Croydon with the 14.23 London Victoria–East Grinstead on 15/10/16. **Robert Pritchard**

▲ London Overground-liveried 378 154 arrives at Honor Oak Park with the 15.13 Highbury & Islington–Crystal Palace on 16/10/16. **Robert Pritchard**

▼ ScotRail Saltire-liveried 380 005 arrives at Motherwell with the 13.50 Glasgow Central–Lanark on 15/09/16. **Stewart Armstrong**

▲ New Hitachi 4-car ScotRail set 385 102 in Shields Road depot, Glasgow during testing on 12/12/16. **Ian Lothian**

▼ Gatwick Express-liveried 387 214, 387 203 and 387 221 pass South Croydon with the 15.15 London Victoria–Gatwick Airport on 13/06/17. **Robert Pritchard**

▲ Virgin Trains-liveried Pendolino 390 039 passes Stafford on 22/04/17 with the 16.40 London Euston–Manchester Piccadilly. **Robert Pritchard**

▼ Southeastern blue-liveried 395 025 is seen near Boxley Tunnel on High Speed 1 with the 14.27 London St Pancras–London St Pancras via Ramsgate/Dover on 27/08/17. **Robert Pritchard**

▲ South West Trains-white liveried 444 044 approaches Southampton Central with the 15.03 Weymouth–London Waterloo on 17/06/17.　**Robert Pritchard**

▼ South West Trains blue-liveried 450 021 and 450 558 overtake SWT red-liveried 5909 and 5750 at Wimbledon on 19/06/17.　**Robert Pritchard**

▲ South West Trains red-liveried 456 004+5728+5707 approach Wimbledon with a service for London Waterloo on 19/06/17. **Robert Pritchard**

▼ South West Trains blue-liveried 458 526 brings up the rear of the 13.53 Windsor & Eton Riverside–London Waterloo (led by 458 510) at Ashford on 19/06/17.
Robert Pritchard

▲ Southeastern suburban-liveried 465 240 approaches Shortlands with the 17.46 Rochester–London Blackfriars empty stock on 19/06/17.　　**Robert Pritchard**

▼ London Transport maroon-liveried 483 004 calls at Ryde St Johns Road with the 15.49 Ryde Pier Head–Shanklin on 16/07/17.　　**Chris Wilson**

▲ Merseyrail-liveried 507 019 arrives at Hooton with the 13.12 Ellesmere Port–Ellesmere Port via Liverpool circular service on 02/09/17. **Cliff Beeton**

▼ Thameslink-liveried 700 007 passes Purley Oaks with the 08.18 Brighton–Bedford on 15/06/17. **Robert Pritchard**

▲ South West Trains red-liveried 707 006 and 707 005 pass Virginia Water with a 14.24 Staines Up Loop–Reading test run on 19/06/17. **Robert Pritchard**

▼ Great Western Railway green-liveried 800 003 and 800 004 pass Biggleswade with a North Pole–Doncaster IEP depot test run on 23/07/17. **Alisdair Anderson**

▲ Virgin Trains East Coast-liveried 800 101 is seen near Claypole on the ECML with a 14.35 Peterborough–Peterborough test run on 07/02/17.　**Bill Atkinson**

▼ New Eurostar-liveried Class 373 3220+3219 exits Boxley Tunnel with the 12.58 London St Pancras–Brussels on 26/08/17.　**Robert Pritchard**

CLASS 377   ELECTROSTAR   BOMBARDIER DERBY

Express and outer suburban units.

Formations: Various.
Systems: 25 kV AC overhead/750 V DC third rail or third rail only with provision for retro-fitting of AC equipment.
Construction: Welded aluminium alloy underframe, sides and roof with steel ends. All sections bolted together.
Traction Motors: Two Bombardier asynchronous of 250 kW.
Wheel Arrangement: 2-Bo + 2-2 + Bo-2 or 2-Bo + 2-Bo + 2-2 + Bo-2 or 2-Bo + 2-Bo + 2-2 + Bo-2 + Bo-2.
Braking: Disc & regenerative.
Bogies: Bombardier P3-25/T3-25.
Gangways: Throughout.
Doors: Sliding plug.

Dimensions: 20.39/20.00 x 2.80 m.
Couplers: Dellner 12.
Control System: IGBT Inverter.
Maximum Speed: 100 mph.

Heating & ventilation: Air conditioning.
Seating Layout: Various, see sub-class headings.
Multiple Working: Within class and with Classes 375, 376, 378, 379 and 387.
Class 377/1. 750 V DC only. DMCO–MSO–TSO–DMCO.
Seating layout: 1: 2+2 facing/unidirectional, 2: 2+2 facing/unidirectional (377 101–119), 3+2/2+2 facing/unidirectional (377 120–139), 3+2 (middle cars and 2+2 (end cars) facing/unidirectional (377 140–164).

DMCO(A). Bombardier Derby 2002–03. 12/48 (s 12/56). 44.8 t.
MSO. Bombardier Derby 2002–03. –/62 (s –/70, t –/69). 1T. 39.0 t.
TSO. Bombardier Derby 2002–03. –/52 (s –/60, t –/57). 1TD 2W. 35.4 t.
DMCO(B). Bombardier Derby 2002–03. 12/48 (s 12/56). 44.8 t.

377 101		**SN**	P	*SN*	SU	78501	77101	78901	78701
377 102		**SN**	P	*SN*	SU	78502	77102	78902	78702
377 103		**SN**	P	*SN*	SU	78503	77103	78903	78703
377 104		**SN**	P	*SN*	SU	78504	77104	78904	78704
377 105		**SN**	P	*SN*	SU	78505	77105	78905	78705
377 106		**SN**	P	*SN*	SU	78506	77106	78906	78706
377 107		**SN**	P	*SN*	SU	78507	77107	78907	78707
377 108		**SN**	P	*SN*	SU	78508	77108	78908	78708
377 109		**SN**	P	*SN*	SU	78509	77109	78909	78709
377 110		**SN**	P	*SN*	SU	78510	77110	78910	78710
377 111		**SN**	P	*SN*	SU	78511	77111	78911	78711
377 112		**SN**	P	*SN*	SU	78512	77112	78912	78712
377 113		**SN**	P	*SN*	SU	78513	77113	78913	78713
377 114		**SN**	P	*SN*	SU	78514	77114	78914	78714
377 115		**SN**	P	*SN*	SU	78515	77115	78915	78715
377 116		**SN**	P	*SN*	SU	78516	77116	78916	78716
377 117		**SN**	P	*SN*	SU	78517	77117	78917	78717
377 118		**SN**	P	*SN*	SU	78518	77118	78918	78718
377 119		**SN**	P	*SN*	SU	78519	77119	78919	78719
377 120	s	**SN**	P	*SN*	SU	78520	77120	78920	78720
377 121	s	**SN**	P	*SN*	SU	78521	77121	78921	78721
377 122	s	**SN**	P	*SN*	SU	78522	77122	78922	78722
377 123	s	**SN**	P	*SN*	SU	78523	77123	78923	78723

377 124	s	**SN**	P	*SN*	SU	78524	77124	78924	78724
377 125	s	**SN**	P	*SN*	SU	78525	77125	78925	78725
377 126	s	**SN**	P	*SN*	SU	78526	77126	78926	78726
377 127	s	**SN**	P	*SN*	SU	78527	77127	78927	78727
377 128	s	**SN**	P	*SN*	SU	78528	77128	78928	78728
377 129	s	**SN**	P	*SN*	SU	78529	77129	78929	78729
377 130	s	**SN**	P	*SN*	SU	78530	77130	78930	78730
377 131	s	**SN**	P	*SN*	SU	78531	77131	78931	78731
377 132	s	**SN**	P	*SN*	SU	78532	77132	78932	78732
377 133	s	**SN**	P	*SN*	SU	78533	77133	78933	78733
377 134	s	**SN**	P	*SN*	SU	78534	77134	78934	78734
377 135	s	**SN**	P	*SN*	SU	78535	77135	78935	78735
377 136	s	**SN**	P	*SN*	SU	78536	77136	78936	78736
377 137	s	**SN**	P	*SN*	SU	78537	77137	78937	78737
377 138	s	**SN**	P	*SN*	SU	78538	77138	78938	78738
377 139	s	**SN**	P	*SN*	SU	78539	77139	78939	78739
377 140	t	**SN**	P	*SN*	SU	78540	77140	78940	78740
377 141	t	**SN**	P	*SN*	SU	78541	77141	78941	78741
377 142	t	**SN**	P	*SN*	SU	78542	77142	78942	78742
377 143	t	**SN**	P	*SN*	SU	78543	77143	78943	78743
377 144	t	**SN**	P	*SN*	SU	78544	77144	78944	78744
377 145	t	**SN**	P	*SN*	SU	78545	77145	78945	78745
377 146	t	**SN**	P	*SN*	SU	78546	77146	78946	78746
377 147	t	**SN**	P	*SN*	SU	78547	77147	78947	78747
377 148	t	**SN**	P	*SN*	SU	78548	77148	78948	78748
377 149	t	**SN**	P	*SN*	SU	78549	77149	78949	78749
377 150	t	**SN**	P	*SN*	SU	78550	77150	78950	78750
377 151	t	**SN**	P	*SN*	SU	78551	77151	78951	78751
377 152	t	**SN**	P	*SN*	SU	78552	77152	78952	78752
377 153	t	**SN**	P	*SN*	SU	78553	77153	78953	78753
377 154	t	**SN**	P	*SN*	SU	78554	77154	78954	78754
377 155	t	**SN**	P	*SN*	SU	78555	77155	78955	78755
377 156	t	**SN**	P	*SN*	SU	78556	77156	78956	78756
377 157	t	**SN**	P	*SN*	SU	78557	77157	78957	78757
377 158	t	**SN**	P	*SN*	SU	78558	77158	78958	78758
377 159	t	**SN**	P	*SN*	SU	78559	77159	78959	78759
377 160	t	**SN**	P	*SN*	SU	78560	77160	78960	78760
377 161	t	**SN**	P	*SN*	SU	78561	77161	78961	78761
377 162	t	**SN**	P	*SN*	SU	78562	77162	78962	78762
377 163	t	**SN**	P	*SE*	SU	78563	77163	78963	78763
377 164	t	**SN**	P	*SE*	SU	78564	77164	78964	78764

Class 377/2. 25 kV AC/750 V DC. DMCO–MSO–PTSO–DMCO. Dual-voltage units. **Seating layout:** 1: 2+2 facing/unidirectional, 2: 2+2 and 3+2 facing/unidirectional (3+2 seating in middle cars only).

DMCO(A). Bombardier Derby 2003–04. 12/48. 44.2 t.
MSO. Bombardier Derby 2003–04. –/69 1T. 39.8 t.
PTSO. Bombardier Derby 2003–04. –/57 1TD 2W. 40.1 t.
DMCO(B). Bombardier Derby 2003–04. 12/48. 44.2 t.

377 201		**SN**	P	*SN*	SU	78571	77171	78971	78771
377 202		**SN**	P	*SN*	SU	78572	77172	78972	78772

377 203	**SN**	P	*SN*	SU	78573	77173	78973	78773
377 204	**SN**	P	*SN*	SU	78574	77174	78974	78774
377 205	**SN**	P	*SN*	SU	78575	77175	78975	78775
377 206	**SN**	P	*SN*	SU	78576	77176	78976	78776
377 207	**SN**	P	*SN*	SU	78577	77177	78977	78777
377 208	**SN**	P	*SN*	SU	78578	77178	78978	78778
377 209	**SN**	P	*SN*	SU	78579	77179	78979	78779
377 210	**SN**	P	*SN*	SU	78580	77180	78980	78780
377 211	**SN**	P	*SN*	SU	78581	77181	78981	78781
377 212	**SN**	P	*SN*	SU	78582	77182	78982	78782
377 213	**SN**	P	*SN*	SU	78583	77183	78983	78783
377 214	**SN**	P	*SN*	SU	78584	77184	78984	78784
377 215	**SN**	P	*SN*	SU	78585	77185	78985	78785

Class 377/3. 750 V DC only. DMCO–TSO–DMCO.
Seating Layout: 1: 2+2 facing/unidirectional, 2: 2+2 facing/unidirectional.

Units built as Class 375, but renumbered in the Class 377/3 range when fitted with Dellner couplers.

377342 was formerly 377442. It had been reformed as a 3-car unit owing to fire damage to MSO vehicle 78842 in November 2016.

DMCO(A). Bombardier Derby 2001–02. 12/48. 43.5 t.
TSO. Bombardier Derby 2001–02. –/56 1TD 2W. 35.4 t.
DMCO(B). Bombardier Derby 2001–02. 12/48. 43.5 t.

377 301	(375 311)	**SN**	P	*SN*	SU	68201	74801	68401
377 302	(375 312)	**SN**	P	*SN*	SU	68202	74802	68402
377 303	(375 313)	**SN**	P	*SN*	SU	68203	74803	68403
377 304	(375 314)	**SN**	P	*SN*	SU	68204	74804	68404
377 305	(375 315)	**SN**	P	*SN*	SU	68205	74805	68405
377 306	(375 316)	**SN**	P	*SN*	SU	68206	74806	68406
377 307	(375 317)	**SN**	P	*SN*	SU	68207	74807	68407
377 308	(375 318)	**SN**	P	*SN*	SU	68208	74808	68408
377 309	(375 319)	**SN**	P	*SN*	SU	68209	74809	68409
377 310	(375 320)	**SN**	P	*SN*	SU	68210	74810	68410
377 311	(375 321)	**SN**	P	*SN*	SU	68211	74811	68411
377 312	(375 322)	**SN**	P	*SN*	SU	68212	74812	68412
377 313	(375 323)	**SN**	P	*SN*	SU	68213	74813	68413
377 314	(375 324)	**SN**	P	*SN*	SU	68214	74814	68414
377 315	(375 325)	**SN**	P	*SN*	SU	68215	74815	68415
377 316	(375 326)	**SN**	P	*SN*	SU	68216	74816	68416
377 317	(375 327)	**SN**	P	*SN*	SU	68217	74817	68417
377 318	(375 328)	**SN**	P	*SN*	SU	68218	74818	68418
377 319	(375 329)	**SN**	P	*SN*	SU	68219	74819	68419
377 320	(375 330)	**SN**	P	*SN*	SU	68220	74820	68420
377 321	(375 331)	**SN**	P	*SN*	SU	68221	74821	68421
377 322	(375 332)	**SN**	P	*SN*	SU	68222	74822	68422
377 323	(375 333)	**SN**	P	*SN*	SU	68223	74823	68423
377 324	(375 334)	**SN**	P	*SN*	SU	68224	74824	68424
377 325	(375 335)	**SN**	P	*SN*	SU	68225	74825	68425
377 326	(375 336)	**SN**	P	*SN*	SU	68226	74826	68426

377 327	(375 337)	**SN**	P	*SN*	SU	68227	74827	68427
377 328	(375 338)	**SN**	P	*SN*	SU	68228	74828	68428
377 342	(377 442)	**SN**	P	*SN*	SU	73442	78642	73842

Class 377/4. 750 V DC only. DMCO–MSO–TSO–DMCO.
Seating Layout: 1: 2+2 facing/two seats longitudinal, 2: 2+2 and 3+2 facing/unidirectional (3+2 seating in middle cars only).

DMCO(A). Bombardier Derby 2004–05. 10/48. 43.1 t.
MSO. Bombardier Derby 2004–05. –/69 1T. 39.3 t.
TSO. Bombardier Derby 2004–05. –/56 1TD 2W. 35.3 t.
DMCO(B). Bombardier Derby 2004–05. 10/48. 43.2 t.

377 401	**SN**	P	*SN*	SU	73401	78801	78601	73801
377 402	**SN**	P	*SN*	SU	73402	78802	78602	73802
377 403	**SN**	P	*SN*	SU	73403	78803	78603	73803
377 404	**SN**	P	*SN*	SU	73404	78804	78604	73804
377 405	**SN**	P	*SN*	SU	73405	78805	78605	73805
377 406	**SN**	P	*SN*	SU	73406	78806	78606	73806
377 407	**SN**	P	*SN*	SU	73407	78807	78607	73807
377 408	**SN**	P	*SN*	SU	73408	78808	78608	73808
377 409	**SN**	P	*SN*	SU	73409	78809	78609	73809
377 410	**SN**	P	*SN*	SU	73410	78810	78610	73810
377 411	**SN**	P	*SN*	SU	73411	78811	78611	73811
377 412	**SN**	P	*SN*	SU	73412	78812	78612	73812
377 413	**SN**	P	*SN*	SU	73413	78813	78613	73813
377 414	**SN**	P	*SN*	SU	73414	78814	78614	73814
377 415	**SN**	P	*SN*	SU	73415	78815	78615	73815
377 416	**SN**	P	*SN*	SU	73416	78816	78616	73816
377 417	**SN**	P	*SN*	SU	73417	78817	78617	73817
377 418	**SN**	P	*SN*	SU	73418	78818	78618	73818
377 419	**SN**	P	*SN*	SU	73419	78819	78619	73819
377 420	**SN**	P	*SN*	SU	73420	78820	78620	73820
377 421	**SN**	P	*SN*	SU	73421	78821	78621	73821
377 422	**SN**	P	*SN*	SU	73422	78822	78622	73822
377 423	**SN**	P	*SN*	SU	73423	78823	78623	73823
377 424	**SN**	P	*SN*	SU	73424	78824	78624	73824
377 425	**SN**	P	*SN*	SU	73425	78825	78625	73825
377 426	**SN**	P	*SN*	SU	73426	78826	78626	73826
377 427	**SN**	P	*SN*	SU	73427	78827	78627	73827
377 428	**SN**	P	*SN*	SU	73428	78828	78628	73828
377 429	**SN**	P	*SN*	SU	73429	78829	78629	73829
377 430	**SN**	P	*SN*	SU	73430	78830	78630	73830
377 431	**SN**	P	*SN*	SU	73431	78831	78631	73831
377 432	**SN**	P	*SN*	SU	73432	78832	78632	73832
377 433	**SN**	P	*SN*	SU	73433	78833	78633	73833
377 434	**SN**	P	*SN*	SU	73434	78834	78634	73834
377 435	**SN**	P	*SN*	SU	73435	78835	78635	73835
377 436	**SN**	P	*SN*	SU	73436	78836	78636	73836
377 437	**SN**	P	*SN*	SU	73437	78837	78637	73837
377 438	**SN**	P	*SN*	SU	73438	78838	78638	73838
377 439	**SN**	P	*SN*	SU	73439	78839	78639	73839

377440	**SN**	P	*SN*	SU	73440	78840	78640	73840
377441	**SN**	P	*SN*	SU	73441	78841	78641	73841
377443	**SN**	P	*SN*	SU	73443	78843	78643	73843
377444	**SN**	P	*SN*	SU	73444	78844	78644	73844
377445	**SN**	P	*SN*	SU	73445	78845	78645	73845
377446	**SN**	P	*SN*	SU	73446	78846	78646	73846
377447	**SN**	P	*SN*	SU	73447	78847	78647	73847
377448	**SN**	P	*SN*	SU	73448	78848	78648	73848
377449	**SN**	P	*SN*	SU	73449	78849	78649	73849
377450	**SN**	P	*SN*	SU	73450	78850	78650	73850
377451	**SN**	P	*SN*	SU	73451	78851	78651	73851
377452	**SN**	P	*SN*	SU	73452	78852	78652	73852
377453	**SN**	P	*SN*	SU	73453	78853	78653	73853
377454	**SN**	P	*SN*	SU	73454	78854	78654	73854
377455	**SN**	P	*SN*	SU	73455	78855	78655	73855
377456	**SN**	P	*SN*	SU	73456	78856	78656	73856
377457	**SN**	P	*SN*	SU	73457	78857	78657	73857
377458	**SN**	P	*SN*	SU	73458	78858	78658	73858
377459	**SN**	P	*SN*	SU	73459	78859	78659	73859
377460	**SN**	P	*SN*	SU	73460	78860	78660	73860
377461	**SN**	P	*SN*	SU	73461	78861	78661	73861
377462	**SN**	P	*SN*	SU	73462	78862	78662	73862
377463	**SN**	P	*SN*	SU	73463	78863	78663	73863
377464	**SN**	P	*SN*	SU	73464	78864	78664	73864
377465	**SN**	P	*SN*	SU	73465	78865	78665	73865
377466	**SN**	P	*SN*	SU	73466	78866	78666	73866
377467	**SN**	P	*SN*	SU	73467	78867	78667	73867
377468	**SN**	P	*SN*	SU	73468	78868	78668	73868
377469	**SN**	P	*SN*	SU	73469	78869	78669	73869
377470	**SN**	P	*SN*	SU	73470	78870	78670	73870
377471	**SN**	P	*SN*	SU	73471	78871	78671	73871
377472	**SN**	P	*SN*	SU	73472	78872	78672	73872
377473	**SN**	P	*SN*	SU	73473	78873	78673	73873
377474	**SN**	P	*SN*	SU	73474	78874	78674	73874
377475	**SN**	P	*SN*	SU	73475	78875	78675	73875
Spare	**SN**	P		ZN		78842		

Class 377/5. 25kV AC/750V DC. DMCO–MSO–PTSO–DMSO. Dual-voltage units. Details as Class 377/2 unless stated.

DMCO. Bombardier Derby 2008–09. 10/48. 43.1t.
MSO. Bombardier Derby 2008–09. –/69 1T. 40.3t.
PTSO. Bombardier Derby 2008–09. –/56 1TD 2W. 40.6 t.
DMSO. Bombardier Derby 2008–09. –/58. 44.9t.

377501	**SB**	P	*SE*	SU	73501	75901	74901	73601
377502	**SB**	P	*SE*	SU	73502	75902	74902	73602
377503	**SB**	P	*SE*	SU	73503	75903	74903	73603
377504	**SB**	P	*SE*	SU	73504	75904	74904	73604
377505	**SB**	P	*SE*	SU	73505	75905	74905	73605
377506	**SB**	P	*SE*	SU	73506	75906	74906	73606
377507	**SB**	P	*SE*	SU	73507	75907	74907	73607

377508	**SB**	P	*SE*	SU	73508	75908	74908	73608
377509	**FB**	P	*SE*	SU	73509	75909	74909	73609
377510	**FB**	P	*SE*	SU	73510	75910	74910	73610
377511	**FB**	P	*SE*	SU	73511	75911	74911	73611
377512	**FB**	P	*SE*	SU	73512	75912	74912	73612
377513	**FB**	P	*SE*	SU	73513	75913	74913	73613
377514	**FB**	P	*SE*	SU	73514	75914	74914	73614
377515	**FB**	P	*SE*	SU	73515	75915	74915	73615
377516	**FB**	P	*SE*	SU	73516	75916	74916	73616
377517	**FB**	P	*SE*	SU	73517	75917	74917	73617
377518	**FB**	P	*SE*	SU	73518	75918	74918	73618
377519	**FB**	P	*SE*	SU	73519	75919	74919	73619
377520	**FB**	P	*SE*	SU	73520	75920	74920	73620
377521	**FB**	P	*SE*	SU	73521	75921	74921	73621
377522	**FB**	P	*SE*	SU	73522	75922	74922	73622
377523	**FB**	P	*SE*	SU	73523	75923	74923	73623

Class 377/6. 750 V DC. DMSO–MSO–TSO–MSO–DMSO. 5-car suburban units fitted with Fainsa seating. Technically the same as the 377/5s but using the slightly modified Class 379-style bodyshell.

Seating Layout: 2+2 facing/unidirectional.

DMSO. Bombardier Derby 2012–13. 24/36. 44.7 t.
MSO. Bombardier Derby 2012–13. –/64 1T. 38.8 t.
TSO. Bombardier Derby 2012–13. –/46(+2) 1TD 2W. 37.8 t.
MSO. Bombardier Derby 2012–13. –/66. 38.3 t.
DMSO. Bombardier Derby 2012–13. –/62. 44.7 t.

377601	**SN**	P	*SN*	SU	70101	70201	70301	70401	70501
377602	**SN**	P	*SN*	SU	70102	70202	70302	70402	70502
377603	**SN**	P	*SN*	SU	70103	70203	70303	70403	70503
377604	**SN**	P	*SN*	SU	70104	70204	70304	70404	70504
377605	**SN**	P	*SN*	SU	70105	70205	70305	70405	70505
377606	**SN**	P	*SN*	SU	70106	70206	70306	70406	70506
377607	**SN**	P	*SN*	SU	70107	70207	70307	70407	70507
377608	**SN**	P	*SN*	SU	70108	70208	70308	70408	70508
377609	**SN**	P	*SN*	SU	70109	70209	70309	70409	70509
377610	**SN**	P	*SN*	SU	70110	70210	70310	70410	70510
377611	**SN**	P	*SN*	SU	70111	70211	70311	70411	70511
377612	**SN**	P	*SN*	SU	70112	70212	70312	70412	70512
377613	**SN**	P	*SN*	SU	70113	70213	70313	70413	70513
377614	**SN**	P	*SN*	SU	70114	70214	70314	70414	70514
377615	**SN**	P	*SN*	SU	70115	70215	70315	70415	70515
377616	**SN**	P	*SN*	SU	70116	70216	70316	70416	70516
377617	**SN**	P	*SN*	SU	70117	70217	70317	70417	70517
377618	**SN**	P	*SN*	SU	70118	70218	70318	70418	70518
377619	**SN**	P	*SN*	SU	70119	70219	70319	70419	70519
377620	**SN**	P	*SN*	SU	70120	70220	70320	70420	70520
377621	**SN**	P	*SN*	SU	70121	70221	70321	70421	70521
377622	**SN**	P	*SN*	SU	70122	70222	70322	70422	70522
377623	**SN**	P	*SN*	SU	70123	70223	70323	70423	70523
377624	**SN**	P	*SN*	SU	70124	70224	70324	70424	70524

| 377625 | **SN** | P | *SN* | SU | 70125 70225 70325 70425 70525 |
| 377626 | **SN** | P | *SN* | SU | 70126 70226 70326 70426 70526 |

Class 377/7. 25 kV AC/750 V DC. DMSO–MSO–TSO–MSO–DMSO. Dual-voltage units, used on both the South Croydon–Milton Keynes cross-London services and on suburban services alongside the Class 377/6s.

DMSO. Bombardier Derby 2013–14. 24/36. 45.6 t.
MSO. Bombardier Derby 2013–14. –/64 1T. 41.0 t.
PTSO. Bombardier Derby 2013–14. –/46(+2) 1TD 2W. 40.9 t.
MSO. Bombardier Derby 2013–14. –/66. 39.6 t.
DMSO. Bombardier Derby 2013–14. –/62. 45.2 t.

377701	**SN**	P	*SN*	SU	65201 70601 65601 70701 65401
377702	**SN**	P	*SN*	SU	65202 70602 65602 70702 65402
377703	**SN**	P	*SN*	SU	65203 70603 65603 70703 65403
377704	**SN**	P	*SN*	SU	65204 70604 65604 70704 65404
377705	**SN**	P	*SN*	SU	65205 70605 65605 70705 65405
377706	**SN**	P	*SN*	SU	65206 70606 65606 70706 65406
377707	**SN**	P	*SN*	SU	65207 70607 65607 70707 65407
377708	**SN**	P	*SN*	SU	65208 70608 65608 70708 65408

CLASS 378   CAPITALSTAR   BOMBARDIER DERBY

These suburban Electrostars are designated Capitalstars by TfL.

Formation: DMSO–MSO–TSO–MSO–DMSO or DMSO–MSO–PTSO–MSO–DMSO.
System: Class 378/1 750 V DC third rail only. Class 378/2 25 kV AC overhead and 750 V DC third rail.
Construction: Welded aluminium alloy underframe, sides and roof with steel ends. All sections bolted together.
Traction Motors: Three Bombardier asynchronous of 200 kW.
Wheel Arrangement: 1A-Bo + 1A-Bo + 2-2 + Bo-1A + Bo-1A.
Braking: Disc & regenerative.   **Dimensions:** 20.46/20.14 x 2.80 m.
Bogies: Bombardier P3-25/T3-25.   **Couplers:** Dellner 12.
Gangways: Within unit + end doors.   **Control System:** IGBT Inverter.
Doors: Sliding.   **Maximum Speed:** 75 mph.
Heating & ventilation: Air conditioning.
Seating Layout: Longitudinal ("tube style") low density.
Multiple Working: Within class and with Classes 375, 376, 377 and 379.

57 extra MSOs (in the 384xx number series) were delivered 2014–15 to make all units up to 5-cars.

Class 378/1. 750 V DC. DMSO–MSO–TSO–MSO–DMSO. Third rail only units used on the East London Line. Provision for retro-fitting as dual voltage.

378 150–154 are fitted with de-icing equipment.

DMSO(A). Bombardier Derby 2009–10. –/36. 43.1 t.
MSO(A). Bombardier Derby 2009–10. –/40. 39.3 t.
TSO. Bombardier Derby 2009–10. –/34(+6) 2W. 34.3 t.
MSO(B). Bombardier Derby 2014–15. –/40. 40.2 t.
DMSO(B). Bombardier Derby 2009–10. –/36. 42.7 t.

378135	**LO**	QW *LO*	NG	38035	38235	38335	38435	38135
378136	**LO**	QW *LO*	NG	38036	38236	38336	38436	38136
378137	**LO**	QW *LO*	NG	38037	38237	38337	38437	38137
378138	**LO**	QW *LO*	NG	38038	38238	38338	38438	38138
378139	**LO**	QW *LO*	NG	38039	38239	38339	38439	38139
378140	**LO**	QW *LO*	NG	38040	38240	38340	38440	38140
378141	**LO**	QW *LO*	NG	38041	38241	38341	38441	38141
378142	**LO**	QW *LO*	NG	38042	38242	38342	38442	38142
378143	**LO**	QW *LO*	NG	38043	38243	38343	38443	38143
378144	**LO**	QW *LO*	NG	38044	38244	38344	38444	38144
378145	**LO**	QW *LO*	NG	38045	38245	38345	38445	38145
378146	**LO**	QW *LO*	NG	38046	38246	38346	38446	38146
378147	**LO**	QW *LO*	NG	38047	38247	38347	38447	38147
378148	**LO**	QW *LO*	NG	38048	38248	38348	38448	38148
378149	**LO**	QW *LO*	NG	38049	38249	38349	38449	38149
378150	**LO**	QW *LO*	NG	38050	38250	38350	38450	38150
378151	**LO**	QW *LO*	NG	38051	38251	38351	38451	38151
378152	**LO**	QW *LO*	NG	38052	38252	38352	38452	38152
378153	**LO**	QW *LO*	NG	38053	38253	38353	38453	38153
378154	**LO**	QW *LO*	NG	38054	38254	38354	38454	38154

Class 378/2. 25kV AC/750V DC. DMSO–MSO–PTSO–MSO–DMSO. Dual-voltage units mainly used on North London Railway services. 378201–224 were built as 3-car units 378001–024 and extended to 4-car units in 2010.

Fitted with tripcocks for operation on the tracks shared with London Underground between Queens Park and Harrow & Wealdstone.

378216–220 are fitted with de-icing equipment.

DMSO(A). Bombardier Derby 2008–11. –/36. 43.4 t.
MSO(A). Bombardier Derby 2008–11. –/40. 39.6 t.
PTSO. Bombardier Derby 2008–11. –/34(+6) 2W. 39.2 t.
MSO(B). Bombardier Derby 2014–15. –/40. 40.4 t.
DMSO(B). Bombardier Derby 2008–11. –/36. 43.1 t.

378201	**LO**	QW *LO*	NG	38001	38201	38301	38401	38101
378202	**LO**	QW *LO*	NG	38002	38202	38302	38402	38102
378203	**LO**	QW *LO*	NG	38003	38203	38303	38403	38103
378204	**LO**	QW *LO*	NG	38004	38204	38304	38404	38104
378205	**LO**	QW *LO*	NG	38005	38205	38305	38405	38105
378206	**LO**	QW *LO*	NG	38006	38206	38306	38406	38106
378207	**LO**	QW *LO*	NG	38007	38207	38307	38407	38107
378208	**LO**	QW *LO*	NG	38008	38208	38308	38408	38108
378209	**LO**	QW *LO*	NG	38009	38209	38309	38409	38109
378210	**LO**	QW *LO*	NG	38010	38210	38310	38410	38110
378211	**LO**	QW *LO*	NG	38011	38211	38311	38411	38111
378212	**LO**	QW *LO*	NG	38012	38212	38312	38412	38112
378213	**LO**	QW *LO*	NG	38013	38213	38313	38413	38113
378214	**LO**	QW *LO*	NG	38014	38214	38314	38414	38114
378215	**LO**	QW *LO*	NG	38015	38215	38315	38415	38115
378216	**LO**	QW *LO*	NG	38016	38216	38316	38416	38116
378217	**LO**	QW *LO*	NG	38017	38217	38317	38417	38117

378218	**LO**	QW *LO*	NG	38018 38218 38318 38418 38118
378219	**LO**	QW *LO*	NG	38019 38219 38319 38419 38119
378220	**LO**	QW *LO*	NG	38020 38220 38320 38420 38120
378221	**LO**	QW *LO*	NG	38021 38221 38321 38421 38121
378222	**LO**	QW *LO*	NG	38022 38222 38322 38422 38122
378223	**LO**	QW *LO*	NG	38023 38223 38323 38423 38123
378224	**LO**	QW *LO*	NG	38024 38224 38324 38424 38124
378225	**LO**	QW *LO*	NG	38025 38225 38325 38425 38125
378226	**LO**	QW *LO*	NG	38026 38226 38326 38426 38126
378227	**LO**	QW *LO*	NG	38027 38227 38327 38427 38127
378228	**LO**	QW *LO*	NG	38028 38228 38328 38428 38128
378229	**LO**	QW *LO*	NG	38029 38229 38329 38429 38129
378230	**LO**	QW *LO*	NG	38030 38230 38330 38430 38130
378231	**LO**	QW *LO*	NG	38031 38231 38331 38431 38131
378232	**LO**	QW *LO*	NG	38032 38232 38332 38432 38132
378233	**LO**	QW *LO*	NG	38033 38233 38333 38433 38133
378234	**LO**	QW *LO*	NG	38034 38234 38334 38434 38134
378255	**LO**	QW *LO*	NG	38055 38255 38355 38455 38155
378256	**LO**	QW *LO*	NG	38056 38256 38356 38456 38156
378257	**LO**	QW *LO*	NG	38057 38257 38357 38457 38157

Names (carried on DMSO(A)):

378204 Professor Sir Peter Hall | 378233   Ian Brown CBE

CLASS 379   ELECTROSTAR   BOMBARDIER DERBY

Express Electrostars used on Liverpool Street–Stansted Airport and Liverpool Street–Cambridge services.

Formation: DMSO–MSO–PTSO–DMCO.
System: 25 kV AC overhead.
Construction: Welded aluminium alloy underframe, sides and roof with steel ends. All sections bolted together.
Traction Motors: Two Bombardier asynchronous of 200 kW.
Wheel Arrangement: 2-Bo + 2-Bo + 2-2 + Bo-2.
Braking: Disc & regenerative.   **Dimensions:** 20.00 x 2.80 m.
Bogies: Bombardier P3-25/T3-25.   **Couplers:** Dellner 12.
Gangways: Throughout.   **Control System:** IGBT Inverter.
Doors: Sliding plug.   **Maximum Speed:** 100 mph.
Heating & ventilation: Air conditioning.
Seating Layout: 1: 2+1 facing. 2: 2+2 facing/unidirectional.
Multiple Working: Within class and with Classes 375, 376, 377 and 378.

DMSO. Bombardier Derby 2010–11. –/60. 42.1 t.
MSO. Bombardier Derby 2010–11. –/62 1T. 38.6 t.
PTSO. Bombardier Derby 2010–11. –/43(+2) 1TD 2W. 40.9 t.
DMCO. Bombardier Derby 2010–11. 20/24. 42.3 t.

379001	**NC**	MQ *GA*	IL	61201 61701 61901 62101
379002	**NC**	MQ *GA*	IL	61202 61702 61902 62102
379003	**NC**	MQ *GA*	IL	61203 61703 61903 62103

379004	**NC**	MQ	*GA*	IL	61204	61704	61904	62104
379005	**NC**	MQ	*GA*	IL	61205	61705	61905	62105
379006	**NC**	MQ	*GA*	IL	61206	61706	61906	62106
379007	**NC**	MQ	*GA*	IL	61207	61707	61907	62107
379008	**NC**	MQ	*GA*	IL	61208	61708	61908	62108
379009	**NC**	MQ	*GA*	IL	61209	61709	61909	62109
379010	**NC**	MQ	*GA*	IL	61210	61710	61910	62110
379011	**NC**	MQ	*GA*	IL	61211	61711	61911	62111
379012	**NC**	MQ	*GA*	IL	61212	61712	61912	62112
379013	**NC**	MQ	*GA*	IL	61213	61713	61913	62113
379014	**NC**	MQ	*GA*	IL	61214	61714	61914	62114
379015	**NC**	MQ	*GA*	IL	61215	61715	61915	62115
379016	**NC**	MQ	*GA*	IL	61216	61716	61916	62116
379017	**NC**	MQ	*GA*	IL	61217	61717	61917	62117
379018	**NC**	MQ	*GA*	IL	61218	61718	61918	62118
379019	**NC**	MQ	*GA*	IL	61219	61719	61919	62119
379020	**NC**	MQ	*GA*	IL	61220	61720	61920	62120
379021	**NC**	MQ	*GA*	IL	61221	61721	61921	62121
379022	**NC**	MQ	*GA*	IL	61222	61722	61922	62122
379023	**NC**	MQ	*GA*	IL	61223	61723	61923	62123
379024	**NC**	MQ	*GA*	IL	61224	61724	61924	62124
379025	**NC**	MQ	*GA*	IL	61225	61725	61925	62125
379026	**NC**	MQ	*GA*	IL	61226	61726	61926	62126
379027	**NC**	MQ	*GA*	IL	61227	61727	61927	62127
379028	**NC**	MQ	*GA*	IL	61228	61728	61928	62128
379029	**NC**	MQ	*GA*	IL	61229	61729	61929	62129
379030	**NC**	MQ	*GA*	IL	61230	61730	61930	62130

Names (carried on end cars):

379005	Stansted Express	379015	City of Cambridge
379011	Ely Cathedral	379025	Go Discover
379012	The West Anglian		

CLASS 380   DESIRO UK   SIEMENS

Used on Strathclyde area services and between Glasgow/Edinburgh and North Berwick.

Formation: DMSO–PTSO–DMSO or DMSO–PTSO–TSO–DMSO.
System: 25 kV AC overhead.
Construction: Welded aluminium with steel ends.
Traction Motors: Four Siemens 1TB2016-0GB02 asynchronous of 250 kW.
Wheel Arrangement: Bo-Bo + 2-2 (+2-2) + Bo-Bo
Braking: Disc & regenerative.   **Dimensions:** 23.78/23.57 x 2.80 m.
Bogies: SGP SF5000.   **Couplers:** Voith.
Gangways: Throughout.   **Control System:** IGBT Inverter.
Doors: Sliding plug.   **Maximum Speed:** 100 mph.
Heating & ventilation: Air conditioning. **Seating Layout:** 2+2 facing/unidirectional.
Multiple Working: Within class.

DMSO(A). Siemens Krefeld 2009–10. –/70. 45.0t.
PTSO. Siemens Krefeld 2009–10. –/57(+12) 1TD 2W. 42.7t.
TSO. Siemens Krefeld 2009–10. –/74 1T. 34.8t.
DMSO(B). Siemens Krefeld 2009–10. –/64(+5). 44.9t.

Class 380/0. 3-car units. **Formation:** DMSO–PTSO–DMSO.

380001	**SR**	E	*SR*	GW	38501	38601	38701
380002	**SR**	E	*SR*	GW	38502	38602	38702
380003	**SR**	E	*SR*	GW	38503	38603	38703
380004	**SR**	E	*SR*	GW	38504	38604	38704
380005	**SR**	E	*SR*	GW	38505	38605	38705
380006	**SR**	E	*SR*	GW	38506	38606	38706
380007	**SR**	E	*SR*	GW	38507	38607	38707
380008	**SR**	E	*SR*	GW	38508	38608	38708
380009	**SR**	E	*SR*	GW	38509	38609	38709
380010	**SR**	E	*SR*	GW	38510	38610	38710
380011	**SR**	E	*SR*	GW	38511	38611	38711
380012	**SR**	E	*SR*	GW	38512	38612	38712
380013	**SR**	E	*SR*	GW	38513	38613	38713
380014	**SR**	E	*SR*	GW	38514	38614	38714
380015	**SR**	E	*SR*	GW	38515	38615	38715
380016	**SR**	E	*SR*	GW	38516	38616	38716
380017	**SR**	E	*SR*	GW	38517	38617	38717
380018	**SR**	E	*SR*	GW	38518	38618	38718
380019	**SR**	E	*SR*	GW	38519	38619	38719
380020	**SR**	E	*SR*	GW	38520	38620	38720
380021	**SR**	E	*SR*	GW	38521	38621	38721
380022	**SR**	E	*SR*	GW	38522	38622	38722

Class 380/1. 4-car units. **Formation:** DMSO–PTSO–TSO–DMSO.

380101	**SR**	E	*SR*	GW	38551	38651	38851	38751
380102	**SR**	E	*SR*	GW	38552	38652	38852	38752
380103	**SR**	E	*SR*	GW	38553	38653	38853	38753
380104	**SR**	E	*SR*	GW	38554	38654	38854	38754
380105	**SR**	E	*SR*	GW	38555	38655	38855	38755
380106	**SR**	E	*SR*	GW	38556	38656	38856	38756
380107	**SR**	E	*SR*	GW	38557	38657	38857	38757
380108	**SR**	E	*SR*	GW	38558	38658	38858	38758
380109	**SR**	E	*SR*	GW	38559	38659	38859	38759
380110	**SR**	E	*SR*	GW	38560	38660	38860	38760
380111	**SR**	E	*SR*	GW	38561	38661	38861	38761
380112	**SR**	E	*SR*	GW	38562	38662	38862	38762
380113	**SR**	E	*SR*	GW	38563	38663	38863	38763
380114	**SR**	E	*SR*	GW	38564	38664	38864	38764
380115	**SR**	E	*SR*	GW	38565	38665	38865	38765
380116	**SR**	E	*SR*	GW	38566	38666	38866	38766

CLASS 385   AT200   HITACHI

New 3- and 4-car units for ScotRail, due to enter service in spring 2018 and financed by Caledonian Rail Leasing. There is an option for a further ten 3-car units.

Formation: DMSO–PTSO–DMSO or DMCO–PTSO–TSO–DMSO.
System: 25 kV AC overhead.
Construction: Aluminium.
Traction Motors: Four Hitachi asynchronous of 250 kW.
Wheel Arrangement: Bo-Bo + 2-2 + Bo-2 or Bo-Bo + 2-2 + 2-2 + Bo-Bo.
Braking: Disc & regenerative.

Dimensions: 23.18/22.08 x 2.74 m.	**Couplers:** Dellner.
Bogies: Hitachi.	**Control System:** IGBT Inverter.
Gangways: Throughout.	**Maximum Speed:** 100 mph.
Doors: Sliding plug.	**Multiple Working:** Within class only.

Heating & ventilation: Air conditioning.
Seating Layout: 1: 2+1 facing. 2: 2+2 facing/unidirectional.

Class 385/0. 3-car units. **Formation:** DMSO–PTSO–DMSO.

DMSO(A): Hitachi Newton Aycliffe/Kasado 2016–18. –/48 (+11) 1TD 2W.
PTSO: Hitachi Newton Aycliffe/Kasado 2016–18. –/80.
DMSO(B): Hitachi Newton Aycliffe/Kasado 2016–18. –62(+5) 1T.

385 001	**SR**	CL	441001	442001	444001
385 002	**SR**	CL	441002	442002	444002
385 003	**SR**	CL	441003	442003	444003
385 004	**SR**	CL	441004	442004	444004
385 005	**SR**	CL	441005	442005	444005
385 006	**SR**	CL	441006	442006	444006
385 007	**SR**	CL	441007	442007	444007
385 008	**SR**	CL	441008	442008	444008
385 009	**SR**	CL	441009	442009	444009
385 010	**SR**	CL	441010	442010	444010
385 011	**SR**	CL	441011	442011	444011
385 012	**SR**	CL	441012	442012	444012
385 013	**SR**	CL	441013	442013	444013
385 014	**SR**	CL	441014	442014	444014
385 015	**SR**	CL	441015	442015	444015
385 016	**SR**	CL	441016	442016	444016
385 017	**SR**	CL	441017	442017	444017
385 018	**SR**	CL	441018	442018	444018
385 019	**SR**	CL	441019	442019	444019
385 020	**SR**	CL	441020	442020	444020
385 021	**SR**	CL	441021	442021	444021
385 022	**SR**	CL	441022	442022	444022
385 023	**SR**	CL	441023	442023	444023
385 024	**SR**	CL	441024	442024	444024
385 025	**SR**	CL	441025	442025	444025
385 026	**SR**	CL	441026	442026	444026
385 027	**SR**	CL	441027	442027	444027

385028	**SR**	CL	441028	442028	444028
385029	**SR**	CL	441029	442029	444029
385030	**SR**	CL	441030	442030	444030
385031	**SR**	CL	441031	442031	444031
385032	**SR**	CL	441032	442032	444032
385033	**SR**	CL	441033	442033	444033
385034	**SR**	CL	441034	442034	444034
385035	**SR**	CL	441035	442035	444035
385036	**SR**	CL	441036	442036	444036
385037	**SR**	CL	441037	442037	444037
385038	**SR**	CL	441038	442038	444038
385039	**SR**	CL	441039	442039	444039
385040	**SR**	CL	441040	442040	444040
385041	**SR**	CL	441041	442041	444041
385042	**SR**	CL	441042	442042	444042
385043	**SR**	CL	441043	442043	444043
385044	**SR**	CL	441044	442044	444044
385045	**SR**	CL	441045	442045	444045
385046	**SR**	CL	441046	442046	444046

Class 385/1. 4-car units. **Formation:** DMCO–PTSO–TSO–DMSO.

DMCO: Hitachi Newton Aycliffe/Kasado 2016–18. 20/15 (+11) 1TD 2W.
PTSO: Hitachi Newton Aycliffe/Kasado 2016–18. –/80.
TSO: Hitachi Newton Aycliffe/Kasado 2016–18. –/80.
DMSO: Hitachi Newton Aycliffe/Kasado 2016–18. –62(+5) 1T.

385101	**SR**	CL	441101	442101	443101	444101
385102	**SR**	CL	441102	442102	443102	444102
385103	**SR**	CL	441103	442103	443103	444103
385104	**SR**	CL	441104	442104	443104	444104
385105	**SR**	CL	441105	442105	443105	444105
385106	**SR**	CL	441106	442106	443106	444106
385107	**SR**	CL	441107	442107	443107	444107
385108	**SR**	CL	441108	442108	443108	444108
385109	**SR**	CL	441109	442109	443109	444109
385110	**SR**	CL	441110	442110	443110	444110
385111	**SR**	CL	441111	442111	443111	444111
385112	**SR**	CL	441112	442112	443112	444112
385113	**SR**	CL	441113	442113	443113	444113
385114	**SR**	CL	441114	442114	443114	444114
385115	**SR**	CL	441115	442115	443115	444115
385116	**SR**	CL	441116	442116	443116	444116
385117	**SR**	CL	441117	442117	443117	444117
385118	**SR**	CL	441118	442118	443118	444118
385119	**SR**	CL	441119	442119	443119	444119
385120	**SR**	CL	441120	442120	443120	444120
385121	**SR**	CL	441121	442121	443121	444121
385122	**SR**	CL	441122	442122	443122	444122
385123	**SR**	CL	441123	442123	443123	444123
385124	**SR**	CL	441124	442124	443124	444124

CLASS 387   ELECTROSTAR   BOMBARDIER DERBY

The first 29 110 mph Class 387/1s were delivered in 2014–15 for Thameslink. In 2016–17 these transferred to Great Northern for services from King's Cross to Cambridge/Kings Lynn and Peterborough.

A further 27 Class 387/2 units were delivered to Southern for Gatwick Express services in 2016.

Great Western Railway has taken delivery of 45 Class 387/1s for services between London Paddington and Reading/Didcot Parkway (and Newbury from late 2018).

Part of a speculative order by Porterbrook Leasing, c2c has six Class 387/3s on lease for 5 years from late 2016. Porterbrook had originally placed an order for 20 speculative units but the other 14 from this order were later incorporated into the GWR fleet.

Formation: DMCO–MSO–PTSO–DMSO.
System: 25 kV AC overhead and 750 V DC third rail.
Construction: Welded aluminium alloy underframe, sides and roof with steel ends. All sections bolted together.
Traction Motors: Two Bombardier asynchronous of 250 kW.
Wheel Arrangement: 2-Bo + 2-Bo + 2-2 + Bo-2.
Braking: Disc & regenerative.   **Dimensions:** 20.39/20.00 x 2.80 m.
Bogies: Bombardier P3-25/T3-25.   **Couplers:** Dellner 12.
Gangways: Throughout.   **Control System:** IGBT Inverter.
Doors: Sliding plug.   **Maximum Speed:** 110 mph.
Heating & ventilation: Air conditioning.
Seating Layout: 2+2 facing/unidirectional.
Multiple Working: Within class and with Class 377.

Class 387/1. Units built for Thameslink, but now used by Great Northern.

DMCO. Bombardier Derby 2014–15. 22/34. 46.0 t.
MSO. Bombardier Derby 2014–15. –/62 1T. 41.3 t.
PTSO. Bombardier Derby 2014–15. –/45(+2) 1TD 2W. 41.6 t.
DMSO. Bombardier Derby 2014–15. –/60. 45.9 t.

387 101	**TG**	P	*GN*	HE	421101	422101	423101	424101
387 102	**TG**	P	*GN*	HE	421102	422102	423102	424102
387 103	**TG**	P	*GN*	HE	421103	422103	423103	424103
387 104	**TG**	P	*GN*	HE	421104	422104	423104	424104
387 105	**TG**	P	*GN*	HE	421105	422105	423105	424105
387 106	**TG**	P	*GN*	HE	421106	422106	423106	424106
387 107	**TG**	P	*GN*	HE	421107	422107	423107	424107
387 108	**TG**	P	*GN*	HE	421108	422108	423108	424108
387 109	**TG**	P	*GN*	HE	421109	422109	423109	424109
387 110	**TG**	P	*GN*	HE	421110	422110	423110	424110
387 111	**TG**	P	*GN*	HE	421111	422111	423111	424111
387 112	**TG**	P	*GN*	HE	421112	422112	423112	424112
387 113	**TG**	P	*GN*	HE	421113	422113	423113	424113
387 114	**TG**	P	*GN*	HE	421114	422114	423114	424114
387 115	**TG**	P	*GN*	HE	421115	422115	423115	424115

387 116	**TG**	P	*GN*	HE	421116	422116	423116	424116
387 117	**TG**	P	*GN*	HE	421117	422117	423117	424117
387 118	**TG**	P	*GN*	HE	421118	422118	423118	424118
387 119	**TG**	P	*GN*	HE	421119	422119	423119	424119
387 120	**TG**	P	*GN*	HE	421120	422120	423120	424120
387 121	**TG**	P	*GN*	HE	421121	422121	423121	424121
387 122	**TG**	P	*GN*	HE	421122	422122	423122	424122
387 123	**TG**	P	*GN*	HE	421123	422123	423123	424123
387 124	**TG**	P	*GN*	HE	421124	422124	423124	424124
387 125	**TG**	P	*GN*	HE	421125	422125	423125	424125
387 126	**TG**	P	*GN*	HE	421126	422126	423126	424126
387 127	**TG**	P	*GN*	HE	421127	422127	423127	424127
387 128	**TG**	P	*GN*	HE	421128	422128	423128	424128
387 129	**TG**	P	*GN*	HE	421129	422129	423129	424129

Name (carried on DMCO): 387 124   Paul McCann

Class 387/1. Great Western Railway units.

DMCO. Bombardier Derby 2016–17. –/56. 46.0 t.
MSO. Bombardier Derby 2016–17. –/62 1T. 41.3 t.
PTSO. Bombardier Derby 2016–17. –/45(+2) 1TD 2W. 41.6 t.
DMSO. Bombardier Derby 2016–17. –/60. 45.9 t.

387 130	**GW**	P	*GW*	RG	421130	422130	423130	424130
387 131	**GW**	P	*GW*	RG	421131	422131	423131	424131
387 132	**GW**	P	*GW*	RG	421132	422132	423132	424132
387 133	**GW**	P	*GW*	RG	421133	422133	423133	424133
387 134	**GW**	P	*GW*	RG	421134	422134	423134	424134
387 135	**GW**	P	*GW*	RG	421135	422135	423135	424135
387 136	**GW**	P	*GW*	RG	421136	422136	423136	424136
387 137	**GW**	P	*GW*	RG	421137	422137	423137	424137
387 138	**GW**	P	*GW*	RG	421138	422138	423138	424138
387 139	**GW**	P	*GW*	RG	421139	422139	423139	424139
387 140	**GW**	P	*GW*	RG	421140	422140	423140	424140
387 141	**GW**	P	*GW*	RG	421141	422141	423141	424141
387 142	**GW**	P	*GW*	RG	421142	422142	423142	424142
387 143	**GW**	P	*GW*	RG	421143	422143	423143	424143
387 144	**GW**	P	*GW*	RG	421144	422144	423144	424144
387 145	**GW**	P	*GW*	RG	421145	422145	423145	424145
387 146	**GW**	P	*GW*	RG	421146	422146	423146	424146
387 147	**GW**	P	*GW*	RG	421147	422147	423147	424147
387 148	**GW**	P	*GW*	RG	421148	422148	423148	424148
387 149	**GW**	P	*GW*	RG	421149	422149	423149	424149
387 150	**GW**	P	*GW*	RG	421150	422150	423150	424150
387 151	**GW**	P	*GW*	RG	421151	422151	423151	424151
387 152	**GW**	P	*GW*	RG	421152	422152	423152	424152
387 153	**GW**	P	*GW*	RG	421153	422153	423153	424153
387 154	**GW**	P	*GW*	RG	421154	422154	423154	424154
387 155	**GW**	P	*GW*	RG	421155	422155	423155	424155
387 156	**GW**	P	*GW*	RG	421156	422156	423156	424156
387 157	**GW**	P	*GW*	RG	421157	422157	423157	424157
387 158	**GW**	P	*GW*	RG	421158	422158	423158	424158

387 159	**GW**	P	*GW*	RG	421159	422159	423159	424159
387 160	**GW**	P	*GW*	RG	421160	422160	423160	424160
387 161	**GW**	P	*GW*	RG	421161	422161	423161	424161
387 162	**GW**	P	*GW*	RG	421162	422162	423162	424162
387 163	**GW**	P	*GW*	RG	421163	422163	423163	424163
387 164	**GW**	P	*GW*	RG	421164	422164	423164	424164
387 165	**GW**	P	*GW*	RG	421165	422165	423165	424165
387 166	**GW**	P	*GW*	RG	421166	422166	423166	424166
387 167	**GW**	P	*GW*	RG	421167	422167	423167	424167
387 168	**GW**	P	*GW*	RG	421168	422168	423168	424168
387 169	**GW**	P	*GW*	RG	421169	422169	423169	424169
387 170	**GW**	P	*GW*	RG	421170	422170	423170	424170
387 171	**GW**	P	*GW*	RG	421171	422171	423171	424171
387 172	**GW**	P	*GW*	RG	421172	422172	423172	424172
387 173	**GW**	P	*GW*	RG	421173	422173	423173	424173
387 174	**GW**	P	*GW*	RG	421174	422174	423174	424174

Class 387/2. Southern units used on Gatwick Express-branded services on the London Victoria–Gatwick Airport–Brighton route.

DMCO. Bombardier Derby 2015–16. 22/34. 46.0 t.
MSO. Bombardier Derby 2015–16. –/60 1T. 41.3 t.
PTSO. Bombardier Derby 2015–16. –/45(+2) 1TD 2W. 41.6 t.
DMSO. Bombardier Derby 2015–16. –/60. 45.9 t.

387 201	**GX**	P	*SN*	SL	421201	422201	423201	424201
387 202	**GX**	P	*SN*	SL	421202	422202	423202	424202
387 203	**GX**	P	*SN*	SL	421203	422203	423203	424203
387 204	**GX**	P	*SN*	SL	421204	422204	423204	424204
387 205	**GX**	P	*SN*	SL	421205	422205	423205	424205
387 206	**GX**	P	*SN*	SL	421206	422206	423206	424206
387 207	**GX**	P	*SN*	SL	421207	422207	423207	424207
387 208	**GX**	P	*SN*	SL	421208	422208	423208	424208
387 209	**GX**	P	*SN*	SL	421209	422209	423209	424209
387 210	**GX**	P	*SN*	SL	421210	422210	423210	424210
387 211	**GX**	P	*SN*	SL	421211	422211	423211	424211
387 212	**GX**	P	*SN*	SL	421212	422212	423212	424212
387 213	**GX**	P	*SN*	SL	421213	422213	423213	424213
387 214	**GX**	P	*SN*	SL	421214	422214	423214	424214
387 215	**GX**	P	*SN*	SL	421215	422215	423215	424215
387 216	**GX**	P	*SN*	SL	421216	422216	423216	424216
387 217	**GX**	P	*SN*	SL	421217	422217	423217	424217
387 218	**GX**	P	*SN*	SL	421218	422218	423218	424218
387 219	**GX**	P	*SN*	SL	421219	422219	423219	424219
387 220	**GX**	P	*SN*	SL	421220	422220	423220	424220
387 221	**GX**	P	*SN*	SL	421221	422221	423221	424221
387 222	**GX**	P	*SN*	SL	421222	422222	423222	424222
387 223	**GX**	P	*SN*	SL	421223	422223	423223	424223
387 224	**GX**	P	*SN*	SL	421224	422224	423224	424224
387 225	**GX**	P	*SN*	SL	421225	422225	423225	424225
387 226	**GX**	P	*SN*	SL	421226	422226	423226	424226
387 227	**GX**	P	*SN*	SL	421227	422227	423227	424227

Class 387/3. c2c units, originally ordered speculatively by Porterbrook Leasing.

DMSO(A). Bombardier Derby 2016. –/56. 46.0 t.
MSO. Bombardier Derby 2016. –/62 1T. 41.3 t.
PTSO. Bombardier Derby 2016. –/45(+2) 1TD 2W. 41.6 t.
DMSO(B). Bombardier Derby 2016. –/60. 45.9 t.

387 301	**C2**	P	*C2*	EM	421301	422301	423301	424301
387 302	**C2**	P	*C2*	EM	421302	422302	423302	424302
387 303	**C2**	P	*C2*	EM	421303	422303	423303	424303
387 304	**C2**	P	*C2*	EM	421304	422304	423304	424304
387 305	**C2**	P	*C2*	EM	421305	422305	423305	424305
387 306	**C2**	P	*C2*	EM	421306	422306	423306	424306

CLASS 390   PENDOLINO   ALSTOM

Tilting units used on the West Coast Main Line.

Formations: As listed below.
Traction Motors: Two Alstom ONIX 800 of 425 kW.
Wheel Arrangement: 1A-A1 + 1A-A1 + 2-2 + 1A-A1 (+ 2-2 + 1A-A1) + 2-2 + 1A-A1 + 2-2 + 1A-A1 + 1A-A1.
Dimensions: 24.80/23.90 x 2.73 m.
Bogies: Fiat-SIG.
Gangways: Within unit.
Doors: Sliding plug.
Seating Layout: 1: 2+1 facing/unidirectional, 2: 2+2 facing/unidirectional.
Multiple Working: Within class. Can also be controlled from Class 57/3 locos.

Construction: Welded aluminium alloy.
Braking: Disc, rheostatic & regenerative.
Couplers: Dellner 12.
Control System: IGBT Inverter.
Maximum Speed: 125 mph.
Heating & ventilation: Air conditioning.

Units up to 390034 were delivered as 8-car sets, without the TSO (688xx). During 2004–05 these units were increased to 9-cars.

62 extra vehicles were built 2010–12 to lengthen 31 sets to 11-cars. On renumbering units were renumbered by adding 100 to the set number. Four new complete 11-car units were also delivered. All these extra vehicles were built at Savigliano, Italy (all original Pendolino vehicles were built at Birmingham).

The 9-car units had their MFO(B) converted to an MSO in 2015 to give them a better balance of Standard to First Class seating.

390033 was written off in the Lambrigg accident of February 2007.

Advertising livery: 390 104 – Black Alstom vinyls on Virgin silver livery.

DMRBFO: Alstom Birmingham/Savigliano 2001–05/2010–12. 18/–. 56.3 t.
MFO(A): Alstom Birmingham/Savigliano 2001–05/2010–12. 37/–(+2) 1TD 1W. 52.3 t.
PTFO: Alstom Birmingham/Savigliano 2001–05/2010–12. 44/– 1T. 51.2 t.
MFO(B: 11-car): Alstom Birmingham/Savigliano 2001–05/2010–12. 46/– 1T. 52.3 t.
MSO(C: 9-car): Alstom Birmingham/Savigliano 2001–05/2010–12. –/76 1T. 52.3 t.
(TSO: 8-car): Alstom Savigliano 2010–12. –/74 1T. 49.2 t.)
(MSO: Alstom Savigliano 2010–12. –/76 1T. 52.2 t.)
TSO: Alstom Birmingham/Savigliano 2001–05/2010–12. –/76 1T. 45.5 t.
MSO(A): Alstom Birmingham/Savigliano 2001–05/2010–12. –/62(+4) 1TD 1W. 52.0 t.
PTSRMB: Alstom Birmingham/Savigliano 2001–05/2010–12. –/48. 53.2 t.
MSO(B): Alstom Birmingham/Savigliano 2001–05/2010–12. –/62(+2) 1TD 1W. 52.5 t.

DMSO: Alstom Birmingham/Savigliano 2001–05/2010–12. –/46 1T. 54.5 t.

Class 390/0. Original build 9-car units.
Formation: DMRFO–MFO–PTFO–MSO–TSO–MSO–PTSRMB–MSO–DMSO.

390 001	**VT**	A	*VW*	MA	69101	69401	69501	69601	68801
					69701	69801	69901	69201	
390 002	**VT**	A	*VW*	MA	69102	69402	69502	69602	68802
					69702	69802	69902	69202	
390 005	**VW**	A	*VW*	MA	69105	69405	69505	69605	68805
					69705	69805	69905	69205	
390 006	**VW**	A	*VW*	MA	69106	69406	69506	69606	68806
					69706	69806	69906	69206	
390 008	**VT**	A	*VW*	MA	69108	69408	69508	69608	68808
					69708	69808	69908	69208	
390 009	**VW**	A	*VW*	MA	69109	69409	69509	69609	68809
					69709	69809	69909	69209	
390 010	**VW**	A	*VW*	MA	69110	69410	69510	69610	68810
					69710	69810	69910	69210	
390 011	**VT**	A	*VW*	MA	69111	69411	69511	69611	68811
					69711	69811	69911	69211	
390 013	**VT**	A	*VW*	MA	69113	69413	69513	69613	68813
					69713	69813	69913	69213	
390 016	**VW**	A	*VW*	MA	69116	69416	69516	69616	68816
					69716	69816	69916	69216	
390 020	**VW**	A	*VW*	MA	69120	69420	69520	69620	68820
					69720	69820	69920	69220	
390 039	**VT**	A	*VW*	MA	69139	69439	69539	69639	68839
					69739	69839	69939	69239	
390 040	**VT**	A	*VW*	MA	69140	69440	69540	69640	68840
					69740	69840	69940	69240	
390 042	**VT**	A	*VW*	MA	69142	69442	69542	69642	68842
					69742	69842	69942	69242	
390 043	**VT**	A	*VW*	MA	69143	69443	69543	69643	68843
					69743	69843	69943	69243	
390 044	**VT**	A	*VW*	MA	69144	69444	69544	69644	68844
					69744	69844	69944	69244	
390 045	**VT**	A	*VW*	MA	69145	69445	69545	69645	68845
					69745	69845	69945	69245	
390 046	**VT**	A	*VW*	MA	69146	69446	69546	69646	68846
					69746	69846	69946	69246	
390 047	**VT**	A	*VW*	MA	69147	69447	69547	69647	68847
					69747	69847	69947	69247	
390 049	**VT**	A	*VW*	MA	69149	69449	69549	69649	68849
					69749	69849	69949	69249	
390 050	**VT**	A	*VW*	MA	69150	69450	69550	69650	68850
					69750	69850	69950	69250	

Class 390/1. Original build 9-car units later extended to 11-cars, except
390 154–157 which were built new (in Italy) as 11-cars.
Formation: DMRFO–MFO–PTFO–MFO–TSO–MSO–TSO–MSO–PTSRMB–
MSO–DMSO.

390 103	**VT**	A	*VW* MA	69103 69403 69503 69603 65303 68903
				68803 69703 69803 69903 69203
390 104	**AL**	A	*VW* MA	69104 69404 69504 69604 65304 68904
				68804 69704 69804 69904 69204
390 107	**VT**	A	*VW* MA	69107 69407 69507 69607 65307 68907
				68807 69707 69807 69907 69207
390 112	**VT**	A	*VW* MA	69112 69412 69512 69612 65312 68912
				68812 69712 69812 69912 69212
390 114	**VT**	A	*VW* MA	69114 69414 69514 69614 65314 68914
				68814 69714 69814 69914 69214
390 115	**VT**	A	*VW* MA	69115 69415 69515 69615 65315 68915
				68815 69715 69815 69915 69215
390 117	**VT**	A	*VW* MA	69117 69417 69517 69617 65317 68917
				68817 69717 69817 69917 69217
390 118	**VT**	A	*VW* MA	69118 69418 69518 69618 65318 68918
				68818 69718 69818 69918 69218
390 119	**VT**	A	*VW* MA	69119 69419 69519 69619 65319 68919
				68819 69719 69819 69919 69219
390 121	**VT**	A	*VW* MA	69121 69421 69521 69621 65321 68921
				68821 69721 69821 69921 69221
390 122	**VT**	A	*VW* MA	69122 69422 69522 69622 65322 68922
				68822 69722 69822 69922 69222
390 123	**VT**	A	*VW* MA	69123 69423 69523 69623 65323 68923
				68823 69723 69823 69923 69223
390 124	**VT**	A	*VW* MA	69124 69424 69524 69624 65324 68924
				68824 69724 69824 69924 69224
390 125	**VT**	A	*VW* MA	69125 69425 69525 69625 65325 68925
				68825 69725 69825 69925 69225
390 126	**VT**	A	*VW* MA	69126 69426 69526 69626 65326 68926
				68826 69726 69826 69926 69226
390 127	**VT**	A	*VW* MA	69127 69427 69527 69627 65327 68927
				68827 69727 69827 69927 69227
390 128	**VT**	A	*VW* MA	69128 69428 69528 69628 65328 68928
				68828 69728 69828 69928 69228
390 129	**VT**	A	*VW* MA	69129 69429 69529 69629 65329 68929
				68829 69729 69829 69929 69229
390 130	**VT**	A	*VW* MA	69130 69430 69530 69630 65330 68930
				68830 69730 69830 69930 69230
390 131	**VT**	A	*VW* MA	69131 69431 69531 69631 65331 68931
				68831 69731 69831 69931 69231
390 132	**VT**	A	*VW* MA	69132 69432 69532 69632 65332 68932
				68832 69732 69832 69932 69232
390 134	**VT**	A	*VW* MA	69134 69434 69534 69634 65334 68934
				68834 69734 69834 69934 69234
390 135	**VT**	A	*VW* MA	69135 69435 69535 69635 65335 68935
				68835 69735 69835 69935 69235
390 136	**VT**	A	*VW* MA	69136 69436 69536 69636 65336 68936
				68836 69736 69836 69936 69236
390 137	**VT**	A	*VW* MA	69137 69437 69537 69637 65337 68937
				68837 69737 69837 69937 69237

390 138	**VT**	A	*VW* MA	69138	69438	69538	69638	65338	68938
				68838	69738	69838	69938	69238	
390 141	**VT**	A	*VW* MA	69141	69441	69541	69641	65341	68941
				68841	69741	69841	69941	69241	
390 148	**VT**	A	*VW* MA	69148	69448	69548	69648	65348	68948
				68848	69748	69848	69948	69248	
390 151	**VT**	A	*VW* MA	69151	69451	69551	69651	65351	68951
				68851	69751	69851	69951	69251	
390 152	**VT**	A	*VW* MA	69152	69452	69552	69652	65352	68952
				68852	69752	69852	69952	69252	
390 153	**VT**	A	*VW* MA	69153	69453	69553	69653	65353	68953
				68853	69753	69853	69953	69253	
390 154	**VT**	A	*VW* MA	69154	69454	69554	69654	65354	68954
				68854	69754	69854	69954	69254	
390 155	**VT**	A	*VW* MA	69155	69455	69555	69655	65355	68955
				68855	69755	69855	69955	69255	
390 156	**VT**	A	*VW* MA	69156	69456	69556	69656	65356	68956
				68856	69756	69856	69956	69256	
390 157	**VT**	A	*VW* MA	69157	69457	69557	69657	65357	68957
				68857	69757	69857	69957	69257	

Names (carried on MFO No. 696xx):

390001 Virgin Pioneer	390 121 Virgin Dream
390002 Stephen Sutton	390 122 Penny the Pendolino
390005 City of Wolverhampton	390 123 Virgin Glory
390006 Rethink Mental Illness	390 124 Virgin Venturer
390008 Virgin King	390 125 Virgin Stagecoach
390010 Cumbrian Spirit	390 126 Virgin Enterprise
390011 City of Lichfield	390 127 Virgin Buccaneer
390013 Virgin Spirit	390 128 City of Preston
390039 Virgin Quest	390 129 City of Stoke-on-Trent
390040 Virgin Radio Star	390 130 City of Edinburgh
390042 City of Bangor/Dinas Bangor	390 131 City of Liverpool
390043 Virgin Explorer	390 132 City of Birmingham
390044 Virgin Lionheart	390 134 City of Carlisle
390045 101 Squadron	390 135 City of Lancaster
390046 Virgin Soldiers	390 136 City of Coventry
390047 CLIC Sargent	390 137 Virgin Difference
390049 Virgin Express	390 138 City of London
390050 Virgin Invader	390 141 City of Chester
390103 Virgin Hero	390 148 Flying Scouseman
390104 Alstom Pendolino	390 151 Virgin Ambassador
390107 Independence Day Resurgence	390 152 Virgin Knight
390112 Virgin Star	390 153 Mission Accomplished
390114 City of Manchester	390 154 Matthew Flinders
390115 Virgin Crusader	390 155 X-MEN Days of Future Past
390117 Virgin Prince	390 156 Stockport 170
390118 Virgin Princess	390 157 Chad Varah
390119 Virgin Warrior	

CLASS 395   JAVELIN   HITACHI JAPAN

6-car dual-voltage units used on Southeastern High Speed trains from London St Pancras.

Formation: PDTSO–MSO–MSO–MSO–MSO–PDTSO.
Systems: 25 kV AC overhead/750 V DC third rail.
Construction: Aluminium.
Traction Motors: Four Hitachi asynchronous of 210 kW.
Wheel Arrangement: 2-2 + Bo-Bo + Bo-Bo + Bo-Bo + Bo-Bo + 2-2.
Braking: Disc, rheostatic & regenerative.
Dimensions: 20.88/20.0 x 2.81 m.   **Couplers:** Scharfenberg.
Bogies: Hitachi.   **Control System:** IGBT Inverter.
Gangways: Within unit.   **Maximum Speed:** 140 mph.
Doors: Single-leaf sliding.   **Multiple Working:** Within class only.
Heating & ventilation: Air conditioning.
Seating Layout: 2+2 facing/unidirectional (mainly unidirectional).

PDTSO(A): Hitachi Kasado, Japan 2006–09. –/28(+12) 1TD 2W. 46.7 t.
MSO: Hitachi Kasado, Japan 2006–09. –/66. 45.0t–45.7 t.
PDTSO(B): Hitachi Kasado, Japan 2006–09. –/48 1T. 46.7 t.

395 001	**SB**	E	*SE*	AD	39011	39012	39013	39014	39015	39016
395 002	**SB**	E	*SE*	AD	39021	39022	39023	39024	39025	39026
395 003	**SB**	E	*SE*	AD	39031	39032	39033	39034	39035	39036
395 004	**SB**	E	*SE*	AD	39041	39042	39043	39044	39045	39046
395 005	**SB**	E	*SE*	AD	39051	39052	39053	39054	39055	39056
395 006	**SB**	E	*SE*	AD	39061	39062	39063	39064	39065	39066
395 007	**SB**	E	*SE*	AD	39071	39072	39073	39074	39075	39076
395 008	**SB**	E	*SE*	AD	39081	39082	39083	39084	39085	39086
395 009	**SB**	E	*SE*	AD	39091	39092	39093	39094	39095	39096
395 010	**SB**	E	*SE*	AD	39101	39102	39103	39104	39105	39106
395 011	**SB**	E	*SE*	AD	39111	39112	39113	39114	39115	39116
395 012	**SB**	E	*SE*	AD	39121	39122	39123	39124	39125	39126
395 013	**SB**	E	*SE*	AD	39131	39132	39133	39134	39135	39136
395 014	**SB**	E	*SE*	AD	39141	39142	39143	39144	39145	39146
395 015	**SB**	E	*SE*	AD	39151	39152	39153	39154	39155	39156
395 016	**SB**	E	*SE*	AD	39161	39162	39163	39164	39165	39166
395 017	**SB**	E	*SE*	AD	39171	39172	39173	39174	39175	39176
395 018	**SB**	E	*SE*	AD	39181	39182	39183	39184	39185	39186
395 019	**SB**	E	*SE*	AD	39191	39192	39193	39194	39195	39196
395 020	**SB**	E	*SE*	AD	39201	39202	39203	39204	39205	39206
395 021	**SB**	E	*SE*	AD	39211	39212	39213	39214	39215	39216
395 022	**SB**	E	*SE*	AD	39221	39222	39223	39224	39225	39226
395 023	**SB**	E	*SE*	AD	39231	39232	39233	39234	39235	39236
395 024	**SB**	E	*SE*	AD	39241	39242	39243	39244	39245	39246
395 025	**SB**	E	*SE*	AD	39251	39252	39253	39254	39255	39256
395 026	**SB**	E	*SE*	AD	39261	39262	39263	39264	39265	39266
395 027	**SB**	E	*SE*	AD	39271	39272	39273	39274	39275	39276
395 028	**SB**	E	*SE*	AD	39281	39282	39283	39284	39285	39286
395 029	**SB**	E	*SE*	AD	39291	39292	39293	39294	39295	39296

Names (carried on end cars):

395001	Dame Kelly Holmes
395002	Sebastian Coe
395003	Sir Steve Redgrave
395004	Sir Chris Hoy
395005	Dame Tanni Grey-Thompson
395006	Daley Thompson
395007	Steve Backley
395008	Ben Ainslie
395009	Rebecca Adlington
395010	Duncan Goodhew
395011	Katherine Grainger
395015	LIVE ON
395017	PASSCHENDAELE Javelin
395018	Mo Farah
395019	Jessica Ennis
395020	Jason Kenny
395021	Ed Clancy MBE
395022	Alistair Brownlee
395023	Ellie Simmonds
395024	Jonnie Peacock
395025	Victoria Pendleton
395026	Marc Woods
395027	Hannah Cockcroft
395028	Laura Trott
395029	David Weir

CLASS 397　　　　　　　　CIVITY　　　　　　　　CAF

New units under construction for TransPennine Express, for delivery 2018–19. Full details awaited.

Formation: DMF–PTS–MS–PTS–DMS.
Construction: Aluminium.
Traction Motors:
Wheel Arrangement:
Braking:
Bogies: CAF.
Gangways: Within unit.
Doors:
Heating & ventilation: Air conditioning.
Seating:
Multiple Working: Within class.

Dimensions:
Couplers:
Control System: IGBT Inverter.
Maximum Speed: 125 mph.

DMFO. CAF Zaragoza 2017–18.
PTSO(A). CAF Zaragoza 2017–18.
MSO. CAF Zaragoza 2017–18.
PTSO(B). CAF Zaragoza 2017–18.
DMSO. CAF Zaragoza 2017–18.

397001	E	471001	472001	473001	474001	475001
397002	E	471002	472002	473002	474002	475002
397003	E	471003	472003	473003	474003	475003
397004	E	471004	472004	473004	474004	475004
397005	E	471005	472005	473005	474005	475005
397006	E	471006	472006	473006	474006	475006
397007	E	471007	472007	473007	474007	475007
397008	E	471008	472008	473008	474008	475008
397009	E	471009	472009	473009	474009	475009
397010	E	471010	472010	473010	474010	475010
397011	E	471011	472011	473011	474011	475011
397012	E	471012	472012	473012	474012	475012

CLASS 399   CITYLINK   VOSSLOH/STADLER

Tram-trains for the Sheffield–Rotherham Parkgate pilot tram-train project, being run jointly by South Yorkshire Passenger Transport Executive, Network Rail, Northern and Stagecoach Supertram. Dual-voltage 750 V DC/25 kV AC (although currently only planned to operate on 750 V DC). For operation on Network Rail lines EMU running numbers 399 201–207 are carried (as well as vehicle numbers in the 999xxx series), as well as Supertram fleet numbers 201–207.

Entered service on the Supertram network in autumn 2017 and due to enter service on the national railway network as tram-trains from September 2018.

Formation: DMSO–MSO–DMSO.
Systems: 750 V DC/25 kV AC overhead.
Construction: Steel.
Traction Motors: Six VEM of 145 kW.
Wheel Arrangement: Bo-2-Bo-Bo.
Braking: Disc, regenerative & emergency track.
Dimensions: 37.20 x 2.65 m (full set). **Couplers:** Albert (emergency use).
Bogies: Vossloh.   **Control System:** IGBT Inverter.
Gangways: Within unit.   **Maximum Speed:** 60 mph.
Doors: Sliding plug.   **Multiple Working:** Within class only.
Seating Layout: 2+2 facing/unidirectional.
Weight: 64 t.

DMSO(A): Vossloh, Valencia 2014–15. –/22(+4).
MSO: Vossloh, Valencia 2014–15. –/44.
DMSO(B): Vossloh, Valencia 2014–15. –/22(+4).

399 201	**SD**	SY	*SY*	NU	999001	999101	999201
399 202	**SD**	SY	*SY*	NU	999002	999102	999202
399 203	**SD**	SY	*SY*	NU	999003	999103	999203
399 204	**SD**	SY	*SY*	NU	999004	999104	999204
399 205	**SD**	SY	*SY*	NU	999005	999105	999205
399 206	**SD**	SY	*SY*	NU	999006	999106	999206
399 207	**SD**	SY	*SY*	NU	999007	999107	999207

Name (carried on end cars): 399 202   Theo – The Children's Hospital Charity

4.2. 750 V DC THIRD RAIL EMUs

These classes use the third rail system at 750 V DC (unless stated). Outer couplers are buckeyes on units built before 1982 with bar couplers within the units. Newer units generally have Dellner outer couplers.

CLASS 442   WESSEX EXPRESS   BREL DERBY

Units built for Waterloo–Bournemouth–Weymouth services. Previously used by South West Trains, used by Southern until 2017 when they were replaced by new Class 387/2s. 18 units are to be refurbished and returned to service with South Western Railway from 2018.

Formation: DTSO(A)–TSO–MBC–TSO(W)–DTSO(B).
Construction: Steel.
Traction Motors: Four EE546 of 300 kW recovered from Class 432s.
Wheel Arrangement: 2-2 + 2-2 + Bo-Bo + 2-2 + 2-2.
Braking: Disc.   **Dimensions:** 23.15/23.00 x 2.74 m.
Bogies: Two BREL P7 motor bogies (MBSO). T3 bogies (trailer cars).
Couplers: Buckeye.   **Control System:** 1986-type.
Gangways: Throughout.   **Maximum Speed:** 100 mph.
Doors: Sliding plug.   **Heating & Ventilation:** Air conditioning.
Seating Layout: 1: 2+1 facing, 2: 2+2 mainly unidirectional.
Multiple Working: Within class and Class 33/1 & 73 locos in an emergency.

DTSO(A). Lot No. 31030 Derby 1988–89. –/74. 38.5 t.
TSO. Lot No. 31032 Derby 1988–89. –/76 2T. 37.5 t.
MBC. Lot No. 31034 Derby 1988–89. 24/28. 55.0 t.
TSO(W). Lot No. 31033 Derby 1988–89. –/66(+4) 1TD 1T 2W. 37.8 t.
DTSO(B). Lot No. 31031 Derby 1988–89. –/74. 37.3 t.

442 401	GV	A	EP	77382	71818	62937	71842	77414
442 402	GV	A	ZG	77383	71819	62938	71843	77407
442 403	GV	A	BM	77384	71820	62941	71844	77408
442 404	GV	A	BM	77385	71821	62939	71845	77409
442 405	GV	A	EH	77386	71822	62944	71846	77410
442 406	GV	A	BM	77389	71823	62942	71847	77411
442 407	GV	A	EP	77388	71824	62943	71848	77412
442 408	GV	A	ZG	77387	71825	62945	71849	77413
442 409	GV	A	BM	77390	71826	62946	71850	77406
442 410	GV	A	ZG	77391	71827	62948	71851	77415
442 411	GV	A	BM	77392	71828	62940	71858	77422
442 412	GV	A	EP	77393	71829	62947	71853	77417
442 413	GV	A	ZG	77394	71830	62949	71854	77418
442 414	GV	A	BM	77395	71831	62950	71855	77419
442 415	GV	A	BM	77396	71832	62951	71856	77420
442 416	GV	A	BM	77397	71833	62952	71857	77421
442 417	GV	A	BM	77398	71834	62953	71852	77416
442 418	GV	A	BM	77399	71835	62954	71859	77423
442 419	GV	A	BM	77400	71836	62955	71860	77424
442 420	GV	A	BM	77401	71837	62956	71861	77425

442421	**GV**	A	EP	77402 71838 62957 71862 77426
442422	**GV**	A	BM	77403 71839 62958 71863 77427
442423	**GV**	A	BM	77404 71840 62959 71864 77428
442424	**GV**	A	EH	77405 71841 62960 71865 77429

CLASS 444   DESIRO UK   SIEMENS

Express units.

Formation: DMCO–TSO–TSO–TSORMB–DMSO.
Construction: Aluminium.
Traction Motors: 4 Siemens 1TB2016-0GB02 asynchronous of 250 kW.
Wheel Arrangement: Bo-Bo + 2-2 + 2-2 + 2-2 + Bo-Bo.
Braking: Disc, rheostatic & regenerative. **Dimensions:** 23.57 x 2.80 m.
Bogies: SGP SF5000.   **Couplers:** Dellner 12.
Gangways: Throughout.   **Control System:** IGBT Inverter.
Doors: Single-leaf sliding plug.   **Maximum Speed:** 100 mph.
Heating & Ventilation: Air conditioning.
Seating Layout: 1: 2+1 facing/unidirectional, 2: 2+2 facing/unidirectional.
Multiple Working: Within class and with Class 450.

DMSO. Siemens Vienna/Krefeld 2003–04. –/76. 51.3t.
TSO 67101–145. Siemens Vienna/Krefeld 2003–04. –/76 1T. 40.3t.
TSO 67151–195. Siemens Vienna/Krefeld 2003–04. –/76 1T. 36.8t.
TSORMB. Siemens Vienna/Krefeld 2003–04. –/47 1T 1TD 2W. 42.1t.
DMCO. Siemens Vienna/Krefeld 2003–04. 35/24. 51.3t.

444001	**ST**	A	*SW*	NT	63801 67101 67151 67201 63851
444002	**ST**	A	*SW*	NT	63802 67102 67152 67202 63852
444003	**ST**	A	*SW*	NT	63803 67103 67153 67203 63853
444004	**ST**	A	*SW*	NT	63804 67104 67154 67204 63854
444005	**ST**	A	*SW*	NT	63805 67105 67155 67205 63855
444006	**ST**	A	*SW*	NT	63806 67106 67156 67206 63856
444007	**ST**	A	*SW*	NT	63807 67107 67157 67207 63857
444008	**ST**	A	*SW*	NT	63808 67108 67158 67208 63858
444009	**ST**	A	*SW*	NT	63809 67109 67159 67209 63859
444010	**ST**	A	*SW*	NT	63810 67110 67160 67210 63860
444011	**ST**	A	*SW*	NT	63811 67111 67161 67211 63861
444012	**ST**	A	*SW*	NT	63812 67112 67162 67212 63862
444013	**ST**	A	*SW*	NT	63813 67113 67163 67213 63863
444014	**ST**	A	*SW*	NT	63814 67114 67164 67214 63864
444015	**ST**	A	*SW*	NT	63815 67115 67165 67215 63865
444016	**ST**	A	*SW*	NT	63816 67116 67166 67216 63866
444017	**ST**	A	*SW*	NT	63817 67117 67167 67217 63867
444018	**ST**	A	*SW*	NT	63818 67118 67168 67218 63868
444019	**ST**	A	*SW*	NT	63819 67119 67169 67219 63869
444020	**ST**	A	*SW*	NT	63820 67120 67170 67220 63870
444021	**ST**	A	*SW*	NT	63821 67121 67171 67221 63871
444022	**ST**	A	*SW*	NT	63822 67122 67172 67222 63872
444023	**ST**	A	*SW*	NT	63823 67123 67173 67223 63873
444024	**ST**	A	*SW*	NT	63824 67124 67174 67224 63874
444025	**ST**	A	*SW*	NT	63825 67125 67175 67225 63875

444026	**ST**	A	*SW*	NT	63826	67126	67176	67226	63876
444027	**ST**	A	*SW*	NT	63827	67127	67177	67227	63877
444028	**ST**	A	*SW*	NT	63828	67128	67178	67228	63878
444029	**ST**	A	*SW*	NT	63829	67129	67179	67229	63879
444030	**ST**	A	*SW*	NT	63830	67130	67180	67230	63880
444031	**ST**	A	*SW*	NT	63831	67131	67181	67231	63881
444032	**ST**	A	*SW*	NT	63832	67132	67182	67232	63882
444033	**ST**	A	*SW*	NT	63833	67133	67183	67233	63883
444034	**ST**	A	*SW*	NT	63834	67134	67184	67234	63884
444035	**ST**	A	*SW*	NT	63835	67135	67185	67235	63885
444036	**ST**	A	*SW*	NT	63836	67136	67186	67236	63886
444037	**ST**	A	*SW*	NT	63837	67137	67187	67237	63887
444038	**ST**	A	*SW*	NT	63838	67138	67188	67238	63888
444039	**ST**	A	*SW*	NT	63839	67139	67189	67239	63889
444040	**SW**	A	*SW*	NT	63840	67140	67190	67240	63890
444041	**ST**	A	*SW*	NT	63841	67141	67191	67241	63891
444042	**ST**	A	*SW*	NT	63842	67142	67192	67242	63892
444043	**ST**	A	*SW*	NT	63843	67143	67193	67243	63893
444044	**ST**	A	*SW*	NT	63844	67144	67194	67244	63894
444045	**ST**	A	*SW*	NT	63845	67145	67195	67245	63895

Names (carried on TSORMB):

444001	NAOMI HOUSE	444018	THE FAB 444
444012	DESTINATION WEYMOUTH	444038	SOUTH WESTERN RAILWAY

CLASS 450   DESIRO UK   SIEMENS

Outer suburban units.

Formation: DMSO–TCO–TSO–DMSO (DMSO–TSO–TCO–DMSO 450111–127).
Construction: Aluminium.
Traction Motors: 4 Siemens 1TB2016-0GB02 asynchronous of 250 kW.
Wheel Arrangement: Bo-Bo + 2-2 + 2-2 + Bo-Bo.
Braking: Disc, rheostatic & regenerative. **Dimensions:** 20.34 x 2.79 m.
Bogies: SGP SF5000. **Couplers:** Dellner 12.
Gangways: Throughout. **Control System:** IGBT Inverter.
Doors: Sliding plug. **Maximum Speed:** 100 mph.
Heating & Ventilation: Air conditioning.
Seating Layout: 1: 2+2 facing/unidirectional, 2: 3+2 facing/unidirectional.
Multiple Working: Within class and with Class 444.

Class 450/0. Standard units.

DMSO(A). Siemens Krefeld/Vienna 2002–06. –/70. 48.0 t.
TCO. Siemens Krefeld/Vienna 2002–06. 24/32(+4) 1T. 35.8 t.
TSO. Siemens Krefeld/Vienna 2002–06. –/61(+9) 1TD 2W. 39.8 t.
DMSO(B). Siemens Krefeld/Vienna 2002–06. –/70. 48.6 t.

450001	**SD**	A	*SW*	NT	63201	64201	68101	63601
450002	**SD**	A	*SW*	NT	63202	64202	68102	63602
450003	**SD**	A	*SW*	NT	63203	64203	68103	63603
450004	**SD**	A	*SW*	NT	63204	64204	68104	63604
450005	**SD**	A	*SW*	NT	63205	64205	68105	63605

450006	**SD**	A	*SW*	NT	63206	64206	68106	63606
450007	**SD**	A	*SW*	NT	63207	64207	68107	63607
450008	**SD**	A	*SW*	NT	63208	64208	68108	63608
450009	**SD**	A	*SW*	NT	63209	64209	68109	63609
450010	**SD**	A	*SW*	NT	63210	64210	68110	63610
450011	**SD**	A	*SW*	NT	63211	64211	68111	63611
450012	**SD**	A	*SW*	NT	63212	64212	68112	63612
450013	**SD**	A	*SW*	NT	63213	64213	68113	63613
450014	**SD**	A	*SW*	NT	63214	64214	68114	63614
450015	**SD**	A	*SW*	NT	63215	64215	68115	63615
450016	**SD**	A	*SW*	NT	63216	64216	68116	63616
450017	**SD**	A	*SW*	NT	63217	64217	68117	63617
450018	**SD**	A	*SW*	NT	63218	64218	68118	63618
450019	**SD**	A	*SW*	NT	63219	64219	68119	63619
450020	**SD**	A	*SW*	NT	63220	64220	68120	63620
450021	**SD**	A	*SW*	NT	63221	64221	68121	63621
450022	**SD**	A	*SW*	NT	63222	64222	68122	63622
450023	**SD**	A	*SW*	NT	63223	64223	68123	63623
450024	**SD**	A	*SW*	NT	63224	64224	68124	63624
450025	**SD**	A	*SW*	NT	63225	64225	68125	63625
450026	**SD**	A	*SW*	NT	63226	64226	68126	63626
450027	**SD**	A	*SW*	NT	63227	64227	68127	63627
450028	**SD**	A	*SW*	NT	63228	64228	68128	63628
450029	**SD**	A	*SW*	NT	63229	64229	68129	63629
450030	**SD**	A	*SW*	NT	63230	64230	68130	63630
450031	**SD**	A	*SW*	NT	63231	64231	68131	63631
450032	**SD**	A	*SW*	NT	63232	64232	68132	63632
450033	**SD**	A	*SW*	NT	63233	64233	68133	63633
450034	**SD**	A	*SW*	NT	63234	64234	68134	63634
450035	**SD**	A	*SW*	NT	63235	64235	68135	63635
450036	**SD**	A	*SW*	NT	63236	64236	68136	63636
450037	**SD**	A	*SW*	NT	63237	64237	68137	63637
450038	**SD**	A	*SW*	NT	63238	64238	68138	63638
450039	**SD**	A	*SW*	NT	63239	64239	68139	63639
450040	**SD**	A	*SW*	NT	63240	64240	68140	63640
450041	**SD**	A	*SW*	NT	63241	64241	68141	63641
450042	**SD**	A	*SW*	NT	63242	64242	68142	63642
450071	**SD**	A	*SW*	NT	63271	64271	68171	63671
450072	**SD**	A	*SW*	NT	63272	64272	68172	63672
450073	**SD**	A	*SW*	NT	63273	64273	68173	63673
450074	**SD**	A	*SW*	NT	63274	64274	68174	63674
450075	**SD**	A	*SW*	NT	63275	64275	68175	63675
450076	**SD**	A	*SW*	NT	63276	64276	68176	63676
450077	**SD**	A	*SW*	NT	63277	64277	68177	63677
450078	**SD**	A	*SW*	NT	63278	64278	68178	63678
450079	**SD**	A	*SW*	NT	63279	64279	68179	63679
450080	**SD**	A	*SW*	NT	63280	64280	68180	63680
450081	**SD**	A	*SW*	NT	63281	64281	68181	63681
450082	**SD**	A	*SW*	NT	63282	64282	68182	63682
450083	**SD**	A	*SW*	NT	63283	64283	68183	63683
450084	**SD**	A	*SW*	NT	63284	64284	68184	63684

450 085	**SD**	A	*SW*	NT	63285	64285	68185	63685
450 086	**SD**	A	*SW*	NT	63286	64286	68186	63686
450 087	**SD**	A	*SW*	NT	63287	64287	68187	63687
450 088	**SD**	A	*SW*	NT	63288	64288	68188	63688
450 089	**SD**	A	*SW*	NT	63289	64289	68189	63689
450 090	**SD**	A	*SW*	NT	63290	64290	68190	63690
450 091	**SD**	A	*SW*	NT	63291	64291	68191	63691
450 092	**SD**	A	*SW*	NT	63292	64292	68192	63692
450 093	**SD**	A	*SW*	NT	63293	64293	68193	63693
450 094	**SD**	A	*SW*	NT	63294	64294	68194	63694
450 095	**SD**	A	*SW*	NT	63295	64295	68195	63695
450 096	**SD**	A	*SW*	NT	63296	64296	68196	63696
450 097	**SD**	A	*SW*	NT	63297	64297	68197	63697
450 098	**SD**	A	*SW*	NT	63298	64298	68198	63698
450 099	**SD**	A	*SW*	NT	63299	64299	68199	63699
450 100	**SD**	A	*SW*	NT	63300	64300	68200	63700
450 101	**SD**	A	*SW*	NT	63701	66851	66801	63751
450 102	**SD**	A	*SW*	NT	63702	66852	66802	63752
450 103	**SD**	A	*SW*	NT	63703	66853	66803	63753
450 104	**SD**	A	*SW*	NT	63704	66854	66804	63754
450 105	**SD**	A	*SW*	NT	63705	66855	66805	63755
450 106	**SD**	A	*SW*	NT	63706	66856	66806	63756
450 107	**SD**	A	*SW*	NT	63707	66857	66807	63757
450 108	**SD**	A	*SW*	NT	63708	66858	66808	63758
450 109	**SD**	A	*SW*	NT	63709	66859	66809	63759
450 110	**SD**	A	*SW*	NT	63710	66860	66810	63760
450 111	**SD**	A	*SW*	NT	63901	66921	66901	63921
450 112	**SD**	A	*SW*	NT	63902	66922	66902	63922
450 113	**SD**	A	*SW*	NT	63903	66923	66903	63923
450 114	**SD**	A	*SW*	NT	63904	66924	66904	63924
450 115	**SD**	A	*SW*	NT	63905	66925	66905	63925
450 116	**SD**	A	*SW*	NT	63906	66926	66906	63926
450 117	**SD**	A	*SW*	NT	63907	66927	66907	63927
450 118	**SD**	A	*SW*	NT	63908	66928	66908	63928
450 119	**SD**	A	*SW*	NT	63909	66929	66909	63929
450 120	**SD**	A	*SW*	NT	63910	66930	66910	63930
450 121	**SD**	A	*SW*	NT	63911	66931	66911	63931
450 122	**SD**	A	*SW*	NT	63912	66932	66912	63932
450 123	**SD**	A	*SW*	NT	63913	66933	66913	63933
450 124	**SD**	A	*SW*	NT	63914	66934	66914	63934
450 125	**SD**	A	*SW*	NT	63915	66935	66915	63935
450 126	**SD**	A	*SW*	NT	63916	66936	66916	63936
450 127	**SD**	A	*SW*	NT	63917	66937	66917	63937

Names (carried on DMSO(B)):

450 015 DESIRO
450 042 TRELOAR COLLEGE

450 114 FAIRBRIDGE investing in the future
450 127 DAVE GUNSON

Class 450/5. 28 units converted 2007–08 with First Class removed and a modified seating layout with more standing room (some Standard Class seats were taken out). First Class was refitted in 2013 but the removed Standard Class seats were not refitted so the units have kept their 450 5xx series numbers.

DMSO(A). Siemens Krefeld/Vienna 2002–04. –/64. 48.0 t.
TCO. Siemens Krefeld/Vienna 2002–04. 24/30(+4) 1T. 35.5 t.
TSO. Siemens Krefeld/Vienna 2002–04. –/56(+9) 1TD 2W. 39.8 t.
DMSO(B). Siemens Krefeld/Vienna 2002–04. –/64. 48.6 t.

450 543	(450 043)	**SD**	A	*SW*	NT	63243	64243	68143	63643
450 544	(450 044)	**SD**	A	*SW*	NT	63244	64244	68144	63644
450 545	(450 045)	**SD**	A	*SW*	NT	63245	64245	68145	63645
450 546	(450 046)	**SD**	A	*SW*	NT	63246	64246	68146	63646
450 547	(450 047)	**SD**	A	*SW*	NT	63247	64247	68147	63647
450 548	(450 048)	**SD**	A	*SW*	NT	63248	64248	68148	63648
450 549	(450 049)	**SD**	A	*SW*	NT	63249	64249	68149	63649
450 550	(450 050)	**SD**	A	*SW*	NT	63250	64250	68150	63650
450 551	(450 051)	**SD**	A	*SW*	NT	63251	64251	68151	63651
450 552	(450 052)	**SD**	A	*SW*	NT	63252	64252	68152	63652
450 553	(450 053)	**SD**	A	*SW*	NT	63253	64253	68153	63653
450 554	(450 054)	**SD**	A	*SW*	NT	63254	64254	68154	63654
450 555	(450 055)	**SD**	A	*SW*	NT	63255	64255	68155	63655
450 556	(450 056)	**SD**	A	*SW*	NT	63256	64256	68156	63656
450 557	(450 057)	**SD**	A	*SW*	NT	63257	64257	68157	63657
450 558	(450 058)	**SD**	A	*SW*	NT	63258	64258	68158	63658
450 559	(450 059)	**SD**	A	*SW*	NT	63259	64259	68159	63659
450 560	(450 060)	**SD**	A	*SW*	NT	63260	64260	68160	63660
450 561	(450 061)	**SD**	A	*SW*	NT	63261	64261	68161	63661
450 562	(450 062)	**SD**	A	*SW*	NT	63262	64262	68162	63662
450 563	(450 063)	**SD**	A	*SW*	NT	63263	64263	68163	63663
450 564	(450 064)	**SD**	A	*SW*	NT	63264	64264	68164	63664
450 565	(450 065)	**SD**	A	*SW*	NT	63265	64265	68165	63665
450 566	(450 066)	**SD**	A	*SW*	NT	63266	64266	68166	63666
450 567	(450 067)	**SD**	A	*SW*	NT	63267	64267	68167	63667
450 568	(450 068)	**SD**	A	*SW*	NT	63268	64268	68168	63668
450 569	(450 069)	**SD**	A	*SW*	NT	63269	64269	68169	63669
450 570	(450 070)	**SD**	A	*SW*	NT	63270	64270	68170	63670

CLASS 455   BREL YORK

Inner suburban units. During 2016–17 the South Western Railway fleet was fitted with new AC traction motors by Vossloh Kiepe.

Formation: DTSO–MSO–TSO–DTSO.
Construction: Steel. Class 455/7 TSO have a steel underframe and an aluminium alloy body and roof.
Traction Motors: Four GEC507-20J of 185 kW, some recovered from Class 405s (* Four TSA010163 AC motors of 240 kW).
Wheel Arrangement: 2-2 + Bo-Bo + 2-2 + 2-2.
Braking: Disc (* and regenerative).   **Dimensions:** 19.92/19.83 x 2.82 m.

Bogies: P7 (motor) and T3 (455/8 & 455/9) BX1 (455/7) trailer.
Gangways: Within unit + end doors (sealed on Southern units).
Couplers: Tightlock.   **Maximum Speed:** 75 mph.
Control System: 1982-type, camshaft (* IGBT Inverter).
Doors: Sliding.   **Heating & Ventilation:** Various.
Seating Layout: All units refurbished. SWR units: 2+2 high-back unidirectional/
facing seating. Southern units: 3+2 high back mainly facing seating.
Multiple Working: Within class and with Class 456.

Class 455/7. South Western Railway units. Second series with TSOs
originally in Class 508s. Pressure heating & ventilation.

DTSO. Lot No. 30976 1984–85. –/50(+4) 1W. 30.8t.
MSO. Lot No. 30975 1984–85. –/68. 45.7t.
TSO. Lot No. 30944 1979–80. –/68. 26.1t.

5701	*	SS	P	SW	WD	77727	62783	71545	77728
5702	*	SS	P	SW	WD	77729	62784	71547	77730
5703	*	SS	P	SW	WD	77731	62785	71540	77732
5704	*	SS	P	SW	WD	77733	62786	71548	77734
5705	*	SS	P	SW	WD	77735	62787	71565	77736
5706	*	SS	P	SW	WD	77737	62788	71534	77738
5707	*	SS	P	SW	WD	77739	62789	71536	77740
5708	*	SS	P	SW	WD	77741	62790	71560	77742
5709	*	SS	P	SW	WD	77743	62791	71532	77744
5710	*	SS	P	SW	WD	77745	62792	71566	77746
5711	*	SS	P	SW	WD	77747	62793	71542	77748
5712	*	SS	P	SW	WD	77749	62794	71546	77750
5713	*	SS	P	SW	WD	77751	62795	71567	77752
5714	*	SS	P	SW	WD	77753	62796	71539	77754
5715	*	SS	P	SW	WD	77755	62797	71535	77756
5716	*	SS	P	SW	WD	77757	62798	71564	77758
5717	*	SS	P	SW	WD	77759	62799	71528	77760
5718	*	SS	P	SW	WD	77761	62800	71557	77762
5719	*	SS	P	SW	WD	77763	62801	71558	77764
5720	*	SS	P	SW	WD	77765	62802	71568	77766
5721	*	SS	P	SW	WD	77767	62803	71553	77768
5722	*	SS	P	SW	WD	77769	62804	71533	77770
5723	*	SS	P	SW	WD	77771	62805	71526	77772
5724	*	SS	P	SW	WD	77773	62806	71561	77774
5725	*	SS	P	SW	WD	77775	62807	71541	77776
5726	*	SS	P	SW	WD	77777	62808	71556	77778
5727	*	SS	P	SW	WD	77779	62809	71562	77780
5728	*	SS	P	SW	WD	77781	62810	71527	77782
5729	*	SS	P	SW	WD	77783	62811	71550	77784
5730	*	SS	P	SW	WD	77785	62812	71551	77786
5731	*	SS	P	SW	WD	77787	62813	71555	77788
5732	*	SS	P	SW	WD	77789	62814	71552	77790
5733	*	SS	P	SW	WD	77791	62815	71549	77792
5734	*	SS	P	SW	WD	77793	62816	71531	77794
5735	*	SS	P	SW	WD	77795	62817	71563	77796
5736	*	SS	P	SW	WD	77797	62818	71554	77798

5737	*	**SS**	P	*SW*	WD	77799	62819	71544	77800
5738	*	**SS**	P	*SW*	WD	77801	62820	71529	77802
5739	*	**SS**	P	*SW*	WD	77803	62821	71537	77804
5740	*	**SS**	P	*SW*	WD	77805	62822	71530	77806
5741	*	**SS**	P	*SW*	WD	77807	62823	71559	77808
5742	*	**SS**	P	*SW*	WD	77809	62824	71543	77810
5750	*	**SS**	P	*SW*	WD	77811	62825	71538	77812

Class 455/8. Southern units. First series. Pressure heating & ventilation. Fitted with in-cab air conditioning systems meaning that the end door has been sealed.

DTSO. Lot No. 30972 York 1982–84. –/74. 33.6 t.
MSO. Lot No. 30973 York 1982–84. –/84. 45.6 t.
TSO. Lot No. 30974 York 1982–84. –/75(+3) 2W. 34.0 t.

455801	**SN**	E	*SN*	SL	77627	62709	71657	77580
455802	**SN**	E	*SN*	SL	77581	62710	71664	77582
455803	**SN**	E	*SN*	SL	77583	62711	71639	77584
455804	**SN**	E	*SN*	SL	77585	62712	71640	77586
455805	**SN**	E	*SN*	SL	77587	62713	71641	77588
455806	**SN**	E	*SN*	SL	77589	62714	71642	77590
455807	**SN**	E	*SN*	SL	77591	62715	71643	77592
455808	**SN**	E	*SN*	SL	77637	62716	71644	77594
455809	**SN**	E	*SN*	SL	77623	62717	71648	77602
455810	**SN**	E	*SN*	SL	77597	62718	71643	77598
455811	**SN**	E	*SN*	SL	77599	62719	71647	77600
455812	**SN**	E	*SN*	SL	77595	62720	71645	77626
455813	**SN**	E	*SN*	SL	77603	62721	71649	77604
455814	**SN**	E	*SN*	SL	77605	62722	71650	77606
455815	**SN**	E	*SN*	SL	77607	62723	71651	77608
455816	**SN**	E	*SN*	SL	77609	62724	71652	77633
455817	**SN**	E	*SN*	SL	77611	62725	71653	77612
455818	**SN**	E	*SN*	SL	77613	62726	71654	77632
455819	**SN**	E	*SN*	SL	77615	62727	71637	77616
455820	**SN**	E	*SN*	SL	77617	62728	71656	77618
455821	**SN**	E	*SN*	SL	77619	62729	71655	77620
455822	**SN**	E	*SN*	SL	77621	62730	71658	77622
455823	**SN**	E	*SN*	SL	77601	62731	71659	77596
455824	**SN**	E	*SN*	SL	77593	62732	71660	77624
455825	**SN**	E	*SN*	SL	77579	62733	71661	77628
455826	**SN**	E	*SN*	SL	77630	62734	71662	77629
455827	**SN**	E	*SN*	SL	77610	62735	71663	77614
455828	**SN**	E	*SN*	SL	77631	62736	71638	77634
455829	**SN**	E	*SN*	SL	77635	62737	71665	77636
455830	**SN**	E	*SN*	SL	77625	62743	71666	77638
455831	**SN**	E	*SN*	SL	77639	62739	71667	77640
455832	**SN**	E	*SN*	SL	77641	62740	71668	77642
455833	**SN**	E	*SN*	SL	77643	62741	71669	77644
455834	**SN**	E	*SN*	SL	77645	62742	71670	77646
455835	**SN**	E	*SN*	SL	77647	62738	71671	77648
455836	**SN**	E	*SN*	SL	77649	62744	71672	77650

456 006	**SS**	P	*SW*	WD	64740	78255
456 007	**SS**	P	*SW*	WD	64741	78256
456 008	**SS**	P	*SW*	WD	64742	78257
456 009	**SS**	P	*SW*	WD	64743	78258
456 010	**SS**	P	*SW*	WD	64744	78259
456 011	**SS**	P	*SW*	WD	64745	78260
456 012	**SS**	P	*SW*	WD	64746	78261
456 013	**SS**	P	*SW*	WD	64747	78262
456 014	**SS**	P	*SW*	WD	64748	78263
456 015	**SS**	P	*SW*	WD	64749	78264
456 016	**SS**	P	*SW*	WD	64750	78265
456 017	**SS**	P	*SW*	WD	64751	78266
456 018	**SS**	P	*SW*	WD	64752	78267
456 019	**SS**	P	*SW*	WD	64753	78268
456 020	**SS**	P	*SW*	WD	64754	78269
456 021	**SS**	P	*SW*	WD	64755	78270
456 022	**SS**	P	*SW*	WD	64756	78271
456 023	**SS**	P	*SW*	WD	64757	78272
456 024	**SS**	P	*SW*	WD	64758	78273

CLASS 458   JUNIPER   ALSTOM BIRMINGHAM

Outer suburban units. Between 2013 and 2016 the fleet of 30 4-car Class 458 units and the former Gatwick Express fleet of eight 8-car Class 460 units was combined to form a fleet of 36 5-car Standard Class only Class 458/5s. The work was carried out at Wabtec Doncaster and Brush Loughborough. Former Class 460 driving cars 67901/903/907/908 were not included in this programme and have been scrapped.

After lengthening each unit was renumbered into the 458 5xx series. All individual vehicles retained their original numbers.

Formation: DMSO–TSO*–TSO–MSO–DMSO (* ex-Class 460 in 458 501–530).
Construction: Steel.   **Dimensions:** 21.16 or 21.06 x 2.80 m.
Traction Motors: Two Alstom ONIX 800 asynchronous of 270 kW.
Wheel Arrangement: 2-Bo + 2-2 + 2-2 + Bo-2 + Bo-2.
Braking: Disc & regenerative.   **Control System:** IGBT Inverter.
Bogies: ACR.   **Doors:** Sliding plug.
Gangways: Throughout.
Couplers: Voith 136.
Maximum Speed: 75 mph.
Heating & Ventilation: Air conditioning. **Multiple Working:** Within class.
Seating Layout: 2+2 facing/unidirectional.

DMSO(A). Alstom 1998–2000. –/60. 45.7 t.
TSO. Alstom 1998–99. 458 501–530 –/56; 458 531–536 –/52 1T. 34.4 t.
TSO. Alstom 1998–2000. –/42 1TD 2W. 34.1 t.
MSO. Alstom 1998–2000. 458 501–530 –56 1T; 458 531–536 –/56. 40.1 t.
DMSO(B). Alstom 1998–2000. –/60. 44.9 t.

| 458 501 | **SD** | P | *SW* | WD | 67601 | 74431 | 74001 | 74101 | 67701 |
| 458 502 | **SD** | P | *SW* | WD | 67602 | 74421 | 74002 | 74102 | 67702 |

458503	**SD**	P	*SW*	WD	67603 74441 74003 74103 67703
458504	**SD**	P	*SW*	WD	67604 74451 74004 74104 67704
458505	**SD**	P	*SW*	WD	67605 74425 74005 74105 67705
458506	**SD**	P	*SW*	WD	67606 74436 74006 74106 67706
458507	**SD**	P	*SW*	WD	67607 74428 74007 74107 67707
458508	**SD**	P	*SW*	WD	67608 74433 74008 74108 67708
458509	**SD**	P	*SW*	WD	67609 74452 74009 74109 67709
458510	**SD**	P	*SW*	WD	67610 74405 74010 74110 67710
458511	**SD**	P	*SW*	WD	67611 74435 74011 74111 67711
458512	**SD**	P	*SW*	WD	67612 74427 74012 74112 67712
458513	**SD**	P	*SW*	WD	67613 74437 74013 74113 67713
458514	**SD**	P	*SW*	WD	67614 74407 74014 74114 67714
458515	**SD**	P	*SW*	WD	67615 74404 74015 74115 67715
458516	**SD**	P	*SW*	WD	67616 74406 74016 74116 67716
458517	**SD**	P	*SW*	WD	67617 74426 74017 74117 67717
458518	**SD**	P	*SW*	WD	67618 74432 74018 74118 67718
458519	**SD**	P	*SW*	WD	67619 74403 74019 74119 67719
458520	**SD**	P	*SW*	WD	67620 74401 74020 74120 67720
458521	**SD**	P	*SW*	WD	67621 74438 74021 74121 67721
458522	**SD**	P	*SW*	WD	67622 74424 74022 74122 67722
458523	**SD**	P	*SW*	WD	67623 74434 74023 74123 67723
458524	**SD**	P	*SW*	WD	67624 74402 74024 74124 67724
458525	**SD**	P	*SW*	WD	67625 74422 74025 74125 67725
458526	**SD**	P	*SW*	WD	67626 74442 74026 74126 67726
458527	**SD**	P	*SW*	WD	67627 74412 74027 74127 67727
458528	**SD**	P	*SW*	WD	67628 74408 74028 74128 67728
458529	**SD**	P	*SW*	WD	67629 74423 74029 74129 67729
458530	**SD**	P	*SW*	WD	67630 74411 74030 74130 67730

The following units were converted entirely from Class 460s.

458531	**SD**	P	*SW*	WD	67913 74418 74446 74458 67912
458532	**SD**	P	*SW*	WD	67904 74417 74447 74457 67905
458533	**SD**	P	*SW*	WD	67917 74413 74443 74453 67916
458534	**SD**	P	*SW*	WD	67914 74414 74444 74454 67918
458535	**SD**	P	*SW*	WD	67915 74415 74445 74455 67911
458536	**SD**	P	*SW*	WD	67906 74416 74448 74456 67902

CLASS 465   NETWORKER

Inner/outer suburban units.

Formation: DMSO–TSO–TSO–DMSO.
Construction: Welded aluminium alloy.
Traction Motors: Hitachi asynchronous of 280 kW (Classes 465/0 and 465/1) or GEC-Alsthom G352BY (Classes 465/2 and 465/9).
Wheel Arrangement: Bo-Bo + 2-2 + 2-2 + Bo-Bo.
Braking: Disc & rheostatic and regenerative (Classes 465/0 and 465/1 only).
Bogies: BREL P3/T3 (465/0 and 465/1), SRP BP62/BT52 (465/2 and 465/9).
Dimensions: 20.89/20.06 x 2.81 m.
Control System: IGBT Inverter (465/0 and 465/1) or 1992-type GTO Inverter.
Gangways: Within unit.   **Couplers:** Tightlock.

Doors: Sliding plug.   **Maximum Speed:** 75 mph.
Seating Layout: 3+2 facing/unidirectional.
Multiple Working: Within class and with Class 466.

64759–808. DMSO(A). Lot No. 31100 BREL York 1991–93. –/86. 39.2t.
64809–858. DMSO(B). Lot No. 31100 BREL York 1991–93. –/86. 39.2t.
65734–749. DMSO(A). Lot No. 31103 Metro-Cammell 1991–93. –/86. 39.2t.
65784–799. DMSO(B). Lot No. 31103 Metro-Cammell 1991–93. –/86. 39.2t.
65800–846. DMSO(A). Lot No. 31130 ABB York 1993–94. –/86. 39.2t.
65847–893. DMSO(B). Lot No. 31130 ABB York 1993–94. –/86. 39.2t.
72028–126 (even nos.) TSO. Lot No. 31102 BREL York 1991–93. –/90. 27.2t.
72029–127 (odd nos.) TSO. Lot No. 31101 BREL York 1991–93. –/86 1T
(* –/67(+7) 1TD 2W). 28.0t.
72787–817 (odd nos.) TSO. Lot No. 31104 Metro-Cammell 1991–92. –/86 1T. 28.0t.
72788–818 (even nos.) TSO. Lot No. 31105 Metro-Cammell 1991–92. –/90. 27.2t.
72900–992 (even nos.) TSO. Lot No. 31102 ABB York 1993–94. –/90. 27.2t.
72901–993 (odd nos.) TSO. Lot No. 31101 ABB York 1993–94. –/86 1T. 28.0t.

Class 465/0. Built by BREL/ABB.

* Fitted with universal access toilet to meet the 2020 accessibilty regulations.

465001		**SE**	E	*SE*	SG	64759	72028	72029	64809
465002	*	**SE**	E	*SE*	SG	64760	72030	72031	64810
465003		**SE**	E	*SE*	SG	64761	72032	72033	64811
465004		**SE**	E	*SE*	SG	64762	72034	72035	64812
465005	*	**SE**	E	*SE*	SG	64763	72036	72037	64813
465006		**SE**	E	*SE*	SG	64764	72038	72039	64814
465007		**SE**	E	*SE*	SG	64765	72040	72041	64815
465008		**SE**	E	*SE*	SG	64766	72042	72043	64816
465009		**SE**	E	*SE*	SG	64767	72044	72045	64817
465010		**SE**	E	*SE*	SG	64768	72046	72047	64818
465011		**SE**	E	*SE*	SG	64769	72048	72049	64819
465012		**SE**	E	*SE*	SG	64770	72050	72051	64820
465013		**SE**	E	*SE*	SG	64771	72052	72053	64821
465014	*	**SE**	E	*SE*	SG	64772	72054	72055	64822
465015		**SE**	E	*SE*	SG	64773	72056	72057	64823
465016		**SE**	E	*SE*	SG	64774	72058	72059	64824
465017		**SE**	E	*SE*	SG	64775	72060	72061	64825
465018		**SE**	E	*SE*	SG	64776	72062	72063	64826
465019		**SE**	E	*SE*	SG	64777	72064	72065	64827
465020		**SE**	E	*SE*	SG	64778	72066	72067	64828
465021		**SE**	E	*SE*	SG	64779	72068	72069	64829
465022		**SE**	E	*SE*	SG	64780	72070	72071	64830
465023		**SE**	E	*SE*	SG	64781	72072	72073	64831
465024		**SE**	E	*SE*	SG	64782	72074	72075	64832
465025		**SE**	E	*SE*	SG	64783	72076	72077	64833
465026		**SE**	E	*SE*	SG	64784	72078	72079	64834
465027		**SE**	E	*SE*	SG	64785	72080	72081	64835
465028		**SE**	E	*SE*	SG	64786	72082	72083	64836
465029		**SE**	E	*SE*	SG	64787	72084	72085	64837
465030		**SE**	E	*SE*	SG	64788	72086	72087	64838
465031		**SE**	E	*SE*	SG	64789	72088	72089	64839

465032		**SE**	E	*SE*	SG	64790	72090	72091	64840
465033		**SE**	E	*SE*	SG	64791	72092	72093	64841
465034		**SE**	E	*SE*	SG	64792	72094	72095	64842
465035		**SE**	E	*SE*	SG	64793	72096	72097	64843
465036		**SE**	E	*SE*	SG	64794	72098	72099	64844
465037		**SE**	E	*SE*	SG	64795	72100	72101	64845
465038		**SE**	E	*SE*	SG	64796	72102	72103	64846
465039		**SE**	E	*SE*	SG	64797	72104	72105	64847
465040		**SE**	E	*SE*	SG	64798	72106	72107	64848
465041		**SE**	E	*SE*	SG	64799	72108	72109	64849
465042		**SE**	E	*SE*	SG	64800	72110	72111	64850
465043		**SE**	E	*SE*	SG	64801	72112	72113	64851
465044		**SE**	E	*SE*	SG	64802	72114	72115	64852
465045		**SE**	E	*SE*	SG	64803	72116	72117	64853
465046	*	**SE**	E	*SE*	SG	64804	72118	72119	64854
465047		**SE**	E	*SE*	SG	64805	72120	72121	64855
465048		**SE**	E	*SE*	SG	64806	72122	72123	64856
465049	*	**SE**	E	*SE*	SG	64807	72124	72125	64857
465050		**SE**	E	*SE*	SG	64808	72126	72127	64858

Class 465/1. Built by BREL/ABB. Similar to Class 465/0 but with detail differences.

465151		**SE**	E	*SE*	SG	65800	72900	72901	65847
465152		**SE**	E	*SE*	SG	65801	72902	72903	65848
465153		**SE**	E	*SE*	SG	65802	72904	72905	65849
465154		**SE**	E	*SE*	SG	65803	72906	72907	65850
465155		**SE**	E	*SE*	SG	65804	72908	72909	65851
465156	*	**SE**	E	*SE*	SG	65805	72910	72911	65852
465157		**SE**	E	*SE*	SG	65806	72912	72913	65853
465158		**SE**	E	*SE*	SG	65807	72914	72915	65854
465159		**SE**	E	*SE*	SG	65808	72916	72917	65855
465160		**SE**	E	*SE*	SG	65809	72918	72919	65856
465161		**SE**	E	*SE*	SG	65810	72920	72921	65857
465162		**SE**	E	*SE*	SG	65811	72922	72923	65858
465163		**SE**	E	*SE*	SG	65812	72924	72925	65859
465164	*	**SE**	E	*SE*	SG	65813	72926	72927	65860
465165		**SE**	E	*SE*	SG	65814	72928	72929	65861
465166		**SE**	E	*SE*	SG	65815	72930	72931	65862
465167		**SE**	E	*SE*	SG	65816	72932	72933	65863
465168		**SE**	E	*SE*	SG	65817	72934	72935	65864
465169		**SE**	E	*SE*	SG	65818	72936	72937	65865
465170		**SE**	E	*SE*	SG	65819	72938	72939	65866
465171		**SE**	E	*SE*	SG	65820	72940	72941	65867
465172		**SE**	E	*SE*	SG	65821	72942	72943	65868
465173		**SE**	E	*SE*	SG	65822	72944	72945	65869
465174		**SE**	E	*SE*	SG	65823	72946	72947	65870
465175		**SE**	E	*SE*	SG	65824	72948	72949	65871
465176		**SE**	E	*SE*	SG	65825	72950	72951	65872
465177		**SE**	E	*SE*	SG	65826	72952	72953	65873
465178		**SE**	E	*SE*	SG	65827	72954	72955	65874
465179		**SE**	E	*SE*	SG	65828	72956	72957	65875

465 180		**SE**	E	*SE*	SG	65829	72958	72959	65876
465 181	*	**SE**	E	*SE*	SG	65830	72960	72961	65877
465 182		**SE**	E	*SE*	SG	65831	72962	72963	65878
465 183		**SE**	E	*SE*	SG	65832	72964	72965	65879
465 184		**SE**	E	*SE*	SG	65833	72966	72967	65880
465 185		**SE**	E	*SE*	SG	65834	72968	72969	65881
465 186		**SE**	E	*SE*	SG	65835	72970	72971	65882
465 187		**SE**	E	*SE*	SG	65836	72972	72973	65883
465 188		**SE**	E	*SE*	SG	65837	72974	72975	65884
465 189		**SE**	E	*SE*	SG	65838	72976	72977	65885
465 190		**SE**	E	*SE*	SG	65839	72978	72979	65886
465 191		**SE**	E	*SE*	SG	65840	72980	72981	65887
465 192		**SE**	E	*SE*	SG	65841	72982	72983	65888
465 193		**SE**	E	*SE*	SG	65842	72984	72985	65889
465 194		**SE**	E	*SE*	SG	65843	72986	72987	65890
465 195		**SE**	E	*SE*	SG	65844	72988	72989	65891
465 196		**SE**	E	*SE*	SG	65845	72990	72991	65892
465 197		**SE**	E	*SE*	SG	65846	72992	72993	65893

Class 465/2. Built by Metro-Cammell. **Dimensions:** 20.80/20.15 x 2.81 m.

* Fitted with universal access toilet to meet the 2020 accessibilty regulations. Full details awaited.

465 235		**SE**	A	*SE*	SG	65734	72787	72788	65784
465 236		**SE**	A	*SE*	SG	65735	72789	72790	65785
465 237	*	**SE**	A	*SE*	SG	65736	72791	72792	65786
465 238		**SE**	A	*SE*	SG	65737	72793	72794	65787
465 239		**SE**	A	*SE*	SG	65738	72795	72796	65788
465 240		**SE**	A	*SE*	SG	65739	72797	72798	65789
465 241		**SE**	A	*SE*	SG	65740	72799	72800	65790
465 242		**SE**	A	*SE*	SG	65741	72801	72802	65791
465 243		**SE**	A	*SE*	SG	65742	72803	72804	65792
465 244		**SE**	A	*SE*	SG	65743	72805	72806	65793
465 245		**SE**	A	*SE*	SG	65744	72807	72808	65794
465 246		**SE**	A	*SE*	SG	65745	72809	72810	65795
465 247		**SE**	A	*SE*	SG	65746	72811	72812	65796
465 248		**SE**	A	*SE*	SG	65747	72813	72814	65797
465 249		**SE**	A	*SE*	SG	65748	72815	72816	65798
465 250		**SE**	A	*SE*	SG	65749	72817	72818	65799

Class 465/9. Built by Metro-Cammell. Refurbished 2005 for longer distance services, with the addition of First Class. Fitted with universal access toilet to meet the 2020 accessibility regulations. Details as Class 465/0 unless stated.

Formation: DMCO–TSO(A)–TSO(B)–DMCO.
Seating Layout: 1: 2+2 facing/unidirectional, 2: 3+2 facing/unidirectional.

65700–733. DMCO(A). Lot No. 31103 Metro-Cammell 1991–93. 12/68. 39.2t.
72719–785 (odd nos.) TSO(A). Lot No. 31104 Metro-Cammell 1991–92. –/65(+7) 1TD 2W. 30.3t.
72720–786 (even nos.) TSO(B). Lot No. 31105 Metro-Cammell 1991–92. –/90. 29.5t.
65750–783. DMCO(B). Lot No. 31103 Metro-Cammell 1991–93. 12/68. 39.2t.

465901	(465201)	**SE**	A	*SE*	SG	65700	72719	72720	65750
465902	(465202)	**SE**	A	*SE*	SG	65701	72721	72722	65751
465903	(465203)	**SE**	A	*SE*	SG	65702	72723	72724	65752
465904	(465204)	**SE**	A	*SE*	SG	65703	72725	72726	65753
465905	(465205)	**SE**	A	*SE*	SG	65704	72727	72728	65754
465906	(465206)	**SE**	A	*SE*	SG	65705	72729	72730	65755
465907	(465207)	**SE**	A	*SE*	SG	65706	72731	72732	65756
465908	(465208)	**SE**	A	*SE*	SG	65707	72733	72734	65757
465909	(465209)	**SE**	A	*SE*	SG	65708	72735	72736	65758
465910	(465210)	**SE**	A	*SE*	SG	65709	72737	72740	65759
465911	(465211)	**SE**	A	*SE*	SG	65710	72739	72740	65760
465912	(465212)	**SE**	A	*SE*	SG	65711	72741	72742	65761
465913	(465213)	**SE**	A	*SE*	SG	65712	72743	72744	65762
465914	(465214)	**SE**	A	*SE*	SG	65713	72745	72746	65763
465915	(465215)	**SE**	A	*SE*	SG	65714	72747	72748	65764
465916	(465216)	**SE**	A	*SE*	SG	65715	72749	72750	65765
465917	(465217)	**SE**	A	*SE*	SG	65716	72751	72752	65766
465918	(465218)	**SE**	A	*SE*	SG	65717	72753	72754	65767
465919	(465219)	**SE**	A	*SE*	SG	65718	72755	72756	65768
465920	(465220)	**SE**	A	*SE*	SG	65719	72757	72758	65769
465921	(465221)	**SE**	A	*SE*	SG	65720	72759	72760	65770
465922	(465222)	**SE**	A	*SE*	SG	65721	72761	72762	65771
465923	(465223)	**SE**	A	*SE*	SG	65722	72763	72764	65772
465924	(465224)	**SE**	A	*SE*	SG	65723	72765	72766	65773
465925	(465225)	**SE**	A	*SE*	SG	65724	72767	72768	65774
465926	(465226)	**SE**	A	*SE*	SG	65725	72769	72770	65775
465927	(465227)	**SE**	A	*SE*	SG	65726	72771	72772	65776
465928	(465228)	**SE**	A	*SE*	SG	65727	72773	72774	65777
465929	(465229)	**SE**	A	*SE*	SG	65728	72775	72776	65778
465930	(465230)	**SE**	A	*SE*	SG	65729	72777	72778	65779
465931	(465231)	**SE**	A	*SE*	SG	65730	72779	72780	65780
465932	(465232)	**SE**	A	*SE*	SG	65731	72781	72782	65781
465933	(465233)	**SE**	A	*SE*	SG	65732	72783	72784	65782
465934	(465234)	**SE**	A	*SE*	SG	65733	72785	72786	65783

CLASS 466   NETWORKER   GEC-ALSTHOM

Inner/outer suburban units.

Formation: DMSO–DTSO.
Construction: Welded aluminium alloy.
Traction Motors: Two GEC-Alsthom G352AY asynchronous of 280 kW.
Wheel Arrangement: Bo-Bo + 2-2. **Couplers:** Tightlock.
Braking: Disc, rheostatic & regen. **Control System:** 1992-type GTO Inverter.
Dimensions: 20.80 x 2.80 m. **Maximum Speed:** 75 mph.
Bogies: BREL P3/T3. **Doors:** Sliding plug.
Gangways: Within unit. **Seating Layout:** 3+2 facing/unidirectional.
Multiple Working: Within class and with Class 465.

DMSO. Lot No. 31128 Birmingham 1993–94. –/86. 40.6t.
DTSO. Lot No. 31129 Birmingham 1993–94. –/82 1T. 31.4t.

466001	**SE**	A	*SE*	SG	64860	78312
466002	**SE**	A	*SE*	SG	64861	78313
466003	**SE**	A	*SE*	SG	64862	78314
466004	**SE**	A	*SE*	SG	64863	78315
466005	**SE**	A	*SE*	SG	64864	78316
466006	**SE**	A	*SE*	SG	64865	78317
466007	**SE**	A	*SE*	SG	64866	78318
466008	**SE**	A	*SE*	SG	64867	78319
466009	**SE**	A	*SE*	SG	64868	78320
466010	**SE**	A	*SE*	SG	64869	78321
466011	**SE**	A	*SE*	SG	64870	78322
466012	**SE**	A	*SE*	SG	64871	78323
466013	**SE**	A	*SE*	SG	64872	78324
466014	**SE**	A	*SE*	SG	64873	78325
466015	**SE**	A	*SE*	SG	64874	78326
466016	**SE**	A	*SE*	SG	64875	78327
466017	**SE**	A	*SE*	SG	64876	78328
466018	**SE**	A	*SE*	SG	64877	78329
466019	**SE**	A	*SE*	SG	64878	78330
466020	**SE**	A	*SE*	SG	64879	78331
466021	**SE**	A	*SE*	SG	64880	78332
466022	**SE**	A	*SE*	SG	64881	78333
466023	**SE**	A	*SE*	SG	64882	78334
466024	**SE**	A	*SE*	SG	64883	78335
466025	**SE**	A	*SE*	SG	64884	78336
466026	**SE**	A	*SE*	SG	64885	78337
466027	**SE**	A	*SE*	SG	64886	78338
466028	**SE**	A	*SE*	SG	64887	78339
466029	**SE**	A	*SE*	SG	64888	78340
466030	**SE**	A	*SE*	SG	64889	78341
466031	**SE**	A	*SE*	SG	64890	78342
466032	**SE**	A	*SE*	SG	64891	78343
466033	**SE**	A	*SE*	SG	64892	78344
466034	**SE**	A	*SE*	SG	64893	78345
466035	**SE**	A	*SE*	SG	64894	78346
466036	**SE**	A	*SE*	SG	64895	78347
466037	**SE**	A	*SE*	SG	64896	78348
466038	**SE**	A	*SE*	SG	64897	78349
466039	**SE**	A	*SE*	SG	64898	78350
466040	**SE**	A	*SE*	SG	64899	78351
466041	**SE**	A	*SE*	SG	64900	78352
466042	**SE**	A	*SE*	SG	64901	78353
466043	**SE**	A	*SE*	SG	64902	78354

CLASS 483 METRO-CAMMELL

Built 1938 onwards for LTE. Converted 1989–90 for the Isle of Wight Line.

Formation: DMSO–DMSO.
System: 660 V DC third rail.
Construction: Steel.
Traction Motors: Two Crompton Parkinson/GEC/BTH LT100 of 125 kW.
Wheel arrangement: A1-1A + A1-1A.
Braking: Tread.   **Dimensions:** 16.15 x 2.69 m.
Bogies: LT design.   **Couplers:** Wedgelock.
Gangways: None. End doors.
Control System: Pneumatic Camshaft Motor (PCM).
Doors: Sliding.   **Maximum Speed:** 45 mph.
Seating Layout: Longitudinal or 2+2 facing/unidirectional.
Multiple Working: Within class.
The last three numbers of the unit number only are carried.

Former London Underground numbers are shown in parentheses.

DMSO (A). Lot No. 31071. –/40. 27.4 t.
DMSO (B). Lot No. 31072. –/42. 27.4 t.

483 002	**LT**	SW		RY (S)	122	(10221)	225	(11142)	RAPTOR
483 004	**LT**	SW	SW	RY	124	(10205)	224	(11205)	
483 006	**LT**	SW	SW	RY	126	(10297)	226	(11297)	
483 007	**LT**	SW	SW	RY	127	(10291)	227	(11291)	
483 008	**LT**	SW	SW	RY	128	(10255)	228	(11255)	
483 009	**LT**	SW	SW	RY	129	(10229)	229	(11229)	

CLASS 507 BREL YORK

Formation: BDMSO–TSO–DMSO.
Construction: Steel underframe, aluminium alloy body and roof.
Traction Motors: Four GEC G310AZ of 82.125 kW.
Wheel Arrangement: Bo-Bo + 2-2 + Bo-Bo.
Braking: Disc & rheostatic.   **Dimensions:** 20.18 x 2.82 m.
Bogies: BX1.   **Couplers:** Tightlock.
Gangways: Within unit + end doors. **Control System:** Camshaft.
Doors: Sliding.   **Maximum Speed:** 75 mph.
Seating Layout: All refurbished with 2+2 high-back facing seating.
Multiple Working: Within class and with Class 508.

Fitted with tripcocks for operating on the Merseyrail Wirral Lines.

Advertising livery: 507 002 Liverpool Hope University (white).

BDMSO. Lot No. 30906 1978–80. –/56(+3) 1W. 37.0 t.
TSO. Lot No. 30907 1978–80. –/74. 25.5 t.
DMSO. Lot No. 30908 1978–80. –/56(+3) 1W. 35.5 t.

507 001	**MY**	A	ME	BD	64367	71342	64405
507 002	**AL**	A	ME	BD	64368	71343	64406

507 003	**MY**	A	*ME*	BD	64369	71344	64407
507 004	**MY**	A	*ME*	BD	64388	71345	64408
507 005	**MY**	A	*ME*	BD	64371	71346	64409
507 006	**MY**	A	*ME*	BD	64372	71347	64410
507 007	**MY**	A	*ME*	BD	64373	71348	64411
507 008	**MY**	A	*ME*	BD	64374	71349	64412
507 009	**MY**	A	*ME*	BD	64375	71350	64413
507 010	**MY**	A	*ME*	BD	64376	71351	64414
507 011	**MY**	A	*ME*	BD	64377	71352	64415
507 012	**MY**	A	*ME*	BD	64378	71353	64416
507 013	**MY**	A	*ME*	BD	64379	71354	64417
507 014	**MY**	A	*ME*	BD	64380	71355	64418
507 015	**MY**	A	*ME*	BD	64381	71356	64419
507 016	**MY**	A	*ME*	BD	64382	71357	64420
507 017	**MY**	A	*ME*	BD	64383	71358	64421
507 018	**MY**	A	*ME*	BD	64384	71359	64422
507 019	**MY**	A	*ME*	BD	64385	71360	64423
507 020	**MY**	A	*ME*	BD	64386	71361	64424
507 021	**MY**	A	*ME*	BD	64387	71362	64425
507 023	**MY**	A	*ME*	BD	64389	71364	64427
507 024	**MY**	A	*ME*	BD	64390	71365	64428
507 025	**MY**	A	*ME*	BD	64391	71366	64429
507 026	**MY**	A	*ME*	BD	64392	71367	64430
507 027	**MY**	A	*ME*	BD	64393	71368	64431
507 028	**MY**	A	*ME*	BD	64394	71369	64432
507 029	**MY**	A	*ME*	BD	64395	71370	64433
507 030	**MY**	A	*ME*	BD	64396	71371	64434
507 031	**MY**	A	*ME*	BD	64397	71372	64435
507 032	**MY**	A	*ME*	BD	64398	71373	64436
507 033	**MY**	A	*ME*	BD	64399	71374	64437

Names:

507 004	Bob Paisley
507 008	Harold Wilson
507 009	Dixie Dean
507 016	Merseyrail – celebrating the first ten years (2003–2013)
507 020	John Peel
507 021	Red Rum
507 023	Operations Inspector Stuart Mason
507 026	Councillor George Howard
507 033	Councillor Jack Spriggs

CLASS 508 BREL YORK

Formation: DMSO–TSO–BDMSO.
Construction: Steel underframe, aluminium alloy body and roof.
Traction Motors: Four GEC G310AZ of 82.125 kW.
Wheel Arrangement: Bo-Bo + 2-2 + Bo-Bo.
Braking: Disc & rheostatic.   **Dimensions:** 20.18 x 2.82 m.
Bogies: BX1.   **Couplers:** Tightlock.
Gangways: Within unit + end doors.   **Control System:** Camshaft.
Doors: Sliding.   **Maximum Speed:** 75 mph.
Seating Layout: All refurbished with 2+2 high-back facing seating.
Multiple Working: Within class and with Class 507.

Fitted with tripcocks for operating on the Merseyrail Wirral Lines.

Advertising livery: 508 111 Beatles Story (blue).

DMSO. Lot No. 30979 1979–80. –/56(+3) 1W. 36.0 t.
TSO. Lot No. 30980 1979–80. –/74. 26.5 t.
BDMSO. Lot No. 30981 1979–80. –/56(+3) 1W. 36.5 t.

508 103	**MY**	A	*ME*	BD	64651	71485	64694
508 104	**MY**	A	*ME*	BD	64652	71486	64695
508 108	**MY**	A	*ME*	BD	64656	71490	64699
508 110	**MY**	A	*ME*	BD	64658	71492	64701
508 111	**AL**	A	*ME*	BD	64659	71493	64702
508 112	**MY**	A	*ME*	BD	64660	71494	64703
508 114	**MY**	A	*ME*	BD	64662	71496	64705
508 115	**MY**	A	*ME*	BD	64663	71497	64706
508 117	**MY**	A	*ME*	BD	64665	71499	64708
508 120	**MY**	A	*ME*	BD	64668	71502	64711
508 122	**MY**	A	*ME*	BD	64670	71504	64713
508 123	**MY**	A	*ME*	BD	64671	71505	64714
508 124	**MY**	A	*ME*	BD	64672	71506	64715
508 125	**MY**	A	*ME*	BD	64673	71507	64716
508 126	**MY**	A	*ME*	BD	64674	71508	64717
508 127	**MY**	A	*ME*	BD	64675	71509	64718
508 128	**MY**	A	*ME*	BD	64676	71510	64719
508 130	**MY**	A	*ME*	BD	64678	71512	64721
508 131	**MY**	A	*ME*	BD	64679	71513	64722
508 134	**MY**	A	*ME*	BD	64682	71516	64725
508 136	**MY**	A	*ME*	BD	64684	71518	64727
508 137	**MY**	A	*ME*	BD	64685	71519	64728
508 138	**MY**	A	*ME*	BD	64686	71520	64729
508 139	**MY**	A	*ME*	BD	64687	71521	64730
508 140	**MY**	A	*ME*	BD	64688	71522	64731
508 141	**MY**	A	*ME*	BD	64689	71523	64732
508 143	**MY**	A	*ME*	BD	64691	71525	64734

Names:

508 111 The Beatles	508 136 Wilfred Owen MC
508 123 William Roscoe	

4.3. DUAL VOLTAGE OR 25 kV AC OVERHEAD UNITS

The Class 7xx series is being used for some new-build EMUs built from 2014 onwards as freight wagons take up many of the remaining potential Class 3xx series'.

CLASS 700   DESIRO CITY   SIEMENS

The Class 700s are a large fleet of EMUs currently entering service with Govia Thameslink. The first unit was delivered in summer 2015, the first entered traffic in spring 2016 and all units will be in traffic by the end of 2018. The units are financed by Cross London Trains (a consortium of Siemens Project Ventures, Innisfree Ltd and 3i Infrastructure Ltd).

Formations (8-car): DMCO–PTSO–MSO–TSO–TSO–MSO–PTSO–DMCO or **(12-car):** DMCO–PTSO–MSO–MSO–TSO–TSO–TSO–TSO–MSO–MSO–PTSO–DMCO.
Systems: 25 kV AC overhead/750 V DC third rail.
Construction: Aluminium.
Traction Motors: Four Siemens asynchronous of 200 kW.
Wheel Arrangement (8-car): Bo-Bo + 2-2 + Bo-Bo + 2-2 + 2-2 + Bo-Bo + 2-2 + Bo-Bo. **(12-car):** Bo-Bo + 2-2 + Bo-Bo + Bo-Bo + 2-2 + 2-2 + 2-2 + 2-2 + Bo-Bo + Bo-Bo + 2-2 + Bo-Bo.
Braking: Disc, tread & regenerative.   **Dimensions:** 20.52/20.16 m x 2.80 m.
Bogies: Siemens SF7000 inside-frame. **Couplers:** Dellner 12.
Gangways: Within unit.   **Control System:** IGBT Inverter.
Doors: Sliding plug.   **Maximum Speed:** 100 mph.
Heating & ventilation: Air conditioning.
Seating Layout: 2+2 facing/unidirectional.
Multiple Working: Within class and with Class 707.

Class 700/0. 8-car units.

DMCO(A). Siemens Krefeld 2014–18. 26/16(+3). 38.5 t.
PTSO. Siemens Krefeld 2014–18. –/54 1T. 33.1 t.
MSO. Siemens Krefeld 2014–18. –/64. 36.2 t.
TSO. Siemens Krefeld 2014–18. –/56(+3). 28.7 t.
TSO(W). Siemens Krefeld 2014–18. –/40(+8) 1TD 2W. 29.1 t.
MSO. Siemens Krefeld 2014–18. –/64. 36.2 t.
PTSO. Siemens Krefeld 2014–18. –/54 1T. 33.2 t.
DMCO(B). Siemens Krefeld 2014–18. 26/16(+3). 38.5 t.

700001	**TL**	CT	*TL*	TB	401001	402001	403001	406001
					407001	410001	411001	412001
700002	**TL**	CT	*TL*	TB	401002	402002	403002	406002
					407002	410002	411002	412002
700003	**TL**	CT	*TL*	TB	401003	402003	403003	406003
					407003	410003	411003	412003
700004	**TL**	CT	*TL*	TB	401004	402004	403004	406004
					407004	410004	411004	412004

700005	**TL** CT *TL* TB	401005	402005	403005	406005
		407005	410005	411005	412005
700006	**TL** CT *TL* TB	401006	402006	403006	406006
		407006	410006	411006	412006
700007	**TL** CT *TL* TB	401007	402007	403007	406007
		407007	410007	411007	412007
700008	**TL** CT *TL* TB	401008	402008	403008	406008
		407008	410008	411008	412008
700009	**TL** CT *TL* TB	401009	402009	403009	406009
		407009	410009	411009	412009
700010	**TL** CT *TL* TB	401010	402010	403010	406010
		407010	410010	411010	412010
700011	**TL** CT *TL* TB	401011	402011	403011	406011
		407011	410011	411011	412011
700012	**TL** CT *TL* TB	401012	402012	403012	406012
		407012	410012	411012	412012
700013	**TL** CT *TL* TB	401013	402013	403013	406013
		407013	410013	411013	412013
700014	**TL** CT *TL* TB	401014	402014	403014	406014
		407014	410014	411014	412014
700015	**TL** CT *TL* TB	401015	402015	403015	406015
		407015	410015	411015	412015
700016	**TL** CT *TL* TB	401016	402016	403016	406016
		407016	410016	411016	412016
700017	**TL** CT *TL* TB	401017	402017	403017	406017
		407017	410017	411017	412017
700018	**TL** CT *TL* TB	401018	402018	403018	406018
		407018	410018	411018	412018
700019	**TL** CT *TL* TB	401019	402019	403019	406019
		407019	410019	411019	412019
700020	**TL** CT *TL* TB	401020	402020	403020	406020
		407020	410020	411020	412020
700021	**TL** CT *TL* TB	401021	402021	403021	406021
		407021	410021	411021	412021
700022	**TL** CT *TL* TB	401022	402022	403022	406022
		407022	410022	411022	412022
700023	**TL** CT *TL* TB	401023	402023	403023	406023
		407023	410023	411023	412023
700024	**TL** CT *TL* TB	401024	402024	403024	406024
		407024	410024	411024	412024
700025	**TL** CT *TL* TB	401025	402025	403025	406025
		407025	410025	411025	412025
700026	**TL** CT *TL* TB	401026	402026	403026	406026
		407026	410026	411026	412026
700027	**TL** CT *TL* TB	401027	402027	403027	406027
		407027	410027	411027	412027
700028	**TL** CT *TL* TB	401028	402028	403028	406028
		407028	410028	411028	412028
700029	**TL** CT *TL* TB	401029	402029	403029	406029
		407029	410029	411029	412029

700030	**TL**	CT	*TL*	TB	401030	402030	403030	406030
					407030	410030	411030	412030
700031	**TL**	CT	*TL*	TB	401031	402031	403031	406031
					407031	410031	411031	412031
700032	**TL**	CT	*TL*	TB	401032	402032	403032	406032
					407032	410032	411032	412032
700033	**TL**	CT	*TL*	TB	401033	402033	403033	406033
					407033	410033	411033	412033
700034	**TL**	CT	*TL*	TB	401034	402034	403034	406034
					407034	410034	411034	412034
700035	**TL**	CT	*TL*	TB	401035	402035	403035	406035
					407035	410035	411035	412035
700036	**TL**	CT	*TL*	TB	401036	402036	403036	406036
					407036	410036	411036	412036
700037	**TL**	CT	*TL*	TB	401037	402037	403037	406037
					407037	410037	411037	412037
700038	**TL**	CT	*TL*	TB	401038	402038	403038	406038
					407038	410038	411038	412038
700039	**TL**	CT	*TL*	TB	401039	402039	403039	406039
					407039	410039	411039	412039
700040	**TL**	CT	*TL*	TB	401040	402040	403040	406040
					407040	410040	411040	412040
700041	**TL**	CT	*TL*	TB	401041	402041	403041	406041
					407041	410041	411041	412041
700042	**TL**	CT	*TL*	TB	401042	402042	403042	406042
					407042	410042	411042	412042
700043	**TL**	CT	*TL*	TB	401043	402043	403043	406043
					407043	410043	411043	412043
700044	**TL**	CT	*TL*	TB	401044	402044	403044	406044
					407044	410044	411044	412044
700045	**TL**	CT	*TL*	TB	401045	402045	403045	406045
					407045	410045	411045	412045
700046	**TL**	CT	*TL*	TB	401046	402046	403046	406046
					407046	410046	411046	412046
700047	**TL**	CT			401047	402047	403047	406047
					407047	410047	411047	412047
700048	**TL**	CT			401048	402048	403048	406048
					407048	410048	411048	412048
700049	**TL**	CT			401049	402049	403049	406049
					407049	410049	411049	412049
700050	**TL**	CT		TB	401050	402050	403050	406050
					407050	410050	411050	412050
700051	**TL**	CT			401051	402051	403051	406051
					407051	410051	411051	412051
700052	**TL**	CT		TB	401052	402052	403052	406052
					407052	410052	411052	412052
700053	**TL**	CT			401053	402053	403053	406053
					407053	410053	411053	412053
700054	**TL**	CT			401054	402054	403054	406054
					407054	410054	411054	412054

700 055	**TL** CT			401055 402055 403055 406055 407055 410055 411055 412055
700 056	**TL** CT			401056 402056 403056 406056 407056 410056 411056 412056
700 057	**TL** CT			401057 402057 403057 406057 407057 410057 411057 412057
700 058	**TL** CT			401058 402058 403058 406058 407058 410058 411058 412058
700 059	**TL** CT			401059 402059 403059 406059 407059 410059 411059 412059
700 060	**TL** CT			401060 402060 403060 406060 407060 410060 411060 412060

Class 700/1. 12-car units.

DMCO(A). Siemens Krefeld 2013–18. 26/20. 38.2 t.
PTSO. Siemens Krefeld 2013–18. –/54 1T. 34.4 t.
MSO. Siemens Krefeld 2013–18. –/60(+3). 36.0 t.
MSO. Siemens Krefeld 2013–18. –/56 1T. 35.8 t.
TSO. Siemens Krefeld 2013–18. –/64. 26.8 t.
TSO. Siemens Krefeld 2013–18. –/56(+3). 28.3 t.
TSO(W). Siemens Krefeld 2013–18. –/38(+9) 1TD 2W. 28.7 t.
TSO. Siemens Krefeld 2013–18. –/64. 27.9 t.
MSO. Siemens Krefeld 2013–18. –/56 1T. 35.6 t.
MSO. Siemens Krefeld 2013–18. –/60(+3). 35.3 t.
PTSO. Siemens Krefeld 2013–18. –/54 1T. 34.4 t.
DMCO(B). Siemens Krefeld 2013–18. 26/20. 38.2 t.

700 101	**TL** CT *TL*	TB	401101 402101 403101 404101 405101 406101 407101 408101 409101 410101 411101 412101
700 102	**TL** CT *TL*	TB	401102 402102 403102 404102 405102 406102 407102 408102 409102 410102 411102 412102
700 103	**TL** CT *TL*	TB	401103 402103 403103 404103 405103 406103 407103 408103 409103 410103 411103 412103
700 104	**TL** CT *TL*	TB	401104 402104 403104 404104 405104 406104 407104 408104 409104 410104 411104 412104
700 105	**TL** CT *TL*	TB	401105 402105 403105 404105 405105 406105 407105 408105 409105 410105 411105 412105
700 106	**TL** CT *TL*	TB	401106 402106 403106 404106 405106 406106 407106 408106 409106 410106 411106 412106
700 107	**TL** CT *TL*	TB	401107 402107 403107 404107 405107 406107 407107 408107 409107 410107 411107 412107
700 108	**TL** CT *TL*	TB	401108 402108 403108 404108 405108 406108 407108 408108 409108 410108 411108 412108
700 109	**TL** CT *TL*	TB	401109 402109 403109 404109 405109 406109 407109 408109 409109 410109 411109 412109
700 110	**TL** CT *TL*	TB	401110 402110 403110 404110 405110 406110 407110 408110 409110 410110 411110 412110
700 111	**TL** CT *TL*	TB	401111 402111 403111 404111 405111 406111 407111 408111 409111 410111 411111 412111
700 112	**TL** CT *TL*	TB	401112 402112 403112 404112 405112 406112 407112 408112 409112 410112 411112 412112

700 113	**TL** CT *TL*	TB	401113	402113	403113	404113	405113	406113
			407113	408113	409113	410113	411113	412113
700 114	**TL** CT *TL*	TB	401114	402114	403114	404114	405114	406114
			407114	408114	409114	410114	411114	412114
700 115	**TL** CT *TL*	TB	401115	402115	403115	404115	405115	406115
			407115	408115	409115	410115	411115	412115
700 116	**TL** CT *TL*	TB	401116	402116	403116	404116	405116	406116
			407116	408116	409116	410116	411116	412116
700 117	**TL** CT *TL*	TB	401117	402117	403117	404117	405117	406117
			407117	408117	409117	410117	411117	412117
700 118	**TL** CT *TL*	TB	401118	402118	403118	404118	405118	406118
			407118	408118	409118	410118	411118	412118
700 119	**TL** CT *TL*	TB	401119	402119	403119	404119	405119	406119
			407119	408119	409119	410119	411119	412119
700 120	**TL** CT *TL*	TB	401120	402120	403120	404120	405120	406120
			407120	408120	409120	410120	411120	412120
700 121	**TL** CT *TL*	TB	401121	402121	403121	404121	405121	406121
			407121	408121	409121	410121	411121	412121
700 122	**TL** CT *TL*	TB	401122	402122	403122	404122	405122	406122
			407122	408122	409122	410122	411122	412122
700 123	**TL** CT *TL*	TB	401123	402123	403123	404123	405123	406123
			407123	408123	409123	410123	411123	412123
700 124	**TL** CT *TL*	TB	401124	402124	403124	404124	405124	406124
			407124	408124	409124	410124	411124	412124
700 125	**TL** CT *TL*	TB	401125	402125	403125	404125	405125	406125
			407125	408125	409125	410125	411125	412125
700 126	**TL** CT	TB	401126	402126	403126	404126	405126	406126
			407126	408126	409126	410126	411126	412126
700 127	**TL** CT	TB	401127	402127	403127	404127	405127	406127
			407127	408127	409127	410127	411127	412127
700 128	**TL** CT *TL*	TB	401128	402128	403128	404128	405128	406128
			407128	408128	409128	410128	411128	412128
700 129	**TL** CT	TB	401129	402129	403129	404129	405129	406129
			407129	408129	409129	410129	411129	412129
700 130	**TL** CT *TL*	TB	401130	402130	403130	404130	405130	406130
			407130	408130	409130	410130	411130	412130
700 131	**TL** CT *TL*	TB	401131	402131	403131	404131	405131	406131
			407131	408131	409131	410131	411131	412131
700 132	**TL** CT	TB	401132	402132	403132	404132	405132	406132
			407132	408132	409132	410132	411132	412132
700 133	**TL** CT *TL*	TB	401133	402133	403133	404133	405133	406133
			407133	408133	409133	410133	411133	412133
700 134	**TL** CT	TB	401134	402134	403134	404134	405134	406134
			407134	408134	409134	410134	411134	412134
700 135	**TL** CT *TL*	TB	401135	402135	403135	404135	405135	406135
			407135	408135	409135	410135	411135	412135
700 136	**TL** CT	TB	401136	402136	403136	404136	405136	406136
			407136	408136	409136	410136	411136	412136
700 137	**TL** CT *TL*	TB	401137	402137	403137	404137	405137	406137
			407137	408137	409137	410137	411137	412137

700 138	**TL** CT		TB	401138 402138 403138 404138 405138 406138
				407138 408138 409138 410138 411138 412138
700 139	**TL** CT	*TL*	TB	401139 402139 403139 404139 405139 406139
				407139 408139 409139 410139 411139 412139
700 140	**TL** CT	*TL*	TB	401140 402140 403140 404140 405140 406140
				407140 408140 409140 410140 411140 412140
700 141	**TL** CT	*TL*	TB	401141 402141 403141 404141 405141 406141
				407141 408141 409141 410141 411141 412141
700 142	**TL** CT	*TL*	TB	401142 402142 403142 404142 405142 406142
				407142 408142 409142 410142 411142 412142
700 143	**TL** CT	*TL*	TB	401143 402143 403143 404143 405143 406143
				407143 408143 409143 410143 411143 412143
700 144	**TL** CT	*TL*	TB	401144 402144 403144 404144 405144 406144
				407144 408144 409144 410144 411144 412144
700 145	**TL** CT	*TL*	TB	401145 402145 403145 404145 405145 406145
				407145 408145 409145 410145 411145 412145
700 146	**TL** CT			401146 402146 403146 404146 405146 406146
				407146 408146 409146 410146 411146 412146
700 147	**TL** CT			401147 402147 403147 404147 405147 406147
				407147 408147 409147 410147 411147 412147
700 148	**TL** CT			401148 402148 403148 404148 405148 406148
				407148 408148 409148 410148 411148 412148
700 149	**TL** CT			401149 402149 403149 404149 405149 406149
				407149 408149 409149 410149 411149 412149
700 150	**TL** CT			401150 402150 403150 404150 405150 406150
				407150 408150 409150 410150 411150 412150
700 151	**TL** CT			401151 402151 403151 404151 405151 406151
				407151 408151 409151 410151 411151 412151
700 152	**TL** CT			401152 402152 403152 404152 405152 406152
				407152 408152 409152 410152 411152 412152
700 153	**TL** CT			401153 402153 403153 404153 405153 406153
				407153 408153 409153 410153 411153 412153
700 154	**TL** CT			401154 402154 403154 404154 405154 406154
				407154 408154 409154 410154 411154 412154
700 155	**TL** CT			401155 402155 403155 404155 405155 406155
				407155 408155 409155 410155 411155 412155

CLASS 707   DESIRO CITY   SIEMENS

These 30 5-car units are currently entering service with South Western Railway on suburban services. Built with the capability to be easily converted to dual voltage units.

Formation: DMSO–TSO–TSO–(P)TSO–DMSO.
Systems: 750 V DC third rail but with 25 kV AC overhead capability.
Construction: Aluminium.
Traction Motors: Four Siemens asynchronous of 200 kW.
Wheel Arrangement: Bo-Bo + 2-2 + 2-2 + 2-2 + Bo-Bo.
Braking: Disc, tread & regenerative.   **Dimensions:** 20.00/20.16 m x 2.80 m.
Bogies: Siemens SF7000 inside-frame.   **Couplers:** Dellner 12.

Gangways: Within unit.
Doors: Sliding plug.
Heating & ventilation: Air conditioning.
Seating Layout: 2+2/2+1 facing/unidirectional.
Multiple Working: Within class and with Class 700.

Control System: IGBT Inverter.
Maximum Speed: 100 mph.

DMSO(A). Siemens Krefeld 2015–17. –/46. 37.9 t.
TSO. Siemens Krefeld 2015–17. –/64. 28.4 t.
TSO. Siemens Krefeld 2015–17. –/53(+4) 2W. 28.5 t.
(P)TSO. Siemens Krefeld 2015–17. –/62. 27.6 t.
DMSO(B). Siemens Krefeld 2015–17. –/46. 37.6 t.

707001	**SS**	A	*SW*	WD	421001	422001	423001	424001	425001
707002	**SS**	A	*SW*	WD	421002	422002	423002	424002	425002
707003	**SS**	A	*SW*	WD	421003	422003	423003	424003	425003
707004	**SS**	A	*SW*	WD	421004	422004	423004	424004	425004
707005	**SS**	A	*SW*	WD	421005	422005	423005	424005	425005
707006	**SS**	A	*SW*	WD	421006	422006	423006	424006	425006
707007	**SS**	A	*SW*	WD	421007	422007	423007	424007	425007
707008	**SS**	A	*SW*	WD	421008	422008	423008	424008	425008
707009	**SS**	A	*SW*	WD	421009	422009	423009	424009	425009
707010	**SS**	A	*SW*	WD	421010	422010	423010	424010	425010
707011	**SS**	A	*SW*	WD	421011	422011	423011	424011	425011
707012	**SS**	A	*SW*	WD	421012	422012	423012	424012	425012
707013	**SS**	A	*SW*	WD	421013	422013	423013	424013	425013
707014	**SS**	A	*SW*	WD	421014	422014	423014	424014	425014
707015	**SS**	A	*SW*	WD	421015	422015	423015	424015	425015
707016	**SS**	A	*SW*	WD	421016	422016	423016	424016	425016
707017	**SS**	A			421017	422017	423017	424017	425017
707018	**SS**	A			421018	422018	423018	424018	425018
707019	**SS**	A			421019	422019	423019	424019	425019
707020	**SS**	A			421020	422020	423020	424020	425020
707021	**SS**	A			421021	422021	423021	424021	425021
707022	**SS**	A			421022	422022	423022	424022	425022
707023	**SS**	A	*SW*	WD	421023	422023	423023	424023	425023
707024	**SS**	A			421024	422024	423024	424024	425024
707025	**SS**	A	*SW*	WD	421025	422025	423025	424025	425025
707026	**SS**	A	*SW*	WD	421026	422026	423026	424026	425026
707027	**SS**	A	*SW*	WD	421027	422027	423027	424027	425027
707028	**SS**	A	*SW*	WD	421028	422028	423028	424028	425028
707029	**SS**	A	*SW*	WD	421029	422029	423029	424029	425029
707030	**SS**	A			421030	422030	423030	424030	425030

CLASS 710   AVENTRA   BOMBARDIER DERBY

These 45 4-car units are under construction for London Overground for use on London Liverpool Street local services, Romford–Upminster, Gospel Oak–Barking and London Euston–Watford Junction. There are a mix of AC only and dual-voltage units. The first trains are due to enter service in spring 2018. There are options for a further 249 Class 710 vehicles. Full details awaited.

Formation: DMSO–MSO–PMSO–DMSO.
Systems: Class 710/1 25 kV AC overhead only. Class 710/2 25 kV AC overhead and 750 V DC third rail.
Construction: Aluminium.
Traction Motors:
Wheel Arrangement: Bo-2 + 2-Bo + Bo-2 + 2-Bo.
Braking: Disc & regenerative   **Dimensions:** 23.62/22.50 m x 2.78 m.
Bogies: Inside-frame.   **Couplers:** Dellner.
Gangways: Within unit.   **Control System:** IGBT Inverter.
Doors: Sliding plug.   **Maximum Speed:**
Heating & ventilation: Air conditioning.
Seating Layout:
Multiple Working: Within class.

DMSO(A). Bombardier Derby 2017–18.   t.
MSO. Bombardier Derby 2017–18.   t.
PMSO. Bombardier Derby 2017–18.   t.
DMSO(B). Bombardier Derby 2017–18.   t.

Class 710/1. 25 kV AC only units.

710 101	431101	431401	431301	431501
710 102	431102	431402	431302	431502
710 103	431103	431403	431303	431503
710 104	431104	431404	431304	431504
710 105	431105	431405	431305	431505
710 106	431106	431406	431306	431506
710 107	431107	431407	431307	431507
710 108	431108	431408	431308	431508
710 109	431109	431409	431309	431509
710 110	431110	431410	431310	431510
710 111	431111	431411	431311	431511
710 112	431112	431412	431312	431512
710 113	431113	431413	431313	431513
710 114	431114	431414	431314	431514
710 115	431115	431415	431315	431515
710 116	431116	431416	431316	431516
710 117	431117	431417	431317	431517
710 118	431118	431418	431318	431518
710 119	431119	431419	431319	431519
710 120	431120	431420	431320	431520
710 121	431121	431421	431321	431521
710 122	431122	431422	431322	431522
710 123	431123	431423	431323	431523
710 124	431124	431424	431324	431524
710 125	431125	431425	431325	431525
710 126	431126	431426	431326	431526
710 127	431127	431427	431327	431527
710 128	431128	431428	431328	431528
710 129	431129	431429	431329	431529
710 130	431130	431430	431330	431530
710 131	431131	431431	431331	431531

Class 710/2. 25 kV AC/750 V DC units.

710 256	432156	432456	432356	432556
710 257	432157	432457	432357	432557
710 258	432158	432458	432358	432558
710 259	432159	432459	432359	432559
710 260	432160	432460	432360	432560
710 261	432161	432461	432361	432561
710 262	432162	432462	432362	432562
710 263	432163	432463	432363	432563
710 264	432164	432464	432364	432564
710 265	432165	432465	432365	432565
710 266	432166	432466	432366	432566
710 267	432167	432467	432367	432567
710 268	432168	432468	432368	432568
710 269	432169	432469	432369	432569

CLASS 717   DESIRO CITY   SIEMENS

These 25 dual-voltage 6-car units are under construction for Govia
Thameslink Railway for use on Great Northern services from London
Moorgate from 2018–19. The design is based on Classes 700/707, but with
emergency end doors. Full details awaited.

Formation: DMSO–TSO–TSO–MSO–PTSO–DMSO.
Systems: 25 kV AC overhead and 750 V DC third rail.
Construction: Aluminium.
Traction Motors:
Wheel Arrangement:
Braking: **Dimensions:**
Bogies: **Couplers:**
Gangways: Within unit + end doors. **Control System:** IGBT Inverter.
Doors: Sliding plug.   **Maximum Speed:** 100 mph.
Heating & ventilation: Air conditioning.
Seating Layout:
Multiple Working:

DMSO(A). Siemens Krefeld 2017–18.   t.
TSO. Siemens Krefeld 2017–18.   t.
TSO. Siemens Krefeld 2017–18.   t.
MSO. Siemens Krefeld 2017–18.   t.
PTSO. Siemens Krefeld 2017–18.   t.
DMSO(B). Siemens Krefeld 2017–18.   t.

717 001	RR	451001	452001	453001	454001	455001	456001
717 002	RR	451002	452002	453002	454002	455002	456002
717 003	RR	451003	452003	453003	454003	455003	456003
717 004	RR	451004	452004	453004	454004	455004	456004
717 005	RR	451005	452005	453005	454005	455005	456005
717 006	RR	451006	452006	453006	454006	455006	456006
717 007	RR	451007	452007	453007	454007	455007	456007
717 008	RR	451008	452008	453008	454008	455008	456008

717009	RR	451009 452009 453009 454009 455009 456009
717010	RR	451010 452010 453010 454010 455010 456010
717011	RR	451011 452011 453011 454011 455011 456011
717012	RR	451012 452012 453012 454012 455012 456012
717013	RR	451013 452013 453013 454013 455013 456013
717014	RR	451014 452014 453014 454014 455014 456014
717015	RR	451015 452015 453015 454015 455015 456015
717016	RR	451016 452016 453016 454016 455016 456016
717017	RR	451017 452017 453017 454017 455017 456017
717018	RR	451018 452018 453018 454018 455018 456018
717019	RR	451019 452019 453019 454019 455019 456019
717020	RR	451020 452020 453020 454020 455020 456020
717021	RR	451021 452021 453021 454021 455021 456021
717022	RR	451022 452022 453022 454022 455022 456022
717023	RR	451023 452023 453023 454023 455023 456023
717024	RR	451024 452024 453024 454024 455024 456024
717025	RR	451025 452025 453025 454025 455025 456025

CLASS 720   AVENTRA   BOMBARDIER DERBY

This large fleet of Aventra EMUs was ordered by Greater Anglia in 2016 to replace its entire Class 317, 321, 360 and 379 fleets on outer suburban and medium-distance services. The units will enter traffic in 2019–20. Full details awaited.

Formations (5-car): DMSO–PMSO–MSO–MSO–DTSO or
(10-car): DMSO–PMSO–MSO–MSO–TSO–MSO–PMSO–MSO–MSO–DTSO.
Systems: 25 kV AC overhead.
Construction: Aluminium.
Traction Motors:
Wheel Arrangement:
Braking: Disc & regenerative   **Dimensions:**
Bogies: Inside-frame.   **Couplers:** Dellner.
Gangways: Within unit.   **Control System:** IGBT Inverter.
Doors: Sliding plug.   **Maximum Speed:**
Heating & ventilation: Air conditioning.
Seating Layout:
Multiple Working: Within class.

Class 720/1. 10-car units.

DMSO. Bombardier Derby 2018–20.   t.
PMSO(A). Bombardier Derby 2018–20.   t.
MSO(A). Bombardier Derby 2018–20.   t.
MSO(B). Bombardier Derby 2018–20.   t.
TSO. Bombardier Derby 2018–20.   t.
MSO(C). Bombardier Derby 2018–20.   t.
PMSO(B). Bombardier Derby 2018–20.   t.
MSO(D). Bombardier Derby 2018–20.   t.
MSO(E). Bombardier Derby 2018–20.   t.
DTSO. Bombardier Derby 2018–20.   t.

720 101	A	450101	451101	452101	453101	454101
		455101	456101	457101	458101	459101
720 102	A	450102	451102	452102	453102	454102
		455102	456102	457102	458102	459102
720 103	A	450103	451103	452103	453103	454103
		455103	456103	457103	458103	459103
720 104	A	450104	451104	452104	453104	454104
		455104	456104	457104	458104	459104
720 105	A	450105	451105	452105	453105	454105
		455105	456105	457105	458105	459105
720 106	A	450106	451106	452106	453106	454106
		455106	456106	457106	458106	459106
720 107	A	450107	451107	452107	453107	454107
		455107	456107	457107	458107	459107
720 108	A	450108	451108	452108	453108	454108
		455108	456108	457108	458108	459108
720 109	A	450109	451109	452109	453109	454109
		455109	456109	457109	458109	459109
720 110	A	450110	451110	452110	453110	454110
		455110	456110	457110	458110	459110
720 111	A	450111	451111	452111	453111	454111
		455111	456111	457111	458111	459111
720 112	A	450112	451112	452112	453112	454112
		455112	456112	457112	458112	459112
720 113	A	450113	451113	452113	453113	454113
		455113	456113	457113	458113	459113
720 114	A	450114	451114	452114	453114	454114
		455114	456114	457114	458114	459114
720 115	A	450115	451115	452115	453115	454115
		455115	456115	457115	458115	459115
720 116	A	450116	451116	452116	453116	454116
		455116	456116	457116	458116	459116
720 117	A	450117	451117	452117	453117	454117
		455117	456117	457117	458117	459117
720 118	A	450118	451118	452118	453118	454118
		455118	456118	457118	458118	459118
720 119	A	450119	451119	452119	453119	454119
		455119	456119	457119	458119	459119
720 120	A	450120	451120	452120	453120	454120
		455120	456120	457120	458120	459120
720 121	A	450121	451121	452121	453121	454121
		455121	456121	457121	458121	459121
720 122	A	450122	451122	452122	453122	454122
		455122	456122	457122	458122	459122

Class 720/5. 5-car units.

DMSO. Bombardier Derby 2018–20.　　　t.
PMSO. Bombardier Derby 2018–20.　　　t.
MSO(A). Bombardier Derby 2018–20.　　t.
MSO(B). Bombardier Derby 2018–20.　　t.
DTSO. Bombardier Derby 2018–20.　　　t.

720501	A	450501	451501	452501	453501	459501
720502	A	450502	451502	452502	453502	459502
720503	A	450503	451503	452503	453503	459503
720504	A	450504	451504	452504	453504	459504
720505	A	450505	451505	452505	453505	459505
720506	A	450506	451506	452506	453506	459506
720507	A	450507	451507	452507	453507	459507
720508	A	450508	451508	452508	453508	459508
720509	A	450509	451509	452509	453509	459509
720510	A	450510	451510	452510	453510	459510
720511	A	450511	451511	452511	453511	459511
720512	A	450512	451512	452512	453512	459512
720513	A	450513	451513	452513	453513	459513
720514	A	450514	451514	452514	453514	459514
720515	A	450515	451515	452515	453515	459515
720516	A	450516	451516	452516	453516	459516
720517	A	450517	451517	452517	453517	459517
720518	A	450518	451518	452518	453518	459518
720519	A	450519	451519	452519	453519	459519
720520	A	450520	451520	452520	453520	459520
720521	A	450521	451521	452521	453521	459521
720522	A	450522	451522	452522	453522	459522
720523	A	450523	451523	452523	453523	459523
720524	A	450524	451524	452524	453524	459524
720525	A	450525	451525	452525	453525	459525
720526	A	450526	451526	452526	453526	459526
720527	A	450527	451527	452527	453527	459527
720528	A	450528	451528	452528	453528	459528
720529	A	450529	451529	452529	453529	459529
720530	A	450530	451530	452530	453530	459530
720531	A	450531	451531	452531	453531	459531
720532	A	450532	451532	452532	453532	459532
720533	A	450533	451533	452533	453533	459533
720534	A	450534	451534	452534	453534	459534
720535	A	450535	451535	452535	453535	459535
720536	A	450536	451536	452536	453536	459536
720537	A	450537	451537	452537	453537	459537
720538	A	450538	451538	452538	453538	459538
720539	A	450539	451539	452539	453539	459539
720540	A	450540	451540	452540	453540	459540
720541	A	450541	451541	452541	453541	459541
720542	A	450542	451542	452542	453542	459542
720543	A	450543	451543	452543	453543	459543
720544	A	450544	451544	452544	453544	459544

720545	A	450545	451545	452545	453545	459545
720546	A	450546	451546	452546	453546	459546
720547	A	450547	451547	452547	453547	459547
720548	A	450548	451548	452548	453548	459548
720549	A	450549	451549	452549	453549	459549
720550	A	450550	451550	452550	453550	459550
720551	A	450551	451551	452551	453551	459551
720552	A	450552	451552	452552	453552	459552
720553	A	450553	451553	452553	453553	459553
720554	A	450554	451554	452554	453554	459554
720555	A	450555	451555	452555	453555	459555
720556	A	450556	451556	452556	453556	459556
720557	A	450557	451557	452557	453557	459557
720558	A	450558	451558	452558	453558	459558
720559	A	450559	451559	452559	453559	459559
720560	A	450560	451560	452560	453560	459560
720561	A	450561	451561	452561	453561	459561
720562	A	450562	451562	452562	453562	459562
720563	A	450563	451563	452563	453563	459563
720564	A	450564	451564	452564	453564	459564
720565	A	450565	451565	452565	453565	459565
720566	A	450566	451566	452566	453566	459566
720567	A	450567	451567	452567	453567	459567
720568	A	450568	451568	452568	453568	459568
720569	A	450569	451569	452569	453569	459569
720570	A	450570	451570	452570	453570	459570
720571	A	450571	451571	452571	453571	459571
720572	A	450572	451572	452572	453572	459572
720573	A	450573	451573	452573	453573	459573
720574	A	450574	451574	452574	453574	459574
720575	A	450575	451575	452575	453575	459575
720576	A	450576	451576	452576	453576	459576
720577	A	450577	451577	452577	453577	459577
720578	A	450578	451578	452578	453578	459578
720579	A	450579	451579	452579	453579	459579
720580	A	450580	451580	452580	453580	459580
720581	A	450581	451581	452581	453581	459581
720582	A	450582	451582	452582	453582	459582
720583	A	450583	451583	452583	453583	459583
720584	A	450584	451584	452584	453584	459584
720585	A	450585	451585	452585	453585	459585
720586	A	450586	451586	452586	453586	459586
720587	A	450587	451587	452587	453587	459587
720588	A	450588	451588	452588	453588	459588
720589	A	450589	451589	452589	453589	459589

CLASS 769   BREL YORK/BRUSH

In 2017 it was announced that Porterbrook would be converting eight Class 319s into bi-mode "Flex" units for Northern, with two new diesel engines being fitted (one under each of the driving trailer cars) to drive ABB alternators. Arriva Trains Wales will also be taking five units (identities to be confirmed). Work on the conversions is taking place at Brush Loughborough and the first units are due into traffic from spring 2018. Full details awaited.

Formation:
Systems: Diesel/25 kV AC overhead/750 V DC third rail (decommissioned).
Construction: Steel.
Engines: Two MAN D2876.
Traction Motors: Four GEC G315BZ of 268 kW.
Wheel Arrangement: 2-2 + Bo-Bo + 2-2 + 2-2.
Braking: Disc.   **Dimensions:** 20.17/20.16 x 2.82 m.
Bogies: P7-4 (MSO), T3-7 (others).   **Couplers:** Tightlock.
Gangways: Within unit + end doors. **Control System:** GTO chopper.
Doors: Sliding.   **Maximum Speed:** 100 mph.
Seating Layout: 2+2/3+2 facing.
Multiple Working:

769 424	**NR**	P		77337	62914	71795	77336
769 431	**NR**	P		77351	62921	71802	77350
769 434	**NR**	P		77357	62924	71805	77356
769 442	**NR**	P		77373	62932	71813	77372
769 448	**NR**	P		77433	62962	71867	77432
769 450	**NR**	P		77437	62964	71869	77436
769 456	**NR**	P		77449	62970	71875	77448
769 458	**NR**	P		77453	62972	71877	77452

4.4. HITACHI IEP UNITS

CLASS 800 INTERCITY EXPRESS PROGRAMME
BI-MODE   HITACHI

In summer 2012 Agility Trains, a consortium of Hitachi and John Laing, signed a deal with the DfT to design, build, finance and maintain the next generation of InterCity rolling stock for the Great Western and East Coast Main Lines, principally to replace ageing High Speed Trains on these routes. A follow-on order in 2013 was placed for 30 9-car trains to replace the Class 91 and Mark 4 carriages on the ECML. This brought the total number of vehicles ordered to 866. Both GWR and VTEC were originally planned to have a mix of 5-car and 9-car units which will be bi-mode and straight electric trains (although the EMUs will also have one diesel engine fitted to each set). However, owing to delays with electrification works on the GWML, in 2016 it was announced that the 21 9-car electric Class 801 units for GWR would be built as 21 9-car bi-mode units, numbered instead in the Class 800/3 series.

The units are broadly based on the Southeastern Class 395s, but have 25 m length bodyshells. They are numbered in the Class 800 (bi-mode) and Class 801 (EMU) number series'. 12 trains (76 vehicles) were fully manufactured in Japan before the new Hitachi factory at Newton Aycliffe, County Durham was up and running. The remaining trains will be assembled at Newton Aycliffe. New maintenance depots for the trains have been built at Stoke Gifford (Bristol), Swansea and North Pole (London, the former Eurostar depot) for the GWR sets and at Doncaster for the VTEC units.

The first trains arrived for testing in 2015. 5-car units entered service on the Great Western Main Line in autumn 2017 and Class 800s and 801s will enter service on the East Coast Main Line from late 2018.

In 2015 GWR ordered a further 22 5-car and seven 9-car IEPs, designated Class 802/0 (5-car) and Class 802/1 (9-car). These will be used on Paddington–West of England services. In 2016 GWR ordered a further seven 9-car Class 802s, TransPennine Express ordered 19 5-car Class 802s and Hull Trains ordered five 5-car Class 802s, for delivery 2019–20. Apart from three pre-series trains, the GWR Class 802s are being constructed in Pistoia, Italy, whilst the TransPennine Express and Hull Trains Class 802s will be mainly built at Newton Aycliffe.

Formations: Various, see class headings for details.
Systems: Diesel/25 kV AC overhead electric.
Construction: Aluminium.
Diesel engines: In the 5-car sets diesel engines are located in cars 2, 3 and 4. In the 9-car sets diesel engines are located in cars 2, 3, 5, 7 and 8.
Engines: MTU 12V 1600 R80L of 700 kW (940 hp).
Traction Motors: Four Hitachi asynchronous of 226 kW.
Wheel Arrangement: 2-2 + Bo-Bo + Bo-Bo + Bo-Bo + 2-2 or
2-2 + Bo-Bo + Bo-Bo + 2-2 + Bo-Bo + 2-2 + Bo-Bo + Bo-Bo + 2-2.

Braking: Disc & regenerative.
Bogies: Hitachi.
Gangways: Within unit.
Doors: Single-leaf sliding.
Heating & ventilation: Air conditioning.
Seating Layout: 1: 2+1 facing/unidirectional; 2+2 facing/unidirectional.
Multiple Working: Within class and with Classes 801 and 802.

Dimensions: 25.35/25.00 m x 2.74 m.
Couplers: Dellner 10.
Control System: IGBT Inverter.
Maximum Speed: 125 mph.

Class 800/0. 5-car units for Great Western Railway entering service first in 2017–18, as replacements for HSTs and Class 180s.
Formation: PDTSO–MSO–MSO–MCO–PDTRBFO.

PDTSO. Hitachi Newton Aycliffe/Kasado 2013–17. –/56 1TD. 47.8 t.
MSO. Hitachi Newton Aycliffe/Kasado 2013–17. –/88. 50.1 t.
MSO. Hitachi Newton Aycliffe/Kasado 2013–17. –/88 2T. 50.3 t.
MCO. Hitachi Newton Aycliffe/Kasado 2013–17. 17/58 1T. 50.6 t.
PDTRBFO. Hitachi Newton Aycliffe/Kasado 2013–17. 18/– 1TD 2W. 51.7 t.

800001		AT		NP	811001	812001	813001	814001	815001
800002		AT		NP	811002	812002	813002	814002	815002
800003	**GW**	AT		NP	811003	812003	813003	814003	815003
800004	**GW**	AT		NP	811004	812004	813004	814004	815004
800005	**GW**	AT	*GW*	NP	811005	812005	813005	814005	815005
800006	**GW**	AT	*GW*	NP	811006	812006	813006	814006	815006
800007		AT		NP	811007	812007	813007	814007	815007
800008	**GW**	AT	*GW*	NP	811008	812008	813008	814008	815008
800009	**GW**	AT	*GW*	NP	811009	812009	813009	814009	815009
800010	**GW**	AT	*GW*	NP	811010	812010	813010	814010	815010
800011	**GW**	AT	*GW*	NP	811011	812011	813011	814011	815011
800012	**GW**	AT	*GW*	NP	811012	812012	813012	814012	815012
800013	**GW**	AT	*GW*	NP	811013	812013	813013	814013	815013
800014	**GW**	AT	*GW*	NP	811014	812014	813014	814014	815014
800015	**GW**	AT	*GW*	NP	811015	812015	813015	814015	815015
800016	**GW**	AT	*GW*	NP	811016	812016	813016	814016	815016
800017	**GW**	AT	*GW*	NP	811017	812017	813017	814017	815017
800018	**GW**	AT	*GW*	NP	811018	812018	813018	814018	815018
800019	**GW**	AT			811019	812019	813019	814019	815019
800020	**GW**	AT	*GW*	NP	811020	812020	813020	814020	815020
800021	**GW**	AT	*GW*	NP	811021	812021	813021	814021	815021
800022	**GW**	AT	*GW*	NP	811022	812022	813022	814022	815022
800023	**GW**	AT	*GW*	NP	811023	812023	813023	814023	815023
800024	**GW**	AT			811024	812024	813024	814024	815024
800025	**GW**	AT			811025	812025	813025	814025	815025
800026		AT			811026	812026	813026	814026	815026
800027		AT			811027	812027	813027	814027	815027
800028		AT			811028	812028	813028	814028	815028
800029		AT			811029	812029	813029	814029	815029
800030		AT			811030	812030	813030	814030	815030
800031		AT			811031	812031	813031	814031	815031
800032		AT			811032	812032	813032	814032	815032
800033		AT			811033	812033	813033	814033	815033
800034		AT			811034	812034	813034	814034	815034

| 800 035 | AT | 811035 | 812035 | 813035 | 814035 | 815035 |
| 800 036 | AT | 811036 | 812036 | 813036 | 814036 | 815036 |

Names (carried on alternative driving cars):

800003	Queen Victoria/Queen Elizabeth II
800004	Isambard Kingdom Brunel/Sir Daniel Gooch
800010	Michael Bond/Paddington Bear

Class 800/1. 9-car units for Virgin Trains East Coast as replacements for HSTs. Full details awaited.
Formation: PDTSO–MSO–MSO–TSO–MSO–TSO–MCO–MFO–PDTRBFO.

PDTSO. Hitachi Newton Aycliffe/Kasado 2013–18.	t.
MSO. Hitachi Newton Aycliffe/Kasado 2013–18.	t.
MSO. Hitachi Newton Aycliffe/Kasado 2013–18.	t.
TSO. Hitachi Newton Aycliffe/Kasado 2013–18.	t.
MSO. Hitachi Newton Aycliffe/Kasado 2013–18.	t.
TSO. Hitachi Newton Aycliffe/Kasado 2013–18.	t.
MCO. Hitachi Newton Aycliffe/Kasado 2013–18.	t.
MFO. Hitachi Newton Aycliffe/Kasado 2013–18.	t.
PDTRBFO. Hitachi Newton Aycliffe/Kasado 2013–18.	t.

800 101	**VE**	AT	811101	812101	813101	814101	815101
			816101	817101	818101	819101	
800 102		AT	811102	812102	813102	814102	815102
			816102	817102	818102	819102	
800 103		AT	811103	812103	813103	814103	815103
			816103	817103	818103	819103	
800 104		AT	811104	812104	813104	814104	815104
			816104	817104	818104	819104	
800 105		AT	811105	812105	813105	814105	815105
			816105	817105	818105	819105	
800 106		AT	811106	812106	813106	814106	815106
			816106	817106	818106	819106	
800 107		AT	811107	812107	813107	814107	815107
			816107	817107	818107	819107	
800 108		AT	811108	812108	813108	814108	815108
			816108	817108	818108	819108	
800 109		AT	811109	812109	813109	814109	815109
			816109	817109	818109	819109	
800 110		AT	811110	812110	813110	814110	815110
			816110	817110	818110	819110	
800 111		AT	811111	812111	813111	814111	815111
			816111	817111	818111	819111	
800 112		AT	811112	812112	813112	814112	815112
			816112	817112	818112	819112	
800 113		AT	811113	812113	813113	814113	815113
			816113	817113	818113	819113	

Class 800/2. 5-car units for Virgin Trains East Coast as replacements for HSTs. Full details awaited.
Formation: PDTSO–MSO–MSO–MCO–PDTRBFO.

PDTSO. Hitachi Newton Aycliffe/Kasado 2018–19.   t.
MSO. Hitachi Newton Aycliffe/Kasado 2018–19.   t.
MSO. Hitachi Newton Aycliffe/Kasado 2018–19.   t.
MCO. Hitachi Newton Aycliffe/Kasado 2018–19.   t.
PDTRBFO. Hitachi Newton Aycliffe/Kasado 2018–19.   t.

800 201	AT	811201	812201	813201	814201	815201
800 202	AT	811202	812202	813202	814202	815202
800 203	AT	811203	812203	813203	814203	815203
800 204	AT	811204	812204	813204	814204	815204
800 205	AT	811205	812205	813205	814205	815205
800 206	AT	811206	812206	813206	814206	815206
800 207	AT	811207	812207	813207	814207	815207
800 208	AT	811208	812208	813208	814208	815208
800 209	AT	811209	812209	813209	814209	815209
800 210	AT	811210	812210	813210	814210	815210

Class 800/3. 9-car units for Great Western Railway as replacements for HSTs. Originally to be built as full electric trains and numbered in the Class 801/0 series. Full details awaited.
Formation: PDTSO–MSO–MSO–TSO–MSO–TSO–MSO–MFO–PDTRBFO.

PDTSO. Hitachi Newton Aycliffe/Kasado 2017–18. –/48 1TD 2W.   t.
MSO. Hitachi Newton Aycliffe/Kasado 2017–18. –/88 1T.   t.
MSO. Hitachi Newton Aycliffe/Kasado 2017–18. –/88 2T.   t.
TSO. Hitachi Newton Aycliffe/Kasado 2017–18. –/88.   t.
MSO. Hitachi Newton Aycliffe/Kasado 2017–18. –/88 2T.   t.
TSO. Hitachi Newton Aycliffe/Kasado 2017–18. –/88 2T.   t.
MSO. Hitachi Newton Aycliffe/Kasado 2017–18. –/88.   t.
MFO. Hitachi Newton Aycliffe/Kasado 2017–18. 56/– 1T.   t.
PDTRBFO. Hitachi Newton Aycliffe/Kasado 2017–18. 15/– 1TD 2W.   t.

800 301	**GW**	AT	821001	822001	823001	824001	825001
			826001	827001	828001	829001	
800 302	**GW**	AT	821002	822002	823002	824002	825002
			826002	827002	828002	829002	
800 303	**GW**	AT	821003	822003	823003	824003	825003
			826003	827003	828003	829003	
800 304	**GW**	AT	821004	822004	823004	824004	825004
			826004	827004	828004	829004	
800 305	**GW**	AT	821005	822005	823005	824005	825005
			826005	827005	828005	829005	
800 306	**GW**	AT	821006	822006	823006	824006	825006
			826006	827006	828006	829006	
800 307	**GW**	AT	821007	822007	823007	824007	825007
			826007	827007	828007	829007	
800 308	**GW**	AT	821008	822008	823008	824008	825008
			826008	827008	828008	829008	

800 309	GW	AT	821009	822009	823009	824009	825009
			826009	827009	828009	829009	
800 310	GW	AT	821010	822010	823010	824010	825010
			826010	827010	828010	829010	
800 311	GW	AT	821011	822011	823011	824011	825011
			826011	827011	828011	829011	
800 312	GW	AT	821012	822012	823012	824012	825012
			826012	827012	828012	829012	
800 313	GW	AT	821013	822013	823013	824013	825013
			826013	827013	828013	829013	
800 314	GW	AT	821014	822014	823014	824014	825014
			826014	827014	828014	829014	
800 315	GW	AT	821015	822015	823015	824015	825015
			826015	827015	828015	829015	
800 316	GW	AT	821016	822016	823016	824016	825016
			826016	827016	828016	829016	
800 317	GW	AT	821017	822017	823017	824017	825017
			826017	827017	828017	829017	
800 318	GW	AT	821018	822018	823018	824018	825018
			826018	827018	828018	829018	
800 319	GW	AT	821019	822019	823019	824019	825019
			826019	827019	828019	829019	
800 320	GW	AT	821020	822020	823020	824020	825020
			826020	827020	828020	829020	
800 321	GW	AT	821021	822021	823021	824021	825021
			826021	827021	828021	829021	

CLASS 801 INTERCITY EXPRESS PROGRAMME
ELECTRIC   HITACHI

The Class 801s are electric units, but will still have one diesel engine fitted per unit for emergency use.

Formations: Various, see class headings for details.
Systems: 25 kV AC overhead electric, plus one diesel engine per set.
Construction: Aluminium.
Diesel engines: In the 5-car sets the single diesel engine is located in car 4 and in the 9-car sets the diesel engine is located in car 8.
Engines: MTU 12V 1600 R80L of 700 kW (940 hp).
Traction Motors: Four Hitachi asynchronous of 226 kW.
Wheel Arrangement: 2-2 + Bo-Bo + Bo-Bo + Bo-Bo + 2-2 or
2-2 + Bo-Bo + Bo-Bo + 2-2 + Bo-Bo + Bo-Bo + Bo-Bo + 2-2.
Braking: Disc & regenerative.   **Dimensions:** 25.35/25.00 m x 2.74 m.
Bogies: Hitachi.   **Couplers:** Dellner 10.
Gangways: Within unit.   **Control System:** IGBT Inverter.
Doors: Single-leaf sliding.   **Maximum Speed:** 125 mph.
Heating & ventilation: Air conditioning.
Seating Layout: 1: 2+1 facing/unidirectional; 2+2 facing/unidirectional.
Multiple Working: Within class and with Classes 800 and 802.

Class 801/1. 5-car units for Virgin Trains East Coast as replacements for HSTs. Full details awaited.
Formation: PDTSO–MSO–MSO–MCO–PDTRBFO.

PDTSO. Hitachi Newton Aycliffe/Kasado 2016–19.   t.
MSO. Hitachi Newton Aycliffe/Kasado 2016–19.   t.
MSO. Hitachi Newton Aycliffe/Kasado 2016–19.   t.
MCO. Hitachi Newton Aycliffe/Kasado 2016–19.   t.
PDTRBFO. Hitachi Newton Aycliffe/Kasado 2016–19.   t.

801 101	AT	821101	822101	823101	824101	825101
801 102	AT	821102	822102	823102	824102	825102
801 103	AT	821103	822103	823103	824103	825103
801 104	AT	821104	822104	823104	824104	825104
801 105	AT	821105	822105	823105	824105	825105
801 106	AT	821106	822106	823106	824106	825106
801 107	AT	821107	822107	823107	824107	825107
801 108	AT	821108	822108	823108	824108	825108
801 109	AT	821109	822109	823109	824109	825109
801 110	AT	821110	822110	823110	824110	825110
801 111	AT	821111	822111	823111	824111	825111
801 112	AT	821112	822112	823112	824112	825112

Class 801/2. 9-car units for Virgin Trains East Coast as replacements for locomotive-hauled Class 91+Mark 4 stock. Full details awaited.
Formation: PDTSO–MSO–MSO–TSO–MSO–TSO–MCO–MFO–PDTRBFO.

PDTSO. Hitachi Newton Aycliffe 2018–19.   t.
MSO. Hitachi Newton Aycliffe 2018–19.   t.
MSO. Hitachi Newton Aycliffe 2018–19.   t.
TSO. Hitachi Newton Aycliffe 2018–19.   t.
MSO. Hitachi Newton Aycliffe 2018–19.   t.
TSO. Hitachi Newton Aycliffe 2018–19.   t.
MCO. Hitachi Newton Aycliffe 2018–19.   t.
MFO. Hitachi Newton Aycliffe 2018–19.   t.
PDTRBFO. Hitachi Newton Aycliffe 2018–19.   t.

801 201	AT	821201	822201	823201	824201	825201
		826201	827201	828201	829201	
801 202	AT	821202	822202	823202	824202	825202
		826202	827202	828202	829202	
801 203	AT	821203	822203	823203	824203	825203
		826203	827203	828203	829203	
801 204	AT	821204	822204	823204	824204	825204
		826204	827204	828204	829204	
801 205	AT	821205	822205	823205	824205	825205
		826205	827205	828205	829205	
801 206	AT	821206	822206	823206	824206	825206
		826206	827206	828206	829206	
801 207	AT	821207	822207	823207	824207	825207
		826207	827207	828207	829207	
801 208	AT	821208	822208	823208	824208	825208
		826208	827208	828208	829208	

801 209	AT	821209	822209	823209	824209	825209
		826209	827209	828209	829209	
801 210	AT	821210	822210	823210	824210	825210
		826210	827210	828210	829210	
801 211	AT	821211	822211	823211	824211	825211
		826211	827211	828211	829211	
801 212	AT	821212	822212	823212	824212	825212
		826212	827212	828212	829212	
801 213	AT	821213	822213	823213	824213	825213
		826213	827213	828213	829213	
801 214	AT	821214	822214	823214	824214	825214
		826214	827214	828214	829214	
801 215	AT	821215	822215	823215	824215	825215
		826215	827215	828215	829215	
801 216	AT	821216	822216	823216	824216	825216
		826216	827216	828216	829216	
801 217	AT	821217	822217	823217	824217	825217
		826217	827217	828217	829217	
801 218	AT	821218	822218	823218	824218	825218
		826218	827218	828218	829218	
801 219	AT	821219	822219	823219	824219	825219
		826219	827219	828219	829219	
801 220	AT	821220	822220	823220	824220	825220
		826220	827220	828220	829220	
801 221	AT	821221	822221	823221	824221	825221
		826221	827221	828221	829221	
801 222	AT	821222	822222	823222	824222	825222
		826222	827222	828222	829222	
801 223	AT	821223	822223	823223	824223	825223
		826223	827223	828223	829223	
801 224	AT	821224	822224	823224	824224	825224
		826224	827224	828224	829224	
801 225	AT	821225	822225	823225	824225	825225
		826225	827225	828225	829225	
801 226	AT	821226	822226	823226	824226	825226
		826226	827226	828226	829226	
801 227	AT	821227	822227	823227	824227	825227
		826227	827227	828227	829227	
801 228	AT	821228	822228	823228	824228	825228
		826228	827228	828228	829228	
801 229	AT	821229	822229	823229	824229	825229
		826229	827229	828229	829229	
801 230	AT	821230	822230	823230	824230	825230
		826230	827230	828230	829230	

CLASS 802   AT300   HITACHI

These units are under construction or on order for Great Western Railway, TransPennine Express and Hull Trains. Technically they are very similar to the Class 800s, with modifications to the roof-mounted brake resistors for operation along the Dawlish seawall and larger fuel tanks. Full details awaited.

Formations: Various, full details awaited.
Systems: Diesel/25 kV AC overhead electric.
Construction: Aluminium.
Diesel engines: In the 5-car sets diesel engines are located in cars 2, 3 and 4. In the 9-car sets diesel engines are located in cars 2, 3, 5, 7 and 8.
Engines: MTU 12V 1600 R80L of 700 kW (940 hp).
Traction Motors: Four Hitachi asynchronous of 226 kW.
Wheel Arrangement: 2-2 + Bo-Bo + Bo-Bo + Bo-Bo + 2-2 or
2-2 + Bo-Bo + Bo-Bo + 2-2 + Bo-Bo + 2-2 + Bo-Bo + Bo-Bo + 2-2.
Braking: Disc & regenerative.   **Dimensions:** 25.35/25.00 m x 2.74 m.
Bogies: Hitachi.   **Couplers:** Dellner 10.
Gangways: Within unit.   **Control System:** IGBT Inverter.
Doors: Single-leaf sliding.   **Maximum Speed:** 125 mph.
Heating & ventilation: Air conditioning.
Seating Layout: 1: 2+1 facing/unidirectional; 2+2 facing/unidirectional.
Multiple Working: Within class and with Classes 800 and 801.

Class 802/0. 5-car units for Great Western Railway. Pre-series units 802 001/002 were built at Kasado and the remainder are being assembled at Pistoia in Italy. Full details awaited.
Formation: PDTSO–MSO–MSO–MCO–PDTRBFO.

PDTSO. Hitachi Pistoia/Kasado 2017–19.   t.
MSO. Hitachi Pistoia/Kasado 2017–19.   t.
MSO. Hitachi Pistoia/Kasado 2017–19.   t.
MCO. Hitachi Pistoia/Kasado 2017–19.   t.
PDTRBFO. Hitachi Pistoia/Kasado 2017–19.   t.

802 001	GW	E		831001	832001	833001	834001	835001
802 002	GW	E		831002	832002	833002	834002	835002
802 003		E		831003	832003	833003	834003	835003
802 004		E		831004	832004	833004	834004	835004
802 005		E		831005	832005	833005	834005	835005
802 006		E		831006	832006	833006	834006	835006
802 007		E		831007	832007	833007	834007	835007
802 008		E		831008	832008	833008	834008	835008
802 009		E		831009	832009	833009	834009	835009
802 010		E		831010	832010	833010	834010	835010
802 011		E		831011	832011	833011	834011	835011
802 012		E		831012	832012	833012	834012	835012
802 013		E		831013	832013	833013	834013	835013
802 014		E		831014	832014	833014	834014	835014
802 015		E		831015	832015	833015	834015	835015
802 016		E		831016	832016	833016	834016	835016
802 017		E		831017	832017	833017	834017	835017

802 018	E	831018	832018	833018	834018	835018
802 019	E	831019	832019	833019	834019	835019
802 020	E	831020	832020	833020	834020	835020
802 021	E	831021	832021	833021	834021	835021
802 022	E	831022	832022	833022	834022	835022

Class 802/1. 9-car units for Great Western Railway. Pre-series unit 802 101 was built at Kasado and the remainder are being assembled at Pistoia in Italy. Full details awaited.

Formation: PDTSO–MSO–MSO–TSO–MSO–TSO–MCO–MFO–PDTRBFO.

PDTSO. Hitachi Pistoia/Kasado 2017–19.   t.
MSO. Hitachi Pistoia/Kasado 2017–19.   t.
MSO. Hitachi Pistoia/Kasado 2017–19.   t.
TSO. Hitachi Pistoia/Kasado 2017–19.   t.
MSO. Hitachi Pistoia/Kasado 2017–19.   t.
TSO. Hitachi Pistoia/Kasado 2017–19.   t.
MCO. Hitachi Pistoia/Kasado 2017–19.   t.
MFO. Hitachi Pistoia/Kasado 2017–19.   t.
PDTRBFO. Hitachi Pistoia/Kasado 2017–19.   t.

802 101	**GW**	E	831101	832101	833101	834101	835101
			836101	837101	838101	839101	
802 102		E	831102	832102	833102	834102	835102
			836102	837102	838102	839102	
802 103		E	831103	832103	833103	834103	835103
			836103	837103	838103	839103	
802 104		E	831104	832104	833104	834104	835104
			836104	837104	838104	839104	
802 105		E	831105	832105	833105	834105	835105
			836105	837105	838105	839105	
802 106		E	831106	832106	833106	834106	835106
			836106	837106	838106	839106	
802 107		E	831107	832107	833107	834107	835107
			836107	837107	838107	839107	
802 108		E	831108	832108	833108	834108	835108
			836108	837108	838108	839108	
802 109		E	831109	832109	833109	834109	835109
			836109	837109	838109	839109	
802 110		E	831110	832110	833110	834110	835110
			836110	837110	838110	839110	
802 111		E	831111	832111	833111	834111	835111
			836111	837111	838111	839111	
802 112		E	831112	832112	833112	834112	835112
			836112	837112	838112	839112	
802 113		E	831113	832113	833113	834113	835113
			836113	837113	838113	839113	
802 114		E	831114	832114	833114	834114	835114
			836114	837114	838114	839114	

Class 802/2. 5-car units for TransPennine Express. Due to enter traffic 2019–20. Full details awaited.

802 201	A	831201	832201	833201	834201	835201
802 202	A	831202	832202	833202	834202	835202
802 203	A	831203	832203	833203	834203	835203
802 204	A	831204	832204	833204	834204	835204
802 205	A	831205	832205	833205	834205	835205
802 206	A	831206	832206	833206	834206	835206
802 207	A	831207	832207	833207	834207	835207
802 208	A	831208	832208	833208	834208	835208
802 209	A	831209	832209	833209	834209	835209
802 210	A	831210	832210	833210	834210	835210
802 211	A	831211	832211	833211	834211	835211
802 212	A	831212	832212	833212	834212	835212
802 213	A	831213	832213	833213	834213	835213
802 214	A	831214	832214	833214	834214	835214
802 215	A	831215	832215	833215	834215	835215
802 216	A	831216	832216	833216	834216	835216
802 217	A	831217	832217	833217	834217	835217
802 218	A	831218	832218	833218	834218	835218
802 219	A	831219	832219	833219	834219	835219

Class 802/3. 5-car units for Hull Trains. Due to enter traffic 2019. Full details awaited.

802 301	A	831301	832301	833301	834301	835301
802 302	A	831302	832302	833302	834302	835302
802 303	A	831303	832303	833303	834303	835303
802 304	A	831304	832304	833304	834304	835304
802 305	A	831305	832305	833305	834305	835305

4.5. EUROSTAR UNITS

The original Eurostar Class 373 units were built for and are normally used on services between Britain and continental Europe via the Channel Tunnel. SNCF-owned units 3225/26 and 3227/28 have been removed from the Eurostar pool and withdrawn. As they are not now permitted through the Channel Tunnel they are not listed here. The trailers from SNCF set 3203/04 were refurbished to run with power cars 3211/12 (original power cars 3203/04 have been scrapped and 3211/12 renumbered 3203/04 to match the trailers).

Each Class 373 train consists of two 10-car units coupled, with a motor car at each driving end. All units are articulated with an extra motor bogie on the coach adjacent to the motor car.

All Class 373 sets can be used between London St Pancras and Paris, Brussels and Disneyland Paris. Certain sets (shown *) are equipped for 1500 V DC operation and are used for the winter service to Bourg Saint Maurice and the summer service to Avignon. All eight units being refurbished will be fitted for operation on 1500 V DC.

Seven 8-car Class 373 sets were built for Regional Eurostar services, but all except one power car (3308) and one half set were on long-term hire to SNCF for use on French internal services so are not listed here. They are now stored in France, apart from power car 3308 which has been preserved at the National Railway Museum, York.

The second generation Eurostar trains, the Siemens Class 374s, are currently being introduced and have already replaced most of the Class 373s, with withdrawn sets now being progressively moved to EMR Kingsbury for disposal. Eight sets are being fully refurbished and retained by Eurostar – 3007/08, 3015/16, 3205/06, 3209/10, 3211/12, 3219/20, 3221/22 and 3229/30.

CLASS 373   "THREE CAPITALS" EUROSTARS

10-car half-sets. Built for services starting from or terminating in London Waterloo (now St Pancras). Individual vehicles in each set are allocated numbers 373xxx0 + 373xxx1 + 373xxx2 + 373xxx3 + 373xxx4 + 373xxx5 + 373xxx6 + 373xxx7 + 373xxx8 + 373xxx9, where 3xxx denotes the set number.

Formation: DM–MSO–4TSO–RB–2TFO–TBFO. Gangwayed within pair of units. Air conditioned.
Construction: Steel.
Supply Systems: 25 kV AC 50 Hz overhead or 3000 V DC overhead (* also equipped for 1500 V DC overhead operation).
Control System: GTO–GTO Inverter on UK 750 V DC and 25 kV AC, GTO Chopper on SNCB 3000 V DC.
Continuous rating: 12 x 240 kW (25 kV AC); 5700 kW (1500 and 3000 V DC).
Wheel Arrangement: Bo-Bo + Bo–2–2–2–2–2–2–2–2–2.
Lengths: 22.15 m (DM), 21.85 m (MSO & TBFO), 18.70 m (other cars).
Couplers: Schaku 10S at outer ends, Schaku 10L at inner end of each DM and outer ends of each sub set.

Maximum Speed: 186 mph (300 km/h).
Built: 1992–93 by GEC-Alsthom/Brush/ANF/De Dietrich/BN Construction/ACEC.

DM vehicles carry the set numbers indicated below.

† Refurbished.
§ Originally numbered 3203/04.

373xxx0 series. DM. Lot No. 31118 1992–95. 68.5 t.
373xxx1 series. MSO. Lot No. 31119 1992–95. –/48 2T. 44.6 t.
373xxx2 series. TSO. Lot No. 31120 1992–95. –/56 1T. 28.1 t.
373xxx3 series. TSO. Lot No. 31121 1992–95. –/56 2T. 29.7 t.
373xxx4 series. TSO. Lot No. 31122 1992–95. –/56 1T. 28.3 t.
373xxx5 series. TSO. Lot No. 31123 1992–95. –/56 2T. 29.2 t.
373xxx6 series. RB. Lot No. 31124 1992–95. 31.1 t.
373xxx7 series. TFO. Lot No. 31125 1992–95. 39/– 1T. 29.6 t.
373xxx8 series. TFO. Lot No. 31126 1992–95. 39/– 1T. 32.2 t.
373xxx9 series. TBFO. Lot No. 31127 1992–95. 25/– 1TD. 39.4 t.

3001	**EU**	EU	*EU*	TI
3002	**EU**	EU	*EU*	TI
3007 *	**ER**	EU	*EU*	TI
3008 *	**ER**	EU	*EU*	TI
3009	**EU**	EU	*EU*	TI
3010	**EU**	EU	*EU*	TI
3011	**EU**	EU	*EU*	TI
3012	**EU**	EU	*EU*	TI
3015 †*	**ER**	EU	*EU*	TI
3016 †*	**ER**	EU	*EU*	TI
3017	**EU**	EU		Valenciennes (S)
3018	**EU**	EU		Valenciennes (S)
3021	**EU**	EU		Dourges (S)
3022	**EU**	EU		Dourges (S)
3105	**EU**	SB		Dourges (S)
3106	**EU**	SB		Dourges (S)
3201 *	**EU**	SF	*EU*	LY
3202 *	**EU**	SF	*EU*	LY
3205	**EU**	SF	*EU*	LY
3206	**EU**	SF	*EU*	LY
3208 *	**EU**	SF		Dourges (S)
3209 *	**EU**	SF	*EU*	LY
3210 *	**EU**	SF	*EU*	LY
3211 †*§	**ER**	SF	*EU*	LY
3212 †*§	**ER**	SF	*EU*	LY
3213 *	**EU**	SF	*EU*	LY
3214 *	**EU**	SF	*EU*	LY
3215 *	**EU**	SF	*EU*	LY
3216 *	**EU**	SF	*EU*	LY
3217	**EU**	SF	*EU*	LY
3218 *	**EU**	SF	*EU*	LY
3219 †*	**ER**	SF	*EU*	LY
3220 †*	**ER**	SF	*EU*	LY
3221 †*	**ER**	SF	*EU*	LY
3222 †*	**ER**	SF	*EU*	LY
3223 *	**EU**	SF	*EU*	LY
3224 *	**EU**	SF	*EU*	LY
3229 †*	**ER**	SF	*EU*	LY
3230 †*	**ER**	SF	*EU*	LY

Spare DM:

3999	**ER**	EU	*EU*	TI

Names:

3001/02	Tread Lightly/Voyage Vert
3009/10	REMEMBERING FROMELLES
3209/10	THE DA VINCI CODE

CLASS 374   SIEMENS VELARO e320

8-car half-sets. These units are similar to the DB Class 407 ICE sets, with distributed power rather than a power car at either end like the Class 373s. The first sets entered service in November 2015, operating initially on the St Pancras–Paris route. They will also be used on the proposed St Pancras–Amsterdam service from 2018.

The initial order was for ten units (4001–20) and this was then increased by another seven (4021–34) in 2014. An option exists for a further six units.

Formation: DMFO–TBFO–MFO–TSO–TSO–MSO–TSO–MSORB.
Gangwayed within pair of units. Air conditioned.
Construction: Aluminium.   **Control System:** IGBT Inverter.
Supply Systems: 25 kV AC 50 Hz overhead, 1500 V DC overhead and 3000 V DC overhead.
Continuous rating: 8000 kW (25 kV AC), 4200 kW (1500 and 3000 V DC).
Wheel Arrangement: Bo-Bo + 2-2 + Bo-Bo + 2-2 + 2-2 + Bo-Bo + 2-2 + Bo-Bo.
Lengths: 26.035 m (DMFO), 24.775 m (other cars).
Couplers: Dellner 12.   **Maximum Speed:** 200 mph (320 km/h).
Built: 2012–17 by Siemens, Krefeld, Germany.

DM vehicles carry the full 12-digit EVNs as indicated below. For example set 4001/02 carries the numbers 93 70 3740 011-9 + 93 70 3740 012-7 + 93 70 3740 013-5 + 93 70 3740 014-3 + 93 70 3740 015-0 + 93 70 3740 016-8 + 93 70 3740 017-6 + 93 70 3740 018-4 + 93 70 3740 028-3 + 93 70 3740 027-5 + 93 70 3740 026-7 + 93 70 3740 025-9 + 93 70 3740 024-2 + 93 70 3740 023-4 + 93 70 3740 022-6 + 93 70 3740 021-8.

93 70 3740 xx1-c series. DMFO. Siemens Krefeld 2012–17. 40/–. 58.0 t.
93 70 3740 xx2-c series. TBFO. Siemens Krefeld 2012–17. 36/– 2T. 59.0 t.
93 70 3740 xx3-c series. MFO. Siemens Krefeld 2012–17. 34/–(+2) 1TD 2W. 59.0 t.
93 70 3740 xx4-c series. TSO. Siemens Krefeld 2012–17. –/76 2T. 53.0 t.
93 70 3740 xx5-c series. TSO. Siemens Krefeld 2012–17. –/76 2T. 53.0 t.
93 70 3740 xx6-c series. MSO. Siemens Krefeld 2012–17. –/76 2T. 58.0 t.
93 70 3740 xx7-c series. TSO. Siemens Krefeld 2012–17. –/76 2T. 57.0 t.
93 70 3740 xx8-c series. MSORB. Siemens Krefeld 2012–17. –/32 2T. 58.0 t.

4001	**ER**	EU	*EU*	TI	4018	**ER**	EU	*EU*	TI
4002	**ER**	EU	*EU*	TI	4019	**ER**	EU	*EU*	TI
4003	**ER**	EU	*EU*	TI	4020	**ER**	EU	*EU*	TI
4004	**ER**	EU	*EU*	TI	4021	**ER**	EU	*EU*	TI
4005	**ER**	EU	*EU*	TI	4022	**ER**	EU	*EU*	TI
4006	**ER**	EU	*EU*	TI	4023	**ER**	EU	*EU*	TI
4007	**ER**	EU	*EU*	TI	4024	**ER**	EU	*EU*	TI
4008	**ER**	EU	*EU*	TI	4025	**ER**	EU	*EU*	TI
4009	**ER**	EU	*EU*	TI	4026	**ER**	EU	*EU*	TI
4010	**ER**	EU	*EU*	TI	4027	**ER**	EU	*EU*	TI
4011	**ER**	EU	*EU*	TI	4028	**ER**	EU	*EU*	TI
4012	**ER**	EU	*EU*	TI	4029	**ER**	EU	*EU*	TI
4013	**ER**	EU	*EU*	TI	4030	**ER**	EU	*EU*	TI
4014	**ER**	EU	*EU*	TI	4031	**ER**	EU	*EU*	TI
4015	**ER**	EU	*EU*	TI	4032	**ER**	EU	*EU*	TI
4016	**ER**	EU	*EU*	TI	4033	**ER**	EU		
4017	**ER**	EU	*EU*	TI	4034	**ER**	EU		

4.6. SERVICE EMUS

The following unit is used by Network Rail for ERTMS testing on the Hertford Loop. It has been heavily modified from its original condition, and now includes a toilet.

313121   **Y**   BN *GB*   WN 62549 71233 62613

4.7. EMU VEHICLES IN INDUSTRIAL SERVICE

This list comprises EMU vehicles that have been withdrawn from active service but continue to be used in industrial service.

Cl. 390	69133	69833	Virgin Trains Training Centre, Westmere Drive, Crewe, Cheshire
Cl. 390	69633	69733	The Fire Service College, Moreton-in-Marsh, Gloucestershire
Cl. 390	69933		Safety & Accident Investigation Centre, Cranfield University, Cranfield, Bedfordshire
Cl. 508	64649	64712	Emergency Services Training Centre, Seacombe, Merseyside
Cl. 508	64681	71511 64724	The Fire Service College, Moreton-in-Marsh, Gloucestershire

4.8. EMUS AWAITING DISPOSAL

This list comprises vehicles awaiting disposal which are stored on the national railway network.

25 kV AC 50 Hz OVERHEAD UNITS:

Cl. 309	**RR**	WC	CS	71758
Cl. 365	**N**	X	ZN	65919
Cl. 365	**N**	X	ZI	72290

5. ON-TRACK MACHINES

These machines are used for maintaining, renewing and enhancing the infrastructure of the national railway network. With the exception of snowploughs all can be self-propelled, controlled either from a cab mounted on the machine or remotely. They are permitted to operate either under their own power or in train formations throughout the network both within and outside engineering possessions. Machines only permitted to be used within engineering possessions, referred to as On-Track Plant, are not included. Also not included are wagons included in OTM consists.

For each machine its Network Rail registered number, owner or responsible custodian and type is given, plus its name if carried. In addition, for snow clearance equipment the berthing location is given. Actual operation of each machine is undertaken by either the owner/responsible custodian or a contracted responsible custodian.

Machines were numbered by British Rail with either six-digit wagon series numbers or in the CEPS (Civil Engineers Plant System) series with five prefixed digits. Recently delivered machines have been numbered in the EVN series. Machines may also carry additional identifying numbers which are shown as "xxxx". Machines are listed here in CEPS/wagon series order. Those with EVN numbers are included where they would have been if allocated CEPS numbers.

(S) after the registered number designates a machine that is currently stored (the storage location of each is given at the end of this section).

DYNAMIC TRACK STABILISERS

| DR 72211 | BB | Plasser & Theurer DGS 62-N |
| DR 72213 | BB | Plasser & Theurer DGS 62-N |

TAMPERS

DR 73108	CS	Plasser & Theurer 09-32-RT	Tiger
DR 73109	SK	Plasser & Theurer 09-3X-RT	
DR 73110	SK	Plasser & Theurer 09-3X-RT	PETER WHITE
DR 73111	NR	Plasser & Theurer 09-3X-Dynamic	
DR 73113	NR	Plasser & Theurer 09-3X-Dynamic	
DR 73114	NR	Plasser & Theurer 09-3X-Dynamic	Ron Henderson
DR 73115	NR	Plasser & Theurer 09-3X-Dynamic	
DR 73116	NR	Plasser & Theurer 09-3X Dynamic	
DR 73117	NR	Plasser & Theurer 09-3X Dynamic	
DR 73118	NR	Plasser & Theurer 09-3X Dynamic	

99 70 9123 120-6	NR	Plasser & Theurer 09-3X Dynamic "DR 73120"
99 70 9123 121-4	NR	Plasser & Theurer 09-2X Dynamic "DR 73121"
99 70 9123 122-2	NR	Plasser & Theurer 09-2X Dynamic "DR 73122"

| DR 73803 | SK | Plasser & Theurer 08-32U-RT | Alexander Graham Bell |

DR 73804	SK	Plasser & Theurer 08-32U-RT	James Watt
DR 73805	CS	Plasser & Theurer 08-16/32U-RT	
DR 73806	CS	Plasser & Theurer 08-16/32U-RT	Karine
DR 73904	SK	Plasser & Theurer 08-4x4/4S-RT	Thomas Telford
DR 73905	CS	Plasser & Theurer 08-4x4/4S-RT	
DR 73906	CS	Plasser & Theurer 08-4x4/4S-RT	Panther
DR 73907	CS	Plasser & Theurer 08-4x4/4S-RT	
DR 73908	CS	Plasser & Theurer 08-4x4/4S-RT	
DR 73909	CS	Plasser & Theurer 08-4x4/4S-RT	Saturn
DR 73910	CS	Plasser & Theurer 08-4x4/4S-RT	Jupiter
DR 73911	CS	Plasser & Theurer 08-16/4x4C-RT	Puma
DR 73912	CS	Plasser & Theurer 08-16/4x4C-RT	Lynx
DR 73913	CS	Plasser & Theurer 08-12/4x4C-RT	
DR 73914	SK	Plasser & Theurer 08-4x4/4S-RT	Robert McAlpine
DR 73915	SK	Plasser & Theurer 08-16/4x4C-RT	William Arrol
DR 73916	SK	Plasser & Theurer 08-16/4x4C-RT	First Engineering
DR 73917	BB	Plasser & Theurer 08-4x4/4S-RT	
DR 73918	BB	Plasser & Theurer 08-4x4/4S-RT	
DR 73919	CS	Plasser & Theurer 08-16/4x4C100-RT	
DR 73920	CS	Plasser & Theurer 08-16/4x4C80-RT	
DR 73921	CS	Plasser & Theurer 08-16/4x4C80-RT	
DR 73922	CS	Plasser & Theurer 08-16/4x4C80-RT	John Snowdon
DR 73923	CS	Plasser & Theurer 08-4x4/4S-RT	Mercury
DR 73924	CS	Plasser & Theurer 08-16/4x4C100-RT	
DR 73925	CS	Plasser & Theurer 08-16/4x4C100-RT	Europa
DR 73926	BB	Plasser & Theurer 08-16/4x4C100-RT	Stephen Keith Blanchard
DR 73927	BB	Plasser & Theurer 08-16/4x4C100-RT	
DR 73928	BB	Plasser & Theurer 08-16/4x4C100-RT	
DR 73929	CS	Plasser & Theurer 08-4x4/4S-RT	
DR 73930	CS	Plasser & Theurer 08-4x4/4S-RT	
DR 73931	CS	Plasser & Theurer 08-16/4x4C100-RT	
DR 73932	SK	Plasser & Theurer 08-4x4/4S-RT	
DR 73933	SK	Plasser & Theurer 08-16/4x4/C100-RT	
DR 73934	SK	Plasser & Theurer 08-16/4x4/C100-RT	
DR 73935	CS	Plasser & Theurer 08-4x4/4S-RT	
DR 73936	CS	Plasser & Theurer 08-4x4/4S-RT	
DR 73937	BB	Plasser & Theurer 08-16/4x4C100-RT	
DR 73938	BB	Plasser & Theurer 08-16/4x4C100-RT	
DR 73939	BB	Plasser & Theurer 08-16/4x4C100-RT	Pat Best
DR 73940	SK	Plasser & Theurer 08-4x4/4S-RT	
DR 73941	SK	Plasser & Theurer 08-4x4/4S-RT	
DR 73942	CS	Plasser & Theurer 08-4x4/4S-RT	
DR 73943	BB	Plasser & Theurer 08-16/4x4C100-RT	
DR 73944	BB	Plasser & Theurer 08-16/4x4C100-RT	
DR 73945	BB	Plasser & Theurer 08-16/4x4C100-RT	
DR 73946	VO	Plasser & Theurer Euromat 08-4x4/4S	
DR 73947	CS	Plasser & Theurer 08-4x4/4S-RT	
DR 73948	CS	Plasser & Theurer 08-4x4/4S-RT	

99 70 9128 001-3	SK	Plasser & Theurer Unimat 09-4x4/4S Dynamic "928001"
99 70 9128 002-1	SK	Plasser & Theurer Unimat 09-4x4/4S Dynamic "DR 74002"

DR 75301	VO	Matisa B 45 UE	
DR 75302	VO	Matisa B 45 UE	
DR 75303	VO	Matisa B 45 UE	Gary Wright
DR 75401	VO	Matisa B 41 UE	
DR 75402	VO	Matisa B 41 UE	
DR 75404	VO	Matisa B 41 UE	
DR 75405	VO	Matisa B 41 UE	
DR 75406	CS	Matisa B 41 UE	
DR 75407	CS	Matisa B 41 UE	Eric Machell
DR 75408	BB	Matisa B 41 UE	
DR 75409	BB	Matisa B 41 UE	
DR 75410	BB	Matisa B 41 UE	
DR 75411	BB	Matisa B 41 UE	
DR 75501	BB	Matisa B 66 UC	
DR 75502	BB	Matisa B 66 UC	

BALLAST CLEANERS

DR 76323	NR	Plasser & Theurer RM95-RT	
DR 76324	NR	Plasser & Theurer RM95-RT	
DR 76501	NR	Plasser & Theurer RM-900-RT	
DR 76502	NR	Plasser & Theurer RM-900-RT	
DR 76503	NR	Plasser & Theurer RM-900-RT	
99 70 9314 504-0	NR	Plasser & Theurer RM-900	"DR 76504"

VACUUM PREPARATION MACHINES

DR 76701	NR	Plasser & Theurer VM80-NR
DR 76702	NR	Plasser & Theurer VM80-NR
DR 76703	NR	Plasser & Theurer VM80-NR
DR 76710 (S)	NR	Plasser & Theurer VM80-TRS
DR 76711 (S)	NR	Plasser & Theurer VM80-TRS

RAIL VACUUM MACHINES

99 70 9515 001-4	RC	Railcare 16000-480-UK RailVac OTM
99 70 9515 002-2	RC	Railcare 16000-480-UK RailVac OTM
99 70 9515 003-0	RC	Railcare 16000-480-UK RailVac OTM
99 70 9515 004-8	RC	Railcare 16000-480-UK RailVac OTM
99 70 9515 005-5	RC	Railcare 16000-480-UK RailVac OTM
99 70 9515 006-3	RC	Railcare 16000-480-UK RailVac OTM

BALLAST FEEDER MACHINE

99 70 9522 020-5	RC	Railcare Ballast Feeder UK

BALLAST TRANSFER MACHINES

DR 76750 NR Matisa D75   *(works with DR 78802/DR 78812/*
                                    DR 78822/DR 78832)
DR 76751 NR Matisa D75   *(works with DR 78801/DR 78811/*
                                    DR 78821/DR 78831)

CONSOLIDATION MACHINES

DR 76801   NR   Plasser & Theurer 09-CM-NR
99 70 9320 802-0   NR   Plasser & Theurer 09-2X-CM "DR 76802"

FINISHING MACHINES & BALLAST REGULATORS

DR 77001 SK Plasser & Theurer AFM 2000-RT Finishing Machine Anthony
                                                               Lou Phillips
DR 77002 SK Plasser & Theurer AFM 2000-RT Finishing Machine

99 70 9125 010-7 NR   Plasser & Theurer USP 6000 Regulator "DR 77010"

DR 77315 (S) BB Plasser & Theurer USP 5000C Regulator
DR 77316 (S) BB Plasser & Theurer USP 5000C Regulator
DR 77322   BB Plasser & Theurer USP 5000C Regulator
DR 77327   CS Plasser & Theurer USP 5000C Regulator
DR 77336 (S) BB Plasser & Theurer USP 5000C Regulator
DR 77801   VO Matisa R 24 S Regulator
DR 77802   VO Matisa R 24 S Regulator
DR 77901   CS Plasser & Theurer USP 5000-RT Regulator
DR 77903   NR Plasser & Theurer USP 5000-RT Regulator
DR 77904   NR Plasser & Theurer USP 5000-RT Regulator
DR 77905   NR Plasser & Theurer USP 5000-RT Regulator
DR 77906   NR Plasser & Theurer USP 5000-RT Regulator
DR 77907   NR Plasser & Theurer USP 5000-RT Regulator
DR 77908   SK Plasser & Theurer USP 5000-RT Regulator

99 70 9125 909-0 NR   Plasser & Theurer USP 5000 Regulator "DR 77909"

TWIN JIB TRACK RELAYERS

DRP 78213   VO Plasser & Theurer Self-Propelled Heavy Duty
DRP 78215   SK Plasser & Theurer Self-Propelled Heavy Duty
DRP 78216   BB Plasser & Theurer Self-Propelled Heavy Duty
DRP 78217 (S) SK Plasser & Theurer Self-Propelled Heavy Duty
DRP 78218 (S) BB Plasser & Theurer Self-Propelled Heavy Duty
DRP 78219   SK Plasser & Theurer Self-Propelled Heavy Duty
DRP 78221   BB Plasser & Theurer Self-Propelled Heavy Duty
DRP 78222   BB Plasser & Theurer Self-Propelled Heavy Duty
DRP 78223 (S) BB Plasser & Theurer Self-Propelled Heavy Duty
DRP 78224 (S) BB Plasser & Theurer Self-Propelled Heavy Duty
DRC 78226   CS Cowans Sheldon Self-Propelled Heavy Duty

DRC 78229   NR Cowans Sheldon Self-Propelled Heavy Duty
DRC 78231   NR Cowans Sheldon Self-Propelled Heavy Duty
DRC 78234   NR Cowans Sheldon Self-Propelled Heavy Duty
DRC 78235   CS Cowans Sheldon Self-Propelled Heavy Duty
DRC 78237 (S) CS Cowans Sheldon Self-Propelled Heavy Duty

NEW TRACK CONSTRUCTION
TRAIN PROPULSION MACHINES

DR 78701   BB Harsco Track Technologies NTC-PW
DR 78702   BB Harsco Track Technologies NTC-PW

TRACK RENEWAL MACHINES

Matisa P95 Track Renewals Trains
DR 78801+DR 78811+DR 78821+DR 78831 NR *(works with DR 76751)*
DR 78802+DR 78812+DR 78822+DR 78832 NR *(works with DR 76750)*

RAIL GRINDING TRAINS

Loram SPML 17
DR 79201A + DR 79201B   NR

Speno RPS-32
DR 79221 + DR 79222 + DR 79223 + DR 79224 + DR 79225 + DR 79226 SI

Loram C21
DR 79231 + DR 79232 + DR 79233 + DR 79234 + DR 79235 + DR 79236 + DR 79237 NR
DR 79241 + DR 79242 + DR 79243 + DR 79244 + DR 79245 + DR 79246 + DR 79247 NR
DR 79251 + DR 79252 + DR 79253 + DR 79254 + DR 79255 + DR 79256 + DR 79257 NR

Names: DR 79241/247   Roger South *(one plate on opposite sides of each)*
        DR 79251/257   Martin Elwood

Harsco Track Technologies RGH20C
DR 79261 + DR 79271   NR
DR 79262 + DR 79272   NR
DR 79263 + DR 79273   NR
DR 79264 + DR 79274   NR
DR 79265   NR   *spare vehicle*
DR 79267 + DR 79277   NR

Loram C44
99 70 9427 038-3 + 99 70 9427 039-1 + 99 70 9427 040-9 + 99 70 9427 041-7
                    NR   "DR 79301/302/303/304"
99 70 9427 042-5 + 99 70 9427 043-3 + 99 70 9427 044-1 + 99 70 9427 045-8
                    NR   "DR 79401/402/403/404"
99 70 9427 046-6 + 99 70 9427 047-4 + 99 70 9427 048-2 + 99 70 9427 049-0
99 70 9427 050-8 + 99 70 9427 051-6 + 99 70 9427 052-4
                    NR   "DR 79501/502/503/504/505/506/507"

STONEBLOWERS

DR 80200 (S)	NR	Pandrol Jackson Plain Line
DR 80201	NR	Pandrol Jackson Plain Line
DR 80202 (S)	NR	Pandrol Jackson Plain Line
DR 80203 (S)	NR	Pandrol Jackson Plain Line
DR 80204 (S)	NR	Pandrol Jackson Plain Line
DR 80205	NR	Pandrol Jackson Plain Line
DR 80206	SK	Pandrol Jackson Plain Line
DR 80207 (S)	NR	Pandrol Jackson Plain Line
DR 80208	NR	Pandrol Jackson Plain Line
DR 80209	NR	Pandrol Jackson Plain Line
DR 80210	NR	Pandrol Jackson Plain Line
DR 80211	NR	Pandrol Jackson Plain Line
DR 80212 (S)	NR	Pandrol Jackson Plain Line
DR 80213	NR	Harsco Track Technologies Plain Line
DR 80214	NR	Harsco Track Technologies Plain Line
DR 80215	NR	Harsco Track Technologies Plain Line
DR 80216	NR	Harsco Track Technologies Plain Line
DR 80217	NR	Harsco Track Technologies Plain Line
DR 80301	NR	Harsco Track Technologies Multi-purpose Stephen Cornish
DR 80302	NR	Harsco Track Technologies Multi-purpose
DR 80303	NR	Harsco Track Technologies Multi-purpose

CRANES

DRP 81505	BB	Plasser & Theurer 12 tonne Heavy Duty Diesel Hydraulic
DRP 81507 (S)	BB	Plasser & Theurer 12 tonne Heavy Duty Diesel Hydraulic
DRP 81508	BB	Plasser & Theurer 12 tonne Heavy Duty Diesel Hydraulic
DRP 81511 (S)	BB	Plasser & Theurer 12 tonne Heavy Duty Diesel Hydraulic
DRP 81513	BB	Plasser & Theurer 12 tonne Heavy Duty Diesel Hydraulic
DRP 81517	BB	Plasser & Theurer 12 tonne Heavy Duty Diesel Hydraulic
DRP 81519 (S)	BB	Plasser & Theurer 12 tonne Heavy Duty Diesel Hydraulic
DRP 81522	BB	Plasser & Theurer 12 tonne Heavy Duty Diesel Hydraulic
DRP 81525	BB	Plasser & Theurer 12 tonne Heavy Duty Diesel Hydraulic
DRP 81532	BB	Plasser & Theurer 12 tonne Heavy Duty Diesel Hydraulic
DRK 81601	VO	Kirow KRC 810UK 100 tonne Heavy Duty Diesel Hydraulic
DRK 81602	BB	Kirow KRC 810UK 100 tonne Heavy Duty Diesel Hydraulic
DRK 81611	BB	Kirow KRC 1200UK 125 tonne Heavy Duty Diesel Hydraulic
DRK 81612	CS	Kirow KRC 1200UK 125 tonne Heavy Duty Diesel Hydraulic
DRK 81613	VO	Kirow KRC 1200UK 125 tonne Heavy Duty Diesel Hydraulic
DRK 81621	VO	Kirow KRC 250UK 25 tonne Diesel Hydraulic
DRK 81622	VO	Kirow KRC 250UK 25 tonne Diesel Hydraulic
DRK 81623	SK	Kirow KRC 250UK 25 tonne Diesel Hydraulic
DRK 81624	SK	Kirow KRC 250UK 25 tonne Diesel Hydraulic
DRK 81625	SK	Kirow KRC 250UK 25 tonne Diesel Hydraulic

99 70 9319 012-9 SK Kirow KRC 250S 25 tonne Diesel Hydraulic "DRK 81626"
99 70 9319 013-7 NR Kirow KRC 1200UK 125 tonne Heavy Duty Diesel Hydraulic

Names:

DRK 81601	Nigel Chester		DRK 81611	Malcolm L. Pearce

LONG WELDED RAIL TRAIN PROPULSION MACHINES

DR 89005	NR	Cowans Boyd PW
DR 89007	NR	Cowans Boyd PW
DR 89008	NR	Cowans Boyd PW

BALLAST SYSTEM PROPULSION MACHINES

DR 92263 (S)	NR	Plasser & Theurer MFS-PW	
DR 92264	NR	Plasser & Theurer NB-PW	
DR 92285	NR	Plasser & Theurer PW-RT	
DR 92286	NR	Plasser & Theurer NPW-RT	
DR 92331	NR	Plasser & Theurer PW-RT	
DR 92332	NR	Plasser & Theurer NPW-RT	
DR 92431	NR	Plasser & Theurer PW-RT	
DR 92432	NR	Plasser & Theurer PW-RT	
99 70 9310 477-3	NR	Plasser & Theurer PW	"DR 92477"
99 70 9310 478-1	NR	Plasser & Theurer NPW	"DR 92478"

BREAKDOWN CRANES

ADRC 96710 (S)	NR	Cowans Sheldon 75 tonne Diesel Hydraulic
ADRC 96713	NR	Cowans Sheldon 75 tonne Diesel Hydraulic
ADRC 96714 (S)	NR	Cowans Sheldon 75 tonne Diesel Hydraulic
ADRC 96715	NR	Cowans Sheldon 75 tonne Diesel Hydraulic

HIGH SPEED 1 MAINTENANCE TRAIN VEHICLES

DR 97001	H1	Eiv de Brieve DU94BA TRAMM with Crane	"DU 94 B 001 URS"
DR 97011	H1	Windhoff MPV (Modular)	
DR 97012	H1	Windhoff MPV (Modular)	
DR 97013	H1	Windhoff MPV (Modular)	
DR 97014	H1	Windhoff MPV (Modular)	

MOBILE MAINTENANCE TRAINS

Robel Type 69.70 Mobile Maintenance System

99 70 9481 001-4 + 99 70 9559 001-1 + 99 70 9580 001-4	NR	"DR 97501/601/801"
99 70 9481 002-2 + 99 70 9559 002-9 + 99 70 9580 002-2	NR	"DR 97502/602/802"
99 70 9481 003-0 + 99 70 9559 003-7 + 99 70 9580 003-0	NR	"DR 97503/603/803"
99 70 9481 004-8 + 99 70 9559 004-5 + 99 70 9580 004-8	NR	"DR 97504/604/804"
99 70 9481 005-5 + 99 70 9559 005-2 + 99 70 9580 005-5	NR	"DR 97505/605/805"
99 70 9481 006-3 + 99 70 9559 006-0 + 99 70 9580 006-3	NR	"DR 97506/606/806"
99 70 9481 007-1 + 99 70 9559 007-8 + 99 70 9580 007-1	NR	"DR 97507/607/807"
99 70 9481 008-9 + 99 70 9559 008-6 + 99 70 9580 008-9	NR	"DR 97508/608/808"

HB HSBC Rail (Oxford blue & white).
HC Heathrow Connect (grey with a broad deep blue bodyside band & orange doors).
HE Heathrow Express (silver with purple doors and black window surrounds.
HN Harry Needle Railroad Company (orange with a black roof and solebar).
IC BR InterCity (dark grey/white/red/white).
K Black.
KB Knorr-Bremse Rail UK (blue, white & light green).
LH BR Loadhaul (black with orange cabsides).
LM London Midland (white/grey & green with black stripe around the windows).
LN London Northwestern Railway (light grey, dark green & light green).
LO London Overground (all over white with a blue solebar & black window surrounds and orange doors).
LT London Transport maroon & cream.
LW LNWR (grey with a red solebar).
M BR maroon (maroon lined out in straw & black).
ML BR Mainline Freight (aircraft blue with a silver stripe).
MY Merseyrail (all over yellow or all over grey (alternate sides)).
N BR Network SouthEast (white & blue with red lower bodyside stripe, grey solebar & cab ends).
NB Northern all over dark blue.
NC National Express white (white with blue doors).
NO Northern (deep blue, purple & white). Some units have area-specific promotional vinyls (see class heading for details).
NR New Northern Rail (white & purple).
NX National Express (white with grey ends).
O Non-standard (see class heading for details).
PB Porterbrook Leasing Company (blue).
PC Pullman Car Company (umber & cream with gold lettering lined out in gold).
RB Riviera Trains Oxford blue.
RG BR Parcels (dark grey & red).
RL RMS Locotec (dark blue with light grey cabsides).
RM Royal Mail revised (all over red).
RO Rail Operations Group (dark blue).
RP Royal Train (claret, lined out in red & black).
RR Regional Railways (dark blue & grey with light blue & white stripes, three narrow dark blue stripes at vehicle ends).
RS Railway Support Services (grey with a red solebar).
RV Riviera Trains Great Briton (Oxford blue & cream lined out in gold).
RX Rail Express Systems (dark grey & red with or without blue markings).
RZ Royal Train revised (plain claret, no lining).
SB Southeastern blue (all over blue with black window surrounds).
SC Strathclyde PTE (carmine & cream lined out in black & gold).
SD Stagecoach/South West Trains outer suburban {Class 450 style} (deep blue with red doors & orange & red cab sides).
SE Southeastern suburban (all over white with black window surrounds, light blue doors and (on some units) dark blue lower bodyside stripe).
SL Silverlink (indigo blue with white stripe, green lower body & yellow doors).
SN Southern (white & dark green with light green semi-circles at one end of each vehicle. Light grey band at solebar level).

SR ScotRail – Scotland's Railways (dark blue with Scottish Saltire flag & white/light blue flashes).

SS South West Trains inner suburban {Class 455 style} (red with blue & orange flashes at unit ends).

ST Stagecoach {long-distance stock} (white & dark blue with dark blue window surrounds and red & orange swishes at unit ends).

SW South Western Railway (two-tone grey with a yellow lower bodyside stripe).

TF TfL Rail (white with blue doors and lower bodyside stripe).

TG Govia Thameslink interim {Class 387} (white with dark green doors).

TL Govia Thameslink Railway (light grey & white with blue doors).

TP TransPennine Express (silver, grey, blue & purple).

TT Transmart Trains (all over green).

V Virgin Trains (red with black doors extending into bodysides, three white lower bodysides stripes).

VE Virgin Trains East Coast (red & white with black window surrounds).

VP Virgin Trains shunters (black with a large black & white chequered flag on the bodyside).

VN Northern Belle (crimson lake & cream lined out in gold).

VT Virgin Trains silver (silver, with black window surrounds, white cantrail stripe & red roof. Red swept down at unit ends).

VI Vivarail (white & green).

WA Wabtec Rail (black).

WC West Coast Railway Company maroon.

WM West Midlands Railway (silver with purple ends & solebar stripe, orange doors).

XC CrossCountry (two-tone silver with deep crimson ends & pink doors).

XR Crossrail (white with black window surrounds and a purple lower bodyside).

Y Network Rail yellow.

YR West Yorkshire PTE/Northern EMUs (red, lilac & grey).

6.2. OWNER CODES

The following codes are used to define the ownership details of the locomotives or rolling stock listed in this book. Codes shown indicate either the legal owner or "responsible custodian" of each vehicle.

20	Class 20189
37	Scottish Thirty-Seven Group
40	Class 40 Preservation Society
47	Stratford 47 Group
50	Class 50 Alliance
56	Class 56 Locomotives
70	7029 Clun Castle
71	71A Locomotives
2L	Class 20 Locomotives
A	Angel Trains
AD	AV Dawson
AF	Arlington Fleet Services

AI	Aggregate Industries
AM	Alstom
AT	Agility Trains
AV	Arriva UK Trains
BB	Balfour Beatty Rail Infrastructure Services
BD	Bardon Aggregates
BE	Belmond (UK)
BN	Beacon Rail
BR	Brodie Leasing
BT	Bombardier Transportation
CA	Caledonian Sleepers Rail Leasing
CL	Caledonian Rail Leasing
CT	Cross London Trains
CS	Colas Rail
DB	DB Cargo (UK)
DC	Devon & Cornwall Railways
DP	Deltic Preservation Society
DR	Direct Rail Services
DT	The Diesel Traction Group
E	Eversholt Rail (UK)
EA	Eastern Rail Services
ED	Ed Stevenson
EL	Electric Traction Limited
EM	East Midlands Trains
EP	Europhoenix
ER	European Metal Recycling
ET	Eurotunnel
EU	Eurostar International
FG	First Group
FL	Freightliner
GB	GB Railfreight
GW	Great Western Railway (assets of the Greater Western franchise)
H1	Network Rail (High Speed)
HA	Hanson UK
HD	Hastings Diesels
HE	Heathrow Airport Holdings
HJ	Howard Johnston
HN	Harry Needle Railroad Company
HT	Hanson Traction
HU	Hunslet Engine Company
KB	Knorr-Bremse Rail UK
LD	Locomotive Diesels
LF	Lombard Finance
LS	Locomotive Services
LN	London Overground
LO	Loram (UK)
MG	Mid Glamorgan County Council
MQ	Macquarie Group
MR	Mendip Rail
NB	Boden Rail Engineering
NM	National Museum of Science & Industry

NN	North Norfolk Railway
NR	Network Rail
NS	Nemesis Rail
NY	North Yorkshire Moors Railway Enterprises
P	Porterbrook Leasing Company
PP	Peter Pan Locomotive Company
PR	The Princess Royal Class Locomotive Trust
QW	QW Rail Leasing
RC	RailCare UK
RL	Rail Management Services (trading as RMS Locotec)
RM	Royal Mail
RO	Rail Operations Group
RP	Rampart Engineering
RR	Rock Rail
RS	Railway Support Services
RU	Russell Logistics
RV	Riviera Trains
SB	SNCB/NMBS (Société Nationale des Chemins de fer Belges/Nationale Maatschappij der Belgische Spoorwegen)
SF	SNCF (Société Nationale des Chemins de fer Français)
SG	South Glamorgan County Council
SI	Speno International
SK	Swietelsky Babcock Rail
SP	The Scottish Railway Preservation Society
SU	SembCorp Utilities UK
SW	South Western Railway
SY	South Yorkshire Passenger Transport Executive
TT	Transmart Trains
UR	UK Rail Leasing
VG	Victoria Group
VI	Vivarail
VO	VolkerRail
VT	Vintage Trains
WA	Wabtec Rail Group
WC	West Coast Railway Company
WM	West Midlands Trains
X	Sold for scrap/further use and awaiting collection
XR	Crossrail

6.3. LOCOMOTIVE POOL CODES

Locomotives are split into operational groups ("pools") for diagramming and maintenance purposes. The codes used to denote these pools are shown in this publication.

AWCA	West Coast Railway Company operational locomotives.
AWCX	West Coast Railway Company stored locomotives.
CFOL	Class 50 Operations locomotives.
CFSL	Class 40 Preservation Society Locomotives.
COFS	Colas Rail Class 56.

COLO	Colas Rail Classes 60, 66 & 70.
COLS	Colas Rail stored locomotives.
COTS	Colas Rail Classes 37 & 67.
DFGI	Freightliner Class 70.
DFHH	Freightliner Class 66/6.
DFIM	Freightliner Class 66/5.
DFIN	Freightliner low emission Class 66.
DFLC	Freightliner Class 90.
DFNC	Freightliner Class 86/6.
DHLT	Freightliner locomotives awaiting maintenance/repair/disposal.
EFOO	Great Western Railway Class 57.
EFPC	Great Western Railway 43.
EHPC	CrossCountry Class 43.
EMPC	East Midlands Trains Class 43.
EPEX	Europhoenix locomotives for export.
EPUK	Europhoenix UK locomotives.
GBBR	GB Railfreight Class 73 for possible rebuilding.
GBBT	GB Railfreight Class 66. Large fuel tanks.
GBCH	GB Railfreight Class 86 & 87.
GBCS	GB Railfreight Class 73/9. Caledonian Sleeper.
GBDF	GB Railfreight Class 47.
GBEB	GB Railfreight Class 66. Ex-European, large fuel tanks.
GBED	GB Railfreight Class 73.
GBEE	GB Railfreight Class 20. On hire from HNRC.
GBEL	GB Railfreight Class 66. New build, small fuel tanks.
GBET	GB Railfreight Class 92. Stored locomotives.
GBFM	GB Railfreight Class 66. RETB fitted.
GBHN	GB Railfreight Class 47. Hired from HNRC.
GBLT	GB Railfreight Class 66. Small fuel tanks.
GBNB	GB Railfreight Class 66. New build.
GBNR	GB Railfreight Class 73/9. Network Rail contracts.
GBOB	GB Railfreight Class 66. Former DB Cargo locomotives; large fuel tanks and buckeye couplers.
GBSL	GB Railfreight Class 92. Caledonian Sleeper.
GBST	GB Railfreight Class 92. Caledonian Sleeper & Channel Tunnel.
GBYH	GB Railfreight Class 59.
GROG	Rail Operations Group operational locomotives.
HAPC	ScotRail Class 43.
HNRL	Harry Needle Railroad Company hire locomotives.
HNRS	Harry Needle Railroad Company stored locomotives.
HTLX	British American Railway Services locomotives.
HYWD	South Western Railway Class 73.
IANA	Greater Anglia Class 90.
IECA	Virgin Trains East Coast Class 91.
IECP	Virgin Trains East Coast Class 43.
MBDL	Non TOC-owned diesel locomotives.
MBED	Non TOC-owned electro-diesel locomotives.
MBEL	Non TOC-owned electric locomotives.
MOLO	Class 20189 Ltd Class 20.
NRLO	Nemesis Rail locomotives.
QADD	Network Rail locomotives.

QCAR	Network Rail New Measurement Train Class 43.
QETS	Network Rail Class 37.
RVLO	Loram (UK) locomotives.
SROG	Rail Operations Group locomotives under overhaul.
UKRL	UK Rail Leasing. Operational locomotives.
UKRM	UK Rail Leasing. Locomotives for overhaul.
UKRS	UK Rail Leasing. Stored locomotives.
WAAC	DB Cargo Class 67.
WABC	DB Cargo Class 67. RETB fitted.
WACC	DB Cargo Class 67.
WAWC	DB Cargo Class 67 for hire to Arriva Trains Wales.
WBAE	DB Cargo Class 66. Locomotives fitted with "stop-start" technology.
WBAR	DB Cargo Class 66. Fitted with remote monitoring equipment.
WBAT	DB Cargo Class 66.
WBBE	DB Cargo Class 66. RETB fitted and fitted with "stop-start" technology.
WBBT	DB Cargo Class 66. RETB fitted.
WBLE	DB Cargo Class 66. Dedicated locomotives for Lickey Incline banking duties. Fitted with "stop-start" technology.
WBLT	DB Cargo Class 66. Dedicated locomotives for Lickey Incline banking duties.
WCAT	DB Cargo Class 60.
WCBT	DB Cargo Class 60. Extended-range fuel tanks.
WDAM	DB Cargo Class 59.
WEAC	DB Cargo Class 90.
WEDC	DB Cargo Class 90 for hire to Virgin Trains East Coast.
WFBC	DB Cargo Class 92 with TVM430 cab signalling equipment for use on High Speed 1.
WQAA	DB Cargo stored locomotives Group 1A (short-term maintenance).
WQAB	DB Cargo stored locomotives Group 1B.
WQBA	DB Cargo stored locomotives Group 2 (unserviceable).
WQCA	DB Cargo stored locomotives Group 3 (unserviceable).
WQDA	DB Cargo stored locomotives Group 4 (awaiting disposal).
XHAC	Direct Rail Services Classes 37/4 & 57/3.
XHCC	Direct Rail Services Class 37/4. Cumbrian Coast passenger.
XHCE	Direct Rail Services Class 68 for hire to Chiltern Railways.
XHCK	Direct Rail Services Class 57/0.
XHIM	Direct Rail Services locomotives – Intermodal traffic.
XHNC	Direct Rail Services locomotives – nuclear traffic/general.
XHSS	Direct Rail Services stored locomotives.
XHTP	Direct Rail Services Class 68 for hire to TransPennine Express.
XHVE	Direct Rail Services Classes 68 & 88.
XHVT	Direct Rail Services Class 57/3 for hire to Virgin Trains West Coast.
XYPA	Mendip Rail Class 59/1.
XYPO	Mendip Rail Class 59/0.

6.4. OPERATOR CODES

Operator codes are used to denote the organisation that facilitates the use of that vehicle, and may not be the actual Train Operating Company which runs the train. Where no operator code is shown, vehicles are currently not in use.

AW	Arriva Trains Wales
BP	Belmond British Pullman
C2	c2c
CA	Caledonian Sleeper
CR	Chiltern Railways
CS	Colas Rail
DB	DB Cargo (UK)
DR	Direct Rail Services
EM	East Midlands Trains
EU	Eurostar (UK)
GA	Greater Anglia
GB	GB Railfreight
GC	Grand Central
GN	Great Northern (part of Govia Thameslink Railway)
GW	Great Western Railway
HC	Heathrow Connect
HD	Hastings Diesels
HE	Heathrow Express
HT	Hull Trains
LO	London Overground
LS	Locomotive Services
ME	Merseyrail
NB	Northern Belle
NO	Northern
NY	North Yorkshire Moors Railway
PR	The Princess Royal Class Locomotive Trust
RG	Rail Operations Group
RS	The Royal Scotsman (Belmond)
RT	Royal Train
RV	Riviera Trains
SE	Southeastern
SN	Southern (part of Govia Thameslink Railway)
SP	The Scottish Railway Preservation Society
SR	ScotRail
SW	South Western Railway
SY	Stagecoach Supertram
TL	Thameslink (part of Govia Thameslink Railway)
TP	TransPennine Express
VE	Virgin Trains East Coast
VT	Vintage Trains
VW	Virgin Trains West Coast
WC	West Coast Railway Company
WM	West Midlands Trains
XC	CrossCountry
XR	Crossrail/Elizabeth Line

6.5. ALLOCATION & LOCATION CODES

Allocation codes are used in this publication to denote the normal maintenance base ("depots") of each operational locomotive, multiple unit or coach. However, maintenance may be carried out at other locations and may also be carried out by mobile maintenance teams. Location codes are used to denote common storage locations whilst the full place name is used for other locations. The designation (S) denotes stored.

Code	Depot	Depot Operator
AD	Ashford (Kent)	Hitachi
AK	Ardwick (Manchester)	Siemens
AL	Aylesbury	Chiltern Railways
AN	Allerton (Liverpool)	Northern
BD	Birkenhead North	Merseyrail
BF	Bedford Cauldwell Walk	Govia Thameslink Railway
BH	Barrow Hill (Chesterfield)	Barrow Hill Engine Shed Society
BI	Brighton Lovers Walk	Govia Thameslink Railway
BL	Shackerstone, Battlefield Line	*Storage location only*
BM	Bournemouth	South Western Railway
BN	Bounds Green (London)	Virgin Trains East Coast
BO	Bo'ness (West Lothian)	The Bo'ness & Kinneil Railway
BQ	Bury (Greater Manchester)	East Lancashire Railway Trust
BS	Bescot (Walsall)	DB Cargo (UK)
BU	Burton-upon-Trent	Nemesis Rail
BY	Bletchley	West Midlands Trains
CB	Crewe Basford Hall	Freightliner Engineering
CE	Crewe International	DB Cargo (UK)
CF	Cardiff Canton	Arriva Trains Wales/Colas Rail
CH	Chester	Alstom
CK	Corkerhill (Glasgow)	ScotRail
CL	Crewe LNWR Heritage	LNWR Heritage Company
CO	Coquelles (France)	Eurotunnel
CP	Crewe Carriage Shed	Arriva TrainCare
CR	Crewe Gresty Bridge	Direct Rail Services
CS	Carnforth	West Coast Railway Company
CY	Crewe South Yard	*Storage location only*
CZ	Central Rivers (Barton-under-Needwood)	Bombardier Transportation
DE	East Dereham (Norfolk)	Mid Norfolk Railway
DM	Dollands Moor	DB Cargo (UK)
DR	Doncaster Belmont Yard	DB Cargo (UK)
DY	Derby Etches Park	East Midlands Trains
EC	Edinburgh Craigentinny	Virgin Trains East Coast
EH	Eastleigh	Arriva TrainCare
EM	East Ham (London)	c2c
EP	Ely (Potter Group)	Potter Group Logistics
EX	Exeter	Great Western Railway
FA	Fawley (Hampshire)	*Storage location only*
FF	Forest (Brussels)	SNCB/NMBS
GW	Glasgow Shields Road	ScotRail

HA	Haymarket (Edinburgh)	ScotRail
HE	Hornsey (London)	Govia Thameslink Railway
HJ	Hoo Junction (Kent)	Colas Rail
HM	Healey Mills (Wakefield)	*Storage location only*
HO	Hope Cement Works	Hope Cement
HT	Heaton (Newcastle-upon-Tyne)	Northern
IL	Ilford (London)	Greater Anglia/Elizabeth Line
IS	Inverness	ScotRail
KM	Carlisle Kingmoor	Direct Rail Services
KR	Kidderminster	Severn Valley Railway
LA	Laira (Plymouth)	Great Western Railway
LB	Loughborough Works	Brush Traction
LD	Leeds Midland Road	Freightliner Engineering
LE	Landore (Swansea)	Great Western Railway
LG	Longsight (Manchester)	Northern
LM	Quinton Rail Technology Centre (Long Marston, Warwickshire)	Motorail Logistics
LR	Leicester	UK Rail Leasing
LW	MoD Longtown (Cumbria)	*Storage location only*
LY	Le Landy (Paris)	SNCF
MA	Alstom Longsight (Manchester)	Alstom
MD	Merehead	Mendip Rail
ME	Mossend Yard	DB Cargo (UK)
ML	Motherwell	Direct Rail Services
MN	Machynlleth	Arriva Trains Wales
NC	Norwich Crown Point	Greater Anglia
NG	New Cross Gate (London)	London Overground
NH	Newton Heath (Manchester)	Northern
NL	Neville Hill (Leeds)	East Midlands Trains/Northern
NM	Nottingham Eastcroft	East Midlands Trains
NN	Northampton King's Heath	Siemens
NO	Weybourne (Norfolk)	North Norfolk Railway
NP	North Pole (London)	Hitachi
NT	Northam (Southampton)	Siemens
NU	Sheffield Nunnery	Stagecoach Supertram
NY	Grosmont (North Yorkshire)	North Yorkshire Moors Railway Enterprises
OH	Old Oak Common Heathrow	Heathrow Express
OO	Old Oak Common HST	Great Western Railway
PM	St Philip's Marsh (Bristol)	Great Western Railway
PO	Polmadie (Glasgow)	Alstom
PZ	Penzance Long Rock	Great Western Railway
RG	Reading	Great Western Railway
RM	Ramsgate	Southeastern
RR	Doncaster Roberts Road	ElectroMotive Diesel Services
RU	Rugby	Colas Rail
RY	Ryde (Isle of Wight)	South Western Railway
SA	Salisbury	South Western Railway
SC	Scunthorpe Steelworks	British Steel
SE	St Leonards (Hastings)	St Leonards Railway Engineering
SG	Slade Green (London)	Southeastern
SH	Southall (London)	West Coast Rly Co/Locomotive Services

SJ	Stourbridge Junction	Parry People Movers
SK	Swanwick Junction (Derbyshire)	Midland Railway Enterprises
SL	Stewarts Lane (London)	Govia Thameslink Railway/Belmond
SO	Soho (Birmingham)	West Midlands Trains
SP	Springs Branch (Wigan)	DB Cargo (UK)
SU	Selhurst (Croydon)	Govia Thameslink Railway
SW	Swanage	Swanage Railway
TB	Three Bridges (Crawley)	Siemens
TI	Temple Mills (London)	Eurostar International
TJ	Tavistock Junction Yard (Plymouth)	*Storage location only*
TM	Tyseley Locomotive Works	Birmingham Railway Museum
TN	Thornton (Fife)	John Cameron
TO	Toton (Nottinghamshire)	DB Cargo (UK)
TS	Tyseley (Birmingham)	West Midlands Trains
WD	Wimbledon (London)	South Western Railway
WE	Willesden Brent sidings	*Storage location only*
WH	Washwood Heath (Birmingham)	Boden Rail Engineering/RMS Locotec
WN	Willesden (London)	London Overground
WO	Wolsingham, Weardale Railway	RMS Locotec
YK	National Railway Museum (York)	National Museum of Science & Industry
ZA	RTC Business Park (Derby)	Loram (UK)
ZB	Doncaster Works	Wabtec Rail
ZC	Crewe Works	Bombardier Transportation UK
ZD	Derby Works	Bombardier Transportation UK
ZG	Eastleigh Works	Arlington Fleet Services
ZH	Springburn Depot (Glasgow)	Knorr-Bremse Rail Systems (UK)
ZI	Ilford Works	Bombardier Transportation UK
ZJ	Stoke-on-Trent Works	Axiom Rail (Stoke)
ZK	Kilmarnock Caledonia Works	Wabtec Rail Scotland
ZM	Kilmarnock Bonnyton Works	Brodie Engineering
ZN	Wolverton Works	Knorr-Bremse Rail Systems (UK)
ZR	Holgate Works (York)	Network Rail

6.6. ABBREVIATIONS

The following general abbreviations are used in this book:

AC	Alternating Current (ie Overhead supply)
AFD	Air Force Department
BAA	British Airports Authority
BR	British Railways
BSI	Bergische Stahl Industrie
CRDC	Component Recovery & Disposal Centre
C&W	Carriage & Wagon
DC	Direct Current (ie Third Rail)
DEMU	Diesel Electric Multiple Unit
DERA	Defence Evaluation & Research Agency
DfT	Department for Transport
Dia	Diagram number
DMU	Diesel Multiple Unit (general term)
DSDC	Defence Storage & Distribution Centre
DRS	Direct Rail Services
ETS	Electric Train Supply
EMU	Electric Multiple Unit (general term)
GWR	Great Western Railway
FLT	Freightliner Terminal
HB	Hunslet-Barclay
hp	Horse power
HNRC	Harry Needle Railroad Company
Hz	Hertz
kN	Kilonewtons
km/h	Kilometres per hour
kW	Kilowatts
lbf	Pounds force
LT	London Transport
LUL	London Underground Limited
m	Metres
mm	Millimetres
mph	Miles per hour
NPCCS	Non Passenger Carrying Coaching Stock
PTE	Passenger Transport Executive
RCH	Railway Clearing House
rpm	Revolutions per minute
RR	Rolls Royce
RSL	Rolling Stock Library
SR	BR Southern Region and Southern Railway
t	Tonnes
T	Toilet
TD	Toilet suitable for use by disabled passengers
TDM	Time Division Multiplex
TOPS	Total Operations Processing System
V	Volts
W	Wheelchair space

6.7 BUILDERS

Builders are shown in class headings. The workshops of British Railways and the pre-nationalisation and pre-grouping companies were first transferred to a wholly-owned subsidiary called British Rail Engineering Ltd (BREL). These workshops were later privatised, BREL then becoming BREL Ltd. Some of the works were then taken over by ABB, which was later merged with Daimler-Benz Transportation to become Adtranz. This has now been taken over by Bombardier Transportation. Bombardier also built vehicles for the British market in Brugge, Belgium.

Other workshops were the subject of separate sales, Springburn, Glasgow and Wolverton becoming "Railcare" and Eastleigh becoming "Wessex Traincare". All three were sold to GEC-Alsthom (now Alstom) but Eastleigh closed in 2006, although the site is now used as a storage and refurbishment location.

Part of Doncaster works was sold to RFS Engineering, which became insolvent and was bought out and renamed RFS Industries. Now part of Wabtec Rail Group.

The builder details in the class headings show the owner at the time of vehicle construction followed by the works as follows:

Ashford	Ashford Works (now Ashford Rail Plant depot, not the same location as the now closed Chart Leacon Works).
Birmingham	The former Metro-Cammell works at Saltley, Birmingham.
Cowlairs	Cowlairs Works, Glasgow.
Derby	Derby Carriage Works (also known as Litchurch Lane).
Doncaster	Doncaster Works.
Eastleigh	Eastleigh Works
Swindon	Swindon Works.
Wolverton	Wolverton Works.
York	York Carriage Works.

Other builders are:

Alexander	Walter Alexander, Falkirk.
Barclay	Andrew Barclay, Caledonia Works, Kilmarnock (now Wabtec).
BRCW	Birmingham Railway Carriage & Wagon, Smethwick.
CAF	Construcciones y Auxiliar de Ferrocarriles (works in Zaragoza, Beasain and Irun, Spain).
Cravens	Cravens, Sheffield.
Gloucester	Gloucester Railway Carriage & Wagon, Gloucester.
Hitachi	Hitachi Rail Europe (Newton Aycliffe, County Durham, Kasado, Japan and Pistoia, Italy).
Hunslet-Barclay	Hunslet-Barclay, Caledonia Works, Kilmarnock (now Wabtec).
Hunslet TPL	Hunslet Transportation Projects, Leeds.
Lancing	SR, Lancing Works.
Leyland Bus	Leyland Bus, Workington.
Metro-Cammell	Metropolitan-Cammell, Saltley, Birmingham
Pressed Steel	Pressed Steel, Linwood.
Charles Roberts	Charles Roberts, Horbury Junction, Wakefield.
SGP	Simmering-Graz-Pauker, Austria (now owned by Siemens).
Siemens	Siemens Transportation Systems (principal works in Krefeld (Germany) and others in Vienna (Austria) and Prague (Czech Rep).
SRP	Specialist Rail Products Ltd (A subsidiary of RFS).
Vossloh	Vossloh Rail Vehicles, Valencia, Spain (sold to Stadler in 2015).